# CHILTON'S REPAIR & TUNE-UP GUIDE
# CHEVROLET
# GMC PICK-UPS
# 1970-80

Chevrolet C-10, C-20, K-10, K-20
GMC C-1500, C-2500, K-1500, K-2500

Managing Editor KERRY A. FREEMAN, S.A.E.
Senior Editor THEODORE COSTANTINO

President WILLIAM A. BARBOUR
Executive Vice President JAMES MIADES
Vice President and General Manager JOHN P. KUSHNERICK

CHILTON BOOK COMPANY
Radnor, Pennsylvania
19089

## SAFETY NOTICE

Proper service and repair procedures are vital to the safe, reliable operation of all motor vehicles, as well as the personal safety of those performing repairs. This book outlines procedures for servicing and repairing vehicles using safe, effective methods. The procedures contain many NOTES, CAUTIONS and WARNINGS which should be followed along with standard safety procedures to eliminate the possibility of personal injury or improper service which could damage the vehicle or compromise its safety.

It is important to note that repair procedures and techniques, tools and parts for servicing motor vehicles, as well as the skill and experience of the individual performing the work vary widely. It is not possible to anticipate all of the conceivable ways or conditions under which vehicles may be serviced, or to provide cautions as to all of the possible hazards that may result. Standard and accepted safety precautions and equipment should be used when handling toxic or flammable fluids, and safety goggles or other protection should be used during cutting, grinding, chiseling, prying, or any other process that can cause material removal or projectiles.

Some procedures require the use of tools specially designed for a specific purpose. Before substituting another tool or procedure, you must be completely satisfied that neither your personal safety, nor the performance of the vehicle will be endangered.

Although information in this guide is based on industry sources and is as complete as possible at the time of publication, the possibility exists that the manufacturer made later changes which could not be included here. While striving for total accuracy, Chilton Book Company cannot assume responsibility for any errors, changes, or omissions that may occur in the compilation of this data.

## PART NUMBERS

Part numbers listed in this reference are not recommendations by Chilton for any product by brand name. They are references that can be used with interchange manuals and aftermarket supplier catalogs to locate each brand supplier's discrete part number.

## ACKNOWLEDGMENTS

Chilton Book Company expresses appreciation to the Chevrolet Motor Division, General Motors Corporation, Detroit, Michigan 48202; and GMC Truck and Coach Division, General Motors Corporation, Pontiac, Michigan 48053 for their generous assistance.

Information has been selected from Chevrolet and GMC shop manuals, owner's manuals, data books, brochures, service bulletins, and technical manuals.

Copyright © 1980 by Chilton Book Company
All Rights Reserved
Published in Radnor, Pa by Chilton Book Company
and simultaneously in Ontario, Canada
by Nelson Canada Limited

Manufactured in the United States of America
    234567890    9876543210


Chilton's Repair & Tune-Up Guide: Chevrolet and GMC Pick-Ups 1970–80
ISBN 0-8019-6936-0 pbk.
Library of Congress Catalog Card No. 79-8304

# CONTENTS

# Quick Reference Specifications For Your Vehicle

Fill in this chart with the most commonly used specifications for your vehicle. Specifications can be found in Chapters 1 through 3 or on the tune-up decal under the hood of the vehicle.

 **Tune-Up**

Firing Order_____

Spark Plugs:

    Type_____

    Gap (in.)_____

Point Gap (in.)_____

Dwell Angle (°)_____

Ignition Timing (°)_____

    Vacuum (Connected/Disconnected)_____

Valve Clearance (in.)

    Intake_____    Exhaust_____

---

# Capacities

Engine Oil (qts)

    With Filter Change_____

    Without Filter Change_____

Cooling System (qts)_____

Manual Transmission (pts)_____

    Type_____

Automatic Transmission (pts)_____

    Type_____

Front Differential (pts)_____

    Type_____

Rear Differential (pts)_____

    Type_____

Transfer Case (pts)_____

    Type_____

---

## FREQUENTLY REPLACED PARTS

Use these spaces to record the part numbers of frequently replaced parts.

| PCV VALVE | OIL FILTER | AIR FILTER |
|---|---|---|
| Manufacturer_____ | Manufacturer_____ | Manufacturer_____ |
| Part No._____ | Part No._____ | Part No._____ |

# General Information and Maintenance

## HOW TO USE THIS BOOK

This book is intended to serve as a guide to the tune-up, repair, and maintenance of ½ and ¾ ton Chevrolet and GMC pick-ups from 1970 to 1980. All of the operations in this book apply to both Chevrolet and GMC trucks unless specified otherwise. It is also understood that a Chevrolet C-10, K-10, C-20, or K-20 is equivalent to its GMC counterpart C-1500, K-1500, C-2500, or K-2500, respectively.

To use this book properly, each operation should be approached logically and the recommended procedures read thoroughly before beginning the work. Before attempting any operation, be sure that you understand exactly what is involved. Naturally, it is considerably easier if you have the necessary tools on hand and a clean place to work.

When reference is made in this book to the "right side" or "left side" of the truck, it should be understood that these positions are to be viewed from the front seat. Thus, the left side of the truck is always the driver's side, even when one is facing the truck, as when working on the engine.

Information in this book is based on factory sources. Special factory tools have been eliminated from repair procedures wherever possible, in order to substitute more readily available tools.

## TOOLS AND EQUIPMENT

It would be impossible to catalog each tool that you would need to perform each or any operation in this book. It would also not be wise for the amateur to rush out and buy an expensive set of tools on the theory that he may need one of them at some time. The best approach is to proceed slowly, gathering together a good quality set of those tools that are used most frequently. Don't be misled by the low cost of bargain tools. Forged wrenches, 12 point sockets and fine tooth ratchets are by far preferable to their less expensive counterparts. As any good mechanic can tell you, there are few worse experiences than trying to work on a car or truck with bad tools. Your monetary savings will be far outweighed by frustration and mangled knuckles.

Begin accumulating those tools that are used most frequently. In addition to a basic assortment of screwdrivers and a pair of pliers, you will need the following tools for routine maintenance and tune-up jobs:

1. Wrenches in inch sizes—sockets and combination open end/box wrenches, up to about 1 inch.

2. A spark plug gap gauge/bending tool.

3. Feeler gauges for breaker points (through 1974 only).

4. Tachometer/dwell meter;

5. Timing light;
6. Grease gun;
7. Oil filter wrench;

For some suspension and engine work, a torque wrench measuring in foot pounds will also be necessary.

## Special Tools

Although a basic collection of hand tools is sufficient for the majority of service procedures in this guide, in a few cases special tools are necessary. Factory-approved tools are available from your dealer, or from:

Service Tool Division
Kent-Moore Corporation
1501 South Jackson Street
Jackson, Michigan 49203

## SERVICING YOUR TRUCK SAFELY

It is virtually impossible to anticipate all of the hazards involved with automotive maintenance and service, but care and common sense will prevent most accidents.

The rules of safety for mechanics range from "don't smoke around gasoline," to "use the proper tool for the job." The trick to avoiding injuries is to develop safe work habits and take every possible precaution.

## Dos

• Do keep a fire extinguisher and first aid kit within easy reach.
• Do wear safety glasses or goggles when cutting, drilling, grinding or prying. If you wear glasses for the sake of vision, they should be made of hardened glass that can serve also as safety glasses, or wear safety goggles over your regular glasses.
• Do shield your eyes whenever you work around the battery. Batteries contain sulphuric acid. In case of contact with the eyes or skin, flush the area with water or a mixture of water and baking soda and get medical attention immediately.
• Do use safety stands for any undercar service. Jacks are for raising vehicles; safety stands are for making sure the vehicle stays raised until you want it to come down. Whenever the truck is raised, block the wheels remaining on the ground and set the parking brake.
• Do use adequate ventilation when work-ing with any chemicals or hazardous materials.
• Do disconnect the negative battery cable when working on the electrical system. The secondary ignition system can contain up to 40,000 volts.
• Do follow manufacturer's directions whenever working with potentially hazardous materials. Both brake fluid and antifreeze are poisonous if taken internally.
• Do properly maintain your tools. Loose hammerheads, mushroomed punches and chisels, frayed or poorly grounded electrical cords, excessively worn screwdrivers, spread wrenches, cracked sockets, slipping ratchets, or faulty droplight sockets can cause accidents.
• Do use the proper size and type of tool for the job being done.
• Do when possible, pull on a wrench handle rather than push on it, and adjust your stance to prevent a fall.
• Do be sure that adjustable wrenches are tightly closed on the nut or bolt and pulled so that the face is on the side of the fixed jaw.
• Do select a wrench or socket that fits the nut or bolt. The wrench or socket should sit straight, not cocked.
• Do strike squarely with a hammer; avoid glancing blows.
• Do set the parking brake and block the drive wheels if the work requires the engine running.

## Don'ts

• Don't run an engine in a garage or anywhere else without proper ventilation—EVER! Carbon monoxide is poisonous; it takes a long time to leave the human body and you can build up a deadly supply of it in your system by simply breathing in a little every day. You may not realize you are slowly poisoning yourself. Always use power vents, windows, fans or open the garage doors.
• Don't work around moving parts while wearing a necktie or other loose clothing. Short sleeves are much safer than long, loose sleeves; hard-toed shoes with neoprene soles protect your toes and give a better grip on slippery surfaces. Jewelry such as watches, fancy belt buckles, beads or body adornment of any kind is not safe working around a truck. Long hair should be hidden under a hat or cap.
• Don't use pockets for toolboxes. A fall or

bump can drive a screwdriver deep into your body. Even a wiping cloth hanging from the back pocket can wrap around a spinning shaft or fan.

• Don't smoke when working around gasoline, cleaning solvent or other flammable material.

• Don't smoke when working around the battery. When the battery is being charged, it gives off explosive hydrogen gas.

• Don't use gasoline to wash your hands; there are excellent soaps available. Gasoline may contain lead, and lead can enter the body through a cut, accumulating in the body until you are very ill. Gasoline also removes all the natural oils from the skin so that bone dry hands will suck up oil and grease.

• Don't service the air conditioning system unless you are equipped with the necessary tools and training. The refrigerant, R-12, is extremely cold when compressed, and when released into the air will instantly freeze any surface it contacts, including your eyes. Although the refrigerant is normally non-toxic, R-12 becomes a deadly poisonous gas in the presence of an open flame. One good whiff of the vapors from burning refrigerant can be fatal.

## HISTORY

The development of today's pick-up truck is firmly rooted in the history of the automobile itself. Actually, the passenger car evolved from the truck, since the very first cars were powered horse-drawn wagons with a platform or cargo area behind the driver.

Trucks were basically work vehicles in the early 1900s. Popular with commercial establishments, they were equipped with rectangular boxes, narrow enough to fit between the rear wheels, with rear fenders bolted on, creating the "stepside" of today. The wide bed, or "fleetside" was actually not available until 1958.

In 1955, pick-up trucks began the long evolvement into their present form, for it was then that Chevrolet overhauled their entire model line and some of the innovations overflowed into the pick-up truck line. The fenders were integral with the bed and for the first time a V8 engine, the venerable 265 cu in. small block, was available as an option.

It was not too long ago that pick-up trucks were commercial vehicles only and four wheel drives were for farm or military use.

But, somewhere around 1970, manufacturers bowed to public pressure and the hope of increased sales and began making trucks for family as well as commercial use. Pick-up trucks are now equally at home at the country club, in the driveways of suburbia, or in commercial use. The 1975 "Gentleman Jim" pick-up is a good example of a highly stylized pick-up for any use.

The latest series of Chevrolet and GMC pick-ups are far removed from the vehicles of the past. Since 1970, they have received such improvements as disc brakes, electronic ignition, and full time four wheel drive. Features such as air conditioning, power steering, adjustable steering columns, automatic transmissions, and softer riding suspensions are now commonplace.

Light duty Chevrolet and GMC pick-ups are now offered in C series (two wheel drive) and K series (four wheel drive) in ½ and ¾ ton capacities with either Stepside or Fleetside cargo beds. In addition, Crew Cab models are available in the 20 and 2500 series. And in 1978, GM introduced the first American made 350 cu in. V8 diesel engine for light duty application. There is no doubt that trucks are becoming more popular. They now account for one out of every three vehicle sales by Chevrolet dealers.

## SERIAL NUMBER IDENTIFICATION

### Vehicle

The Vehicle Identification Number (V.I.N.) is on a plate attached to the left hand door pillar. The gross vehicle weight (GVW), or maximum safe total weight of the truck, cargo, and passengers, is also given on the plate.

```
MFD. BY GENERAL MOTORS CORPORATION
                              GVWR [          ]
GAWR FRONT [          ]        GAWR REAR [          ]

VIN [                    ]
   CAMPER LOADING DATA
CWR [        ] DIM A [        ] DIM B [        ]
   INFLATION DATA FOR TIRES FURNISHED WITH VEHICLE
FRONT [          ]              PRESSURE [     ]
REAR  [          ]              PRESSURE [     ]
   WARRANTY VOIDED IF LOADED IN EXCESS OF RATINGS [ ]
   SEE OWNERS MANUAL FOR OTHER LOADING AND INFLATION DATA
```

**Typical vehicle identification plate (© Chevrolet Motor Div.)**

**1970**

The first letter indicates the vehicle type, C for two wheel drive, K for four wheel drive. The second letter indicates the engine type, S for six cylinder, or E for V8. The first number is for the GVW range, either a 1, indicating ½ ton, or a 2, indicating ¾ ton. The second and third numbers are for the body type: 04 for fenderside, or Stepside; 34 for wideside, or Fleetside. The third letter indicates the assembly plant. The fourth letter is for the model year (Z is for 1970). The last five digits are the serial numbers.

**1971**

The plate is essentially the same as 1970, except that either a hyphen or a letter indicating the type of state certification appears between the body type numbers and the assembly plant letter. The model year number is 1.

**1972–78**

The plates for these years are the same, with the exception of the engine codes, and the model years, of course. The first letter indicates a Chevrolet (C) or GMC (T) vehicle. The second letter is the vehicle type, C or K. The third letter is the engine type. For 1972 this would be an S or an E. Later years are covered below. The first number is the GVW range, 1 (½ ton) or 2 (¾ ton). The second number is the model type, 4 for cab and pick-up box. The third number is for the year, 2 for 1972, for example. The fourth letter indicates the assembly plant. The last six numbers are the serial numbers.

1973 Engine Codes:
| | |
|---|---|
| Q | 250 six |
| T | 292 six |
| X | 307 V8 |
| Y | 350 V8 |
| Z | 454 V8 |

1974 Engine Codes:
Same except:
| | |
|---|---|
| V | 350 V8 two barrel |
| Y | 350 V8 four barrel |

1975 Engine Codes:
Same except: M 400 V8 Four barrel

1976 and 1977 Engine Codes:
| | |
|---|---|
| D | 250 six |
| T | 292 six |

| | |
|---|---|
| V | 350 V8 two barrel |
| L | 350 V8 four barrel |
| V | 400 V8 (R in 1977) |
| S | 454 V8 |

1978 Engine Codes:
| | |
|---|---|
| D | 250 six |
| T | 292 six |
| U | 305 V8 |
| L | 350 V8 |
| R | 400 V8 |
| S | 454 V8 |
| Z | 350 V8 Diesel |

**1979–80**

The VIN is on a plate attached to the upper left-hand side of the instrument number panel. The plate is visible through the windshield. The interpretation for the VIN code is the same as outlined for 1972–78, except for the engine codes, which are:

| | |
|---|---|
| D | 250 six |
| T | 292 six |
| U | 305 V8 |
| L | 350 V8 four barrel |
| M | 350 V8 two barrel |
| R | 400 V8 |
| S | 454 V8 |
| Z | 350 V8 Diesel |

## Engine

The engine number is located as follows:

6 Cylinder: On a pad on the right-hand side of the cylinder block, at the rear of the distributor.

V8: On a pad at the front right-hand side of the cylinder block, except for 1979 and 1980 454 V8s, which have the code on a pad at the front top center of the engine block immediately forward of the intake manifold; and diesel engines, which have the code on a label

**Six cylinder engine serial number location (© Chevrolet Motor Div.)**

Gasoline V8 engine serial number location (© Chevrolet Motor Div.)

attached to the rear face of the left valve cover.

Example—F1210TFA

F—Manufacturing Plant. F-Flint and T-Tonawanda

12—Month of Manufacture (December)

10—Day of Manufacture (Tenth)

T—Truck

FA—Transmission and Engine Combination

## Transmission

The Muncie or Saginaw three speed manual transmission serial number is located on the lower left side of the case adjacent to the rear of the cover. The three speed Tremec transmission (1976–80 only) has the number on the upper forward mounting flange. The four speed transmission is numbered on the rear of the case, above the output shaft. The Turbo Hydra-Matic 350 serial number is on the right rear vertical surface of the fluid pan. The Turbo Hydra-Matic 400 is identified by a light blue plate attached to the right side, which is stamped with the serial number. The Powerglide transmission (through 1972 only) is stamped in the same location as the Turbo Hydra-Matic 350.

Three and four speed transmission serial number location—lower left side of the case adjacent to the rear cover (© Chevrolet Motor Div.)

## Transfer Case

The New Process 203 and 205 transfer cases have a build date tag attached to the front of the case. Muncie Model 203 transfer cases have a build date on the front of the case above the output shaft.

## Axles

From 1970 to 1973, the axle serial number for Series 10 Chevrolet and 1500 GMC trucks can be found on the bottom flange of the carrier housing. For Series 20 and 2500, the number is stamped on the forward upper surface of the carrier. For all trucks, 1974–80, the rear axle numbers are on the front of the right rear axle tube inboard of the upper control arm bracket, except for Dana-built axles, which are stamped on the rear surface of the right axle tube. Front axles are marked on the front of the left axle tube.

## Service Parts Identification Plate

The service parts identification plate, commonly known as the option list, is usually located on the inside of the glove compart-

Rear axle serial number location (© Chevrolet Motor Div.)

Alternator serial number location (© Chevrolet Motor Div.)

**Starter serial number location (© Chevrolet Motor Div.)**

**Powerglide serial number location (© Chevrolet Motor Div.)**

**Turbo Hydra-Matic serial number location (© Chevrolet Motor Div.)**

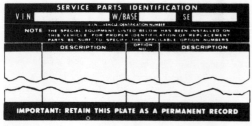

**Service parts identification plate (© Chevrolet Motor Div.)**

ment door. On some trucks, you may have to look for it on an inner fender panel. The plate lists the vehicle serial number, wheelbase, all regular production options (RPOs) and all special equipment. Probably the most valuable piece of information on this plate is the paint code, a useful item when you have occasion to need paint.

## ROUTINE MAINTENANCE

The accompanying chart gives the recommended maintenance intervals for the components covered here. Refer to the text for the applicable procedures.

## Air Cleaner

Two types of air cleaners are available for early models; a paper element type and an oil bath type for heavy-duty use. Normally, the oil bath type is available as an option only. Later models have paper element types only.

### PAPER ELEMENT TYPE

Loosen the wing nut on top of the cover and remove the cover from the air cleaner housing. The element should be replaced when it has become oil saturated or filled with dirt. If the filter is equipped with a wetted wrapper, remove the wrapper and wash it in kerosene or similar solvent. Shake or blot dry. Saturate the wrapper in 10W-30 engine oil and squeeze it tightly in an absorbent towel to remove the excess oil. Leave the wrapper moist. Clean the dirt from the filter by lightly tapping it against a workbench to dislodge the dirt particles. Wash the top of the air cleaner housing and wipe it dry. If equipped, replace the crankcase ventilation filter, located in the air filter housing, if it appears excessively dirty. Replace the oiled wrapper on the air cleaner element and reinstall the element in the housing, repositioning it 180° from its original position.

### OIL BATH TYPE

Oil bath air cleaners are recommended for use in extremely dusty or off-road areas.

To service the oil bath type air cleaner, remove the wing nut at the top and remove the cover and element. Drain all of the oil from the reservoir. Clean all of the parts and dry thoroughly, but do not use compressed air on the element.

Reinstall the reservoir and fill to the mark

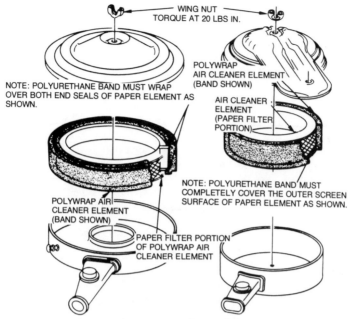

WING NUT
TORQUE AT 20 LBS IN.

POLYWRAP
AIR CLEANER ELEMENT
(BAND SHOWN)

AIR CLEANER
ELEMENT
(PAPER FILTER
PORTION)

NOTE: POLYURETHANE BAND MUST WRAP
OVER BOTH END SEALS OF PAPER ELEMENT AS
SHOWN.

NOTE: POLYURETHANE BAND MUST
COMPLETELY COVER THE OUTER SCREEN
SURFACE OF PAPER ELEMENT AS SHOWN.

POLYWRAP AIR
CLEANER ELEMENT
(BAND SHOWN)

PAPER FILTER PORTION
OF POLYWRAP AIR
CLEANER ELEMENT

**Air cleaner element with polyurethane wrap (© Chevrolet Motor Div.)**

with SAE 50 engine oil (above freezing) or SAE 20 engine oil (below freezing). Install the element in the reservoir and replace the cover and tighten the wing nut.

## PCV Valve

The PCV valve is located on top of the valve cover. Its function is to purge the crankcase of harmful vapors through a system using engine vacuum to draw fresh air through the crankcase. The system reburns crankcase vapors, rather than exhausting them. Proper operation of the PCV valve depends on a sealed engine. If the oil begins to form sludge, which will be obvious as it is drained, and the PCV system is functioning properly, check the engine for possible causes.

Engine operating conditions that would indicate a malfunctioning PCV system are rough idle, oil present in the air cleaner, oil leaks or excessive oil sludging.

The simplest check for the PCV valve is to remove it from its rubber grommet on top of the valve cover and shake it. If it rattles, it is functioning; if not replace it. In any event, it should be replaced at the recommended interval whether it rattles or not. While you are about it, check the PCV hoses for breaks or restrictions. As necessary, the hoses should also be replaced. The plastic T-fittings used in this system break easily, so be careful.

To replace the PCV valve:

1. Pull the valve, with the hose still attached to the valve, from the rubber grommet in the rocker cover.

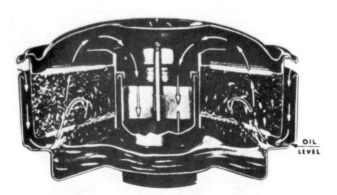

OIL
LEVEL

**Oil level in the oil bath air cleaner case (© Chevrolet Motor Div.)**

## Maintenance Intervals

See text for procedures concerning regular maintenance.

NOTE: *Heavy-duty operation (trailer towing, prolonged idling, severe stop-and-start driving) should be accompanied by a 50% increase in maintenance. Cut the interval in half for these conditions. Figures given are maintenance intervals when service should be performed.*

| Maintenance | 1970 | 1971–74 | 1975–80 |
|---|---|---|---|
| **Air Cleaner (Check and Clean)** | | | |
| Oil bath | 12,000 mi | 12,000 mi | |
| Paper element ① | 24,000 mi (replace) | 24,000 mi (replace) | 30,000 mi (replace) ⑥ |
| **PCV Valve (Replace)** | 12 mo/12,000 mi | 12 mo/12,000 mi | 12 mo/15,000 mi ⑦⑧ |
| **Evaporative Canister** | | | |
| Replace filter | — | 12 mo/12,000 mi | 24 mo/30,000 mi ⑧ |
| **Engine Oil** | | | |
| Check | Each fuel stop | Each fuel stop | Each fuel stop |
| Replace | 4 mo/6,000 mi | 4 mo/6,000 mi | 6 mo/7,500 mi ⑨⑬ |
| **Engine Oil Filter (Replace)** | At 1st oil change; then every 2nd | At 1st oil change; then every 2nd | At 1st oil change; then every 2nd⑬ |
| **Fuel Filter** | | | |
| Replace | 12,000 mi | 12,000 mi | 12 mo/15,000 mi ⑥⑫ |
| **Powerglide Transmission Fluid** | | | |
| Check | 6,000 mi | 6,000 mi | — |
| Replace | 24,000 mi ⑤ | 24,000 mi | |
| **Turbo Hydra-Matic Fluid & Filter** | | | |
| Check fluid | 6,000 mi | 6,000 mi | Each oil change |
| Change fluid | 24,000 mi | 24,000 mi | 30,000 mi |
| Replace filter | 24,000 mi | 24,000 mi | 30,000 mi ⑧⑩ |
| **Manual transmission (All)** | | | |
| Check lubricant | 6,000 mi | 4 mo/6,000 mi | 6 mo/7,500 mi ⑨ |
| Add lubricant | As necessary | As necessary | As necessary |
| **Battery** | | | |
| Lubricate terminal felt washer | 6,000 mi ④ | — | — |
| Clean terminals | 6,000 mi | As necessary | As necessary |
| Check electrolyte level | Twice monthly | Twice monthly | Twice monthly |
| **Coolant Level** | Each fuel stop | Each fuel stop | Each fuel stop |
| **Front Wheel Bearings** | | | |
| Lubricate | 30,000 mi | 30,000 mi ③ | 30,000 mi ⑧⑪ |
| **Front and Rear Axle Lube** | | | |
| Check | 6,000 mi | 6,000 mi | 6 mo/7,500 mi ⑨ |
| Replace | 24,000 mi | 24,000 mi | 1st 15,000 mi w/Positraction |
| **Brake Fluid (Master Cylinder)** | | | |
| Check fluid level | 6,000 mi | 6,000 mi | 6 mo/7,500 mi ⑨ |
| Add fluid | As necessary | As necessary | As necessary |

## Maintenance Intervals (cont'd)

| Maintenance | 1970 | 1971–74 | 1975–80 |
|---|---|---|---|
| **Manual Steering Gear Lubricant** | | | |
| Check level | 36,000 mi ② | 36,000 mi ② | 30,000 mi |
| Add lubricant | As necessary ② | ② | ② |
| **Power Steering Reservoir** | | | |
| Check fluid level | At each oil change | At each oil change | 6 mo/7,500 mi |
| Add fluid | As necessary | As necessary | As necessary |
| **Rotate Tires** | 6,000 mi | 6,000 mi | Radial—1st 7,500 mi, then every 15,000 mi Bias Belted—every 7,500 mi |
| **Chassis Lubrication** | See Chassis Lubrication charts | See Chassis Lubrication charts | See Chassis Lubrication charts |
| **Drive Belts** | | | |
| Check and adjust (as necessary) | 6,000 mi | 6,000 mi | 6 mo/7,500 mi |
| **Transfer Case** | | | |
| Check | 4 mo/6,000 mi | 4 mo/6,000 mi | 4 mo/6,000 mi |
| Add | As necessary | As necessary | As necessary |
| **Driveshaft Centering Ball** | | | |
| Lubricate (4WD only) | 6,000 mi | 6,000 mi | 7,500 mi ⑨ |

—Not applicable
mi—Miles
mo—Months
① Paper element air cleaners should be rotated 180° each time they are checked
② From 1970 on, no lubrication of the manual steering gear is recommended. The gear should be inspected for leaks at the seal (lubricant leaks, not filmy oil leaks). Seasonal change of the lubricant is not required and the housing should not be drained.
③ 24,000 miles in 1972–74
④ May be equipped with a felt terminal washer
⑤ 20 Series—every 12,000 miles
⑥ 12,000 mi in heavy duty emissions vehicles (C 10 or C-1500 over 6000 lbs GVW; all K models)
⑦ 24 mo/30,000 mi 1976–80
⑧ 24,000 mi in heavy duty emission vehicles
⑨ 4 mo/6,000 mi in heavy duty emissions vehicles
⑩ 60,000 mi 1976–78, 100,000 mi 1979–80, light duty emissions vehicles
⑪ 12,000 mi in four wheel drive vehicles
⑫ 24 mo/24,000 mi in California 350 and 400 engines through 1977; 12,000 mi on 1979–80 heavy duty emissions vehicles
⑬ Change at 3,000 mile intervals for 350 Diesel

2. Use a pair of pliers to release the hose clamp; remove the PCV valve from the hose.

3. Install the new valve into the hose, slide the clamp into position, and install the valve into the rubber grommet.

## Evaporative Canister

The only regular maintenance that need be performed on the evaporative emission canister is to regularly change the filter and check the condition of the hoses. If any hoses need replacement, use only hoses which are marked "EVAP." No other types should be used. Whenever the vapor vent hose is replaced, the restrictor adjacent to the canister should also be replaced.

The evaporative emission canister is located on the left side of the engine compartment, with a filter located in its bottom. The filter should be replaced according to the scheduled maintenance.

To service the canister filter:

1. Note the installed positions of the

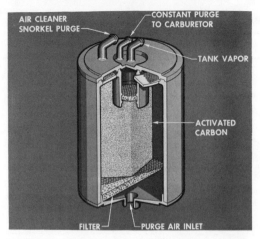

**Typical evaporative canister (© Chevrolet Motor Div.)**

hoses, tagging them as necessary, in case any have to be removed.

2. Loosen the clamps and remove the bottom of the canister.

3. Pull the filter out and throw it away.

4. Install a new canister filter.

5. Install the bottom of the canister and tighten the clamps.

6. Check the hoses for cracks, restrictions or hose connection openings.

## Heat Riser

The heat riser is a thermostatically or vacuum operated valve in the exhaust manifold. Not all engines have one. Heat riser-equipped V8s have only one valve, located in the right manifold. The valve opens when the engine is warming up, to direct hot exhaust gases to the intake manifold, in order to preheat the incoming fuel/air mixture. If it sticks shut, the result will be frequent stalling during warmup, especially in cold and damp weather. If it sticks open, the result will be a rough idle after the engine is warm. The heat riser should move freely. If it sticks, apply GM Manifold Heat Control Solvent or something similar (engine cool) to the ends of the shaft. Sometimes rapping the end of the shaft sharply with a hammer (engine hot) will

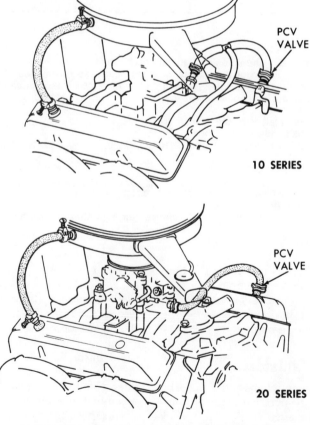

**Typical PCV valve locations (© Chevrolet Motor Div.)**

Typical heater riser valve (six cylinder shown) (© Chevrolet Motor Div.)

break it loose. If this fails, components must be removed for further repairs.

## Drive Belts

### BELT TENSION

At the interval specified in the "Maintenance Intervals" chart, check the water pump, alternator, power steering pump (if equipped), air conditioning compressor (if equipped) and air pump (if equipped) drive belts for proper tension. Also look for signs of wear, fraying, separation, glazing, and so on, and replace the belts as required.

Belt tension should be checked with a gauge made for the purpose. If a tension gauge is not available, tension can be checked with moderate thumb pressure applied to the belt at its longest span midway between pulleys. If the belt has a free span

less than twelve inches, it should deflect approximately ⅛–¼ inch. If the span is longer than twelve inches, deflection can range between ⅛ and ⅜ inches.

To adjust or replace belts:

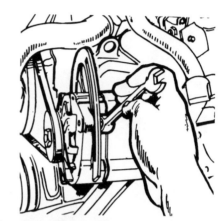

To adjust belt tension or to replace belts, first loosen the component's mounting and adjusting bolts slightly

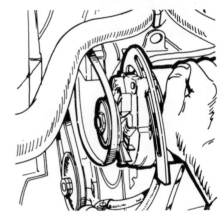

Push the component toward the engine and slip off the belt

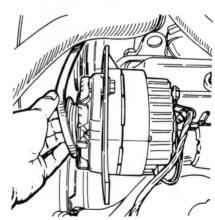

Slip the new belt over the pulley

A gauge is recommended, but you can check belt tension with thumb pressure (© Chevrolet Motor Div.)

7" TO 10"
1/4" DEFLECTION

13" TO 16"
1/2" DEFLECTION

## How To Spot Worn V-Belts

V-Belts are vital to efficient engine operation—they drive the fan, water pump and other accessories. They require little maintenance (occasional tightening) but they will not last forever. Slipping or failure of the V-belt will lead to overheating. If your V-belt looks like any of these, it should be replaced.

This belt has deep cracks, which cause it to flex. Too much flexing leads to heat build-up and premature failure. These cracks can be caused by using the belt on a pulley that is too small. Notched belts are available for small diameter pulleys.

**Cracking or weathering**

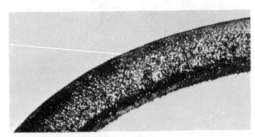

Oil and grease on a belt can cause the belt's rubber compounds to soften and separate from the reinforcing cords that hold the belt together. The belt will first slip, then finally fail altogether.

**Softening (grease and oil)**

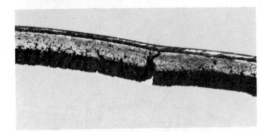

Glazing is caused by a belt that is slipping. A slipping belt can cause a run-down battery, erratic power steering, overheating or poor accessory performance. The more the belt slips, the more glazing will be built up on the surface of the belt. The more the belt is glazed, the more it will slip. If the glazing is light, tighten the belt.

**Glazing**

The cover of this belt is worn off and is peeling away. The reinforcing cords will begin to wear and the belt will shortly break. When the belt cover wears in spots or has a rough jagged appearance, check the pulley grooves for roughness.

**Worn cover**

This belt is on the verge of breaking and leaving you stranded. The layers of the belt are separating and the reinforcing cords are exposed. It's just a matter of time before it breaks completely.

**Separation**

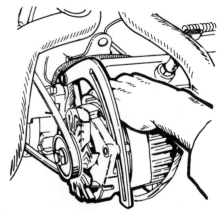

**Pull outward on the component and tighten the mounting bolts**

1. Loosen the driven accessory's pivot and mounting bolts.

2. Move the accessory toward or away from the engine until the tension is correct. You can use a wooden hammer handle, a broomstick, or the like as a lever, but do not use anything metallic, such as a prybar.

3. Tighten the bolts and recheck the tension. If new belts have been installed, run the engine for a few minutes, then recheck and readjust as necessary.

It is better to have belts too loose than too tight, because overtight belts will lead to bearing failure, particularly in the water pump and alternator. However, loose belts place an extremely high impact load on the driven component due to the whipping action of the belt.

## Air Conditioning

Regular maintenance for the air conditioning system includes periodic checks of the compressor drive belt tension, covered in the previous section. In addition, the system should be operated for at least five minutes every month. This ensures an adequate supply of lubricant to the bearings, and helps prevent the seals and hoses from drying out. To do this comfortably in winter, set the air conditioning lever to "Norm," the temperature lever to "Hot," and turn on the blower. This will engage the compressor, circulating lubricating oils within the system, but prevent the discharge of cold air.

The system can be checked for proper refrigerant charge using the appropriate procedure given below. Note that these procedures apply only to the factory-installed systems. If your truck has an aftermarket

unit, you should consult the manufacturer of the unit for system checks.

If the system does not seem to be properly charged, take the truck to a trained professional for service. Do *not* attempt to charge the air conditioning system yourself unless you are thoroughly familiar with its operation and the hazards involved. Escaping refrigerant evaporates at subzero temperatures, and is cold enough to freeze any surface it contacts, including your skin and eyes.

### SYSTEM CHECKS

#### 1970–72

All Chevrolet and GMC pick-ups in these years have an air conditioning sight glass for checking the refrigerant charge.

1. Start the engine and set it on fast idle.

2. Set the controls for maximum cold with the blower on high.

3. If bubbles are present in the sight glass, the system is low on charge. If no bubbles are present in the sight glass, the system is either fully charged or empty.

4. Feel the high and low pressure lines at the compressor. The high pressure line should be warm and the low pressure line should be cool. If no appreciable temperature difference is felt, the system is empty or nearly empty.

NOTE: *Do not attempt to charge the refrigerant system unless thoroughly familiar with its operation and the procedures involved.*

Even though there is a noticeable temperature difference, there is a possibility of overcharge. If the refrigerant in the sight glass remains clear for more than 45 seconds before foaming and then settling away from the sight glass, an overcharge is indicated.

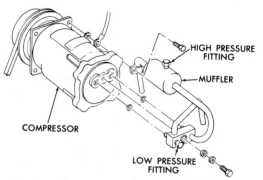

**High and low pressure lines on the 1970–72 factory-installed air conditioning compressor (© Chevrolet Motor Div.)**

CAUTION: *No attempt should be made to discharge the system. Severe injury could result.*

If the refrigerant foams and then settles away from the sight glass in less than 45 seconds, it can be assumed that the system is properly charged.

**1973–80**

These air conditioning systems have no sight glass for checking.

1. Warm the engine to normal operating temperature.

2. Open the hood and doors.

3. Set the selector lever at A/C.

4. Set the temperature lever at the first detent to the right of COLD (outside air).

5. Set the blower on HI.

6. Idle the engine at 1,000 rpm.

7. Feel the temperature of the evaporator inlet and the accumulator outlet with the compressor engaged.

Both lines should be cold. If the inlet pipe is colder than the outlet pipe the system is low on charge.

Do not attempt to charge the system yourself.

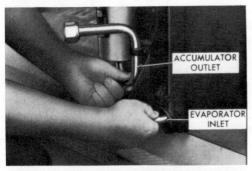

Checking evaporator inlet and accumulator outlet line temperatures, 1973–80 (© Chevrolet Motor Div.)

## Fluid Level Checks

### ENGINE OIL

The engine oil should be checked on a regular basis, ideally at each fuel stop. If the truck is used for trailer towing or for heavy-duty use, it would be safer to check it more often.

When checking the oil level it is best that the oil be at operating temperature, although checking the level immediately after stopping will give a false reading because all of the oil will not yet have drained back into the crankcase. Be sure that the truck is resting on

a level surface, allowing time for the oil to drain back into the crankcase.

1. Open the hood and locate the dipstick. Remove it from the tube. The oil dipstick is located on the passenger's side of 6 cylinder engines and on the driver's side of V8s.

2. Wipe the dipstick with a clean rag.

3. Insert the dipstick fully into the tube, and remove it again. Hold the dipstick horizontally and read the oil level. The level should be between the FULL and ADD OIL marks. If the oil level is at or below the ADD OIL mark, oil should be added as necessary. Oil is added through the capped opening on the valve cover(s) on gasoline engines. Diesel engines have a capped oil fill tube at the front of the engine. See "Oil and Fuel Recommendations" for the proper viscosity and oil to use.

4. Replace the dipstick and check the level after adding oil. Be careful not to overfill the crankcase. Approximately one quart of oil will raise the level from ADD to FULL.

### MANUAL TRANSMISSION

Check the lubricant level at the interval specified in the maintenance chart.

1. With the truck parked on a level surface, remove the filler plug from the side of the transmission case. Be careful not to take out the drain plug at the bottom.

2. If lubricant begins to trickle out of the hole, there is enough. If not, carefully insert a finger (watch out for sharp threads) and check that the level is up to the edge of the hole.

3. If not, add sufficient lubricant with a funnel and tube, or a squeeze bulb to bring it

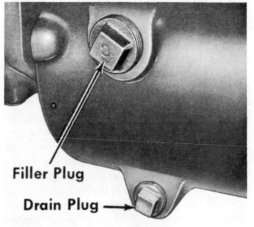

**Filler Plug**

**Drain Plug ⟶**

Manual transmission fill and drain plugs (© Chevrolet Motor Div.)

to the proper level. The correct lubricant to use is SAE 80W-90 GL-5 Gear Lubricant, or SAE 80W GL-5 for cold climates.

4. Replace the plug and check for leaks.

## AUTOMATIC TRANSMISSION

Check the level of the fluid at the specified interval. The fluid level should be checked with the engine at normal operating temperature and running. If the truck has been running at high speed for a long period, in city traffic on a hot day, or pulling a trailer, let it cool down for about thirty minutes before checking the level.

1. Park on the level with the engine running and the shift lever in Park.

2. Remove the dipstick at the rear of the engine compartment. Cautiously feel the end of the dipstick with your fingers. Wipe it off and replace it, then pull it again and check the level of the fluid on the dipstick.

3. If the fluid felt cool, the level should be between the two dimples below ADD. If it was too hot to hold, the level should be between the ADD and FULL marks.

4. If the fluid is at or below the ADD mark, add fluid through the dipstick tube. One pint raises the level from ADD to FULL when the fluid is hot. The correct fluid to use is DEXRON® II. Be certain that the transmission is not overfilled; this will cause foaming, fluid loss, and slippage.

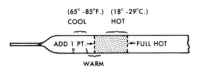

(65° -85°F.) (18° -29°C.)
COOL     HOT

ADD 1 PT.→     ←FULL HOT

WARM

NOTE: DO NOT OVERFILL. It takes only one pint to raise level from ADD to FULL with a hot transmission.

**Automatic transmission dipstick markings (© Chevrolet Motor Div.)**

## TRANSFER CASE

Check the four wheel drive transfer case lubricant level every 4 months or 6,000 miles.

1. With the truck parked on a level surface, remove the filler plug from the rear of the transfer case (behind the transmission). Be careful not to take out the drain plug at the bottom.

2. If lubricant trickles out, there is enough. If not, carefully insert a finger and check that the level is up to the edge of the hole, EXCEPT in full time four wheel drive systems. The lubricant level in full time four

wheel drive cases should be ½ in. below the hole.

Lubricant may be added, if necessary, with a funnel and tube, or a squeeze bulb. Conventional transfer cases require SAE 80W or SAE 80W-90 GL-5 gear lubricant; full time systems use SAE 10W-30 or 10W-40 engine oil. The full time system (1973–79) is the one with the H LOC and L LOC positions on the shifter.

## BRAKE MASTER CYLINDER

Chevrolet and GMC trucks are equipped with a dual braking system, allowing a vehicle to be brought to a safe stop in the event of failure in either the front or rear brakes. The dual master cylinder has two entirely separate reservoirs, one connected to the front brakes and the other connected to the rear brakes. In the event of failure in either portion, the remaining part is not affected.

1. Clean all of the dirt from around the cover of the master cylinder.

2. Be sure that the vehicle is resting on a level surface.

3. Carefully pry the clip from the top of the master cylinder to release the cover.

4. The fluid level should be approximately ⅛ in. from the top of the master cylinder. If not, add fluid until the level is correct. Only high quality brake fluids, such as General Motors Supreme No. 11 Hydraulic Brake Fluid, or fluids meeting DOT 3 specifications should be used.

NOTE: *It is normal for the fluid level to fall slightly as the disc brake pads wear, on 1971 and later trucks. However, if the level drops significantly between fluid level checks, or if the level is chronically low, the system should be examined for leakage.*

**Pry the bail from the master cylinder reservoir cap to check the fluid level**

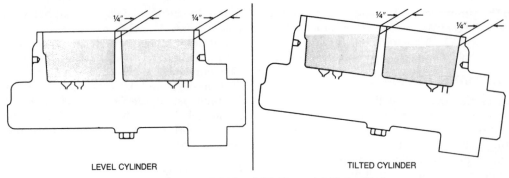

LEVEL CYLINDER          TILTED CYLINDER

**Master cylinder fluid level (© Chevrolet Motor Div.)**

5. Install the cover of the master cylinder. On most models there is a rubber gasket under the cover, which fits into two slots on the cover. Be sure that this is seated properly.

6. Push the clip back into place and be sure that it seats in the groove on the top of the cover.

CAUTION: *Brake fluid dissolves paint. It also absorbs moisture from the air; never leave a container or the master cylinder uncovered any longer than necessary. All parts in contact with the brake fluid (i.e. master cylinder, and its lid, hoses, plunger assemblies, etc.) must be kept scrupulously clean, since any contamination of the brake fluid will adversely affect braking performance.*

## COOLANT SERVICE

The coolant level should be checked at each fuel stop, ideally, to prevent the possibility of overheating and serious engine damage. If not, it should at least be checked once each month.

The cooling system was filled at the factory with a high quality coolant solution that is good for year around operation and protects the system from freezing down to $-20°$ F. ($-32°$ F in Canada). It is good for two full calendar years or 24,000 miles, whichever occurs first, provided that the proper concentration of coolant is maintained.

The 1973–80 cooling system differs slightly from those used on 1970–72 trucks. The 1973–80 system incorporates a plastic expansion tank connected to the radiator by a hose from the base of the radiator filler neck. The hot coolant level on 1973–80 trucks should be at the FULL HOT mark on the expansion tank and the cold coolant level should be at the FULL COLD mark on the tank. Do not remove the radiator cap to check the coolant level on 1973–80 trucks.

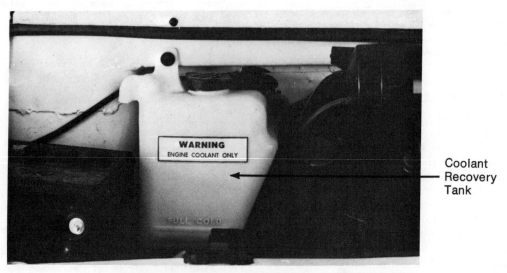

WARNING
ENGINE COOLANT ONLY

FULL COLD

Coolant Recovery Tank

**Typical coolant recovery tank (© Chevrolet Motor Div.)**

On 1970–72 trucks, the cold coolant level should be approximately three inches below the bottom of the filler neck, and the hot level should be 1–1½ in. below the bottom of the filler neck.

To check the coolant level:

1. On 1973–80 models, check the level on the see-through expansion tank. On earlier models it will be necessary to CAREFULLY remove the radiator cap.

CAUTION: *The radiator coolant is under pressure when hot. To avoid the danger of physical harm, coolant level should be checked or replenished only when the engine is cold. To remove the radiator cap when the engine is hot, first cover the cap with a thick rag, or wear a heavy glove for protection. Press down on the cap slightly and slowly turn it counterclockwise until it reaches the first stop. Allow all the pressure to vent (indicated when the hissing sound stops). When the pressure is released, press down on the cap and continue to rotate it counterclockwise. Some radiator caps have a lever for venting the pressure; lifting the lever will release the pressure, but you should still exercise extreme caution when removing the cap.*

2. Check the level and, as necessary, add coolant to the proper level. Use a 50/50 mix of ethylene glycol antifreeze and water for coolant additions. Alcohol or methanol base coolants are not recommended. Anti-freeze solutions should be used, even in summer, to prevent rust and to take advantage of the solution's higher boiling point compared to plain water. This is imperative on air conditioned trucks; the heater core can freeze if it isn't protected. On 1974–80 models, coolant should be added through the coolant recovery tank, not the radiator filler neck.

CAUTION: *Never add large quantities of cold coolant to a hot engine. A cracked engine block may result.*

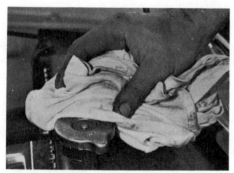
If you must remove the radiator cap when hot, cover the cap with a thick rag

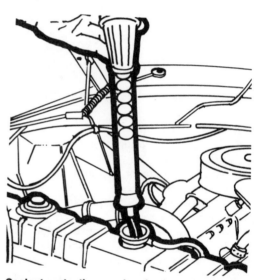
Coolant protection can be checked with a simple float-type tester

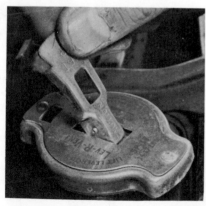
Some radiator caps have levers to vent pressure before the cap is removed

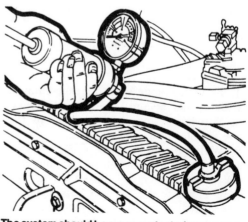
The system should be pressure tested once a year

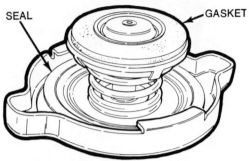

SEAL — GASKET

**Check the radiator cap's rubber gasket and metal seal for deterioration at least once a year**

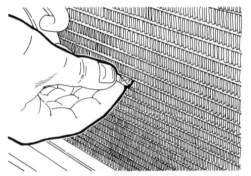

**Remove any debris from the radiator's cooling fins**

3. Replace the cap.

Each year the cooling system should be serviced as follows:

1. Wash the radiator cap and filler neck with clean water.

2. Check the coolant for proper level and freeze protection.

3. Have the system pressure tested (15 psi). If a replacement cap is installed, be sure that it conforms to the original specifications.

4. Tighten the hose clamps and inspect all hoses. Replace hoses that are swollen, cracked or otherwise deteriorated.

5. Clean the frontal area of the radiator core and the air conditioning condenser, if so equipped.

Every 2 years or 24,000 miles, which ever occurs first, the system should be drained and filled as follows:

1. Run the engine with the cap removed and the heater on until operating temperature is reached (indicated by heat in the upper radiator hose).

2. With the engine stopped, open the radiator drain cock located at the bottom of the radiator, and (to speed the draining) the engine block drains, if any. Six cylinder engines have a coolant drain plug on the left side of the engine block; V8s have one on

each side. Some trucks are not equipped with a radiator drain. These radiators can be emptied by siphoning, using the type of siphon used for pilfering gasoline, or coolant can be drained by removing the lower radiator hose.

NOTE: *Do not attempt to siphon coolant by sucking on the end of a hose. The coolant is poisonous and can cause death or serious illness if swallowed.*

3. Completely drain the coolant, and close the drain cocks.

4. Add sufficient clean water to fill the system. Run the engine and drain and refill the system as often as necessary until the drained water is nearly colorless.

5. Add sufficient ethylene glycol coolant to provide the required freezing and corrosion protection (at least a 44% solution protecting to −20° F). Fill the radiator to the cold level. Run the engine with the cap removed until normal operating temperature is reached.

6. Check the hot level.

7. Install the cap.

For problems with engine overheating, see Chapter 3.

## *AXLES*

Locking front hubs should be run in the LOCK position for at least 10 miles each month to assure proper lubrication to the front axle.

Lubricant levels in both axles should be checked as specified in the "Maintenance" chart. To check the lubricant level in both front and rear axles:

1. Park on the level.

2. Remove the filler plug from the differential housing cover.

3. If lubricant trickles out, there is enough. If not, carefully insert a finger and check that the level is up to the bottom of the hole. Front axles should be full up to the level of the hole when warm, and ½ in. below when cold.

4. Lubricant may be added with a funnel and hose or a squeeze bulb. Front axles use SAE 80W-90 GL-5 gear lubricant. Rear axles use SAE 80 GL-5 in cold climates, SAE 90 normally, and SAE 140 in very hot climates.

Positraction® limited slip axles must use a special lubricant available from dealers. If the special fluid is not used, noise, uneven operation, and damage will result. There is also a Positraction® additive to cure noise and slippage. Positraction® axles have an iden-

## How To Spot Bad Hoses

Both the upper and lower radiator hoses are called upon to perform difficult jobs in an inhospitable environment. They are subject to nearly 18 psi at under hood temperatures often over 280°F., and must circulate nearly 7500 gallons of coolant an hour—3 good reasons to have good hoses.

**Swollen hose**

A good test for any hose is to feel it for soft or spongy spots. Frequently these will appear as swollen areas of the hose. The most likely cause is oil soaking. This hose could burst at any time, when hot or under pressure.

**Cracked hose**

Cracked hoses can usually be seen but feel the hoses to be sure they have not hardened; a prime cause of cracking. This hose has cracked down to the reinforcing cords and could split at any of the cracks.

**Frayed hose end (due to weak clamp)**

Weakened clamps frequently are the cause of hose and cooling system failure. The connection between the pipe and hose has deteriorated enough to allow coolant to escape when the engine is hot.

**Debris in cooling system**

Debris, rust and scale in the cooling system can cause the inside of a hose to weaken. This can usually be felt on the outside of the hose as soft or thinner areas.

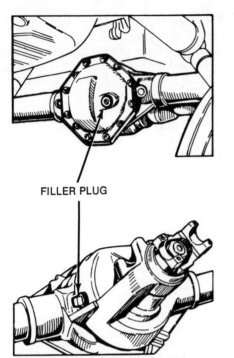

FILLER PLUG

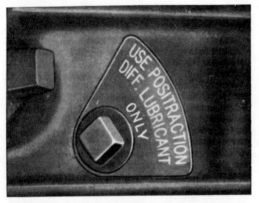

**The rear axle filler plug may be in either of the two locations shown here**

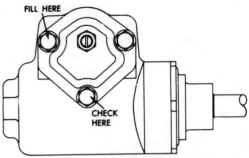

FILL HERE

CHECK HERE

**Steering box lubrication points (© Chevrolet Motor Div.)**

the gear should be filled with Part No. 1051052, which is a 13 oz container of Steering Gear lubricant which meets GM Specification GM 4673M, or its equivalent. Do not use EP Chassis Lube to lubricate the gear and do not overfill.

## POWER STEERING RESERVOIR

The reservoir is part of the belt-driven power steering pump at the front of the engine.

1. Wipe off the cap and surrounding area, after stopping the engine with the wheels straight. On 1970–71 models, the wheels should be all the way to the left.

2. Remove the cap and attached dipstick.

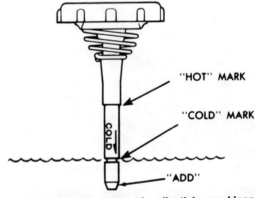

"HOT" MARK

"COLD" MARK

COLD

"ADD"

**Power steering reservoir dipstick markings (© Chevrolet Motor Div.)**

**Positraction® rear axle identification tag (© Chevrolet Motor Div.)**

tifying tag, as well as a warning sticker near the jack or on the rear wheel well.

## STEERING GEAR

The steering gear is factory-filled with a lubricant which does not require seasonal change. The housing should not be drained; no lubrication is required for the life of the gear.

The gear should be inspected for seal leakage when specified in the "Maintenance" chart. Look for solid grease, not an oily film. If a seal is replaced or the gear overhauled,

3. Wipe the dipstick off with a clean, lint-free rag, replace the cap, and take a reading. If the fluid is hot, the level should be between HOT and COLD; if it is cold, it should be between COLD and ADD.

4. Either GM Power Steering Fluid or DEXRON® II Automatic Transmission Fluid may be used.

## Battery

Check the battery fluid level (except in Maintenance Free batteries) at least once a month, more often in hot weather or during extended periods of travel. The electrolyte level should be up to the bottom of the split ring in each cell. All batteries on Chevrolet and GMC trucks are equipped with an "eye" in the cap of one cell. If the "eye" glows or has an amber color to it, this means that the level is low and only distilled water should be added. Do not add anything else to the battery. If the "eye" has a dark appearance the battery electrolyte level is high enough. It is wise to also check each cell individually.

At least once a year, check the specific gravity of the battery. It should be between 1.20–1.26. Clean and tighten the clamps and apply a thin coat of petroleum jelly to the terminals. This will help to retard corrosion. The terminals can be cleaned with a stiff wire brush or with an inexpensive terminal cleaner designed for this purpose.

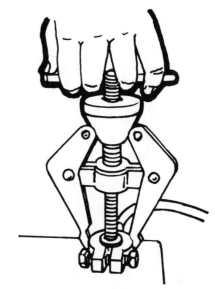

Special pullers are available to remove cable clamps

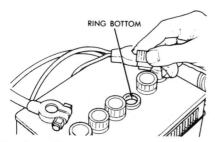

Fill each battery cell to the bottom of the split ring with distilled water

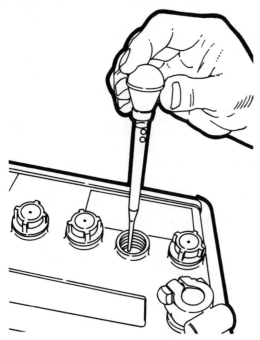

The specific gravity of the battery can be checked with a simple float-type hydrometer

Clean the battery posts with a wire brush, or the special tool shown

Clean the inside of the cable clamp with a wire brush

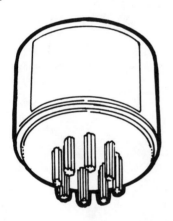

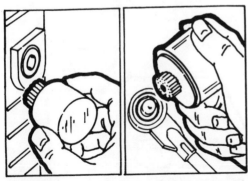

Special tools are available for cleaning the terminals and cable clamps on side terminal batteries

If water is added during freezing weather, the truck should be driven several miles to allow the electrolyte and water to mix. Otherwise the battery could freeze.

If the battery becomes corroded, a solution

## Battery State of Charge at Room Temperature

| Specific Gravity Reading | Charged Condition |
|---|---|
| 1.260–1.280 | Fully Charged |
| 1.230–1.250 | ¾ Charged |
| 1.200–1.220 | ½ Charged |
| 1.170–1.190 | ¼ Charged |
| 1.140–1.160 | Almost no Charge |
| 1.110–1.130 | No Charge |

of baking soda and water will neutralize the corrosion. This should be washed off after making sure that the caps are securely in place. Rinse the solution off with cold water.

Some batteries were equipped with a felt terminal washer. This should be saturated with engine oil approximately every 6,000 miles. This will also help to retard corrosion.

If a "fast" charger is used while the battery is in the truck, disconnect the battery before connecting the charger.

NOTE: *Keep flame or sparks away from the battery; it gives off explosive hydrogen gas.*

### TESTING THE MAINTENANCE-FREE BATTERY

All later model trucks are equipped with maintenance-free batteries, which do not require normal attention as far as fluid level checks are concerned. However, the terminals require periodic cleaning, which should be performed at least once a year.

The sealed-top battery cannot be checked for charge in the normal manner, since there is no provision for access to the electrolyte. To check the condition of the battery:

1. If the indicator eye on top of the battery is dark, the battery has enough fluid. If the eye is light, the electrolyte fluid is too low and the battery must be replaced.

2. If a green dot appears in the middle of the eye, the battery is sufficiently charged. Proceed to Step 4. If no green dot is visible, charge the battery as in Step 3.

3. Charge the battery at this rate:

| Charging Rate Amps | Time |
|---|---|
| 75 | 40 min |
| 50 | 1 hr |
| 25 | 2 hr |
| 10 | 5 hr |

CAUTION: *Do not charge the battery for more than 50 amp/hours. If the green dot appears, or if electrolyte squirts out of the vent hole, stop the charge and proceed to Step 4.*

It may be necessary to tip the battery from side to side to get the green dot to appear after charging.

4. Connect a battery load tester and a voltmeter across the battery terminals (the battery cables should be disconnected from the battery). Apply a 300 amp load to the battery for 15 seconds to remove the surface charge. Remove the load.

5. Wait 15 seconds to allow the battery to recover. Apply the appropriate test load, as specified in the following chart:

| Battery | Test Load |
|---------|-----------|
| Y85-4 | 130 amps |
| R85-5 | 170 amps |
| R87-5 | 210 amps |
| R89-5 | 230 amps |

Apply the load for 15 seconds while reading the voltage. Disconnect the load.

6. Check the results against the following chart. If the battery voltage is at or above the specified voltage for the temperature listed, the battery is good. If the voltage falls below what's listed, the battery should be replaced.

| Temperature (° F) | Minimum Voltage |
|-------------------|-----------------|
| 70 or above | 9.6 |
| 60 | 9.5 |
| 50 | 9.4 |
| 40 | 9.3 |
| 30 | 9.1 |
| 20 | 8.9 |
| 10 | 8.7 |
| 0 | 8.5 |

## Tires and Wheels

The tires should be rotated as specified in the "Maintenance Intervals" chart. Refer to the accompanying illustrations for the recommended rotation patterns.

The tires on your truck should have built-in tread wear indicators, which appear as ½ in. bands when the tread depth gets as low as ¹/₁₆ in. When the indicators appear in 2 or

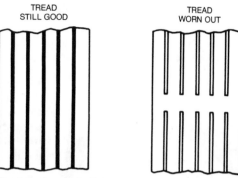

TREAD STILL GOOD    TREAD WORN OUT

**Tire tread wear indicators appear as solid bands when the tire is worn out (© Chevrolet Motor Div.)**

**Tread depth can be checked with a penny; when the top of Lincoln's head is visible, it's time for new tires**

**Tread depth can also be checked with an inexpensive gauge made for the purpose**

more adjacent grooves, it's time for new tires.

For optimum tire life, you should keep the tires properly inflated, rotate them often and have the wheel alignment checked periodically.

Some late models have the maximum load pressures listed on the V.I.N. plate on the left door frame. In general, pressure of 28–32 psi would be suitable for highway use with moderate loads and passenger car type tires (load range B, non-flotation) of original

## How to Read Tire Wear

The way your tires wear is a good indicator of other parts of your car. Abnormal wear patterns are often caused by the need for simple tire maintenance, or for front end alignment.

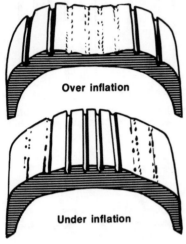

**Over inflation**

Excessive wear at the center of the tread indicates that the air pressure in the tire is consistently too high. The tire is riding on the center of the tread and wearing it prematurely. Occasionally, this wear pattern can result from outrageously wide tires on narrow rims. The cure for this is to replace either the tires or the wheels.

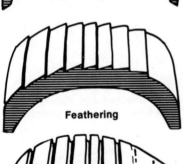

**Under inflation**

This type of wear usually results from consistent under-inflation. When a tire is under inflated, there is too much contact with the road by the outer treads, which wear prematurely. When this type of wear occurs, and the tire pressure is known to be consistently correct, a bent or worn steering component or the need for wheel alignment could be indicated.

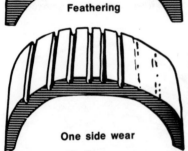

**Feathering**

Feathering is a condition when the edge of each tread rib develops a slightly rounded edge on one side and a sharp edge on the other. By running your hand over the tire, you can usually feel the sharper edges before you'll be able to see them. The most common causes of feathering are incorrect toe-in setting or deteriorated bushings in the front suspension.

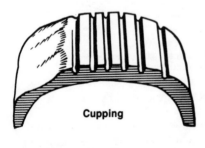

**One side wear**

When an inner or outer rib wears faster than the rest of the tire, the need for wheel alignment is indicated. There is excessive camber in the front suspension, causing the wheel to lean too much putting excessive load on one side of the tire. Misalignment could also be due to sagging springs, worn ball joints, or worn control arm bushings. Be sure the vehicle is loaded the way it's normally driven when you have the wheels aligned.

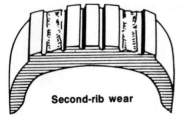

**Cupping**

Cups or scalloped dips appearing around the edge of the tread almost always indicate worn (sometimes bent) suspension parts. Adjustment of wheel alignment alone will seldom cure the problem. Any worn component that connects the wheel to the car can cause this type of wear. Occasionally, wheels that are out of balance will wear like this, but wheel imbalance usually shows up as bald spots between the outside edges and center of the tread.

**Second-rib wear**

Second-rib wear is normally found only in radial tires, and appears where the steel belts end in relation to the tread. Normally, it can be kept to a minimum by paying careful attention to tire pressure and frequently rotating the tires. This is frequently considered normal wear but excessive amounts indicate that the tires are too wide for the wheels.

equipment size. Pressures should be checked before driving, since pressure can increase as much as 6 psi due to heat. It is a good idea to have an accurate gauge and to check pressures weekly. Not all gauges on service station air pumps are to be trusted. In general, truck-type tires require higher pressures and flotation-type tires, lower pressures.

## TIRE ROTATION

It is recommended that you have the tires rotated every 6,000 miles. There is no way to give a tire rotation diagram for every combination of tires and vehicles, but the accompanying diagrams are a general rule to follow. Radial tires should not be cross-switched; they last longer if their direction of rotation is not changed. Truck tires sometimes have directional tread, indicated by arrows on the sidewalls; the arrow shows the direction of rotation. They will wear very rapidly if reversed. Studded snow tires will lose their studs if their direction of rotation is reversed.

NOTE: *Mark the wheel position or direction of rotation on radial tires or studded snow tires before removing them.*

If your truck is equipped with tires having different load ratings on the front and the rear, the tires should not be rotated front to rear. Rotating these tires could affect tire life (the tires with the lower rating will wear faster, and could become overloaded), and upset the handling of the truck.

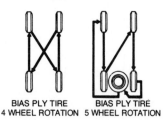

BIAS PLY TIRE          BIAS PLY TIRE
4 WHEEL ROTATION   5 WHEEL ROTATION

**This rotation pattern is for bias or bias-belted tires only (© Chevrolet Motor Div.)**

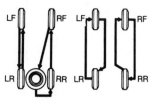

5 WHEEL ROTATION      4 WHEEL ROTATION

**This rotation pattern is for radial tires; it can also be used for bias or bias-belted tires, if you wish. The radial spare can be used on the left side, too, but don't change its direction of rotation, once used (© Chevrolet Motor Div.)**

## TIRE USAGE

The tires on your truck were selected to provide the best all-around performance for normal operation when inflated as specified. Oversize tires (Load Range D) will not increase the maximum carrying capacity of the vehicle, although they will provide an extra margin of tread life. Be sure to check overall height before using larger size tires which may cause interference with suspension components or wheel wells. When replacing conventional tire sizes with other tire size designations, be sure to check the manufacturer's recommendations. Interchangeability is not always possible because of differences in load ratings, tire dimensions, wheel well clearances, and rim size. Also due to differences in handling characteristics, "70 Series" and "60 Series" tires should be used only in pairs on the same axle; radial tires should be used only in sets of four.

The wheels must be the correct width for the tire. Tire dealers have charts of tire and rim compatibility. A mismatch can cause sloppy handling and rapid tread wear. The old rule of thumb is that the tread width should match the rim width (inside bead to inside bead) within an inch. For radial tires, the rim width should be 80% or less of the tire (not tread) width.

The height (mounted diameter) of the new tires can greatly change speedometer accuracy, engine speed at a given road speed, fuel mileage, acceleration, and ground clearance. Tire manufacturers furnish full measurement specifications. Speedometer drive gears are available for correction.

NOTE: *Dimensions of tires marked the same size may vary significantly, even among tires from the same manufacturer.*

The spare tire should be usable, at least for low speed operation, with the new tires.

## TIRE TYPES

For maximum satisfaction, tires should be used in sets of five. Mixing or different types (radial, bias-belted, fiberglass belted) should be avoided. Conventional bias tires are constructed so that the cords run bead-to-bead at an angle. Alternate plies run at an opposite angle. This type of construction gives rigidity to both tread and sidewall. Bias-belted tires are similar in construction to conventional bias ply tires. Belts run at an angle and also at a 90° angle to the bead, as in the radial tire.

## Capacities

| Year | Model | Engine Displacement (cu in.) | Engine Crankcase (qts) | | Transmission (pts) | | | Drive Axle (pts) | | Fuel Tank (gals) | Transfer Case (pts) | Cooling System (qts) | | |
|---|---|---|---|---|---|---|---|---|---|---|---|---|---|---|
| | | | With Filter | Without Filter | Manual 3-spd | 4-spd | Auto (Refill) | Front | Rear | | | w/o A/C | w/A/C | HD |
| 1970 | All w/ | 250 | 5 | 4 | 1.75[1] | 8.0 | [2] | 5 | [3] | 21.5 | 5 | 12.5 | — | — |
| | All w/ | 292 | 6 | 5 | 1.75[1] | 8.0 | [2] | 5 | [3] | 21.5 | 5 | 12.5 | 13.0 | 13.5 |
| | All w/ | 307 | 5 | 4 | 1.75[1] | 8.0 | [2] | 5 | [3] | 21.5 | 5 | 17.5 | 18.5 | 18.0 |
| | All w/ | 350 | 5 | 4 | 1.75[1] | 8.0 | [2] | 5 | [3] | 21.5 | 5 | 17.0 | 18.5 | 18.5 |
| | All w/ | 396 | 5 | 4 | 1.75[1] | 8.0 | [2] | 5 | [3] | 21.5 | 5 | 24.0 | — | 24.5 |
| 1971–72 | All w/ | 250 | 5 | 4 | 3.5 | 7.0 | [2] | 5 | [3] | 20.2[4] | 5 | 12.2 | 12.9 | 12.9 |
| | All w/ | 292 | 6 | 5 | 3.5 | 7.0 | [2] | 5 | [3] | 20.2[4] | 5 | 12.6 | 13.3 | 13.3 |
| | All w/ | 307 | 5 | 4 | 3.5 | 7.0 | [2] | 5 | [3] | 20.2[4] | 5 | 16.0 | 16.0 | 16.0 |
| | All w/ | 350 | 5 | 4 | 3.5 | 7.0 | [2] | 5 | [3] | 20.2[4] | 5 | 16.2 | 17.7 | 17.7 |
| | All w/ | 402 | 5 | 4 | 3.5 | 7.0 | [2] | 5 | [3] | 20.2[4] | 5 | 23.2 | 24.7 | 24.7 |
| 1973–74 | All w/ | 250 | 5 | 4 | 3.5 | 7.0 | [2] | 5 | [6] | 20[10] | 5[5] | 12.2 | 12.5 | 12.5 |
| | All w/ | 292 | 6 | 5 | 3.5 | 7.0 | [2] | 5 | [6] | 20[10] | 5[5] | 12.6 | 13.3 | 13.3 |
| | All w/ | 307 | 5 | 4 | 3.5 | 7.0 | [2] | 5 | [6] | 20[10] | 5[5] | 16.0 | 16.0 | 16.0 |
| | All w/ | 350, 400 | 5 | 4 | 3.5 | 7.0 | [2] | 5 | [6] | 20[10] | 5[5] | 16.2 | 17.7 | 17.7 |
| | All w/ | 454 | 5 | 4 | 3.5 | 7.0 | [2] | 5 | [6] | 20[10] | 5[5] | 18.5 | 21.0 | 21.0 |

| | | | | | | | | | | | | |
|---|---|---|---|---|---|---|---|---|---|---|---|---|
| **1975** | | | | | | | | | | | | |
| All w/ 250 | 5 | 4 | 3.2 ⑦ | 8.3 | ② | 5 | ⑥ | 20 ⑩ | 5 ⑤ | 14.8 | 15.4 | 14.8 |
| All w/ 292 | 6 | 5 | 3.2 ⑦ | 8.3 | ② | 5 | ⑥ | 20 ⑩ | 5 ⑤ | 14.8 | 15.6 | 14.8 |
| All w/ 350 | 5 | 4 | 3.2 ⑦ | 8.3 | ② | 5 | ⑥ | 20 ⑩ | 5 ⑤ | 17.6 | 18.0 | 18.0 |
| All w/ 400 | 5 | 4 | 3.2 ⑦ | 8.3 | ② | 5 | ⑥ | 20 ⑩ | 5 ⑤ | 19.6 | 20.4 | 20.4 |
| All w/ 454 | 5 | 4 | 3.2 ⑦ | 8.3 | ② | 5 | ⑥ | 20 ⑩ | 5 ⑤ | 24.8 | 24.8 | 24.8 |
| **1976–80** | | | | | | | | | | | | |
| All w/ 250 | 5 | 4 | 3.2 ⑦ | 8.0 | ② | 5 ⑧ | ⑥ | 20 ⑩ | 5 ⑤ | 15.0 | 15.6 | 15.0 |
| All w/ 292 | 6 | 5 | 3.2 ⑦ | 8.0 | ② | 5 ⑧ | ⑥ | 20 ⑩ | 5 ⑤ | 14.8 | 15.4 | 14.8 |
| All w/ 305 | 5 | 4 | 3.2 ⑦ | 8.0 | ② | 5 ⑧ | ⑥ | 20 ⑩ | 5 ⑤ | 17.6 | 18.0 | 18.0 |
| All w/ 350 | 5 | 4 | 3.2 ⑦ | 8.0 | ② | 5 ⑧ | ⑥ | 20 ⑩ | 5 ⑤ | 17.6 | 18.0 | 18.0 |
| All w/ 350 Diesel | 7 | 6 | — | — | 5.0 | — | ⑥ | 20 ⑩ | — | 18.0 | 18.0 | 18.0 |
| All w/ 400 | 5 | 4 | 3.2 ⑦ | 8.0 | ② | 5 ⑧ | ⑥ | 20 ⑩ | 5 ⑤ | 20.4 | 20.4 | 20.4 |
| All w/ 454 | 5 ⑪ | 4 ⑪ | 3.2 ⑦ | 8.0 | ② | 5 ⑧ | ⑥ | 20 ⑩ | 5 ⑤ | 24.4 ⑨ | 24.7 | 24.7 |

① Heavy-duty 3-speed—3.5 pts
② Powerglide—4.0 pts
   Turbo Hydra-Matic 350—5.0 pts
   Turbo Hydra-Matic 400—7.5 pts
③ 3,300 and 3,500 lb Chevrolet axles—4.5 pts
   5,200 and 7,200 lb Chevrolet axles—6.5 pts
   5,500 lb Dana axles—6.0 pts
   11,000 lb Chevrolet axles—14.0 pts
④ 20 Series—21.0 gals
⑤ Full-time 4 wd—8.25 pts

⑥ 8½ in. ring gear—4.2 pts
   8⅞ in. ring gear (Chevrolet)—4.5 pts (3.5 pts 1977–78)
   10½ in. ring gear (Chevrolet)—5.4 pts
   10½ in. ring gear (Dana)—7.2 pts
   12½ in. ring gear (Chevrolet)—14.0 pts
⑦ Tremec 3-spd—4.0 pts
   Muncie 3-spd—3.0 pts
⑧ 8½ in. ring gear—4.25 pts (1977–80)
⑨ 22.8—1979–80
⑩ 16.0 gal—short wheelbase models
⑪ 6 qts with filter, 5 qts without filter, 1978–80

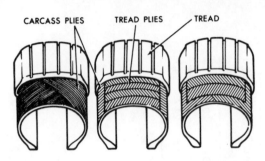

CARCASS PLIES    TREAD PLIES    TREAD

BIAS    BELTED RADIAL    BELTED BIAS

Types of tire construction (© Chevrolet Motor Div.)

## Wheel Nut Torque Chart
All specifications in ft lbs

| Year | C-10, C-1500 | K-10, K-1500 | C-20, C-2500 K-20, K-2500 |
|---|---|---|---|
| 1970 | 55–75 | 55–75 | 65–90 |
| 1971–74 | 65–90 | 55–75 | 90–120 |
| 1975–80 | 75–100 | 70–90 | 90–120 |

Tread life is improved considerably over the conventional bias tire. The radial tire differs in construction, but instead of the carcass plies running at an angle of 90° to each other, they run at an angle of 90° to the bead. This gives the tread a great deal of rigidity and the sidewall a great deal of flexibility and accounts for the characteristic bulge associated with radial tires.

Chevrolet and GMC trucks are capable of using radial tires and they are recommended in some years. If they are used, tire sizes and wheel diameters should be selected to maintain ground clearance and tire load capacity equivalent to the minimum specified tire. Radial tires should always be used in sets of five, but in an emergency radial tires can be used with caution on the rear axle only. If this is done, both tires on the rear should be of radial design.

NOTE: *Radial tires should never be used on only the front axle.*

CAUTION: *Radial tires must not be mounted on 16.5 in. rims unless the rims are stamped with the word "Radial". Ordinary rims are not strong enough to withstand the additional side loads.*

Snow tires should not be operated at sustained speeds over 70 mph.

On four wheel drive trucks, all tires must be of the same size, type, and tread pattern, to provide even traction on loose surfaces, to prevent driveline bind when conventional four wheel drive is used, and to prevent excessive wear on the center differential with full time four wheel drive.

### WHEEL NUT TORQUES

On a new vehicle, or after the wheels have been changed or rotated, the wheel nut torque should be checked at 100, 1,000, and 6,000 mile intervals. To avoid distortion of brake rotors on disc brake models, torque the wheels to the figures given in the chart above. Tighten the wheels in a criss-cross pattern.

## Fuel Filter

### Gasoline Engines

The fuel filter should be serviced at the interval given on the "Maintenance Interval" chart. Two types of fuel filters are used in the carburetor body, a bronze type and a paper element type. Either one may be encountered at any given time. However, the replacement filter should be of the same type as the one removed. Inline fuel filters may be used on some engines which should be changed at the same time as the filter in the carburetor body. Filter replacement should be attempted only when the engine is cold. Additionally, it is a good idea to place some absorbent rags under the fuel fittings to catch the gasoline which will spill out when the lines are loosened. To replace the filter found in the carburetor body:

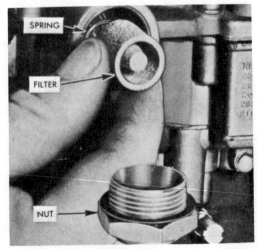

SPRING

FILTER

NUT

A bronze fuel filter is used on earlier trucks (© Chevrolet Motor Div.)

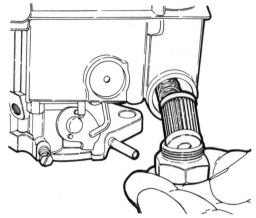

**Most carburetors use a paper element fuel filter**

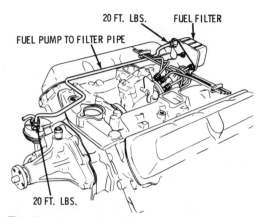

**The diesel engine fuel filter is located at the rear of the engine (© Chevrolet Motor Div.)**

1. Disconnect the fuel line connection at the intake fuel filter nut. Plug the opening to prevent loss of fuel.

2. Remove the intake fuel filter nut from the carburetor with a 1 in. box wrench or socket.

3. Remove the filter element and spring.

4. Check the element for restrictions by blowing on the cone end. Air should pass freely.

5. Clean or replace the element, as necessary.

6. Install the element spring, then the filter element in the carburetor. Bronze filters should have the small section of the cone facing out.

7. Install a new gasket on the intake fuel nut. Install the nut in the carburetor body and tighten securely.

8. Install the fuel line and tighten the connector.

Some trucks may have an inline filter. This is a can-shaped device located in the fuel line between the pump and the carburetor. It may be made of either plastic or metal. To replace the filter:

1. Place some absorbent rags under the filter; remember, it will be full of gasoline when removed.

2. Use a pair of pliers to expand the clamp on one end of the filter, then slide the clamp down past the point to which the filter pipe extends in the rubber hose. Do the same with the other clamp.

3. Gently twist and pull the hoses free of the filter pipes. Remove and discard the old filter.

4. Install the new filter into the hoses, slide the clamps back into place, and check for leaks with the engine idling.

### Diesel Engines

The diesel fuel filter is mounted on a bracket at the top rear of the engine. It is replaced as a unit every 24,000 miles.

1. Unbolt the fuel pump line at the filter inlet (upper corner of the filter).

2. Unbolt the injector pump line at the lower corner of the fuel filter.

3. Loosen the center bolt holding the filter to the bracket, and remove the filter.

Installation is the reverse of removal. Tighten the two fuel line nuts to 20 ft lbs, and check for leaks.

## LUBRICATION

### Oil and Fuel Recommendations
#### Engine Oil

The SAE grade number indicates the viscosity of the engine oil, or its ability to lubricate under a given temperature. The lower the SAE grade number, the lighter the oil; the lower the viscosity, the easier it is to crank the engine in cold weather.

The API (American Petroleum Institute) designation indicates the classification of engine oil for use under given operating conditions. Only oils designated for "Service SE" (old designation MS) should be used. These oils provide maximum engine protection. Both the SAE grade number and the API designation can be found on the top of a can of oil.

NOTE: *Non-detergent or straight mineral oils should not be used.*

Oil viscosities should be chosen from those oils recommended for the lowest anticipated temperatures during the oil change interval.

The oil sequence test symbol can be found on the top of the can; all engines must use SE quality oil. Diesels must use SE/CC

The multi-viscosity oils offer the important advantage of being adaptable to temperature extremes. They allow easy starting at low temperatures, yet give good protection at high speeds and engine temperatures. This is a decided advantage in changeable climates or in long distance touring.

NOTE: *If your gasoline engine takes a long time to build up oil pressure after starting in warm weather, when using either 10W-30 or 10W-40 oil, the problem can often be solved by switching to 20W-40.*

## Gasoline Engine Oil Viscosity Chart

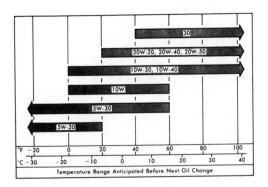

(© Chevrolet Motor Div.)

NOTES: 1. SAE 5W and 5W-20 are not recommended for sustained high speed driving.
2. SAE 5W-30 is recommended for all seasons in Canada

Diesel engines also require SE engine oil. In addition, the oil must qualify for a CC rating. The API has a number of different diesel engine ratings, including CB, CC, and CD. The diesel engine in the Chevrolet and GMC pick-ups requires SE/CC rated oil. DO NOT use an oil if the designation CD appears anywhere on the oil can. Use SE/CC engine oil

only. Do not use an oil labeled only SE or only CC. Both designations must appear.

For recommended oil viscosities, refer to the chart. Note that 10W-30 grade oils are not recommended for sustained high speed driving when temperatures rise above freezing.

## Fuels

### GASOLINE ENGINES

**1970–74 and 1975–80 Models Without Catalytic Converter**

Chevrolet and GMC trucks are designed to operate on regular grades of fuel (1970–71) commonly sold in the U.S. and Canada. In 1972–74 (and 1975–80 models without a catalytic converter), unleaded or low-lead fuels of approximately 91 octane (Research Octane) or higher are recommended. General Motors recommends the use of low-leaded or unleaded fuels (0–0.5 grams per gallon) to reduce particulate and hydrocarbon pollutants. In states using the Gasoline Performance and Information system of fuel designation, unleaded or low-lead fuels with an anti-knock designation of "2" or higher are recommended.

Use of a fuel which is too low in anti-knock quality will result in "spark knock." Since many factors affect operating efficiency, such as altitude, terrain and air temperature, knocking may result even though you are using the recommended fuel. If persistent knocking occurs, it may be necessary to switch to a slightly higher grade of gasoline to correct the problem. In the case of late model engines, switching to a premium fuel would be an unnecessary expense. In these engines, a slightly higher grade of gasoline (regular) should be used only when persistent knocking occurs. Continuous or excessive knocking may result in engine damage, for which Chevrolet (or GMC) is not responsible.

NOTE: *Your engine's fuel requirement can change with time, mainly due to carbon buildup, which changes the compression ratio. If your engine pings, knocks, or runs on, switch to a higher grade of fuel and check the ignition timing as soon as possible. If you must use unleaded fuel, sometimes a change of brands will cure the*

## Diesel Engine Oil Viscosity Chart

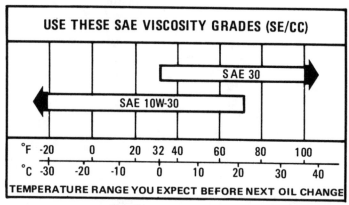

(© Chevrolet Motor Div.)

*problem. If it is necessary to retard the timing from specifications, don't change it more than about four degrees. Retarded timing will reduce power output and fuel mileage, and it will increase engine temperature.*

### 1975–80 Models With Catalytic Converter

Chevrolet and GMC trucks with Gross Vehicle Weight Ratings (GVWR) which place them in the heavy-duty emissions class do not require a catalytic converter. However, almost all 1975 and later light-duty emissions trucks have a catalytic converter. The light-duty classification applies to all trucks with a GVWR under 6,000 lbs through 1978, except for 1978 trucks sold in California. 1978 California models and all 1979 models with GVWR's under 8,500 lbs fall into the light-duty category. In 1980, the light-duty classification applies to all trucks with GVWR's under 8,600 lbs.

The catalytic converter is a muffler-shaped device installed in the exhaust system. It contains platinum and palladium coated pellets which, through catalytic action, oxidize hydrocarbon and carbon monoxide gases into harmless hydrogen, oxygen, and carbon dioxide.

The design of the converter requires the exclusive use of unleaded fuel. Leaded fuel renders the converter inoperative, raising exhaust emissions to illegal levels. In addition, the lead in the gasoline coats the pellets in the converter, blocking the flow of exhaust gases. This raises exhaust back pressure and severely reduces engine performance. In extreme cases, the exhaust system becomes so blocked that the engine will not run.

Converter-equipped trucks are delivered with the label "Unleaded Fuel Only" conspicuously placed next to the fuel gauge on the instrument panel and next to the gas tank filler opening. In general, any unleaded fuel is suitable for use in these trucks as long as the gas has an octane rating of 87 or more. Octane ratings are posted on the gas pumps. However, in some cases, knocking may occur even though the recommended fuel is being used. The only practical solution for this is to switch to a slightly higher grade of unleaded fuel, or to switch brands of unleaded gasoline.

### DIESEL ENGINES

Diesel-engined pick-ups require the use of diesel fuel. Two grades of diesel fuel are manufactured, #1 and #2, although #2 grade is generally the only grade available. Better fuel economy results from the use of #2 grade fuel. In some northern parts of the U.S., and in most parts of Canada, #1 grade fuel is available in winter, or a winterized blend of #2 grade is supplied in winter months. If #1 grade is available, it should be used whenever temperatures fall below 20° F (−7° C). Winterized #2 grade may also be used at these temperatures. However, unwinterized #2 grade should *not* be used below 20° F (−7° C). Cold temperatures cause unwinterized #2 grade to thicken (it actually gels), blocking the fuel lines and preventing the engine from running.

Do not use home heating oil or gasoline in the diesel pick-up. Do not attempt to "thin" unwinterized #2 diesel fuel with gasoline. Gasoline or home heating oil will damage the engine and void the manufacturer's warranty.

## Operation in Foreign Countries

### GASOLINE ENGINES

If you plan to drive your truck outside the United States or Canada, there is a possibility that fuels will be too low in anti-knock quality and could produce engine damage. Send Chevrolet or GMC Owner Relations Department the Vehicle Identification Number, compression ratio of your engine and the countries in which you plan to operate and they will send you details of adjustments or modifications that can be made to your engine. It is also wise to consult with local authorities upon arrival in a foreign country to determine the best fuels available.

## Lubricant Changes

### ENGINE OIL

Engine oil should be changed according to the schedule in the "Maintenance Interval Chart." Under conditions such as:
  —Driving in dusty conditions,
  —Continuous trailer pulling or RV use,
  —Extensive or prolonged idling,
  —Extensive short trip operation in freezing temperatures (when the engine is not thoroughly warmed-up),
  —Frequent long runs at high speeds and high ambient temperatures, and
  —Stop-and-go service such as delivery trucks,
the oil change interval and filter replacement interval should be cut in half. Operation of the engine in severe conditions such as a dust storm may require an immediate oil and filter change.

Except for the first oil change, the factory recommends that the oil filter be replaced every other oil change (except for diesels). But, if you do this you are leaving 1 quart of dirty oil in the system for at least 12,000 miles.

To change the oil, the truck should be on a level surface, and the engine should be at operating temperature. This is to ensure that the foreign matter will be drained away along with the oil, and not left in the engine to form sludge, which would happen if the oil is drained cold. Oil that is slightly brownish when drained is a good sign that the contaminants are being drained away. You should have available a container that will hold a minimum of 8 quarts of liquid, a wrench to fit the oil drain plug, a spout for pouring in new oil, and a rag or two, which

you will always need. If the filter is being replaced, you will also need a band wrench or filter wrench to fit the end of the filter.

NOTE: *If the engine is equipped with an oil cooler, this will also have to be drained, using the drain plug. Be sure to add enough oil to fill the cooler in addition to the engine.*

1. Position the truck on a level surface and set the parking brake or block the wheels. Slide a drain pan under the oil drain plug.

2. From under the truck, loosen, but do not remove the oil drain plug. Cover your hand with a heavy rag or glove and slowly unscrew the drain plug, pushing the plug against the threads to prevent oil from leaking past the threads.

CAUTION: *The engine oil will be HOT. Keep your arms, face and hands clear of the oil as it drains out.*

3. As the drain plug comes to the end of the threads, whisk it away from the hole, letting the oil drain into the pan, which hopefully is still under the drain hole. This method usually avoids the messy task of reaching into a tub of hot, dirty oil to retrieve a drain plug, which is never where you think it is. Crawl out from under the truck and wait for the oil to drain.

4. When all of the oil has drained, clean off the drain plug and put it back into the hole. Torque it to 20 ft lbs (30 ft lbs on diesels).

The oil drain plug is located at the lowest point of the engine oil pan

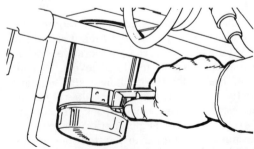

Use a strap wrench to loosen the oil filter; install the new filter by hand

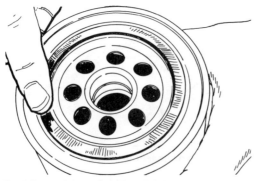

**Coat the gasket on the new oil filter with a film of oil**

5. Change the filter as necessary or desired. Loosen the filter with a band wrench or special oil filter cap wrench. On most Chevrolet engines, especially the V8s, the oil filter is next to the exhaust pipes. Stay clear of these, since even a passing contact will result in a painful burn.

NOTE: *On trucks equipped with catalytic converters stay clear of the converter. The outside temperature of a hot catalytic converter can approach 1200° F.*

If someone has put the filter on so tightly that it collapses under the pressure of the wrench, drive a punch or a long nail across the diameter of the filter near its end, and use this as a lever to remove it.

If a replaceable element filter is used, remove the bolt holding the housing and carefully remove the housing and element. Throw the element away and clean the housing, and install a new element. Reinstall the housing.

6. Cover your hand with a heavy rag, the same one you used previously will do, and spin the filter off by hand, being careful of the 1 quart of hot oil which inevitably overflows the filter.

7. Coat the rubber gasket on a new filter with a light film of clean engine oil. Screw the filter onto the mounting stud and tighten according to the directions on the filter (usually hand-tight one turn past the point where the gasket contacts the mounting base). Don't overtighten the filter or you'll be punching holes in it to remove it the next time.

8. Refill the engine with the specified amount of clean engine oil. Oil is poured into the engine through the openings in the valve cover(s), or the capped oil fill tube on diesel engines.

9. Run the engine for several minutes, checking for leaks. Check the level of the oil

and compensate (as necessary) for oil absorbed by a new filter.

When you have finished this job, you will notice that you now possess four or five quarts of rather filthy oil. The best thing to do with it is to pour it into plastic jugs, such as milk or antifreeze containers. Then, if you are on good terms with your gas station man, he might let your pour it into his used oil container for recycling. Otherwise, the only thing to do with it is to put the containers into the trash barrel.

## MANUAL TRANSMISSION

No intervals are specified for changing the transmission lubricant, but it is a good idea on a used vehicle, one that has been worked hard, or one driven in deep water. The vehicle should be on a level surface and the lubricant should be at operating temperature.

1. Position the truck on a level surface.
2. Place a pan of sufficient capacity under the transmission drain plug.
3. Remove the upper (fill) plug to provide a vent opening.
4. Remove the lower (drain) plug and let the lubricant drain out. The 1976–80 Tremec top-cover three speed is drained by removing the lower extension housing bolt.
5. Replace the drain plug.
6. Add lubricant with a suction gun or squeeze bulb. The correct lubricant is SAE 80W-90 GL-5 Gear Lubricant, or SAE 80W GL-5 for cold climates.
7. Reinstall the filler plug. Run the engine and check for leaks.

## AUTOMATIC TRANSMISSION

The fluid should be drained with the transmission warm. It is easier to change the fluid if the truck is raised somewhat from the ground, but this is not always easy without a lift. The transmission must be level for it to drain properly.

1. Place a shallow pan underneath to catch the transmission fluid (about 5 pints). On earlier models, the transmission pan has a drain plug. Remove this and drain the fluid. For later models, loosen all the pan bolts, then pull one corner down to drain most of the fluid. If it sticks, VERY CAREFULLY pry the pan loose with a screwdriver. You can buy aftermarket drain plug kits that make this operation a bit less messy, once installed.

NOTE: *If the fluid removed smells burnt, serious transmission troubles, probably due to overheating, should be suspected.*

2. Remove the pan screws and empty out the pan. On some models, there may not be much room to get at the screws at the front of the pan.

3. Clean the pan without solvent and allow it to air dry. If you use a rag to wipe it out, you risk leaving bits of lint and threads in the transmission.

4. Remove the filter or strainer retaining bolts. On the Turbo Hydra-Matic 400, there are two screws securing the filter or screen to the valve body. A reusable strainer may be found on some models. The strainer may be cleaned in solvent and air dried thoroughly. The filter and gasket must be replaced.

5. Install a new gasket and filter.

6. Install a new gasket on the pan, and tighten the bolts evenly to 12 foot pounds in a criss-cross pattern.

**Install the new gasket to the pan**

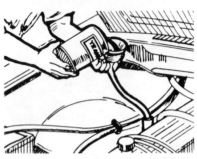

**Transmission fluid is added through the dipstick tube**

7. Add DEXRON® or DEXRON® II transmission fluid through the dipstick tube. The correct amount is in the Capacities Chart. Do not overfill.

8. With the gearshift lever in PARK, start the engine and let it idle. Do not race the engine.

9. Move the gearshift lever through each position, holding the brakes. Return the lever to PARK, and check the fluid level with the engine idling. The level should be between the two dimples on the dipstick, about ¼ in. below the ADD mark. Add fluid, if necessary.

10. Check the fluid level after the truck has been driven enough to thoroughly warm up the transmission. Details are given under Fluid Level Checks earlier in the Chapter. If the transmission is overfilled, the excess must be drained off. Overfilling causes aerated fluid, resulting in transmission slippage and probable damage.

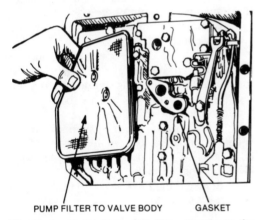

PUMP FILTER TO VALVE BODY          GASKET

**The Turbo Hydra-Matic 350 filter mounts to the valve body**

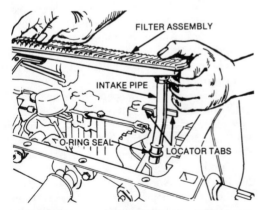

FILTER ASSEMBLY

INTAKE PIPE

O-RING SEAL          LOCATOR TABS

**The Turbo Hydra-Matic 400 filter has an O-ring on the intake pipe; check the condition of this O-ring, and replace as necessary**

### TRANSFER CASE

#### Part Time Systems

No intervals are specified for changing transfer case lubricant, but it is a good idea for trucks that are worked hard or driven in deep water.

1. With the transfer case warmed up, park on a level surface.

2. Slide a pan of at least 6 pts. capacity under the case drain plug.

3. Remove the filler plug from the rear of the transfer case (behind the transmission). Remove the drain plug from the bottom.

4. Wipe the area clean and replace the drain plug.

5. Add lubricant with a suction gun or squeeze bulb. Conventional transfer cases require SAE 80W or SAE 80W-90 GL-5 Gear Lubricant (SAE 80W GL-5 in cold climates).

6. When the lubricant level is up to the bottom of the filler hole, replace the plug.

### Full Time Four Wheel Drive

The full time system requires oil changes at regular intervals, according to the amount and type of work done by the unit. Trucks used for normal on-off road work should have the transfer case oil changed at 24,000 mile intervals. When used for heavy duty work, trailer towing, snowplowing, and the like, the interval should be halved to 12,000 miles. If the truck is exposed to extremely dusty or muddy conditions, as in mining operations, the oil should be changed at 1,000 mile intervals. Chevrolet and GMC recommend that the oil be changed immediately after use in rice fields, deep water, or extreme wet conditions.

The transfer case oil must be hot before changing. Drive the truck until the engine has reached normal operating temperature, and park on a level surface.

1. Slide a pan of at least 8 pts. capacity under the case drain plug.

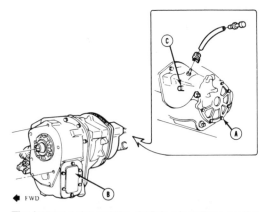

The letters point out the draining locations on the full time four wheel drive transfer case. Letter A indicates the lowest bolt in the rear cover, B indicates the P.T.O. cover, and C shows the location of the speedometer driven gear. Use a suction gun at locations B and C (© Chevrolet Motor Div.)

2. Remove the filler plug.

3. Remove the lowest bolt from the front output shaft rear bearing retainer cover, and allow the lubricant to drain, Be careful—the oil will be hot. There may be a drain plug. If so, remove that instead.

4. Remove the six bolts on the left (driver's) side of the case whch secure the P.T.O. (power take-off) cover. Remove this cover and allow the lubricant to drain out.

5. Remove the speedometer driven gear from the upper left rear corner of the case.

6. Use a suction gun to remove as much lubricant as possible from the case cover location and the speedometer gear location.

7. Install the speedometer driven gear, the P.T.O. cover, and the lowest bolt or drain plug.

8. Add approximately seven pints of oil through the filler plug opening. The proper oil to use is 10W-30 or 10W-40 engine oil.

9. Check the fluid level and add sufficient oil to raise the level to ½ in. below the filler plug opening. Replace the plug, and wipe the surfaces of the case and skid plate to remove any excess oil. Drive the truck and check for leaks.

### AXLES

No intervals are specified for changing axle lubricant, but it is a good idea, especially if you have driven in water over the axle vents. If you got in this deep, you probably got your feet wet.

1. Park the vehicle on the level with the axles at normal operating temperature.

2. Place a pan of at least 6 pints capacity under the differential housing.

3. Remove the filler plug.

4. If you have a drain plug, remove it. If not, unbolt and remove the differential cover.

5. Replace the drain plug, or differential cover with a new gasket.

6. Lubricant may be added with a suction gun or squeeze bulb. Front axles use SAE 90 GL-5 Gear Lubricant; in cold climates, SAE 80. Fill front axles to ½ in. below the filler plug opening. Rear axles use SAE 80 in cold climates, SAE 90 normally, and SAE 140 in very hot climates. Positraction limited slip axles must use special lubricant available from dealers. If the special fluid is not used, noise, uneven operation, and damage will result. There is also a Positraction additive used to cure noise and slippage. Positraction axles have an identifying tag, as well as a

warning sticker near the jack or on the rear wheel well. Rear axle lubricant level should be up to the bottom of the filler plug opening.

NOTE: *The 1974–80 locking differential does not require special lubricant.*

## CHASSIS GREASING

The lubrication charts show the points to be lubricated. Not all vehicles have all the fittings illustrated. For example, most trucks don't have grease fittings on the driveshaft universal joints; the fittings on the shafts are for lubricating the sliding splines.

The four wheel drive front driveshaft requires special attention for lubrication. The large constant velocity joint at the front of the transfer case has a special grease fitting in the centering ball; a special needle nose adapter for a flush type fitting is required, as well as a special lubricant, GM part no. 1050679. You can only get at this fitting when it is facing up toward the floorboards, so you need a flexible hose, too. To lubricate the sliding splines in the Dana type front driveshaft properly, first unscrew and slide back the spline seal collar. Pump chassis grease into the fitting until it oozes out the vent hole, then plug the vent hole with your finger and pump in grease until it comes out past the seal. This isn't necessary on the GM style driveshaft, which has the grease fitting closer to the seal collar.

Water resistant EP chasis lubricant (grease) conforming to GM specification 6031-M should be used for all chassis grease points.

## WHEEL BEARINGS

Only front wheel bearings require periodic service. A premium high melting point grease meeting GM specification 6031-M must be used. Long fiber or viscous type greases should not be used. This service is recommended at the intervals in the Maintenance Intervals chart or whenever the truck has been driven in water up to the hubs.

### Two Wheel Drive

1. Remove the wheel and tire assembly, and the brake drum or brake caliper. See Chapter 9 for details.

2. Remove the hub and disc as an assembly. Remove the caliper mounting bolts and insert a block between the brake pads as the caliper is removed. Remove the caliper and wire it out of the way.

3. Pry out the grease cap, remove the cotter pin, spindle nut, and washer, and then remove the hub. Be careful that you do not drop the wheel bearings.

4. Remove the outer roller bearing assembly from the hub. The inner bearing assembly will remain in the hub and may be removed after prying out the inner seal. Discard this seal.

5. Clean all parts in solvent and allow to air dry. Check the parts for excessive wear or damage.

6. If the bearing cups are worn or scored, they must be replaced. Using a hammer and a drift, remove the bearing cups from the hub. When installing new cups, make sure that they are not cocked, and that they are fully seated against the hub shoulder.

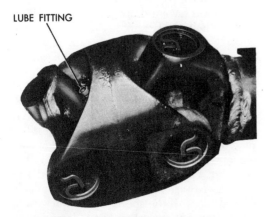

The front driveshaft constant velocity joint grease fitting must face up (toward the underbody) so that a needle nose adapter can be inserted (© Chevrolet Motor Div.)

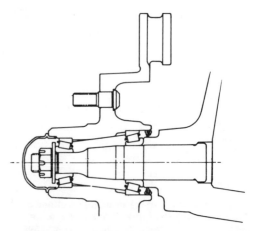

Cut away view of two wheel drive front wheel bearings. The dust cap is on the left, and the grease seal on the right (© Chevrolet Motor Div.)

7. Pack both wheel bearings using high melting point wheel bearing grease made for disc brakes. Ordinary grease will melt and ooze out, ruining the pads. Use this grease even if you have drum brakes; its high temperature capability provides an extra margin of protection. Place a healthy glob of grease in the palm of one hand and force the edge of the bearing into it so that the grease fills the bearing. Do this until the whole bearing is packed. Grease packing tools are available to make this job a lot less messy. There are also tools which make it possible to grease the inner bearing without removing it or the disc from the spindle.

8. Place the inner bearing in the hub and install a new inner seal, making sure that the seal flange faces the bearing cup.

9. Carefully install the wheel hub over the spindle.

10. Using your hands, firmly press the outer bearing into the hub. Install the spindle washer and nut.

11. To adjust the bearings on 1970–71 models, tighten the adjusting nut to 15 ft lbs while rotating the hub. Back the nut off one flat ($1/6$ turn) and insert a new cotter pin. If the nut and spindle hole do not align, back the nut off slightly. There should be 0.001–0.008 in. end play in the bearing. This can be measured with a dial indicator, if you wish. Install the dust cap, wheel, and tire.

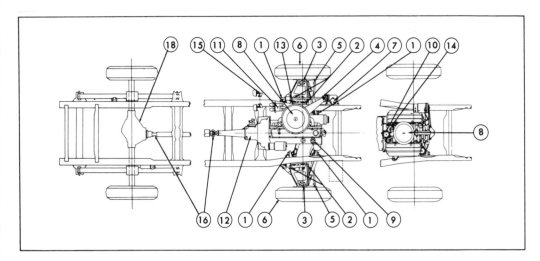

| No. | Lubrication Points | Lubrication Period | Type of Lubrication | Quantity | Remarks |
|---|---|---|---|---|---|
| 1 | Lower Control Arms | 6,000 Miles | Chassis Lubricant | 4 places as required | |
| 2 | Upper Control Arms | 6,000 Miles | Chassis Lubricant | 4 places as required | |
| 3 | Upper and Lower Control Arm Ball Joints | 6,000 Miles | Chassis Lubricant | 4 places as required | |
| 4 | Intermediate Steering Shaft (PA10) | 6,000 Miles | Chassis Lubricant | 2 places as required | |
| 5 | Tie Rod Ends | 6,000 Miles | Chassis Lubricant | 4 places as required | |
| 6 | Wheel Bearings | 24,000 Miles | Whl. Brg. Lubricant | 2 places as required | |
| 7 | Steering Gear | 36,000 Miles | | | Check for Grease Leak— Do not Lubricate |
| 8 | Air Cleaner — Element | 12,000 Miles | | | See Vehicle Maintenance Schedule |
| 9 | Distributor — L-6 | 24,000 Miles | | | Replace cam lubricator* |
| 10 | Distributor — V-8 | 24,000 Miles | | | Replace cam lubricator* |
| 11 | Master Cylinder | 6,000 Miles | Delco Supreme No. 11 or DOT-3 fluids | As required | Check — add fluid when necessary |
| 12 | Transmission — Manual — Automatic | 6,000 Miles 6,000 Miles | GL-5 Dexron® or equivalent | As required As required | Keep even w/filler plug. See Lubrication Section |
| 13 | Throttle Bell Crank — L-6 | 12,000 Miles | Engine Oil | As required | |
| 14 | Carburetor Linkage — V-8 | 12,000 Miles | Engine Oil | As required | |
| 15 | Brake and Clutch Pedal Springs | 6,000 Miles | Engine Oil | As required | |
| 16 | Universal Joints | 6,000 Miles | Chassis Lubricant | As required | |
| 17 | Propeller Shaft Slip Joint | 6,000 Miles | Chassis Lubricant | As required | Not shown |
| 18 | Rear Axle | 6,000 Miles | GL-5 | As required | Check See Lubrication section |

*Replace Points at 12,000 mile intervals.

**Typical lubrication diagram—two wheel drive models (© CHEVROLET Motor Div.)**

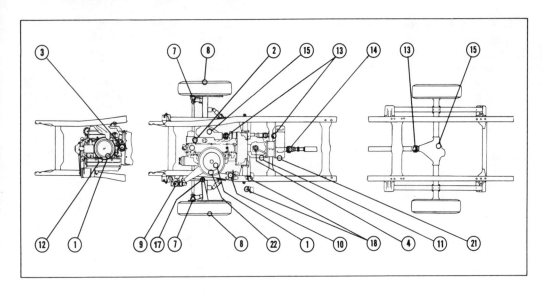

| No. | Lubrication Points | Lubrication Period | Type of Lubrication | Quantity | Remarks |
|---|---|---|---|---|---|
| 1 | Air Cleaner | 12,000 Miles | | | See Vehicle Maintenance Schedule |
| 2 | Distributor – L-6 | 24,000 Miles | | | Replace Cam Lubricator* |
| 3 | Distributor – V-8 | 24,000 Miles | | | Replace Cam Lubricator* |
| 4 | Control Linkage Points | 12,000 Miles | Engine Oil | As required | Brush or Spray to apply |
| 7 | Tie Rod Ends | 6,000 Miles | Chassis Lubricant | 2 places as required | |
| 8 | Wheel Bearings | 24,000 Miles | Wheel Bearing Grease | 2 places as required | |
| 9 | Steering Gear | 36,000 Miles | | | Check for Grease Leak Do not Lubricate |
| 10 | Master Cylinder | 6,000 Miles | Delco Supreme No.11 or DOT-3 fluids | As required | Check – add fluid when necessary |
| 11 | Transmission – Manual | 6,000 Miles | GL-5 | As required | Keep even w/filler plug |
| | – Automatic | 6,000 Miles | Dexron® or equivalent | As required | See Lubrication Section |
| 12 | Carburetor Linkage – V-8 | 12,000 Miles | Engine Oil | As required | |
| 13 | Universal Joints | 6,000 Miles | Chassis Lubricant | As required | See Lubrication Section |
| 14 | Propeller Shaft Slip Joints | 6,000 Miles | Chassis Lubricant | 3 places as required | |
| 15 | Front and Rear Axle | 6,000 Miles | GL-6 | As required | Check See Lubrication Section |
| 17 | Drag Link | 6,000 Miles | Chassis B | 2 places as required | |
| 18 | Brake and Clutch Pedal Springs | 6,000 Miles | Engine Oil | As required | |
| 21 | Transfer Case | 6,000 Miles | GL-5 | As required | Check See Lubrication Section |
| 22 | Throttle Bell Crank – L-6 | 12,000 Miles | Engine Oil | As required | |

*Replace Points at 12,000 mile intervals.

**Typical lubrication diagram—four wheel drive models (© Chevrolet Motor Div.)**

12. To adjust the bearings on 1972 through 1980 models, spin the wheel hub by hand and tighten the nut until it is just snug (12 ft lbs). Back off the nut until it is loose, then tighten it finger tight. Loosen the nut until either hole in the spindle lines up with a slot in the nut, and insert a new cotter pin. There should be 0.001–0.008 in. end play in the bearing through 1973, and 0.001–0.005 in. from 1974–80. This can be measured with a dial indicator, if you wish. Replace the dust cap, wheel, and tire.

**Four Wheel Drive**

NOTE: *This procedure requires snap ring pliers and a special hub nut wrench. It is not very easy without them.*

1. Remove the wheel and tire.

2. For K-10 or K-1500 models 1970–80, and K-20 or K-2500 models 1977–80 with locking front hubs: Lock the hubs. Remove the outer retaining plate Allen head bolts and take off the plate, O-ring, and knob. Take out the large snap ring inside the hub and re-

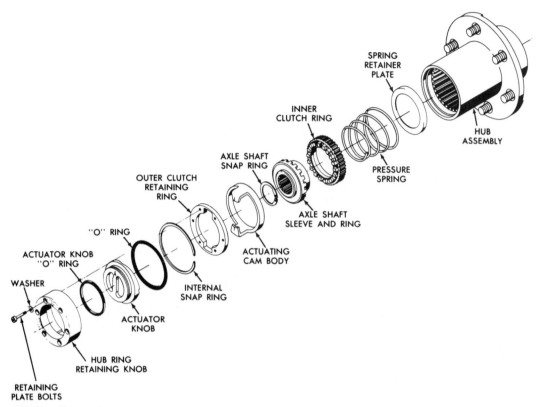

**SPRING RETAINER PLATE**

**INNER CLUTCH RING**

**HUB ASSEMBLY**

**AXLE SHAFT SNAP RING**

**PRESSURE SPRING**

**OUTER CLUTCH RETAINING RING**

**AXLE SHAFT SLEEVE AND RING**

**"O" RING**

**ACTUATING CAM BODY**

**ACTUATOR KNOB "O" RING**

**WASHER**

**INTERNAL SNAP RING**

**ACTUATOR KNOB**

**HUB RING RETAINING KNOB**

**RETAINING PLATE BOLTS**

**Details of the locking hubs for K-10 and K-1500 models, 1970–80, and K-20 and K-2500 models, 1977–80 (© Chevrolet Motor Div.)**

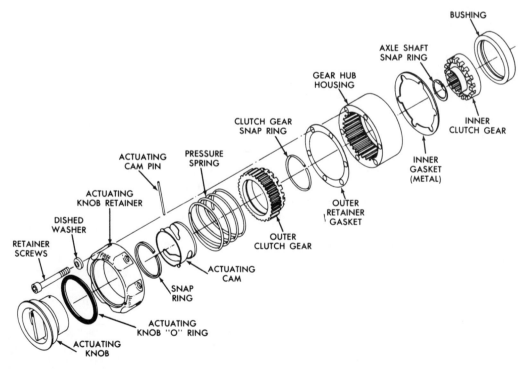

**BUSHING**

**AXLE SHAFT SNAP RING**

**GEAR HUB HOUSING**

**CLUTCH GEAR SNAP RING**

**INNER CLUTCH GEAR**

**PRESSURE SPRING**

**ACTUATING CAM PIN**

**INNER GASKET (METAL)**

**ACTUATING KNOB RETAINER**

**OUTER RETAINER GASKET**

**DISHED WASHER**

**RETAINER SCREWS**

**OUTER CLUTCH GEAR**

**ACTUATING CAM**

**SNAP RING**

**ACTUATING KNOB "O" RING**

**ACTUATING KNOB**

**Details of locking hubs for K-20 and K-2500 models, 1970–76 (© Chevrolet Motor Div.)**

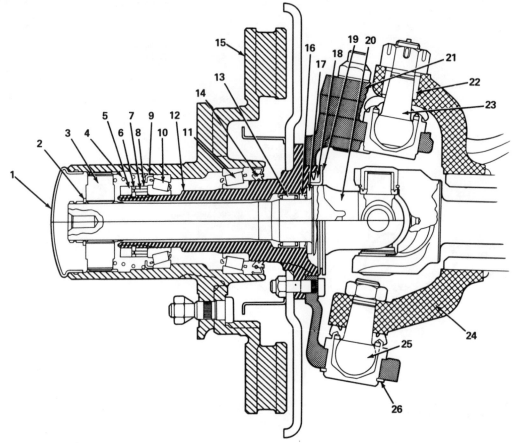

1. Hub cap
2. Snap ring
3. Hub drive gear
4. Spring
5. Lock nut
6. Lock nut for adjusting nut
7. Pin for adjusting nut
8. Adjusting nut
9. Pressure plate (spring retainer plate)
10. Outer wheel bearing
11. Inner wheel bearing
12. Spindle
13. Spindle bearing
14. Seal
15. Hub and brake disc assembly
16. Oil seal
17. Spacer
18. Dust seal
19. Deflector (slinger)
20. Axle outer shaft
21. Knuckle
22. Adjusting sleeve
23. Upper ball joint
24. Yoke
25. Lower ball joint
26. Retaining ring

**Cutaway view of four wheel drive front wheel bearings. This axle does not have locking hubs (© Chevrolet Motor Div.)**

move the outer clutch retaining ring and actuating cam body. This is a lot easier with snap ring pliers. Relieve pressure on the axle shaft snap ring and remove it. Take out the axle shaft sleeve and clutch ring assembly and the inner clutch ring and bushing assembly. Remove the spring and retainer plate.

3. For K-20 and K-2500 models 1970–76, with locking front hubs, turn the hub key to the Free position. Remove the Allen head bolts securing the retainer cap assembly to the wheel hub. Pull off the hub cap assembly and gasket, and the exterior sleeve extension housing and its gasket.

NOTE: *You will have to modify this procedure for either of the models mentioned above if you have non-factory installed locking hubs.*

4. If you don't have locking front hubs, remove the hub cap and snap ring. Next, remove the drive gear and pressure spring. To prevent the spring from popping out, place a hand over the drive gear and use a screwdriver to pry the gear out. Remove the spring.

5. Remove the wheel bearing outer lock nut, lock ring, and wheel bearing inner adjusting nut. A special wrench is required.

6. Remove the brake disc assembly and

outer wheel bearing. Remove the spring retainer plate if you don't have locking hubs. See Chapter 9 for details on brake drum or disc and caliper removal.

7. Remove the oil seal and inner bearing cone from the hub using a brass drift and hammer. Discard the oil seal. Use the drift to remove the inner and outer bearing cups.

8. Check the condition of the spindle bearing. If you have drum brakes, remove the grease retainer, gasket, and backing plate after removing the bolts. Unbolt the spindle and tap it with a soft hammer to break it loose. Remove the spindle and check the condition of the thrust washer, replacing it if worn. Now you can remove the oil seal and spindle roller bearing.

NOTE: *The spindle bearings must be greased each time the wheel bearings are serviced.*

9. Clean all parts in solvent, dry, and check for wear or damage.

10. Pack both wheel bearings (and the spindle bearing) using wheel bearing grease. Place a healthy glob of grease in the palm of one hand and force the edge of the bearing into it so that grease fills the bearing. Do this until the whole bearing is packed. Grease packing tools are available to make this job a lot less messy.

11. To reassemble the spindle: drive the repacked bearing into the spindle and install the grease seal onto the slinger with the lip toward the spindle. It would be best to replace the axle shaft slinger when the spindle seal is replaced. See Axle Shaft Removal and Overhaul in Chapter 7 for details.

NOTE: *An improved spindle seal (no. 376855) and axle seal (no. 376851) were introduced during the 1976 model year. These can be installed on earlier (late 1972 and up) models. See the note under Axle Shaft Removal and Installation in Chapter 7 for details on identifying late 1972 models.*

**The special four wheel drive bearing adjusting wrench; these are available at four wheel drive suppliers and truck parts outlets (© Chevrolet Motor Div.)**

**Driving out the bearing cups (© Chevrolet Motor Div.)**

**Removing the spindle (© Chevrolet Motor Div.)**

**Replacing the spindle thrust washer and spindle; the components are removed from the truck for clarity (© Chevrolet Motor Div.)**

If you are using the improved seals, fill the seal end of the spindle with grease. If not, apply grease only to the lip of the seal. Install the thrust washer over the axle shaft. On late 1972 through 1980 models, the chamfered side of the thrust washer should be toward the slinger. Replace the spindle and torque the nuts to 45 ft lbs through 1976, 25 ft lbs, 1977–78, and 33 ft lbs, 1979–80.

12. To reassemble the wheel bearings: drive the outer bearing cup into the hub, replace the inner bearing cup, and insert the repacked bearing.

13. Install the disc or drum and outer wheel bearing to the spindle.

14. Adjust the bearings by rotating the hub and torquing the inner adjusting nut to 50 ft lbs, then loosening it and retorquing to 35 ft lbs. Next, back the nut off ⅜ turn or less. Turn the nut to the nearest hole in the lockwasher. Install the outer locknut and torque to a minimum of 50 ft lbs through 1978, or 80 ft lbs, 1979–80. There should be 0.001–0.010 in. bearing end play. This can be measured with a dial indicator.

15. Replace the brake components.

16. Lubricate the locking hub components with high temperature grease. Lubrication must be applied to prevent component failure. For K-10 or K-1500 models, 1970–80, and K-20 and K-2500 models, 1977–80, install the spring retainer plate with the flange side facing the bearing over the spindle nuts and seat it against the bearing outer cup. Install the pressure spring with the large end against the spring retaining plate. The spring is an interference fit; when seated, its end extends past the spindle nuts by approximately ⅞ in. Place the inner clutch ring and bushing assembly into the axle shaft sleeve and clutch ring assembly and install that as an assembly onto the axle shaft. Press in on this assembly and install the axle shaft ring. If there are two axle shaft snap ring grooves (1976–79), use the inner one.

NOTE: *You can install a ⁷/₁₆ in. bolt in the axle shaft end and pull outward on it to aid in seating the snap ring.*

Install the actuating cam body in the cams facing outward, the outer clutch retaining ring, and the internal snap ring. Install a new O-ring on the retaining plate, and then install the actuating knob in the Lock position. Install the retaining plate. The grooves in the knob must fit into the actuator cam body. Install the seals and six cover bolts and torque them to 30 ft lbs. Turn the knob to the Free position and check for proper operation.

17. For K-20 or K-2500 models, 1970–76, apply grease generously to the axle splines and teeth of the inner and outer clutch gears.

NOTE: *Remove the head from a 5 in. long ⅜ in. bolt and use this to align the hub assembly.*

Install the headless bolt into one of the hub housing bolt holes. Install a new exterior sleeve extension housing gasket, the housing, and a new hub retainer cap assembly gasket, and the cap assembly. Install the six Allen head bolts and their washers, and torque them to 30 ft lbs. Turn the knob to Lock and check engagement.

18. Without locking hubs, replace the snap ring and hub cap. If there are two axle shaft snap ring grooves (1976–79), use the inner one.

## PUSHING AND TOWING

### Pushing

Chevrolet and GMC trucks with manual transmissions can be push started, but this is not recommended if you value the appearance of your truck.

To push start, make sure that both bumpers are in reasonable alignment. Bent sheet metal and inflamed tempers are both common results from misaligned bumpers when push starting. Turn the ignition key to ON and engage High gear. Depress the clutch pedal. When a speed of about 10 mph is reached, slightly depress the gas pedal and slowly release the clutch. The engine should start.

Never get an assist by having your vehicle towed.

Automatic transmission equipped trucks cannot be started by pushing.

Push starting is specifically not recommended for 1975–80 trucks with catalytic converters. Doing so could cause the converter to explode.

### Towing
#### TWO WHEEL DRIVE

Chevrolet and GMC trucks can be towed on all four wheels (flat towed) at speeds of less than 35 mph for distances less than 50 miles, providing that the axle, driveline and engine/transmission are normally operable. The transmission should be in Neutral, the engine should be off, the steering column unlocked, and the parking brake released.

Do not attach chains to the bumpers or

TOWING FOUR WHEEL DRIVE

| FRONT WHEELS OFF THE GROUND | |
|---|---|
| FULL TIME ( 4 X 4 )<br>AUTOMATIC TRANSMISSION | PART TIME (4 X 4)<br>MANUAL TRANSMISSION |
| 1. TRANSFER CASE IN NEUTRAL<br>2. TRANSMISSION IN PARK<br>3. MAXIMUM SPEED 35 MPH<br>4. MAXIMUM DISTANCE 50 MILES<br>NOTE: For distances over 50 miles, disconnect rear propshaft at rear axle carrier and secure in safe position. | 1. TRANSFER CASE IN 2 H<br>2. TRANSMISSION IN NEUTRAL<br>3. MAXIMUM SPEED 35 MPH<br>4. MAXIMUM DISTANCE 50 MILES<br>NOTE: For distances over 50 miles, disconnect the rear propshaft at rear axle carrier and secure in safe position. |
| REAR WHEELS OFF THE GROUND | |
| CAUTION: When towing a vehicle in this position, the steering wheel should be secured to keep the front wheels in a straight ahead position. | |
| FULL TIME (4 X 4) | PART TIME (4 X 4) |
| 1. TRANSFER CASE IN NEUTRAL<br>2. TRANSMISSION IN PARK<br>3. MAXIMUM SPEED 35 MPH<br>4. MAXIMUM DISTANCE 50 MILES<br>NOTE: For distances over 50 miles, disconnect front propshaft at front axle carrier and secure in safe position. | 1. TRANSFER CASE IN 2 H<br>2. TRANSMISSION IN NEUTRAL<br>3. MAXIMUM SPEED 35 MPH<br>4. MAXIMUM DISTANCE 50 MILES<br>NOTE: For distances over 50 miles, disconnect the front propshaft at front axle carrier and secure in safe position. |
| ALL FOUR WHEELS ON GROUND | |
| FULL TIME (4 X 4) | PART TIME (4 X 4) |
| 1. TRANSFER CASE IN NEUTRAL<br>2. TRANSMISSION IN PARK<br>NOTE: Do not exceed speed as per State laws for towing vehicles. | 1. TRANSFER CASE IN 2 H<br>2. TRANSMISSION IN NEUTRAL<br>3. MAXIMUM SPEED 35 MPH<br>4. MAXIMUM DISTANCE 50 MILES<br>NOTE: For speeds or distances greater than above, both propshafts must be disconnected at the axle carrier end and secured in a safe position. It is recommended that both propshafts be removed and stored in the vehicle.<br>NOTE: Do not exceed speeds as per State laws for towing vehicles. |

(© Chevrolet Motor Div.)

bracketing. All attachments must be made to the structural members. Safety chains should be used. It should also be remembered that power steering and brake assists will not be working with the engine off.

The rear wheels must be raised off the ground or the driveshaft disconnected when the transmission is not operating properly, or when speeds of over 35 mph will be used or when towing more than 50 miles.

CAUTION: *If a truck is towed on its front wheels only, the steering wheel must be secured with the wheels in a straight ahead position.*

## FOUR WHEEL DRIVE

Details for towing procedures are given in the Towing Four Wheel Drive Chart.

Remember that the power steering and power brakes will not have their power assist with the engine off. The only safe way to tow is with a tow bar. The steering column must be unlocked and the parking brake released. Attachments should be made to the frame and not to the bumper or its brackets. Safety chains are also required.

NOTE: *When towing a full time four wheel drive manual transmission truck with all four wheels on the ground, the transfer case must be in Neutral and the transmission in high gear. There is no speed restriction.*

## JUMP STARTING

The following procedure is recommended by the manufacturer. Be sure that the booster battery is 12 volt with negative ground.

CAUTION: *Do not attempt this procedure on a frozen battery; it will probably explode. Do not attempt it on a sealed Delco Freedom battery showing a light color in the charge indicator. Be certain to observe correct polarity connections. Failure to do so will result in almost immediate alternator and regulator destruction. Never allow the jumper cable ends to touch each other.*

1. Position the vehicles so that they are not touching. Set the parking brake and place automatic transmissions in Park and manual transmissions in Neutral. Turn off the lights, heater and other electrical loads.

2. Remove the vent caps from both the booster and discharged battery. Lay a cloth over the open vent cells of each battery. This isn't necessary on batteries equipped with sponge type flame arrestor caps, and

(© Chevrolet Motor Div.)

The ground connection of the booster battery's jumper cable should be made to a metal part of the truck to be jump started, such as the alternator bracket, not to the negative battery post (© Chevrolet Motor Div.)

**Make Connections in Numerical Order**

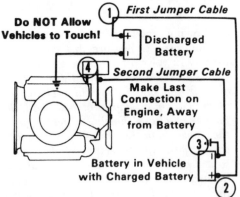

Jump starting connections (© Chevrolet Motor Div.)

it isn't possible on sealed Freedom batteries.

3. Attach one cable to the positive (+) terminal of the booster battery and the other end to the positive terminal of the discharged battery. If you are attempting to start a Chevrolet or GMC pick-up with the diesel engine, it is suggested that this connection be made to the battery on the driver's side of the truck, because this battery is closer to the starter, and thus the resistance of the electrical cables is lower. From this point on, ignore the other battery in the truck.

CAUTION: *Do not attempt to jump start the truck with a 24 volt power source.*

4. Attach one end of the remaining cable to the negative (−) terminal of the booster battery and the other end to the lift bracket of 6 cylinder engines or the alternator bracket of V8 engines. Do not attach to the negative terminal of discharged batteries. Do not lean over the battery when making this last connection.

5. Start the engine of the truck with the booster battery. Start the engine of the truck with the discharged battery. If the engine will not start, disconnect the batteries as soon as possible. If this is not done, the two batteries will soon reach a state of equilibrium, with both too weak to start an engine. This will not be a problem if the engine of the booster truck is kept running fast enough. Lengthy cranking can also overheat and damage the starter.

6. Reverse the above steps to disconnect the booster and discharged batteries. Be certain to remove negative connections first.

7. Reinstall the vent caps. Dispose of the cloths; they may have battery acid on them.

## JACKING AND HOISTING

The jack supplied with the truck was meant for changing tires. It was not meant to support a truck while you crawl under it and work. Whenever it is necessary to get under a truck to perform service operations, always be sure that it is adequately supported, preferably by jackstands at the proper points. Always block the wheels when changing tires.

If your truck is equipped with a Positraction rear axle, do not run the engine for any reason with one rear wheel off the ground. Power will be transmitted through the rear wheel remaining on the ground, possibly causing the vehicle to drive itself off the jack.

Some of the service operations in this book require that one or both ends of the truck be raised and supported safely. The best arrangement for this, of course, is a grease pit or a vehicle lift, but these items are seldom found in the home garage. However, small hydraulic, screw, or scissors jacks are satisfactory for raising the truck.

Heavy wooden blocks or adjustable jackstands should be used to support the truck while it is being worked on. Drive-on trestles, or ramps, are also a handy and a safe way to raise the truck, assuming their capacity is adequate. These can be bought or con-structed from suitable heavy timbers or steel.

In any case, it is always best to spend a little extra time to make sure that the truck is lifted and supported safely.

CAUTION: *Concrete blocks are not rec-ommended. They may crumble if the load is not evenly distributed. Boxes and milk crates of any description must not be used.*

# Tune-Up

## TUNE-UP PROCEDURES

Neither tune-up nor troubleshooting can be considered independently since each has a direct relationship with the other.

It is advisable to follow a definite and thorough tune-up procedure. Tune-up consists of three separate steps: Analysis, the process of determining whether normal wear is responsible for performance loss, and whether parts require replacement or service; parts replacement or service; and adjustment, where engine adjustments are performed.

The manufacturer's recommended interval for tune-ups is every 12,000 miles or 12 months, whichever comes first for 1970–74, and 22,500 miles or 18 months for 1975–80, except for heavy duty emission models, which use the 12 mo/12,000 mi schedule in all years. These intervals should be shortened if the truck is subjected to severe operating conditions such as trailer pulling or off-road driving, or if starting and running problems are noticed. It is assumed that the routine maintenance described in Chapter 1 has been kept up, as this will have an effect on the results of the tune-up. All the applicable tune-up steps should be followed, as each adjustment complements the effects of the others. If the tune-up (emission control) sticker in the engine compartment disagrees with the information presented in the "Tune-up Specifications" chart in this chapter, the sticker figures must be followed. The sticker information reflects running changes made by the manufacturer during production. The light duty sticker is usually found on the underhood sheet metal above the grille. The heavy duty sticker is usually on top of the air cleaner.

Diesel engines do not require tune-ups *per se*, as there is no ignition system.

Troubleshooting is a logical sequence of procedures designed to locate a particular cause of trouble. The "Troubleshooting" chapter of this book is general in nature (applicable to most vehicles), yet specific enough to locate the problem.

It is advisable to read the entire chapter before beginning a tune-up, although those who are more familiar with tune-up procedures may wish to go directly to the instructions.

## Spark Plugs

Rough idle, hard starting, frequent engine miss at high speeds and physical deterioration are all indications that the plugs should be replaced.

The electrode end of a spark plug is a good indicator of the internal condition of your

# Tune-Up Specifications

| Year | Engine Displacement (cu in.) | Spark Plugs Type | Gap (in.) | Distributor Point Dwell (deg) | Point Gap (in.) ▲ | Ignition Timing (deg) MT | AT | Fuel Pump Pressure (psi) | Compression Pressure (psi) ● | Idle Speed (rpm)* MT | AT | Valve Clearance (in.) Ex | In |
|---|---|---|---|---|---|---|---|---|---|---|---|---|---|
| 1970 | 250 | R46T | 0.035 | 31–34 | 0.019 | TDC | 4B | 3.5–4.5 | 130 | See Text | See Text | Hyd | Hyd |
| | 292 | R46T | 0.035 | 31–34 | 0.019 | TDC | 4B | 3.5–4.5 | 130 | See Text | See Text | Hyd | Hyd |
| | 307 | R44 | 0.035 | 28–32 | 0.019 | 2B | 8B | 5.0–6.5 | 150 | See Text | See Text | Hyd | Hyd |
| | 350 (2 bbl) | R43 | 0.035 | 28–32 | 0.019 | 4B | — | 7.0–8.5 | 150 | See Text | See Text | Hyd | Hyd |
| | 350 (4 bbl) | R43 | 0.035 | 28–32 | 0.019 | TDC | 4B | 7.0–8.5 | 150 | See Text | See Text | Hyd | Hyd |
| | 396 | R43T | 0.035 | 28–32 | 0.019 | 4B | — | 7.0–8.5 | 150 | See Text | See Text | Hyd | Hyd |
| 1971 | 250 | R46TS | 0.035 | 31–34 | 0.019 | 4B | 4B | 3.5–4.5 | 130 | 550 | 500 | Hyd | Hyd |
| | 292 | R44T | 0.035 | 31–34 | 0.019 | 4B | 4B | 3.5–4.5 | 130 | 550 | 500 | Hyd | Hyd |
| | 307 (200 HP) | R45TS | 0.035 | 28–32 | 0.019 | 4B | 8B | 5.0–6.5 | 150 | 600 | 550 | Hyd | Hyd |
| | 307 (215 HP) | R45TS | 0.035 | 28–32 | 0.019 | 4B | 4B | 7.0–8.5 | 150 | 550 | 550 | Hyd | Hyd |
| | 350 | R44TS | 0.035 | 28–32 | 0.019 | 4B | 8B | 7.0–8.5 | 150 | 600 | 550 | Hyd | Hyd |
| | 402 | R44TS | 0.035 | 28–32 | 0.019 | 8B | 8B | 7.0–8.5 | 150 | 600 | 600 | Hyd | Hyd |
| 1972 | 250 | R46T | 0.035 | 31–34 | 0.019 | 4B | 4B | 3.5–4.5 | 130 | 700 | 600 | Hyd | Hyd |
| | 292 | R44T | 0.035 | 31–34 | 0.019 | 4B | 4B | 3.5–4.5 | 130 | 700 | 700 | Hyd | Hyd |

# 48    TUNE-UP

## Tune-Up Specifications (cont.)

| Year | Engine Displacement (cu in.) | Spark Plugs | | Distributor | | Ignition Timing (deg) | | Fuel Pump Pressure (psi) | Compression Pressure (psi) ● | Idle Speed (rpm)* | | Valve Clearance (in.) | |
|---|---|---|---|---|---|---|---|---|---|---|---|---|---|
| | | Type | Gap (in.) | Point Dwell (deg) | Point Gap (in.) ▲ | MT | AT | | | MT | AT | Ex | In |
| 1972 | 307 | R44T | 0.035 | 28–32 | 0.019 | 4B | 8B① | 5.0–6.5 | 150 | 900② | 600 | Hyd | Hyd |
| | 350 | R44T | 0.035 | 28–32 | 0.019 | 4B | 8B | 7.0–8.5 | 150 | 800 | 600 | Hyd | Hyd |
| | 402 | R44T | 0.035 | 28–32 | 0.019 | 8B | 8B | 7.0–8.5 | 150 | 750 | 600 | Hyd | Hyd |
| 1973 | 250 (LD) | R46T | 0.035 | 31–34 | 0.019 | 6B | 6B | 3.5–4.5 | 130 | 700 | 600 | Hyd | Hyd |
| | 250 (HD) | R46T | 0.035 | 31–34 | 0.019 | 4B | 4B | 3.5–4.5 | 130 | 700 | 700 | Hyd | Hyd |
| | 292 (Fed) | R44T | 0.035 | 31–34 | 0.019 | 4B | 4B | 3.5–4.5 | 130 | 700 | 700 | Hyd | Hyd |
| | 292 (Calif) | R44T | 0.035 | 31–34 | 0.019 | 8B | 8B | 3.5–4.5 | 130 | 600 | 600 | Hyd | Hyd |
| | 307 (LD) | R44T | 0.035 | 28–32 | 0.019 | 4B | 8B | 5.0–6.5 | 150 | 900 | 600 | Hyd | Hyd |
| | 307 (HD) | R44T | 0.035 | 28–32 | 0.019 | TDC | TDC | 5.0–6.5 | 150 | 600 | 600 | Hyd | Hyd |
| | 350 (LD) | R44T | 0.035 | 28–32 | 0.019 | 8B | 12B | 7.0–8.5 | 150 | 900 | 600 | Hyd | Hyd |
| | 350 (HD) | R44T | 0.035 | 28–32 | 0.019 | 4B | 4B | 7.0–8.5 | 150 | 600 | 600 | Hyd | Hyd |
| | 454 (LD) | R44T | 0.035 | 28–32 | 0.019 | 10B | 10B | 7.0–8.5 | 150 | 900 | 600 | Hyd | Hyd |
| | 454 (HD) | R44T | 0.035 | 28–32 | 0.019 | ③ | ④ | 7.0–8.5 | 150 | 700 | 700 | Hyd | Hyd |
| 1974 | 250 (LD, Fed) | R46T | 0.035 | 31–34 | 0.019 | 8B | 8B | 3.5–4.5 | 130 | 850 | 600 | Hyd | Hyd |

| Model | | | | | | | | | | | |
|---|---|---|---|---|---|---|---|---|---|---|---|
| 250 (LD, Calif) | R46T | 0.035 | 31–34 | 0.019 | 8B | — | 3.5–4.5 | 130 | 850 | — | Hyd | Hyd |
| 250 (HD) | R44T | 0.035 | 31–34 | 0.019 | 6B | 6B | 3.5–4.5 | 130 | 600 | 600 | Hyd | Hyd |
| 292 (HD) | R44T | 0.035 | 31–34 | 0.019 | 8B | 8B | 3.5–4.5 | 130 | 600 | 600 | Hyd | Hyd |
| 350 (2 bbl) | R44T | 0.035 | 29–31 | 0.019 | 4B | 8B | 7.0–8.5 | 150 | 900 | 600 | Hyd | Hyd |
| 350 (4 bbl, Calif) | R44T | 0.035 | 29–31 | 0.019 | 4B | 8B | 7.0–8.5 | 150 | 900 | 600 | Hyd | Hyd |
| 350 (4 bbl, Fed) | R44T | 0.035 | 29–31 | 0.019 | 6B | 12B | 7.0–8.5 | 150 | 900 | 600 | Hyd | Hyd |
| 350 (4 bbl, HD) | R44T | 0.035 | 29–31 | 0.019 | 8B | 8B | 7.0–8.5 | 150 | 700 | 700 | Hyd | Hyd |
| 454 (LD) | R44T | 0.035 | 29–31 | 0.019 | 10B | 10B | 7.0–8.5 | 150 | 800 | 600 | Hyd | Hyd |
| 454 (HD) | R44T | 0.035 | 29–31 | 0.019 | 8B | 8B | 7.0–8.5 | 150 | 700 | 700 | Hyd | Hyd |
| 1975 250 | R46TX | 0.060 | — | — | 10B | 10B | 3.5–4.5 | 130 | 900 | 550 | Hyd | Hyd |
| 292 (HD) | R44TX | 0.060 | — | — | 8B | 8B | 3.5–4.5 | 130 | 600 | 600 | Hyd | Hyd |
| 350 (2 bbl) | R44TX | 0.060 | — | — | — | 6B | 7.0–8.5 | 150 | — | 600 | Hyd | Hyd |
| 350 (4 bbl) | R44TX | 0.060 | — | — | 6B | 6B | 7.0–8.5 | 150 | 800 | 600 | Hyd | Hyd |
| 350 (HD, Fed) | R44TX | 0.060 | — | — | 8B | 8B | 7.0–8.5 | 150 | 600 | 600 | Hyd | Hyd |
| 350 (HD, Calif) | R44TX | 0.060 | — | — | 2B | 2B | 7.0–8.5 | 150 | 700 | 700 | Hyd | Hyd |
| 400 (HD, Fed) | R44TX | 0.060 | — | — | 4B | 4B | 7.0–8.5 | 150 | 700 | 700 | Hyd | Hyd |
| 400 (HD, Calif) | R44TX | 0.060 | — | — | 2B | 2B | 7.0–8.5 | 150 | 700 | 700 | Hyd | Hyd |

# Tune-Up Specifications (cont.)

| Year | Engine Displace-ment (cu in.) | Spark Plugs | | Distributor | | Ignition Timing (deg) | | Fuel Pump Pressure (psi) | Compression Pressure (psi) ● | Idle Speed (rpm)* | | Valve Clearance (in.) | |
|---|---|---|---|---|---|---|---|---|---|---|---|---|---|
| | | Type | Gap (in.) | Point Dwell (deg) | Point Gap (in.) ▲ | MT | AT | | | MT | AT | Ex | In |
| 1975 | 454 (LD) | R44TX | 0.060 | — | — | — | 16B | 7.0–8.5 | 150 | — | 650 | Hyd | Hyd |
| | 454 (HD, Fed) | R44TX | 0.060 | — | — | 8B | 8B | 7.0–8.5 | 150 | 700 | 700 | Hyd | Hyd |
| | 454 (HD, Calif) | R44TX | 0.060 | — | — | 8B | 8B | 7.0–8.5 | 150 | 600 | 600 | Hyd | Hyd |
| 1976 | 250 | R46TS | 0.035 | — | — | 10B | 10B | 3.5–4.5 | 130 | 900 | 550 | Hyd | Hyd |
| | 250 (Calif) | R46TS | 0.035 | — | — | 6B | 10B | 3.5–4.5 | 130 | 1000 | 600 | Hyd | Hyd |
| | 250 (HD) | R46T | 0.035 | — | — | 6B | 6B | 3.5–4.5 | 130 | 600 | 600(N) | Hyd | Hyd |
| | 292 (HD) | R44T | 0.035 | — | — | 8B | 8B | 3.5–4.5 | 130 | 600 | 600(N) | Hyd | Hyd |
| | 350 | R45TS | 0.045 | — | — | 2B | 6B | 7–8.5 | 150 | 800 | 600 | Hyd | Hyd |
| | 350 (4 bbl) | R45TS | 0.045 | — | — | 8B | 8B | 7–8.5 | 150 | 800 | 600 | Hyd | Hyd |
| | 350 (4 bbl Calif) | R45TS | 0.045 | — | — | 6B | 6B | 7–8.5 | 150 | 800 | 600 | Hyd | Hyd |
| | 350 (HD) | R44TX | 0.060 | — | — | 8B | 8B | 7–8.5 | 150 | 600 | 600(N) | Hyd | Hyd |
| | 350 (HD Calif) | R44TX | 0.060 | — | — | 2B | 2B | 7–8.5 | 150 | 700 | 700(N) | Hyd | Hyd |
| | 400 (HD) | R44TX | 0.060 | — | — | 4B | 4B | 7–8.5 | 150 | — | 700(N) | Hyd | Hyd |
| | 400 (HD Calif) | R44TX | 0.060 | — | — | 2B | 2B | 7–8.5 | 150 | — | 700(N) | Hyd | Hyd |

| Year | Engine | | | | | | | | | | | |
|------|--------|--|--|--|--|--|--|--|--|--|-----|-----|
| | 454 (w/cat) | R45TS | 0.045 | — | | 12B | 12B | 7–8.5 | 150 | — | 600 | Hyd | Hyd |
| | 454 (w/o cat) | R45TS | 0.045 | — | 8B | 8B | 7–8.5 | 150 | — | 600 | Hyd | Hyd |
| | 454 (HD) | R44T | 0.045 | — | 8B | 8B | 7–8.5 | 150 | 700 | 700(N) | Hyd | Hyd |
| 1977 | 250 | R46TS | 0.035 | — | 8B | 12B | 3.5–4.5 | 130 | 750 | 550 | Hyd | Hyd |
| | 250 (High Alt) | R46TS | 0.035 | — | 8B | 12B | 3.5–4.5 | 130 | 750 | 600 | Hyd | Hyd |
| | 250 (Calif) | R46TS | 0.035 | — | 6B | 10B | 3.5–4.5 | 130 | 850 | 600 | Hyd | Hyd |
| | 250 (HD) | R46T | 0.035 | — | 6B | 6B | 3.5–4.5 | 130 | 600 | 600(N) | Hyd | Hyd |
| | 292 | R44T | 0.035 | — | 8B | 8B | 3.5–4.5 | 130 | 600 | 600(N) | Hyd | Hyd |
| | 305 | R45TS | 0.045 | — | 8B | 8B | 7–8.5 | 150 | 600 | 500 | Hyd | Hyd |
| | 305 (HD) | R44T | 0.045 | — | 6B | 6B | 7–8.5 | 150 | 700 | 700(N) | Hyd | Hyd |
| | 350 | R45TS | 0.045 | — | 8B | 8B | 7–8.5 | 150 | 700 | 500 | Hyd | Hyd |
| | 350 (High Alt) | R45TS | 0.045 | — | — | 6B | 7–8.5 | 150 | — | 600 | Hyd | Hyd |
| | 350 (Calif) | R45TS | 0.045 | — | 6B | 6B | 7–8.5 | 150 | 700 | 500 | Hyd | Hyd |
| | 350 (HD) | R44T | 0.045 | — | 8B | 8B | 7–8.5 | 150 | 700 | 700(N) | Hyd | Hyd |
| | 350 (HD Calif) | R44TX | 0.060 | — | 2B | 2B | 7–8.5 | 150 | 700 | 700(N) | Hyd | Hyd |
| | 400 (HD) | R44T | 0.045 | — | — | 4B | 7–8.5 | 150 | — | 700(N) | Hyd | Hyd |
| | 400 (HD Calif) | R44T | 0.045 | — | — | 2B | 7–8.5 | 150 | — | 700(N) | Hyd | Hyd |
| | 454 | R45TS | 0.045 | — | — | 4B | 7–8.5 | 150 | — | 600 | Hyd | Hyd |

# Tune-Up Specifications (cont.)

| Year | Engine Displacement (cu in.) | Spark Plugs | | Distributor | | Ignition Timing (deg) | | Fuel Pump Pressure (psi) | Compression Pressure (psi) ● | Idle Speed (rpm)* | | Valve Clearance (in.) | |
|---|---|---|---|---|---|---|---|---|---|---|---|---|---|
| | | Type | Gap (in.) | Point Dwell (deg) | Point Gap (in.) ▲ | MT | AT | | | MT | AT | Ex | In |
| 1977 | 454 (HD) | R44T | 0.045 | — | — | 8B | 8B | 7–8.5 | 150 | 700 | 700(N) | Hyd | Hyd |
| 1978 | 250 (LD Fed) | R46TS | 0.035 | — | — | 8B | 8B | 4.5–6.0 | 130 | 750 | 550 | Hyd | Hyd |
| | 250 (LD Calif) | R46TS | 0.035 | — | — | 8B | 8B | 4.5–6.0 | 130 | 750 | 750 | Hyd | Hyd |
| | 250 (LD High Alt) | R46TS | 0.035 | — | — | 8B | 12B | 4.5–6.0 | 130 | 750 | 600 | Hyd | Hyd |
| | 250 (HD) | R46T | 0.035 | — | — | 6B | 6B | 4.5–6.0 | 130 | 600 | 600(N) | Hyd | Hyd |
| | 292 (HD) | R44T | 0.035 | — | — | 8B | 8B | 4.5–6.0 | 130 | 600 | 600(N) | Hyd | Hyd |
| | 305 (LD) | R45TS | 0.045 | — | — | 4B | 4B | 7.5–9.0 | 150 | 600 | 500 | Hyd | Hyd |
| | 305 (HD) | R44T | 0.045 | — | — | 6B | 6B | 7.5–9.0 | 150 | 700 | 700(N) | Hyd | Hyd |
| | 350 (LD) | R45TS | 0.045 | — | — | 8B | 8B | 7.5–9.0 | 150 | 600 ⑤ | 500 | Hyd | Hyd |
| | 350 (HD Fed) | R44T | 0.045 | — | — | 8B | 8B | 7.5–9.0 | 150 | 700 | 700(N) | Hyd | Hyd |
| | 350 (HD Calif) | R44TX | 0.060 | — | — | 2B | 2B | 7.5–9.0 | 150 | 700 | 700(N) | Hyd | Hyd |
| | 400 (LD) | R45TS | 0.045 | — | — | — | 4B | 7.5–9.0 | 150 | — | 500 | Hyd | Hyd |
| | 400 (HD Fed) | R44T | 0.045 | — | — | — | 4B | 7.5–9.0 | 150 | — | 700(N) | Hyd | Hyd |
| | 400 (HD Calif) | R44T | 0.045 | — | — | — | 2B | 7.5–9.0 | 150 | — | 700(N) | Hyd | Hyd |

| Year | Model | Plug | Gap | | | | | | | | | |
|---|---|---|---|---|---|---|---|---|---|---|---|---|
| | 454 (LD Fed) | R45TS | 0.045 | — | — | 8B | 7.5–9.0⑥ | 150 | — | 550 | Hyd | Hyd |
| | 454 (LD Calif) | R45TS | 0.045 | — | — | 8B | 7.5–9.0⑥ | 150 | — | 700(N) | Hyd | Hyd |
| | 454 (HD) | R44T | 0.045 | — | 8B | 8B | 7.5–9.0⑥ | 150 | 700 | 700(N) | Hyd | Hyd |
| 1979 | 250 (LD Fed) | R46TS | 0.035 | — | 10B | 10B | 4.5–6.0 | 130 | 750 | 600 | Hyd | Hyd |
| | 250⑦ | R46TS | 0.035 | — | 6B | 8B | 4.5–6.0 | 130 | 750 | 600 | Hyd | Hyd |
| | 292 | R44T | 0.035 | — | 8B | 8B | 4.5–6.0 | 130 | 700 | 700 | Hyd | Hyd |
| | 305 | R45TS | 0.045 | — | 6B | 6B | 7.5–9.0 | 150 | 600 | 500 | Hyd | Hyd |
| | 350 (LD) | R45TS | 0.045 | — | 8B | 8B | 7.5–9.0 | 150 | 700 | 500 | Hyd | Hyd |
| | 350 (HD) | R44T | 0.045 | — | 4B | 4B | 7.5–9.0 | 150 | 700 | 700(N) | Hyd | Hyd |
| | 400 | R45TS | 0.045 | — | — | 4B | 7.5–9.0 | 150 | — | 500 | Hyd | Hyd |
| | 454 (LD) | R45TS | 0.045 | — | 8B | 8B | 7.5–9.0⑥ | 150 | 700 | 500 | Hyd | Hyd |
| | 454 (HD) | R44T | 0.045 | — | — | 4B | 7.5–9.0⑥ | 150 | — | 700(N) | Hyd | Hyd |
| 1980 | 250 (LD Fed) | R46TS | 0.035 | — | 10B | 10B | 4.5–6.0 | 130 | 750 | 650 | Hyd | Hyd |
| | 250 (LD Calif) | R46TS | 0.035 | — | 10B | 10B | 4.5–6.0 | 130 | 750 | 600 | Hyd | Hyd |
| | 250⑦ | R46TS | 0.035 | — | — | 8B | 4.5–6.0 | 130 | — | 600 | Hyd | Hyd |
| | 292 | R44T | 0.035 | — | 8B | 8B | 4.5–6.0 | 130 | 700 | 700(N) | Hyd | Hyd |
| | 305 | R45TS | 0.045 | — | 8B | 8B | 7.5–9.0 | 150 | 600 | 500 | Hyd | Hyd |
| | 350 (LD) | R45TS | 0.045 | — | 8B | 8B | 7.5–9.0 | 150 | 700 | 500 | Hyd | Hyd |

# Tune-Up Specifications (cont.)

| Year | Engine Displacement (cu in.) | Spark Plugs Type | Spark Plugs Gap (in.) | Distributor Point Dwell (deg) | Distributor Point Gap (in.) ▲ | Ignition Timing (deg) MT | Ignition Timing (deg) AT | Fuel Pump Pressure (psi) | Compression Pressure (psi) ● | Idle Speed (rpm)* MT | Idle Speed (rpm)* AT | Valve Clearance (in.) Ex | Valve Clearance (in.) In |
|---|---|---|---|---|---|---|---|---|---|---|---|---|---|
| 1980 | 350 (HD Fed) | R44T | 0.045 | — | — | 4B | 4B | 7.5–9.0 | 150 | 700 | 700(N) | Hyd | Hyd |
| | 350 (HD Calif) | R44T | 0.045 | — | — | 6B | 6B | 7.5–9.0 | 150 | 700 | 700(N) | Hyd | Hyd |
| | 400 (HD Fed) | R44T | 0.045 | — | — | — | 4B | 7.5–9.0 | 150 | — | 700(N) | Hyd | Hyd |
| | 400 (HD Calif) | R44T | 0.045 | — | — | — | 6B | 7.5–9.0 | 150 | — | 700(N) | Hyd | Hyd |
| | 454 | R44T | 0.045 | — | — | 4B | 4B | 7.5–9.0⑥ | 150 | 700 | 700(N) | Hyd | Hyd |

▲ 0.016 in. for used points
● Maximum variation among cylinders—20 psi
B Before Top Dead Center
LD Light-duty
HD Heavy-duty
Fed Federal (49 states)
Calif California only
MT Manual transmission
AT Automatic transmission
N Neutral
*Automatic transmission idle speed set in Drive unless otherwise indicated

NA Not available
—Not applicable
Hyd Hydraulic
① 4B–20 Series
② 950 rpm—California trucks
③ Federal—10B; California—5B
④ Federal—10B; California—8B
⑤ 700 rpm—California
⑥ 5.5–7.0 with vapor return line
⑦ California C-20, C-2500 only

Part numbers in this chart are not recommendations by Chilton for any product by brand name.

engine. If a spark plug is fouled, causing the engine to misfire, the problem will have to be found and corrected. Often, "reading" the plugs will lead you to the cause of the problem. Spark plug conditions and probable causes are listed in the "Troubleshooting" chapter.

NOTE: *A small amount of light tan or rust red colored deposits at the electrode end of the plug is normal. These plugs need not be renewed unless they are severely worn.*

Heat range is a term used to describe the cooling characteristics of spark plugs. Plugs with longer nosed insulators take a longer time to dissipate heat than plugs with shorter nosed insulators. These are termed "hot" or "cold" plugs, respectively. It is generally advisable to use the factory recommended plugs. However, in conditions of extremely hard use (cross-country driving in summer) going to the next cooler heat range may be advisable. If most driving is done in the city or over short distances, go to the next hotter heat range plug to eliminate fouling. If in doubt concerning the substitution of spark plugs, consult your Chevrolet or GMC dealer.

Spark plugs should be gapped when they are checked or newly installed. Never assume that new plugs are correctly gapped.

1. Before removing the spark plugs, number the plug wires so that the correct wire goes on the plug when replaced. This can be done with pieces of adhesive tape.

2. Next, clean the area around the plugs by brushing or blowing with compressed air. You can also loosen the plugs a few turns and crank the engine to blow the dirt away.

3. Disconnect the plug wires by twisting and pulling on the rubber cap, not on the

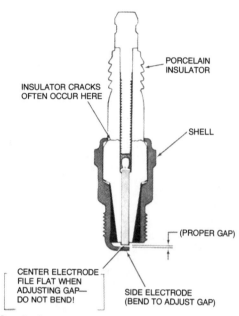

Spark plug cutaway (© Chevrolet Motor Div.)

wire. On H.E.I. systems, twist the plug caps ½ turn in either direction to break the seal before removing the wire. Never remove the wires from H.E.I. systems when the engine is running. Severe shock could result.

4. Remove each plug with a rubber-insert spark plug socket, ⅝ in. for tapered seat plugs (designated with a letter T), $^{13}/_{16}$ in. for the rest. The tapered seat plugs are used in some engines in 1970 and all engines thereafter. Make sure that the socket is all the way down on the plug to prevent it from slipping and cracking the porcelain insulator. On some V8s the plugs are more accessible from under the truck.

5. After removing each plug, evaluate its condition. A spark plug's useful life is about 12,000 miles (optimistically 22,500 with H.E.I.). Thus, it would make sense to replace a plug if it has been in service that long. If the plug is to be replaced, refer to the

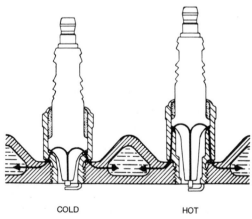

Heat range (© Chevrolet Motor Div.)

Pull on the spark plug boot, not on the wire

Larger (¹³/₁₆) plug on the right and the smaller (⅝) plug on the left. The ⅝ inch plug needs no gasket (© Chevrolet Motor Div.)

Bend the side electrode to adjust the gap. Never bend the center electrode

"Tune-up Specifications" chart for the proper spark plug type.

The letter codes on the General Motors original equipment type plugs are read this way:

R    resistor
S    extended tip
T    tapered seat
X    wide gap

The numbers indicate heat range; hotter running plugs have higher numbers.

6. If the plugs are to be reused, file the center and side electrodes flat with a fine, flat points file. Heavy or baked on deposits can be carefully scraped off with a small knife blade or the scraper tool on a combination spark plug tool. It is often suggested that plugs be tested and cleaned on a service station sandblasting machine; however, this piece of equipment is becoming rare. Check the gap between the electrodes with a round wire spark plug gapping gauge. Do not use a flat feeler gauge; it will give an inaccurate reading. If the gap is not as specified, use the bending tool on the spark plug gap gauge to bend the outside electrode. Be careful not to bend the electrode too far or too often, because excessive bending may cause the electrode to break off and fall into the combustion chamber. This would require removing the cylinder head to reach the broken piece, and could also result in cylinder wall, piston ring, or valve damage.

CAUTION: *Never bend the center electrode of the spark plug. This will break the insulator and render the plug useless.*

7. Clean the plug threads with a wire brush. Lubricate the threads with a drop of oil.

8. Screw the plugs in finger tight, and then tighten them with the spark plug socket. Be very careful not to overtighten them. Just snug them in. If a torque wrench is available, torque them to 15 ft lbs for plug designations with a T, 25 ft lbs for all the rest.

9. Reinstall the wires. If, by chance, you have forgotten to number the plug wires, refer to the "Firing Order" illustrations in Chapter 3.

NOTE: *On 1975–77 six cylinder engines with HEI, the coil is not integral with the distributor cap. It is important that the coil wires be properly routed on these engines. On 250s, the coil wire goes in the wire loom clip above the plug wires. On 292s, the coil wire goes in the clip below the plug wires.*

## Breaker Points and Condenser—Dwell Angle

### 1970–74

The usual procedure is to replace the condenser each time the point set is replaced.

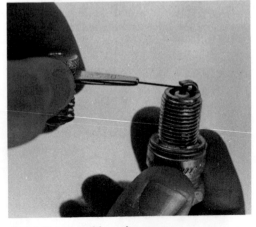

Check the gap with a wire gauge

Although this is not always necessary, it is easy to do at this time and the cost is negligible. Every time you adjust or replace the breaker points, the ignition timing must be checked and, if necessary, adjusted. No special equipment other than a feeler gauge is required for point replacement or adjustment, but a dwell meter is strongly advised. A magnetic screwdriver is handy to prevent the small points and condenser screws from falling down into the distributor.

Point sets using the push-in type wiring terminal should be used on those distributors equipped with an R.F.I. (Radio Frequency Interference) shield (1970–74). Points using a lockscrew-type terminal may short out due to contact between the shield and the screw.

1. Push down on the spring-loaded V8 distributor cap retaining screws and give them a half-turn to release. Unscrew the captive six-cylinder cap retaining screws. Remove the cap. You might have to unclip or detach some or all of the plug wires to remove the cap. If so, number the wires and the cap before removal.

2. Clean the cap inside and out with a clean rag. Check for cracks and carbon paths. A carbon path shows up as a dark line, usually from one of the cap sockets or inside terminals to a ground. Check the condition of

**The six cylinder distributor cap is retained by two captive screws**

**The eight cylinder distributor cap has latches**

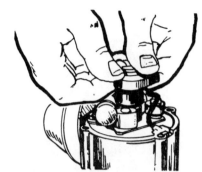

**Pull the six cylinder rotor straight up to remove**

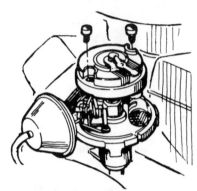

**The eight cylinder rotor is held on by two screws**

the carbon button inside the center of the cap and the inside terminals. Replace the cap as necessary. Carbon paths usually cannot be successfully scraped off. It is better to replace the cap.

3. Pull the six-cylinder rotor up and off the shaft. Remove the two screws and lift the round V8 rotor off. There is less danger of losing the screws if you just back them out all the way and lift them off with the rotor. Clean off the metal outer tip if it is burned or corroded. Don't file it. Replace the rotor as necessary or if one came with your tune-up kit.

4. Remove the radio frequency interference shield if your distributor has one. Watch out for those little screws! The factory says that the points don't need to be replaced if they are only slightly rough or pitted. However, sad experience shows that it is more economical and reliable in the long run to replace the point set while the distributor is open, than to have to do this at a later (and possibly more inconvenient) time.

5. Pull off the two wire terminals from the point assembly. One wire comes from the condenser and the other comes from within the distributor. The terminals are usually held in place by spring tension only. There

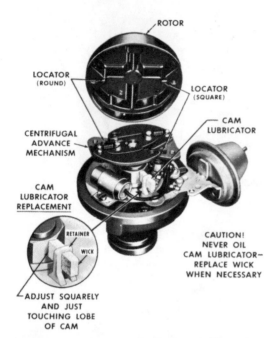

ROTOR

LOCATOR (ROUND)

LOCATOR (SQUARE)

CENTRIFUGAL ADVANCE MECHANISM

CAM LUBRICATOR

CAM LUBRICATOR REPLACEMENT

RETAINER

WICK

ADJUST SQUARELY AND JUST TOUCHING LOBE OF CAM

CAUTION! NEVER OIL CAM LUBRICATOR— REPLACE WICK WHEN NECESSARY

Typical V8 point-type distributor (© Chevrolet Motor Div.)

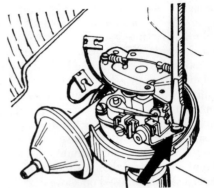

The points are retained by screws; use a magnetic screwdriver to avoid losing them

might be a clamp screw securing the terminals on some older versions. There is also available a one-piece point/condenser assembly for V8s. The radio frequency interference shield isn't needed with this set. Loosen the point set hold-down screw(s). Be very careful not to drop any of these little screws inside the distributor. If this happens, the distribu-

tor will probably have to be removed to get at the screw. If the hold-down screw is lost elsewhere, it must be replaced with one that is no longer than the original to avoid interference with the distributor workings. Remove the point set, even if it is to be reused.

6. If the points are to be reused, clean them with a few strokes of a special point file. This is done with the points removed to prevent tiny metal filings from getting into the distributor. Don't use sandpaper or emery cloth; they will cause rapid point burning.

7. Loosen the condenser hold-down screw and slide the condenser out of the clamp. This will save you a struggle with the clamp, condenser, and the tiny screw when you install the new one. If you have the type

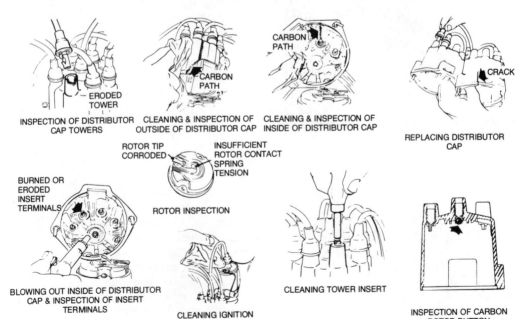

INSPECTION OF DISTRIBUTOR CAP TOWERS

ERODED TOWER

CLEANING & INSPECTION OF OUTSIDE OF DISTRIBUTOR CAP

CARBON PATH

CLEANING & INSPECTION OF INSIDE OF DISTRIBUTOR CAP

CARBON PATH

REPLACING DISTRIBUTOR CAP

CRACK

BURNED OR ERODED INSERT TERMINALS

ROTOR TIP CORRODED

INSUFFICIENT ROTOR CONTACT SPRING TENSION

ROTOR INSPECTION

BLOWING OUT INSIDE OF DISTRIBUTOR CAP & INSPECTION OF INSERT TERMINALS

CLEANING IGNITION COIL

CLEANING TOWER INSERT

INSPECTION OF CARBON ROTOR BUTTON

Inspection points for the distributor, rotor, cap, and coil (© Chevrolet Motor Div.)

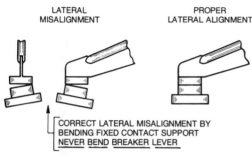

LATERAL MISALIGNMENT   PROPER LATERAL ALIGNMENT

CORRECT LATERAL MISALIGNMENT BY BENDING FIXED CONTACT SUPPORT NEVER BEND BREAKER LEVER

**Breaker point alignment (© Chevrolet Motor Div.)**

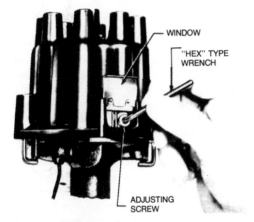

WINDOW

"HEX" TYPE WRENCH

ADJUSTING SCREW

**Setting the dwell on a 1970–74 V8 distributor (© Chevrolet Motor Div.)**

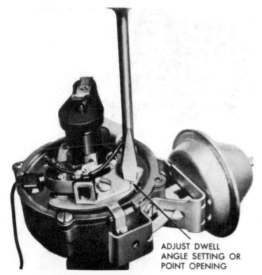

ADJUST DWELL ANGLE SETTING OR POINT OPENING

**Adjusting the point gap (and therefore the dwell) on a six cylinder distributor (© Chevrolet Motor Div.)**

of clamp that is permanently fastened to the condenser, remove the screw and the condenser. Don't lose the screw.

8. Attend to the distributor cam lubrica-

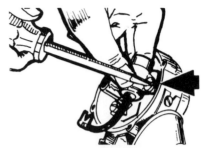

**The condenser is also retained by a screw**

tor. If you have the round kind, turn it around on its shaft at the first tune-up and replace it at the second. If you have the long kind, switch ends at the first tune-up and replace it at the second.

NOTE: *Don't oil or grease the lubricator. The foam is impregnated with a special lubricant.*

If you didn't get any lubricator at all, or if it looks like someone took it off, don't worry. You don't really need it. Just rub a match-head size dab of grease on the cam lobes.

9. Install the new condenser. If you left the clamp in place, just slide the new condenser into the clamp.

10. Replace the point set and tighten the screws on a V8. Leave the screw slightly loose on a six. Replace the two wire terminals, making sure that the wires don't interfere with anything. Some V8 distributors have a ground wire that must go under one of the screws.

11. Check that the contacts meet squarely. If they don't, bend the tab supporting the fixed contact.

NOTE: *If you are installing preset points on a V8, go ahead to Step 16. If they are preset, it will say so on the package. It would be a good idea to make a quick check on point gap, anyway. Sometimes those preset points aren't.*

**The points have a locating tab which fits into a hole in the breaker plate**

12. Turn the engine until a high point on the cam that opens the points contacts the rubbing block on the point arm. You can turn the engine by hand if you can get a wrench on the crankshaft pulley nut, or you can grasp the fan belt and turn the engine with the spark plugs removed.

CAUTION: *If you try turning the engine by hand, be very careful not to get your fingers pinched in the pulleys.*

On a stick-shift you can push it forward in High gear. Another alternative is to bump the starter switch or use a remote starter switch.

13. On a six, there is a screwdriver slot near the contacts. Insert a screwdriver and lever the points open or closed until they appear to be at about the gap specified in the "Tune-Up Specifications." On a V8, simply insert a ⅛ in. Allen wrench into the adjustment screw and turn. The wrench sometimes comes with a tune-up kit.

14. Insert the correct size feeler gauge and adjust the gap until you can push the gauge in and out between the contacts with a slight drag, but without disturbing the point

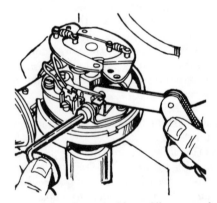

**V8 point gap is adjusted with an Allen wrench**

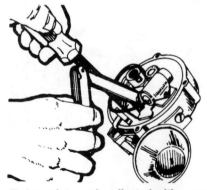

**Six cylinder point gap is adjusted with a screwdriver**

arm. This operation takes a bit of experience to obtain the correct feel. Check by trying the gauges 0.001–0.002 larger and smaller than the setting size. The larger one should disturb the point arm, while the smaller one should not drag at all. Tighten the six-cylinder point set hold-down screw. Recheck the gap, because it often changes when the screw is tightened.

15. After all the point adjustments are complete, pull a white business card through (between) the contacts to remove any traces of oil. Oil will cause rapid contact burning.

NOTE: *You can adjust six-cylinder dwell at this point, if you wish. Refer to Step 18.*

16. Replace the radio frequency interference shield, if any. You don't need it if you are installing the one-piece point/condenser set. Push the rotor firmly down into place. It will only go on one way. Tighten the V8 rotor screws. If the rotor is not installed properly, it will probably break when the starter is operated.

17. Replace the distributor cap.

18. If a dwell meter is available, check the dwell. The dwell meter hookup is shown in the "Troubleshooting" Section.

NOTE: *This hookup may not apply to electronic, capacitive discharge, or other special ignition systems. Some dwell meters won't work at all with such systems.*

Dwell can be checked with the engine running or cranking. Decrease dwell by increasing the point gap; increase by decreasing the gap. Dwell angle is simply the number of degrees of distributor shaft rotation during which the points stay closed. Theoretically, if the point gap is correct, the dwell should also be correct or nearly so. Adjustment with a dwell meter produces more exact, consistent results since it is a dynamic adjustment. If dwell varies more than 3 degrees from idle speed to 1,750 engine rpm, the distributor is worn.

19. To adjust dwell on a six, trial and error point adjustments are required. On a V8, simply open the metal window on the distributor and insert a ⅛ in. Allen wrench. Turn until the meter shows the correct reading. Be sure to snap the window closed.

20. An approximate dwell adjustment can be made without a meter on a V8. Turn the adjusting screw clockwise until the engine begins to misfire, then turn it out ½ turn.

21. If the engine won't start, check:

a. That all the spark plug wires are in place.

b. That the rotor has been installed.

c. That the two (or three) wires inside the distributor are connected.

d. That the points open and close when the engine turns.

e. That the gap is correct and the hold-down screw (on a six) is tight.

22. After the first 200 miles or so on a new set of points, the point gap often closes up due to initial rubbing block wear. For best performance, recheck the dwell (or gap) at this time. This quick initial wear is the reason why the factory recommends 0.003 in. more gap on new points.

23. Since changing the gap affects the ignition timing, the timing should be checked and adjusted as necessary after each point replacement or adjustment.

### 1975–80

These engines use the breakerless HEI (High Energy Ignition) system. Since there is no mechanical contact, there is no wear or need for periodic service. There is an item in the distributor that resembles a condenser; it is a radio interference suppression capacitor which requires no service.

## HIGH ENERGY IGNITION (HEI) SYSTEM

The General Motors HEI system is a pulse-triggered, transistor-controlled, inductive discharge ignition system. Except on inline six-cylinder models through 1977, the entire HEI system is contained within the distributor cap. Inline six-cylinder engines through 1977 have an external coil. Otherwise, the systems are the same.

The distributor, in addition to housing the mechanical and vacuum advance mechanisms, contains the ignition coil (except on some inline six engines), the electronic control module, and the magnetic triggering device. The magnetic pick-up assembly contains a permanent magnet, a pole piece with internal "teeth," and a pick-up coil (not to be confused with the ignition coil).

In the HEI system, as in other electronic ignition systems, the breaker points have been replaced with an electronic switch—a transistor—which is located *within* the control module. This switching transistor performs the same function the points did in a conventional ignition system; it simply turns coil primary current on and off at the correct

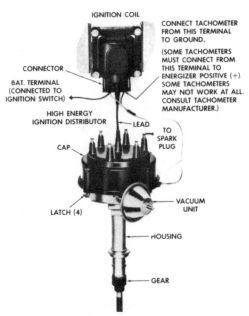

**Six cylinder HEI distributor, 1975–77. 1978–80 models have the coil in the distributor cap (© Chevrolet Motor Div.)**

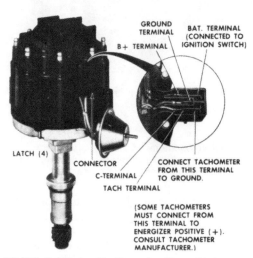

**V8 HEI distributor (© Chevrolet Motor Div.)**

time. Essentially then, electronic and conventional ignition systems operate on the same principle.

The module which houses the switching transistor is controlled (turned on and off) by a magnetically generated impulse induced in the pick-up coil. When the teeth of the rotating timer align with the teeth of the pole piece, the induced voltage in the pick-up coil signals the electronic module to open the coil primary circuit. The primary current then decreases, and a high voltage is induced in the ignition coil secondary windings which is

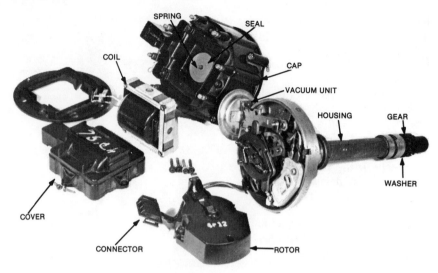

**V8 HEI distributor components**

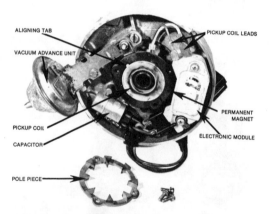

**Internal components of the HEI distributor; later
models have slightly different connectors at the
module, but the wiring is the same**

### Timing Light Use

Inductive pick-up timing lights are the best
kind to use with HEI. Timing lights which
connect between the spark plug and the
spark plug wire occasionally (not always) give
false readings.

### Spark Plug Wires

The plug wires used with HEI systems are of
a different construction than conventional
wires. When replacing them, make sure you
get the correct wires, since conventional
wires won't carry the voltage. Also, handle
them carefully to avoid cracking or splitting
them and *never* pierce them.

then directed through the rotor and high
voltage leads (spark plug wires) to fire the
spark plugs.

In essence then, the pick-up coil module
system simply replaces the conventional
breaker points and condenser. The condenser found within the distributor is for
radio suppression purposes only and has
nothing to do with the ignition process. The
module automatically controls the dwell
period, increasing it with increasing engine
speed. Since dwell is automatically controlled, it cannot be adjusted. The module itself is non-adjustable and non-repairable and
must be replaced if found defective.

## HEI System Precautions

Before going on to troubleshooting, it might
be a good idea to take note of the following
precautions:

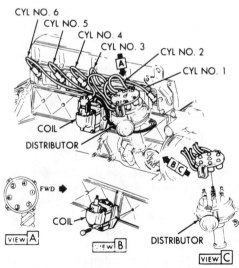

**Six cylinder HEI wiring with non-integral coil
(© Chevrolet Motor Div.)**

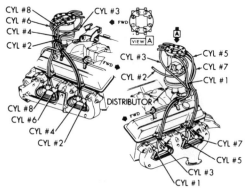

CYL #8
CYL #6
CYL #4
CYL #2
CYL #3
FWD
VIEW A
A
CYL #3
CYL #5
CYL #7
CYL #2
CYL #1
DISTRIBUTOR
FWD
CYL #8
CYL #6
CYL #4
CYL #2
CYL #7
CYL #5
CYL #3
CYL #1

**V8 HEI wiring (© Chevrolet Motor Div.)**

### Tachometer Use

Not all tachometers will operate or indicate correctly when used on a HEI system. While some tachometers may give a reading, this does not necessarily mean the reading is correct. In addition, some tachometers hook up differently from others. If you can't figure out whether or not your tachometer will work on your truck, check with the tachometer manufacturer. Dwell readings, of course, have no significance at all.

### HEI System Testers

Instruments designed specifically for testing HEI systems are available from several tool manufacturers. Some of these will even test the module itself. However, the tests given in the following section will require only an ohmmeter and a voltmeter.

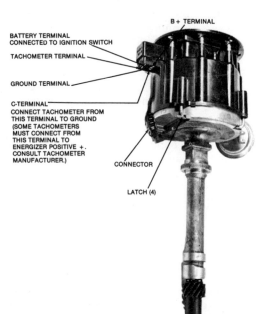

B+ TERMINAL
BATTERY TERMINAL
CONNECTED TO IGNITION SWITCH
TACHOMETER TERMINAL
GROUND TERMINAL
C-TERMINAL
CONNECT TACHOMETER FROM
THIS TERMINAL TO GROUND
(SOME TACHOMETERS
MUST CONNECT FROM
THIS TERMINAL TO
ENERGIZER POSITIVE +.
CONSULT TACHOMETER
MANUFACTURER.)
CONNECTOR
LATCH (4)

**HEI distributor connections**

## Troubleshooting the HEI System

The symptoms of a defective component within the HEI system are exactly the same as those you would encounter in a conventional system. Some of these symptoms are:

- Hard or no Starting
- Rough Idle
- Poor Fuel Economy
- Engine misses under load or while accelerating

If you suspect a problem in the ignition system, there are certain preliminary checks which you should carry out before you begin to check the electronic portions of the system. First, it is extremely important to make sure the vehicle battery is in a good state of charge. A defective or poorly charged battery will cause the various components of the ignition system to read incorrectly when they are being tested. Second, make sure all wiring connections are clean and tight, not only at the battery, but also at the distributor cap, ignition coil, and at the electronic control module.

Since the only change between electronic and conventional ignition systems is in the distributor component area, it is imperative to check the secondary ignition circuit first. If the secondary circuit checks out properly, then the engine condition is probably not the fault of the ignition system. To check the secondary ignition system, perform a simple spark test. Remove one of the plug wires and insert some sort of extension in the plug socket. An old spark plug with the ground electrode removed makes a good extension. Hold the wire and extension about ¼ in. away from the block and crank the engine. If a normal spark occurs, then the problem is most likely *not* in the ignition system. Check for fuel system problems, or fouled spark plugs.

If, however, there is no spark or a weak spark, then further ignition system testing will have to be done. Troubleshooting techniques fall into two categories, depending on the nature of the problem. The categories are (1) Engine cranks, but won't start or (2) Engine runs, but runs rough or cuts out. To begin with, let's consider the first case.

### ENGINE FAILS TO START

If the engine won't start, perform a spark test as described earlier. This will narrow the problem area down considerably. If no spark occurs, check for the presence of normal battery voltage at the battery (BAT) terminal in the distributor cap. The ignition switch must be in the "on" position for this test. Either a voltmeter or a test light may be used for this test. Connect the test light wire to ground and the probe end to the BAT terminal at the distributor. If the light comes on, you have voltage to the distributor. If the light fails to come on, this indicates an open circuit in the ignition primary wiring leading to the distributor. In this case, you will have to check wiring continuity back to the ignition switch using a test light. If there is battery voltage at the BAT terminal, but no spark at the plugs, then the problem lies within the distributor assembly. Go on to the distributor components test section.

### ENGINE RUNS, BUT RUNS ROUGH OR CUTS OUT

1. Make sure the plug wires are in good shape first. There should be no obvious cracks or breaks. You can check the plug wires with an ohmmeter, but *do not* pierce the wires with a probe. Check the chart for the correct plug wire resistance.

One lead from the ohmmeter connects to the rotor button when checking coil secondary resistance

### HEI Plug Wire Resistance Chart

| Wire Length | Minimum | Maximum |
|---|---|---|
| 0–15 inches | 3000 ohms | 10,000 ohms |
| 15–25 inches | 4000 ohms | 15,000 ohms |
| 25–35 inches | 6000 ohms | 20,000 ohms |
| Over 35 inches | | 25,000 ohms |

2. If the plug wires are OK, remove the cap assembly, and check for moisture, cracks, chips, or carbon tracks, or any other high voltage leaks or failures. Replace the cap if you find any defects. Make sure the timer wheel rotates when the engine is cranked. If everything is all right so far, go on to the distributor components test section.

### DISTRIBUTOR COMPONENTS TESTING

If the trouble has been narrowed down to the units within the distributor, the following tests can help pinpoint the defective component. An ohmmeter with both high and low ranges should be used. These tests are made with the cap assembly removed and the battery wire disconnected.

1. Connect an ohmmeter between the TACH and BAT terminals in the distributor cap. The primary coil resistance should be less than one ohm (zero or nearly zero).

2. To check the coil secondary resistance, connect an ohmmeter between the rotor button and the BAT terminal. Then connect the ohmmeter between the ground terminal and the rotor button. The resistance in both cases should be between 6,000 and 30,000 ohms.

3. Replace the coil *only* if the readings in step one and two are infinite.

NOTE: *These resistance checks will not disclose shorted coil windings. This condition can be detected only with scope analysis or a suitably designed coil tester. If these instruments are unavailable, replace the coil with a known good coil as a final coil test.*

4. To test the pick-up coil, first disconnect the white and green module leads. Set the ohmmeter on the high scale and connect it between a ground and either the white or green lead. Any resistance measurement *less* than infinity requires replacement of the pick-up coil.

5. Pick-up coil continuity is tested by connecting the ohmmeter (on low range) between the white and green leads. Normal resistance is between 650 and 850 ohms, or 500 and 1500 ohms on 1977 and later models. Move the vacuum advance arm while performing this test. This will detect any break in coil continuity. Such a condition can cause intermittent misfiring. Replace the pick-up coil if the reading is outside the specified limits.

6. If no defects have been found at this time, and you still have a problem, then the module will have to be checked. If you do not have access to a module tester, the only possible alternative is a substitution test. If the module fails the subsitution test, replace it.

## COMPONENT REPLACEMENT

### Integral Ignition Coil

1. Disconnect the feed and module wire terminal connectors from the distributor cap.
2. Remove the ignition set retainer.
3. Remove the 4 coil cover-to-distributor cap screws and the coil cover.
4. Remove the 4 coil-to-distributor cap screws.
5. Using a blunt drift, press the coil wire spade terminals up out of distributor cap.
6. Lift the coil up out of the distributor cap.
7. Remove and clean the coil spring, rubber seal washer and coil cavity of the distributor cap.
8. Coat the rubber seal with a dielectric lubricant furnished in the replacement ignition coil package.
9. Reverse the above procedures to install.

### Distributor Cap

1. Remove the feed and module wire terminal connectors from the distributor cap.
2. Remove the retainer and spark plug wires from the cap.
3. Depress and release the 4 distributor cap-to-housing retainers and lift off the cap assembly.
4. Remove the 4 coil cover screws and cover.
5. Using a finger or a blunt drift, push the spade terminals up out of the distributor cap.
6. Remove all 4 coil screws and lift the coil, coil spring and rubber seal washer out of the cap coil cavity.
7. Using a new distributor cap, reverse the above procedures to assemble being sure to clean and lubricate the rubber seal washer with dielectric lubricant.

### Rotor

1. Disconnect the feed and module wire connectors from the distributor.
2. Depress and release the 4 distributor cap to housing retainers and lift off the cap assembly.
3. Remove the two rotor attaching screws and rotor.
4. Reverse the above procedure to install.

### Vacuum Advance

1. Remove the distributor cap and rotor as previously described.
2. Disconnect the vacuum hose from the vacuum advance unit.
3. Remove the two vacuum advance retaining screws, pull the advance unit outward, rotate and disengage the operating rod from its tang.
4. Reverse the above procedure to install.

### Module

1. Remove the distributor cap and rotor as previously described.
2. Disconnect the harness connector and pick-up coil spade connectors from the module. Be careful not to damage the wires when removing the connector.
3. Remove the two screws and module from the distributor housing.
4. Coat the bottom of the new module with dielectric lubricant supplied with the new module. Reverse the above procedure to install.

## Ignition Timing

Timing should be checked at each tune-up and any time the points are adjusted or replaced. It isn't likely to change much with HEI. The timing marks consist of a notch on the rim of the crankshaft pulley or vibration damper and a graduated scale attached to the engine front (timing) cover. A stroboscopic flash (dynamic) timing light must be used, as a static light is too inaccurate for emission controlled engines.

There are three basic types of timing light

**Typical ignition timing marks (© Chevrolet Motor Div.)**

available. The first is a simple neon bulb with two wire connections. One wire connects to the spark plug terminal and the other plugs into the end of the spark plug wire for the No. 1 cylinder, thus connecting the light in series with the spark plug. This type of light is pretty dim and must be held very closely to the timing marks to be seen. Sometimes a dark corner has to be sought out to see the flash at all. This type of light is very inexpensive. The second type operates from the vehicle battery—two alligator clips connect to the battery terminals, while an adapter enables a third clip to be connected to the No. 1 spark plug and wire. This type is a bit more expensive, but it provides a nice bright flash that you can see even in bright sunlight. It is the type most often seen in professional shops. The third type replaces the battery power source with 110 volt current.

Some timing lights have other features built into them, such as dwell meters or tachometers. These are convenient, in that they reduce the tangle of wires under the hood when you're working, but may duplicate the functions of tools you already have. One worthwhile feature, which is becoming more of a necessity with higher voltage ignition systems, is an inductive pickup. The inductive pickup clamps around the No. 1 spark plug wire, sensing the surges of high voltage electricity as they are sent to the plug. The advantage is that no mechanical connection is inserted between the wire and the plug, which eliminates false signals to the timing light. A timing light with an inductive pickup should be used on HEI systems.

To check and adjust the timing:

1. Warm up the engine to normal operating temperature. Stop the engine and connect the timing light to the No. 1 (left front on V8, front on six) spark plug wire. You can also use the No. 6 wire, if it is more convenient. No. 6 is the rear cylinder on a six, and the third cylinder back on the right bank of a V8. Numbering is illustrated in Chapter 3. Under no circumstances should the spark plug wire be pierced to hook up a timing light. Clean off the timing marks and mark the pulley or damper notch and timing scale with white chalk. If you don't have any chalk handy, an aspirin tablet can be used. The timing notch on the pulley or damper can be elusive. The best way to get it to an accessible position for marking is to "bump" the engine around using either the ignition key or a remote starter.

2. Disconnect and plug the vacuum line at the distributor. This is done to prevent any distributor vacuum advance. The vacuum line is the rubber hose connected to the metal cone-shaped canister on the side of the distributor. The hose must be plugged to prevent an air leak into the carburetor. A short screw, pencil, or a golf tee can be used to plug the line.

3. Start the engine and adjust the idle speed to that specified in the "Tune-Up Specifications" chart. With automatic transmission, set the specified idle speed in Park. It will be too high, since it is normally (in most cases) adjusted in Drive. However, it is safer to adjust the timing in Park and to reset the idle speed after all timing work is done. Some trucks require that the timing be set with the transmission in Neutral. Refer to the "Tune-up Specifications" chart or the underhood sticker for details. You can disconnect the idle solenoid, if any, to get the speed down. Otherwise, adjust the idle speed screw. This is done to prevent any centrifugal (mechanical) advance.

The tachometer hookup for 1970–74 models is the same as the dwell meter hookup shown in the "Tune-Up and Troubleshooting" sections. On 1975–77 HEI systems, the tachometer connects to the TACH terminal on the distributor (V8) or on the coil (six) and to a ground. For 1978–80, all tachometer connections are to the TACH terminal. Some tachometers must connect to the TACH terminal and to the positive battery terminal. Some tachometers won't work with HEI.

CAUTION: *Never ground the HEI TACH terminal; serious system damage will result.*

4. Aim the timing light at the pointer marks. Be careful not to touch the fan, because it may appear to be standing still. Keep the timing light wires clear of the fan, belts, and pulleys. If the pulley or damper notch isn't aligned with the proper timing mark (see the "Tune-Up Specifications" chart), the timing will have to be adjusted.

NOTE: *TDC or Top Dead Center corresponds to 0 degrees. B, or BTDC, or Before Top Dead Center may be shown as BEFORE. A, or ATDC, or After Top Dead Center may be shown as AFTER.*

5. Loosen the distributor base clamp locknut. You can buy trick wrenches which make this task a lot easier on V8s. Turn the distributor slowly to adjust the timing, holding it by

the body and not the cap. Turn the distributor in the direction of rotor rotation (found in the "Firing Order" illustration in Chapter 3) to retard, and against the direction of rotation to advance.

6. Tighten the locknut. Check the timing again, in case the distributor moved slightly as you tightened it.

7. Replace the distributor vacuum line. Correct the idle speed.

8. Stop the engine and disconnect the timing light.

## Carburetor

1976 and later models, except as noted in the procedures, have sealed idle mixture screws. In most cases, the mixture screws have limiter caps, but in later years the mixture screws are concealed under staked-in plugs. Idle mixture is adjustable only during carburetor overhaul, and requires the addition of propane as an artificial mixture enrichener. For these reasons, mixture adjustments are not covered here for affected models.

See the emission control label in the engine compartment for procedures and specifications not supplied here.

### *IDLE SPEED AND MIXTURE*

#### 1970

On all vehicles, disconnect the "FUEL TANK" line from the vapor canister. Remember to reconnect the line after setting the idle speed and mixture. The engine should be at operating temperature with the choke valve and air cleaner damper door fully open, air conditioning OFF and parking brake ON.

250–292 Engines, 10 and 1500 Series: Disconnect and plug the vacuum advance line.

**Adjusting the idle solenoid, 1970 (© Chevrolet Motor Div.)**

Turn the mixture screw in until it lightly contacts the seat, then back out 4 turns. Adjust the solenoid screw to obtain 800 rpm with mannual transmission in Neutral or 630 rpm with automatic transmission in drive. Adjust the mixture screw to obtain 750 rpm with manual transmission in Neutral or automatic in Drive. Electrically, disconnect the solenoid and set the carburetor idle speed screw to obtain 400 rpm and connect the solenoid. Reconnect the vacuum line.

292 Engine, 20 and 2500 Series: Disconnect and plug the distributor vacuum line. Turn the mixture screws in until they lightly contact the seats and back the screw(s) out 4 turns. On manual transmission models, adjust the carburetor idle speed screw to obtain 600 rpm in Neutral. Then adjust the mixture screw to obtain 550 rpm in Neutral. On automatic transmission models, adjust the solenoid screw to obtain 550 rpm with transmission in Drive. Adjust the mixture screw to obtain 500 rpm with transmission in Drive. Disconnect the solenoid and set the carburetor idle speed screw to obtain 400 rpm and connect the solenoid. Reconnect the distributor vacuum line on all models.

307 V8, 10 Series: Disconnect and plug the distributor vacuum line. Turn the mixture screws in until they lightly contact the seats then back them out 4 turns. Adjust the carburetor idle speed screw to obtain 800 rpm with manual transmission in Drive. Adjust the mixture screw to obtain 630 rpm with automatic transmission in Drive. Adjust the mixture screws in equally to obtain 700 rpm with manual transmission in Neutral or 600 rpm with automatic transmission in Drive. Disconnect the solenoid and set the carburetor idle speed screw to obtain 450 rpm and reconnect the solenoid. Reconnect the vacuum line.

307 V8, 20 and 2500 Series: Disconnect and plug the distributor vacuum line. Set the mixture screws for maximum idle rpm and adjust the idle speed screw to obtain 700 rpm with manual transmission in Neutral or 600 rpm with automatic transmission in Drive. Adjust the mixture screws equally to obtain a 200 rpm drop, then back the screws out ¼ turn. As necessary, adjust the idle screw on manual transmission models to obtain 700 rpm with the transmission in Neutral. On automatic transmission models, adjust the solenoid screw to obtain 600 rpm with the transmission in Drive. Disconnect the solenoid electrically and set the carburetor idle screw

to obtain 450 rpm and reconnect the sole-noid. Reconnect the vacuum line.

350 V8, 10 and 1500 Series: Disconnect and plug the distributor vacuum line. Turn the mixture screws in until they lightly contact the seats. Back the screws out 4 turns. Adjust the idle speed screw to obtain 650 rpm with manual transmission in Neutral or 550 rpm with automatic transmission in Drive. Adjust the mixture screws equally to obtain 600 rpm with manual transmission in Neutral or automatic transmission in Drive. Reconnect the vacuum advance line.

350 and 396 V8, 20 and 2500 Series: Disconnect and plug the distributor vacuum line. Turn the mixture screws in until they lightly contact the seats and back them out 4 turns. Adjust the carburetor idle speed screw to obtain 775 rpm (manual transmission in Neutral) or 630 rpm (automatic transmission in Drive). Adjust the mixture screws equally to obtain 700 rpm (manual transmission in Neutral) or 600 rpm (automatic transmission in Drive). Reconnect the vacuum line.

### 1971

The engine should be running at operating temperature, choke valve fully open, parking brake ON and drive wheels blocked.

250–292 Engines, 10 and 1500 Series: Disconnect the "FUEL TANK" line from the evaporative canister. Disconnect the vacuum advance line and plug the vacuum source. Adjust the carburetor speed screw to obtain 550 rpm with manual transmission in Neutral or 550 rpm with automatic transmission in Drive. Do not adjust the solenoid screw.

CAUTION: *Use the C.E.C. solenoid screw to adjust the idle speed could result in a decrease in engine braking.*

Reconnect the "FUEL TANK" line and the vacuum advance line.

307 V8, 10 and 1500 Series: Disconnect the "FUEL TANK" line from the evaporative canister. Disconnect the vacuum source opening. Adjust the carburetor speed screw to obtain 600 rpm with manual transmission in Neutral or 550 rpm with automatic transmission in Drive and air conditioner ON. Do not adjust the solenoid. See the previous "Caution." Reconnect the "FUEL TANK" line and the vacuum advance line.

350 and 402 V8, 10 and 1500 Series: Disconnect the "FUEL TANK" line from the evaporative canister. Disconnect the vacuum advance line and plug the vacuum source opening. Turn the air conditioner OFF and adjust the carburetor speed screw to obtain

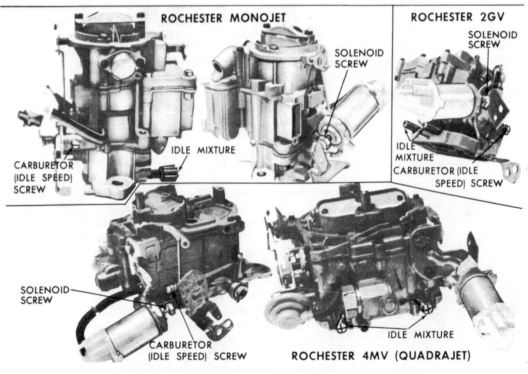

**Idle speed and mixture screws, 1971 (© Chevrolet Motor Div.)**

600 rpm with manual transmission in Neutral or 550 rpm (600 rpm on 402 V8) with automatic transmission in Drive. Do not adjust the solenoid screw, or a decrease in engine braking could result. Place the fast idle cam follower on the second step of the fast idle cam and turn the air conditioner OFF. Adjust the fast idle to 1,350 rpm with manual transmission in Neutral or 1,500 rpm with automatic transmission in PARK. Reconnect the "FUEL TANK" and vacuum advance lines.

292 and 307 V8, 20 and 2500 Series: Disconnect the vacuum advance line and plug the vacuum source opening. Turn the air conditioner ON. Turn the mixture screws in until they lightly contact the seats and back them out 4 turns. Adjust the carburetor speed screw to obtain 600 rpm with manual transmission in Neutral and 500 rpm with automatic in Drive. Reconnect the vacuum advance hose.

350 and 402 V8, 20 and 2500 Series: Disconnect the distributor vacuum advance hose and plug the vacuum source opening. Turn the air conditioner off. Turn the mixture screws in until they contact the seats lightly. Back the screws out 4 turns. Adjust the carburetor speed screw to obtain 650 rpm with manual transmission in Neutral or 550 rpm with automatic transmission in Drive. Reconnect the vacuum advance hose.

**1972**

The engine should be at normal operating temperature with the choke valve fully open, parking brake ON and the drive wheels blocked. All carburetors are equipped with idle mixture limiter caps, which provide for only a small adjustment range. Normally, these should not be removed. However, if they are removed, the CO content of the exhaust should be checked to be sure that it meets Federal Emission Control limits.

250 and 292: Disconnect the "FUEL TANK" line from the vapor canister. Remember to reconnect it after making the adjustment. Disconnect and plug the vacuum line source. Adjust the idle stop solenoid to obtain 700 rpm with manual transmission in Neutral or 600 rpm with automatic transmission in Drive. Do not adjust the CEC solenoid screw.

CAUTION: *If the CEC solenoid screw is adjusted out of limits, a decrease in engine braking may result.*

Reconnect the vacuum line.

307 V8: Disconnect the "FUEL TANK" line from the vapor canister and remove and plug the vacuum line source. Adjust the idle stop solenoid screw to obtain 900 rpm (950 on California trucks) with manual transmission in Neutral or 600 rpm with automatic transmission in Drive. On trucks without TCS,

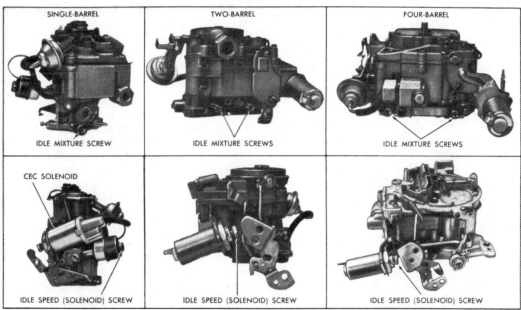

ROCHESTER CARBURETORS

SINGLE-BARREL     TWO-BARREL     FOUR-BARREL

IDLE MIXTURE SCREW     IDLE MIXTURE SCREWS     IDLE MIXTURE SCREWS

CEC SOLENOID

IDLE SPEED (SOLENOID) SCREW     IDLE SPEED (SOLENOID) SCREW     IDLE SPEED (SOLENOID) SCREW

**Idle speed and mixture screws, 1972–75 (© Chevrolet Motor Div.)**

adjust speed screw for 600 rpm with transmission in Neutral. With transmission in Park or Neutral, adjust the fast idle speed to obtain 1850 rpm. Reconnect the "FUEL TANK" line and the vacuum line.

350 V8: Disconnect the "FUEL TANK" line and disconnect and plug the vacuum line. On vehicles with TCS, turn the air conditioner OFF and adjust the idle solenoid screw to obtain 800 rpm with manual transmission in Neutral or 600 rpm with automatic transmission in Drive. On vehicles without TCS, adjust the carburetor speed screw to obtain 600 rpm with transmission in Neutral. Place the fast idle cam, turn the air conditioner OFF and adjust the fast idle to 1,350 rpm with manual transmission in Neutral or automatic transmission in Drive. Reconnect the "FUEL TANK" and vacuum lines.

402 V8: Disconnect the "FUEL TANK" line from the evaporative canister. Disconnect the vacuum advance hose and plug the vacuum source opening. On trucks with TCS, turn the air conditioning OFF and adjust the idle stop solenoid screw to obtain 750 rpm with manual transmission in Neutral or 600 rpm with automatic in Drive. On trucks without TCS, adjust the carburetor speed screw to obtain 600 rpm with transmission in Neutral. Place the fast idle cam follower on the second step of the fast idle cam, turn the air conditioner OFF and adjust the fast idle speed to 1,350 rpm with manual transmission in Neutral or 1,500 rpm with automatic transmission in Drive. Reconnect the "FUEL TANK" line and the vacuum advance line.

### 1973–75

Emission system requirements necessitate the division of trucks as follows:
- Light-Duty: All 10 and 1500 Series
- Heavy-Duty: All 20 and 2500 Series

All adjustments should be made with the engine at operating temperature, choke valve fully open, air conditioner OFF, parking brake ON and drive wheels blocked.

250: Disconnect the "FUEL TANK" line and the vacuum source opening. Plug the vacuum line. Adjust the idle stop solenoid by turning the hex nut to obtain:

700 rpm (1973) or 600 rpm (1974) on all heavy-duty vehicles with manual transmission in Neutral;

600 rpm (1973–74) on all light-duty vehicles with automatic transmission in Drive.

850 rpm (1974–75) on all light duty trucks with manual transmission.

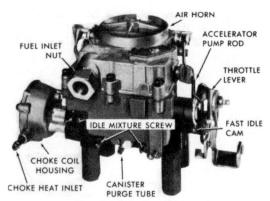

**Rochester 2GC, 1975 (© Chevrolet Motor Div.)**

Do not adjust the CEC solenoid on 1973 vehicles or a decrease in engine braking may result. Place automatic transmissions in Park and manual transmissions in Neutral and adjust the fast idle to 1800 rpm, on the top step of the fast idle cam. Reconnect the "FUEL TANK" and vacuum lines.

292: Disconnect the vacuum advance line and plug the vacuum source opening. Adjust the idle stop solenoid screw to obtain 600 rpm on California (and all 1974–75) trucks or 700 rpm on all other trucks. Reconnect the vacuum advance line.

1973 307 V8: On light-duty vehicles, disconnect the "FUEL TANK" line from the vapor canister and plug the vacuum source opening. Adjust the idle stop solenoid to obtain 600 rpm with automatic transmission in Park or 900 rpm with manual transmission in Neutral. Disconnect the idle stop solenoid and adjust the low idle screw located inside the solenoid hex nut, to obtain 450 rpm in Neutral or Drive. Reconnect the idle stop solenoid, the "FUEL TANK" line, and the vacuum line.

350 V8: On light-duty vehicles, disconnect the "FUEL TANK" line from the vapor canister. Disconnect and plug the vacuum line. On heavy-duty vehicles, adjust the carburetor idle speed screw to obtain 600 rpm with automatic transmission in Park or manual transmission in Neutral. On light-duty vehicles, adjust the idle stop solenoid screw to obtain 600 rpm with automatic transmission in Drive or 900 rpm with manual transmission in Neutral. On light-duty vehicles with automatic transmission, reconnect the vacuum line and adjust the fast idle to 1600 rpm on the top step of the fast idle cam. On light-duty vehicles with manual transmission, adjust the fast idle screw to obtain 1300 rpm

with the screw on the top step of the fast idle cam and the vacuum line disconnected. Reconnect the "FUEL TANK" line and the vacuum line.

454 V8: On light-duty trucks, disconnect the "FUEL TANK" line from the evaporative canister. Disconnect the vacuum advance line and plug the vacuum source opening. Adjust the idle speed with the idle stop solenoid screw to obtain:

700 rpm on all heavy-duty trucks with automatic transmission in Park and manual transmission in Neutral.

600 rpm on light-duty trucks with automatic transmission in Drive.

900 rpm (1973) or 800 rpm (1974–75) on light-duty trucks with manual transmission in Neutral.

On light-duty trucks with automatic transmission, reconnect the vacuum advance line. Adjust the fast idle screw to obtain 1,600 rpm with the screw on the top step of the fast idle cam.

On light-duty trucks with manual transmission, adjust the fast idle screw to obtain 1,600 rpm (1973) or 1,500 rpm (1974–75) with the screw on the top step of the fast idle cam and the vacuum hose disconnected.

Reconnect the "FUEL TANK" line and the vacuum advance line.

### 1976 IDLE SPEED ADJUSTMENT

All adjustments should be made with the engine at normal operating temperature, air cleaner on, choke open, and air conditioning off, unless otherwise noted. Set the parking brake and block the rear wheels.

250 and 292 Engines: Disconnect and plug the carburetor and PCV hoses at the vapor canister on the 250. On heavy duty emissions 250s and all 292s, disconnect the "FUEL TANK" hose at the vapor canister. If the engine has a solenoid located between the carburetor and the distributor on the vacuum hose line, disconnect and plug the vacuum line. Otherwise, leave the vacuum hose connected. On heavy duty 250s and all 292s turn the air conditioning on, if so equipped. With manual transmissions in Neutral, 250 automatics in Drive, and heavy duty 250 and 292 automatics in Neutral, turn the solenoid body in or out to set the idle speed to specified rpm. Disconnect the electrical wire from the carburetor solenoid, and turn the air conditioner off. Turn the ⅛ in. hex (Allen head) screw located in the end of the solenoid body to set the low idle to 425 rpm for 250s and 450 rpm for heavy duty 250s and 292s. Reconnect the electrical wire and any hoses that were disconnected.

350, 400, and 454 Engines: On California emissions engines, disconnect and plug the "FUEL TANK" hose at the vapor canister. On heavy duty emissions 350s and 400s, turn the air conditioning on. Place the automatic transmission in Drive, manuals in Neutral, unless otherwise noted in the "Tune-Up Specifications" chart. Adjust the carburetor idle speed to the specified rpm by turning the idle speed screw. Reconnect the "FUEL TANK" hose on California engines. On engines equipped with four barrel carburetors, place the transmission in Park for automatics, and leave manual transmissions in Neutral. Disconnect and plug the vacuum hose at the EGR valve if so equipped. On 454

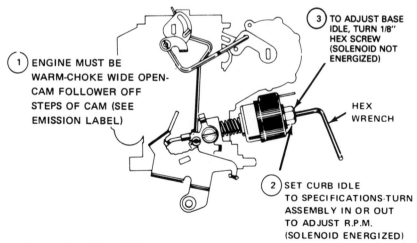

1. ENGINE MUST BE WARM-CHOKE WIDE OPEN-CAM FOLLOWER OFF STEPS OF CAM (SEE EMISSION LABEL)

3. TO ADJUST BASE IDLE, TURN 1/8" HEX SCREW (SOLENOID NOT ENERGIZED)

HEX WRENCH

2. SET CURB IDLE TO SPECIFICATIONS-TURN ASSEMBLY IN OR OUT TO ADJUST R.P.M. (SOLENOID ENERGIZED)

**Idle speed adjustment for 250 and 292 sixes, 1976–78, and 292 sixes, 1979–80 (© Chevrolet Motor Div.)**

engines with electric chokes, disconnect and plug the vacuum hose to the front vacuum break unit located in front of the choke coil housing. Position the cam follower lever of the fast idle unit on the proper step on the cam, as specified on the underhood emissions sticker. Turn the fast idle screw to obtain the specified rpm on the sticker. Reconnect any hoses that were disconnected.

### 1977–78 IDLE SPEED ADJUSTMENT

All adjustments should be made with the engine at normal operating temperature, air cleaner on, choke open, and air conditioning off, unless otherwise noted. Set the parking brake and block the rear wheels. Automatics should be placed in Drive, manuals in Neutral, except as noted in the "Tune-Up Specifications" chart.

250 and 292 Engines: Make certain that the fast idle follower is not on any of the steps marked "H", "2", or "L" on the cam. It should be resting against the first step below "L". Set the idle to specifications by turning the solenoid in or out. Do this with a wrench on the nut attached to the end of the solenoid body. Disconnect the electrical connector from the solenoid. The engine speed will drop. With a ⅛ in. hex (Allen head) wrench, turn the screw located inside the nut attached to the solenoid body, and set the idle speed to 425 rpm for light duty emissions trucks, 450 rpm for heavy duty 250s and 292s. Reconnect the solenoid wire and check idle speed.

305, 350, 400, and 454 Engines: Check the underhood emissions sticker to determine which hoses, if any, must be disconnected. On carburetors not equipped with a solenoid: For two barrel carburetors, make sure that the idle speed screw is on the low ("L") step of the fast idle cam. Then, for all engines except 1978 2bbl models with a solenoid but without air conditioning: Turn the idle speed screw to adjust idle speed to the specification found in the "Tune-Up Specifications" chart or on the underhood emissions sticker.

On 1978 trucks with a two barrel carburetor which have a solenoid, but without air conditioning, open the throttle slightly to allow the solenoid plunger to extend. Turn the solenoid screw to adjust the curb idle to specification, as given in the chart or on the emission control sticker in the engine compartment. Then disconnect the electrical connector from the solenoid. The idle speed will drop. Turn the idle speed screw to set the slow engine idle to the figure given on the emission control sticker in the engine compartment. Reconnect the solenoid and shut off the engine.

On carburetors equipped with a solenoid and air conditioning: Turn the idle speed screw to set the idle to specifications. Then, disconnect the air conditioner compressor electrical lead at the compressor, and turn the air conditioner on. Open the throttle slightly to allow the solenoid plunger to fully extend. Turn the solenoid screw and adjust to 650 rpm, except light duty emissions trucks with manual transmissions, which should be set to 700 rpm. Reconnect the air conditioner compressor lead.

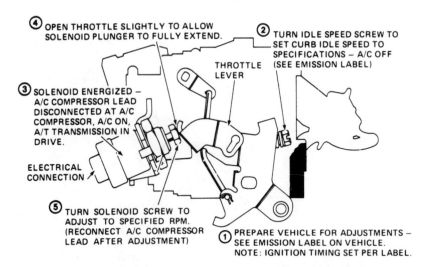

**Idle speed adjustment for V8 4 bbl carburetors with solenoid, 1977 (© Chevrolet Motor Div.)**

### 1979–80 IDLE SPEED ADJUSTMENT

Idle mixture is not adjustable in these years, except for the heavy-duty emission 292 six-cylinder equipped with the 1ME carburetor, and heavy-duty emission V8s equipped with the four barrel M4MC.

All adjustments should be made with the engine at normal operating temperature, air cleaner on, choke open, and air conditioning off, unless otherwise noted. Set the parking brake and block the rear wheels. Automatic transmissions should be set in Drive, manuals in Neutral, unless otherwise noted in the procedures or in the "Tune-Up Specifications" chart, or on the emission control label in the engine compartment.

250 Engine: Check the emission control label in the engine compartment for any special preparatory instructions. Open the throttle slightly to allow the solenoid plunger to extend. Turn the solenoid screw to adjust the curb idle to the figure given in the "Tune-Up Specifications" chart or on the emission control label. Disconnect the electrical connector from the solenoid. The idle speed will drop. Adjust the idle to the basic idle speed figure given on the emission control label by means of the idle speed screw. Connect the solenoid lead and shut off the engine.

292 Engine: See the procedure given for 1977–78. Check the idle figures given against the emission control label in the engine compartment; the label figures must be used if different.

Idle mixture is adjustable on this carburetor (model 1ME):

1. Set the parking brake and block the rear wheels.

2. Remove the air cleaner but do not disconnect any of the hoses. Disconnect and plug the other hoses as directed on the emission control label in the engine compartment.

3. The engine should be at normal operating temperature, choke open, and air conditioning off (if equipped). Connect an accurate tachometer to the engine.

4. Disconnect and plug the vacuum advance hose at the distributor and check the ignition timing. Correct as necessary. Reconnect the vacuum advance hose.

5. Carefully remove the limiter cap from the idle mixture screw. Lightly seat the screw, then back it out just enough to allow the engine to run.

6. Place the transmission in Neutral.

7. Back the mixture screw out ⅛ turn at a time until the maximum idle speed is obtained. Adjust the idle speed to the figure given on the emission control label by means of the idle speed screw. Repeat this step until you are certain that the maximum speed has been obtained with the mixture screw.

8. Turn the mixture screw in ⅛ turn at a time until the idle speed drops to the figure given on the emission control label.

9. Reset the idle speed to the figure given on the emission control label by means of the idle speed screw. Check and adjust the fast

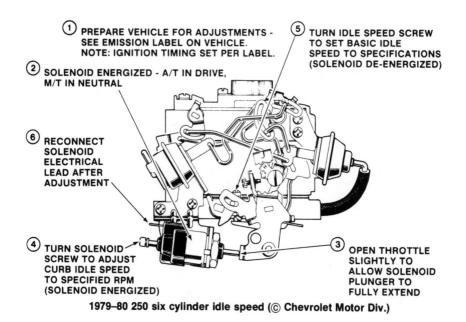

1. PREPARE VEHICLE FOR ADJUSTMENTS - SEE EMISSION LABEL ON VEHICLE. NOTE: IGNITION TIMING SET PER LABEL.

2. SOLENOID ENERGIZED - A/T IN DRIVE, M/T IN NEUTRAL

5. TURN IDLE SPEED SCREW TO SET BASIC IDLE SPEED TO SPECIFICATIONS (SOLENOID DE-ENERGIZED)

6. RECONNECT SOLENOID ELECTRICAL LEAD AFTER ADJUSTMENT

4. TURN SOLENOID SCREW TO ADJUST CURB IDLE SPEED TO SPECIFIED RPM (SOLENOID ENERGIZED)

3. OPEN THROTTLE SLIGHTLY TO ALLOW SOLENOID PLUNGER TO FULLY EXTEND

**1979–80 250 six cylinder idle speed (© Chevrolet Motor Div.)**

idle as directed on the emission control label. Reconnect any vacuum hoses removed in Step 2, install the air cleaner, and recheck the idle speed. Correct, if necessary, by means of the idle speed screw.

305 Engine: Check the emission control label in the engine compartment to determine which hoses, if any, must be disconnected. Make sure the idle speed screw is on the low ("L") step of the fast idle cam. Turn the idle speed screw to adjust the idle speed to the figure given in the "Tune-Up Specifications" chart, or on the emission control label.

On carburetors equipped with a solenoid (air conditioned trucks): turn the idle speed screw to set the idle to specifications, as in the previous paragraph. Then, disconnect the air conditioner compressor electrical lead at the compressor. Turn the air conditioning on. Open the throttle slightly to allow the solenoid plunger to fully extend. Turn the solenoid screw and adjust to 700 rpm with manual transmission (Neutral), or 600 rpm with automatic transmission (Drive). Reconnect the air conditioner electrical lead.

350, 400, and 454 Engines: The idle speed procedure is the same as given for 1977–78 models. Check the emission control label and the "Tune-Up Specifications" chart to determine the proper idle speeds.

Mixture is adjustable on heavy duty emis-

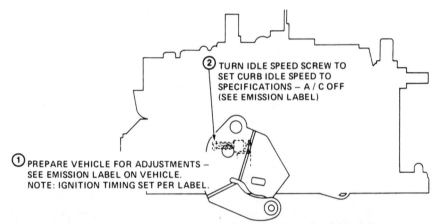

2 TURN IDLE SPEED SCREW TO SET CURB IDLE SPEED TO SPECIFICATIONS – A / C OFF (SEE EMISSION LABEL)

1 PREPARE VEHICLE FOR ADJUSTMENTS – SEE EMISSION LABEL ON VEHICLE. NOTE: IGNITION TIMING SET PER LABEL.

**1979–80 4 bbl adjustments without solenoid; 1978 4 bbl and 1979–80 V8 2 bbl (M2MC) models similar (© Chevrolet Motor Div.)**

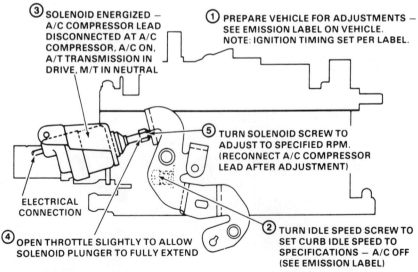

3 SOLENOID ENERGIZED – A/C COMPRESSOR LEAD DISCONNECTED AT A/C COMPRESSOR, A/C ON, A/T TRANSMISSION IN DRIVE, M/T IN NEUTRAL

1 PREPARE VEHICLE FOR ADJUSTMENTS – SEE EMISSION LABEL ON VEHICLE. NOTE: IGNITION TIMING SET PER LABEL.

5 TURN SOLENOID SCREW TO ADJUST TO SPECIFIED RPM. (RECONNECT A/C COMPRESSOR LEAD AFTER ADJUSTMENT)

ELECTRICAL CONNECTION

4 OPEN THROTTLE SLIGHTLY TO ALLOW SOLENOID PLUNGER TO FULLY EXTEND

2 TURN IDLE SPEED SCREW TO SET CURB IDLE SPEED TO SPECIFICATIONS – A/C OFF (SEE EMISSION LABEL)

**1979–80 4 bbl adjustments with solenoid; 1978 4 bbl and 1979 V8 2 bbl (M2MC) similar (© Chevrolet Motor Div.)**

sions V8s with the four barrel M4MC carburetor. This procedure will not work on light-duty emissions trucks.

1. The engine must be at normal operating temperature, choke open, parking brake applied, and the transmission in Park or Neutral. Block the rear wheels and do not stand in front of the truck when making adjustments.

2. Remove the air cleaner. Connect a tachometer and a vacuum gauge to the engine.

3. Turn the idle mixture screws in lightly until they seat, then back them out two turns. Be careful not to tighten the mixture screw against its seat, which will result in damage to the parts.

4. Adjust the idle speed screw to obtain the engine rpm figure specified on the emission control label in the engine compartment.

5. Adjust the idle mixture screws equally to obtain the highest engine speed.

6. Repeat Steps 4 and 5 until the best idle is obtained.

7. Shut off the engine, remove the tachometer and vacuum gauge, and install the air cleaner.

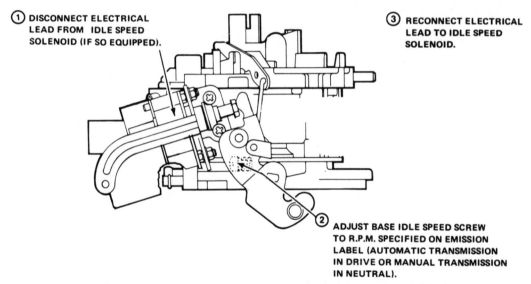

① DISCONNECT ELECTRICAL LEAD FROM IDLE SPEED SOLENOID (IF SO EQUIPPED).

③ RECONNECT ELECTRICAL LEAD TO IDLE SPEED SOLENOID.

② ADJUST BASE IDLE SPEED SCREW TO R.P.M. SPECIFIED ON EMISSION LABEL (AUTOMATIC TRANSMISSION IN DRIVE OR MANUAL TRANSMISSION IN NEUTRAL).

1980 V8 2 bbl (M2MC) idle speed adjustment with solenoid (© Chevrolet Motor Div.)

# Engine and Engine Rebuilding

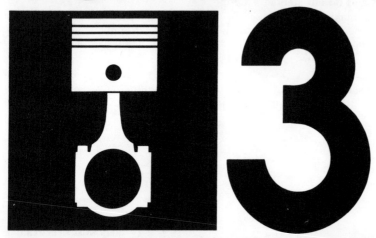

## ENGINE ELECTRICAL

### Distributor

#### *REMOVAL AND INSTALLATION—1970–74*

1. Remove the distributor cap and position it out of the way.

2. Disconnect the primary coil wire and the vacuum advance line.

3. Scribe a mark on the distributor body and the engine block showing their relationship. Mark the distributor housing to show the direction in which the rotor is pointing. Note the positioning of the vacuum advance unit.

4. Remove the hold-down bolt and clamp and remove the distributor.

To install the distributor with the engine undisturbed:

5. Reinsert the distributor into its opening, aligning the previously-made marks on the housing and the engine block.

6. The rotor may have to be turned either way a slight amount to align the rotor-to-housing marks.

7. Install the retaining clamp and bolt. Install the distributor cap, primary wire, and the vacuum hose.

8. Start the engine and check the ignition timing.

To install the distributor with the engine disturbed:

9. Turn the engine so the No. 1 piston is at the top of its compression stroke. This may be determined by covering the No. 1 spark plug hole with your thumb and slowly turning the engine over. When the timing mark on the crankshaft pulley aligns with the 0 on the timing scale and your thumb is pushed out by compression, No. 1 piston is at top-dead-center (TDC).

10. Install the distributor to the engine block so that the vacuum advance unit points in the correct direction.

11. Turn the rotor so that it will point to the No. 1 terminal in the cap.

12. Install the distributor into the engine block. It may be necessary to turn the rotor a little in either direction in order to engage the gears.

13. Tap the starter a few times to ensure that the oil pump shaft is mated to the distributor shaft.

14. Bring the engine to No. 1 TDC again and check to see that the rotor is indeed pointing toward the No. 1 terminal of the cap.

15. After correct positioning is assured, turn the distributor housing so that the points are just opening. Tighten the retaining clamp.

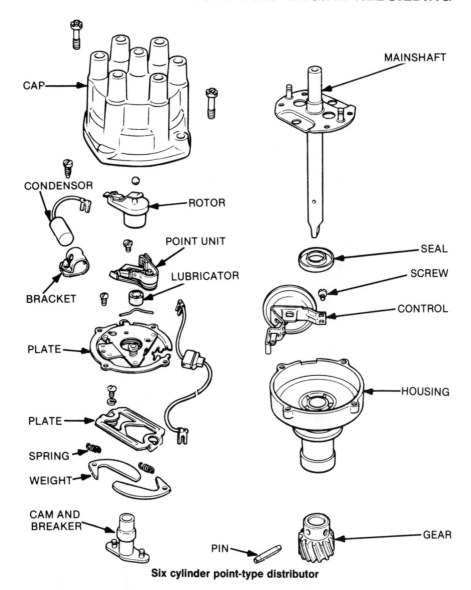

CAP

CONDENSOR

ROTOR

POINT UNIT

LUBRICATOR

BRACKET

PLATE

PLATE

SPRING

WEIGHT

CAM AND BREAKER

PIN

MAINSHAFT

SEAL

SCREW

CONTROL

HOUSING

GEAR

**Six cylinder point-type distributor**

16. Install the cap and primary wire. Check the ignition timing. Install the vacuum hose.

### REMOVAL AND INSTALLATION— 1975–80

1. Disconnect the wiring harness connectors at the side of the distributor cap.
2. Remove the distributor cap and lay it aside.
3. Disconnect the vacuum advance line.
4. Scribe a mark on the engine in line with the rotor and note the approximate position of the vacuum advance unit in relation to the engine.
5. Remove the distributor hold-down clamp and nut.

6. Lift the distributor from the engine.
7. Installation is the same as for the standard (1970–74) distributor.

## Alternator

Three basic alternators are used; the 5.5 in. Series 1D Delcotron, the 6.2 in. Series 150 Delcotron and the integral regulator 10 SI Delcotron.

### ALTERNATOR PRECAUTIONS

1. When installing a battery, ensure that the ground polarity of the battery and the ground polarity of the alternator and regulator are the same.
2. When connecting a jumper battery, be

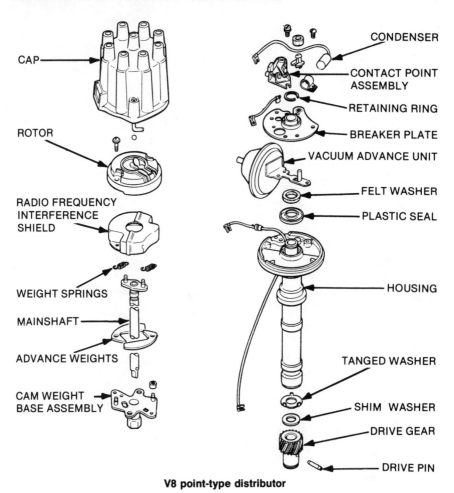

CAP

ROTOR

RADIO FREQUENCY INTERFERENCE SHIELD

WEIGHT SPRINGS

MAINSHAFT

ADVANCE WEIGHTS

CAM WEIGHT BASE ASSEMBLY

CONDENSER

CONTACT POINT ASSEMBLY

RETAINING RING

BREAKER PLATE

VACUUM ADVANCE UNIT

FELT WASHER

PLASTIC SEAL

HOUSING

TANGED WASHER

SHIM WASHER

DRIVE GEAR

DRIVE PIN

**V8 point-type distributor**

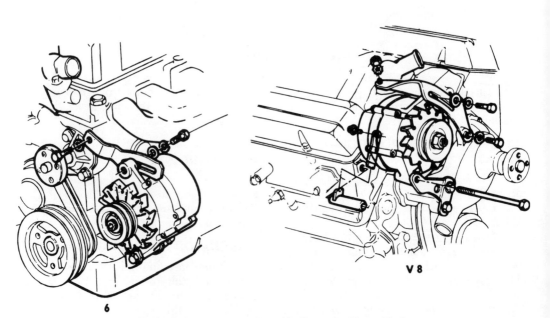

6

V 8

**Typical alternator mounting (© Chevrolet Motor Div.)**

certain that the correct terminals are connected.

3. When charging, connect the correct charger leads to the battery terminals.

4. Never operate the alternator on an open circuit. Be sure that all connections in the charging circuit are tight.

5. Do not short across or ground any of the terminals on the alternator or regulator.

6. Never polarize an AC system.

### REMOVAL AND INSTALLATION

1. Disconnect the battery ground cable to prevent diode damage.

2. Disconnect and tag all wiring to the alternator.

3. Remove the alternator brace bolt. If the truck is equipped with power steering, loosen the pump brace and mount nuts.

4. Remove the drive belt(s).

5. Support the alternator and remove the mounting bolts. Remove the alternator from the truck.

6. Install the unit on the truck using the reverse procedure of removal. Adjust the belt(s) to have ¼–½ in. depression under thumb pressure on its longest run.

## Firing Order

To avoid possible cross-wiring, replace spark plug wires one at a time.

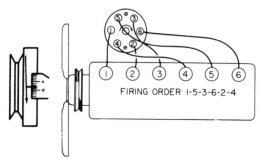

FIRING ORDER 1-5-3-6-2-4

**Six cylinder (© Chevrolet Motor Div.)**

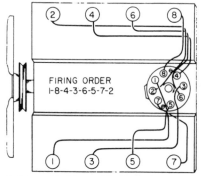

FIRING ORDER 1-8-4-3-6-5-7-2

**V8 point-type (© Chevrolet Motor Div.)**

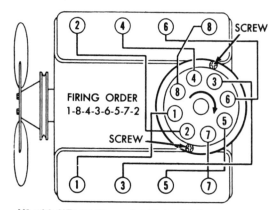

FIRING ORDER 1-8-4-3-6-5-7-2

**V8 with HEI (© Chevrolet Motor Div.)**

## Regulator

### REMOVAL AND INSTALLATION, 1970–72

1. Disconnect the ground cable from the battery.

2. Disconnect the wiring harness from the regulator.

3. Remove the mounting screws and remove the regulator.

4. Make sure that the regulator base gasket is in place before installation.

5. Clean the attaching area for proper grounding.

6. Install the regulator. Do not overtighten the mounting screws, as this will cancel the cushioning effect of the rubber grommets.

### VOLTAGE ADJUSTMENT

The standard voltage regulator from 1970–72 is a conventional double contact unit, al-

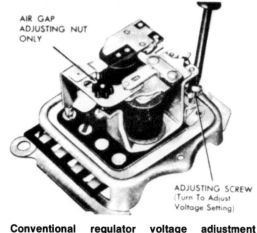

AIR GAP
ADJUSTING NUT
ONLY

ADJUSTING SCREW
(Turn To Adjust
Voltage Setting)

**Conventional regulator voltage adjustment (© Chevrolet Motor Div.)**

## Alternator and Regulator Specifications

| Year | Alternator | | | | Regulator | | | | | |
|---|---|---|---|---|---|---|---|---|---|---|
| | | | | | Field Relay | | | Regulator | | |
| | Part No. or Manufacturer | Field Current @ 12 V | Output (amps) | Part No. or Manufacturer | Air Gap (in.) | Point Gap (in.) | Volts to Close | Air Gap (in.) | Point Gap (in.) | Volts at 75° F |
| 1970 | 1100834, 38 | 2.2–2.6 | 37 | 1119515 | 0.015 | 0.030 | 2.3–2.7 | 0.067 | 0.014 | 13.8–14.8 |
| | 1100839, 41, 42 | 2.2–2.6 | 42 | 1119515 | 0.015 | 0.030 | 2.3–2.7 | 0.067 | 0.014 | 13.8–14.8 |
| | 1100843, 49 | 2.2–2.6 | 61 | 1119515 | 0.015 | 0.030 | 2.3–2.7 | 0.067 | 0.014 | 13.8–14.8 |
| | — | 3.7–4.4 | 62 | 1116378 | 0.011–0.018 | 0.020–0.030 | 2.5–3.5 | NA | NA | 13.8–14.8 |
| | 1100825 | 2.2–2.6 | 61 | 1119515 | 0.015 | 0.030 | 2.3–2.7 | 0.067 | 0.014 | 13.8–14.8 |
| | 1100833 ① | 2.2–2.6 | 61 | Integral with the Alternator | | | | | | |
| 1971 | 1100566 | 2.2–2.6 | 37 | 1119515 | 0.015 | 0.030 | 2.3–3.7 | 0.067 | 0.014 | 13.8–14.8 |
| | 1100838 | 2.2–2.6 | 37 | 1119515 | 0.015 | 0.030 | 2.3–3.7 | 0.067 | 0.014 | 13.8–14.8 |
| | 1100842 | 2.2–2.6 | 42 | 1119515 | 0.015 | 0.030 | 2.3–3.7 | 0.067 | 0.014 | 13.8–14.8 |
| 1972 | 1102452 | 2.2–2.6 | 37 | 1119515 | 0.015 | 0.030 | 2.3–3.7 | 0.067 | 0.014 | 13.8–14.8 |
| | 1102453 | 2.2–2.6 | 37 | 1119515 | 0.015 | 0.030 | 2.3–3.7 | 0.067 | 0.014 | 13.8–14.8 |
| | 1102456 | 2.2–2.6 | 37 | 1119515 | 0.015 | 0.030 | 2.3–3.7 | 0.067 | 0.014 | 13.8–14.8 |
| | 1102458 | 2.2–2.6 | 42 | 1119515 | 0.015 | 0.030 | 2.3–3.7 | 0.067 | 0.014 | 13.8–14.8 |

| | 1102455 | 2.2–2.6 | 61 | 1119515 | 0.015 | 0.030 | 2.3–3.7 | 0.067 | 0.014 | 13.8–14.8 |
|---|---|---|---|---|---|---|---|---|---|---|
| **1973–1977** | 1100497 | 4.4–4.9 | 37 | | | Integral with the Alternator | | | | |
| | 1100934 | 4.4–4.5 | 37 | | | Integral with the Alternator | | | | |
| | 1102394 1102483, 91 1102889 | 4.0–4.5 | 37 | | | Integral with the Alternator | | | | |
| | 1102346, 49, 82 1102485 1102841, 87 1100573 | 4.0–4.5 | 42 | | | Integral with the Alternator | | | | |
| | 1100560, 75 1102478, 79, 93 | 4.0–4.5 | 55 | | | Integral with the Alternator | | | | |
| | 1100597 1102347, 50, 83 1102480, 86, 90 1102886, 88 | 4.0–4.5 | 61 | | | Integral with the Alternator | | | | |
| **1978–1980** | 1102394 1102491 1102889 | 4.0–4.5 | 37 | | | Integral with the Alternator | | | | |
| | 1102485 1102841, 87 | 4.0–4.5 | 42 | | | Integral with the Alternator | | | | |
| | 1102480, 86 1102886, 88 | 4.0–4.5 | 61 | | | Integral with the Alternator | | | | |
| | 1101016, 28 | 4.0–4.5 | 80 | | | Integral with the Alternator | | | | |

—Not available    NA Not applicable    ⊙ 10 SI Integral Alternator

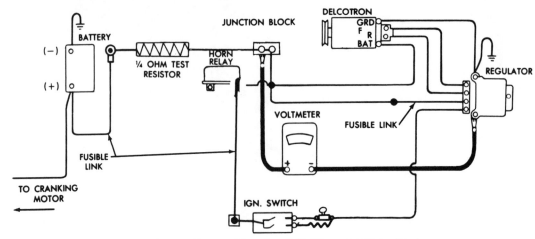

**Regulator voltage setting circuit (© Chevrolet Motor Div.)**

though an optional transistorized regulator was available. Voltage adjustment procedures are the same for both types except for the point of adjustment. The double contact adjusting screw is located under the cover and the transistorized regulator is adjusted externally after removing an allen screw from the adjustment hole. On 1973–80 models, the 10 SI Delcotron is used which is equipped with an integral regulator that cannot be adjusted.

1. Insert a ¼ ohm—25 watt fixed resistor into the charging circuit at the horn relay junction block, between both leads and the terminal. Use a ½ ohm-25 watt resistor for 1971–72.

2. Install a voltmeter as shown in the figure.

3. Warm the engine by running it for several minutes at 1,500 rpm or more.

4. Cycle the voltage regulator by discon-

necting and reconnecting the regulator connector.

5. Read the voltage on the voltmeter. If it is between 13.5 and 15.2, the regulator does not need adjustment or replacement. If the voltage is not within these limits, leave the engine running at 1,500 rpm.

6. Disconnect the four-terminal connector and remove the regulator cover (except on transistorized regulators). Reconnect the four-terminal connector and adjust the voltage to between 14.2 and 14.6 volts by turning the adjusting screw while observing the voltmeter.

7. Disconnect the terminal, install the cover, and then reconnect the terminal.

8. Continue running the engine at 1,500 rpm to re-establish the regulator internal temperature.

9. Cycle the regulator by disconnecting/reconnecting the regulator connector. Check the voltage. If the voltage is between 13.5 and 15.2, the regulator is good.

CAUTION: *Always disconnect the regulator before removing or installing the cover in order to prevent damage by short-circuiting.*

## Starter

No periodic lubrication of the starting motor or solenoid is required. Since the starting motor and brushes cannot be inspected without disassembling the unit, no service is required on these units.

### REMOVAL AND INSTALLATION

The following is a general procedure for all trucks, and may vary slightly depending on model and series.

**Transistorized regulator voltage adjustment (© Chevrolet Motor Div.)**

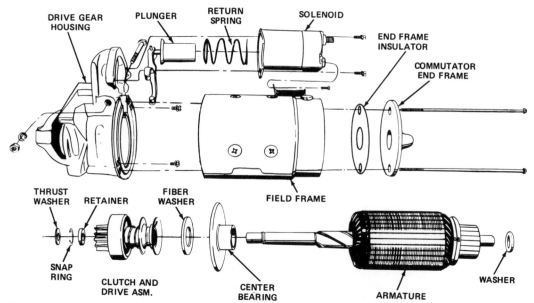

Exploded view of the 20 MT starter motor used on the diesel. Gasoline engine starters are almost identical; the only real difference is that they do not have the center bearing (© Oldsmobile Motor Div.)

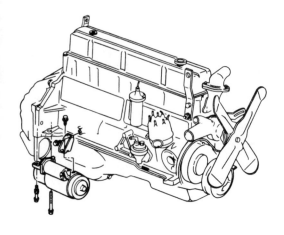

6

V 8

Typical starter mountings (© Chevrolet Motor Div.)

1. Disconnect the battery ground cable at the battery.

2. Raise and support the vehicle.

3. Disconnect and tag all wires at the solenoid terminal.

NOTE: *1975–80 starters no longer require the "R" terminal. The High Energy Ignition System does not need a cable from solenoid to ignition coil.*

4. Reinstall all nuts as soon as they are removed, since the thread sizes are different.

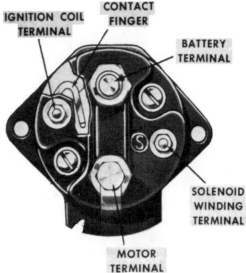

Starter solenoid terminals through 1974 (© Chevrolet Motor Div.)

## Battery and Starter Specifications

| | Battery | | | Starter ④ | | | |
| | | | | | | No Load Test | |
| Year | Amp Hour Capacity | Volts | Ground Terminal | Identification | Volts | Amps ① | rpm |
|---|---|---|---|---|---|---|---|
| 1970 | 53 | 12 | Neg | 1108365, 67, 68 | 9 | 50–80 | 5500–10,500 |
| | 61 | 12 | Neg | 1108338, 60, 61, 62 1107375 1107370, 71, 72, 1108357, 50, 63, 1108364, 69 | 9 9 | 55–80 35–75 | 3500–6000 6000–9000 |
| 1971–72 | 53 ② | 12 | Neg | 108367, 65, 68 | 9 | 50–80 | 5500–10,500 |
| | 61 | 12 | Neg | 1108338, 60 1108350, 63 1108385, 1108418 1108425 | 9 9 9 9 | 55–80 35–75 65–95 40–105 | 3500–6000 6000–9000 7500–10,500 3500–6500 |
| 1973 | 45 61 | 12 12 | Neg Neg | 1108479 | 9 | 50–80 | 5500–10,500 |
| | 76 | 12 | Neg | 1108367 1108427 1108480 | 9 9 9 | 50–80 55–80 65–95 | 5500–10,500 3500–6000 7500–10,500 |
| 1974 | 45 | 12 | Neg | 1108365, 67 | 9 | 50–80 | 5500–10,500 |
| | 61 | 12 | Neg | 1108427, 360 | 9 | 55–80 | 3500–6000 |
| | 76 | 12 | Neg | 1108430 1108480 1108502 | 9 9 9 | 65–95 50–80 65–95 | 7500–10,500 5500–10,500 7500–10,500 |
| 1975 | 60 | 12 | Neg | 1108744 1108788 ③ | 9 | 50–80 | 5500–10,500 |
| | 80 | 12 | Neg | 1108747 1108780 ③ 1108748 1108781 ③ | 9 9 | 50–80 65–90 | 3500–6000 7500–10,500 |
| | 125 | 12 | Neg | 1108748 1108781 ③ | 9 | 65–90 | 7500–10,500 |
| 1976 | 60 | 12 | Neg | 1108778 ③ | 9 | 50–80 | 5500–10,500 |
| | 80 | 12 | Neg | 1108780 ③ 1108781 ③ | 9 9 | 50–80 65–90 | 3500–6000 7500–10,500 |
| | 125 | 12 | Neg | 1108781 ③ | 9 | 65–90 | 7500–10,500 |
| 1977–80 | 60 | 12 | Neg | 1108778 ③ | 9 | 50–80 | 5500–10,500 |

## Battery and Starter Specifications (cont'd)

| | Battery | | | Starter ④ | | | |
| | | | | | | No Load Test | |
| Year | Amp Hour Capacity | Volts | Ground Terminal | Identification | Volts | Amps ① | rpm |
|---|---|---|---|---|---|---|---|
| 1977–80 (cont'd) | 80 | 12 | Neg | 1108780 ③ | 9 | 50–80 | 3500–6000 |
| | | | | 1109056 ③ | 9 | 50–80 | 5500–10,500 |
| | | | | 1109052 ③ | 9 | 65–95 | 7500–10,500 |
| | | | | 1108776 ③ | 9 | 65–95 | 7500–10,500 |
| | 125 | 12 | Neg | 1108776 ③ | 9 | 65–95 | 7500–10,500 |

① Solenoid included
② 45 amp hrs—1972
③ "R" terminal removed
④ Brush spring tension is 35 oz for all starters. Lock tests are not recommended.

5. Remove the front bracket from the starter and the two mounting bolts. On engines with a solenoid heat shield, remove the front bracket upper bolt and detach the bracket from the starter.

6. Remove the front bracket bolt or nut. Lower the starter front end first, and then remove the unit from the truck.

7. Reverse the removal procedures to install the starter. Torque the two mounting bolts to 25–35 ft lbs.

### STARTER DRIVE REPLACEMENT

1. Remove the drive housing by removing the through bolts.

2. Remove the thrust collar from the end of the retaining shaft.

3. Using a ½ in. pipe or another suitable tool, drive the retainer toward the armature end of the snap-ring.

4. Remove the snap-ring from the groove in the shaft using pliers. If the snap-ring is badly distorted, it will have to be replaced.

5. Slide the drive mechanism off the armature shaft.

To assemble the starter drive, use the following procedure.

1. Slide the drive assembly onto the armature shaft after it has been lubricated with a silicone lubricant.

2. The retainer is positioned on the shaft with the cupped surface facing away from the pinion.

3. Place the snap-ring on the end of the shaft and slide it into its groove.

4. Place the thrust collar on the shaft with its shoulder next to the snap-ring.

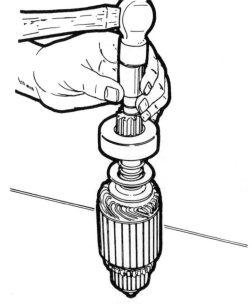

Use a piece of pipe to drive the retainer toward the snap-ring

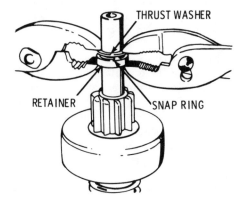

THRUST WASHER
RETAINER
SNAP RING

Snap-ring installation

5. Using two pliers, one on either side, force the snap-ring into the retainer.

6. Lubricate the drive housing bushing and slide the armature shaft into the starter housing.

7. Assemble the commutator end of the starter after lubricating the bushing and placing the leather brake washer in position.

### SOLENOID REPLACEMENT

1. Remove the screw and washer from the motor connector strap terminal.

2. Remove the two solenoid retaining screws.

3. Twist the solenoid housing clockwise to remove the flange key from the keyway in the housing. Then remove the housing.

4. To re-install the unit, place the return spring on the plunger and place the solenoid body on the drive housing. Turn counterclockwise to engage the flange key. Place the two retaining screws in position and install the screw and washer which secures the strap terminal. Install the unit on the starter.

## Battery

Refer to Chapter 1 for battery maintenance. Battery installation and removal varies with the truck model and series, making it impossible to detail all installations in this space. However, observe the following precautions when dealing with batteries:

1. Always disconnect the grounded (negative) terminal first and install it last to avoid short circuits and sparks. Special pullers are available to remove clamp-type battery terminals.

2. Be sure that the battery tray is clean and free of debris, so that the battery will seat squarely.

3. When installing batteries, tighten the hold-down strap or clamp snugly, but not with such force that it cracks the cover or case.

4. Be sure that the cables are in good condition and that the terminal clamps are clean and tight. Wire brushes are available to clean these items. Make sure that the ground cable is clean and tight at the engine block or frame. When installing cables, never hammer them in place. The terminals should be coated lightly with grease after installation to reduce corrosion.

5. Always check the battery polarity before installing cables. Reversed connections will destroy an alternator almost instantaneously.

NOTE: *On air conditioned vehicles, it may be necessary to remove air conditioning equipment to provide access to other components. Never, under any circumstances, disconnect any air conditioning lines. These lines are under pressure and can cause serious burns. It is best to unbolt the desired component, usually the compressor, and lay it aside with the lines attached.*

## ENGINE MECHANICAL

### Design

All Chevrolet and GMC truck engines, whether six or V8, are water-cooled, overhead valve powerplants. All engines use cast iron cylinder blocks and heads.

The 250 and 292 cu in. inline six-cylinder engines are all very similar in design although some 250 cu in. sixes have an integral cylinder head and intake manifold beginning 1975. Crankshafts are supported in seven main bearings, with the thrust taken by No. 7. The camshaft is low in the block and driven by the crankshaft gear; no timing chain is used. Relatively long pushrods actuate the valves through ball-jointed rocker arms.

The small-block family of engines, which includes the 283, 305, 307, 327, 350, and 400 cu in. blocks, have all sprung from the basic design of the 1955 265 cu in. engine. Only the 305, 307, 350, and 400 cu in. engines are used in Chevrolet and GMC trucks. It was this engine that introduced the balljoint rocker arm design which is now used by many car makers. This line of engines features a great deal of interchangeability, and later parts may be utilized on earlier engines for increased reliability and/or performance. In 1968, rod and main bearings were increased in size on the small-block family. The 283 was also dropped in that year and replaced by the 307, which is in effect a 327 crankshaft in a 283 block. The 327 and 350 engines share the same cylinder block, with the difference in displacement being provided by a longer stroke crankshaft. The 305 engine, introduced into the truck line in 1977, is essentially a de-bored and lighter version of the 350.

The 396, 402, and 454 cu in. engines are

known as the Mark IV engines or big-blocks. These engines feature unusual cylinder heads, in that the intake and exhaust valves are canted at the angle at which their respective port enters the cylinder. The 396 was first used on the 1965 Corvette, and through bore and stroke increases has developed into 454 cu ins. The big-block cylinder heads use balljoint rockers similar to those on the small block engines.

The General Motors Diesel, first used in 1978 in the Chevrolet C-10 pick-up, is based on, and is similar in construction to the Oldsmobile 350 cu in. gasoline V8. The major difference between the two engines is in the cylinder heads, combustion chamber, fuel distribution system, air intake manifold, and method of ignition. The cylinder block, crankshaft, main bearings, rods, pistons, pins, and rings are all made heavier to withstand the considerably higher pressures and stresses common to diesel engines. Diesel ignition occurs because of heat developed in the combustion chamber during compression. This is the reason for the diesel's high compression ratio (22.5:1). Because the fuel ignites under compression, the need for spark plugs and high voltage ignition is eliminated.

Intake and exhaust valves are of the bridged pivot design, and operate in the same manner as in a gasoline engine. The cylinder head combustion chambers feature pre-chamber inserts made of stainless steel. Glow plugs are threaded in the same way as spark plugs, but the injection nozzles are retained by a bolt and a clamp. The injection nozzles are spring loaded and calibrated to open at a specific fuel pressure.

## Engine Removal and Installation

The factory recommended procedure for engine removal is to remove the engine/transmission as a unit on two wheel drive models, except for the diesel. Only the engine should be removed on diesels and four wheel drive models.

1. Disconnect and remove the battery, negative cable first. On diesels, disconnect the negative cables at the batteries and ground wires at the inner fender panel.
2. Drain the cooling system.
3. Drain the engine oil.
4. Remove the air cleaner and ducts.
5. Scribe alignment marks around the hood hinges, and remove the hood.
6. Remove the radiator and hoses, and the fan shroud if so equipped.
7. Disconnect and label the wires at:
   a. Starter solenoid.
   b. Alternator.
   c. Temperature switch.

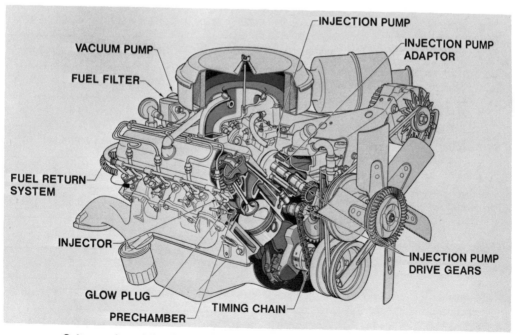

Cutaway view of the General Motors diesel (Courtesy Oldsmobile Motor Div.)

## General Engine Specifications

| Year | Engine No. Cyl Displacement Cu In. | Carburetor Type | Advertised Horsepower @ rpm ■ | Advertised Torque @ rpm (ft lbs) ■ | Bore and Stroke (in.) | Advertised Compression Ratio | Oil Pressure @ 2000 rpm |
|------|-----|------|------|------|------|------|------|
| 1970 | 6—250 | 1 bbl | 155 @ 4200 | 235 @ 1600 | 3.875 × 3.530 | 8.5 : 1 | 40 |
| | 6—292 | 1 bbl | 170 @ 4000 | 275 @ 1600 | 3.875 × 4.120 | 8.0 : 1 | 40 |
| | 8—307 | 2 bbl | 200 @ 4600 | 300 @ 2400 | 3.875 × 3.250 | 9.0 : 1 | 40 |
| | 8—350 | 2 bbl | 215 @ 4400 | 320 @ 2400 | 4.000 × 3.480 | 8.0 : 1 | 40 |
| | 8—350 | 4 bbl | 225 @ 4600 | 355 @ 3000 | 4.000 × 3.480 | 9.0 : 1 | 40 |
| | 8—396 | 4 bbl | 310 @ 4800 | 400 @ 3200 | 4.125 × 3.760 | 9.0 : 1 | 40 |
| 1971 | 6—250 | 1 bbl | 145 @ 4200 | 235 @ 1600 | 3.875 × 3.530 | 8.5 : 1 | 40 |
| | 6—292 | 1 bbl | 165 @ 4000 | 270 @ 1600 | 3.875 × 4.120 | 8.0 : 1 | 40 |
| | 8—307 | 2 bbl | 200 @ 4600 | 300 @ 2400 | 3.875 × 3.250 | 9.0 : 1 | 40 |
| | 8—307 | 2 bbl | 215 @ 4800 | 305 @ 2800 | 3.875 × 3.250 | 8.5 : 1 | 40 |
| | 8—350 | 4 bbl | 250 @ 4600 | 350 @ 3000 | 4.000 × 3.480 | 8.5 : 1 | 40 |
| | 8—402 | 4 bbl | 300 @ 4800 | 400 @ 3200 | 4.125 × 3.760 | 8.5 : 1 | 40 |
| 1972 | 6—250 | 1 bbl | 110 @ 3800 | 185 @ 1600 | 3.875 × 3.530 | 8.5 : 1 | 40 |
| | 6—292 | 1 bbl | 125 @ 3600 | 225 @ 2400 | 3.875 × 4.120 | 8.0 : 1 | 40 |
| | 8—307 | 2 bbl | 135 @ 4000 | 230 @ 2400 | 3.875 × 3.250 | 8.5 : 1 | 40 |
| | 8—350 | 4 bbl | 175 @ 4000 | 290 @ 2400 | 4.000 × 3.480 | 8.5 : 1 | 40 |
| | 8—402 | 4 bbl | 210 @ 4000 | 320 @ 2800 | 4.125 × 3.760 | 8.5 : 1 | 40 |
| 1973 | 6—250 | 1 bbl | 100 @ 3800 | 175 @ 2000 | 3.875 × 3.530 | 8.25 : 1 | 40 |
| | 6—292 | 1 bbl | 120 @ 3600 | 225 @ 2000 | 3.875 × 4.120 | 8.0 : 1 | 40 |
| | 8—307 | 2 bbl | 115 @ 3600 | 205 @ 2000 | 3.875 × 3.250 | 8.5 : 1 | 40 |
| | 8—307 | 2 bbl | 130 @ 4000 | 220 @ 2200 | 3.875 × 3.250 | 8.5 : 1 | 40 |
| | 8—350 | 4 bbl | 155 @ 4000 | 255 @ 2400 | 4.000 × 3.480 | 8.5 : 1 | 40 |
| | 8—454 | 4 bbl | 240 @ 4000 | 355 @ 2800 | 4.125 × 4.000 | 8.25 : 1 | 40 |
| | 8—454 | 4 bbl | 250 @ 4000 | 365 @ 2800 | 4.125 × 4.000 | 8.25 : 1 | 40 |

## General Engine Specifications (cont'd)

| Year | Engine No. Cyl Displacement Cu In. | Carburetor Type | Advertised Horsepower @ rpm ■ | Advertised Torque @ rpm (ft lbs) ■ | Bore and Stroke (in.) | Advertised Compression Ratio | Oil Pressure @ 2000 rpm |
|------|------|------|------|------|------|------|------|
| 1974 | 6—250 | 1 bbl | 100 @ 3600 | 175 @ 1800 | 3.875 × 3.530 | 8.25 : 1 | 40 |
| | 6—292 | 1 bbl | 120 @ 3600 | 215 @ 2000 | 3.875 × 4.120 | 8.0 : 1 | 40 |
| | 8—350 | 2 bbl | 145 @ 3800 | 250 @ 2200 | 4.000 × 3.480 | 8.5 : 1 | 40 |
| | 8—350 | 4 bbl | 160 @ 3800 | 250 @ 2400 | 4.000 × 3.480 | 8.5 : 1 | 40 |
| | 8—454 | 4 bbl | 230 @ 4000 | 350 @ 2800 | 4.125 × 4.000 | 8.25 : 1 | 40 |
| | 8—454 | 4 bbl | 245 @ 4000 | 365 @ 2800 | 4.125 × 4.000 | 8.25 : 1 | 40 |
| 1975 | 6—250 | 1 bbl | 105 @ 3800 | 185 @ 1200 | 3.875 × 3.530 | 8.25 : 1 | 40 |
| | 6—292 | 1 bbl | 120 @ 3600 | 213 @ 2000 | 3.875 × 4.120 | 8.0 : 1 | 40 |
| | 8—350 | 4 bbl | 160 @ 3800 | 250 @ 2400 | 4.000 × 3.480 | 8.5 : 1 | 40 |
| | 8—400 | 4 bbl | 175 @ 3600 | 290 @ 2800 | 4.125 × 3.750 | 8.5 : 1 | 40 |
| | 8—454 | 4 bbl | 245 @ 4000 | 355 @ 3000 ① | 4.125 × 4.000 | 8.25 : 1 | 40 |
| 1976 | 6—250 | 1 bbl | 105 @ 3800 | 185 @ 1200 | 3.875 × 3.530 | 8.25 : 1 | 40–60 |
| | 6—250 HD | 1 bbl | 100 @ 3600 | 175 @ 1800 | 3.875 × 3.530 | 8.25 : 1 | 40–60 |
| | 6—292 | 1 bbl | 120 @ 3600 | 215 @ 2000 | 3.870 × 4.120 | 8.0 : 1 | 40–60 |
| | 8—350 | 2 bbl | 145 @ 3800 | 250 @ 2200 | 4.000 × 3.480 | 8.5 : 1 | 40 |
| | 8—350 | 4 bbl | 165 @ 3800 | 260 @ 2400 ② | 4.000 × 3.480 | 8.5 : 1 | 40 |
| | 8—400 | 4 bbl | 175 @ 3600 | 290 @ 2800 | 4.125 × 3.750 | 8.5 : 1 | 40 |
| | 8—454 | 4 bbl | 245 @ 3800 | 365 @ 2800 | 4.251 × 4.000 | 8.25 : 1 | 40 |
| | 8—454 HD | 4 bbl | 240 @ 3800 ③ | 370 @ 2800 ④ | 4.251 × 4.000 | 8.15 : 1 | 40 |
| 1977 | 6—250 | 1 bbl | 110 @ 3800 | 195 @ 1600 | 3.875 × 3.530 | 8.3 : 1 | 40–60 |
| | 6—250 HD | 1 bbl | 100 @ 3600 | 175 @ 1800 | 3.875 × 3.530 | 8.0 : 1 | 40–60 |
| | 6—292 | 1 bbl | 120 @ 3600 | 215 @ 2000 | 3.870 × 4.120 | 8.0 : 1 | 40–60 |
| | 8—305 ⑤ | 2 bbl | 145 @ 3800 | 245 @ 2200 | 3.740 × 3.480 | 8.5 : 1 | 40 |
| | 8—305 HD ⑤ | 2 bbl | 140 @ 3800 | 235 @ 2000 | 3.740 × 3.480 | 8.5 : 1 | 40 |

## General Engine Specifications (cont'd)

| Year | Engine No. Cyl Displacement Cu In. | Carburetor Type | Advertised Horsepower @ rpm ▪ | Advertised Torque @ rpm (ft lbs) ▪ | Bore and Stroke (in.) | Advertised Compression Ratio | Oil Pressure @ 2000 rpm |
|---|---|---|---|---|---|---|---|
| 1977 | 8—350 | 4 bbl | 165 @ 3800 | 260 @ 2400 ② | 4.000 × 3.480 | 8.5 : 1 | 40 |
| | 8—400 | 4 bbl | 175 @ 3600 | 290 @ 2800 | 4.125 × 3.750 | 8.5 : 1 | 40 |
| | 8—454 | 4 bbl | 245 @ 3800 | 365 @ 2800 | 4.251 × 4.000 | 8.25 : 1 | 40 |
| | 8—454 HD | 4 bbl | 240 @ 3800 ③ | 370 @ 2800 ④ | 4.251 × 4.000 | 8.15 : 1 | 40 |
| 1978 | 6—250 LD | 1 bbl | 115 @ 3800 | 195 @ 1600 | 3.870 × 3.530 | 8.0 : 1 | 40–60 |
| | 6—250 Calif | 1 bbl | 100 @ 3800 | 185 @ 1600 | 3.870 × 3.530 | 8.1 : 1 | 40–60 |
| | 6—250 HD | 1 bbl | 100 @ 3600 | 175 @ 1800 | 3.870 × 3.530 | 8.1 : 1 | 40–60 |
| | 6—292 | 1 bbl | 120 @ 3600 | 215 @ 2000 | 3.870 × 4.120 | 8.0 : 1 | 40–60 |
| | 8—305 | 2 bbl | 145 @ 3800 | 245 @ 2400 | 3.740 × 3.480 | 8.4 : 1 | 45 |
| | 8—350 LD | 4 bbl | 165 @ 3800 | 260 @ 2400 | 4.000 × 3.480 | 8.2 : 1 | 45 |
| | 8—350 HD | 4 bbl | 165 @ 3800 | 255 @ 2800 | 4.000 × 3.480 | 8.3 : 1 | 45 |
| | 8—350 Diesel | FI | 120 @ 3600 | 220 @ 1600 | 4.057 × 3.385 | 22.5 : 1 | 35 |
| | 8—400 | 4 bbl | 175 @ 3600 | 290 @ 2800 | 4.125 × 3.750 | 8.3 : 1 | 40 |
| | 8—400 Calif | 4 bbl | 165 @ 3600 | 290 @ 2000 | 4.125 × 3.750 | 8.2 : 1 | 40 |
| | 8—454 LD | 4 bbl | 205 @ 3600 | 335 @ 2800 | 4.250 × 4.000 | 8.0 : 1 | 40 |
| | 8—454 HD | 4 bbl | 240 @ 3800 | 370 @ 2800 | 4.250 × 4.000 | 7.9 : 1 | 40 |
| | 8—454 HD Calif | 4 bbl | 250 @ 3800 | 385 @ 2800 | 4.250 × 4.000 | 7.9 : 1 | 40 |
| 1979 | 6—250 LD | 2 bbl | 130 @ 3800 | 210 @ 2400 | 3.870 × 3.530 | 8.3 : 1 | 40–60 |
| | 6—250 Calif | 2 bbl | 125 @ 4000 | 205 @ 2000 | 3.870 × 3.530 | 8.3 : 1 | 40–60 |
| | 6—250 HD | 2 bbl | 130 @ 4000 | 205 @ 2000 | 3.870 × 3.530 | 8.3 : 1 | 40–60 |
| | 6—292 | 1 bbl | 115 @ 3400 | 215 @ 1600 | 3.870 × 4.120 | 7.8 : 1 | 40–60 |
| | 8—305 | 2 bbl | 140 @ 4000 | 240 @ 2000 | 3.740 × 3.480 | 8.4 : 1 | 45 |
| | 8—350 LD | 4 bbl | 165 @ 3600 | 270 @ 2000 | 4.000 × 3.480 | 8.2 : 1 | 45 |
| | 8—350 Hi Alt | 4 bbl | 155 @ 3600 | 260 @ 2000 | 4.000 × 3.480 | 8.2 : 1 | 45 |

## General Engine Specifications (cont'd)

| Year | Engine No. Cyl Displacement Cu In. | Carburetor Type | Advertised Horsepower @ rpm ■ | Advertised Torque @ rpm (ft lbs) ■ | Bore and Stroke (in.) | Advertised Compression Ratio | Oil Pressure @ 2000 rpm |
|---|---|---|---|---|---|---|---|
| | 8—350 HD | 4 bbl | 165 @ 3800 | 255 @ 2800 | 4.000 × 3.480 | 8.3 : 1 | 45 |
| | 8—350 Diesel | FI | 120 @ 3600 | 220 @ 1600 | 4.057 × 3.385 | 22.5 : 1 | 35 |
| | 8—400 HD | 4 bbl | 180 @ 3600 | 310 @ 2400 | 4.125 × 3.750 | 8.2 : 1 | 40 |
| | 8—454 LD | 4 bbl | 205 @ 3600 | 335 @ 2800 | 4.250 × 4.000 | 8.0 : 1 | 40 |
| | 8—454 HD | 4 bbl | 210 @ 3800 | 340 @ 2800 | 4.250 × 4.000 | 7.9 : 1 | 40 |
| 1980 | 6—250 | 2 bbl | 130 @ 4000 | 210 @ 2000 | 3.870 × 3.530 | 8.3 : 1 | 40–60 |
| | 6—250 Calif | 2 bbl | 130 @ 4000 | 205 @ 2000 | 3.870 × 3.530 | 8.3 : 1 | 40–60 |
| | 6—292 | 1 bbl | 115 @ 3400 | 215 @ 1600 | 3.870 × 4.120 | 7.8 : 1 | 40–60 |
| | 8—305 | 2 bbl | 135 @ 4200 | 235 @ 2400 | 3.740 × 3.480 | 8.5 : 1 | 45 |
| | 8—350 LD | 4 bbl | 175 @ 4000 | 275 @ 2400 | 4.000 × 3.480 | 8.2 : 1 | 45 |
| | 8—350 LD Calif | 4 bbl | 170 @ 4000 | 275 @ 2000 | 4.000 × 3.480 | 8.2 : 1 | 45 |
| | 8—350 HD | 4 bbl | 165 @ 3800 | 255 @ 2800 | 4.000 × 3.480 | 8.3 : 1 | 45 |
| | 8—350 Diesel | FI | 125 @ 3600 | 225 @ 1600 | 4.057 × 3.385 | 22.5 : 1 | 35 |
| | 8—400 HD | 4 bbl | 180 @ 3600 | 310 @ 2400 | 4.125 × 3.750 | 8.3 : 1 | 40 |
| | 8—454 HD | 4 bbl | 210 @ 3800 | 340 @ 2800 | 4.250 × 4.000 | 7.9 : 1 | 40 |

■Starting 1972, horsepower and torque are SAE net figures. They are measured at the rear of the transmission with all accessories installed and operating. Since the figures vary when a given engine is installed in different models, some are representative rather than exact.
① 375 @ 2800—Calif.
② 255 @ 2800 HD
③ 250 @ 3800—Calif.
④ 385 @ 2800—Calif.
⑤ Not available in California
FI—Fuel Injection

## Torque Specifications
(ft lbs)

| Usage | 6—292 | 6—250 | 8—305 | 8—307 | 8—350 | 8—396 | 8—400 | 8—402 | 8—454 | 350 Diesel |
|---|---|---|---|---|---|---|---|---|---|---|
| Camshaft Thrust Plate | 6–7 | 6–7 | — | — | — | — | — | — | — | — |
| Crankcase Front Cover | 6–7 | 6–7 | 6–7 | 6–7 | 6–7 | 6–7 | 6–7 | 6–7 | 6–7 | 35 |
| Oil Pan-to-Crankcase | 6–7 | 6–7 | 6–7 | 6–7 | 6–7 | 11–12 | 6–7 | 11–12 | 11–12 | 10 |
| Connecting Rod Bearing Cap | 35 | 35 | 45 | 45 | 45 | 50 | 45 | 50 | 50 | 42 |
| Camshaft Sprocket | — | — | 20 | 20 | 20 | 20 | 20 | 20 | 20 | 65 |
| Oil Pump | 9–10 | 9–10 | 65 | 65 | 65 | 65 | 65 | 65 | 65 | 35 |
| Water Pump | 15 | 15 | 30 | 30 | 30 | 30 | 30 | 30 | 30 | 13 |
| Exhaust Manifold | — | — | 20① | 20① | 20① | 20 | 20① | 20 | 20 | 25 |

| | | | | | | | | | |
|---|---|---|---|---|---|---|---|---|---|
| Intake Manifold | 40③ | 30 | 30 | 30 | 30 | 30 | 30 | — | — |
| Exhaust-to-Intake Manifold | — | — | — | — | — | — | — | 25⑤ | 25⑤ |
| Thermostat Housing | 20 | 30 | 30 | 30 | 30 | 30 | 30 | 30 | 30 |
| Cylinder Head | 130③ | 80 | 80 | 65 | 80 | 65 | 65 | 95 | 95 |
| Main Bearing Cap | 120 | 110 | 110 | 70 | 110 | 70 | 70 | 65 | 65 |
| Oil Drain Plug | 30 | 20 | 20 | 20 | 20 | 20 | 20 | 20 | 20 |
| Spark Plug | 12④ | 15 | 15 | 15 | 25② | 15 | 15 | 25② | 25② |
| Flywheel-to-Crankshaft | 60 | 65 | 65 | 60 | 65 | 60 | 60 | 60 | 110 |

① Inside bolts—30 ft lbs
② $5/8$ in. (small) plug—15 ft lbs
   $13/16$ in. (large) plug—25 ft lbs
— Not applicable
③ Clean and dip in engine oil before installation
④ Glow plug
⑤ 45—1978 and later

## Crankshaft and Connecting Rod Specifications

All measurements are given in in.

| Year | Engine No. Cyl Displacement (cu in.) | Crankshaft | | | | Connecting Rod | | |
| --- | --- | --- | --- | --- | --- | --- | --- | --- |
| | | Main Brg Journal Dia | Main Brg Oil Clearance | Shaft End-Play | Thrust on No. | Journal Diameter | Oil Clearance | Side Clearance |
| 1970 | 6—250 | 2.2983–2.2993 | .0003–.0029 | .002–.006 | 7 | 1.999–2.000 | .0007–.0027 | .009–.014 |
| | 6—292 | 2.2983–2.2993 | .0008–.0034 | .002–.006 | 7 | 1.999–2.100 | .0007–.0028 | .009–.014 |
| | 8—307, 350 | 2.4484–2.4493 ② | .0008–.0020 ⑤ | .002–.006 | 5 | 2.199–2.200 | .0007–.0028 | .008–.014 |
| | 8—396 | ⑥ | ⑦ | .006–.010 | 5 | 2.199–2.200 | .0009–.0025 | .008–.014 |
| 1971 | 6—250 | 2.2983–2.2993 | .0003–.0029 | .002–.006 | 7 | 1.999–2.000 | .0007–.0027 | .009–.014 |
| | 6—292 | 2.2983–2.2993 | .0008–.0034 | .002–.006 | 7 | 2.099–2.100 | .0007–.0027 | .009–.014 |
| | 8—307, 350 | 2.4484–2.4493 ② | .0008–.0015 ⑤ | .002–.006 | 5 | 2.199–2.200 | .0007–.0028 | .008–.014 |
| | 8—402 | ⑥ | ⑧ | .006–.010 | 5 | 2.1985–2.1995 | .0009–.0025 | .013–.023 |
| 1972 | 6—250 | 2.2983–2.2993 | .0003–.0029 | .002–.006 | 7 | 1.999–2.000 | .0007–.0027 | .009–.014 |
| | 6—292 | 2.2983–2.2993 | .0008–.0034 | .002–.006 | 7 | 2.099–2.100 | .0007–.0027 | .009–.014 |
| | 8—307, 350 | 2.4484–2.4493 ② | .0008–.0020 ⑤ | .002–.006 | 5 | 2.199–2.200 | .0007–.0028 | .008–.014 |
| | 8—402 | ⑥ | ⑧ | .006–.010 | 5 | 2.1985–2.1995 | .0009–.0025 | .013–.023 |
| 1973–1977 | 6—250 | 2.2983–2.2993 | .0003–.0029 | .002–.006 | 7 | 1.999–2.000 | .0007–.0027 | .006–.017 |

| Engine | Main Brg Journal Dia | Main Brg Oil Clearance | Shaft End-Play | Thrust on No. | Journal Dia | Oil Clearance | Side Clearance |
|---|---|---|---|---|---|---|---|
| 6—292 | 2.2983–2.2993 | .0008–.0034 | .002–.006 | 7 | 2.099–2.100 | .0007–.0027 | .006–.017 |
| 8—305, 307 350, 400 | 2.4484–2.4493 ②⑪ | .0008–.0020 ⑤ | .002–.006 | 5 | 2.199–2.200 | .0013–.0035 | .008–.014 |
| 8—454 | ⑨ | ⑩ | .006–.010 | 5 | 2.1985–2.1995 | .0009–.0025 | .013–.023 |
| **1978– 1980** | | | | | | | |
| 6—250 | 2.2979–2.2994 | Nos. 1–6 .0010–.0024 No. 7 .0016–.0035 | .002–.006 | 7 | 1.999–2.000 | .0010–.0026 | .006–.017 |
| 6—292 | 2.2979–2.2994 | Nos. 1–6 .0010–.0024 No. 7 .0016–.0035 | .002–.006 | 7 | 2.099–2.100 | .0010–.0026 | .006–.017 |
| 8—305, 350, 400 | ⑪ | .0008–.0020 ⑤ | .002–.006 | 5 | 2.199–2.200 ⑫ | .0013–.0035 | .008–.014 |
| 8—454 | ⑨ | ⑩ | .006–.010 | 5 | 2.1985–2.1995 | .0009–.0025 | .013–.023 |
| 8—350 Diesel | 2.9993–3.0003 | Nos. 1–4 .0005–.0021 No. 5 .0015–.0031 | .0035–.0135 | 5 | 2.1238–2.1248 | .0005–.0026 | .006–.020 |

② No. 5—2.4479–2.4488
⑤ Nos. 2–4—.0011–.0023
   No. 5—.0017–.0033
⑥ Nos. 1–2—2.7487–2.7496
   Nos. 3–4—2.7481–2.7490
   No. 5—2.7478–2.7488
⑦ No. 1—.0007–.0019
   Nos. 2–4—.0013–.0025
   No. 5—.0024–.0040
⑧ No. 1—.0007–.0019
   Nos. 2–4—.0013–.0025
   No. 5—.0019–.0033

⑨ No. 1—2.7485–2.7494
   Nos. 2–4—2.7481–2.7490
   No. 5—2.7478–2.7488
⑩ Nos. 1–4—.0013–.0025
   No. 5—.0024–.0040
⑪ 1977–80 only: 305, 350—No. 1—2.4484–2.4493
   Nos. 2–4—2.4481–2.4490
   No. 5—2.4479–2.4488
   400—Nos. 1–4—2.6484–2.6493
   No. 5—2.6479–2.6488
⑫ 1978–80: 2.0988–2.0998

## Valve Specifications

| Year | Engine No. Cyl Displacement (cu in.) | Seat Angle (deg) | Face Angle (deg) | Spring Test Pressure (lbs @ in.) | Spring Installed Height (in.) ① | Stem to Guide Clearance (in.) | | Stem Diameter (in.) | |
|---|---|---|---|---|---|---|---|---|---|
| | | | | | | Intake | Exhaust | Intake | Exhaust |
| 1970 | 6—250 | 46 | 45 | 60 @ 1.66 | $1^{21}/_{32}$ | 0.0010–0.0027 | 0.0015–0.0032 | 0.3414 | 0.3414 |
| | 6—292 | 46 | 45 | 89 @ 1.69 | $1^5/_8$ | 0.0010–0.0027 | 0.0015–0.0032 | 0.3414 | 0.3414 |
| | 8—307 | 46 | 45 | 80 @ 1.70 | $1^{23}/_{32}$ | 0.0010–0.0027 | 0.0010–0.0027 | 0.3414 | 0.3414 |
| | 8—350 | 46 | 45 | 80 @ 1.70 | $1^{23}/_{32}$ | 0.0010–0.0027 | 0.0010–0.0027 | 0.3414 | 0.3414 |
| | 8—396 | 46 | 45 | 100 @ 1.88 | $1^7/_8$ | 0.0017–0.0020 | 0.0019–0.0022 | 0.3414 | 0.3414 |
| 1971 | 6—250 | 46 | 45 | 60 @ 1.66 | $1^{21}/_{32}$ | 0.0010–0.0027 | 0.0015–0.0032 | 0.3414 | 0.3414 |
| | 6—292 | 46 | 45 | 89 @ 1.69 | $1^5/_8$ | 0.0010–0.0027 | 0.0015–0.0032 | 0.3414 | 0.3414 |
| | 8—307 | 46 | 45 | 80 @ 1.70 | $1^{23}/_{32}$ | 0.0010–0.0027 | 0.0010–0.0027 | 0.3414 | 0.3414 |
| | 8—350 | 46 | 45 | 80 @ 1.70 | $1^{23}/_{32}$ | 0.0010–0.0027 | 0.0010–0.0027 | 0.3414 | 0.3414 |
| | 8—402 | 46 | 45 | 75 @ 1.88 | $1^7/_8$ | 0.0010–0.0027 | 0.0012–0.0029 | 0.3414 | 0.3414 |
| 1972 | 6—250 | 46 | 45 | 60 @ 1.66 · | $1^{21}/_{32}$ | 0.0010–0.0027 | 0.0015–0.0032 | 0.3414 | 0.3414 |
| | 6—292 | 46 | 45 | 89 @ 1.69 | $1^5/_8$ | 0.0010–0.0027 | 0.0015–0.0032 | 0.3414 | 0.3414 |
| | 8—307 | 46 | 45 | 80 @ 1.70 | $1^{23}/_{32}$ | 0.0010–0.0027 | 0.0010–0.0027 | 0.3414 | 0.3414 |
| | 8—350 | 46 | 45 | 80 @ 1.70 | $1^{23}/_{32}$ | 0.0010–0.0027 | 0.0010–0.0027 | 0.3414 | 0.3414 |
| | 8—402 | 46 | 46 | 75 @ 1.88 | $1^7/_8$ | 0.0010–0.0027 | 0.0010–0.0029 | 0.3414 | 0.3414 |
| 1973 | 6—250 | 46 | 45 | 60 @ 1.66 | $1^{21}/_{32}$ | 0.0010–0.0027 | 0.0015–0.0032 | 0.3414 | 0.3414 |
| | 6—292 | 46 | 45 | 89 @ 1.69 | $1^5/_8$ | 0.0010–0.0027 | 0.0015–0.0032 | 0.3414 | 0.3414 |
| | 8—307 | 46 | 45 | 80 @ 1.70② | $1^5/_8$ | 0.0010–0.0027 | 0.0010–0.0027 | 0.3414 | 0.3414 |
| | 8—350 | 46 | 45 | 80 @ 1.70② | $1^{23}/_{32}$ | 0.0010–0.0027 | 0.0010–0.0027 | 0.3414 | 0.3414 |
| | 8—454 | 46 | 45 | 80 @ 1.88 | $1^7/_8$ | 0.0010–0.0027 | 0.0012–0.0029 | 0.3414 | 0.3414 |
| 1974 | 6—250 | 46 | 45 | 60 @ 1.66 | $1^{21}/_{32}$ | 0.0010–0.0027 | 0.0015–0.0032 | 0.3414 | 0.3414 |
| | 6—292 | 46 | 45 | 89 @ 1.69 | $1^5/_8$ | 0.0010–0.0027 | 0.0015–0.0032 | 0.3414 | 0.3414 |
| | 8—350 | 46 | 45 | 80 @ 1.70② | $1^{23}/_{32}$ | 0.0010–0.0027 | 0.0010–0.0027 | 0.3414 | 0.3414 |
| | 8—454 | 46 | 45 | 80 @ 1.88 | $1^7/_8$ | 0.0010–0.0027 | 0.0012–0.0029 | 0.3414 | 0.3414 |

## Valve Specifications (cont'd)

| Year | Engine No. Cyl Displacement (cu in.) | Seat Angle (deg) | Face Angle (deg) | Spring Test Pressure (lbs @ in.) | Spring Installed Height (in.) ① | Stem to Guide Clearance (in.) | | Stem Diameter (in.) | |
|---|---|---|---|---|---|---|---|---|---|
| | | | | | | Intake | Exhaust | Intake | Exhaust |
| 1975–1980 | 6—250 | 46 | 45 | 60 @ 1.66 | $1^{21}/_{32}$ | 0.0010–0.0027 | 0.0015–0.0032 | 0.3414 | 0.3414 |
| | 6—292 | 46 | 45⑤ | 89 @ 1.69⑥ | $1^{5}/_{8}$⑦ | 0.0010–0.0027 | 0.0015–0.0032 | 0.3414 | 0.3414 |
| | 8—305 | 46 | 45 | 80 @ 1.70② | ③ | 0.0010–0.0027 | 0.0010–0.0027 | 0.3414 | 0.3414 |
| | 8—350 | 46 | 45 | 80 @ 1.70② | ③ | 0.0010–0.0027 | 0.0010–0.0027 | 0.3414 | 0.3414 |
| | 8—400 | 46 | 45 | 80 @ 1.70② | ③ | 0.0010–0.0027 | 0.0012–0.0029 | 0.3414 | 0.3414 |
| | 8—454 | 46 | 45 | 80 @ 1.88 | $1^{7}/_{8}$ | 0.0010–0.0027 | 0.0012–0.0029 | 0.3719 | 0.3719 |
| | 8—350 Diesel | ⑧ | ④ | 80 @ 1.67 | $1^{43}/_{64}$ | 0.0010–0.0027 | 0.0015–0.0032 | — | — |

① ± $^{1}/_{32}$ in.
② Exhaust—80 @ 1.61
③ Intake—$1^{23}/_{32}$
　Exhaust—$1^{19}/_{32}$
④ Intake 44°
　Exhaust 30°
⑤ 1978–80: 46°
⑥ 1978–80: 82 @ 1.66
⑦ 1978–80: $1^{21}/_{32}$
⑧ Intake 45°
　Exhaust 31°

## Ring Side Clearance
(in.)

| Year | Engine | Top Compression | Bottom Compression |
|---|---|---|---|
| 1970–73 | 8—307 | 0.0012–0.0027 | 0.0012–0.0032 |
| 1970–80 | 6—250 | 0.0012–0.0027 | 0.0012–0.0032 |
| 1970–80 | 6—292 | 0.0020–0.0040 | 0.0020–0.0040 |
| 1970–80 | 8—350 | 0.0012–0.0032 | 0.0012–0.0032 |
| 1975–80 | 8—400 | 0.0012–0.0032 | 0.0012–0.0032 |
| 1970 | 8—396 | 0.0012–0.0032 | 0.0012–0.0032 |
| 1971–72 | 8—402 | 0.0017–0.0032 | 0.0017–0.0032 |
| 1973–80 | 8—454 | 0.0017–0.0032 | 0.0017–0.0032 |
| 1977–80 | 8—305 | 0.0012–0.0032 | 0.0012–0.0032 |
| 1978–80 | 8—350 Diesel | 0.0040–0.0060 | 0.0018–0.0038 |

## Ring Side Clearance (cont'd)
(in.)

| Year | Engine | Oil Control |
|---|---|---|
| 1970–73 | 6—250, 8—307 | 0.0000–0.0050 |
| 1974–80 | 6—250 | 0.0000–0.0050 |
| 1970–80 | 8—350 | 0.002–0.007 |
| 1970–80 | 6—292 | 0.0050–0.0055 |
| 1970 | 8—396 | 0.0012–0.0060 |

| Year | Engine | Oil Control |
|---|---|---|
| 1971–72 | 8—402 | 0.0005–0.0065 |
| 1973–80 | 8—454 | 0.0005–0.0065 |
| 1975–80 | 8—400 | 0.002–0.007 |
| 1977–80 | 8—305 | 0.002–0.007 |
| 1978–80 | 8—350 Diesel | 0.001–0.005 |

## Ring Gap
(in.)

| Year | Engine | Top Compression | Bottom Compression | Oil Control |
|---|---|---|---|---|
| 1970–80 | 6—250 | 0.010–0.020 | 0.010–0.020 | 0.015–0.055 |
| 1970–80 | 6—292 | 0.010–0.020 | 0.010–0.020 | 0.015–0.055 |
| 1970–72 | 8—307 | 0.010–0.020 | 0.010–0.020 | 0.015–0.055 |
| 1970–80 | 8—350 | 0.010–0.020 | 0.013–0.025 ② | 0.015–0.055 |
| 1975–80 | 8—400 | 0.010–0.020 | 0.010–0.025 | 0.010–0.035 ① |
| 1970 | 8—396 | 0.010–0.020 | 0.010–0.020 | 0.010–0.030 |
| 1971–72 | 8—402 | 0.010–0.020 | 0.010–0.020 | 0.010–0.030 |
| 1973–80 | 8—454 | 0.010–0.020 | 0.010–0.020 | 0.010–0.030 ① |
| 1977–80 | 8—305 | 0.010–0.020 | 0.010–0.025 | 0.015–0.055 |
| 1978–80 | 8—350 Diesel | 0.015–0.025 | 0.015–0.025 | 0.015–0.055 |

① 0.015–0.055—1977–80
② 0.010–0.025—1977–80

## Piston Clearance

| Year | Engine | Piston-to-Bore Production Clearance (in.) | Year | Engine | Piston-to-Bore Production Clearance (in.) |
|------|--------|-------------------------------------------|------|--------|-------------------------------------------|
| 1970 | 6—250 | 0.0005–0.0015 | 1974–76 | 6—250 | 0.0005–0.0015 |
|      | 6—292 | 0.0025–0.0031 |         | 6—292 | 0.0026–0.0036 |
|      | 8—307 | 0.0005–0.0011 |         | 8—350 | 0.0007–0.0013 |
|      | 8—350 | 0.0012–0.0022 |         | 8—400 | 0.0014–0.0024 |
|      | 8—396 | 0.0018–0.0026 |         | 8—454 | 0.0018–0.0028 |
| 1971–72 | 6—250 | 0.0005–0.0015 | 1977–80 | 6—250 | 0.0005–0.0015 ① |
|      | 6—292 | 0.0025–0.0031 |         | 6—292 | 0.0026–0.0036 |
|      | 8—307 | 0.0012–0.0018 |         | 8—305 | 0.0007–0.0017 |
|      | 8—350 | 0.0007–0.0013 |         | 8—350 | 0.0007–0.0017 |
|      | 8—402 | 0.0018–0.0026 |         | 8—350 Diesel | 0.0050–0.0060 |
| 1973 | 6—250 | 0.0005–0.0015 |         | 8—400 | 0.0014–0.0024 |
|      | 6—292 | 0.0026–0.0036 |         | 8—454 | 0.0014–0.0024 |
|      | 8—307 | 0.0012–0.0018 |   |   |   |
|      | 8—350 | 0.0007–0.0013 |   |   |   |
|      | 8—454 | 0.0018–0.0028 |   |   |   |

① 0.0010–0.0020—1978–80

d. Oil pressure switch.

e. Transmission controlled spark solenoid.

f. CEC solenoid.

g. Coil.

h. Neutral safety switch.

8. Disconnect:

a. Accelerator linkage (hairpin at bellcrank, throttle and T.V. cables at intake manifold brackets on diesels. Position away from the engine.).

b. Choke cable at carburetor (if so equipped).

c. Fuel line to fuel pump.

d. Heater hoses at engine.

e. Air conditioning compressor with hoses attached. Do not remove the hoses from the air conditioning compressor. Remove it as a unit and set it aside. Its contents are under pressure, and can freeze body tissue on contact.

f. Transmission dipstick and tube on automatic transmission models, except for diesel. Plug the tube hole.

g. Oil dipstick and tube. Plug the hole.

h. Vacuum lines.

i. Oil pressure line to gauge, if so equipped.

j. Parking brake cable.

k. Power steering pump. This can be removed as a unit and set aside, without removing any of the hoses.

l. Engine ground straps.

m. Exhaust pipe (support if necessary).

9. Loosen and remove the fan belt, remove the fan blades and pulley. If you have the finned aluminum viscous drive fan clutch, keep it upright in its normal position. If the fluid leaks out, the unit will have to be replaced.

10. Remove the clutch cross-shaft.

11. Attach a chain or lifting device to the engine. If your engine doesn't have any lifting eyes, the usual locations are under the intake manifold bolts on V8s, or under the cylinder head bolts at either end on the sixes. You may have to remove the carburetor. Take the engine weight off the engine mounts, and unbolt the mounts. On all models except the gas-engined C-10, 1500, C-20, and 2500, support and disconnect the transmission. With automatic transmission, remove the torque converter underpan and starter, unbolt the converter from the flywheel, detach the throttle linkage and vacuum modulator line, and unbolt the engine from the transmission. Be certain that the converter does not fall out. With manual transmission, unbolt the clutch housing from the engine. Further details are in Chapter 6.

12. On two wheel drive models, remove the driveshaft. See details in Chapter 7. Either drain the transmission or plug the driveshaft opening. Disconnect the speedometer cable at the transmission. Disconnect the TCS switch wire, if so equipped. Disconnect the shift linkage or lever, or the clutch linkage. Disconnect the transmission cooler lines, if so equipped. If you have an automatic or a four speed transmission, the rear

crossmember must be removed. With the three speed, unbolt the transmission from the crossmember. Raise the engine/transmission assembly and pull it forward.

13. On diesels, remove the three bolts, transmission, right side; disconnect the wires to the starter and remove the starter.

14. On four wheel drive, raise and pull the engine forward until it is free of the transmission. On diesels, slightly raise the transmission, remove the three left transmission to engine bolts, and remove the engine.

15. On all trucks, lift the engine out slowly, making certain as you go that all lines between the engine and the truck have been disconnected.

Installation is as follows:

1. On four wheel drive and diesels, lower the engine into place and align it with the transmission. Push the engine back gently and turn the crankshaft until the manual transmission shaft and clutch engage. Bolt the transmission to the engine. With automatic transmission, align the converter with the flywheel, bolt the transmission to the engine, bolt the converter to the flywheel, replace the underpan and starter, and connect the throttle linkage and vacuum modulator line. See Chapter 6 for details.

2. On two wheel drive, lower the engine/transmission unit into place. Replace the rear crossmember if removed. Bolt the three speed transmission back to the crossmember. Replace the driveshaft.

3. Install the engine mounts.

4. Replace all transmission connections and the clutch cross-shaft. Replace the fan, pulley, and belts.

5. Replace all the items removed from the engine earlier. Connect all the wires which were detached.

6. Replace the radiator and fan shroud, air cleaner, and battery or battery cables. Fill the cooling system and check the automatic transmission fuel level. Fill the crankcase with oil. Check for leaks.

## Cylinder Head
### REMOVAL AND INSTALLATION
#### Six Cylinder

1. Disconnect the battery cable clamp at the negative terminal.

2. Drain the cooling system and remove the air cleaner. Disconnect the PCV hose. If equipped, disconnect the air injection hose at the check valve.

3. Disconnect the accelerator pedal rod at the bellcrank on the manifold, and the fuel and vacuum lines at the carburetor.

4. Disconnect the exhaust pipe at the manifold flange, then remove the manifold bolts and clamps and remove the manifolds and carburetor as an assembly. There is a round ring gasket at the exhaust manifold flange, and a gasket for each of the manifolds at the cylinder head. These will have to be replaced. On 1975 and later engines with an integral manifold head, remove the carburetor at the intake manifold, and remove the exhaust manifold.

5. Remove the fuel and vacuum line retaining clip from the water outlet. Then disconnect the wire harness from the heat sending unit and coil, leaving the harness clear of clips on the rocker arm cover.

6. Disconnect the radiator hose at the water outlet housing and the battery ground strap at the head.

7. Number the spark plug wires, then remove the wires and the spark plugs. Disconnect the coil-to-distributor primary wire lead at the coil and remove the coil on models without HEI.

8. Remove the rocker arm cover. Back off the rocker arm nuts, pivot the rocker arms to clear the pushrods, and remove the pushrods. Be certain to keep the pushrods in the order in which they came out. They must be reinstalled in their original order.

9. Remove the cylinder head bolts, cylinder head, and gasket. The bolts should be loosened a little at a time, to prevent the head from warping.

To install:

1. Clean the mating surfaces of the cylinder block and head thoroughly. They can be scraped with a razor blade. Vacuum out any bits that fall onto the pistons, being careful not to nick the cylinder walls. As long as you have the head off, it is a good practice to replace the core (freeze) plugs in the head, as they are subject to corrosion and can cause leaks. They can be driven out with a punch. New plugs can be driven in with a hammer and a socket slightly smaller in diameter than the plugs.

2. Place a new cylinder head gasket over the dowel pins on the cylinder block with the head up. Steel gaskets should not be painted or sprayed with copper head gasket paint. Composition steel/asbestos gaskets should not be used.

3. Guide and lower the cylinder head

# Torque Sequences

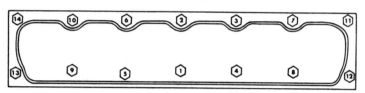

Six cylinder head (© Chevrolet Motor Div.)

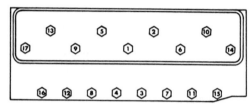

**Small block V8 head (© Chevrolet Motor Div.)**

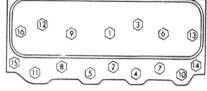

**Big block V8 head (© Chevrolet Motor Div.)**

into place over the dowels and gasket. This may require the help of a strong friend.

4. Clean and oil the cylinder head bolts. Install and tighten them down until their heads contact the cylinder head.

5. Tighten the cylinder head bolts a little at a time with a torque wrench. Torque them in the sequence shown in the accompanying diagram. You should go around at least three times, increasing the amount of torque applied each time until the specified value is reached.

6. Coat the ends of the pushrods with pre-lube and install them in their respective cylinder head openings. Seat them in their lifter sockets. You will be able to feel them click into place when they are correctly installed.

7. Coat the rocker arm assemblies with pre-lube, and install the rocker arms, balls and nuts in their respective places. Tighten the rocker arm nuts until all pushrod play is taken up.

8. Connect the radiator hose.

9. Connect the engine ground strap.

10. Connect temperature sending unit wires and install fuel and vacuum lines in clip at water outlet.

11. Clean the spark plugs, or install new ones. Use new gaskets if necessary, and torque to specifications.

12. Install the coil and coil wire, and install the spark plug wires.

13. Clean the surfaces of the manifold(s) and install a new gasket or gaskets over the manifold studs. Install the manifold(s). Clean and oil the bolts, then install and torque them in sequence to the specified values.

Connect exhaust pipe to manifold, using a new ring gasket.

14. Install the carburetor if it was removed, and reconnect the carburetor linkage.

15. Fill the cooling system and check for leaks.

16. Adjust the valves as explained later.

17. Install the rocker arm cover and position the wiring harness in the clips. Earlier model engines have rocker arm covers sealed by gaskets; later models use RTV (room temperature vulcanizing) silicone seal. Do not use the sealer in place of a gasket, or conversely, use a gasket instead of the sealer. If the cover uses sealer, remove any loose pieces of sealer, then clean and dry the mating surfaces. It is not necessary to remove every last bit of old sealer, because the new sealer will adhere to the old. Apply a 3/16 inch bead of RTV sealer, G.M. #1052366 or the equivalent, to the sealing surface on the cylinder head. Run the bead to the inside of the bolt holes. Install the cover and tighten the bolts within 10 minutes of the sealer application (while the sealer is still wet).

18. Clean and install the air cleaner. Connect PCV, fuel, and vacuum hoses.

19. Connect battery cable to ground terminal.

## V8 Gasoline Engines

1. Remove the intake manifold as described later.

2. Remove the exhaust manifolds as described later and tie out of the way.

3. Back off the rocker arm nuts and pivot the rocker arms out of the way so that the

pushrods can be removed. Identify the pushrods so that they can be installed in their original positions.

4. Remove the cylinder head bolts and remove the heads.

5. Install the cylinder heads using new gaskets. Install the gaskets with the bead up.

NOTE: *Coat a steel gasket on both sides with sealer. If a composition gasket is used, do not use sealer.*

6. Clean the bolts, apply sealer to the threads, and install them hand tight.

7. Tighten the head bolts a little at a time in the sequence shown. Head bolt torque is listed in the "Torque Specifications" chart.

8. Install the intake and exhaust manifolds.

9. Adjust the valves.

### Diesel

It is strongly recommended that the cylinder heads not be removed on diesels. The procedure requires that the intake manifold and rocker arms be removed, which, in turn, requires removal of the valve lifters, disassembly, and reassembly while submerged in kerosene or diesel fuel. The valve lifters must then be bled down using a specially weighted press. In addition, removal of the intake manifold requires re-timing of the injection pump, which involves grinding off the old timing marks and using a special timing tool to scribe new marks while the pump is torqued to specification. It is advised that any work of this nature be performed by a qualified dealer or mechanic, as the tools involved are expensive and not generally available.

However, if the necessary tools are available, the cylinder heads may be removed and installed as follows:

1. Remove the intake manifold, using the procedure outlined later in this chapter.

2. Remove the rocker arm cover(s), after removing any accessory brackets which interfere with cover removal.

3. Disconnect and label the glow plug wiring.

4. If the right cylinder head is being removed, remove the ground strap from the head.

5. Remove the rocker arm bolts, the bridge pivots, the rocker arms, and the pushrods, keeping all the parts in order so that they can be returned to their original positions. It is a good practice to number or mark the parts to avoid interchanging them.

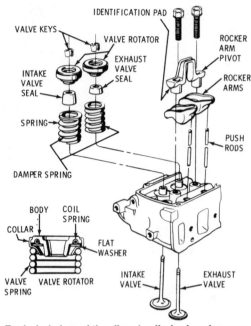

Exploded view of the diesel cylinder head components (© Chevrolet Motor Div.)

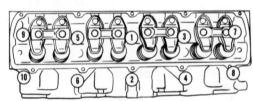

Diesel head torque sequence (© Chevrolet Motor Div.)

6. Remove the fuel return lines from the nozzles.

7. Remove the exhaust manifold(s), using the procedure outlined later in this chapter.

8. Remove the engine block drain plug on the side of the engine from which the cylinder head is being removed.

9. Remove the head bolts. Remove the cylinder head.

10. To install, first clean the mating surfaces thoroughly. Install new head gaskets on the engine block. Do NOT coat the gaskets with any sealer. The gaskets have a special coating that eliminates the need for sealer. The use of sealer will interfere with this coating and cause leaks. Install the cylinder head onto the block.

11. Clean the head bolts thoroughly. Dip the bolts in clean engine oil and install into the cylinder block until the heads of the bolts lightly contact the cylinder head.

12. Tighten the bolts, in the sequence il-

lustrated, to 100 ft lbs. When all bolts have been tightened to this figure, begin the tightening sequence again, and torque all bolts to 130 ft lbs.

13. Install the engine block drain plug(s), the exhaust manifold(s), the fuel return lines, the glow plug wiring, and the ground strap for the right cylinder head.

14. After disassembling, cleaning, and reassembling the valve lifters, bleed them down using the appropriate procedure outlined later in this chapter, and install them into the engine. Install the pushrods, rocker arms, and pivots into their original locations.

15. Install the intake manifold.

16. Install the rocker cover(s). The covers do not use gaskets, but are sealed with a bead of RTV (room temperature vulcanizing) silicone sealer instead. Apply a $^3/_{32}$ inch bead of RTV sealer, G.M. #1052289 or the equivalent, to the clean and dry mating surface of the rocker arm cover. Run the bead of sealer to the inside of the bolt holes. Install the cover to the head within 10 minutes (while the sealer is still wet).

## VALVE GUIDES

Valve guides are integral with the cylinder head on all engines. Valve guide bores may be reamed to accommodate oversize valves. If wear permits, valve guides can be knurled to allow the retention of standard valves. Maximum allowable valve stem-to-guide bore clearances are listed under "Valve Specifications."

## VALVE LASH ADJUSTMENT— GASOLINE ENGINES

All engines described in this book use hydraulic lifters, which require no periodic adjustment. In the event of cylinder head removal or any operation that requires disturbing the rocker arms, the rocker arms will have to be adjusted.

### 1970–71

Normalize the engine temperature by running it for several minutes. Shut the engine off and remove the valve cover(s). After valve cover removal, torque the cylinder heads to specification. The use of oil stopper clips, readily available on the market, is recommended to prevent oil splatter when adjusting valve lash. Restart the engine. Valve lash is set with the engine warm and idling.

Turn the rocker arm nut counterclockwise until the rocker arm begins to clatter. Re-

**Oil splash stopper clips will prevent splatter when adjusting valves with the engine running (© Chevrolet Motor Div.)**

verse the direction and turn the rocker arm down slowly until the clatter just stops. This is the zero lash position. Turn the nut down an additional ¼ turn and wait ten seconds until the engine runs smoothly. Continue with additional ¼ turns, waiting ten seconds each time, until the nut has been turned down one full turn from the zero lash position. This one turn, pre-load adjustment must be performed to allow the lifter to adjust itself and prevents possible interference between the valves and pistons. Noisy lifters should be cleaned or replaced.

### 1972–80

1. Remove the rocker covers and gaskets.

2. Adjust the valves on six cylinder engines as follows:

a. Mark the distributor housing with a piece of chalk at No. 1 and 6 plug wire positions. Remove the distributor cap with the plug wires attached.

b. Crank the engine until the distributor rotor points to No. 1 cylinder and No. 1 cylinder is in firing position (both valves closed). At this point, adjust the following valves as outlined in Step c:

No. 1—Exhaust and Intake
No. 2—Intake
No. 3—Exhaust
No. 4—Intake
No. 5—Exhaust

c. Back out the adjusting nut until lash is felt at the pushrod, then turn the adjusting nut in until all lash is removed. This can be determined by checking pushrod end-play while turning the adjusting nut. When all play has been removed, turn the adjusting nut in 1 full turn.

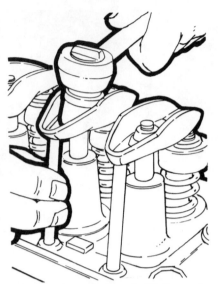

**Six cylinder valve adjustment with the engine off**

**Adjusting V8 valves with the engine off (© Chevrolet Motor Div.)**

d. Crank · the engine until the distributor rotor points to No. 6 cylinder. The following valves can be adjusted with the engine in the No. 6 firing position (both No. 6 valves closed):

No. 2—Exhaust
No. 3—Intake
No. 4—Exhaust
No. 5—Intake
No. 6—Intake and Exhaust

3. Adjust the valves on V8 engines as follows:

a. Crank the engine until the mark on the damper aligns with the TDC or 0° mark on the timing tab and the engine is in No. 1 firing position. This can be determined by placing the fingers on the No. 1 cylinder valves as the marks align. If the valves do not move, it is in No. 1 firing position. If the valves move, it is in No. 6 firing position and the crankshaft should be rotated one more revolution to the No. 1 firing position.

b. The adjustment is made in the same manner as six cylinder engines (see Step c of the six cylinder procedure).

c. With the engine in No. 1 firing position, the following valves can be adjusted:

Exhaust—1,3,4,8
Intake—1,2,5,7

d. Crank the engine 1 full revolution until the marks are again in alignment. This is No. 6 firing position. The following valves can now be adjusted:

Exhaust—2,5,6,7
Intake—3,4,6,8

4. Reinstall the rocker arm covers using new gaskets or RTV silicone sealer (see Step 17 of the six cylinder head installation procedure).

5. Install the distributor cap and wire assembly.

6. Adjust the carburetor idle speed (see Chapter 2).

### DIESEL

Valve lash adjustment in diesel engines is controlled by the valve lifters, rather than through adjustments to the rocker arms. If the intake manifold has been removed, or if the heads have been removed, it will be necessary to remove those valve lifters affected, disassemble, reassemble, and bleed them down under pressure from a specially weighted testing press. It is for this reason that removal of the valve lifters, intake manifold, or cylinder heads is specifically not recommended. The procedure is complicated and requires expensive tools not generally available.

If the intake manifold has not been removed but rocker arms have been loosened or removed, valve lifters can be bled down by the following procedure:

1. For cylinders no. 3,5,7,2,4 and 8, turn the crankshaft so the saw slot on the harmonic balancer is at 0° on the timing indicator. For cylinders no. 1,3,7,2,4 and 6, turn the crankshaft so that the saw slot on the harmonic balancer is at 4 o'clock.

2. Tighten the rocker arm pivot bolts to 25 ft lbs.

NOTE: *It will take up to 45 minutes at*

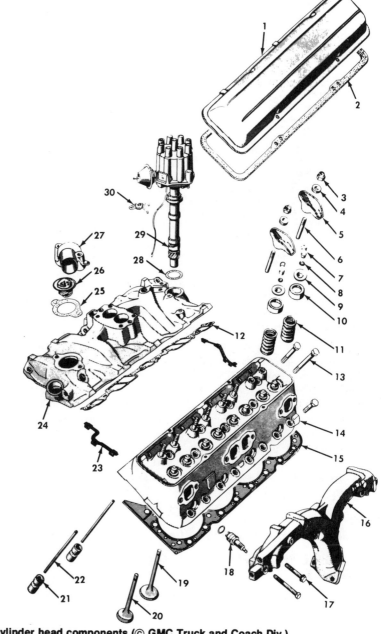

1. Rocker arm cover
2. Gasket
3. Nut
4. Ball
5. Rocker arms
6. Rocker arm studs
7. Valve keeper locks
8. O-ring seals
9. Valve spring cap
10. Shield
11. Spring
12. Gasket
13. Bolts
14. Cylinder head
15. Head gasket
16. Exhaust manifold
17. Bolts
18. Spark plug and gasket
19. Intake valve
20. Exhaust valve
21. Hydraulic lifters
22. Push rods
23. Intake manifold gaskets
24. Intake manifold
25. Gasket
26. Thermostat
27. Thermostat housing
28. Gasket
29. Distributor
30. Clamp

**Small block cylinder head components (© GMC Truck and Coach Div.)**

*each position for the valve lifters to be completely bled down.*

CAUTION: *Do not rotate the engine until the valve lifters have been bled down, or damage to the valve train could occur.*

3. If any additional lifters need to be bled, rotate the crankshaft to the second position. Again, you must wait at least 45 minutes before rotating the crankshaft.

4. Finish reassembling the engine as the lifters are being bled.

## Rocker Arms

### REMOVAL AND INSTALLATION– GASOLINE ENGINES

Rocker arms are removed by removing the adjusting nut. Be sure to adjust the valve lash after replacing the rocker arms. Coat the replacement rocker arm and ball with SAE 90 gear oil before installation.

Rocker arm studs on sixes and small block V8s that have damaged threads or are loose

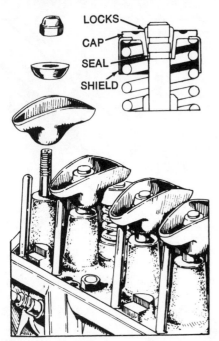

**Six cylinder rocker arm components—V8s similar**

in the cylinder heads may be replaced by reaming the bore and installing oversize studs. Oversizes available are 0.003 and 0.013 in. The bores may also be tapped and screw-in studs installed. Several aftermarket companies produce complete rocker arm stud kits with installation tools. Late high-performance small-block engines and Mark IV V8s use screw-in studs and pushrod guide plates.

## OVERHAUL

See the "Engine Rebuilding Section."

## REMOVAL AND INSTALLATION–DIESEL ENGINES

1. Remove the air cleaner, high pressure fuel lines to the injectors, and the rocker arm cover.

2. Remove the arm pivot bolts and the pivot(s). Remove the rocker arms. The use of bridged pivots requires that the rocker arms be removed in pairs.

3. To install, position the set of rocker arms in the original locations.

4. Lubricate the pivot contact surfaces and install the pivot(s).

5. Install the pivot bolts. Tighten the bolts alternately and evenly to 25 ft lbs, following the bleed down procedure outlined previously under "Valve Lash Adjustment" for diesel engines.

6. Install the rocker arm cover as outlined in Step 16 of the diesel engine cylinder head removal and installation procedure. Install the fuel lines and the air cleaner.

## VALVE LIFTER REMOVAL, INSTALLATION, DISASSEMBLY, AND BLEED DOWN–DIESEL ENGINES

Whenever the rocker arms have been removed and the intake manifold removed, the valve lifters must be removed, disassembled, assembled while submerged in diesel fuel or kerosene, and bled down using a specially-weighted press. The lifters also must be disassembled, reassembled while submerged, and bled down on the press whenever they are removed. Note that if the rocker arms have been removed but the intake manifold has not been disturbed, the lifters can be bled down as outlined in the "Valve Lash Adjustment" procedure for diesel engines. The following procedure is to be used for lifter removal and installation, or whenever both the rocker arms and the intake manifold have been disturbed.

1. Remove the intake manifold.

2. Remove the rocker covers, the rocker arms, and the pushrods. Keep all the parts in order so that they may be installed in their original locations.

3. Remove the valve lifters.

To disassemble the lifters:

4. Remove the retainer ring with a small screwdriver.

5. Remove the pushrod seat. Remove the oil metering valve. Remove the plunger and plunger spring. Remove the check valve retainer from the plunger, and remove the valve and its spring.

6. Clean all parts in a safe solvent. Check for burrs, nicks, scoring, or excessive wear, and replace as necessary.

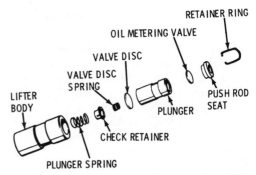

**Exploded view of the diesel valve lifter (© Chevrolet Motor Div.)**

7. Check the lifter foot for excessive wear:

a. Place a straightedge across the lifter foot.

b. Hold the lifter at eye level. Check for light appearing between the lifter foot and the straightedge.

c. If light is visible, indicating a concave surface, the lifter should be replaced and the camshaft inspected. If the cam lobe is worn across the full width of the cam base circle (opposite the high lobe of the cam), the camshaft should be replaced. Wear at the center of the cam base circle is normal. Wear across the full width of the nose of the lobe is also normal.

8. After the lifter parts have been cleaned, assemble the valve disc spring and retainer into the plunger. Be sure the retainer flange is pressed tightly against the bottom of the recess in the plunger.

9. Install the plunger spring over the check retainer.

10. Hold the plunger with the spring up. Insert into the lifter body. Hold the plunger vertically while doing this to avoid cocking the spring.

11. Fill the reservoir of G.M. tool no. J-5790 with kerosene to within ½ inch of the top of the reservoir. This tool is a specially weighted press with provision for reservoir rotation.

12. Place the valve lifter assembly into the reservoir. Position the oil control valve and the pushrod seat onto the plunger.

13. Install a ¼ inch steel ball onto the pushrod seat. Lower the tester ram until it contacts the steel ball. Do not press on the ram. Allow the ram to move downward by its own weight, until the air bubbles expelled from the lifter assembly disappear.

14. Raise the ram, then allow it to lower by its own weight. Repeat this operation until all air is expelled from the lifter. Do not attempt to hasten the process by pumping the ram up and down.

15. After all air has been expelled, allow the ram to descend, bleeding the lifter, until the retaining ring groove is exposed. Install the retaining ring.

16. Adjust the ram screw so that it contacts the steel ball in the pushrod seat at the same time as the pointer is at the start line.

17. Raise the arm of the tester, then start the bleed down test by resting the ram on the steel ball and starting a timer. Rotate the reservoir one revolution every two seconds, and time the indicator from the start line to the stop line. Acceptable leak down time is 6 seconds minimum for used lifters, and from 9 to 60 seconds for a new lifter.

18. If the lifter leak down rate falls within the specified limit, the lifter may be reused. If not, new lifters should be installed in the engine.

19. If new lifters are to be installed, they must first be filled with kerosene or diesel fuel. Install the lifter in the tester. Fill the reservoir to within ½ inch of the top, and fill the lifter as outlined in Steps 13, 14, and 15 of this procedure.

To install the lifters:

20. Coat the foot of the lifter with G.M. lubricant #562458 or the equivalent.

21. Install the lifters into their original positions. Install the pushrods into their original positions.

22. Install the intake manifold.

23. Install the rocker arms and pivots.

24. Bleed down the lifters as outlined under "Valve Lash Adjustment" for the diesel engine.

25. Install the rocker covers.

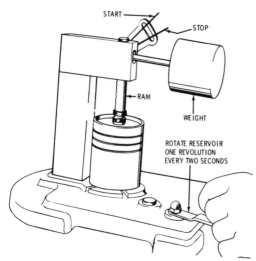

**A specially-weighted press must be used to assemble and test diesel valve lifters (© Chevrolet Motor Div.)**

## Intake Manifold
### *REMOVAL AND INSTALLATION*
#### Six Cylinder

Most 1975–80 sixes have an intake manifold cast as one piece with the cylinder head. Other sixes require the intake and exhaust manifolds removed as an assembly. For these engines:

1. Remove the air cleaner.

2. Disconnect the throttle rods at the bellcrank and remove the throttle return spring.

3. Disconnect the fuel and vacuum lines at the carburetor. Plug the fuel line. Disconnect the choke cable at the carburetor.

4. Disconnect the crankcase ventilation hose at the carburetor.

5. Disconnect the exhaust pipe at the manifold flange and discard the packing.

6. Disconnect the EGR valve hose (if equipped).

7. Remove the manifold attaching bolts and clamps and remove the manifold assembly. Discard the gaskets.

8. The manifold assembly can be separated by removing 1 bolt and 2 nuts at the center.

9. Check the manifold for straightness along the exhaust port faces. If it is distorted more than 0.015 in. it should be replaced. Clean all mounting faces.

10. Installation is the reverse of removal. Use all new gaskets. The exhaust pipe-to-manifold mounting studs and nuts should be scraped clean with a wire brush and lightly oiled. The manifolds should be torqued in sequence to specifications.

### V8 Except Diesel

1. Remove the air cleaner.

2. Drain the radiator.

3. Disconnect:

   a. Battery cables at the battery.

   b. Upper radiator and heater hoses at the manifolds.

   c. Crankcase ventilation hoses as required.

   d. Fuel line and choke cable at the carburetor.

   e. Accelerator linkage at the carburetor.

   f. Vacuum hose at the distributor.

   g. Power brake hose at the carburetor base or manifold, if applicable.

   h. Ignition coil (point-type ignition) and temperature sending switch wires.

   i. Water pump by-pass at the water pump (Mark IV only).

4. Remove the distributor cap and scribe the rotor position relative to the distributor body.

5. Remove the distributor.

6. As required, remove the oil filler

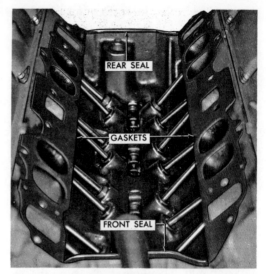

**Gasoline V8 intake manifold gasket and seal location (© Chevrolet Motor Div.)**

bracket, air cleaner bracket, air compressor and bracket and accelerator bellcrank.

7. Remove the manifold-to-head attaching bolts then remove the manifold and carburetor as an assembly.

8. If the manifold is to be replaced, transfer the carburetor (and mounting studs), water outlet and thermostat (use a new gasket) heater hose adapter, EGR valve (use new gasket) and, if applicable, TVS switch and the choke coil. 1975–80 engines use a new carburetor heat choke tube which must be transferred to a new manifold.

9. Before installing the manifold, thoroughly clean the gasket and seal surfaces of the cylinder heads and manifold.

10. Install the manifold end seals, folding the tabs if applicable, and the manifold/head gaskets, using a sealing compound around the water passages. 1978 and later models use RTV (Room Temperature Vulcanizing) silicone seal at the front and rear ridges of the cylinder block, instead of seals. On these models, remove any loose RTV from the sealing surfaces. Apply a $^3/_{16}$ inch bead of RTV sealer, G.M. #1052366 or the equivalent, on the front and rear ridges, extending the bead up ½ inch on the cylinder heads to seal and retain the intake manifold side gaskets.

NOTE: *1974–75 350 V8 engines require a new intake manifold side gasket on 4-bbl engines. The new gasket has restricted cross-over ports. The 350 2-bbl uses a restricted cross-over gasket on the right-hand side and an open gasket on the left. The*

*350 4-bbl uses restricted cross-over gaskets on both sides.*

11. When installing the manifold, care should be taken not to dislocate the end seals. It is helpful to use a pilot in the distributor opening. Tighten the manifold bolts to 30 ft lbs in the sequence illustrated.

12. Install the ignition coil (point-type ignitions).

13. Install the distributor with the rotor in its original location as indicated by the scribe line. If the engine has been disturbed, refer to the "Distributor Removal and Installation" section.

14. If applicable, install the alternator upper bracket and adjust the belt tension.

15. Connect all components disconnected in Steps 3 and 6.

16. Filling the cooling system, start the engine, check for leaks and adjust the ignition timing and carburetor idle speed and mixture.

## Torque Sequences

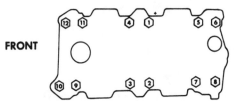

**Small block V8 intake manifold (© Chevrolet Motor Div.)**

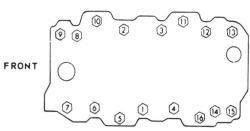

**Mark IV intake manifold (© Chevrolet Motor Div.)**

### Diesel

It is not recommended that the intake manifold be removed on diesel engines. The procedure requires re-timing of the injection pump. This involves grinding off the old timing mark and scribing a new mark with a special timing tool while re-torqueing the pump to specification. It is strongly advised that any work of this nature be performed only by a qualified mechanic or dealer.

If the necessary tools are available, the intake manifold can be removed and installed using the following procedure.

1. Remove the air cleaner.

2. Drain the radiator. Loosen the upper bypass hose clamp, remove the thermostat housing bolts, and remove the housing and the thermostat from the intake manifold.

3. Remove the breather pipes from the rocker covers and the air crossover. Remove the air crossover. It is a good idea to cover the air intakes in the manifold to prevent nuts and bolts from falling down into the engine, if dropped. The intake passages can simply be taped over.

4. Disconnect the throttle rod and the return spring. If equipped with cruise control, remove the servo.

5. Remove the hairpin clip at the bellcrank and disconnect the cables. Remove the throttle cable from the bracket on the manifold; position the cable away from the engine. Disconnect and label any wiring as necessary.

6. Remove the alternator bracket as necessary. If the truck is equipped with air conditioning, remove the compressor mounting bolts and move the compressor aside, without disconnecting any of the hoses. Remove the compressor mounting bracket from the intake manifold.

7. Disconnect the fuel line from the pump and the fuel filter. Remove the fuel filter and bracket.

8. Disconnect the fuel return line from the injection pump. Using two wrenches to prevent the lines from being twisted, disconnect the injection pump lines at the nozzles.

CAUTION: *Do not bend the injection pump lines!*

9. Remove the three nuts retaining the injection pump, using G.M. special tool no. J-26987 or the equivalent. Remove the pump and cap all open lines and nozzles.

10. Disconnect the vacuum lines at the vacuum pump. Remove the bolt and the bracket holding the pump to the block and remove the pump.

11. Remove the intake manifold drain tube clamp and remove the drain tube.

12. Remove the intake manifold bolts and remove the manifold. Remove the adapter seal. Remove the injection pump adapter.

13. Clean the mating surfaces of the cylinder heads and the intake manifold using a putty knife. Be extremely careful not to scratch or gouge the surfaces. Clean and dry the surfaces with solvent.

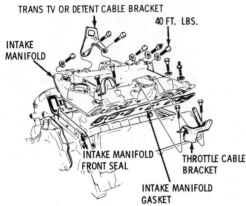

Diesel intake manifold installation (© Oldsmobile Motor Div.)

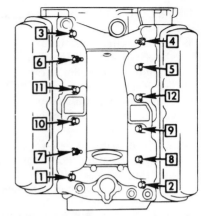

Diesel intake manifold torque sequence (© Oldsmobile Motor Div.)

To install the manifold:

NOTE: *If the rocker arms have been removed, the valve lifters must be removed, disassembled, then reassembled while submerged in kerosene or diesel fuel, then bled down using the specially weighted press. See the procedure earlier in this chapter. Do not install the manifold until the affected lifters have been serviced.*

14. Coat both sides of the gasket surface that seal the intake manifold to the cylinder heads with G.M. sealer #1050805 or the equivalent. Position the intake manifold gaskets on the cylinder heads. Install the end seals, making sure that the ends are positioned under the cylinder heads.

15. Carefully lower the intake manifold into place on the engine.

16. Clean the intake manifold bolts thoroughly, then dip them in clean engine oil. Install the bolts and tighten to 15 ft lbs in the sequence shown. Next, tighten all the bolts to 30 ft lbs, in sequence, and finally tighten to 40 ft lbs in sequence.

17. Install the intake manifold drain tube and clamp.

18. File the mark from the injection pump adapter.

CAUTION: *Do not file the mark from the injection pump.*

19. Place the engine on TDC for the No. 1 cylinder. The mark on the harmonic balancer on the crankshaft will be aligned with the zero mark on the timing tab, and both valves for No. 1 cylinder will be closed. The index mark on the injection pump driven gear should be offset to the right when No. 1 is at TDC. Check that all these conditions are met before continuing.

20. Apply chassis grease to the seal area

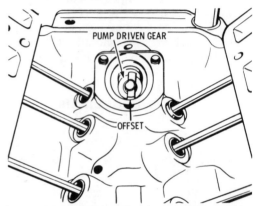

The index mark on the injection pump driven gear will be offset to the right when the No. 1 cylinder is at TDC (© Oldsmobile Motor Div.)

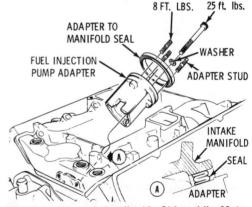

Adapter and seal details (© Oldsmobile Motor Div.)

on the adapter, the tapered edge and the seal area on the intake manifold. Install the adapter but leave the bolts loose.

21. Apply chassis grease to the inside and outside diameters of the adapter seal, and to

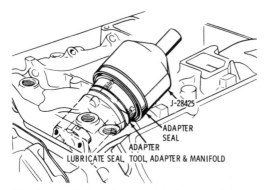

**Adapter seal installation with the special tool (© Oldsmobile Motor Div.)**

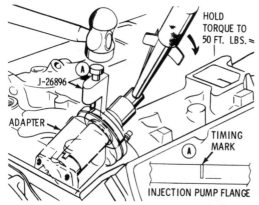

**Injection pump adapter timing mark application (© Oldsmobile Motor Div.)**

the seal installing tool, G.M. no. J-28425. Install the seal onto the tool.

22. Push the seal onto the injection pump adapter, using the tool (no. J-28425 or the equivalent). Remove the tool and inspect the seal to see if it is properly positioned.

23. Tighten the adapter bolts to 25 ft lbs.

24. Install a timing tool, G.M. no. J-26896 or the equivalent, into the injection pump adapter. Tighten the tool toward No. 1 cylinder to 50 ft lbs. While holding the tool and adapter at this torque, mark the injection pump adapter by striking the marking pin with a hammer. Remove the tool.

25. Remove the protective caps from the lines. Line up the offset tang on the injection pump driveshaft with the pump driven gear. Install the pump.

26. Install the three retaining nuts and lockwashers for the injection pump but do not tighten the nuts. Connect the injection pump lines to the nozzles. Use two wrenches to tighten the lines (25 ft lbs).

CAUTION: *Do not bend or twist the injection pump lines.*

27. Connect the fuel return lines to the pump.

28. Align the injection pump mark with the adapter mark and tighten the nuts. Use a ¾ inch open end wrench on the boss at the front of the injection pump to aid in rotating the pump to align the marks. Tighten the nuts to 18 ft lbs.

29. Adjust the throttle rod and return spring. See the procedure in Chapter 4.

30. Install the fuel filter and bracket and install the fuel line to the pump and the filter.

31. Install the vacuum pump and the vacuum lines. Do not operate the engine without the vacuum pump installed—it is the drive for the engine oil pump.

32. Connect the wiring.

33. Install the alternator and air conditioning compressor brackets.

34. Install the cable in the bracket and bellcrank, then install the bellcrank.

35. Connect the throttle rod and the return spring.

36. Remove the tape from the air intakes and install the air crossover. Install the breather tubes and the flow control valve at the air crossover. Connect the upper radiator hose and the heater hose, install the thermostat and thermostat housing, fill the cooling system, start the engine and check for leaks.

## Exhaust Manifold

### REMOVAL AND INSTALLATION

**1970–80 Six Cylinder, Non-Integral Head**

See the "Intake Manifold Removal and Installation" section.

**1975–80 Six Cylinder With Integral Head**

1. Remove the air cleaner. Disconnect negative battery terminal.

2. Remove the power steering pump and, if equipped, the AIR pump.

3. Remove the EFE (Early Fuel Evaporation) valve bracket.

4. Disconnect the throttle controls and the throttle return spring.

5. Disconnect the exhaust pipe at the manifold flange. Disconnect the converter bracket at the transmission mount, if so equipped. If equipped with manifold converter, disconnect the exhaust pipe from the converter, and remove the converter.

6. Remove the manifold attaching bolts and remove the manifold. Discard the gasket.

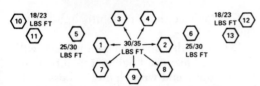

**1975–80 integral cylinder head exhaust manifold torque sequence (© Chevrolet Motor Div.)**

7. Check for cracks in the manifold before it is replaced.

8. Install a new gasket on the exhaust manifold.

9. Clean and oil the bolts and install the bolts, torquing them to specifications.

10. Connect the exhaust pipe, throttle controls, and return spring. Install the air cleaner, start the engine, and check for leaks.

### V8 Except Diesel

1. If equipped with AIR, remove the air injector assembly. The ¼ in. pipe threads in the manifold are straight cut threads. Do not use a ¼ in. tapered pipe tap to clean the threads.

2. Disconnect the battery.

3. If equipped, remove the carburetor heat stove pipe.

4. Remove the spark plug wire heat shields. On Mark IV, remove spark plugs.

5. On the left exhaust manifold, disconnect and remove the alternator.

6. Disconnect the exhaust pipe from the manifold and hang it from the frame out of the way.

7. Bend the locktabs and remove the end bolts, then the center bolts. Remove the manifold.

NOTE: *A ⁹/₁₆ in. thin wall 6-point socket, sharpened at the leading edge and tapped onto the head of the bolt, simplifies bending the locktabs.*

8. Installation is the reverse of removal. Clean all mating surfaces and use new gaskets. Torque all bolts to specifications from the inside working out.

### Diesel

*LEFT SIDE*

1. Remove the air cleaner.

2. Remove the lower alternator bracket.

3. Raise the truck and remove the exhaust pipe from the manifold flange.

4. Lower the truck. Bend the locktabs away from the manifold mounting bolts. Remove the bolts and remove the manifold from above. Do not lose the locktabs, and do not lose the washers for the bolts, which go under the locktabs.

5. Installation is the reverse. Tighten the manifold bolts to 25 ft lbs in two stages, working in a circular pattern from the center to the ends. Then tighten the front bolt to 30 ft lbs.

*RIGHT SIDE*

1. Raise and support the truck. Remove the bolts retaining the exhaust pipe to the manifold flange.

2. Bend the locktabs away from the manifold mounting bolts. Remove the bolts and remove the manifold. Do not lose the locktabs and the washers for the bolts, which go under the locktabs.

3. Installation is the reverse. Tighten the bolts to 25 ft lbs in two progressive steps, working in a circular pattern from the center to the ends.

## Timing Gear Cover

### REMOVAL AND INSTALLATION—SIX CYLINDER

1. Drain the oil and remove the oil pan on 1970–72 models.

2. Remove the radiator after draining it.

3. Remove the fan, pulley, and belt. Remove any power steering and/or AIR pump drive belts. Remove any braces for the above pumps which will interfere with cover removal and position the pumps out of the way.

4. Remove the crankshaft pulley and damper. Use a puller to remove the damper. Do not attempt to pry or hammer the damper off, or it will be damaged.

5. Remove the retaining bolts, and remove the cover of 1970–72 models.

6. On all 1973–78 models, and on all 1979–80 250 sixes, pull the cover forward slightly and cut the oil pan front seal off flush with the block. Remove the cover. 1979–80 292 sixes have RTV (room Temperature Vulcanizing) silicone seal at the oil pan to front cover junction; no front rubber seal is used.

7. On 1973–80 models using a rubber seal, cut the tabs from a new oil pan front seal

CUT THIS PORTION
FROM NEW SEAL

**When the timing gear cover is replaced on most 1973–80 sixes, the oil pan front seal must be modified (© Chevrolet Motor Div.)**

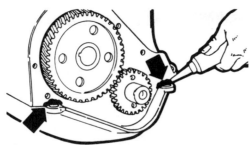

Use sealer at the timing cover-to-oil pan, and oil pan-to-cylinder block joints

and install the seal to the front cover, pressing the tips into the holes provided in the cover. On 1979–80 models using no rubber seal, apply a $3/16$ inch bead of RTV silicone seal on the cover sealing surface.

8. On all models, coat the front cover gasket with sealer and use a ⅛ in. bead of silicone sealer at the oil pan to cylinder block joint. Replace the damper before tightening the cover bolts down, so that the cover seal will align. The damper must be drawn into place. Hammering it will destroy it.

9. Replace the oil pan if it was removed, and fill the crankcase with oil.

### REMOVAL—SMALL BLOCK V8 (1970–80) AND 1970–72 MARK IV

1. Drain the oil and remove the oil pan. The pan need not be removed on 1974 and later engines.

2. Drain and remove the raditor.

3. Remove the fan, pulley and belt. Remove any power steering and/or AIR pump drive belts. Remove any braces for these pumps which will interfere with cover removal and position the pumps out of the way.

4. Remove the water pump.

5. Remove the crankshaft pulley and damper. Use a puller on the damper. Do not attempt to pry or hammer the damper off.

6. Remove the retaining bolts, and remove the timing cover.

### INSTALLATION—SMALL BLOCK V8 (1970–74) AND 1970–72 MARK IV

1. Reverse the preceding steps to install the cover. Use a damper installation tool to pull the damper on. Apply an ⅛ in. bead of silicone rubber sealer to the oil pan and cylinder block joint faces. Lightly coat the bottom of the seal with engine oil.

Refill the engine with oil.

### INSTALLATION—SMALL BLOCK V8 (1975–76)

1. Clean the gasket mating surfaces.

2. Remove any oil pan gasket material that may still be adhering to the oil pan-engine block joint face.

3. Apply a ⅛ in. bead of silicone sealant (Part No. 1051435) or the equivalent to the joint formed by the oil pan and cylinder block, as well as to the entire oil pan front lip.

4. Coat the cover gasket with gasket sealer and place it in position on the front cover.

5. Apply a bead of sealant to the bottom of the lower seal and install it on the cover. Loosely install the front cover on the block. Install the 4 top bolts loosely (about 3 turns). Install two ¼–20 x ½ in. screws in the hole at each side of the front cover.

6. Tighten the screws evenly while aligning the dowel pins and holes in the front cover.

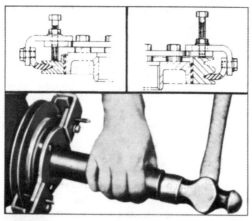

Installing the drive-on torsional damper (© Chevrolet Motor Div.)

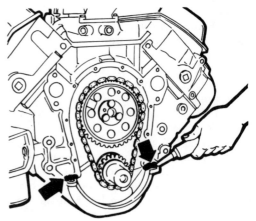

Apply sealer to the front pads at the area shown (gasoline V8s)

7. Remove the ¼–20 x ½ in. screws and install the rest of the cover screws.

8. Further installation is the reverse of removal. Refill the engine with oil.

### INSTALLATION—SMALL BLOCK V8 (1977–80)

1. Clean the gasket surfaces on the block and the front cover.

2. Use a sharp knife to trim any excess oil pan gasket material which protrudes from the oil pan-to-engine block junction.

3. Apply a ⅛ inch bead of RTV silicone sealer, G.M. #1052366 or the equivalent, to the joint of the oil pan and cylinder block.

4. Coat the front cover gasket with sealer and install the gasket onto the cover.

5. Install the front cover-to-oil pan seal. Lightly coat the bottom of the seal with clean engine oil and position over the crankshaft end.

6. Loosely install the front cover upper attaching bolts.

7. Press downward on the cover so that the dowels in the block are aligned with the holes in the cover. While holding the cover in position, tighten the upper attaching bolts alternately and evenly.

8. Install the remaining bolts and tighten all the bolts to specification.

9. Install the torsional damper and the water pump.

### REMOVAL AND INSTALLATION 1973–80 MARK IV

1. Remove the torsional damper and water pump.

2. Remove the two oil pan-to-front cover attaching screws.

3. Remove the front cover-to-block attaching screws.

4. Pull the cover slightly forward to permit cutting the oil pan front seal.

5. Using a sharp knife, cut the oil pan front seal flush with the cylinder block at both sides of the cover.

6. Remove the front cover and the portion of the oil pan front seal. Remove the front cover gasket.

7. Clean the gasket mating surfaces.

8. Cut the tabs from a new oil pan front seal, using a sharp knife to get a clean cut.

9. Install the seal on the front cover pressing the tips into the holes in the front cover.

10. Coat a new gasket with gasket sealer and install the gasket on the cover.

CUT THIS PORTION FROM NEW SEAL

Oil pan front seal (© Chevrolet Motor Div.)

11. Apply a ⅛ in. bead of sealant to the joint formed at the junction of the oil pan and cylinder block.

12. Place the front cover in position.

13. Align the cover over the dowel pins in the block.

14. Further installation is the reverse of removal.

### REMOVAL AND INSTALLATION—DIESEL

1. Drain cooling system. Disconnect radiator hoses and bypass hose.

2. Remove all belts, fan and fan pulley, crankshaft pulley and harmonic balancer, and accessory brackets. The harmonic balancer must be removed with a puller which pulls from the rear center of the balancer. Any other type of puller, such as a universal claw type which pulls on the outside of the hub, can destroy the balancer. The outside ring of the balancer is bonded in rubber to the hub; by pulling on the outside, it is possible to break that bond.

3. Remove cover-to-block attaching bolts and remove the cover, timing indicator and water pump assembly.

4. Remove the front cover and dowel pins. It may be necessary to grind a flat on the pins to get a rough surface for gripping.

To install:

5. Grind a chamfer on one end of each dowel pin.

6. Cut excess material from front end of oil pan gasket on each side of engine block.

7. Clean block, oil pan, and front cover mating surfaces with solvent.

8. Trim about ⅛ in. from each end of a new front pan seal, using a sharp knife to insure a straight cut.

9. Install new front cover gasket on engine block and new front seal on front cover. Apply sealer to gasket around coolant holes and place on block.

10. Apply silicone sealer at junction of block, pan, and front cover.

11. Place cover on block and press downward to compress the seal. Rotate cover left and right and guide pan seal into cavity using a small screwdriver.

12. Apply engine oil to bolts (threads and

heads). Install two bolts finger tight to hold cover in place.

13. Install two dowel pins chamfered end first.

14. Install timing indicator and water pump assembly. Torque bolts evenly to 13 ft lbs for the water pump bolts, and 35 ft lbs for cover bolts.

15. Apply lubricant to balancer seal surface. Install balancer and balancer bolt. Torque to approximately 250 ft lbs.

16. Install brackets. Connect bypass hose and radiator hoses. Install crankshaft pulley and four attaching bolts. Torque to 20 ft lbs.

17. Install fan pulley, fan, and four attaching bolts. Torque to 20 ft lbs. Install belts and adjust tension. Fill radiator. Road test and check for leaks.

### TIMING GEAR COVER OIL SEAL REPLACEMENT

#### All Engines

The seal may be replaced with the cover either on or off the engine. With the cover removed:

1. Pry the old seal from the cover using a wooden or plastic pick to prevent damage to the sealing lip. A plastic knitting needle makes a good removal tool.

2. Oil the lip of the new seal. Place a support under the cover so that it is not damaged when the seal is installed.

3. Install the seal so that the open side of the seal is toward the inside of the cover. Drive the seal into place with a tool made for the purpose (G.M. tool no. J-23042 or the equivalent).

The seal can also be replaced with the cover in place on the engine:

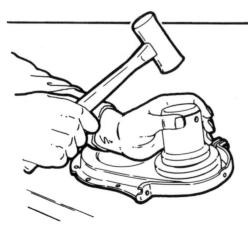

Seal installation with the cover removed

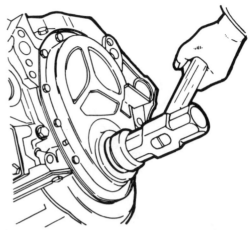

Seal installation with the cover installed

1. Remove the torsional damper. Pry the old seal from the cover, as outlined in Step 1 of the removal procedure with the cover removed.

2. Oil the lip of the new seal and place it into position, with the open side of the seal toward the engine. Drive the seal into position with a tool designed for the purpose (G.M. tool no. J-23042 or the equivalent).

3. Install the damper.

## Timing Chain or Gear
### REMOVAL AND INSTALLATION
#### Six Cylinder

The six-cylinder camshaft is gear driven. To remove the camshaft gear, remove the camshaft and press the gear off.

CAUTION: *The thrust plate must be positioned so that the woodruff key in the shaft does not damage it when the shaft is pressed out of the gear. Support the hub of the gear or the gear will be seriously damaged.*

The crankshaft gear may be removed with a gear puller while in place in the block.

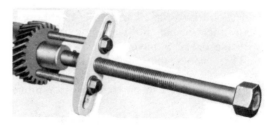

The six cylinder crankshaft gear is removed with a puller (© Chevrolet Motor Div.)

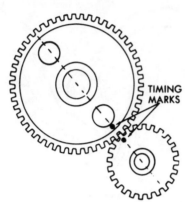

Six cylinder timing gear alignment (© Chevrolet Motor Div.)

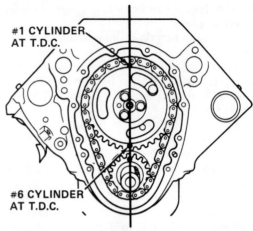

#1 CYLINDER AT T.D.C.

#6 CYLINDER AT T.D.C.

V8 timing sprocket alignment, 1979–80 (© Chevrolet Motor Div.)

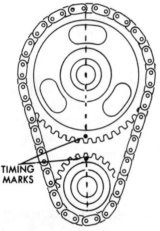

TIMING MARKS

V8 timing sprocket alignment through 1978 (© Chevrolet Motor Div.)

Gasoline V8 crankshaft sprocket removal (© Chevrolet Motor Div.)

### V8 Except Diesel

V8 models are equipped with a timing chain. To replace the chain, remove the radiator core, water pump harmonic balancer, and the crankcase front cover. This will allow access to the timing chain. Crank the engine until the zero marks punched on both sprockets are closest to one another and in line between the shaft centers. Then, take out the three bolts that hold the camshaft gear to the camshaft. This gear is a light press fit on the camshaft and will come off readily. It is located by a dowel.

The chain comes off with the camshaft gear.

A gear puller will be required to remove the crankshaft gear.

Without disturbing the position of the engine, mount the new crank gear on the shaft, then mount the chain over the cam-shaft gear. Arrange the camshaft gear in such a way that the timing marks will line up between the shaft centers and the camshaft locating dowel will enter the dowel hole in the cam sprocket.

Place the cam sprocket, with its chain mounted over it, in position on the front of the camshaft and pull up with the three bolts that hold it to the camshaft.

After the gears are in place, turn the engine two full revolutions to make certain that the timing marks are in correct alignment between the shaft centers.

### Diesel

It is not recommended that the timing chain and gears be removed or replaced, because this requires that the engine be re-timed. Re-timing of the engine requires removal of the injection pump and fuel lines, and the injection pump adapter. The timing mark must be filed off the injection pump adapter, and a new mark must be scribed with a special timing tool. It is recommended that all such work be left to a qualified dealer or mechanic who has access to such equipment.

If the necessary tools are available, the timing chain and gears may be replaced as follows:

1. Remove the crankshaft pulley, harmonic balancer and front cover, using the procedure outlined earlier in this chapter. Be certain to use the correct tool for balancer removal, to avoid damaging the part.

2. Align the timing marks on the crankshaft and camshaft sprockets by rotating the crankshaft in the direction of normal engine rotation. The marks should be closest to one another and in line between the shaft centers, as shown in the accompanying diagram. Do not disturb the position of the engine.

3. Remove the oil slinger from the crankshaft. Remove the camshaft sprocket retaining nut.

4. Remove the crankshaft sprocket. The sprocket-to-crankshaft fit is such that a puller may be necessary. If possible, the crankshaft key should be removed before using the puller. If this is not possible, align the puller so that the fingers of the tool do not overlap the end of the key when the sprocket is removed. The keyway is machined only partway in the crankshaft sprocket, and breakage can occur if the sprocket is improperly removed.

5. Remove the timing chain and camshaft sprocket.

6. The fuel pump eccentric is behind the crankshaft sprocket, and may be removed if necessary.

7. Install the key in the crankshaft, if removed. Install the fuel pump eccentric, if removed.

8. Install the camshaft sprocket, crankshaft sprocket, and the timing chain together, with the timing marks aligned. Tighten the camshaft sprocket retaining bolt to 65 ft lbs.

NOTE: *When the two timing marks are in alignment and closest together, the No. 6 cylinder is at TDC. To obtain TDC for No. 1 cylinder, slowly rotate the crankshaft one full revolution. This will move the camshaft sprocket timing mark to the top. No. 1 cylinder will then be at TDC.*

9. Install the oil slinger.

10. The injection pump must be re-timed. Follow Steps 1, 2, 3, 4, 5, 7, 8, and 9 of the intake manifold removal and installation procedure. Remove the injection pump adapter and the seal from the injection pump adapter.

11. Follow Steps 18, 19, 20, 21, 22, 23, 24, 25, 26, 27, 28, 29, 30, 32, 34, 35, and 36 of the intake manifold removal and installation procedure.

12. Install the front cover, harmonic balancer, and the crankshaft pulley.

## Camshaft

### REMOVAL AND INSTALLATION

NOTE: *Whenever a new camshaft is installed, it is recommended that all valve lifters be replaced, to insure the durability of the camshaft lobes and the valve lifter feet.*

#### Six Cylinder

1. In addition to removing the timing gear cover, remove the grille and radiator. If the truck has air conditioning, the condenser must be moved to provide room for camshaft removal. It may be possible to unbolt the condenser and move it aside, far enough for clearance. Otherwise, the air conditioning system must be discharged and the condenser removed. Do not disconnect any of the air conditioning lines unless you are thoroughly familiar with A/C systems and the hazards involved. It is recommended that

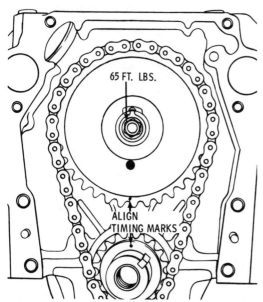

65 FT. LBS.

ALIGN TIMING MARKS

**Diesel V8 timing sprocket alignment (© Oldsmobile Motor Div.)**

TIMING
MARKS

THRUST
PLATE
SCREWS

**Access holes in the six cylinder camshaft gear for the camshaft thrust plate screws (© Chevrolet Motor Div.)**

you have the system discharged by a professional.

WARNING: *Compressed refrigerant expands (boils) into the atmosphere at a temperature of −21° F or less. It will freeze any surface it contacts, including your skin or eyes.*

2. Remove the valve cover and gasket, loosen all the valve rocker arm nuts and pivot the arms clear of the pushrods.

3. Remove the distributor and fuel pump.

4. Remove the coil (through 1977), side covers and gaskets. Remove the pushrods and valve lifters.

5. Align the timing gear marks and remove the two camshaft thrust plate retaining screws by working through the holes in the camshaft gear.

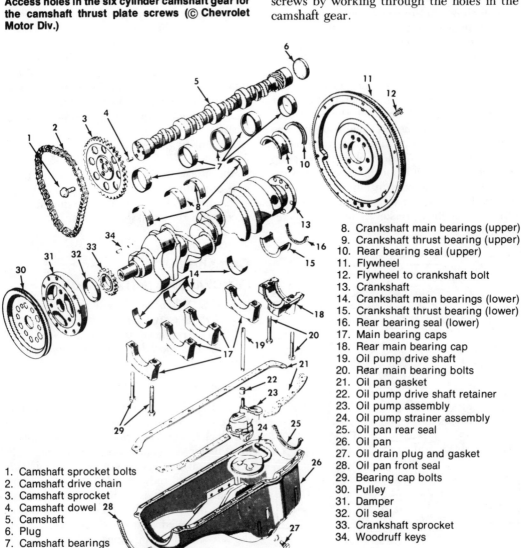

1. Camshaft sprocket bolts
2. Camshaft drive chain
3. Camshaft sprocket
4. Camshaft dowel
5. Camshaft
6. Plug
7. Camshaft bearings
8. Crankshaft main bearings (upper)
9. Crankshaft thrust bearing (upper)
10. Rear bearing seal (upper)
11. Flywheel
12. Flywheel to crankshaft bolt
13. Crankshaft
14. Crankshaft main bearings (lower)
15. Crankshaft thrust bearing (lower)
16. Rear bearing seal (lower)
17. Main bearing caps
18. Rear main bearing cap
19. Oil pump drive shaft
20. Rear main bearing bolts
21. Oil pan gasket
22. Oil pump drive shaft retainer
23. Oil pump assembly
24. Oil pump strainer assembly
25. Oil pan rear seal
26. Oil pan
27. Oil drain plug and gasket
28. Oil pan front seal
29. Bearing cap bolts
30. Pulley
31. Damper
32. Oil seal
33. Crankshaft sprocket
34. Woodruff keys

**Internal components of the gasoline V8 engine (© GMC Truck and Coach Div.)**

1. Extension cover
2. Under pan
3. Bell housing
4. Dowel
5. Ring set
6. Piston
7. Piston pin
8. Piston rod and rod bolts
9. Rod bearing cap
10. Rod nuts
11. Dipstick
12. Dipstick tube (upper)
13. Plug
14. Dipstick tube (lower)
15. Gasket
16. Adapter
17. Gasket
18. Element
19. Oil filter housing
20. Gasket
21. Front cover
22. Gasket
23. Dowel
24. Gasket
25. Plug
26. Water pump
27. Pulley
28. Cylinder block assembly

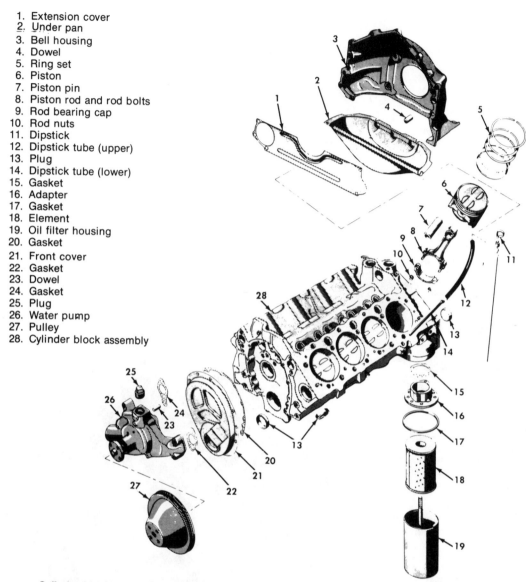

**Cylinder block and related components of the gasoline V8 (© GMC Truck and Coach Div.)**

6. Remove the camshaft and gear assembly by pulling it out through the front of the block. Be careful not to dislodge the camshaft bearings.

NOTE: *If renewing either camshaft or camshaft gear, the gear must be pressed off the camshaft. Install press plates under the camshaft gear and press the camshaft from the gear. The thrust plate must be positioned so that the woodruff key in the camshaft does not damage the shaft when the camshaft is pressed from the gear. Support the hub of the gear to prevent damage to the part. The replacement parts must be assembled in the same manner (under pressure). In placing the gear on the camshaft,* *press the gear onto the shaft until it bottoms against the gear spacer ring. The end clearance of the thrust plate should be .001 to .005 in.*

7. Install the camshaft assembly in the engine.

NOTE: *Pre-lube the cam lobes with E.O.S. or SAE 90 gear lubricant. Do not dislodge the cam bearings when inserting the camshaft.*

8. Turn the crankshaft and camshaft to align and bring the timing marks together. Push the camshaft into this aligned position.

9. Runout on either crankshaft or camshaft gear should not exceed .003 in.

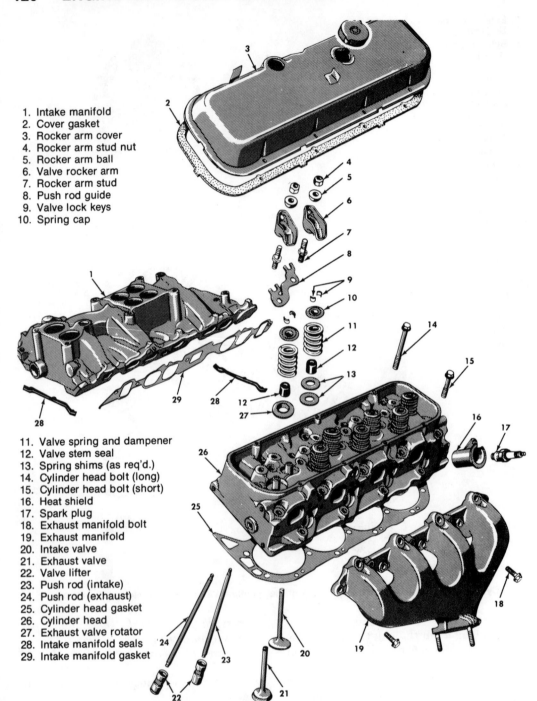

1. Intake manifold
2. Cover gasket
3. Rocker arm cover
4. Rocker arm stud nut
5. Rocker arm ball
6. Valve rocker arm
7. Rocker arm stud
8. Push rod guide
9. Valve lock keys
10. Spring cap

11. Valve spring and dampener
12. Valve stem seal
13. Spring shims (as req'd.)
14. Cylinder head bolt (long)
15. Cylinder head bolt (short)
16. Heat shield
17. Spark plug
18. Exhaust manifold bolt
19. Exhaust manifold
20. Intake valve
21. Exhaust valve
22. Valve lifter
23. Push rod (intake)
24. Push rod (exhaust)
25. Cylinder head gasket
26. Cylinder head
27. Exhaust valve rotator
28. Intake manifold seals
29. Intake manifold gasket

**Mark IV cylinder head components (© GMC Truck and Coach Div.)**

10. Backlash between the two gears should be between .004 and .006 in.

11. Install the timing gear cover and gasket.

12. Install the oil pan and gaskets.

13. Install the harmonic balancer.

14. Line up the keyway in the balancer with the key on the crankshaft and drive the balancer onto the shaft until it bottoms against the crankshaft gear.

15. Install the valve lifters and pushrods. Install the side covers with new gaskets. Later models use RTV sealer instead of gaskets. Attach the coil wires; install the fuel pump.

16. Install the distributor and set the tim-

ing as described under the "Distributor Removal and Installation" section at the beginning of the chapter.

17. Pivot the rocker arms over the pushrods and adjust the valves.

18. Add oil to the engine. Install and adjust the fan belt.

19. Install the radiator or shroud.

20. Install the grille assembly.

21. Fill the cooling system, start the engine and check for leaks.

22. Check and adjust the timing.

### V8 Except Diesel

1. Remove the intake manifold, valve lifters and timing chain cover as previously described.

2. Remove the grille and radiator. If the truck has air conditioning, the condenser must be moved to provide room for camshaft removal. It may be possible to unbolt the condenser and move it aside, far enough for clearance. Otherwise, the air conditioning system must be discharged and the condenser removed. Do not disconnect any of the air conditioning lines unless you are thoroughly familiar with A/C systems and the hazards involved. It is recommended that you have the system discharged by a professional.

WARNING: *Compressed refrigerant expands (boils) into the atmosphere at a temperature of −21° F or less. It will freeze any surface it contacts, including your skin or eyes.*

3. Remove the fuel pump and pump pushrod.

4. Remove the camshaft sprocket bolts, sprocket and timing chain. A light blow to the lower edge of a tight sprocket should free it (use a plastic mallet).

5. Install two 5/16–18 x 14 in. bolts in the cam bolt holes and pull the cam from the block.

6. To install, reverse the removal procedure aligning the timing marks.

NOTE: *Pre-lube the cam lobes with E.O.S. or SAE 90 gear lubricant. Do not dislodge the cam bearings when installing the camshaft.*

### Diesel

Removal of the camshaft also requires removal of the injection pump drive and driven gears, removal of the intake manifold, disassembly of the valve lifters, and re-timing of the injection pump.

1. Disconnect the negative battery cables. Drain the coolant. Remove the radiator.

2. Remove the intake manifold and gasket and the front and rear intake manifold seals. Refer to the intake manifold removal and installation procedure.

3. Remove the balancer pulley and the balancer. Refer to the procedure earlier in this chapter. Remove the engine front cover using the appropriate procedure.

4. Remove the valve covers. Remove the rocker arms, pushrods and valve lifters; see the procedures earlier in this chapter. Be sure to keep the parts in order so that they may be returned to their original positions.

5. If the truck has air conditioning, the condenser must be moved to provide room for camshaft removal. It may be possible to unbolt the condenser and move it aside far enough for clearance. Otherwise, the air conditioning system must be discharged and the condenser removed. Do not disconnect any of the air conditioning lines unless you are thoroughly familiar with A/C systems and the hazards involved. It is recommended that you have the system discharged by a professional.

WARNING: *Compressed refrigerant expands (boils) into the atmosphere at a temperature of −21° F or less. It will freeze any surface it contacts, including your skin or eyes.*

6. Remove the camshaft sprocket retaining bolt, and remove the timing chain and sprockets, using the procedure outlined earlier in this chapter.

7. Position the camshaft dowel pin at the 3 o'clock position.

8. Push the camshaft rearward and hold it there, being careful not to dislodge the oil gallery plug at the rear of the engine. Remove the pump drive gear by sliding it from the camshaft while rocking the pump driven gear.

9. To remove the pump driven gear, remove the injection pump adapter, remove the snap ring, and remove the selective washer. Remove the driven gear and spring.

10. Remove the camshaft by sliding it out the front of the engine. Be extremely careful not to allow the cam lobes to contact any of the bearings, or the journals to dislodge the bearings during camshaft removal. Do not force the camshaft, or bearing damage will result.

11. Coat the camshaft and the cam bearings with G.M. lubricant #562458 or the equivalent.

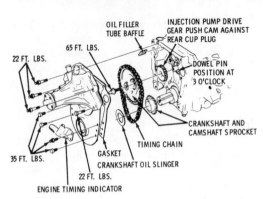

Pump drive gear installation—diesel engine
(© Oldsmobile Motor Div.)

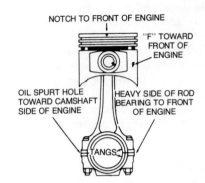

Six cylinder piston-to-connecting rod relationship
(© Chevrolet Motor Div.)

12. Carefully slide the camshaft into position in the engine.

13. Install the timing chain and sprockets, aligning the marks as shown in the procedure earlier in the chapter.

14. Check the injection pump driven gear bushing and replace as necessary.

15. Install the injection pump driven gear, spring, shim, and snap ring. Check the gear end play. If the end play is not within 0.002–0.005 in., replace the shim to obtain the specified clearance. Shims are available in 0.003 in. increments, from 0.080 to 0.115 in.

16. Position the camshaft dowel pin at the 3 o'clock position. Align the zero marks on the pump drive gear and pump driven gear. Hold the camshaft in the rearward position and slide the pump drive gear onto the camshaft.

17. Disassemble, assemble, and bleed the valve lifters as outlined earlier. Install the lifters, pushrods, rocker arms, and pivots. Install the injection pump adapter and injection pump, re-timing the engine as outlined in the intake manifold removal and installation procedure.

18. Install the intake manifold, as outlined earlier. Install the rocker covers.

19. Install the engine front cover, balancer and pulley.

20. Install the radiator. Install the air conditioning condenser, if equipped. Fill the cooling system. Check the automatic transmission fluid level. Connect the negative battery cables.

## Piston and Connecting Rods

Piston and connecting rod removal, installation and piston ring removal/installation are

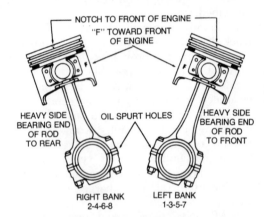

Small block V8 piston-to-connecting rod relationship (© Chevrolet Motor Div.)

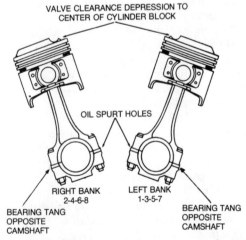

Mark IV piston-to-connecting rod relationship (© Chevrolet Motor Div.)

detailed in the "Engine Rebuilding" section at the end of this chapter. Removal and installation is outlined with the engine out of the truck, but the same procedures may be

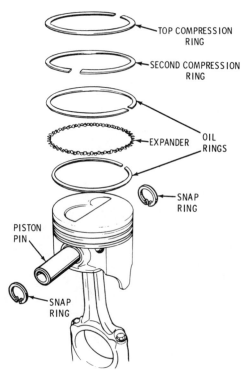

**Diesel piston and rings** (© Oldsmobile Motor Div.)

**Support the engine for oil pan removal** (© Chevrolet Motor Div.)

used with block in the chassis. Remove the cylinder heads and oil pan for piston and connecting rod removal. Piston and connecting rod positioning is illustrated in the accompanying figures.

On diesel engines, the valve depression in the top of the piston faces the inner side of the engine. On the forward half of the engine (cylinders 1, 2, 3, and 4), the large valve depression goes toward the front of the engine. On the rearward half of the engine (cylinders 5, 6, 7, and 8), the large valve depression goes to the rear of the engine.

# ENGINE LUBRICATION

## Oil Pan

### REMOVAL AND INSTALLATION

#### Six Cylinder

1. Disconnect the battery ground cable.
2. Raise and support the vehicle. Disconnect the starter leaving the wires attached and swing it out of the way.
3. If there is not enough clearance, remove the bolts securing the engine mounts to the crossmember and raise the engine high enough to insert a 2 in. × 4 in. piece of wood between the engine mounts and the crossmember brackets.

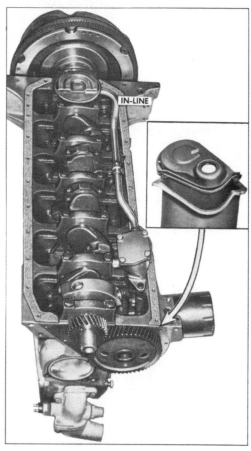

**Six cylinder oil pan and gasket seals** (© Chevrolet Motor Div.)

4. Drain the engine oil.
5. Remove the flywheel or converter cover.
6. Remove the oil pan.

**Engine blocked for oil pan removal (© Chevrolet Motor Div.)**

7. Clean all gasket surfaces and install a new seal in the rear main bearing groove and a new seal in the crankcase front cover. Installation is the reverse of removal. Install new side gaskets on the block, but do not use sealer. Fill the engine with oil and run the engine, checking for leaks.

### V8 Except Diesel

1. Drain the engine oil.
2. Remove the oil dipstick and tube.
3. If necessary, remove the exhaust crossover. On 454s, remove the air cleaner, fan shroud, and distributor cap.
4. Remove the flywheel or converter cover. Remove the starter. On 454s, remove the oil pressure line from the block. On four wheel drive models with automatic transmission, remove the strut rods at the motor mounts.
5. On 454s only, remove the engine mount through bolts and raise the engine.
6. Remove the oil pan and discard the gaskets.
7. Installation is the reverse of removal. Clean all gasket surfaces and use new gaskets to assemble. Use gasket sealer to retain the side gaskets to the cylinder block. Install a new oil pan rear seal in the rear main bearing cap slot with the ends butting the side gaskets. Install a new front seal in the crankcase front cover with the ends butting the side gaskets. Fill the engine with oil and check for leaks.

### Diesel

1. Remove the drive and vacuum pump.
2. Disconnect the battery cables.

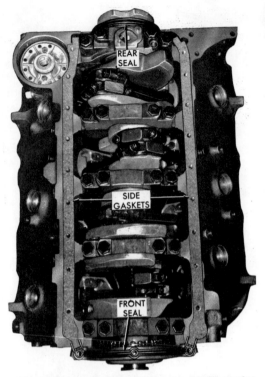

**Gasoline V8 oil pan and gasket seals (© Chevrolet Motor Div.)**

3. Remove the fan shroud attaching screws and pull the shroud up from the clips.
4. Block the rear wheels and jack up the front of the truck. Drain the oil.
5. Remove the flywheel cover.
6. Remove the starter and solenoid.
7. Remove both of the engine mount through bolts and raise the engine. Loosen the right hand mount and remove the left hand mount.
8. Unbolt and remove the oil pan.
NOTE: *If extended work is to be done, the mounts should be reinstalled and the engine lowered to the frame brackets.*
To install:
1. After cleaning the mounting surfaces thoroughly, apply sealer to both sides of the pan gaskets and install the gaskets on the block.
2. Install the front and rear rubber seals.
3. Apply a thin coat of all purpose grease on the seals, and install the oil pan. Torque the bolts to 10 ft lbs in a circular sequence, starting in the middle and working out.
4. Further installation is the reverse of removal. Fill the engine with oil and check for leaks.

## Oil Pump

### REMOVAL AND INSTALLATION

NOTE: *Before installing an oil pump, fill it with clean oil.*

### Six Cylinder

1. Drain the oil and remove the oil pan.
2. Remove the 2 flanged mounting bolts and remove the pickup pipe bolt.
3. Remove the pump and screen as an assembly.
4. To install, align the oil pump driveshafts with the distributor tang and install the oil pump. Position the flange over the distributor lower bushing, using no gasket. The oil pump should slide easily into place. If not, remove it and reposition the slot to align with the distributor tang.
5. Reinstall the oil pan and fill the engine with oil.

### V8 and Diesel

1. Drain the oil and remove the oil pan.
2. Remove the bolt (two bolts on diesels) holding the pump to the rear main bearing cap. Remove the pump and extension shaft.
3. To install, assemble the pump and extension shaft to the rear main bearing cap aligning the slot on the top of the extension shaft with the drive tang on the distributor driveshaft. The installed position of the oil pump screen is with the bottom edge parallel to the oil pan rails. Further installation is the reverse of removal.

## Rear Main Oil Seal Replacement

### All Engines Except Diesel

Both halves of the rear main oil seal can be replaced without removing the crankshaft. Always replace the upper and lower seal together. The lip should face the front of the engine. Be very careful that you do not break the sealing bead in the channel on the outside portion of the seal while installing it. An installation tool can be fabricated to protect the seal bead.

1. Remove the oil pan, oil pump and rear main bearing cap.
2. Remove the oil seal from the bearing cap by prying it out with a small screwdriver.
3. Remove the upper half of the seal with a small punch. Drive it around far enough to be gripped with pliers.
4. Clean the crankshaft and bearing cap.

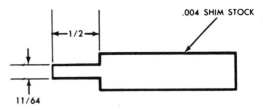

**Fabricated oil seal installation tool (© Chevrolet Motor Div.)**

**Removing the lower half of the oil seal (© Chevrolet Motor Div.)**

5. Coat the lips and bead of the seal with light engine oil, keeping oil from the ends of the seal.
6. Position the fabricated tool between the crankshaft and seal seat.
7. Position the seal between the crankshaft and tip of the tool so that the seal bead contacts the tip of the tool. The oil seal lip should face forward.
8. Roll the seal around the crankshaft using the tool to protect the seal bead from the sharp corners of the crankcase.
9. The installation tool should be left installed until the seal is properly positioned with both ends flush with the block.
10. Remove the tool.
11. Install the other half of the seal in the bearing cap using the tool in the same manner as before. Light thumb pressure should install the seal.
12. Install the bearing cap with sealant applied to the mating areas of the cap and block. Keep sealant from the ends of the seal.

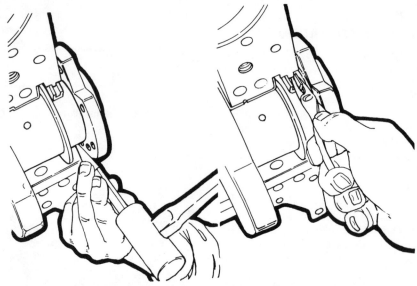

**Removing the upper half of the oil seal**

APPLY
SEALANT
TO SHADED
AREAS ONLY

**Sealing the bearing cap (© Chevrolet Motor Div.)**

13. Torque the main bearing cap retaining bolts to 10–12 ft lbs. Tap the end of the crankshaft first rearward, then forward with a lead hammer. This will line up the rear main bearing and the crankshaft thrust surfaces. Tighten the main bearing cap to specification.

14. Further installation is the reverse of removal.

### Diesel

It is not necessary to remove the crankshaft to correct seal leaks at the rear main bearing.

1. Drain oil and remove oil pan as previously outlined. Remove rear main bearing cap.

2. Insert a packing tool such as a screwdriver or a punch against one end of the seal in the cylinder block and drive the old seal gently into the groove until it is packed tight. This varies from ¼ in. to ¾ in., depending on

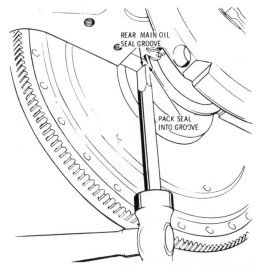

REAR MAIN OIL
SEAL GROOVE

PACK SEAL
INTO GROOVE

**Pack the old seal into the groove (© Oldsmobile Motor Div.)**

the pack required. Be careful not to nick the main bearing when packing the seal.

3. Repeat this procedure on the other end of the cylinder block seal.

4. Measure the amount the seal was driven up on one side. Add ¹/₁₆ in., then use a razor blade to cut this length from the old seal removed from the bearing cap. Repeat for the other side.

5. Place a drop of sealer on each end of the cut pieces of seal.

6. Work these two pieces of seal into the cylinder block with two small screwdrivers. Pack them into the block firmly. Trim the ends of the seal flush with the block.

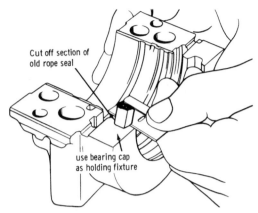

Cut off section of old rope seal

use bearing cap as holding fixture

**Use the bearing cap as a holding fixture for cutting the old rope seal (© Oldsmobile Motor Div.)**

NOTE: *Place a piece of shim stock or strip of metal between the seal and the crankshaft to protect the bearing surface before trimming.*

7. Clean the bearing cap and seal grooves.

8. Install a new seal into the bearing cap, packing by hand.

9. Using a seal installer, pack the seal firmly into the groove. These tools are generally available in automotive parts stores.

10. Cut the seal flush with the mating surface of the bearing cap. Pack the seal end fibers away from the edges, toward the center with a screwdriver.

11. Clean the bearing insert and install in the bearing cap.

12. Clean the crankshaft bearing journal, and the mating surface of the bearing cap. Place a dab of sealer on the mating surface of the cap.

13. Install the bearing cap, lubricate the bolt threads with engine oil, and install. Torque the bolts to 120 ft lbs.

14. Install the oil pan as previously outlined.

## ENGINE COOLING

The cooling system consists of a radiator, belt-driven fan, thermostat and a mechanical water pump. Air conditioned vehicles, diesels, and all 1980 models are equipped with a viscous drive fan that restricts operation at 1,500 rpm in cold weather and 3,500 rpm in hot weather. This fan requires less horsepower to drive it during high rpm operation and restricts noise from the fan.

Refer to Chapter 1 for the coolant level checking procedure and to the Appendix for "Antifreeze" charts. The coolant should periodically be drained and the system flushed with clean water, at the intervals specified in Chapter 1. Service stations have reverse flushing equipment available; there are also permanently-installed do-it-yourself reverse flushing attachments available.

There is a coolant drain cock at the bottom of most radiators. Six-cylinder engines have a coolant drain plug on the left side of the engine block; V8s have one on each side. Some engines don't have any.

The coolant should always be maintained at a minimum of $-20°$ F freezing protection, regardless of the prevailing temperature. This concentration assures rust protection and the highest possible boiling point. It also prevents the heater core from freezing on air-conditioned models.

Some simple modifications can be made to the cooling system for improved performance under severe conditions. The fan can be replaced with either a high-output unit, a clutch type designed for air conditioned models, or a flex-type. The flex unit flattens out at high rpm, moving less air and reducing the horsepower required to drive it. The clutch type is regulated to a set maximum speed, varying with temperature. An overflow tank maintains the proper coolant level in the radiator by storing water which escapes out the radiator overflow tube for return to the engine as it cools. It also keeps the system free of air, a major cause of rust.

NOTES: *The factory does not recommend the use of a front mounted spare tire carrier unless the truck has either the heavy duty radiator or air conditioning.*

*You can get an increase in cooling at the expense of slightly more fan noise on models with the thermostatically controlled viscous drive fan. This modification eliminates the thermostatic control, placing the fan in the high temperature mode at all times; it can save you the considerable price of a new fan clutch unit should your thermostatic control fail. Simply disconnect the thermostatic spring coil outer end tab on the front of the fan unit and let it move slightly counterclockwise (facing it). You will probably have to remove the fan shroud for access. Do not remove the coil entirely or the fan will freewheel, causing overheating. If you have the type of fan clutch with a flat metal spring on the front, you can do the same thing by taking ⅜ in. off the length of the pin behind the spring.*

Two common causes of corrosion are air suction and exhaust gas leakage. Air may be drawn into the system due to low coolant level in the radiator, a leaky water pump, loose hose connections, a defective radiator pressure cap, or a leaky overflow hose connection to the radiator on the coolant recovery bottle. Exhaust gas may be blown into the cooling system past the cylinder head gasket or through cracks in the cylinder head and block.

## Radiator

All pick-up trucks are equipped with cross-flow type radiators.

### REMOVAL AND INSTALLATION

**1970–72**

1. Drain the radiator and remove the hoses.
2. Disconnect and plug the transmission cooler line (if equipped).
3. On six cyl. engines, remove the finger guard.
4. Remove the upper retainers with the fan shroud attached (V8 models) and rest the fan shroud over the engine.
5. Lift the radiator out of the lower retainers.
6. Installation is the reverse of removal. Fill the cooling system, check the automatic transmission fluid level and run the engine, checking for leaks.

**1973–80**

1. Drain the radiator. On some 1973 models, you will have to siphon the coolant out of the filler neck or detach the lower radiator hose. 1974–80 models are equipped with a drain cock.

   CAUTION: *Do not attempt to start the siphoning process with your mouth. The coolant is poisonous and can cause death.*

2. Disconnect the hoses and automatic transmission cooler line (if equipped). Plug the cooler lines. Diesels have transmission cooler and oil cooler lines.
3. Disconnect the coolant recovery system hose.
4. If the vehicle is equipped with a fan shroud, detach the shroud and hang it over the fan to provide clearance.

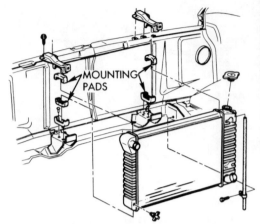

**Typical radiator mounting (© Chevrolet Motor Div.)**

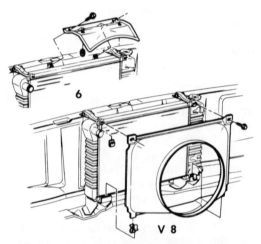

**Typical radiator, shroud, and finger guard. The finger guard is usually found on trucks with six cylinder engines (© Chevrolet Motor Div.)**

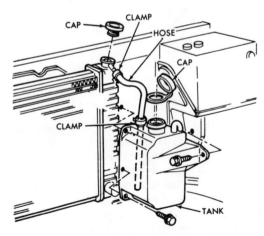

**Coolant recovery tank (© Chevrolet Motor Div.)**

5. On six cylinder engines, remove the finger guard.

6. Remove the mounting panel from the radiator support and remove the upper mounting pads.

7. Lift the radiator up and out of the truck. Lift the shroud out if necessary.

8. Installation is the reverse of removal. Fill the cooling system and check the automatic transmission fluid level, and run the engine, checking for leaks.

## Water Pump

### REMOVAL AND INSTALLATION

1. Drain the radiator and loosen the fan pulley bolts.

2. Disconnect the heater hose and radiator. Disconnect the lower radiator hose at the water pump.

3. Loosen the alternator swivel bolt and remove the fan belt. Remove the fan bolts, fan and pulley.

4. Remove the water pump attaching bolts and remove the pump and gasket from the engine. On inline engines, remove the water pump straight out of the block to avoid damaging the impeller.

NOTE: *Do not store viscous drive (thermostatic) fan clutches in any other position than the normal installed position. They should be supported so that the clutch disc remains vertical; otherwise, silicone fluid may leak out.*

5. Installation is the reverse of removal. Clean the gasket surfaces and install new gaskets. Coat the gasket with sealer. A $5/16$ in. x 24 x 1 in. guide stud installed in one hole of the fan will make installing the fan onto the hub easier. It can be removed after

the other 3 bolts are started. Fill the cooling system and adjust the fan belt tension.

## Thermostat

The factory installed thermostat is a 195° F unit.

NOTE: *Poor heater output and slow warm-up is often caused by a thermostat stuck in the open position; occasionally one sticks shut causing immediate overheating. Do not attempt to correct a chronic overheating condition by permanently removing the thermostat. Thermostat flow restriction is designed into the system; without it, localized overheating due to turbulence may occur.*

### REMOVAL AND INSTALLATION

1. Drain approximately ⅓ of the coolant. This will reduce the coolant level to below the level of the thermostat housing.

2. It is not necessary to remove the upper radiator hose from the thermostat housing. Remove the 2 retaining bolts from the thermostat housing (located on the front top of V8 intake manifolds and directly in front of the valve cover on six cylinder engines) and remove the thermostat.

3. To test the thermostat, place it in hot water or a solution of 33% glycol, 25° above the temperature stamped on the valve. Submerge the valve and agitate the solution. The valve should open fully. Remove the thermostat and place it in the same solution 10° below the temperature stamped on the valve. The valve should close completely.

4. Installation is the reverse of removal. Use a new gasket and sealer. Refill the cooling system and run the engine, checking for leaks.

**Typical thermostat installation (© Chevrolet Motor Div.)**

## ENGINE REBUILDING

Most procedures involved in rebuilding an engine are fairly standard, regardless of the type of engine involved. This section is a guide to accepted rebuilding procedures. Examples of standard rebuilding practices are illustrated and should be used along with specific details concerning your particular engine, found earlier in this chapter.

The procedures given here are those used by any competent rebuilder. Obviously some of the procedures cannot be performed by the do-it-yourself mechanic, but are provided so that you will be familiar with the services that should be offered by rebuilding or machine shops. As an example, in most instances, it is more profitable for the home mechanic to remove the cylinder heads, buy the necessary parts (new valves, seals, keepers, keys, etc.) and deliver these to a machine shop for the necessary work. In this way you will save the money to remove and install the cylinder head and the mark-up on parts.

On the other hand, most of the work involved in rebuilding the lower end is well within the scope of the do-it-yourself mechanic. Only work such as hot-tanking, actually boring the block or Magnafluxing (invisible crack detection) need be sent to a machine shop.

### Tools

The tools required for basic engine rebuilding should, with a few exceptions, be those included in a mechanic's tool kit. An accurate torque wrench, and a dial indicator (reading in thousandths) mounted on a universal base should be available. Special tools, where required, are available from the major tool suppliers. The services of a competent automotive machine shop must also be readily available.

### Precautions

Aluminum has become increasingly popular for use in engines, due to its low weight and excellent heat transfer characteristics. The following precautions must be observed when handling aluminum (or any other) engine parts:
—Never hot-tank aluminum parts.
—Remove all aluminum parts (identification tags, etc.) from engine parts before hot-tanking (otherwise they will be removed during the process).

—Always coat threads lightly with engine oil or anti-seize compounds before installation, to prevent seizure.
—Never over-torque bolts or spark plugs in aluminum threads. Should stripping occur, threads can be restored using any of a number of thread repair kits available (see next section).

### Inspection Techniques

Magnaflux and Zyglo are inspection techniques used to locate material flaws, such as stress cracks. Magnaflux is a magnetic process, applicable only to ferrous materials. The Zyglo process coats the material with a fluorescent dye penetrant, and any material may be tested using Zyglo. Specific checks of suspected surface cracks may be made at lower cost and more readily using spot check dye. The dye is sprayed onto the suspected area, wiped off, and the area is then sprayed with a developer. Cracks then will show up brightly.

### Overhaul

The section is divided into two parts. The first, Cylinder Head Reconditioning, assumes that the cylinder head is removed from the engine, all manifolds are removed, and the cylinder head is on a workbench. The camshaft should be removed from overhead cam cylinder heads. The second section, Cylinder Block Reconditioning, covers the block, pistons, connecting rods and crankshaft. It is assumed that the engine is mounted on a work stand, and the cylinder head and all accessories are removed.

Procedures are identified as follows:
*Unmarked*—Basic procedures that must be performed in order to successfully complete the rebuilding process.
*Starred* (*)—Procedures that should be performed to ensure maximum performance and engine life.
*Double starred* (**)—Procedures that may be performed to increase engine performance and reliability.

When assembling the engine, any parts that will be in frictional contact must be pre-lubricated, to provide protection on initial start-up. Any product specifically formulated for this purpose may be used. NOTE: *Do not use engine oil.* Where semi-permanent (locked but removable) installation of bolts or nuts is desired, threads should be cleaned and located with Loctite® or a similar product (non-hardening).

## Repairing Damaged Threads

Several methods of repairing damaged threads are available. Heli-Coil® (shown here), Keenserts® and Microdot® are among the most widely used. All involve basically the same principle—drilling out stripped threads, tapping the hole and installing a pre-wound insert—making welding, plugging and oversize fasteners unnecessary.

Two types of thread repair inserts are usually supplied—a standard type for most Inch Coarse, Inch Fine, Metric Coarse and Metric Fine thread sizes and a spark plug type to fit most spark plug port sizes. Consult the individual manufacturer's catalog to determine exact applications. Typical thread repair kits will contain a selection of pre-wound threaded inserts, a tap (corresponding to the outside diameter threads of the insert) and an installation tool. Spark plug inserts usually differ because they require a tap equipped with pilot threads and a combined reamer/tap section. Most manufacturers also supply blister-packed thread repair inserts separately in addition to a master kit containing a variety of taps and inserts plus installation tools.

Before effecting a repair to a threaded hole, remove any snapped, broken or damaged bolts or studs. Penetrating oil can be used to free frozen threads; the offending item can be removed with locking pliers or with a screw or stud extractor. After the hole is clear, the thread can be repaired, as follows:

Drill out the damaged threads with specified drill. Drill completely through the hole or to the bottom of a blind hole

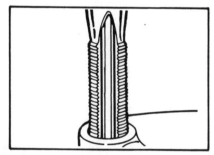

With the tap supplied, tap the hole to receive the thread insert. Keep the tap well oiled and back it out frequently to avoid clogging the threads

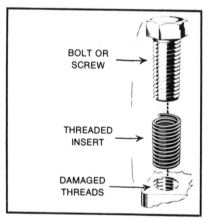

BOLT OR SCREW

THREADED INSERT

DAMAGED THREADS

Damaged bolt holes can be repaired with thread repair inserts

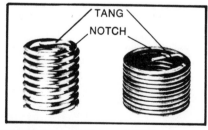

TANG

NOTCH

Standard thread repair insert (left) and spark plug thread insert (right)

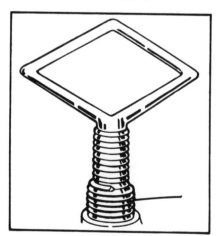

Screw the threaded insert onto the installation tool until the tang engages the slot. Screw the insert into the tapped hole until it is ¼–½ turn below the top surface. After installation break off the tang with a hammer and punch

## Standard Torque Specifications and Fastener Markings

The Newton-metre has been designated the world standard for measuring torque and will gradually replace the foot-pound and kilogram-meter. In the absence of specific torques, the following chart can be used as a guide to the maximum safe torque of a particular size/grade of fastener.

- There is no torque difference for fine or coarse threads.
- Torque values are based on clean, dry threads. Reduce the value by 10% if threads are oiled prior to assembly.
- The torque required for aluminum components or fasteners is considerably less.

### U. S. BOLTS

| SAE Grade Number | 1 or 2 | | | 5 | | | 6 or 7 | | |
|---|---|---|---|---|---|---|---|---|---|

Bolt Markings

Manufacturer's marks may vary—number of lines always 2 less than the grade number.

| Usage | Frequent | | | Frequent | | | Infrequent | | |
|---|---|---|---|---|---|---|---|---|---|
| Bolt Size (inches)—(Thread) | Maximum Torque | | | Maximum Torque | | | Maximum Torque | | |
| | Ft-Lb | kgm | Nm | Ft-Lb | kgm | Nm | Ft-Lb | kgm | Nm |
| ¼—20 | 5 | 0.7 | 6.8 | 8 | 1.1 | 10.8 | 10 | 1.4 | 13.5 |
| —28 | 6 | 0.8 | 8.1 | 10 | 1.4 | 13.6 | | | |
| 5⁄16—18 | 11 | 1.5 | 14.9 | 17 | 2.3 | 23.0 | 19 | 2.6 | 25.8 |
| —24 | 13 | 1.8 | 17.6 | 19 | 2.6 | 25.7 | | | |
| 3⁄8—16 | 18 | 2.5 | 24.4 | 31 | 4.3 | 42.0 | 34 | 4.7 | 46.0 |
| —24 | 20 | 2.75 | 27.1 | 35 | 4.8 | 47.5 | | | |
| 7⁄16—14 | 28 | 3.8 | 37.0 | 49 | 6.8 | 66.4 | 55 | 7.6 | 74.5 |
| —20 | 30 | 4.2 | 40.7 | 55 | 7.6 | 74.5 | | | |
| ½—13 | 39 | 5.4 | 52.8 | 75 | 10.4 | 101.7 | 85 | 11.75 | 115.2 |
| —20 | 41 | 5.7 | 55.6 | 85 | 11.7 | 115.2 | | | |
| 9⁄16—12 | 51 | 7.0 | 69.2 | 110 | 15.2 | 149.1 | 120 | 16.6 | 162.7 |
| —18 | 55 | 7.6 | 74.5 | 120 | 16.6 | 162.7 | | | |
| 5⁄8—11 | 83 | 11.5 | 112.5 | 150 | 20.7 | 203.3 | 167 | 23.0 | 226.5 |
| —18 | 95 | 13.1 | 128.8 | 170 | 23.5 | 230.5 | | | |
| ¾—10 | 105 | 14.5 | 142.3 | 270 | 37.3 | 366.0 | 280 | 38.7 | 379.6 |
| —16 | 115 | 15.9 | 155.9 | 295 | 40.8 | 400.0 | | | |
| 7⁄8— 9 | 160 | 22.1 | 216.9 | 395 | 54.6 | 535.5 | 440 | 60.9 | 596.5 |
| —14 | 175 | 24.2 | 237.2 | 435 | 60.1 | 589.7 | | | |
| 1— 8 | 236 | 32.5 | 318.6 | 590 | 81.6 | 799.9 | 660 | 91.3 | 894.8 |
| —14 | 250 | 34.6 | 338.9 | 660 | 91.3 | 849.8 | | | |

### METRIC BOLTS

NOTE: *Metric bolts are marked with a number indicating the relative strength of the bolt. These numbers have nothing to do with size.*

| Description | Torque ft-lbs (Nm) | | | |
|---|---|---|---|---|
| Thread size x pitch (mm) | Head mark—4 | | Head mark—7 | |
| 6 x 1.0 | 2.2–2.9 | (3.0–3.9) | 3.6–5.8 | (4.9–7.8) |
| 8 x 1.25 | 5.8–8.7 | (7.9–12) | 9.4–14 | (13–19) |
| 10 x 1.25 | 12–17 | (16–23) | 20–29 | (27–39) |
| 12 x 1.25 | 21–32 | (29–43) | 35–53 | (47–72) |
| 14 x 1.5 | 35–52 | (48–70) | 57–85 | (77–110) |
| 16 x 1.5 | 51–77 | (67–100) | 90–120 | (130–160) |
| 18 x 1.5 | 74–110 | (100–150) | 130–170 | (180–230) |
| 20 x 1.5 | 110–140 | (150–190) | 190–240 | (160–320) |
| 22 x 1.5 | 150–190 | (200–260) | 250–320 | (340–430) |
| 24 x 1.5 | 190–240 | (260–320) | 310–410 | (420–550) |

NOTE: *This engine rebuilding section is a guide to accepted rebuilding procedures. Typical examples of standard rebuilding procedures are illustrated. Use these procedures along with the detailed instructions earlier in this chapter, concerning your particular engine.*

## Cylinder Head Reconditioning

| Procedure | Method |
|---|---|
| **Remove the cylinder head:** | See the engine service procedures earlier in this chapter for details concerning specific engines. |
| **Identify the valves:** | Invert the cylinder head, and number the valve faces front to rear, using a permanent felt-tip marker. |
| **Remove the rocker arms:** | Remove the rocker arms with shaft(s) or balls and nuts. Wire the sets of rockers, balls and nuts together, and identify according to the corresponding valve. |
| **Remove the valves and springs:** | Using an appropriate valve spring compressor (depending on the configuration of the cylinder head), compress the valve springs. Lift out the keepers with needlenose pliers, release the compressor, and remove the valve, spring, and spring retainer. See the engine service procedures earlier in this chapter for details concerning specific engines. |
| **Check the valve stem-to-guide clearance:** 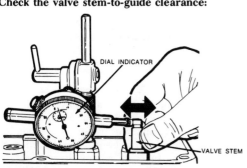 Check the valve stem-to-guide clearance | Clean the valve stem with lacquer thinner or a similar solvent to remove all gum and varnish. Clean the valve guides using solvent and an expanding wire-type valve guide cleaner. Mount a dial indicator so that the stem is at 90° to the valve stem, as close to the valve guide as possible. Move the valve off its seat, and measure the valve guide-to-stem clearance by rocking the stem back and forth to actuate the dial indicator. Measure the valve stems using a micrometer, and compare to specifications, to determine whether stem or guide wear is responsible for excessive clearance. NOTE: *Consult the Specifications tables earlier in this chapter.* |

## Cylinder Head Reconditioning

| Procedure | Method |
|---|---|
| De-carbon the cylinder head and valves: 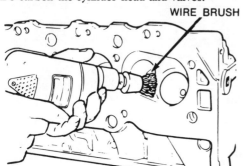 WIRE BRUSH **Remove the carbon from the cylinder head with a wire brush and electric drill** | Chip carbon away from the valve heads, combustion chambers, and ports, using a chisel made of hardwood. Remove the remaining deposits with a stiff wire brush. NOTE: *Be sure that the deposits are actually removed, rather than burnished.* |
| Hot-tank the cylinder head (cast iron heads only): CAUTION: *Do not hot-tank aluminum parts.* | Have the cylinder head hot-tanked to remove grease, corrosion, and scale from the water passages. NOTE: *In the case of overhead cam cylinder heads, consult the operator to determine whether the camshaft bearings will be damaged by the caustic solution.* |
| Degrease the remaining cylinder head parts: | Clean the remaining cylinder head parts in an engine cleaning solvent. Do not remove the protective coating from the springs. |
| Check the cylinder head for warpage: 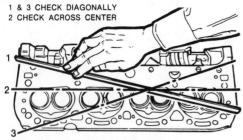 1 & 3 CHECK DIAGONALLY 2 CHECK ACROSS CENTER **Check the cylinder head for warpage** | Place a straight-edge across the gasket surface of the cylinder head. Using feeler gauges, determine the clearance at the center of the straight-edge. If warpage exceeds .003″ in a 6″ span, or .006″ over the total length, the cylinder head must be resurfaced. NOTE: *If warpage exceeds the manufacturer's maximum tolerance for material removal, the cylinder head must be replaced.* When milling the cylinder heads of V-type engines, the intake manifold mounting position is altered, and must be corrected by milling the manifold flange a proportionate amount. |
| *Knurl the valve guides: 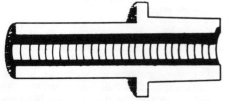 **Cut-away view of a knurled valve guide** | *Valve guides which are not excessively worn or distorted may, in some cases, be knurled rather than replaced. Knurling is a process in which metal is displaced and raised, thereby reducing clearance. Knurling also provides excellent oil control. The possibility of knurling rather than replacing valve guides should be discussed with a machinist. |
| Replace the valve guides: NOTE: *Valve guides should only be replaced if damaged or if an oversize valve stem is not available.* | See the engine service procedures earlier in this chapter for details concerning specific engines. Depending on the type of cylinder head, valve guides may be pressed, hammered, or shrunk in. In cases where the guides are shrunk into the head, replacement should be left to an equipped machine shop. In other |

## Cylinder Head Reconditioning

| Procedure | Method |
|---|---|

A—VALVE GUIDE I.D.    B—LARGER THAN THE VALVE GUIDE O.D.

WASHERS

A—VALVE GUIDE I.D.    B—LARGER THAN THE VALVE GUIDE O.D.

**Valve guide installation tool using washers for installation**

cases, the guides are replaced using a stepped drift (see illustration). Determine the height above the boss that the guide must extend, and obtain a stack of washers, their I.D. similar to the guide's O.D., of that height. Place the stack of washers on the guide, and insert the guide into the boss.

**NOTE:** *Valve guides are often tapered or beveled for installation.* Using the stepped installation tool (see illustration), press or tap the guides into position. Ream the guides according to the size of the valve stem.

---

**Replace valve seat inserts:**

Replacement of valve seat inserts which are worn beyond resurfacing or broken, if feasible, must be done by a machine shop.

---

**Resurface (grind) the valve face:**

FOR DIMENSIONS, REFER TO SPECIFICATIONS

CHECK FOR BENT STEM

DIAMETER

VALVE FACE ANGLE

1/32″ MINIMUM

THIS LINE PARALLEL WITH VALVE HEAD

**Critical valve dimensions**

Using a valve grinder, resurface the valves according to specifications given earlier in this chapter.

**CAUTION:** *Valve face angle is not always identical to valve seat angle.* A minimum margin of $1/32″$ should remain after grinding the valve. The valve stem top should also be squared and resurfaced, by placing the stem in the V-block of the grinder, and turning it while pressing lightly against the grinding wheel.

**NOTE:** *Do not grind sodium filled exhaust valves on a machine. These should be hand lapped.*

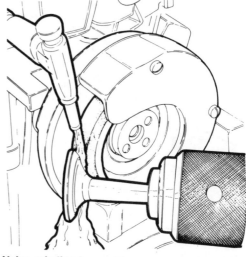

**Valve grinding by machine**

## Cylinder Head Reconditioning

| Procedure | Method |
|---|---|
| Resurface the valve seats using reamers or grinder: | Select a reamer of the correct seat angle, slightly larger than the diameter of the valve seat, and assemble it with a pilot of the correct size. Install the pilot into the valve guide, and using steady pressure, turn the reamer clockwise. |

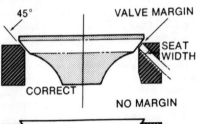
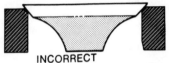

**Valve seat width and centering**

**CAUTION:** *Do not turn the reamer counterclockwise.* Remove only as much material as necessary to clean the seat. Check the concentricity of the seat (following). If the dye method is not used, coat the valve face with Prussian blue dye, install and rotate it on the valve seat. Using the dye marked area as a centering guide, center and narrow the valve seat to specifications with correction cutters.

**NOTE:** *When no specifications are available, minimum seat width for exhaust valves should be 5/64", intake valves 1/16".*

After making correction cuts, check the position of the valve seat on the valve face using Prussian blue dye.

**Reaming the valve seat with a hand reamer**

To resurface the seat with a power grinder, select a pilot of the correct size and coarse stone of the proper angle. Lubricate the pilot and move the stone on and off the valve seat at 2 cycles per second, until all flaws are gone. Finish the seat with a fine stone. If necessary the seat can be corrected or narrowed using correction stones.

Check the valve seat concentricity:

Coat the valve face with Prussian blue dye, install the valve, and rotate it on the valve seat. If the entire seat becomes coated, and the valve is known to be concentric, the seat is concentric.

\* Install the dial gauge pilot into the guide, and rest of the arm on the valve seat. Zero the gauge, and rotate the arm around the seat. Run-out should not exceed .002".

**Check the valve seat concentricity with a dial gauge**

## Cylinder Head Reconditioning

| Procedure | Method |
|---|---|

**\*Lap the valves:**
NOTE: *Valve lapping is done to ensure efficient sealing of resurfaced valves and seats.*

Invert the cylinder head, lightly lubricate the valve stems, and install the valves in the head as numbered. Coat valve seats with fine grinding compound, and attach the lapping tool suction cup to a valve head.
NOTE: *Moisten the suction cup.* Rotate the tool between the palms, changing position and lifting the tool often to prevent grooving. Lap the valve until a smooth, polished seat is evident. Remove the valve and tool, and rinse away all traces of grinding compound.

\*\* Fasten a suction cup to a piece of drill rod, and mount the rod in a hand drill. Proceed as above, using the hand drill as a lapping tool.
CAUTION: *Due to the higher speeds involved when using the hand drill, care must be exercised to avoid grooving the seat.* Lift the tool and change direction of rotation often.

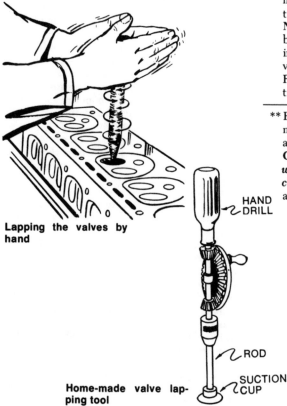

Lapping the valves by hand

HAND DRILL

ROD

SUCTION CUP

**Home-made valve lapping tool**

---

**Check the valve springs:**

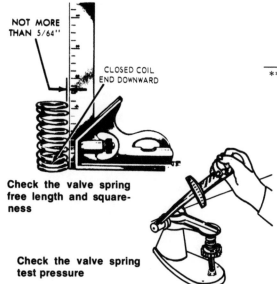

NOT MORE THAN 5/64"

CLOSED COIL END DOWNWARD

Check the valve spring free length and squareness

Check the valve spring test pressure

Place the spring on a flat surface next to a square. Measure the height of the spring, and rotate it against the edge of the square to measure distortion. If spring height varies (by comparison) by more than $1/16''$ or if distortion exceeds $1/16''$, replace the spring.

\*\* In addition to evaluating the spring as above, test the spring pressure at the installed and compressed (installed height minus valve lift) height using a valve spring tester. Springs used on small displacement engines (up to 3 liters) should be $\mp$ 1 lb of all other springs in either position. A tolerance of $\mp$ 5 lbs is permissible on larger engines.

## Cylinder Head Reconditioning

| *Procedure* | *Method* |
|---|---|
| *** Install valve stem seals:** 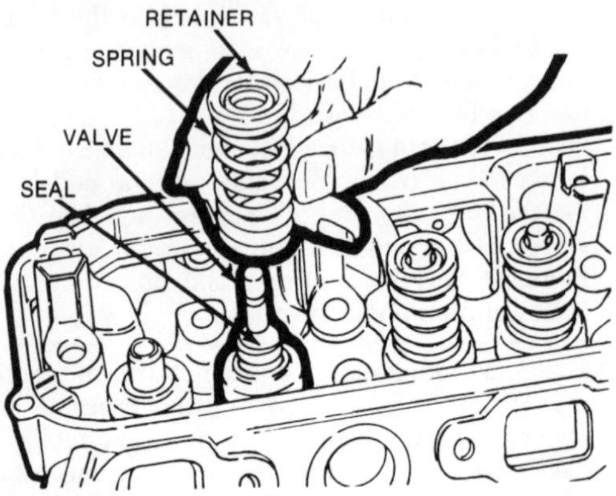  **Install valve stem seals** | * Due to the pressure differential that exists at the ends of the intake valve guides (atmospheric pressure above, manifold vacuum below), oil is drawn through the valve guides into the intake port. This has been alleviated somewhat since the addition of positive crankcase ventilation, which lowers the pressure above the guides. Several types of valve stem seals are available to reduce blow-by. Certain seals simply slip over the stem and guide boss, while others require that the boss be machined. Recently, Teflon guide seals have become popular. Consult a parts supplier or machinist concerning availability and suggested usages.<br>**NOTE: *When installing seals, ensure that a small amount of oil is able to pass the seal to lubricate the valve guides; otherwise, excessive wear may result.*** |
| **Install the valves:** | See the engine service procedures earlier in this chapter for details concerning specific engines.<br>Lubricate the valve stems, and install the valves in the cylinder head as numbered. Lubricate and position the seals (if used) and the valve springs. Install the spring retainers, compress the springs, and insert the keys using needlenose pliers or a tool designed for this purpose.<br>**NOTE: *Retain the keys with wheel bearing grease during installation.*** |
| **Check valve spring installed height:** 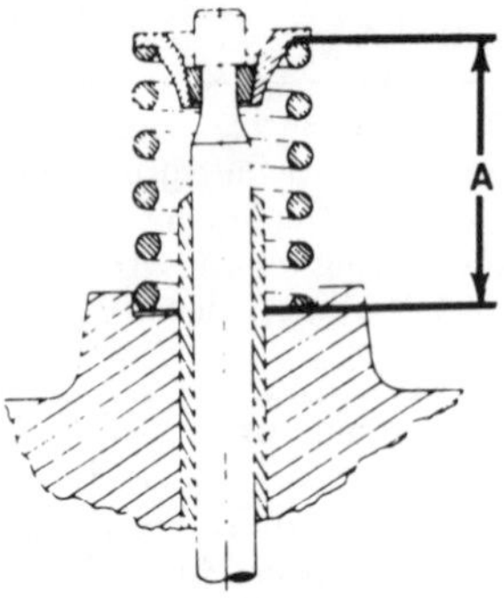  **Valve spring installed height (A)** 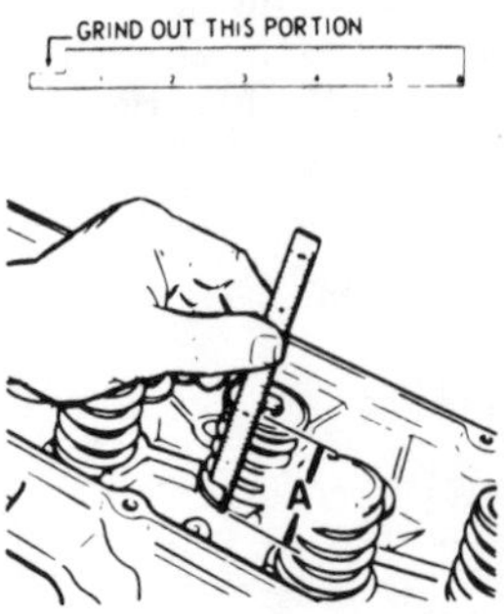  **Measure the valve spring installed height (A) with a modified steel rule** | Measure the distance between the spring pad the lower edge of the spring retainer, and compare to specifications. If the installed height is incorrect, add shim washers between the spring pad and the spring.<br>**CAUTION: *Use only washers designed for this purpose.*** |

## Cylinder Head Reconditioning

| Procedure | Method |
|---|---|
| Inspect the rocker arms, balls, studs, and nuts: 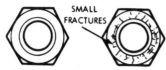 **Stress cracks in the rocker nuts** | Visually inspect the rocker arms, balls, studs, and nuts for cracks, galling, burning, scoring, or wear. If all parts are intact, liberally lubricate the rocker arms and balls, and install them on the cylinder head. If wear is noted on a rocker arm at the point of valve contact, grind it smooth and square, removing as little material as possible. Replace the rocker arm if excessively worn. If a rocker stud shows signs of wear, it must be replaced (see below). If a rocker nut shows stress cracks, replace it. If an exhaust ball is galled or burned, substitute the intake ball from the same cylinder (if it is intact), and install a new intake ball. **NOTE:** *Avoid using new rocker balls on exhaust valves.* |
| Replace rocker studs: 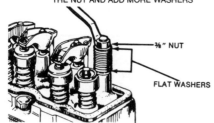 **Extracting a pressed-in rocker stud** 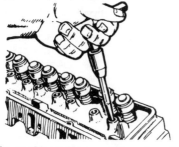 **Ream the stud bore for oversize rocker studs** | In order to remove a threaded stud, lock two nuts on the stud, and unscrew the stud using the lower nut. Coat the lower threads of the new stud with Loctite, and install. Two alternative methods are available for replacing pressed in studs. Remove the damaged stud using a stack of washers and a nut (see ilustration). In the first, the boss is reamed .005–.006″ oversize, and an oversize stud pressed in. Control the stud extension over the boss using washers, in the same manner as valve guides. Before installing the stud, coat it with white lead and grease. To retain the stud more positively drill a hole through the stud and boss, and install a roll pin. In the second method, the boss is tapped, and a threaded stud installed. |
| Inspect the rocker shaft(s) and rocker arms: 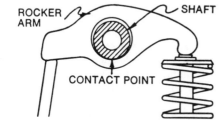 **Check the rocker arm-to-rocker shaft contact area** | Remove the rocker arms, springs and washers from rocker shaft. **NOTE:** *Lay out parts in the order as they are removed.* Inspect rocker arms for pitting or wear on the valve contact point, or excessive bushing wear. Bushings need only be replaced if wear is excessive, because the rocker arm normally contacts the shaft at one point only. Grind the valve contact point of rocker arm smooth if necessary, removing as little material as possible. If excessive material must be removed to smooth and square the arm, it should be replaced. Clean out all oil holes and passages in rocker shaft. If shaft is grooved or worn, replace it. Lubricate and assemble the rocker shaft. |

## Cylinder Head Reconditioning

| Procedure | Method |
|---|---|
| Inspect the pushrods: | Remove the pushrods, and, if hollow, clean out the oil passages using fine wire. Roll each pushrod over a piece of clean glass. If a distinct clicking sound is heard as the pushrod rolls, the rod is bent, and must be replaced. |
| | *The length of all pushrods must be equal. Measure the length of the pushrods, compare to specifications, and replace as necessary. |
| *Inspect the valve lifters:<br><br>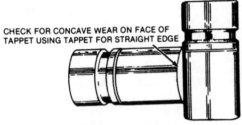<br>CHECK FOR CONCAVE WEAR ON FACE OF TAPPET USING TAPPET FOR STRAIGHT EDGE<br><br>**Check the lifter face for squareness** | Remove lifters from their bores, and remove gum and varnish, using solvent. Clean walls of lifter bores. Check lifters for concave wear as illustrated. If face is worn concave, replace lifter, and carefully inspect the camshaft. Lightly lubricate lifter and insert it into its bore. If play is excessive, an oversize lifter must be installed (where possible). Consult a machinist concerning feasibility. If play is satisfactory, remove, lubricate, and reinstall the lifter. |
| *Testing hydraulic lifter leak down: | Submerge lifter in a container of kerosene. Chuck a used pushrod or its equivalent into a drill press. Position container of kerosene so pushrod acts on the lifter plunger. Pump lifter with the drill press, until resistance increases. Pump several more times to bleed any air out of lifter. Apply very firm, constant pressure to the lifter, and observe rate at which fluid bleeds out of lifter. If the fluid bleeds very quickly (less than 15 seconds), lifter is defective. If the time exceeds 60 seconds, lifter is sticking. In either case, recondition or replace lifter. If lifter is operating properly (leak down time 15–60 seconds), lubricate and install it. |

## Cylinder Block Reconditioning

| Procedure | Method |
|---|---|
| Checking the main bearing clearance:<br><br>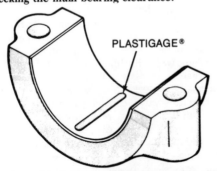<br>PLASTIGAGE®<br><br>**Plastigage® installed on the lower bearing shell** | Invert engine, and remove cap from the bearing to be checked. Using a clean, dry rag, thoroughly clean all oil from crankshaft journal and bearing insert.<br>NOTE: *Plastigage® is soluble in oil; therefore, oil on the journal or bearing could result in erroneous readings.* Place a piece of Plastigage along the full length of journal, reinstall cap, and torque to specifications.<br>NOTE: **Specifications are given in the engine specifications earlier in this chapter.**<br>Remove bearing cap, and determine bearing clearance by comparing width of Plastigage to the scale on Plastigage envelope. Journal taper is determined by comparing width of the Plas- |

## Cylinder Block Reconditioning

| Procedure | Method |
|---|---|

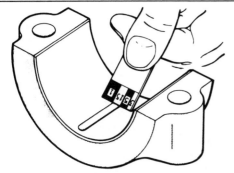

**Measure Plastigage® to determine main bearing clearance**

tigage strip near its ends. Rotate crankshaft 90° and retest, to determine journal eccentricity. **NOTE:** *Do not rotate crankshaft with Plastigage installed.* If bearing insert and journal appear intact, and are within tolerances, no further main bearing service is required. If bearing or journal appear defective, cause of failure should be determined before replacement.

\* Remove crankshaft from block (see below). Measure the main bearing journals at each end twice (90° apart) using a micrometer, to determine diameter, journal taper and eccentricity. If journals are within tolerances, reinstall bearing caps at their specified torque. Using a telescope gauge and micrometer, measure bearing I.D. parallel to piston axis and at 30° on each side of piston axis. Subtract journal O.D. for bearing I.D. to determine oil clearance. If crankshaft journals appear defective, or do not meet tolerances, there is no need to measure bearings; for the crankshaft will require grinding and/or undersize bearings will be required. If bearing appears defective, cause for failure should be determined prior to replacement.

**Check the connecting rod bearing clearance:**

Connecting rod bearing clearance is checked in the same manner as main bearing clearance, using Plastigage. Before removing the crankshaft, connecting rod side clearance also should be measured and recorded.

\* Checking connecting rod bearing clearance, using a micrometer, is identical to checking main bearing clearance. If no other service is required, the piston and rod assemblies need not be removed.

**Remove the crankshaft:**

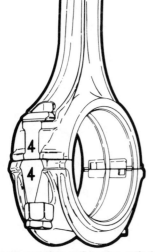

**Match the connecting rod to the cylinder with a number stamp**

Using a punch, mark the corresponding main bearing caps and saddles according to position (i.e., one punch on the front main cap and saddle, two on the second, three on the third, etc.). Using number stamps, identify the corresponding connecting rods and caps, according to cylinder (if no numbers are present). Remove the main and connecting rod caps, and place

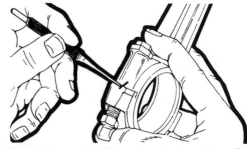

**Match the connecting rod and cap with scribe marks**

## Cylinder Block Reconditioning

| Procedure | Method |
|-----------|--------|
| | sleeves of plastic tubing or vacuum hose over the connecting rod bolts, to protect the journals as the crankshaft is removed. Lift the crankshaft out of the block. |
| **Remove the ridge from the top of the cylinder:**<br><br>RIDGE CAUSED BY CYLINDER WEAR<br><br><br><br>CYLINDER WALL<br>TOP OF PISTON<br><br>**Cylinder bore ridge** | In order to facilitate removal of the piston and connecting rod, the ridge at the top of the cylinder (unworn area; see illustration) must be removed. Place the piston at the bottom of the bore, and cover it with a rag. Cut the ridge away using a ridge reamer, exercising extreme care to avoid cutting too deeply. Remove the rag, and remove cuttings that remain on the piston.<br>**CAUTION:** *If the ridge is not removed, and new rings are installed, damage to rings will result.* |
| **Remove the piston and connecting rod:**<br><br><br><br>**Push the piston out with a hammer handle** | Invert the engine, and push the pistons and connecting rods out of the cylinders. If necessary, tap the connecting rod boss with a wooden hammer handle, to force the piston out.<br>**CAUTION:** *Do not attempt to force the piston past the cylinder ridge* (see above). |
| **Service the crankshaft:** | Ensure that all oil holes and passages in the crankshaft are open and free of sludge. If necessary, have the crankshaft ground to the largest possible undersize. |
| | ** Have the crankshaft Magnafluxed, to locate stress cracks. Consult a machinist concerning additional service procedures, such as surface hardening (e.g., nitriding, Tuftriding) to improve wear characteristics, cross drilling and chamfering the oil holes to improve lubrication, and balancing. |
| **Removing freeze plugs:** | Drill a small hole in the middle of the freeze plugs. Thread a large sheet metal screw into the hole and remove the plug with a slide hammer. |
| **Remove the oil gallery plugs:** | Threaded plugs should be removed using an appropriate (usually square) wrench. To remove soft, pressed in plugs, drill a hole in the plug, and thread in a sheet metal screw. Pull the plug out by the screw using pliers. |

## Cylinder Block Reconditioning

| Procedure | Method |
|---|---|
| Hot-tank the block:<br>NOTE: *Do not hot-tank aluminum parts.* | Have the block hot-tanked to remove grease, corrosion, and scale from the water jackets.<br>**NOTE:** *Consult the operator to determine whether the camshaft bearings will be damaged during the hot-tank process.* |
| Check the block for cracks: | Visually inspect the block for cracks or chips. The most common locations are as follows:<br>  Adjacent to freeze plugs.<br>  Between the cylinders and water jackets.<br>  Adjacent to the main bearing saddles.<br>  At the extreme bottom of the cylinders.<br>Check only suspected cracks using spot check dye (see introduction). If a crack is located, consult a machinist concerning possible repairs. |
|  | ** Magnaflux the block to locate hidden cracks. If cracks are located, consult a machinist about feasibility of repair. |
| Install the oil gallery plugs and freeze plugs: | Coat freeze plugs with sealer and tap into position using a piece of pipe, slightly smaller than the plug, as a driver. To ensure retention, stake the edges of the plugs. Coat threaded oil gallery plugs with sealer and install. Drive replacement soft plugs into block using a large drift as a driver. |
|  | * Rather than reinstalling lead plugs, drill and tap the holes, and install threaded plugs. |
| Check the bore diameter and surface:<br>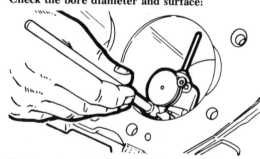<br>**Measure the cylinder bore with a dial gauge** | Visually inspect the cylinder bores for roughness, scoring, or scuffing. If evident, the cylinder bore must be bored or honed oversize to eliminate imperfections, and the smallest possible oversize piston used. The new pistons should be given to the machinist with the block, so that the cylinders can be bored or honed exactly to the piston size (plus clearance). If no flaws are evident, measure the bore diameter using a telescope gauge and micrometer, or dial gauge, parallel and perpendicular to the engine centerline, at the top (below the ridge) and bottom of the bore. Subtract the bottom measurements from the top to determine taper, and the parallel to |

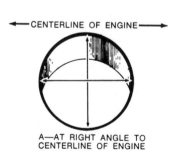

← CENTERLINE OF ENGINE →

A—AT RIGHT ANGLE TO CENTERLINE OF ENGINE
B—PARALLEL TO CENTERLINE OF ENGINE

**Cylinder bore measuring points**

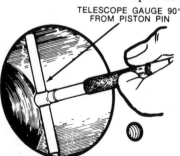

TELESCOPE GAUGE 90°
FROM PISTON PIN

**Measure the cylinder bore with a telescope gauge**

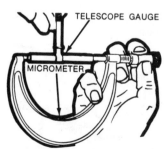

TELESCOPE GAUGE

MICROMETER

**Measure the telescope gauge with a micrometer to determine the cylinder bore**

## Cylinder Block Reconditioning

| Procedure | Method |
|---|---|
| | the centerline measurements from the perpendicular measurements to determine eccentricity. If the measurements are not within specifications, the cylinder must be bored or honed, and an oversize piston installed. If the measurements are within specifications the cylinder may be used as is, with only finish honing (see below). <br> NOTE: *Prior to submitting the block for boring, perform the following operation(s).* |
| Check the cylinder block bearing alignment: <br><br> 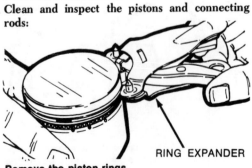 <br> **Check the main bearing saddle alignment** | Remove the upper bearing inserts. Place a straightedge in the bearing saddles along the centerline of the crankshaft. If clearance exists between the straightedge and the center saddle, the block must be alignbored. |
| *Check the deck height: | The deck height is the distance from the crankshaft centerline to the block deck. To measure, invert the engine, and install the crankshaft, retaining it with the center main cap. Measure the distance from the crankshaft journal to the block deck, parallel to the cylinder centerline. Measure the diameter of the end (front and rear) main journals, parallel to the centerline of the cylinders, divide the diameter in half, and subtract it from the previous measurement. The results of the front and rear measurements should be identical. If the difference exceeds .005″, the deck height should be corrected. <br> NOTE: *Block deck height and warpage should be corrected at the same time.* |
| Check the block deck for warpage: | Using a straightedge and feeler gauges, check the block deck for warpage in the same manner that the cylinder head is checked (see Cylinder Head Reconditioning). If warpage exceeds specifications, have the deck resurfaced. <br> NOTE: *In certain cases a specification for total material removal (cylinder head and block deck) is provided. This specification must not be exceeded.* |
| Clean and inspect the pistons and connecting rods: <br><br> **RING EXPANDER** <br> **Remove the piston rings** | Using a ring expander, remove the rings from the piston. Remove the retaining rings (if so equipped) and remove piston pin. <br> NOTE: *If the piston pin must be pressed out, determine the proper method and use the proper tools; otherwise the piston will distort.* <br> Clean the ring grooves using an appropriate tool, exercising care to avoid cutting too deeply. Thoroughly clean all carbon and varnish from the piston with solvent. <br> CAUTION: *Do not use a wire brush or caustic solvent on pistons.* Inspect the pistons for scuffing, scoring, cracks, pitting, or excessive ring |

## Cylinder Block Reconditioning

| Procedure | Method |
|---|---|

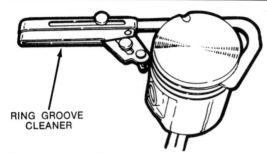

RING GROOVE
CLEANER

**Clean the piston ring grooves**

groove wear. If wear is evident, the piston must be replaced. Check the connecting rod length by measuring the rod from the inside of the large end to the inside of the small end using calipers (see illustration). All connecting rods should be equal length. Replace any rod that differs from the others in the engine.

\* Have the connecting rod alignment checked in an alignment fixture by a machinist. Replace any twisted or bent rods.

\* Magnaflux the connecting rods to locate stress cracks. If cracks are found, replace the connecting rod.

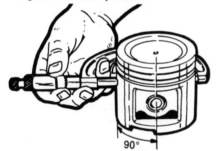

**Check the connecting rod length (arrow)**

**Fit the pistons to the cylinders:**

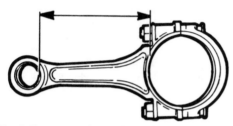

90°

**Measure the piston prior to fitting**

Using a telescope gauge and micrometer, or a dial gauge, measure the cylinder bore diameter perpendicular to the piston pin, 2½″ below the deck. Measure the piston perpendicular to its pin on the skirt. The difference between the two measurements is the piston clearance. If the clearance is within specifications or slightly below (after boring or honing), finish honing is all that is required. If the clearance is excessive, try to obtain a slightly larger piston to bring clearance within specifications. Where this is not possible, obtain the first oversize piston, and hone (or if necessary, bore) the cylinder to size.

**Assemble the pistons and connecting rods:**

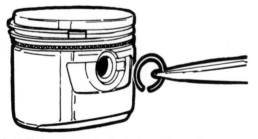

**Install the piston pin lock-rings (if used)**

Inspect piston pin, connecting rod small end bushing, and piston bore for galling, scoring, or excessive wear. If evident, replace defective part(s). Measure the I.D. of the piston boss and connecting rod small end, and the O.D. of the piston pin. If within specifications, assemble piston pin and rod.
**CAUTION:** *If piston pin must be pressed in, determine the proper method and use the proper tools; otherwise the piston will distort.*
    Install the lock rings; ensure that they seat properly. If the parts are not within specifications, determine the service method for the type of engine. In some cases, piston and pin are serviced as an assembly when either is defective. Others specify reaming the piston and connecting rods for an oversize pin. If the connecting rod bushing is worn, it may in many cases be replaced. Reaming the piston and replacing the rod bushing are machine shop operations.

## Cylinder Block Reconditioning

| Procedure | Method |
|---|---|
| Clean and inspect the camshaft: | Degrease the camshaft, using solvent, and clean out all oil holes. Visually inspect cam lobes and bearing journals for excessive wear. If a lobe is questionable, check all lobes as indicated below. If a journal or lobe is worn, the camshaft must be regrounded or replaced. **NOTE:** *If a journal is worn, there is a good chance that the bushings are worn.* If lobes and journals appear intact, place the front and rear journals in V-blocks, and rest a dial indicator on the center journal. Rotate the camshaft to check straightness. If deviation exceeds .001″, replace the camshaft. |

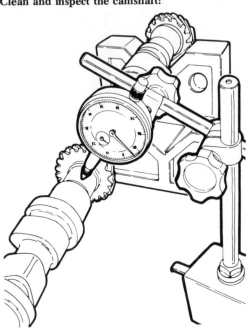

**Check the camshaft for straightness**

*Check the camshaft lobes with a micrometer, by measuring the lobes from the nose to base and again at 90° (see illustration). The lift is determined by subtracting the second measurement from the first. If all exhaust lobes and all intake lobes are not identical, the camshaft must be reground or replaced.

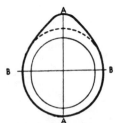

**Camshaft lobe measurement**

**Replace the camshaft bearings:**

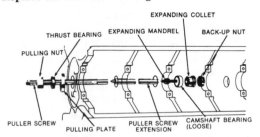

**Camshaft bearing removal and installation tool (OHV engines only)**

If excessive wear is indicated, or if the engine is being completely rebuilt, camshaft bearings should be replaced as follows: Drive the camshaft rear plug from the block. Assemble the removal puller with its shoulder on the bearing to be removed. Gradually tighten the puller nut until bearing is removed. Remove remaining bearings, leaving the front and rear for last. To remove front and rear bearings, reverse position of the tool, so as to pull the bearings in toward the center of the block. Leave the tool in this position, pilot the new front and rear bearings on the installer, and pull them into position: Return the tool to its original position and pull remaining bearings into position. **NOTE:** *Ensure that oil holes align when installing bearings.* Replace camshaft rear plug, and stake it into position to aid retention.

**Finish hone the cylinders:**

Chuck a flexible drive hone into a power drill, and insert it into the cylinder. Start the hone, and remove it up and down in the cylinder at a rate which will produce approximately a 60° cross-hatch pattern. **NOTE:** *Do not extend the hone below the cylinder bore.* After developing the pattern, remove

## Cylinder Block Reconditioning

| Procedure | Method |
| --- | --- |

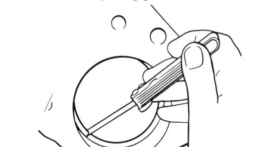

CROSS HATCH
PATTERN

50°-60°

**Cylinder bore after honing**

the hone and recheck piston fit. Wash the cylinders with a detergent and water solution to remove abrasive dust, dry, and wipe several times with a rag soaked in engine oil.

**Check piston ring end-gap:**

Compress the piston rings to be used in a cylinder, one at a time, into that cylinder, and press them approximately 1″ below the deck with an inverted piston. Using feeler gauges, measure the ring end-gap, and compare to specifications. Pull the ring out of the cylinder and file the ends with a fine file to obtain proper clearance.
**CAUTION:** *If inadequate ring end-gap is utilized, ring breakage will result.*

**Check the piston ring end gap**

**Install the piston rings:**

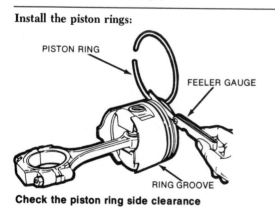

PISTON RING

FEELER GAUGE

RING GROOVE

**Check the piston ring side clearance**

Inspect the ring grooves in the piston for excessive wear or taper. If necessary, recut the groove(s) for use with an overwidth ring or a standard ring and spacer. If the groove is worn uniformly, overwidth rings, or standard rings and spacers may be installed without recutting. Roll the outside of the ring around the groove to check for burrs or deposits. If any are found, remove with a fine file. Hold the ring in the groove, and measure side clearance. If necessary, correct as indicated above.
**NOTE:** *Always install any additional spacers above the piston ring.*
  The ring groove must be deep enough to allow the ring to seat below the lands (see illustration). In many cases, a "go-no-go" depth gauge will be provided with the piston rings. Shallow grooves may be corrected by recutting, while deep grooves require some type of filler or expander

## Cylinder Block Reconditioning

| Procedure | Method |
|---|---|
| | behind the piston. Consult the piston ring supplier concerning the suggested method. Install the rings on the piston, lowest ring first, using a ring expander. <br> NOTE: *Position the rings as specified by the manufacturer.* Consult the engine service procedures earlier in this chapter for details concerning specific engines. |
| Install the camshaft: | Liberally lubricate the camshaft lobes and journals, and install the camshaft. <br> CAUTION: *Exercise extreme care to avoid damaging the bearings when inserting the camshaft.* <br> Install and tighten the camshaft thrust plate retaining bolts. |
| | See the engine service procedures earlier in this chapter for details concerning specific engines. |
| Check camshaft end-play (OHV engines only): <br><br> **Check the camshaft end-play with a feeler gauge** | Using feeler gauges, determine whether the clearance between the camshaft boss (or gear) and backing plate is within specifications. Install shims behind the thrust plate, or reposition the camshaft gear and retest endplay. In some cases, adjustment is by replacing the thrust plate. <br> See the engine service procedures earlier in this chapter for details concerning specific engines. |
| DIAL INDICATOR <br> CAMSHAFT <br><br> **Check the camshaft end-play with a dial indicator** | * Mount a dial indicator stand so that the stem of the dial indicator rests on the nose of the camshaft, parallel to the camshaft axis. Push the camshaft as far in as possible and zero the gauge. Move the camshaft outward to determine the amount of camshaft endplay. If the endplay is not within tolerance, install shims behind the thrust plate, or reposition the camshaft gear and retest. <br> See the engine service procedures earlier in this chapter for details concerning specific engines. |
| Install the rear main seal: | See the engine service procedures earlier in this chapter for details concerning specific engines. |
| Install the crankshaft: <br><br> 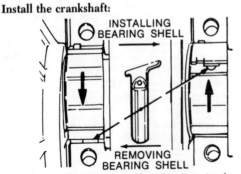 <br> **Remove or install the upper bearing insert using a roll-out pin** | Thoroughly clean the main bearing saddles and caps. Place the upper halves of the bearing inserts on the saddles and press into position. <br> NOTE: *Ensure that the oil holes align.* Press the corresponding bearing inserts into the main bearing caps. Lubricate the upper main bearings, and lay the crankshaft in position. Place a strip of Plastigage on each of the crankshaft journals, install the main caps, and torque to specifications. Remove the main caps, and compare the Plastigage to the scale on the Plastigage envelope. If clearances are within tolerances, remove the Plastigage, turn the crankshaft 90°, wipe off all oil and retest. If all clearances are correct, |

## Cylinder Block Reconditioning

| Procedure | Method |
|---|---|

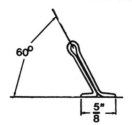

**Home-made bearing roll-out pin**

remove all Plastigage, thoroughly lubricate the main caps and bearing journals, and install the main caps. If clearances are not within tolerance, the upper bearing inserts may be removed, without removing the crankshaft, using a bearing roll out pin (see illustration). Roll in a bearing that will provide proper clearance, and retest. Torque all main caps, excluding the thrust bearing cap, to specifications. Tighten the thrust bearing cap finger tight. To properly align the thrust bearing, pry the crankshaft the extent of its axial travel several times, the last movement held toward the front of the engine, and torque the thrust bearing cap to specifications. Determine the crankshaft end-play (see below), and bring within tolerance with thrust washers.

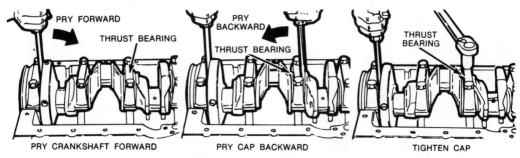

**Aligning the thrust bearing**

**Measure crankshaft end-play:**

Mount a dial indicator stand on the front of the block, with the dial indicator stem resting on the nose of the crankshaft, parallel to the crankshaft axis. Pry the crankshaft the extent of its travel rearward, and zero the indicator. Pry the crankshaft forward and record crankshaft end-play.
NOTE: *Crankshaft end-play also may be measured at the thrust bearing, using feeler gauges* (see illustration).

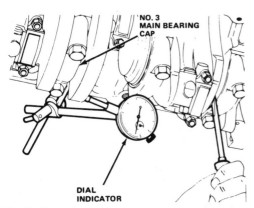

**Check the crankshaft end-play with a dial indicator**

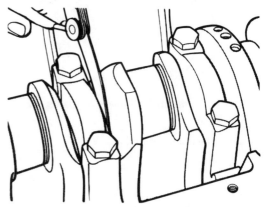

**Check the crankshaft end-play with a feeler gauge**

## Cylinder Block Reconditioning

| *Procedure* | *Method* |
|---|---|
| Install the pistons: | Press the upper connecting rod bearing halves into the connecting rods, and the lower halves into the connecting rod caps. Position the piston ring gaps according to specifications (see car section), and lubricate the pistons. Install a ring compresser on a piston, and press two long (8″) pieces of plastic tubing over the rod bolts. Using the tubes as a guide, press the pistons into the bores and onto the crankshaft with a wooden hammer handle. After seating the rod on the crankshaft journal, remove the tubes and install the cap finger tight. Install the remaining pistons in the same manner. Invert the engine and check the bearing clearance at two points (90° apart) on each journal with Plastigage. |

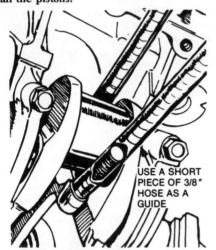

USE A SHORT PIECE OF 3/8″ HOSE AS A GUIDE

**Use lengths of vacuum hose or rubber tubing to protect the crankshaft journals and cylinder walls during piston installation**

NOTE: *Do not turn the crankshaft with Plastigage installed.* If clearance is within tolerances, remove *all* Plastigage, thoroughly lubricate the journals, and torque the rod caps to specifications. If clearance is not within specifications, install different thickness bearing inserts and recheck.

CAUTION: *Never shim or file the connecting rods or caps.* Always install plastic tube sleeves over the rod bolts when the caps are not installed, to protect the crankshaft journals.

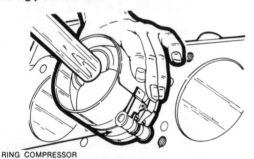

RING COMPRESSOR

**Install the piston using a ring compressor**

| Check connecting rod side clearance: | Determine the clearance between the sides of the connecting rods and the crankshaft using feeler gauges. If clearance is below the minimum tolerance, the rod may be machined to provide adequate clearance. If clearance is excessive, substitute an unworn rod, and recheck. If clearance is still outside specifications, the crankshaft must be welded and reground, or replaced. |

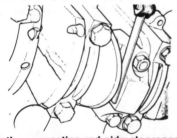

**Check the connecting rod side clearance with a feeler gauge**

| Inspect the timing chain (or belt): | Visually inspect the timing chain for broken or loose links, and replace the chain if any are found. If the chain will flex sideways, it must be replaced. Install the timing chain as specified. Be sure the timing belt is not stretched, frayed or broken. |

NOTE: *If the original timing chain is to be reused, install it in its original position.*

## Cylinder Block Reconditioning

| Procedure | Method |
|---|---|
| Check timing gear backlash and runout (OHV engines): | Mount a dial indicator with its stem resting on a tooth of the camshaft gear (as illustrated). Rotate the gear until all slack is removed, and zero the indicator. Rotate the gear in the opposite direction until slack is removed, and record gear backlash. Mount the indicator with its stem resting on the edge of the camshaft gear, parallel to the axis of the camshaft. Zero the indicator, and turn the camshaft gear one full turn, recording the runout. If either backlash or runout exceed specifications, replace the worn gear(s). |

Check the camshaft gear backlash

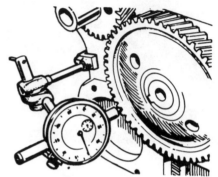

Check the camshaft gear run-out

## Completing the Rebuilding Process

Follow the above procedures, complete the rebuilding process as follows:

Fill the oil pump with oil, to prevent cavitating (sucking air) on initial engine start up. Install the oil pump and the pickup tube on the engine. Coat the oil pan gasket as necessary, and install the gasket and the oil pan. Mount the flywheel and the crankshaft vibration damper or pulley on the crankshaft. NOTE: *Always use new bolts when installing the flywheel.* Inspect the clutch shaft pilot bushing in the crankshaft. If the bushing is excessively worn, remove it with an expanding puller and a slide hammer, and tap a new bushing into place.

Position the engine, cylinder head side up. Lubricate the lifters, and install them into their bores. Install the cylinder head, and torque it as specified. Insert the pushrods and install the rocker shaft(s) or position the rocker arms on the pushrods. Adjust the valves.

Install the intake and exhaust manifolds, the carburetor(s), the distributor and spark plugs. Adjust the point gap and the static ignition timing. Mount all accessories and install the engine in the car. Fill the radiator with coolant, and the crankcase with high quality engine oil.

## Break-in Procedure

Start the engine, and allow it to run at low speed for a few minutes, while checking for leaks. Stop the engine, check the oil level, and fill as necessary. Restart the engine, and fill the cooling system to capacity. Check the point dwell angle and adjust the ignition timing and the valves. Run the engine at low to medium speed (800–2500 rpm) for approximately ½ hour, and retorque the cylinder head bolts. Road test the car, and check again for leaks.

Follow the manufacturer's recommended engine break-in procedure and maintenance schedule for new engines.

# Emission Controls and Fuel System

## EMISSION CONTROLS

The emission control devices required in Chevrolet and GMC pick-ups are determined by weight classification. Light duty emission models use the same controls as cars. These are all 1970–74 trucks; all 1975–78 two wheel drive trucks under 6000 lbs. Gross Vehicle Weight; all 1979 trucks under 8500 lbs. GVW; and all 1980 trucks under 8600 lbs. GVW. Heavy duty models use fewer emission controls and include all four wheel drive trucks, 1970–74; all trucks over 6000 lbs. GVW, 1975–78; all trucks over 8500 lbs. GVW, 1979; and all trucks over 8600 lbs. GVW, 1980.

The exception to these rules is the diesel-powered C-10 and C-1500. 1978–79 diesel engines have only a PCV valve for emission control purposes. Some 1980 models add an EGR valve to the PCV system.

PCV (Positive Crankcase Ventilation) was the earliest form of automotive emission control, dating back to 1955 on Chevrolet vehicles. Still in use today, it routes cylinder blowby gases from the crankcase through a PCV valve and back into the combustion chamber for reburning.

In 1966, the AIR (Air Injector Reactor) system was introduced on Chevrolet vehicles to satisfy the California emission requirements.

This system pumps oxygen to the exhaust gases as they exit from the cylinder, where they are ignited and burned more completely to further reduce hydrocarbon and carbon monoxide exhaust emissions.

General Motors introduced the CCS (Controlled Combustion System) in 1968, which uses various components and design calibrations to further reduce pollutants.

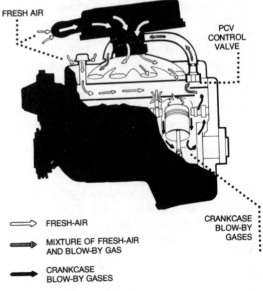

FRESH AIR

PCV CONTROL VALVE

CRANKCASE BLOW-BY GASES

⇨ FRESH-AIR

⇦ MIXTURE OF FRESH-AIR AND BLOW-BY GAS

➡ CRANKCASE BLOW-BY GASES

**PCV system (© Chevrolet Motor Div.)**

The CEC (Combined Emission Control) and TCS (Transmission Controlled Spark) have been used since 1970 and basically do not allow distributor vacuum advance in Low gear.

In 1973, the EGR (Exhaust Gas Recirculation) system was developed in response to more stringent Federal exhaust emission standards regarding $NO_x$ (oxides of nitrogen). Oxides of nitrogen are formed at higher combustion chamber temperatures and increase with higher temperatures. The EGR system is designed to reduce combustion temperature thereby reducing the formation of $NO_x$.

In addition to controlling the engine emissions, the ECS (Evaporative Control System) is designed to control fuel vapors that escape from the fuel tank through evaporation. When the fuel vapors combine with the atmosphere and sunlight they form photochemical smog. This system seals the fuel tank to retain vapors in a charcoal canister. The canister is purged and the vapors burned during engine operation.

In 1975, a catalytic converter was added to the emission control system on some light duty models, and its use has slowly spread through the line in succeeding years. Through catalytic action (that is, causing a chemical reaction without taking part in the reaction itself) the platinum and palladium coated beads in the converter oxidize unburnt hydrocarbons (HC) and carbon monoxide (CO) into carbon dioxide ($CO_2$) and water ($H_2O$). The converter itself is a muffler-shaped device installed in the exhaust system of the truck. Converter-equipped trucks require the use of unleaded fuel.

With emission level maintenance standards getting stricter on state and Federal levels, proper testing and service of each system becomes more important. Much confusion results from the variety and combinations of systems used in any year. Consult the following chart to determine the systems used in each year. The following sections are devoted to the description and service of each separate system.

## Positive Crankcase Ventilation (PCV)

PCV is the earliest form of emission control. Prior to its use, crankcase vapors were vented into the atmosphere through a road draft tube or crankcase breather. The PCV system first appeared on Chevrolets in 1955.

In 1958, it was used on the 348 cu in. truck engine as standard equipment. Two years later the six cyl. 261 cu in. engine also used it as standard. Beginning 1961, the PCV system was used on all California models and in 1963 the system became standard on all models.

This system draws crankcase vapors that are formed through normal combustion into the intake manifold and subsequently into the combustion chambers to be burned. Fresh air is introduced to the crankcase by way of a hose connected to the carburetor air cleaner or a vented oil filler cap on older models. Manifold vacuum is used to draw the vapors from the crankcase through a PCV valve and into the intake manifold. Vented and nonvented filler caps were used on various models until 1968, after which only nonvented caps were used.

### SERVICE

The PCV system should be inspected as stated in the "Maintenance Interval" chart in Chapter 1. Other than checking and replacing the PCV valve and associated hoses, there is no other service required. Engine operating conditions that would direct suspicion to the PCV system are rough idle, oil present in the air cleaner, oil leaks and excessive oil sludging or dilution. If any of the above conditions exist, remove the PCV valve and shake it. A clicking sound indicates

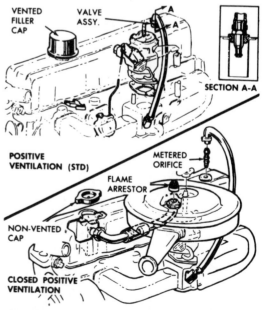

Closed and positive PCV systems (© Chevrolet Motor Div.)

## Emission Control Application Chart

| Year/Engine | 1970 | 1971 | 1972 | 1973 | 1974 | 1975 | 1976 | 1977 | 1978 | 1979 | 1980 |
|---|---|---|---|---|---|---|---|---|---|---|---|
| 6-250 | PCV—CCS— CHA① TSC② ECS②③ | PCV—CCS— CHA① TCS② ECS② | PCV—AIR③ CCS④— CHA—TCS— ECS | PCV—AIR CCS④⑥ EGR② TCS② ECS⑥ | PCV—TCS⑧ CCS CHA— EGR②— AIR②— | PCV—TCS⑧ CCS—CHA— EGR②— AIR② EFE②— CAT⑧ TRC③ | PCV—EGR— CCS—ECS— EFE—CHA— CAT—ISS | PCV—EGR— CCS—ECS— EFE—CHA— CAT—ISS | PCV—EGR CCS—ECS EFE—CHA CAT—ISS | PCV—EGR—ECS— CCS—CHA—CAT— EFE—CHA—CAT— PAIR—TVSS—ISS | PCV—EGR—ECS— EFE—CHA—CAT— PAIR—TVSS—ISS |
| 6-292 | PCV—CCS— CHA① TCS② ECS②⑦ | PCV—CCS— CHA① TCS② ECS② | PCV—AIR③ CCS—CHA— TCS②— ECS② | PCV—AIR③⑥ CCS④⑤ CHA— EGR②— ECS②⑥ | PCV—TCS⑧ CCS— CHA— EGR②— AIR②— | PCV—TCS⑧ CCS—CHA— EGR②— AIR②— EFE②— CAT⑧ TRC③ | PCV—CCS— ECS③—CHA— ISS | PCV—CCS— ECS③— TRC③—CHA— ISS | PCV—CCS— ECS③— TRC③—CHA— ISS—CAT③ | PCV—ECS—TRC— CHA—AIR—TVSS—ISS | PCV—ECS—TRC— CHA—AIR—TVSS—ISS |
| V8-305 | — | — | — | — | — | — | — | PCV—EGR— CCS—ECS— EFE—CHA— CAT | PCV—EGR CCS—ECS EFE—CHA CAT | PCV—EGR—CCS—ECS— EFE—CHA—CAT— TVSS—ISS | PCV—EGR—CCS—ECS— EFE—CHA—CAT— TVSS—ISS |
| V8-307 | PCV—AIR⑦— CCS② CHA①② TCS② ECS②⑧ | PCV—CCS— CHA① TCS② ECS② | PCV—CCS CHA— TCS②— ECS② | PCV—AIR② CCS③— CHA②⑦⑤ EGR② TCS② ECS②⑥ | — | — | — | — | — | — | — |
| V8-350 | PCV—CCS— CHA① TCS② ECS②③ | PCV—CCS— CHA① TCS② ECS② | PCV— AIR②③ CCS⑦②④ CHA— TCS② ECS② | PCV—AIR② CCS⑤— CHA②③⑤ EGR② TCS⑧— ECS②⑥ | PCV—TCS⑧ CCS— CHA— EGR②— AIR②— | PCV—TCS⑧ CCS—CHA— EGR②— AIR② EFE②— CAT⑧— TRC③ | PCV—EGR— CCS—ECS— EFE—CHA— CAT—AIR③— TRC⑤ | PCV—EGR— CCS④—ECS— EFE—CHA— CAT— AIR③⑬— TRC③⑤ | PCV—EGR— CCS④—ECS EFE—CHA— CAT— AIR③⑬ TRC③⑤ | PCV—EGR⑫—ECS— CCS③⑬—EFE— CHA—CAT⑫—AIR⑬— TVSS—ISS⑫—TRC⑬ | PCV—EGR⑫—ECS— CCS③⑬—EFE— CHA—CAT⑫—AIR⑬— TVSS—ISS⑫—TRC⑬ |

**V8—396**
PCV—CCS—
CHA①—
TCS②—
ECS②⑨

**V8—400**
PCV—TCS⑧  PCV—CCS—  PCV—CCS④  PCV—CCS④  PCV—EGR⑫—CCS④⑫  PCV—EGR⑫—CCS④⑫—
CCS—CHA—  ECS③—  ECS③—  ECS③—  ECS—EFE—CHA—  ECS—EFE—CHA—
EGR②—  TRC③—CHA—  TRC③—  TRC③—  CAT⑫—AIR⑬—TVSS  CAT⑫—AIR⑬—
AIR②—  AIR③  CHA—AIR③  CHA—AIR③  ISS⑫  TVSS—ISS⑫
EFE⑥—  CAT③
CAT⑥—
TRC③

**V8—402**
PCV—CCS—  PCV—AIR②④—
CHA①—  CCS⑦—
TCS②—  CHA—
ECS②  TCS②—
ECS②

**V8—454**
PCV—AIR②⑩⑤  PCV—TCS⑧  PCV—EGR—  PCV—EGR—  PCV—EGR—  PCV—EGR⑬—ECS—  PCV—EGR—ECS—
CCS④⑩—  CCS—  ECS—EFE—  ECS—EFE—  ECS—EFE—  EFE—CHA—CAT⑫—  EFE—CHA—AIR—
CHA②⑩⑤—  CHA—  CHA—AIR⑩  CCS④⑥—  CCS④⑥—  AIR—TVSS—ISS⑫  TVSS
EGR②—  EGR②—  CCS②—  CHA—AIR⑩  CHA—AIR⑩
TCS⑧—  AIR②—  TRC②⑥  TRC②⑥  TRC②⑥
ECS②⑩  CAT③

**Legend:**
① Except oil bath air cleaner
② All 10 Series
③ Except California
④ California only
⑤ Trucks with GVW greater than 6,000 lbs
⑥ California heavy-duty built after 1/1/73
⑦ All 20 Series trucks only
⑧ All 10 Series with manual transmission
⑨ Under 6,000 lbs GVW
⑩ Except non-California HD emissions
⑪ High Altitude only
⑫ Under 8,500 lbs GVW
⑬ Over 8,500 lbs GVW
⑭ California, and trucks over 8,500 lbs GVW

— Engine Not Available
PCV Positive Crankcase Ventilation
AIR Air Injector Reactor
CCS Controlled Combustion System—this is a design feature and cannot be serviced
TCS Transmission Controlled Spark
ECS Evaporation Control System
CHA Carburetor Heated Air
EGR Exhaust Gas Recirculation
EFE Early Fuel Evaporation Valve
TRC Throttle Return Control
CAT Catalytic Converter
ISS Idle Stop Solenoid
TVSS Trapped Vacuum Spark System
PAIR Pulse Air Injection Reactor

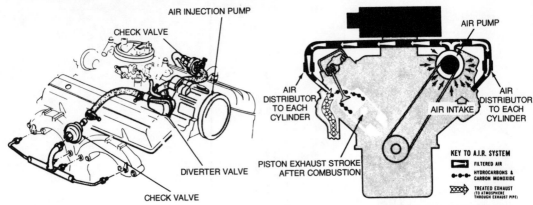

**AIR system schematic (© Chevrolet Motor Div.)**

**AIR system operation (© Chevrolet Motor Div.)**

that the valve is free. If no clicking sound is heard, replace the valve. Inspect the PCV breather in the air cleaner. Replace the breather if it is so dirty that it will not allow gases to pass through. Check all the PCV hoses for condition and tight connections. Replace any hoses that have deteriorated.

## Air Injector Reactor (AIR)

This system was first introduced on California vehicles in 1966. The AIR system injects compressed air into the exhaust system, near enough to the exhaust valves to continue the burning of the normally unburned segment of the exhaust gases. To do this it employs an air injection pump and a system of hoses, valves, tubes, etc., necessary to carry the compressed air from the pump to the exhaust manifolds. Carburetors and distributors for AIR engines have specific modifications to adapt them to the air injection system. These components should not be interchanged with those intended for use on engines that do not have the system.

A diverter valve is used to prevent backfir-

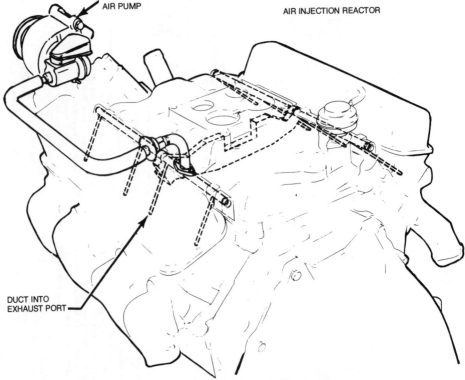

**Air pump and nozzles—V8 (© Chevrolet Motor Div.)**

ing. The valve senses sudden increases in manifold vacuum and ceases the injection of air during fuel-rich periods. During coasting, this valve diverts the entire air flow through a muffler and during high engine speeds, expels it through a relief valve. Check valves in the system prevent exhaust gases from entering the pump.

## TESTING

### Check Valve

To test the check valve, disconnect the hose at the diverter valve. Blow into the hose and suck on it. Air should flow only into the engine.

### Diverter Valve

Pull off the vacuum line to the top of the valve with the engine running. There should be vacuum in the line. Replace the line. No air should be escaping with the engine running at a steady idle. Open and quickly close the throttle. A blast of air should come out of the valve muffler for at least one second. If the valve must be replaced, use a new gasket at the valve mounting on the pump and torque the bolts to 85 in. lbs.

### Air Pump

Disconnect the hose from the diverter valve. Start the engine and accelerate it to about 1,500 rpm. The airflow should increase as the engine is accelerated. If no airflow is noted or it remains constant, check the following:

1. Drive belt tension.
2. Listen for a leaking pressure relief valve. If it is defective, replace the whole relief/diverter valve.
3. Foreign matter in pump filter openings. If the pump is defective or excessively noisy, it must be replaced.

## SERVICE

The AIR system's effectiveness depends on correct engine idle speed, ignition timing, and dwell. These settings should be strictly adhered to and checked frequently. All hoses and fittings should be inspected for condition and tightness of connections. Check the drive belt for wear and tension every 12 months or 12,000 miles (4 months/6,000 miles 1974–75). If, after completion of a tune-up and/or individual inspection of components, a malfunction still exists, the vehicle should be serviced by qualified mechanics.

The AIR system is not completely noiseless. Under normal conditions, noise rises in pitch as engine speed increases. To determine if excessive noise is the fault of the AIR system, operate the engine with the pump drive belt removed. If the noise does not exist with the belt removed:

1. Check for a seized pump.
2. Check hoses, tubes and connections for leaks and kinks.
3. Check diverter valve.
4. Check pump for proper mounting.
CAUTION: *Do not oil AIR pump.*
If no irregularities exist and the AIR pump noise is still excessive, replace the pump.

### Air Pump Removal and Installation

1. Disconnect the output hose.
2. Hold the pump from turning by squeezing the drive belt.
3. Loosen the pulley bolts.
4. Loosen the alternator so the belt can be removed.
5. Remove the pulley.
6. Remove the pump mounting bolts and the pump.
7. Install the pump with the mounting bolts loose.
8. Install the pulley and tighten the bolts finger-tight.
9. Install and adjust the drive belt.
10. Squeeze the drive belt to prevent the pump from turning.
11. Torque the pulley bolts to 25 ft lbs. Tighten the pump mountings.
12. Check and adjust the belt tension again, if necessary.
13. Connect the hose.
14. If any hose leaks are suspected, pour soapy water over the suspected area with the engine running. Bubbles will form wherever air is escaping.

### Filter Replacement

1. Disconnect the air and vacuum hoses from the diverter valve.
2. Loosen the pump pivot and adjusting bolts and remove the drive belt.
3. Withdraw the pivot and adjusting bolts from the pump. Remove the pump and the diverter valve as an assembly.
CAUTION: *Do not clamp the pump in a vise or use a hammer or pry bar on the pump housing.*
4. To change the filter, break the plastic fan from the hub. It is seldom possible to remove the fan without breaking it.

## Air Injection System Diagnosis Chart

| Problem | Cause | Cure |
|---|---|---|
| 1. Noisy drive belt | 1a Loose belt<br>1b Seized pump | 1a Tighten belt<br>1b Replace |
| 2. Noisy pump | 2a Leaking hose<br>2b Loose hose<br>2c Hose contacting other parts<br>2d Diverter or check valve failure<br>2e Pump mounting loose<br>2g Defective pump | 2a Trace and fix leak<br>2b Tighten hose clamp<br>2c Reposition hose<br>2d Replace<br>2e Tighten securing bolts<br>2g Replace |
| 3. No air supply | 3a Loose belt<br>3b Leak in hose or at fitting<br>3c Defective anti-backfire valve<br>3d Defective check valve<br>3e Defective pump | 3a Tighten belt<br>3b Trace and fix leak<br>3c Replace<br>3d Replace<br>3e Replace |
| 4. Exhaust backfire | 4a Vacuum or air leaks<br>4b Defective anti-backfire valve<br>4c Sticking choke<br>4d Choke setting rich | 4a Trace and fix leak<br>4b Replace<br>4c Service choke<br>4d Adjust choke |

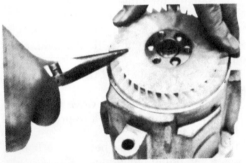

**Removing the air pump filter (© Chevrolet Motor Div.)**

5. Remove the remaining portion of the fan filter from the pump hub. Be careful that filter fragments do not enter the air intake hole.

6. Position the new centrifugal fan filter on the pump hub. Place the pump pulley against the fan filter and install the securing screws. Torque the screws alternately to 95 in. lbs and the fan filter will be pressed onto the pump hub.

7. Install the pump on the engine and adjust its drive belt.

NOTE: *A slight amount of interference between the fan filter and the pump housing bore is normal. After a new fan filter has been installed, it may squeal upon initial operation or until its outside diameter sealing lip is worn in. This may require a short period of pump operation at various engine speeds.*

## Pulse Air Injection System (PAIR)

The PAIR system is used on 1979–80 250 six cylinder engines. The system utilizes exhaust system pulses to siphon fresh air into the exhaust manifold. The injected air supports continued combustion of the hot exhaust gases in the exhaust manifold, reducing exhaust emissions.

Air is drawn into the PAIR plenums through a hose connected to the air cleaner case. There are two plenums, mounted on the rocker arm cover. The air passes through a check valve (there are four check valves—two at each plenum), then through a manifold pipe to the exhaust manifold. All manifold pipes are the same length, to prevent uneven pulsation. The check valves open during pulses of negative exhaust back pressure, admitting air into the manifold pipe and the exhaust manifold. During pulses of positive exhaust back pressure, the check valves close, preventing backfiring into the plenums and air cleaner.

### REMOVAL AND INSTALLATION

1. Remove the air cleaner. Disconnect the rubber hose from the plenum connecting pipe.

2. Disconnect the four manifold pipes at the exhaust manifold. Remove the check valves from the plenum grommets.

3. Unbolt the check valve from the manifold pipe, if necessary.

4. To install, assemble the check valves to the pipes before the pipes are installed on the exhaust manifold.

5. Install the manifold pipe fittings to the exhaust manifold, but tighten the fittings only finger tight.

6. Use a 1 inch open end wrench, or something similar, as a lever to align the check valve on the "A" pipe assemblies (see the illustration) with the plenum grommet. Use the palm of your hand to press the check valve into the grommet. A rubber lubricant can be used to ease assembly.

7. Repeat this operation on the "B" pipe assembly.

8. After all the check valves have been installed in the rubber grommets, tighten the manifold pipe-to-exhaust manifold fittings to 28 ft lbs. Connect the rubber hose to the plenum pipe and install the air cleaner.

## Controlled Combustion System (CCS)

The CCS system is a combination of systems and calibrations. Many of these are not visible or serviceable, but are designed into the engine. Originally, in 1968–69, the system was comprised of special carburetion and distributor settings, higher engine operating temperatures and a thermostatically-controlled air cleaner. In later years, the thermostatically-controlled air cleaner (CHA) was used independently of the other settings on some engines. Likewise, some engines used the special settings without CHA. In 1970, the TCS system was incorporated and the entire system was renamed CEC in 1971. The name reverted to TCS in 1972. In 1973, EGR was also added to the system.

The various systems, CHA, TCS, CEC and EGR are all part of the Controlled Combustion System.

### SERVICE

Refer to the CHA, TCS, CEC or EGR Sections for maintenance and service (if applicable). In addition be sure that the ignition timing, dwell and carburetor settings are correct.

## Carburetor Heated Air (CHA)

The use of carburetor heated air dates back to 1960 when it was first used on heavy trucks.

This system is designed to warm the air entering the carburetor when underhood temperatures are low. This allows more precise calibration of the carburetor.

The thermostatically-controlled air cleaner

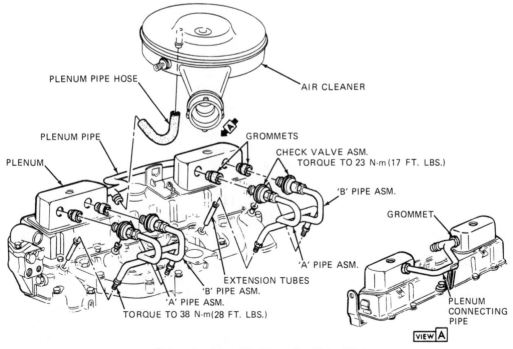

**Pulse air system (© Chevrolet Motor Div.)**

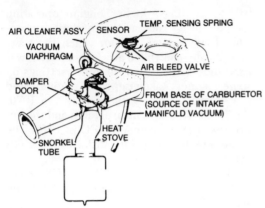

AIR CLEANER ASSY. / SENSOR — TEMP. SENSING SPRING

VACUUM DIAPHRAGM

AIR BLEED VALVE

DAMPER DOOR

FROM BASE OF CARBURETOR (SOURCE OF INTAKE MANIFOLD VACUUM)

HEAT STOVE

SNORKEL TUBE

**Thermostatically-controlled air cleaner case** (© Chevrolet Motor Div.)

is composed of the air cleaner body, a filter, sensor unit, vacuum diaphragm, damper door and associated hoses and connections. Heat radiating from the exhaust manifold is trapped by a heat stove and is ducted to the air cleaner to supply heated air to the carburetor. A moveable door in the air cleaner snorkel allows air to be drawn in from the heat stove (cold operation) or from the underhood air (warm operation). Periods of extended idling, climbing a grade or high-speed operation is followed by a considerable increase in engine compartment temperature. Excessive fuel vapors enter the intake manifold causing an over-rich mixture, resulting in a rough idle. To overcome this, some engines may be equipped with a hot idle compensator.

## SERVICE

1. Either start with a cold engine or remove the air cleaner from the engine for at least half an hour. While cooling the air cleaner, leave the engine compartment hood open.

2. Tape a thermometer, of known accuracy, to the inside of the air cleaner so that it is near the temperature sensor unit. Install the air cleaner on the engine but do not fasten its securing nut.

3. Start the engine. With the engine cold and the outside temperature less than 90° F., the door should be in the "heat on" position (closed to outside air).

NOTE: *Due to the position of the air cleaner on some trucks, a mirror may be necessary when observing the position of the air door.*

4. Operate the throttle lever rapidly to ½–¾ of its opening and release it. The air

door should open to allow outside air to enter and then close again.

5. Allow the engine to warm up to normal temperature. Watch the door. When it opens to the outside air, remove the cover from the air cleaner. The temperature should be over 90° F and no more than 130° F; 115° F is about normal. If the door does not work within these temperature ranges, or fails to work at all, check for linkage or door binding.

If binding is not present and the air door is not working, proceed with the vacuum tests, given below. If these indicate no faults in the vacuum motor and the door is not working, the temperature sensor is defective and must be replaced.

### Vacuum Motor Test

NOTE: *Be sure that the vacuum hose which runs between the temperature switch and the vacuum motor is not pinched by the retaining clip under the air cleaner. This could prevent the air door from closing.*

1. Check all of the vacuum lines and fittings for leaks. Correct any leaks. If none are found, proceed with the test.

2. Remove the hose which runs from the sensor to the vacuum motor. Run a hose directly from the manifold vacuum source to the vacuum motor.

3. If the motor closes the air door, it is functioning properly and the temperature sensor is defective.

4. If the motor does *not* close the door and no binding is present in its operation, the vacuum motor is defective and must be replaced.

NOTE: *If an alternate vacuum source is applied to the motor, insert a vacuum gauge in the line by using a T-fitting. Apply at least 9 in. Hg of vacuum in order to operate the motor.*

## Transmission Controlled Spark (TCS)

Introduced in 1970, this system controls exhaust emissions by eliminating vacuum advance in the lower forward gears.

The 1970 system consists of a transmission switch, solenoid vacuum switch, time delay relay, and a thermostatic water temperature switch. The solenoid vacuum switch is de-energized in the lower gears via the transmission switch and closes off distributor vacuum. The two-way transmission switch is activated by the shifter shaft on manual transmissions, and by oil pressure on automatic transmissions. The switch energizes the solenoid in High gear, the plunger extends and uncovers the vacuum port, and the distributor receives full vacuum. The temperature switch overrides the system, until the engine temperature reaches 82° F. This allows vacuum advance in all gears, thereby preventing stalling after starting. A time delay relay opens fifteen seconds after the ignition is switched on. Full vacuum advance during this delay eliminated the possibility of stalling.

The 1971 system is similar, except that the vacuum solenoid (now called a Combination Emissions Control solenoid) serves two functions. One function is to control distributor vacuum; the added function is to act as a deceleration throttle stop in High gear. This cuts down on emissions when the vehicle is coming to a stop in High gear. Two throttle settings are necessary; one for curb idle and one for emission control on coast. Both settings are described in the tune-up section.

The 1972 six cyl. system is similar to that used in 1971, except that an idle stop solenoid has been added to the system and the name is changed back to TCS. In the energized position, the solenoid maintains engine speed at a predetermined fast idle. When de-energized the solenoid allows the throttle plates to close beyond the normal idle position; thus cutting off the air supply and preventing engine run-on. The 6 is the only 1972 engine with a CEC valve, which serves the same deceleration function as in 1971. The time delay relay now delays full vacuum twenty seconds after the transmission is shifted into High gear. 1972 V8 engines use a vacuum advance solenoid similar to that used in 1970. The solenoid controls distributor vacuum advance and performs no throttle positioning function. The idle stop solenoid used on V8s operates in the same manner as the one on six cyl. engines. All air conditioned cars have an additional antidiesel (run-on) solenoid which engages the compressor clutch for three seconds after the ignition is switched off.

The 1973 TCS system on the six cyl. engine is identical to that on 1972 6, except for recalibration of the temperature switch. The system used on small block 1973 engines changed slightly from 1972. In place of the CEC solenoid on the 6, the V8 continues to use a vacuum advance solenoid. The other

differences are: the upshift delay relay, previously located under the instrument panel has been done away with; a 20 second time delay relay identical to the one on six cyl. engines is now used; small block V8s use manifold vacuum with TCS and ported vacuum without TCS.

The six cyl. TCS system was revised for 1974–75 by replacing the CEC solenoid with a vacuum advance solenoid. Otherwise the system remains the same as 1973.

## TESTING

If there is a TCS system malfunction, first connect a vacuum gauge in the hose between the solenoid valve and the distributor vacuum unit. Drive the vehicle or raise it on a frame lift and observe the vacuum gauge. If full vacuum is available in all gears, check for the following:

1. Blown fuse.
2. Disconnected wire at solenoid-operated vacuum valve.
3. Disconnected wire at transmission switch.
4. Temperature override switch energized due to low engine temperature.
5. Solenoid failure.

If no vacuum is available in any gear, check the following:

1. Solenoid valve vacuum lines switched.
2. Clogged solenoid vacuum valve.
3. Distributor or manifold vacuum lines leaking or disconnected.
4. Transmission switch or wire grounded.

Test for individual components are as follows:

### Idle Stop Solenoid

This unit may be checked simply by observing it while an assistant switches the ignition on and off. It should extend further with the current switched on. The unit is not repairable.

### Solenoid Vacuum Valve

Check that proper manifold vacuum is available. Connect the vacuum gauge in the line between the solenoid valve and the distributor. Apply 12 volts to the solenoid. If vacuum is still not available, the valve is defective, either mechanically or electrically. The unit is not repairable. If the valve is satisfactory, check the relay next.

### Relay

1. With the engine at normal operating temperature and the ignition on, ground the

solenoid vacuum valve terminal with the black lead. The solenoid should energize (no vacuum) if the relay is satisfactory.

2. With the solenoid energized as in Step 1, connect a jumper from the relay terminal with the green/white stripe lead to ground. The solenoid should deenergize (vacuum available) if the relay is satisfactory.

3. If the relay worked properly in Steps 1 and 2, check the temperature switch. The relay unit is not repairable.

### Temperature Switch

The vacuum valve solenoid should be de-energized (vacuum available) with the engine cold. If it is not, ground the green/white stripe wire from the switch. If the solenoid now de-energizes, replace the switch. If the switch was satisfactory, check the transmission switch.

### Transmission Switch

With the engine at normal operating temperature and the transmission in one of the no-vacuum gears, the vacuum valve solenoid should be energized (no vacuum). If not, remove and ground the switch electrical lead. If the solenoid energizes, replace the switch.

## Exhaust Gas Recirculation (EGR)

The EGR system and valve were introduced in 1973. Its purpose is to control oxides of nitrogen which are formed during the peak combustion temperatures. The end products of combustion are relatively inert gases derived from the exhaust gases which are directed into the EGR valve to help lower peak combustion temperatures.

The EGR valve contains a vacuum diaphragm operated by manifold vacuum. The vacuum signal port is located in the carburetor body and is exposed to engine vacuum in the off-idle, part-throttle, and wide-open throttle operation. In 1974, a thermo-delay switch was added to delay operation of the valve during engine warm-up, when $NO_x$ levels are already at a minimum.

There are actually three types of EGR systems: Vacuum Modulated, Positive Exhaust Backpressure Modulated, and Negative Exhaust Backpressure Modulated. The principle of all the systems is the same; the only difference is in the method used to control how far the EGR valve opens.

In the Vacuum Modulated system, which is used on all trucks through 1976, and some models thereafter, the amount of exhaust gas admitted into the intake manifold depends on a ported vacuum signal. A ported vacuum signal is one taken from the carburetor above the throttle plates. Thus, the vacuum signal (amount of vacuum) is dependent on how far the throttle plates are opened. When the throttle is closed (idle or deceleration) there is no vacuum signal. Thus, the EGR valve is closed, and no exhaust gas enters the intake manifold. As the throttle is opened, a vacuum is produced, which opens the EGR valve, admitting exhaust gas into the intake manifold.

In the Exhaust Backpressure Modulated system, a transducer is installed in the EGR valve body, reacting to either positive or negative backpressure, depending on design. The vacuum used is still ported vacuum, but the transducer uses exhaust gas backpressure to control an air bleed within the valve to modify this vacuum signal. Backpressure valves are used on all light duty emissions California and High Altitude engines in 1977 and 1978, and on most engines, 1979–80. The choice of either a positive or negative backpressure valve is determined by measurement of the engine's normal backpressure output. Negative valves are used on engines with relatively low backpressure; positive valves are used on engines with relatively high backpressure. The choice of valve usage is made at the factory, and is nothing

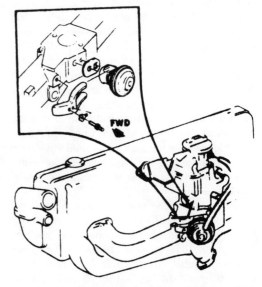

**Six cylinder EGR valve (© Chevrolet Motor Div.)**

The diesel EGR valve is installed in the air intake

Small block V8 EGR valve (© Chevrolet Motor Div.)

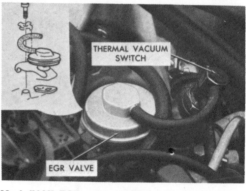

Mark IV V8 EGR valve (© Chevrolet Motor Div.)

for the backyard mechanic to worry about; however, if the valve is replaced, it is important to install the same type as the original. The difference between the three valves (ported, positive, or negative) can be determined by the shape of the diaphragm plate; your Chevrolet or GMC dealer will be able to match the old valve to a new one.

On six cylinder engines, the EGR valve is located on the intake manifold adjacent to the carburetor. On small block V8 engines, the valve is located on the right rear side of the intake manifold adjacent to the rocker arm cover. Mark IV V8 EGR valves are located in the left front corner of the intake manifold in front of the carburetor. The diesel engine EGR valve is located in the air intake in the intake manifold, and is visible when the air cleaner case cover is removed.

## SERVICE

The EGR valve is not serviceable, except for replacement. To check the ported vacuum signal valve, proceed as follows:

1. Connect a tachometer to the engine.

2. With the engine running at normal operating temperature, with the choke valve fully open, set the engine rpm at 2,000. The transmission should be in Park (automatic) or

Neutral (manual) with the parking brake on and the wheels blocked.

3. Disconnect the vacuum hose at the valve. Make sure that vacuum is available at the valve and look at the tachometer to see if the engine speed increases. If it does, a malfunction of the valve is indicated.

4. If necessary, replace the valve.

A back pressure EGR valve is used on all light duty emissions California and High Altitude six and V8 engines in 1977 and 1978, and most 1979–80 models.

The system can be tested as follows:

1. Remove air cleaner so that the EGR valve diaphragm movement can be observed. The choke secondary vacuum break TVS can be unclipped and removed from the air cleaner body, rather than removing hoses.

2. Plug the intake manifold air cleaner vacuum fitting. Connect a tachometer.

3. Start the engine and warm to operating temperature. Open the throttle part way and release. Watch or feel the EGR diaphragm for movement. The valve should open slightly when the throttle is opened and close when it is released.

4. Remove the EGR hose from the EGR valve and plug the hose. Place the carburetor cam follower on the second step of the fast idle cam and note the speed.

5. Attach a vacuum hose between the air cleaner vacuum fitting and the EGR valve. Note the speed change. The speed should drop at least 200 rpm with automatic transmissions, or at least 150 with manuals.

If the EGR valve does not meet the criteria specified in these tests, it must be replaced.

## Evaporation Control System (ECS)

Introduced on California vehicles in 1970, and nationwide in 1971, this system reduces the amount of escaping gasoline vapors. Float bowl emissions are controlled by internal carburetor modifications. Redesigned bowl vents, reduced bowl capacity, heat shields, and improved intake manifold-to-carburetor insulation serve to reduce vapor loss into the atmosphere. The venting of fuel tank vapors into the air has been stopped. Fuel vapors are now directed through lines to a canister containing an activated charcoal filter. Unburned vapors are trapped here until the

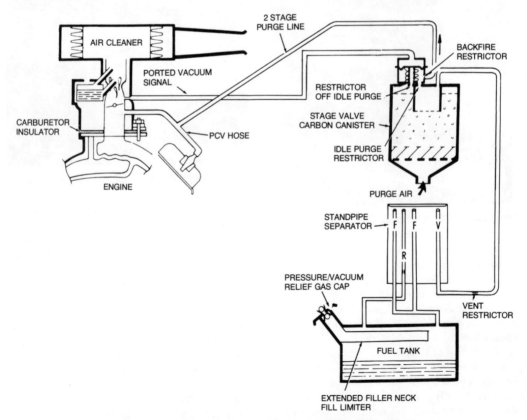

**Evaporation Control System (ECS) (© Chevrolet Motor Div.)**

engine is started. When the engine is running, the canister is purged by air drawn in by manifold vacuum. The air and fuel vapors are directed into the engine to be burned.

### SERVICE

Replace the filter in the engine compartment canister as specified in the "Maintenance Intervals Chart" in Chapter 1. If the fuel tank cap requires replacement, ensure that the new cap is the correct part for your truck.

## Early Fuel Evaporation System (EFE)

The six cylinder and 1975 Mark IV V8 EFE systems consist of an EFE valve mounted at the flange of the exhaust manifold, and actuator, a thermal vacuum switch (TVS) and a vacuum solenoid. The TVS is located on the right-hand side of the engine forward of the oil pressure switch on six cyl. engines and directly above the oil filter on the Mark IV V8. The TVS is normally closed and sensitive to oil temperature.

The small block V8 and 1976 and later Mark IV EFE system consists of an EFE valve at the flange of the exhaust manifold, an actuator, and a thermal vacuum switch. The TVS is located in the coolant outlet housing and directly controls vacuum.

In both systems, manifold vacuum is applied to the actuator, which in turn, closes the EFE valve. This routes hot exhaust gases to the base of the carburetor. When coolant or oil temperatures reach a set limit, vacuum is denied to the actuator allowing an internal

spring to return the actuator to its normal position, opening the EFE valve.

## Throttle Return Control System (TRC)

Two different throttle return control systems are used. The first is used from 1975 to 1978 (consult the chart earlier in this chapter for specific applications). It consists of a control valve and a throttle lever actuator. When the truck is coasting against the engine, the control valve is open to allow vacuum to operate the throttle lever actuator. The throttle lever actuator then pushes the throttle lever slightly open reducing the HC (hydrocarbon) emission level during coasting. When manifold vacuum drops below a predetermined level, the control valve closes, the throttle lever retracts, and the throttle lever closes to the idle position.

The second TRC system is used in 1979 and 1980. It consists of a throttle lever actuator, a solenoid vacuum control valve, and an electronic speed sensor. The throttle lever actuator, mounted on the carburetor, opens the primary throttle plates a preset amount, above normal engine idle speed, in response to a signal from the solenoid vacuum control valve. The valve, mounted at the left rear of the engine above the intake manifold on the six cylinder, or on the thermostat housing mounting stud on the V8, is held open in response to a signal from the electronic speed sensor. When open, the valve allows a vacuum signal to be sent to the throttle lever actuator. The speed sensor monitors engine speed at the distributor. It supplies an electrical signal to the solenoid valve, as long as a preset engine speed is exceeded. The object of this system is the same as that of the earlier system.

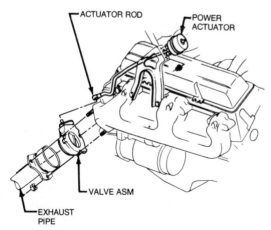

**Typical EFE valve installation (© Chevrolet Motor Div.)**

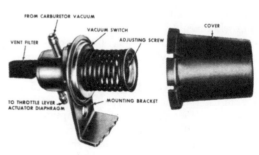

**Throttle return control valve through 1978 (© Chevrolet Motor Div.)**

*SERVICE*

**Control Valve**

*1975–76*

1. Disconnect the valve-to-carburetor hose and connect it to an external vacuum source with a vacuum gauge.

2. Disconnect the valve-to-actuator hose at the connector and connect it to a vacuum gauge.

3. Place a finger firmly over the end of the bleed fitting.

4. Apply a minimum of 23 in. Hg vacuum to the control valve and seal off the vacuum source. The gauge on the actuator side should read the same as the gauge on the source side. If not, the valve needs adjustment. If vacuum drops off on either side (with the finger still on the bleed fitting), the valve is defective and should be replaced.

5. With a minimum of 23 in. Hg vacuum in the valve, remove the finger from the bleed fitting. The vacuum level in the actuator side will drop to zero and the reading on the source side will drop to a value that will be the value set point. If the value is not within ½ in. Hg vacuum of the specified valve set point, adjust the valve.

6. Gently pry off the conical plastic cover.

7. Turn the adjusting screw in (clockwise) to raise the set point or out (counterclockwise) to lower the set point.

8. Recheck the valve set point.

9. If necessary, repeat the adjustment until the valve set point is attained ±½ in. Hg. vacuum.

*1977–78*

1. Disconnect the valve-to-carburetor hose at the carburetor. Connect the hose to an external vacuum source, with an accurate vacuum gauge connected into the line near the valve.

2. Apply a minimum of 25 in. Hg. of vacuum to the control valve vacuum supply fitting while sealing off the vacuum supply between the gauge and the vacuum source. The vacuum gauge will indicate the set point value of the valve.

3. If the gauge reading is not within 0.5 in. Hg. of the specified value (see the chart), the valve must be adjusted. If the trapped vacuum drops off faster than 0.1 in. Hg. per second, the valve is leaking and must be replaced.

4. To adjust the valve set point, follow

## TRS Control Valve Set Points

| Engine | Set Point (in. Hg) |
|---|---|
| 292 | 22.5 |
| 305 | 22.5 |
| 350 | 21.5 |
| 400 | 21.5 |
| 454 (1975–76) | 21.0 |
| 454 (1977–78) | 23.0 |

## TRC Speed

| Engine | Setting (rpm) |
|---|---|
| 292 | 1600 |
| 305 | 1600 |
| 350 | 1500 |
| 400 | 1500 |
| 454 (1975–76) | 1400 |
| 454 (1977–78) | 1500 |

Steps 6–9 of the 1975–76 adjustment procedure.

**Throttle Valve**

*1975–78*

1. Disconnect the valve-to-actuator hose at the valve and connect it to an external vacuum source.

2. Apply 20 in. Hg vacuum to the actuator and seal the vacuum source. If the vacuum gauge reading drops, the valve is leaking and should be replaced.

3. Check the throttle lever, shaft, and linkage for freedom of operation.

4. Start the engine and warm it to operating temperature.

5. Note the idle rpm.

6. Apply 20 in. Hg vacuum to the actuator and manually operate the throttle. Allow it to close against the extended actuator plunger. Note the engine rpm.

7. Release and reapply 20 in. Hg vacuum to the actuator and note the rpm at which engine speed increases (do not assist the actuator).

8. If the engine speed obtained in Step 7 is not within 150 rpm of that obtained in Step 6, then the actuator may be binding,. If the binding cannot be corrected, replace the actuator.

9. Release the vacuum from the actuator

and the engine speed should return to within 50 rpm of the speed noted in Steps 4 and 5.

To adjust the actuator:

10. Turn the screw on the actuator plunger until the specified TRC speed range is obtained.

### TRC System Check

*1979–80*

1. Connect a tachometer to the distributor "TACH" terminal. Start the engine and raise the engine speed to 1890 rpm. The throttle lever actuator on the carburetor should extend.

2. Reduce the engine speed to 1700 rpm. The lever actuator should retract.

3. If the actuator operates outside of the speed limits, the speed switch is faulty and must be replaced. It cannot be adjusted.

4. If the actuator does not operate at all:

a. Check for voltage at the vacuum solenoid and the speed switch with a voltmeter. Connect the negative probe of the voltmeter to the engine ground and the positive probe to the voltage source wire on the component. The positive probe can be inserted on the connector body at the wire side; it is not necessary to unplug the connector. Voltage should be 12 to 14 volts in both cases.

b. If the correct voltage is present at one component but not the other, the engine wiring harness is faulty.

c. If voltage is not present at all, check the engine harness connections at the distributor and the bulkhead connector and repair as necessary.

d. If the correct voltage is present at both components, check the solenoid operation: ground the solenoid-to-speed switch connecting wire terminal at the solenoid connector with a jumper wire. This should cause the throttle lever actuator to extend, with the engine running.

e. If the lever actuator does not extend, remove the hose from the solenoid side port which connects to the actuator hose. Check the port for obstructions or blockage. If the port is not plugged, replace the solenoid.

f. If the actuator extends in Step d, ground the solenoid-to-speed switch wire terminal at the switch. If the actuator does not extend, the wire between the speed switch and the solenoid is open and must be repaired. If the actuator does extend, check the speed switch ground wire for a

ground; it should read zero volts with the engine running. Check the speed switch-to-distributor wire for a proper connection. If the ground and distributor wires are properly connected and the actuator still does not extend when the engine speed is above 1890 rpm, replace the speed switch.

5. If the actuator is extended at all speeds:

a. Remove the connector from the vacuum solenoid.

b. If the actuator remains extended, check the solenoid side port orifice for blockage. If plugged, clear and reconnect the system and recheck. If the actuator is still extended, remove the solenoid connector; if the actuator does not retract, replace the vacuum solenoid.

c. If the actuator retracts with the solenoid connector off, reconnect it and remove the speed switch connector. If the actuator retracts, the problem is in the speed switch, which should be replaced. If the actuator does not retract, the solenoid-to-speed switch wire is shorted to ground in the wiring harness. Repair the short.

### Throttle Lever Actuator

*1979–80*

The checking procedure is the same as for earlier years. Follow Steps 1–9 of the "Throttle Valve" procedure. Adjustment procedures are covered in the carburetor adjustments section, later in this chapter.

## Oxidizing Catalytic Converter (CAT)

Starting 1975 an underfloor oxidizing catalytic converter is used to control hydrocarbon and carbon monoxide emissions on some models. Control is accomplished by placing a catalyst in the exhaust system in such a way as to enable all exhaust gas flow from the engine to pass through it and undergo a chemical reaction before passing into the atmosphere. The chemical reaction involved is the oxidizing of hydrocarbons and carbon monoxide into water vapor and carbon dioxide.

### REMOVAL AND INSTALLATION

WARNING: *Catalytic converter operating temperatures are extremely high. Outside converter temperatures can go well over 1,000°F. Use extreme care when working*

## Basic Emission Control System Checks

| System | Condition | Check(s) |
|---|---|---|
| Positive Crankcase Ventilation | Oil leaks, Rough idle | Plugged system Improper hose routing |
| Air Injector Reactor | Noise | Loose belt or hose Worn pump Diverter valve stuck open Misaligned pump Improper hose mounting |
| | "Pop" on deceleration | Diverter valve stuck closed |
| Controlled Combustion System | Rough idle, stumble or stall | Vacuum hose leak Air cleaner damper stuck:    Defective thermostat    Defective vacuum diaphragm General tune-up |
| Transmission Controlled Spark/ Combined Emission Control | Rough idle, stumble or stall Dieseling Poor fuel economy No vacuum advance | Vacuum leak Idle stop solenoid stuck ① Vacuum solenoid stuck ① Relay, transmission and temperature   switch operation ① |
| Carburetor Heated Air | Rough idle, stumble or stall | Vacuum hose leak Air cleaner damper stuck:    Defective thermostat    Defective vacuum diaphragm |
| Exhaust Gas Recirculation | Rough idle, stumble or stall | Corroded valve shaft Defective valve diaphragm |
| Evaporative Emission Control | Fuel odor Bulged or collapsed fuel tank | Leak in the fuel system Missing, plugged or incorrect gas cap Incorrect hose routing Plugged line or separator |

① Use a test wire from the battery to the solenoid or switch to check for mechanical movement

on the catalytic converter or when working anywhere around it.

1. Raise and support the truck.

2. Remove the clamps at the front and rear of the converter.

3. Cut the converter pipes at the front and rear of the converter and remove it.

4. Remove the support from the transmission or transfer case.

5. Remove the converter pipe-to-exhaust pipe and the converter pipe-to-tailpipe.

To install the converter:

6. Install the exhaust pipe and tailpipe into the converter with sealer.

7. Loosely install the support on the transmission or transfer case.

8. Install new U-bolts and clamps, check all clearances and tighten the clamps.

9. Lower the truck.

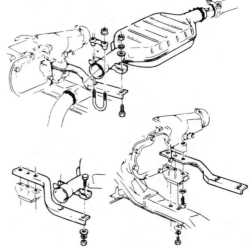

**Catalytic converter—C-10 and C-1500 (© Chevrolet Motor Div.)**

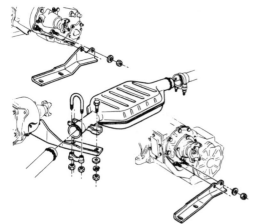

Catalytic converter—K-10 and K-1500 (© Chevrolet Motor Div.)

## Trapped Vacuum Spark System (TVSS)

This system is used to prevent a drop in vacuum to the distributor vacuum advance during cold engine operation, when the engine is accelerating. A thermal vacuum switch (TVS) is used to sense engine coolant temperature. A check valve is installed in the vacuum line to the distributor. The other side of the check valve has two connections: one to manifold vacuum (at the carburetor base), and the other to the thermal vacuum switch.

When the engine is cold, the TVS vacuum ports are closed. Manifold vacuum is routed through the check valve to the distributor. The check valve keeps the vacuum to the distributor at a high vacuum level, so that when the engine is accelerated, the vacuum to the distributor does not drop. This results in a constant spark advance.

When the engine temperature reaches a predetermined value, the TVS ports open to allow manifold vacuum to the distributor, and the check valve operates only as a connector.

## FUEL SYSTEM

### Mechanical Fuel Pump

The fuel pump is a single action AC diaphragm type. All fuel pumps used on inline and V8 engines in trucks are diaphragm type and because of design are serviced by replacement only. No adjustments or repairs are possible.

The pump is operated by an eccentric on the camshaft on gasoline engines, or on the crankshaft on diesels. On six cylinder and diesel V8 engines, the eccentric acts directly on the pump rocker arm. On V8 gasoline engines, a pushrod between the camshaft eccentric and the fuel pump operates the pump rocker arm.

Some trucks have a fuel pump which has a metering outlet for a vapor return system. Any vapor which forms is returned to the fuel tank along with hot fuel through a separate line. This greatly reduces any possibility of vapor lock by keeping cool fuel from the tank constantly circulating through the fuel pump.

### TESTING THE FUEL PUMP

Fuel pumps should always be tested on the vehicle. The larger line between the pump and tank is the suction side of the system and the smaller line, between the pump and carburetor or fuel injection pump is the pressure side. A leak in the pressure side would be apparent because of dripping fuel. A leak in the suction side is usually only apparent because of a reduced volume of fuel delivered to the pressure side.

1. Tighten any loose line connections and look for any kinks or restrictions.

2. Disconnect the fuel line at the carburetor or fuel injection pump. Disconnect the distributor-to-coil primary wire (gasoline engines). Place a container at the end of the fuel line and crank the engine a few revolutions. If little or no fuel flows from the line, either the fuel pump is inoperative or the line is plugged. Blow through the lines with compressed air and try the test again. Reconnect the line.

3. If fuel flows in good volume, check the fuel pump pressure to be sure (pressure tests are possible only on gasoline engines).

4. Attach a pressure gauge to the pressure side of the fuel line. On trucks equipped with a vapor return system, squeeze off the return hose.

5. Run the engine at idle and note the reading on the gauge. Stop the engine and compare the reading with the specifications listed in the "Tune-Up Specifications" chart. If the pump is operating properly, the pressure will be as specified and will be constant at idle speed. If pressure varies sporadically or is too high or low, the pump should be replaced.

6. Remove the pressure gauge.

The following flow test can also be performed:

1. Disconnect fuel line from carburetor or fuel injection pump. Run fuel line into a suitable measuring container.

2. Run the engine at idle until there is one pint of fuel in the container. One pint should be pumped in 30 seconds or less.

3. If flow is below minimum, check for a restriction in the line.

The only way to check fuel pump pressure is by connecting an accurate pressure gauge to the fuel line at the carburetor level. Never replace a fuel pump without performing this simple test. If the engine seems to be starving out, check the ignition system first. Also check for a plugged fuel filter or a restricted fuel line before replacing the pump.

### REMOVAL AND INSTALLATION

NOTE: *When you connect the fuel pump outlet fitting, always use two wrenches to avoid damaging the pump.*

1. Disconnect the fuel intake and outlet lines at the pump and plug the pump intake line.

2. On small-block V8 engines, remove the upper bolt from the right front mounting

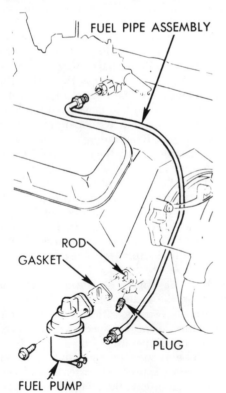

FUEL PIPE ASSEMBLY

ROD

GASKET

PLUG

FUEL PUMP

Mark IV fuel pump installation; other engines similar (© Chevrolet Motor Div.)

boss. Insert a long bolt (⅜–16 x 2 in.) in this hole to hold the fuel pump pushrod.

3. Remove the two pump mounting bolts and lockwashers; remove the pump and its gasket.

4. If the rocker arm pushrod is to be removed from gasoline V8s, remove the two adapter bolts and lockwashers and remove the adapter and its gasket from small blocks and remove the pipe plug and pushrod from 454 cu in. engines.

5. Install the fuel pump with a new gasket reversing the removal procedure. Coat the mating surfaces with sealer. Heavy grease can be used to hold the fuel pump pushrod up while installing the pump.

6. Connect the fuel lines and check for leaks.

## Carburetor
### REMOVAL AND INSTALLATION

1. Remove the air cleaner and its gasket.

2. Disconnect the fuel and vacuum lines from the carburetor.

3. Disconnect the choke coil rod or heated air line tube.

4. Disconnect the throttle linkage.

5. On automatic transmission trucks, disconnect the throttle valve linkage.

6. Remove the CEC valve vacuum hose and electrical connector.

7. Remove the idle stop electrical wiring from the idle stop solenoid, if so equipped.

8. Remove the carburetor attaching nuts and/or bolts, gasket or insulator, and remove the carburetor.

9. Install the carburetor using a reverse of the removal procedure. Use a new gasket and fill the float bowl with gasoline to ease starting the engine.

### IDENTIFICATION

Carburetor identification numbers will generally be found in the following locations:

1 MV, ME: Stamped on the vertical portion of the float bowl, adjacent to the fuel inlet nut.

2 GV, GC: Stamped on the flat section of the float bowl next to the fuel inlet nut.

2SE: Stamped on the vertical surface of the float bowl adjacent to the vacuum tube.

M2MC: Stamped on the vertical surface of the left rear corner of the float bowl.

4 MV, M4MC, M4ME: Stamped on the vertical section of the float bowl, near the secondary throttle lever.

### OVERHAUL

Efficient carburetion depends greatly on careful cleaning and inspection during overhaul, since dirt, gum, water, or varnish in or on the carburetor parts are often responsible for poor performance.

Overhaul your carburetor in a clean, dust-free area. Carefully disassemble the carburetor, referring often to the exploded views and directions packaged with the rebuilding kit. Keep all similar and look-alike parts segregated during disassembly and cleaning to avoid accidental interchange during assembly. Make a note of all jet sizes.

When the carburetor is disassembled, wash all parts (except diaphragms, electric choke units, pump plunger, and any other plastic, leather, fiber, or rubber parts) in clean carburetor solvent. Do not leave parts in the solvent any longer than is necessary to sufficiently loosen the deposits. Excessive cleaning may remove the special finish from the float bowl and choke valve bodies, leaving these parts unfit for service. Rinse all parts in clean solvent, and blow them dry with compressed air or allow them to air dry. Wipe clean all cork, plastic, leather, and fiber parts with a clean, lint-free cloth.

Blow out all passages and jets with compressed air and be sure that there are no restrictions or blockages. Never use wire or similar tools to clean jets, fuel passages, or air bleeds. Clean all jets and valves separately to avoid accidental interchange.

Check all parts for wear or damage. If wear or damage is found, replace the defective parts. Especially check the following:

1. Check the float needle and seat for wear. If wear is found, replace the complete assembly.

2. Check the float hinge pin for wear and the float(s) for dents or distortion. Replace the float if fuel has leaked into it.

3. Check the throttle and choke shaft bores for wear or an out-of-round condition. Damage or wear to the throttle arm, shaft, or shaft bore will often require replacement of the throttle body. These parts require a close tolerance of it; wear may allow air leakage, which could affect starting and idling.

NOTE: *Throttle shafts and bushings are not included in overhaul kits. They can be purchased separately.*

4. Inspect the idle mixture adjusting needles for burrs or grooves. Any such condition requires replacement of the needle,

since you will not be able to obtain a satisfactory idle.

5. Test the accelerator pump check valves. They should pass air one way but not the other. Test for proper seating by blowing and sucking on the valve. Replace the valve as necessary. If the valve is satisfactory, wash the valve again to remove breath moisture.

6. Check the bowl cover for warped surfaces with a straightedge.

7. Closely inspect the valves and seats for wear and damage, replacing as necessary.

8. After the carburetor is assembled, check the choke valve for freedom of operation.

Carburetor overhaul kits are recommended for each overhaul. These kits contain all gaskets and new parts to replace those which deteriorate most rapidly. Failure to replace all parts supplied with the kit (especially gaskets) can result in poor performance later.

Some carburetor manufacturers supply overhaul kits of three basic types: minor repair; major repair; and gasket kits.

After cleaning and checking all components, reassemble the carburetor, using new parts and referring to the exploded view. When reassembling, make sure that all screws and jets are tight in their seats, but do not overtighten as the tips will be distorted. Tighten all screws gradually, in rotation. Do not tighten needle valves into their seats; uneven jetting will result. Always use new gaskets. Be sure to adjust the float level when reassembling.

## Carburetor Adjustments

The following chart gives the various carburetor applications. Determine which carburetor you are dealing with and refer to the following sections for adjustments. Adjustments are divided by carburetor type.

### PRELIMINARY CHECKS (ALL CARBURETORS)

The following should be observed before attempting any adjustments.

1. Thoroughly warm the engine. If the engine is cold, be sure that it reaches operating temperature.

2. Check the torque of all carburetor mounting nuts. Also check the intake manifold-to-cylinder head bolts. If air is leaking at any of these points, any attempts at adjustment will inevitably lead to frustration.

## Carburetor Applications

| Year | Engine | Carburetor |
|------|--------|-----------|
| 1970 | 6—250 | Rochester MV |
| | 6—292 | Rochester MV |
| | V8—307 | Rochester 2GV (1¼) |
| | V8—350 | Rochester 4MV (Quadrajet) |
| | V8—396 | Rochester 4MV (Quadrajet) |
| 1971 | 6—250 | Rochester MV |
| | 6—292 | Rochester MV |
| | V8—307 | Rochester 2GV |
| | V8—350 | Rochester 4MV (Quadrajet) |
| | V8—402 | Rochester 4MV (Quadrajet) |
| 1972 | 6—250 | Rochester MV |
| | 6—292 | Rochester MV |
| | V8—307 | Rochester 2GV |
| | V8—350 | Rochester 4MV (Quadrajet) |
| | V8—402 | Rochester 4MV (Quadrajet) |
| 1973 | 6—250 | Rochester MV |
| | 6—292 | Rochester MV |
| | V8—307 | Rochester 2GV |
| | V8—350 | Rochester 4MV (Quadrajet) |
| | V8—454 | Rochester 4MV (Quadrajet) |
| 1974 | 6—250 | Rochester MV |
| | 6—292 | Rochester MV |
| | V8—350 | Rochester 2GV |
| | V8—350 | Rochester 4MV (Quadrajet) |
| | V8—454 | Rochester 4MV (Quadrajet) |
| 1975 | 6—250 | Rochester MV |
| | 6—292 | Rochester MV |
| | V8—350 | Rochester 2GC (C-10, 1500 only) |
| | V8—350 | Rochester M4MC (C-10, 1500 only) |
| | V8—350 | Rochester 4MV (Quadrajet) (CK-10, 1500, 20, 2500) |
| | V8—400 | Rochester 4MV (Quadrajet) (K10, 1500, 20, 2500) |
| | V8—454 | Rochester 4MV (Quadrajet) (C-10, 1500, 20, 2500) |
| | V8—454 | Rochester M4MC (C-10, 1500 only) |
| | V8—454 | Rochester M4MCA (C-10, 1500, 20, 2500) |
| 1976 | 6—250 | Rochester MV |
| | 6—292 | Rochester MV |
| | V8—350 | Rochester 2GC (C-10, 1500 only) |
| | V8—350 | Rochester 4MVMC (C-10, 1500, 20, 2500 only) |
| | V8—350 | Rochester 4MV (Quadrajet) (HD only) |
| | V8—400 | Rochester 4MV (Quadrajet) (K-10, 1500, 20, 2500 only) |
| | V8—454 | Rochester M4ME (C-10, 1500 only) |
| | V8—454 | Rochester 4MV (Quadrajet) (C-10, 1500 HD, C-20, 2500 HD only) |

## Carburetor Applications

| Year | Engine | Carburetor |
|------|--------|-----------|
| | V8—454 | Rochester M4MC (C-10, 1500, 20, 2500 HD California only) |
| 1977– 1978 | 6—250 | Rochester ME |
| | 6—292 | Rochester ME |
| | V8—305 | Rochester 2GC |
| | V8—350 | Rochester M4MC (C-10, 1500 only) |
| | V8—350 | Rochester 4MV/M4MC |
| | V8—400 | Rochester M4MC (K-10, 1500, 20, 2500 only) |
| | V8—454 | Rochester M4ME (C-10, 1500 only) |
| | V8—454 | Rochester 4MV/M4MC (C-20, 2500 only) |
| 1979– 1980 | 6—250 | Rochester 2SE |
| | 6—292 | Rochester 1ME |
| | 8—305 | Rochester M2MC |
| | 8—350 | Rochester M4MC |
| | 8—400 | Rochester M4MC |
| | 8—454 | Rochester M4MC |

3. Check the manifold heat control valve (if used) to be sure that it is free.

4. Check and adjust the choke as necessary.

5. Adjust the idle speed and mixture. If any adjustments are performed that might possibly change the idle speed or mixture, adjust the idle and mixture again when you are finished.

### ROCHESTER MV (1970–74)

#### Fast Idle

NOTE: *The fast idle adjustment must be made with the transmission in Neutral.*

1. Position the fast idle lever on the high step of the fast idle cam.

2. Be sure that the choke is properly adjusted and in the wide open position with the engine warm. Disconnect the vacuum advance on 1974 manual transmission models.

3. Bend the fast idle lever until the specified speed is obtained.

#### Choke Rod (Fast Idle Cam)

NOTE: *Adjust the fast idle before making choke rod adjustments.*

1. Place the fast idle cam follower on the second step of the fast idle cam and hold it firmly against the rise to the high step.

2. Rotate the choke valve in the direction

of a closed choke by applying force to the choke coil lever.

3. Bend the choke rod, at the point shown in the illustration, to give the specified opening between the lower edge of the choke valve and the inside air horn wall.

NOTE: *Measurement must be made at the center of the choke valve.*

### Choke Vacuum Break

The adjustment of the vacuum break diaphragm unit insures correct choke valve opening after engine starting.

1. Remove the air cleaner on vehicles with Therm AC air cleaner; plug the sensor's vacuum take off port.

2. Using an external vacuum source, apply vacuum to the vacuum break diaphragm until the plunger is fully seated.

3. When the plunger is seated, push the choke valve toward the closed position.

4. Holding the choke valve in this position, place the specified gauge between the lower edge of the choke valve and the air horn wall.

5. If the measurement is not correct, bend the vacuum break rod at the point shown in the illustration.

### Choke Unloader

1. Apply pressure to the choke valve and hold it in the closed position.

2. Open the throttle valve to the wide open position.

3. Check the dimension between the lower edge of the choke plate and the air horn wall; if adjustment is needed, bend the unloader tang on the throttle lever to adjust to specification.

### Choke Coil Rod

1. Disconnect the coil rod from the upper choke lever and hold the choke valve closed.

2. Push down on the coil rod to the end of its travel.

3. The top of the rod should be even with the bottom hole in the choke lever.

4. To make adjustments, bend the rod at the point shown in the illustration.

### Float

1. Hold the float retainer in place and the float arm against the top of the float needle by pushing down on the float arm at the outer end toward the float bowl casting.

2. Using an adjustable T scale, measure the distance from the toe of the float to the float bowl gasket surface.

NOTE: *The float bowl gasket should be removed and the gauge held on the index point on the float for accurate measurement.*

3. Adjust the float level by bending the float arm up or down at the float arm junction.

### Metering Rod

1. Hold the throttle valve wide-open and push down on the metering rod against spring tension, then remove the rod from the main metering jet.

2. In order to check adjustment, the slow idle screw must be backed out and the fast idle cam rotated so that the fast idle cam follower does not contact the steps on the cam.

3. With the throttle valve closed, push down on the power piston until it contacts its stop.

4. With the power piston depressed, swing the metering rod holder over the flat surface of the bowl casting next to the carburetor bore.

5. Insert a specified size drill between the bowl casting sealing bead and the lower surface of the metering rod holder. The drill should slide smoothly between both surfaces.

6. If adjustment is needed, carefully bend the metering rod holder up or down at the point shown. After adjustment, reinstall the metering rod.

### C.E.C. Solenoid Adjustment

Do not set the C.E.C. valve to the idle rpm. This adjustment should only be made after replacement of the solenoid, carburetor overhaul, or after the throttle body is replaced.

1. With the engine running, and transmission in Neutral (manual) or Drive (Automatic), air conditioner OFF, distributor vacuum hose removed and plugged, and fuel tank vapor hose disconnected, manually extend the C.E.C. valve plunger to contact the throttle lever.

2. Adjust the plunger length to obtain the C.E.C. valve rpm.

3. Reconnect the vapor hose and vacuum hose.

### *ROCHESTER MV (1975–76), ME (1977–80)*

### Fast Idle

1. Check and adjust the idle speed.

2. With the engine at normal operating temperature, air cleaner ON, EGR valve sig-

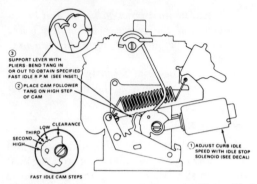

**MV fast idle adjustment (© Chevrolet Motor Div.)**

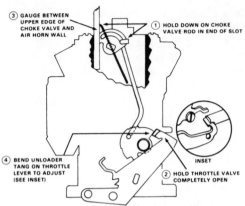

**MV choke unloader adjustment (© Chevrolet Motor Div.)**

nal line disconnected and plugged and the air conditioning OFF, connect a tachometer.

3. Disconnect the vacuum advance hose at the distributor and plug the line.

4. With the transmission in Neutral, start the engine and set the fast idle cam follower on the high step of the cam.

5. Bend the tang in or out to obtain the fast idle speed.

### Fast Idle Cam

1. Check and adjust the fast idle speed.

2. Set the fast idle cam follower on the second step of the cam.

3. Apply force to the choke coil rod and hold the choke valve toward the closed position.

4. Measure the clearance between the lower edge of the choke valve and the inside of the air horn wall. For 1976–77, insert the gauge between the upper edge of the choke valve and the inside of the air horn wall.

5. Bend the cam to choke rod to obtain clearance.

### Choke Unloader

1. Hold the choke valve down by applying light force to the choke coil lever.

2. Open the throttle valve to wide open.

3. Measure the clearance between the upper edge of the choke valve and the air horn wall. Measure at the lower edge of the choke valve on 1978–80 models only.

4. If adjustment is necessary, bend the tang on the throttle lever.

### Choke Coil Rod—1975

1. Pull the rod up to the end of its travel to completely close the choke valve.

2. The bottom of the rod should be even with the top of the lever.

3. If adjustment is necessary, bend the rod.

### 1976

1. Disconnect the upper end of the choke coil rod at the choke valve.

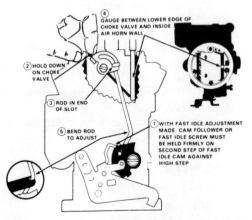

**MV fast idle cam adjustment (© Chevrolet Motor Div.)**

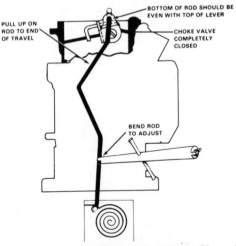

**MV choke coil rod adjustment—1975 (© Chevrolet Motor Div.)**

## Rochester MV Adjustments

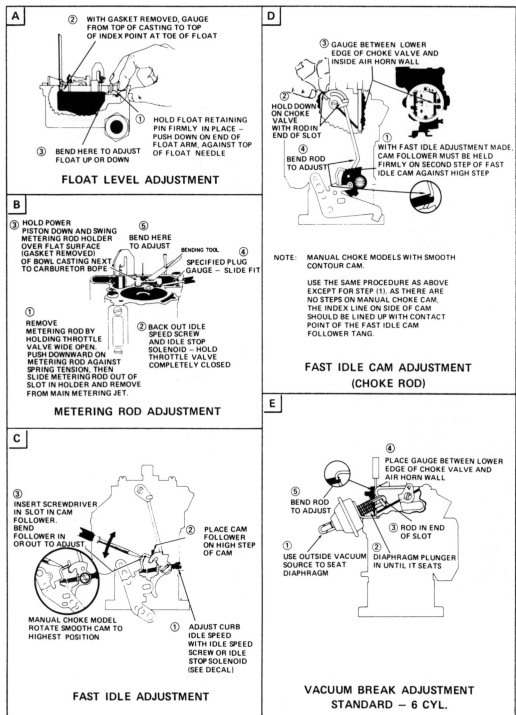

**A**

② WITH GASKET REMOVED, GAUGE FROM TOP OF CASTING TO TOP OF INDEX POINT AT TOE OF FLOAT

① HOLD FLOAT RETAINING PIN FIRMLY IN PLACE — PUSH DOWN ON END OF FLOAT ARM, AGAINST TOP OF FLOAT NEEDLE

③ BEND HERE TO ADJUST FLOAT UP OR DOWN

### FLOAT LEVEL ADJUSTMENT

**B**

③ HOLD POWER PISTON DOWN AND SWING METERING ROD HOLDER OVER FLAT SURFACE (GASKET REMOVED) OF BOWL CASTING NEXT TO CARBURETOR BOPE

⑤ BEND HERE TO ADJUST

BENDING TOOL

④ SPECIFIED PLUG GAUGE — SLIDE FIT

① REMOVE METERING ROD BY HOLDING THROTTLE VALVE WIDE OPEN. PUSH DOWNWARD ON METERING ROD AGAINST SPRING TENSION, THEN SLIDE METERING ROD OUT OF SLOT IN HOLDER AND REMOVE FROM MAIN METERING JET.

② BACK OUT IDLE SPEED SCREW AND IDLE STOP SOLENOID — HOLD THROTTLE VALVE COMPLETELY CLOSED

### METERING ROD ADJUSTMENT

**C**

③ INSERT SCREWDRIVER IN SLOT IN CAM FOLLOWER. BEND FOLLOWER IN OR OUT TO ADJUST.

② PLACE CAM FOLLOWER ON HIGH STEP OF CAM

MANUAL CHOKE MODEL ROTATE SMOOTH CAM TO HIGHEST POSITION

① ADJUST CURB IDLE SPEED WITH IDLE SPEED SCREW OR IDLE STOP SOLENOID (SEE DECAL)

### FAST IDLE ADJUSTMENT

**D**

③ GAUGE BETWEEN LOWER EDGE OF CHOKE VALVE AND INSIDE AIR HORN WALL

② HOLD DOWN ON CHOKE VALVE WITH ROD IN END OF SLOT

④ BEND ROD TO ADJUST

① WITH FAST IDLE ADJUSTMENT MADE, CAM FOLLOWER MUST BE HELD FIRMLY ON SECOND STEP OF FAST IDLE CAM AGAINST HIGH STEP

NOTE:    MANUAL CHOKE MODELS WITH SMOOTH CONTOUR CAM.

USE THE SAME PROCEDURE AS ABOVE EXCEPT FOR STEP (1). AS THERE ARE NO STEPS ON MANUAL CHOKE CAM, THE INDEX LINE ON SIDE OF CAM SHOULD BE LINED UP WITH CONTACT POINT OF THE FAST IDLE CAM FOLLOWER TANG.

### FAST IDLE CAM ADJUSTMENT
### (CHOKE ROD)

**E**

④ PLACE GAUGE BETWEEN LOWER EDGE OF CHOKE VALVE AND AIR HORN WALL

⑤ BEND ROD TO ADJUST

③ ROD IN END OF SLOT

① USE OUTSIDE VACUUM SOURCE TO SEAT DIAPHRAGM

② DIAPHRAGM PLUNGER IN UNTIL IT SEATS

### VACUUM BREAK ADJUSTMENT
### STANDARD — 6 CYL.

(© Chevrolet Motor Div.)

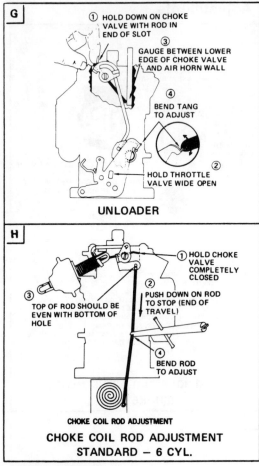

**G**
① HOLD DOWN ON CHOKE VALVE WITH ROD IN END OF SLOT
③ GAUGE BETWEEN LOWER EDGE OF CHOKE VALVE AND AIR HORN WALL
④ BEND TANG TO ADJUST
② HOLD THROTTLE VALVE WIDE OPEN

**UNLOADER**

**H**
① HOLD CHOKE VALVE COMPLETELY CLOSED
② PUSH DOWN ON ROD TO STOP (END OF TRAVEL)
③ TOP OF ROD SHOULD BE EVEN WITH BOTTOM OF HOLE
④ BEND ROD TO ADJUST

CHOKE COIL ROD ADJUSTMENT

**CHOKE COIL ROD ADJUSTMENT STANDARD – 6 CYL.**

(© Chevrolet Motor Div.)

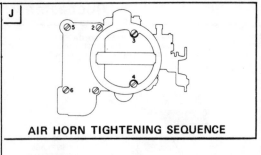

**J**

**AIR HORN TIGHTENING SEQUENCE**

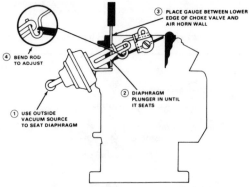

③ PLACE GAUGE BETWEEN LOWER EDGE OF CHOKE VALVE AND AIR HORN WALL
④ BEND ROD TO ADJUST
② DIAPHRAGM PLUNGER IN UNTIL IT SEATS
① USE OUTSIDE VACUUM SOURCE TO SEAT DIAPHRAGM

**MV primary vacuum break adjustment—1975 (© Chevrolet Motor Div.)**

2. Measure the clearance between the choke valve and the air horn wall.

3. Bend the vacuum break rod to adjust the clearance. Be sure that there is no binding or interference.

### 1976–80

1. Place cam follower on high step of cam.

2. Plug purge bleed hole with masking tape over vacuum break end cover. Not all 1977–80 models will have this hole.

3. Using an outside vacuum source, apply vacuum to primary vacuum break diaphragm until the plunger is fully seated.

4. Push up on choke coil lever rod in the end of the slot. Push down on the choke valve for 1978–80.

5. Insert a specified gauge between the upper edge of the choke valve and the air horn wall. Measure at the lower edge of the choke valve, 1978–80 only.

6. Bend vacuum break rod for adjustment.

7. After adjustment, check for binding or interference. Remove tape.

### Auxiliary Vacuum Break (1975–76 Only)

1. With an outside vacuum source, apply vacuum to the auxiliary vacuum break diaphragm until the plunger is seated.

2. Place the cam follower on the high step of the fast idle cam.

---

2. Completely close the choke valve.

3. Push up on the choke coil rod to its end of travel.

4. Bottom of rod should be even with the top of the lever.

5. Bend the rod for adjustment.

6. Connect rod to choke valve.

### 1977–80

1. Place the cam follower on the high step of the cam.

2. Hold the choke valve completely closed.

3. A .120 in. plug gauge must pass through the hole in the lever attached to the choke coil housing and enter the hole in the casting.

4. Bend link to adjust.

### Primary Vacuum Break—1975

1. With an outside vacuum source, apply vacuum to the primary vacuum break diaphragm until the plunger is fully seated.

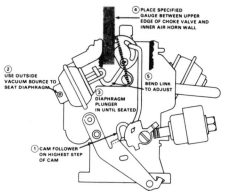

**MV auxiliary vacuum break adjustment** (© Chevrolet Motor Div.)

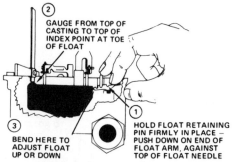

**MV and ME float level adjustment** (© Chevrolet Motor Div.)

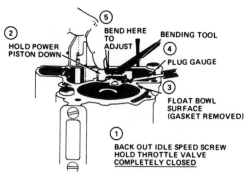

**MV metering rod adjustment—1975-76** (© Chevrolet Motor Div.)

3. Measure the clearance between the upper edge of the choke valve and the air horn wall. Bend the link between the vacuum break and the choke valve to adjust.

### Metering Rod Adjustment—1977-80

1. Remove metering rod by holding throttle valve wide open. Push downward on metering rod against spring tension, then slide metering rod out of slot in holder and remove from main metering jet.

2. Back out idle stop solenoid—hold throttle valve completely closed.

3. Hold power piston down and swing metering rod holder over flat surface (gasket removed) of bowl casting next to carburetor bore.

4. Insert specified gauge.

5. Bend the metering rod holder as necessary.

## ROCHESTER 2GV (1970–74)

These procedures are for both the 1¼ and 1½ models. Where there are differences these are noted. The 1½ model has larger throttle bores and an additional fuel feed circuit to make it suitable for use on the 350 V8.

### Fast Idle Cam

1. Turn the idle screw onto the second step of the fast idle cam, abutting against the top step.

2. Hold the choke valve toward the closed position and check the clearance between the upper edge of the choke valve and the air horn wall.

3. If this measurement varies from specifications, bend the tang on the choke lever.

### Choke Vacuum Break

1. Apply vacuum to the diaphragm to fully seat the plunger.

2. Push the choke valve in toward the closed position and hold it there.

3. Check the distance between the lower edge of the choke valve and the air horn wall.

4. If this dimension is not within specifications, bend the vacuum break rod to adjust.

### Choke Unloader

1. Hold the throttle valves wide-open and use a rubber band to hold the choke valve toward the closed position.

2. Measure the distance between the upper edge of the choke valve and the air horn wall.

3. If this measurement is not within specifications, bend the unloader tang on the throttle lever to correct it.

### Choke Coil Rod

1. Hold the choke valve completely open.

2. With the choke coil rod disconnected from the upper lever, push downward on the end of the rod to the end of its travel.

3. With the rod pushed fully downward, the bottom of the rod should be even with the bottom of the slotted hole in the lever.

4. To adjust the lever, bend it as shown.

## Rochester 2GV Adjustments

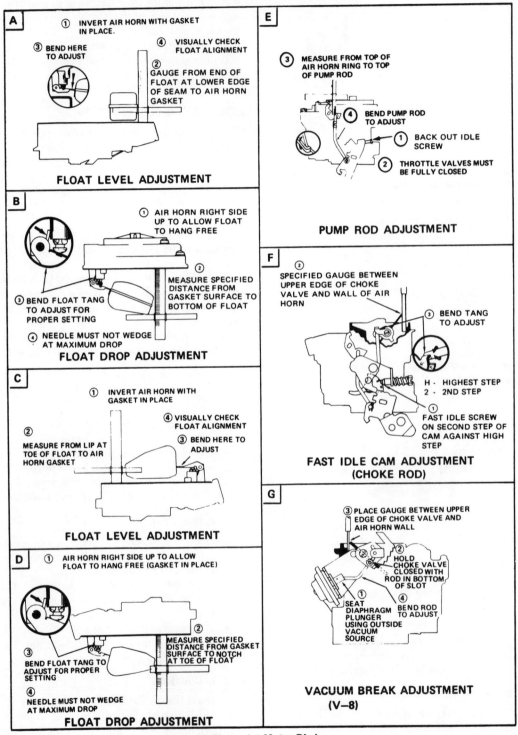

**A**
① INVERT AIR HORN WITH GASKET IN PLACE.
③ BEND HERE TO ADJUST
④ VISUALLY CHECK FLOAT ALIGNMENT
② GAUGE FROM END OF FLOAT AT LOWER EDGE OF SEAM TO AIR HORN GASKET

**FLOAT LEVEL ADJUSTMENT**

**B**
① AIR HORN RIGHT SIDE UP TO ALLOW FLOAT TO HANG FREE
② MEASURE SPECIFIED DISTANCE FROM GASKET SURFACE TO BOTTOM OF FLOAT
③ BEND FLOAT TANG TO ADJUST FOR PROPER SETTING
④ NEEDLE MUST NOT WEDGE AT MAXIMUM DROP

**FLOAT DROP ADJUSTMENT**

**C**
① INVERT AIR HORN WITH GASKET IN PLACE
④ VISUALLY CHECK FLOAT ALIGNMENT
③ BEND HERE TO ADJUST
② MEASURE FROM LIP AT TOE OF FLOAT TO AIR HORN GASKET

**FLOAT LEVEL ADJUSTMENT**

**D**
① AIR HORN RIGHT SIDE UP TO ALLOW FLOAT TO HANG FREE (GASKET IN PLACE)
② MEASURE SPECIFIED DISTANCE FROM GASKET SURFACE TO NOTCH AT TOE OF FLOAT
③ BEND FLOAT TANG TO ADJUST FOR PROPER SETTING
④ NEEDLE MUST NOT WEDGE AT MAXIMUM DROP

**FLOAT DROP ADJUSTMENT**

**E**
③ MEASURE FROM TOP OF AIR HORN RING TO TOP OF PUMP ROD
④ BEND PUMP ROD TO ADJUST
① BACK OUT IDLE SCREW
② THROTTLE VALVES MUST BE FULLY CLOSED

**PUMP ROD ADJUSTMENT**

**F**
② SPECIFIED GAUGE BETWEEN UPPER EDGE OF CHOKE VALVE AND WALL OF AIR HORN
③ BEND TANG TO ADJUST
H - HIGHEST STEP
2 - 2ND STEP
① FAST IDLE SCREW ON SECOND STEP OF CAM AGAINST HIGH STEP

**FAST IDLE CAM ADJUSTMENT (CHOKE ROD)**

**G**
③ PLACE GAUGE BETWEEN UPPER EDGE OF CHOKE VALVE AND AIR HORN WALL
② HOLD CHOKE VALVE CLOSED WITH ROD IN BOTTOM OF SLOT
① SEAT DIAPHRAGM PLUNGER USING OUTSIDE VACUUM SOURCE
BEND ROD TO ADJUST

**VACUUM BREAK ADJUSTMENT (V-8)**

(© Chevrolet Motor Div.)

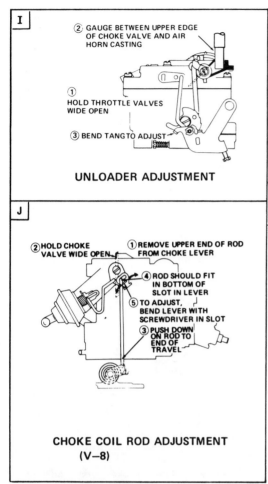

UNLOADER ADJUSTMENT

CHOKE COIL ROD ADJUSTMENT
(V-8)

(© Chevrolet Motor Div.)

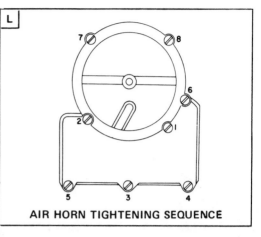

AIR HORN TIGHTENING SEQUENCE

## Accelerator Pump Rod

1. Back the idle stop screw out and close the throttle valves in their bores.

2. Measure the distance from the top of the air horn to the top of the pump rod.

3. Bend the pump rod at a lower angle to correct this dimension.

## Float Level

Invert the air horn, and with the gasket in place and the needle seated, measure the level as follows:

On nitrophyl floats, measure from the air horn gasket to the lip on the toe of the float.

On brass floats, measure from the air horn gasket to the lower edge of the float seam.

Bend the float tang to adjust the level.

## Float Drop

Holding the air horn right side up, measure float drop as follows:

On nitrophyl floats, measure from the air horn gasket to the lip at the toe of the float.

On brass floats, measure from the air horn gasket to the bottom of the float.

Bend the float tang to adjust either type float.

## ROCHESTER 2GC (1975–78)

### Pump Rod

1. Back out the idle speed adjusting screw.

2. Hold the throttle valve completely closed.

3. Measure the distance from the top of the air horn ring to the top of the pump rod.

4. If necessary, bend the pump rod to adjust.

### Fast Idle Cam

1. Turn the idle speed screw in until it contacts the low step of the fast idle cam. Then turn the screw in one full turn.

2. Place the idle speed screw on the second step of the fast idle cam against the highest step.

3. Measure the clearance between the upper edge of the choke valve and the air horn wall.

4. Bend the choke lever tang to adjust.

### Choke Unloader

1. With the throttle valves wide open, place the choke valve in the closed position.

2. Measure the clearance between the upper edge of the choke valve and the air horn casting.

3. Bend the throttle lever tang to adjust.

### Intermediate Choke Rod

1. Remove the thermostatic cover coil, gasket, and inside baffle plate.

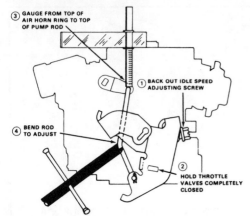

**2GC pump rod adjustment (© Chevrolet Motor Div.)**

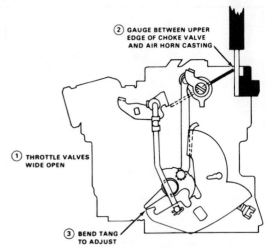

**2GC choke unloader adjustment (© Chevrolet Motor Div.)**

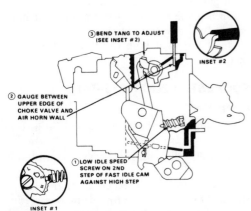

**2GC fast idle cam adjustment (© Chevrolet Motor Div.)**

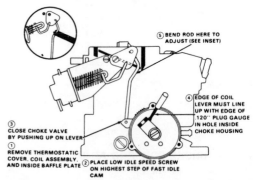

**2GC intermediate choke rod adjustment (© Chevrolet Motor Div.)**

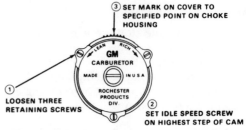

**2GC automatic choke coil adjustment (© Chevrolet Motor Div.)**

2. Place the idle screw on the high step of the fast idle cam.

3. Close the choke valve by pushing up on the intermediate choke lever.

4. The edge of the choke lever inside the choke housing must align with the edge of the plug gauge.

5. Bend the intermediate choke lever to adjust.

6. Replace the cover and set as in the following adjustment.

### Automatic Choke Coil

1. Place the idle screw on the high step of the fast idle cam.

2. Loosen the thermostatic choke coil cover retaining screws.

3. Rotate the choke cover against coil tension until the choke valve begins to close. Continue rotating it until the index mark aligns with the specified point on the choke housing. On models with slotted coil pick-up

lever, make sure coil tang is installed in slot in lever. This will have to be checked with the choke coil cover removed.

4. Tighten the choke cover retaining screws.

### Vacuum Break

1. Disconnect the vacuum hose. Using an outside vacuum source, seat the vacuum diaphragm.

2. Cover the vacuum break bleed hole

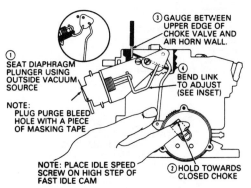

**2GC vacuum break adjustment (© Chevrolet Motor Div.)**

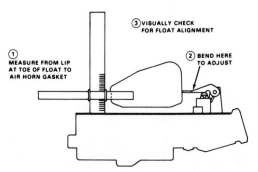

**2GC float level adjustment (© Chevrolet Motor Div.)**

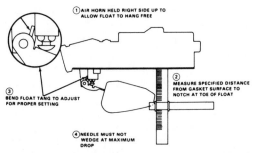

**2GC float drop adjustment (© Chevrolet Motor Div.)**

with a small piece of tape so that the diaphragm will be held inward.

3. Place the idle speed screw on the high step of the fast idle cam.

4. 1975–76: Remove the thermostatic coil and cover; hold the choke coil lever inside the choke coil housing towards the closed choke position. 1977–78: Pull out the stem from the vacuum diaphragm to the vacuum break rod until seated.

5. Measure the clearance between the upper edge of the choke valve and the air horn wall.

6. Bend the vacuum break rod to adjust.

7. After adjustment, remove the piece of tape and reconnect the vacuum hose.

## ROCHESTER 2SE (1979–80)

### Float Adjustment

1. Remove the air horn from the throttle body.

2. Use your fingers to hold the retainer in place, and to push the float down into light contact with the needle.

3. Measure the distance from the toe of the float (furthest from the hinge) to the top of the carburetor (gasket removed).

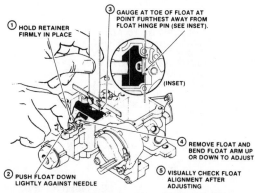

**2SE float adjustment (© Chevrolet Motor Div.)**

4. To adjust, remove the float and gently bend the arm to specification. After adjustment, check the float alignment in the chamber.

### Pump Adjustment

1. With the throttle closed and the fast idle screw off the steps of the fast idle cam, measure the distance from the air horn casting to the top of the pump stem.

2. To adjust, remove the retaining screw and washer and remove the pump lever. Bend the end of the lever to correct the stem height. Do not twist the lever or bend it sideways.

3. Install the lever, washer and screw and check the adjustment. When correct, open and close the throttle a few times to check the linkage movement and alignment.

### Fast Idle Adjustment

1. Set the ignition timing and curb idle speed, and disconnect and plug hoses as directed on the emission control decal.

2. Place the fast idle screw on the highest step of the cam.

3. Start the engine and adjust the engine

> **NOTE:**
> THE PUMP ADJUSTMENT SHOULD NOT BE CHANGED FROM ORIGINAL FACTORY SETTING UNLESS GAUGING SHOWS OUT OF SPECIFICATION. THE PUMP LEVER IS MADE FROM HEAVY DUTY, HARDENED STEEL MAKING BENDING DIFFICULT. DO NOT REMOVE PUMP LEVER FOR BENDING UNLESS ABSOLUTELY NECESSARY.

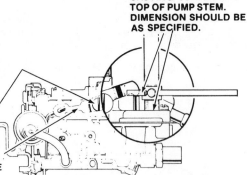

② GAUGE FROM AIR HORN CASTING SURFACE TO TOP OF PUMP STEM. DIMENSION SHOULD BE AS SPECIFIED.

① THROTTLE VALVES COMPLETELY CLOSED. MAKE SURE FAST IDLE SCREW IS OFF STEPS OF FAST IDLE CAM.

③ IF NECESSARY TO ADJUST, REMOVE PUMP LEVER RETAINING SCREW AND WASHER AND REMOVE PUMP LEVER BY ROTATING LEVER TO REMOVE FROM PUMP ROD. PLACE LEVER IN A VISE, PROTECTING LEVER FROM DAMAGE, AND BEND END OF LEVER (NEAREST NECKED DOWN SECTION).

NOTE: DO NOT BEND LEVER IN A SIDEWAYS OR TWISTING MOTION.

⑤ OPEN AND CLOSE THROTTLE VALVES CHECKING LINKAGE FOR FREEDOM OF MOVEMENT AND OBSERVING PUMP LEVER ALIGNMENT.

④ REINSTALL PUMP LEVER, WASHER AND RETAINING SCREW. RECHECK PUMP ADJUSTMENT ① AND ②. TIGHTEN RETAINING SCREW SECURELY AFTER THE PUMP ADJUSTMENT IS CORRECT.

2SE pump adjustment (© Chevrolet Motor Div.)

speed to specification with the fast idle screw.

### Choke Coil Lever Adjustment

1. Remove the three retaining screws and remove the choke cover and coil. On models with a riveted choke cover, drill out the three rivets and remove the cover and choke coil.

NOTE: *A choke stat cover retainer kit is required for reassembly.*

2. Place the fast idle screw on the high step of the cam.

3. Close the choke by pushing in on the intermediate choke lever. The intermediate choke lever is behind the choke vacuum diaphragm.

4. Insert a drill or gauge of the specified size into the hole in the choke housing. The choke lever in the housing should be up against the side of the gauge.

5. If the lever does not just touch the gauge, bend the intermediate choke rod to adjust.

### Fast Idle Cam (Choke Rod) Adjustment

NOTE: *A special angle gauge should be used.*

1. Adjust the choke coil lever and fast idle first.

2. Rotate the degree scale until it is zeroed.

3. Close the choke and install the degree scale onto the choke plate. Center the leveling bubble.

4. Rotate the scale so that the specified degree is opposite the scale pointer.

5. Place the fast idle screw on the second step of the cam (against the high step). Close the choke by pushing in the intermediate lever.

6. Push on the vacuum break lever in the direction of opening choke until the lever is against the rear tang on the choke lever.

7. Bend the fast idle cam rod at the U to adjust angle to specifications.

### Air Valve Rod Adjustment

1. Seat the vacuum diaphragm with an outside vacuum source. Tape over the purge bleed hole if present.

2. Close the air valve.

3. Insert the specified gauge between the rod and the end of the slot in the air valve.

4. Bend the rod to adjust the clearance.

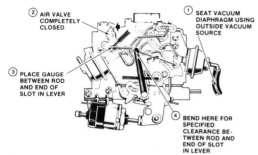

**2SE air valve rod adjustment (© Chevrolet Motor Div.)**

## Primary Side Vacuum Break Adjustment

1. Follow Steps 1–4 of the Fast Idle Cam Adjustment.
2. Seat the choke vacuum diaphragm with an outside vacuum source.
3. Push in on the intermediate choke lever to close the choke valve, and hold closed during adjustment.
4. Adjust by bending the vacuum break rod until the bubble is centered.

## Secondary Vacuum Break Adjustment

1. Follow Steps 1–4 of the Fast Idle Cam Adjustment.
2. Seat the choke vacuum diaphragm with an outside vacuum source.
3. Push in on the intermediate choke lever to close the choke valve, and hold closed during adjustment. Make sure the plunger spring is compressed and seated, if present.
4. Bend the vacuum break rod at the U next to the diaphragm until the bubble is centered.

## Electric Choke Setting

This procedure is only for those carburetors with choke covers retained by screws. Riveted choke covers are preset and nonadjustable.

1. Loosen the three retaining screws.
2. Place the fast idle screw on the high step of the cam.
3. Rotate the choke cover to align the cover mark with the specified housing mark.

## Choke Unloader Adjustment

1. Follow Steps 1–4 of the Fast Idle Cam Adjustment.
2. Install the choke cover and coil, if removed, aligning the marks on the housing and cover as specified.
3. Hold the primary throttle wide open.

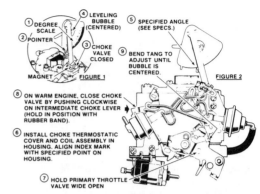

**2SE unloader adjustment (© Chevrolet Motor Div.)**

4. If the engine is warm, close the choke valve by pushing in on the intermediate choke lever.
5. Bend the unloader tang until the bubble is centered.

## Secondary Lockout Adjustment

1. Pull the choke wide open by pushing out on the intermediate choke lever.
2. Open the throttle until the end of the secondary actuating lever is opposite the toe of the lockout lever.
3. Gauge clearance between the lockout lever and secondary lever should be as specified.
4. To adjust, bend the lockout lever where it contacts the fast idle cam.

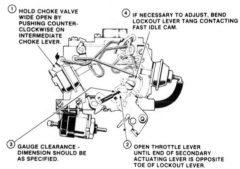

**2SE secondary lockout adjustment (© Chevrolet Motor Div.)**

## ROCHESTER M2MC (1979–80)

### Float Adjustment

1. Remove the air horn from the throttle body.
2. Use your fingers to hold the retainer in place, and to push the float down into light contact with the needle.
3. Gauge from the top of the casting to the

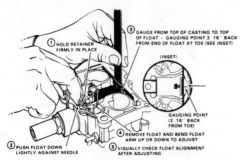

**M2MC float adjustment (© Chevrolet Motor Div.)**

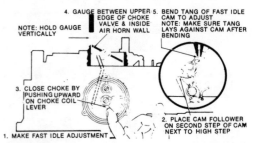

**M2MC fast idle cam adjustment (© Chevrolet Motor Div.)**

top of the float, at a point ³/₁₆ in. back from the end of the toe of the float (gasket removed).

4. To adjust, remove the float and gently bend the arm to specification. After adjustment, check the float alignment in the chamber.

**Fast Idle Speed**

1. Place the fast idle lever on the high step of the fast idle cam.

2. Turn the fast idle screw out until the throttle valves are closed.

3. Turn the screw in to contact the lever, then turn it in two more turns. Check this preliminary setting against the sticker figure.

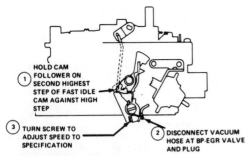

**M2MC fast idle adjustment on the bench (© Chevrolet Motor Div.)**

**Fast Idle Cam Adjustment**

1. Adjust the fast idle speed.

2. Place the cam follower lever on the second step of the fast idle cam, holding it firmly against the rise of the high step.

3. Close the choke valve by pushing upward on the choke coil lever inside the choke housing.

4. Gauge between the upper edge of the choke valve and the inside of the air horn wall.

5. Bend the tang on the fast idle cam to adjust.

**Pump Adjustment**

1. With the fast idle cam follower off the steps of the fast idle cam, back out the idle speed screw until the throttle valves are completely closed.

2. Place the pump rod in the proper hole of the lever.

3. Measure from the top of the choke valve wall, next to the vent stack, to the top of the pump stem.

4. Bend the pump lever to adjust.

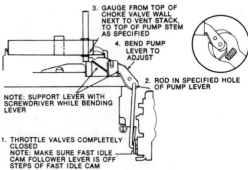

**M2MC pump adjustment (© Chevrolet Motor Div.)**

**Choke Coil Lever Adjustment**

1. Remove the choke cover and thermostatic coil from the choke housing.

2. Push up on the coil tang (counterclockwise) until the choke valve is closed.

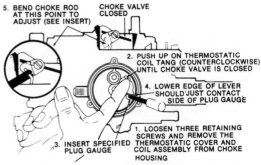

**M2MC choke coil lever adjustment (© Chevrolet Motor Div.)**

The top of the choke rod should be at the bottom of the slot in the choke valve lever. Place the fast idle cam follower on the high step of the cam.

3. Insert a 0.120 in. plug gauge in the hole in the choke housing.

4. The lower edge of the choke coil lever should just contact the side of the plug gauge.

5. Bend the choke rod to adjust.

### Front Vacuum Break Adjustment

1. Seat the choke vacuum diaphragm, using an outside vacuum source. If there is an air bleed hole on the diaphragm, tape it over.

2. Remove the choke cover and coil. Rotate the inside coil lever counterclockwise.

3. Check that the specified gap is present between the top of the choke valve and the air horn wall.

4. Turn the vacuum break adjusting screw to adjust.

### Automatic Choke Coil Adjustment

1. Place the cam follower on the highest step of the fast idle cam.

2. Loosen the three choke cover retaining screws.

3. Rotate the cover and coil assembly counterclockwise until the choke valve just closes.

4. Align the mark on the choke cover with the specified mark on the housing. Make sure the slot in the lever is engaged with the coil tang. Tighten the cover retaining screws.

### Unloader Adjustment

1. With the choke valve completely closed, hold the throttle valves wide open.

2. Measure between the upper edge of the choke valve and the air horn wall.

3. Bend the tang on the fast idle lever to obtain the proper measurement.

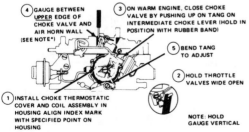

**M2MC unloader adjustment (© Chevrolet Motor Div.)**

### Air Conditioning Idle Speed-Up Solenoid Adjustment

1. With the engine at normal operating temperature and automatic transmissions in drive, manual transmissions in neutral, adjust the curb idle to specifications by means of the idle speed screw (air conditioning off).

2. Turn the air conditioning on and disconnect the compressor clutch electrical lead at the connector. The solenoid should be energized. Open the throttle slightly to allow the solenoid plunger to fully extend.

3. Turn the solenoid screw (plunger) to adjust the engine idle to the specified rpm: 600 for automatics (drive); 700 for manuals (neutral).

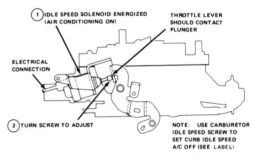

**M2MC A/C idle speed-up solenoid adjustment (© Chevrolet Motor Div.)**

## ROCHESTER 4MV (1970–78)

### Fast Idle

1. Position the fast idle lever on the high step of the fast idle cam.

2. Be sure that the choke is wide-open and the engine warm. On 1974 models, with manual transmission, disconnect the vacuum advance. On 1976 California 454s and all 1977–78 models, disconnect and plug vacuum hose at EGR valve.

3. Turn the fast idle screw to gain the proper fast idle rpm.

### Choke Rod (Fast Idle Cam)

1. Place the cam follower on the second step of the fast idle cam.

2. Close the choke valve by exerting counterclockwise pressure on the external choke lever.

3. Insert a gauge of the proper size between the lower edge of the choke valve and the inside air horn wall. For 1976–78, measure between the upper edge of the choke valve and the inside air horn wall.

4. To adjust, bend the choke rod.

## Rochester 4MV Quadrajet Adjustments

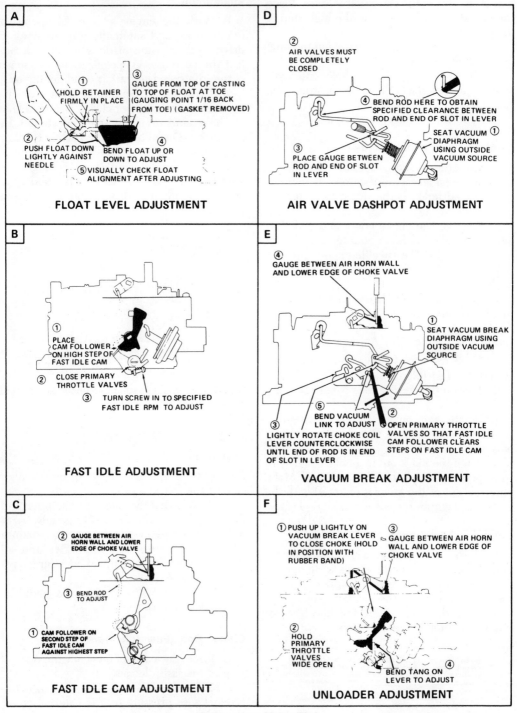

**A**

① HOLD RETAINER FIRMLY IN PLACE

③ GAUGE FROM TOP OF CASTING TO TOP OF FLOAT AT TOE (GAUGING POINT 1/16 BACK FROM TOE) (GASKET REMOVED)

② PUSH FLOAT DOWN LIGHTLY AGAINST NEEDLE

④ BEND FLOAT UP OR DOWN TO ADJUST

⑤ VISUALLY CHECK FLOAT ALIGNMENT AFTER ADJUSTING

**FLOAT LEVEL ADJUSTMENT**

**D**

② AIR VALVES MUST BE COMPLETELY CLOSED

④ BEND ROD HERE TO OBTAIN SPECIFIED CLEARANCE BETWEEN ROD AND END OF SLOT IN LEVER

① SEAT VACUUM DIAPHRAGM USING OUTSIDE VACUUM SOURCE

③ PLACE GAUGE BETWEEN ROD AND END OF SLOT IN LEVER

**AIR VALVE DASHPOT ADJUSTMENT**

**B**

① PLACE CAM FOLLOWER ON HIGH STEP OF FAST IDLE CAM

② CLOSE PRIMARY THROTTLE VALVES

③ TURN SCREW IN TO SPECIFIED FAST IDLE RPM TO ADJUST

**FAST IDLE ADJUSTMENT**

**E**

④ GAUGE BETWEEN AIR HORN WALL AND LOWER EDGE OF CHOKE VALVE

① SEAT VACUUM BREAK DIAPHRAGM USING OUTSIDE VACUUM SOURCE

⑤ BEND VACUUM LINK TO ADJUST

② OPEN PRIMARY THROTTLE VALVES SO THAT FAST IDLE CAM FOLLOWER CLEARS STEPS ON FAST IDLE CAM

③ LIGHTLY ROTATE CHOKE COIL LEVER COUNTERCLOCKWISE UNTIL END OF ROD IS IN END OF SLOT IN LEVER

**VACUUM BREAK ADJUSTMENT**

**C**

② GAUGE BETWEEN AIR HORN WALL AND LOWER EDGE OF CHOKE VALVE

③ BEND ROD TO ADJUST

① CAM FOLLOWER ON SECOND STEP OF FAST IDLE CAM AGAINST HIGHEST STEP

**FAST IDLE CAM ADJUSTMENT**

**F**

① PUSH UP LIGHTLY ON VACUUM BREAK LEVER TO CLOSE CHOKE (HOLD IN POSITION WITH RUBBER BAND)

③ GAUGE BETWEEN AIR HORN WALL AND LOWER EDGE OF CHOKE VALVE

② HOLD PRIMARY THROTTLE VALVES WIDE OPEN

④ BEND TANG ON LEVER TO ADJUST

**UNLOADER ADJUSTMENT**

(© Chevrolet Motor Div.)

### Vacuum Break

1. Fully seat the vacuum break diaphragm using an outside vacuum source.

2. Open the throttle valve enough to allow the fast idle cam follower to clear the fast idle cam.

3. The end of the vacuum break rod should be at the outer end of the slot in the vacuum break diaphragm plunger.

**55 WAYS TO IMPROVE FUEL ECONOMY**

# CHILTON'S
# FUEL ECONOMY
# & TUNE-UP TIPS

### Tune-Up • Spark Plug Diagnosis • Emission Controls
### Fuel System • Cooling System • Tires and Wheels
### General Maintenance

# CHILTON'S FUEL ECONOMY & TUNE-UP TIPS

Fuel economy is important to everyone, no matter what kind of vehicle you drive. The maintenance-minded motorist can save both money and fuel using these tips and the periodic maintenance and tune-up procedures in this Repair and Tune-Up Guide.

There are more than 130,000,000 cars and trucks registered for private use in the United States. Each travels an average of 10-12,000 miles per year, and, in total they consume close to 70 billion gallons of fuel each year. This represents nearly ⅔ of the oil imported by the United States each year. The Federal government's goal is to reduce consumption 10% by 1985. A variety of methods are either already in use or under serious consideration, and they all affect your driving and the cars you will drive. In addition to "down-sizing", the auto industry is using or investigating the use of electronic fuel delivery, electronic engine controls and alternative engines for use in smaller and lighter vehicles, among other alternatives to meet the federally mandated Corporate Average Fuel Economy (CAFE) of 27.5 mpg by 1985. The government, for its part, is considering rationing, mandatory driving curtailments and tax increases on motor vehicle fuel in an effort to reduce consumption. The government's goal of a 10% reduction could be realized — and further government regulation avoided — if every private vehicle could use just 1 less gallon of fuel per week.

## How Much Can You Save?

Tests have proven that almost anyone can make at least a 10% reduction in fuel consumption through regular maintenance and tune-ups. When a major manufacturer of spark plugs sur-

## TUNE-UP

1. Check the cylinder compression to be sure the engine will really benefit from a tune-up and that it is capable of producing good fuel economy. A tune-up will be wasted on an engine in poor mechanical condition.

2. Replace spark plugs regularly. New spark plugs alone can increase fuel economy 3%.

3. Be sure the spark plugs are the correct type (heat range) for your vehicle. See the Tune-Up Specifications.

Heat range refers to the spark plug's ability to conduct heat away from the firing end. It must conduct the heat away in an even pattern to avoid becoming a source of pre-ignition, yet it must also operate hot enough to burn off conductive deposits that could cause misfiring.

The heat range is usually indicated by a number on the spark plug, part of the manufacturer's designation for each individual spark plug. The numbers in bold-face indicate the heat range in each manufacturer's identification system.

Periodically, check the spark plugs to be sure they are firing efficiently. They are excellent indicators of the internal condition of your engine.

| Manufacturer | Typical Designation |
|---|---|
| AC | R **45** TS |
| Bosch (old) | WA **145** T30 |
| Bosch (new) | HR **8** Y |
| Champion | RBL **15** Y |
| Fram/Autolite | **4**15 |
| Mopar | P-**62** PR |
| Motorcraft | BR**F**-**42** |
| NGK | BP **5** ES-15 |
| Nippondenso | W **16** EP |
| Prestolite | 14GR **5** 2A |

On AC, Bosch (new), Champion, Fram/Autolite, Mopar, Motorcraft and Prestolite, a higher number indicates a hotter plug. On Bosch (old), NGK and Nippondenso, a higher number indicates a colder plug.

4. Make sure the spark plugs are properly gapped. See the Tune-Up Specifications in this book.

5. Be sure the spark plugs are firing efficiently. The illustrations on the next 2 pages show you how to "read" the firing end of the spark plug.

6. Check the ignition timing and set it to specifications. Tests show that almost all cars

veyed over 6,000 cars nationwide, they found that a tune-up, on cars that needed one, increased fuel economy over 11%. Replacing worn plugs alone, accounted for a 3% increase. The same test also revealed that 8 out of every 10 vehicles will have some maintenance deficiency that will directly affect fuel economy, emissions or performance. Most of this mileage-robbing neglect could be prevented with regular maintenance.

Modern engines require that all of the functioning systems operate properly for maximum efficiency. A malfunction anywhere wastes fuel. You can keep your vehicle running as efficiently and economically as possible, by being aware of your vehicles operating and performance characterics. If your vehicle suddenly develops performance or fuel economy problems it could be due to one or more of the following:

| PROBLEM | POSSIBLE CAUSE |
|---------|----------------|
| Engine Idles Rough | Ignition timing, idle mixture, vacuum leak or something amiss in the emission control system. |
| Hesitates on Acceleration | Dirty carburetor or fuel filter, improper accelerator pump setting, ignition timing or fouled spark plugs. |
| Starts Hard or Fails to Start | Worn spark plugs, improperly set automatic choke, ice (or water) in fuel system. |
| Stalls Frequently | Automatic choke improperly adjusted and possible dirty air filter or fuel filter. |
| Performs Sluggishly | Worn spark plugs, dirty fuel or air filter, ignition timing or automatic choke out of adjustment. |

Check spark plug wires on conventional point type ignition for cracks by bending them in a loop around your finger.

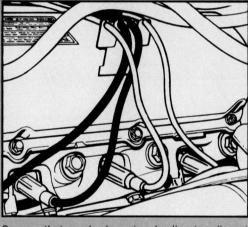
Be sure that spark plug wires leading to adjacent cylinders do not run too close together. (Photo courtesy Champion Spark Plug Co.)

have incorrect ignition timing by more than 2°.

7. If your vehicle does not have electronic ignition, check the points, rotor and cap as specified.

8. Check the spark plug wires (used with conventional point-type ignitions) for cracks and burned or broken insulation by bending them in a loop around your finger. Cracked wires decrease fuel efficiency by failing to deliver full voltage to the spark plugs. One misfiring spark plug can cost you as much as 2 mpg.

9. Check the routing of the plug wires. Misfiring can be the result of spark plug leads to adjacent cylinders running parallel to each

other and too close together. One wire tends to pick up voltage from the other causing it to fire "out of time".

10. Check all electrical and ignition circuits for voltage drop and resistance.

11. Check the distributor mechanical and/or vacuum advance mechanisms for proper functioning. The vacuum advance can be checked by twisting the distributor plate in the opposite direction of rotation. It should spring back when released.

12. Check and adjust the valve clearance on engines with mechanical lifters. The clearance should be slightly loose rather than too tight.

# SPARK PLUG DIAGNOSIS

## Normal

APPEARANCE: This plug is typical of one operating normally. The insulator nose varies from a light tan to grayish color with slight electrode wear. The presence of slight deposits is normal on used plugs and will have no adverse effect on engine performance. The spark plug heat range is correct for the engine and the engine is running normally.

CAUSE: Properly running engine.

RECOMMENDATION: Before reinstalling this plug, the electrodes should be cleaned and filed square. Set the gap to specifications. If the plug has been in service for more than 10-12,000 miles, the entire set should probably be replaced with a fresh set of the same heat range.

## Oil Deposits

APPEARANCE: The firing end of the plug is covered with a wet, oily coating.

CAUSE: The problem is poor oil control. On high mileage engines, oil is leaking past the rings or valve guides into the combustion chamber. A common cause is also a plugged PCV valve, and a ruptured fuel pump diaphragm can also cause this condition. Oil fouled plugs such as these are often found in new or recently overhauled engines, before normal oil control is achieved, and can be cleaned and reinstalled.

RECOMMENDATION: A hotter spark plug may temporarily relieve the problem, but the engine is probably in need of work.

## Incorrect Heat Range

APPEARANCE: The effects of high temperature on a spark plug are indicated by clean white, often blistered insulator. This can also be accompanied by excessive wear of the electrode, and the absence of deposits.

CAUSE: Check for the correct spark plug heat range. A plug which is too hot for the engine can result in overheating. A car operated mostly at high speeds can require a colder plug. Also check ignition timing, cooling system level, fuel mixture and leaking intake manifold.

RECOMMENDATION: If all ignition and engine adjustments are known to be correct, and no other malfunction exists, install spark plugs one heat range colder.

Photos Courtesy Champion Spark Plug Co.

## Carbon Deposits

APPEARANCE: Carbon fouling is easily identified by the presence of dry, soft, black, sooty deposits.

CAUSE: Changing the heat range can often lead to carbon fouling, as can prolonged slow, stop-and-start driving. If the heat range is correct, carbon fouling can be attributed to a rich fuel mixture, sticking choke, clogged air cleaner, worn breaker points, retarded timing or low compression. If only one or two plugs are carbon fouled, check for corroded or cracked wires on the affected plugs. Also look for cracks in the distributor cap between the towers of affected cylinders.

RECOMMENDATION: After the problem is corrected, these plugs can be cleaned and reinstalled if not worn severely.

## MMT Fouled

APPEARANCE: Spark plugs fouled by MMT (Methycyclopentadienyl Maganese Tricarbonyl) have reddish, rusty appearance on the insulator and side electrode.

CAUSE: MMT is an anti-knock additive in gasoline used to replace lead. During the combustion process, the MMT leaves a reddish deposit on the insulator and side electrode.

RECOMMENDATION: No engine malfunction is indicated and the deposits will not affect plug performance any more than lead deposits ( see Ash Deposits). MMT fouled plugs can be cleaned, regapped and reinstalled.

## High Speed Glazing

APPEARANCE: Glazing appears as shiny coating on the plug, either yellow or tan in color.

CAUSE: During hard, fast acceleration, plug temperatures rise suddenly. Deposits from normal combustion have no chance to fluff-off; instead, they melt on the insulator forming an electrically conductive coating which causes misfiring.

RECOMMENDATION: Glazed plugs are not easily cleaned. They should be replaced with a fresh set of plugs of the correct heat range. If the condition recurs, using plugs with a heat range one step colder may cure the problem.

## Ash (Lead) Deposits

APPEARANCE: Ash deposits are characterized by light brown or white colored deposits crusted on the side or center electrodes. In some cases it may give the plug a rusty appearance.

CAUSE: Ash deposits are normally derived from oil or fuel additives burned during normal combustion. Normally they are harmless, though excessive amounts can cause misfiring. If deposits are excessive in short mileage, the valve guides may be worn.

RECOMMENDATION: Ash-fouled plugs can be cleaned, gapped and reinstalled.

## Detonation

APPEARANCE: Detonation is usually characterized by a broken plug insulator.

CAUSE: A portion of the fuel charge will begin to burn spontaneously, from the increased heat following ignition. The explosion that results applies extreme pressure to engine components, frequently damaging spark plugs and pistons.

Detonation can result by over-advanced ignition timing, inferior gasoline (low octane) lean air/fuel mixture, poor carburetion, engine lugging or an increase in compression ratio due to combustion chamber deposits or engine modification.

RECOMMENDATION: Replace the plugs after correcting the problem.

Photos Courtesy Fram Corporation

# EMISSION CONTROLS

13. Be aware of the general condition of the emission control system. It contributes to reduced pollution and should be serviced regularly to maintain efficient engine operation.

14. Check all vacuum lines for dried, cracked or brittle conditions. Something as simple as a leaking vacuum hose can cause poor performance and loss of economy.

15. Avoid tampering with the emission control system. Attempting to improve fuel econ-

# FUEL SYSTEM

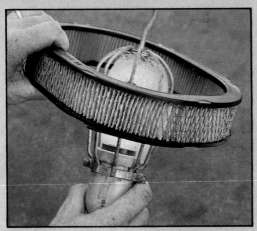

Check the air filter with a light behind it. If you can see light through the filter it can be reused.

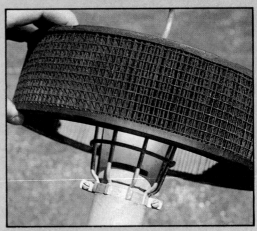

Extremely clogged filters should be discarded and replaced with a new one.

18. Replace the air filter regularly. A dirty air filter richens the air/fuel mixture and can increase fuel consumption as much as 10%. Tests show that ⅓ of all vehicles have air filters in need of replacement.

19. Replace the fuel filter at least as often as recommended.

20. Set the idle speed and carburetor mixture to specifications.

21. Check the automatic choke. A sticking or malfunctioning choke wastes gas.

22. During the summer months, adjust the automatic choke for a leaner mixture which will produce faster engine warm-ups.

# COOLING SYSTEM

29. Be sure all accessory drive belts are in good condition. Check for cracks or wear.

30. Adjust all accessory drive belts to proper tension.

31. Check all hoses for swollen areas, worn spots, or loose clamps.

32. Check coolant level in the radiator or expansion tank.

33. Be sure the thermostat is operating properly. A stuck thermostat delays engine warm-up and a cold engine uses nearly twice as much fuel as a warm engine.

34. Drain and replace the engine coolant at least as often as recommended. Rust and scale

# TIRES & WHEELS

38. Check the tire pressure often with a pencil type gauge. Tests by a major tire manufacturer show that 90% of all vehicles have at least 1 tire improperly inflated. Better mileage can be achieved by over-inflating tires, but never exceed the maximum inflation pressure on the side of the tire.

39. If possible, install radial tires. Radial tires deliver as much as ½ mpg more than bias belted tires.

40. Avoid installing super-wide tires. They only create extra rolling resistance and decrease fuel mileage. Stick to the manufacturer's recommendations.

41. Have the wheels properly balanced.

omy by tampering with emission controls is more likely to worsen fuel economy than improve it. Emission control changes on modern engines are not readily reversible.

16. Clean (or replace) the EGR valve and lines as recommended.

17. Be sure that all vacuum lines and hoses are reconnected properly after working under the hood. An unconnected or misrouted vacuum line can wreak havoc with engine performance.

23. Check for fuel leaks at the carburetor, fuel pump, fuel lines and fuel tank. Be sure all lines and connections are tight.

24. Periodically check the tightness of the carburetor and intake manifold attaching nuts and bolts. These are a common place for vacuum leaks to occur.

25. Clean the carburetor periodically and lubricate the linkage.

26. The condition of the tailpipe can be an excellent indicator of proper engine combustion. After a long drive at highway speeds, the inside of the tailpipe should be a light grey in color. Black or soot on the insides indicates an overly rich mixture.

27. Check the fuel pump pressure. The fuel pump may be supplying more fuel than the engine needs.

28. Use the proper grade of gasoline for your engine. Don't try to compensate for knocking or "pinging" by advancing the ignition timing. This practice will only increase plug temperature and the chances of detonation or pre-ignition with relatively little performance gain.

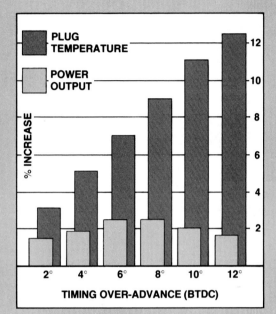

*Increasing ignition timing past the specified setting results in a drastic increase in spark plug temperature with increased chance of detonation or preignition. Performance increase is considerably less. (Photo courtesy Champion Spark Plug Co.)*

that form in the engine should be flushed out to allow the engine to operate at peak efficiency.

35. Clean the radiator of debris that can decrease cooling efficiency.

36. Install a flex-type or electric cooling fan, if you don't have a clutch type fan. Flex fans use curved plastic blades to push more air at low speeds when more cooling is needed; at high speeds the blades flatten out for less resistance. Electric fans only run when the engine temperature reaches a predetermined level.

37. Check the radiator cap for a worn or cracked gasket. If the cap does not seal properly, the cooling system will not function properly.

42. Be sure the front end is correctly aligned. A misaligned front end actually has wheels going in different directions. The increased drag can reduce fuel economy by .3 mpg.

43. Correctly adjust the wheel bearings. Wheel bearings that are adjusted too tight increase rolling resistance.

*Check tire pressures regularly with a reliable pocket type gauge. Be sure to check the pressure on a cold tire.*

# GENERAL MAINTENANCE

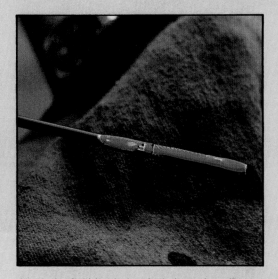

Check the fluid levels (particularly engine oil) on a regular basis. Be sure to check the oil for grit, water or other contamination.

A vacuum gauge is another excellent indicator of internal engine condition and can also be installed in the dash as a mileage indicator.

44. Periodically check the fluid levels in the engine, power steering pump, master cylinder, automatic transmission and drive axle.

45. Change the oil at the recommended interval and change the filter at every oil change. Dirty oil is thick and causes extra friction between moving parts, cutting efficiency and increasing wear. A worn engine requires more frequent tune-ups and gets progressively worse fuel economy. In general, use the lightest viscosity oil for the driving conditions you will encounter.

46. Use the recommended viscosity fluids in the transmission and axle.

47. Be sure the battery is fully charged for fast starts. A slow starting engine wastes fuel.

48. Be sure battery terminals are clean and tight.

49. Check the battery electrolyte level and add distilled water if necessary.

50. Check the exhaust system for crushed pipes, blockages and leaks.

51. Adjust the brakes. Dragging brakes or brakes that are not releasing create increased drag on the engine.

52. Install a vacuum gauge or miles-per-gallon gauge. These gauges visually indicate engine vacuum in the intake manifold. High vacuum = good mileage and low vacuum = poorer mileage. The gauge can also be an excellent indicator of internal engine conditions.

53. Be sure the clutch is properly adjusted. A slipping clutch wastes fuel.

54. Check and periodically lubricate the heat control valve in the exhaust manifold. A sticking or inoperative valve prevents engine warm-up and wastes gas.

55. Keep accurate records to check fuel economy over a period of time. A sudden drop in fuel economy may signal a need for tune-up or other maintenance.

© 1980 Chilton Book Company, Radnor, PA 19089

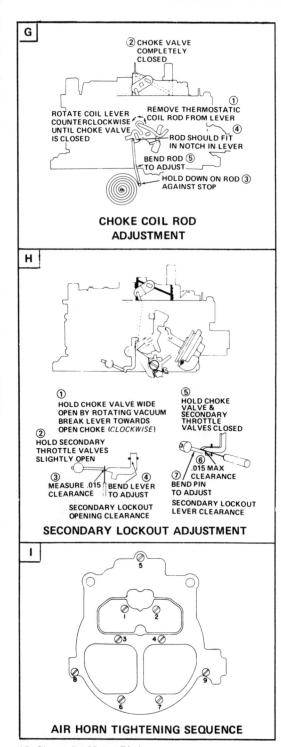

**G**

② CHOKE VALVE COMPLETELY CLOSED

①

ROTATE COIL LEVER COUNTERCLOCKWISE UNTIL CHOKE VALVE IS CLOSED

REMOVE THERMOSTATIC COIL ROD FROM LEVER

④ ROD SHOULD FIT IN NOTCH IN LEVER

BEND ROD ⑤ TO ADJUST

HOLD DOWN ON ROD ③ AGAINST STOP

**CHOKE COIL ROD ADJUSTMENT**

**H**

①
HOLD CHOKE VALVE WIDE OPEN BY ROTATING VACUUM BREAK LEVER TOWARDS OPEN CHOKE (*CLOCKWISE*)

⑤
HOLD CHOKE VALVE & SECONDARY THROTTLE VALVES CLOSED

②
HOLD SECONDARY THROTTLE VALVES SLIGHTLY OPEN

⑥
.015 MAX CLEARANCE

③
MEASURE .015 CLEARANCE

④
BEND LEVER TO ADJUST

⑦
BEND PIN TO ADJUST

SECONDARY LOCKOUT OPENING CLEARANCE

SECONDARY LOCKOUT LEVER CLEARANCE

**SECONDARY LOCKOUT ADJUSTMENT**

**I**

5

1    2

3    4

8    9

6    7

**AIR HORN TIGHTENING SEQUENCE**

(© Chevrolet Motor Div.)

4. The specified clearance should register from the lower end of the choke valve to the inside air horn wall. For 1976–78, measure between the upper edge of the choke valve to the inside air horn wall.

5. If the clearance is not correct, bend the vacuum break line at the point shown in the illustration.

## Secondary Vacuum Break (1970–75 Only)

1. Using an outside vacuum source, seat the auxiliary vacuum break diaphragm plunger.

2. Rotate the choke lever in the closed position until the spring-loaded diaphragm plunger is fully extended.

3. Holding the choke valve closed, check the distance between the lower edge of the choke valve and the air horn wall.

4. To adjust to specifications, bend the vacuum break link.

## Choke Unloader

1. Push up on the vacuum break lever and fully open the throttle valves. (1976–78: push up or down to close choke).

2. Measure the distance from the lower edge of the choke valve to the air horn wall (1976–78: measure from upper edge of choke valve).

3. To adjust, bend the tang on the fast idle lever.

## Choke Coil Rod

Before making this adjustment, check choke mechanism for free operation. Any binding caused by gum on shaft or linkage should be cleaned off. Do not oil linkage.

1. Close the choke valve by rotating the choke coil lever counterclockwise.

2. Disconnect the thermostatic coil rod from the upper lever.

3. Push down on the rod until it contacts the bracket of the coil.

4. The rod must fit in the notch of the upper lever.

5. If it does not, it must be bent on the curved portion just below the upper lever.

## Secondary Closing Adjustment

This adjustment assures proper closing of the secondary throttle plates.

1. Set the slow idle as per instructions in Chapter 2. Make sure that the fast idle cam follower is not resting on the fast idle cam. The choke valve should be wide open.

2. There should be the specified clearance between the secondary throttle actuating rod and the front of the slot on the secondary throttle lever with the closing tang on the throttle lever resting against the actuating lever.

3. Bend the tang on the primary throttle actuating rod to adjust.

### Secondary Opening Adjustment

1. Open the primary throttle valves until the actuating link contacts the upper tang on the secondary lever.
2. With two point linkage, the bottom of the link should be in the center of the secondary lever slot.
3. With three point linkage, there should be the specified clearance between the link and the middle tang.
4. Bend the upper tang on the secondary lever to adjust as necessary.

### Float Level

With the air horn assembly upside down, measure the distance from the air horn gasket surface (gasket removed) to the top of the float at the toe.

NOTE: *Make sure that the retaining pin is firmly held in place and that the tang of the float is firmly against the needle and seat assembly.*

### Accelerator Pump

1. Close the primary throttle valves by backing out the slow idle screw and making sure that the fast idle cam follower is off the steps of the fast idle cam.
2. Bend the secondary throttle closing tang away from the primary throttle lever, if necessary.
3. With the pump in the appropriate hole in the pump lever, measure from the top of the choke valve wall to the top of the pump stem.
4. To adjust, bend the pump lever.
5. After adjusting, readjust the secondary throttle tang and the slow idle screw.

### Air Valve Spring Adjustment

To adjust the air valve spring windup, loosen the allen head lockscrew and turn the adjusting screw counterclockwise to remove all spring tension. Hold the air valve closed, and turn the adjusting screw clockwise the specified number of turns after the torsion spring contacts the pin on the shaft. Hold the adjusting screw in this position and tighten the lockscrew.

### Secondary Lockout Adjustment

For 1970–75, see the illustration in this section. For 1976–78, refer to the secondary throttle lock-out adjustment in the next section.

### ROCHESTER M4MC AND M4MCA (1975) M4MC AND M4ME (1976–78)

NOTE: *The illustrations in this section apply to all M4MC, M4MCA, and M4ME carburetors unless otherwise indicated.*

### Pump Rod

1. Take the fast idle cam follower off the fast idle cam steps.
2. Back out the idle speed screw until the throttle valves are completely closed.
3. Be sure that the secondary actuating rod is not preventing the throttle from closing completely. If the primary throttle valves do not close completely, bend the secondary closing tang out of position, then readjust later.
4. Place the pump rod in the specified hole in the lever.
5. Measure the clearance from the top of the choke valve wall, next to the vent stack, and the top of the pump stem.
6. To adjust the dimension, support the pump lever and bend the pump lever.
7. Adjust the idle speed.
8. If necessary, readjust the secondary actuating rod.

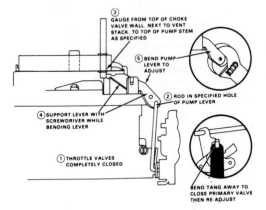

**M4MC and M4ME pump rod adjustment (© Chevrolet Motor Div.)**

### Fast Idle—1975–77

NOTE: *This procedure is to be used only when the carburetor is off the truck, as a means of roughly setting the fast idle speed before the carburetor is reinstalled. For normal adjustment of fast idle speed, refer to the idle adjustment section in Chapter 2.*

1. Hold the cam follower on the high step of the fast idle cam.

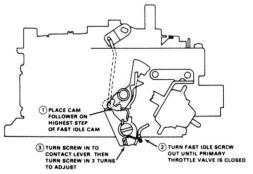

**M4MC and M4ME fast idle adjustment (© Chevrolet Motor Div.)**

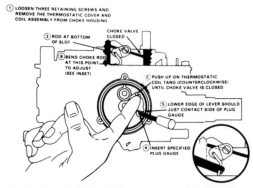

**M4MC and M4ME choke coil lever adjustment (© Chevrolet Motor Div.)**

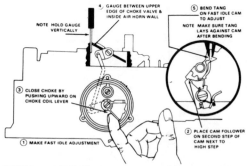

**M4MC and M4ME choke rod adjustment (© Chevrolet Motor Div.)**

2. Turn the fast idle screw out until the primary throttle valves are closed (1975), or until it pulls away from the fast idle cam follower (1976–77).

3. Turn the fast idle screw in to contact the lever, then turn the screw in three turns.

4. Recheck the fast idle speed.

## Choke Coil Lever

1. Loosen the three retaining screws and remove the cover and coil assembly from the choke housing. On the 1978–80 models, also place the fast idle cam follower on the high step of the cam.

2. Push up on the thermostatic coil tang (counterclockwise) until the choke valve closes.

3. Insert the specified gauge into the hole in the choke housing.

4. The lower edge of the choke coil lever should just contact the side of the gauge.

5. Bend the choke rod to adjust.

## Choke Rod

The choke coil lever adjustment must be made before making the following adjustment. The thermostatic cover and coil will remain off for this adjustment.

1. Adjust the fast idle.

2. Place the cam follower on the second step of the fast idle cam firmly against the rise of the high step.

3. Close the choke valve by pushing up on the choke coil lever inside the choke housing.

4. Measure the clearance between the upper edge of the choke valve and the inside of the air horn wall.

5. Bend the tang on the fast idle cam to adjust the clearance. Be sure that the tang lies against the cam after bending it.

6. Recheck the fast idle.

## Air Valve Dashpot

1. Seat the front vacuum diaphragm using an outside vacuum source. Plug the purge bleed hole with masking tape on models where used. Remove tape after making adjustment.

2. The air valves must be completely closed.

3. Measure the clearance between the air valve dashpot and the end of the slot in the air valve lever.

4. Bend the air valve dashpot rod to adjust the clearance.

## Front Vacuum Break

1. Remove the thermostatic cover and coil assembly from the choke housing.

2. Place the cam follower on the high step of the fast idle cam.

3. Seat the front vacuum diaphragm using an outside vacuum source.

4. Push up on the inside choke coil lever until the tang on the vacuum break lever contacts the tang on the vacuum break plunger.

5. Measure the clearance between the upper edge of the choke valve and the air horn wall.

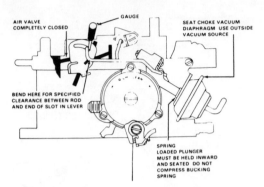

**M4MC and M4ME air valve dashpot adjustment (© Chevrolet Motor Div.)**

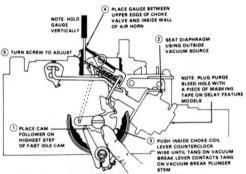

**M4MC and M4ME front vacuum break adjustment (© Chevrolet Motor Div.)**

6. Turn the adjusting screw on the vacuum break plunger lever to adjust.

7. Reconnect the vacuum hose after adjustment.

### Rear Vacuum Break (All 1975; 1976–78 M4ME; 1979–80 M4MC)

1. Remove the thermostatic cover and coil assembly from the choke housing.

2. Place the cam follower on the high step of the fast idle cam.

3. Plug the bleed hose in the vacuum break unit cover with tape.

4. Seat the rear vacuum diaphragm using an outside vacuum source.

5. Push up the choke coil lever inside the choke housing toward the closed position. Diaphragm should be pulled out until seated, bucking spring compressed (where used) on 1976–80.

6. With the choke rod in the bottom slot of the choke lever, measure the clearance between the upper edge of the choke valve and air horn wall.

7. Bend the vacuum break rod if necessary to adjust.

8. After adjustment, remove the tape and install the vacuum hose.

### Automatic Choke Coil, M4MC

1. Install the thermostatic coil and cover with a gasket between the choke cover and choke housing. On all models except the 1976 454 cu in. V8, the thermostatic coil must be installed in the slot in the inside of the choke coil lever pick-up arm.

2. Place the fast idle cam follower on the high step of the fast idle cam.

3. Rotate the cover and coil assembly counterclockwise until the choke valve just closes.

4. Align the index point on the cover with the specified mark on the choke housing.

5. Tighten the retaining screws.

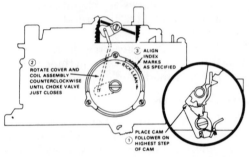

**M4MC automatic choke coil adjustment (© Chevrolet Motor Div.)**

### Automatic Choke Coil, 1976–78 M4ME

1. Install the electric choke assembly in choke housing, making sure coil tang contacts bottom side of inside choke coil lever pick-up arm.

2. Place fast idle cam follower on high step of cam.

3. Rotate cover and coil assembly counterclockwise until choke valve just closes.

4. Align index point on cover with specified mark on housing.

5. Install cover retainers and screws.

NOTE: *Ground contact for the electric choke is provided by a metal plate located at the rear of the choke assembly. Do not install a choke cover gasket between the electric choke assembly and the choke housing. Do not immerse the electric choke assembly in any cleaning solution. Severe damage can result.*

### Unloader

1. Perform Step 1 of the appropriate automatic choke coil procedure.

2. Hold the throttle valves wide open with the choke valve completely closed. On a

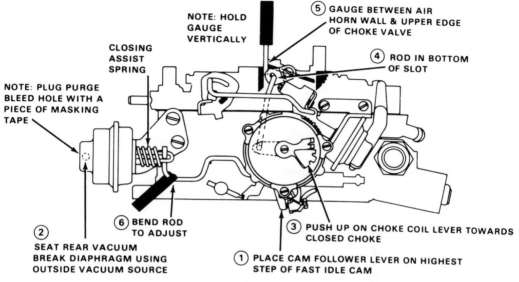

## (ALL EXCEPT 454 ENGINE)

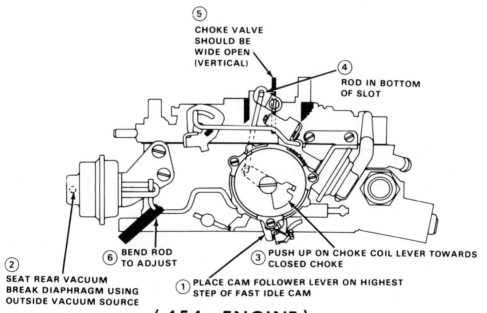

## (454 ENGINE)

M4MC and M4MCA rear vacuum break adjustment. Refer to the upper illustration for 1976–78 M4ME (© Chevrolet Motor Div.)

warm engine, close the choke valve by pushing on the tang of the intermediate choke lever which contacts the fast idle cam. A rubber band will hold it in position.

3. Measure the distance between the upper edge of the choke valve and the air horn wall.

4. Bend the tang on the fast idle lever to adjust the clearance. Check to be sure that the tang on the fast idle cam lever is contact-

ing the center of the fast idle cam after adjustment.

### Secondary Throttle Lock-Out

SECONDARY LEVER CLEARANCE

1. Hold the choke valve and secondary throttle valves closed.

2. Measure the clearance between the lock-out pin and the lock-out lever.

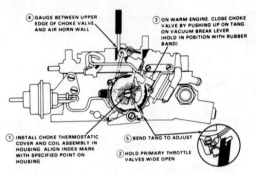

**M4MC and M4ME choke unloader adjustment**
**(© Chevrolet Motor Div.)**

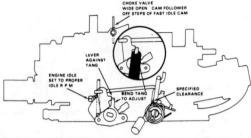

**M4MC and M4ME secondary closing adjustment**
**(© Chevrolet Motor Div.)**

4. Bend the secondary closing tang on the primary throttle lever to adjust to .020 in. clearance.

## Secondary Opening

1. Lightly, crack the primary throttle lever until the link just contacts the tang on the secondary lever.

2. With the link against the tang, the link should be in the center of the slot in the secondary lever.

3. Bend the tang on the secondary lever to adjust.

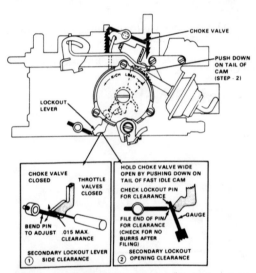

**M4MC and M4ME secondary throttle lock-out adjustment (© Chevrolet Motor Div.)**

3. If necessary, bend the lock-out pin to adjust to .015 in.

*OPENING CLEARANCE*

4. Hold the choke valve wide open by pushing down on the fast idle cam.

5. Hold the secondary throttle valves slightly open.

6. Measure the clearance between the end of the lock-out pin and the toe of the lock-out lever.

7. If necessary, file off the end of the lock-out pin to obtain .015 in. clearance.

## Secondary Closing

1. Set the idle speed to specification.

2. Hold the choke valve wide open with the cam follower lever off the steps of the fast idle cam.

3. Measure the clearance between the slot in the secondary throttle valve pickup lever and the secondary actuating rod.

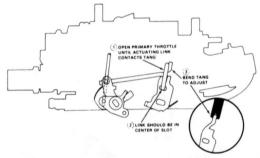

**M4MC and M4ME secondary opening adjustment**
**(© Chevrolet Motor Div.)**

## Air Valve Spring Wind-Up

1. Remove the front vacuum break diaphragm and the air valve dashpot rod.

2. Loosen the lockscrew.

3. Turn the tension adjusting screw counterclockwise until the air valve opens partway.

4. Turn the tension adjusting screw clockwise while tapping lightly on the casting with the handle of a screwdriver.

5. When the air valve just closes, turn the tension adjusting screw clockwise the specified number of turns after the spring contacts the pin.

6. Tighten the lockscrew and reinstall the diaphragm and dashpot rod.

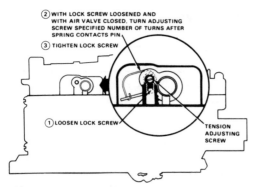

M4MC and M4ME air valve spring wind-up (© Chevrolet Motor Div.)

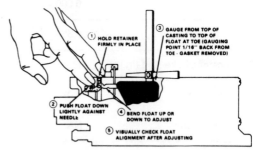

M4MC and M4ME deceleration throttle stop (© Chevrolet Motor Div.)

## Deceleration Throttle Stop

1. Adjust the idle speed.
2. Push the hex end of the throttle stop plunger in (toward the throttle lever) until the plunger stem hits the stop inside the diaphragm.
3. With the plunger against the stop, turn the plunger adjusting screw in or out to obtain the specified deceleration rpm.

M4MC and M4ME float level adjustment (© Chevrolet Motor Div.)

## CARBURETOR SPECIFICATIONS

Specifications for all carburetors can be found on pages 194–202:

## DIESEL FUEL INJECTION

A description of the fuel injection system, and procedures for checking and adjusting timing, linkage adjustments, and specifications can be found on pages 203–204.

## Carburetor Specifications

*ROCHESTER MV (1970–74)*

| | 1970 | 1971 | 1972 | 1973 | 1974 |
|---|---|---|---|---|---|
| Float Level (in.) | ¼ | ¼ | ¼ | ¼ | ¼ ⑮ |
| Fast Idle Mechanical (in.) | 0.100 | 0.100 | — | — | — |
| Running (rpm) | 2400 | 2400 | 2400 | 2400 | 1800⑯ |
| Choke Rod (in.) | 0.180 ① | 0.180 ④ | ⑦ | ⑪ | .0245⑰ |
| Vacuum Break (in.) | 0.260 ② | 0.350 ⑤ | 0.190 ⑧ | 0.430⑫ | 0.300⑱ |
| Choke Unloader (in.) | 0.350 | 0.350 | 0.500 | 0.600⑬ | 0.500⑲ |
| Thermostat Choke Rod (in.) | ③ | — | — | — | — |
| Metering Rod (in.) | 0.070 | 0.070 ⑥ | 0.070 ⑨ | 0.070⑭ | 0.080⑳ |
| CEC Valve (rpm) | NA | ㉑ | ⑩ | ⑩ | — |

—Not applicable
① W/292 cu in. engine—0.275 in.
② W/292 cu in. engine—0.350 in.
③ Bottom of the rod even with top of hole
④ 0.300 in. w/carb No. 7021022
  0.275 in. w/carb No. 7041026
⑤ 0.230 in. w/carb No. 7041021
  0.260 in. w/carb No. 7041025
⑥ 0.080 in. w/carb No. 7041021
⑦ 0.150 in. w/carb No. 7042021, 7042921
  0.125 in. w/carb No. 7042022, 7042922
  0.180 in. w/carb No. 7042025
  0.275 in. w/carb No. 7042026
⑧ 0.225 in. w/carb No. 7042021, 7042921
  0.260 in. w/carb No. 7042025
  0.350 in. w/carb No. 7042026
⑨ 0.076 in. w/carb No. 7042991
  0.078 in. w/carb No. 7042021
  0.079 in. w/carb No. 7042022
⑩ 250 cu in. only—1000 (manual/Neutral)
  —650 (automatic/Drive)

⑪ 0.245 in. w/carb No. 7043022
  0.275 in. w/carb No. 7043021
  0.350 in. w/carb No. 7043025
  0.375 in. w/carb No. 7043026
⑫ 0.300 in. w/carb No. 7043022
  0.350 in. w/carb No. 7043021
⑬ 0.500 in. w/carb No. 7043022, 3021
⑭ 0.080 in. w/carb No. 7043022, 3021
⑮ 0.295 in. w/carb No. 7044021, 4022, 4321
⑯ 2400 rpm w/carb No. 7044025, 4026
⑰ 0.275 in. w/carb No. 7044021, 4026
  0.300 in. w/carb No. 7044321
⑱ 0.350 in. w/carb No. 7044021, 4026
  0.375 in. w/carb No. 7044321
⑲ 0.521 in. w/carb No. 7044025, 4026
  measured at top of choke blade
⑳ 0.070 in. w/carb No. 7044025, 4026
㉑ 250, 292, 307 Manual—1000 rpm
  350V8 Manual—900 rpm
  402V8 Manual—850 rpm
  250, 292 Automatic—750
  350, 307V8 Automatic—650
  402V8 Automatic—650

*ROCHESTER MV (1975)*

| | | | | |
|---|---|---|---|---|
| Float Level (in.) | ¹¹/₃₂ | | Primary Vacuum Break (in.) | 0.300 ② |
| Metering Rod (in.) | 0.080 | | Auxiliary Vacuum Break (in.) | ③ |
| Choke Rod (in.) | ① | | Choke Unloader (in.) | 0.325 ④ |

① 0.245 w/carb No. 7045004, 302, 304
  0.260 w/carb No. 7045002
  0.275 w/carb No. 7045003, 005, 303, 305
② 0.350 w/carb No. 7045005, 303, 305

③ 0.150 w/carb No. 7045004, 302
  0.170 w/carb No. 7045303
  0.290 w/carb No. 7045002, 003, 005, 304, 305
④ 0.275 w/carb No. 7045302, 303

## Carburetor Specifications (cont.)

### *ROCHESTER MV (1976)*

| Carburetor Number | Float Level (in.) | Metering Rod (in.) | Choke Rod (Fast Idle Cam) (in.) | Primary Vacuum Break (in.) | Auxiliary Vacuum Break (in.) | Choke Unloader (in.) |
|---|---|---|---|---|---|---|
| 17056002 | 11/32 | 0.080 | 0.130 | 0.165 | 0.265 | 0.335 |
| 6003 | 11/32 | 0.080 | 0.145 | 0.180 | W.O. | 0.335 |
| 6302 | 11/32 | 0.080 | 0.155 | 0.190 | W.O. | 0.325 |
| 6303 | 11/32 | 0.080 | 0.180 | 0.225 | W.O. | 0.325 |
| 6004 | 11/32 | 0.080 | 0.130 | 0.165 | 0.265 | 0.335 |
| 6006 | 1/4 | 0.080 | 0.130 | 0.165 | — | 0.270 |
| 6007 | 1/4 | 0.070 | 0.130 | 0.165 | — | 0.275 |
| 6008, 6009, 6308, 6309 | 1/4 | 0.070 | 0.150 | 0.190 | — | 0.275 |

### *ROCHESTER ME (1977)*

| Carburetor Number | Float Level (in.) | Metering Rod (in.) | Choke Rod (Fast Idle Cam) (in.) | Primary Vacuum Break (in.) | Auxiliary Vacuum Break (in.) | Choke Unloader (in.) |
|---|---|---|---|---|---|---|
| 17057001 | 3/8 | 0.080 | 0.125 | 0.150 | — | 0.325 |
| 7002, 7004, 7010, 7302 | 3/8 | 0.080 | 0.110 | 0.135 | — | 0.325 |
| 7005 | 3/8 | 0.080 | 0.125 | 0.180 | — | 0.325 |
| 7006, 7007 | 5/16 | 0.070 | 0.150 | 0.180 | — | 0.275 |
| 7008, 7009, 7308, 7309 | 5/16 | 0.065 | 0.150 | 0.180 | — | 0.275 |
| 7303 | 3/8 | 0.090 | 0.125 | 0.150 | — | 0.325 |

### *ROCHESTER ME (1978)*

| Carburetor Number | Float Level (in.) | Metering Rod (in.) | Choke Rod (Fast Idle Cam) (in.) | Primary Vacuum Break (in.) | Auxiliary Vacuum Break (in.) | Choke Unloader (in.) |
|---|---|---|---|---|---|---|
| 17058008, 8009, 8308, 8309, 8358, 8359 | 5/16 | 0.065 | 0.275 | 0.275 | — | 0.520 |
| 8006, 8007 | 5/16 | 0.070 | 0.275 | 0.275 | — | 0.520 |
| 8310, 8312, 8320, 8322 | 5/16 | 0.080 | 0.190 | 0.250 | — | 0.600 |
| 8311, 8313, 8323 | 5/16 | 0.100 | 0.190 | 0.250 | — | 0.600 |
| 8021, 8022, 8024, 8081, 8082, 8084 | 5/16 | — | 0.200 | 0.250 | — | 0.450 |

## Carburetor Specifications (cont.)

### ROCHESTER ME (1979)

| Carburetor Number | Float Level (in.) | Metering Rod (in.) | Choke Rod (Fast Idle Cam) (in.) | Primary Vacuum Break (in.) | Auxiliary Vacuum Break (in.) | Choke Unloader (in.) |
|---|---|---|---|---|---|---|
| 17059009, 9309, 9359 | $5/16$ | 0.065 | 0.275 | 0.400 | — | 0.521 |

### ROCHESTER ME (1980)

| Carburetor Number | Float Level (in.) | Metering Rod (in.) | Choke Rod (Fast Idle Cam) (in.) | Primary Vacuum Break (in.) | Auxiliary Vacuum Break (in.) | Choke Unloader (in.) |
|---|---|---|---|---|---|---|
| 17080009, 0309, 0359 | $11/32$ | 0.090 | 0.275 | 0.400 | — | 0.520 |

### ROCHESTER 2GV, 2GC

| | (2GV) 1970 | (2GV) 1971 | (2GV) 1972 | (2GV) 1973 | (2GV) 1974 | (2GC) 1975 | (2GC) 1976 | (2GC) 1977–78 |
|---|---|---|---|---|---|---|---|---|
| Float Level (in.) | $23/32$ ⑦ | $21/32$ ① | $21/32$ ㉒ | $21/32$ ⑬ | $19/32$ | $21/32$ | $21/32$ | $19/32$ |
| Float Drop (in.) | $1 3/4$ | $1 3/4$ ② | $1 9/32$ | $1 9/32$ | $1 9/32$ | $31/32$ | $1 9/32$ | $1 9/32$ |
| Pump Rod (in.) | — | $1 3/64$ ③ | $1 5/16$ ㉓ | $1 5/16$ ⑭ | $1 9/32$ ⑱ | $1 5/8$ | $1 11/16$ | $1 21/32$ |
| Choke Rod (in.) (Fast Idle Cam) | 0.060 | 0.040 ④ | 0.040 ⑩ | 0.150 ⑮ | 0.200 ⑲ | 0.400 | 0.260 | 0.260 |
| Vacuum Break (in.) | 0.140 ⑧ | 0.080 ⑤ | 0.080 ⑪ | 0.080 ⑯ | 0.140 ⑳ | 0.130 | 0.130 | 0.130 ㉕㉖ |
| Choke Unloader (in.) | 0.215 | 0.215 ⑥ | 0.210 ㉔ | 0.215 ⑰ | 0.250 ㉑ | 0.350 | 0.325 | 0.325 |
| Thermostatic Choke Rod | ⑨ | — | — | — | — | — | — | — |
| CEC Valve (rpm) | ⑫ | ⑫ | — | — | — | — | — | — |
| Fast Idle (rpm) | 2200– 2400 | — | 1850 ($1 1/4$) 2200 ($1 1/2$) | 1600 | 1600 | — | — | — |

① $23/32$ in. w/carb No. 7041138, 139
② $1 1/4$ in. w/carb No. 7041138, 139
③ $1 5/32$ in. w/carb No. 7041138, 139
④ 0.100 in. w/carb No. 7041138, 139
⑤ 0.170 in. w/carb No. 7041138
   0.180 in. w/carb No. 7041139
⑥ 0.325 in. w/carb No. 7041138, 139
⑦ $27/32$ in. w/carb No. 7040108
⑧ 0.130 in. w/carb No. 7040108
⑨ Bottom of rod even with top of hole
⑩ 0.075 in. w/carb No. 7042824, 825
   0.100 in. w/carb No. 7042108
⑪ 0.110 in. w/carb No. 7042824, 825
   0.170 in. w/carb No. 7042108
⑫ 1000 w/Manual
   650 w/Automatic
NOTE: *2 versions of the 2GV are available: $1 1/2$ in. diameter and $1 1/4$ in. diameter venturi.*

⑬ $25/32$ in. w/carb No. 7043108
⑭ $1 7/16$ in. w/carb No. 7043108
⑮ 0.200 in. w/carb No. 7043108
⑯ 0.140 in. w/carb No. 7043108
⑰ 0.250 in. w/carb No. 7043108
⑱ $1 3/16$ in. w/carb No. 7041114
⑲ 0.245 in. w/carb No. 7044114
⑳ 0.130 in. w/carb No. 7044114
㉑ 0.325 in. w/carb No. 7044114
㉒ $25/32$ in. w/carb No. 7042108
㉓ $1 1/2$ in. w/carb No. 7042108
㉔ 0.325 in. w/carb No. 7042108
㉕ Below 22,500 mi
   0.160 above 22,500 mi
㉖ 0.190 in. w/carb No. 17056137
—Not applicable

## Carburetor Specifications (cont.)

### ROCHESTER 2SE (1979–80)

| Carburetor Identification | Float Level (in.) | Pump Rod (in.) | Fast Idle (rpm) | Choke Coil Lever (in.) | Fast Idle Cam (deg./in.) | Air Valve Rod (in.) | Primary Vacuum Break (deg./in.) | Secondary Vacuum Break (deg./in.) | Choke Unloader (deg./in.) | Secondary Lockout (in.) |
|---|---|---|---|---|---|---|---|---|---|---|
| 17059640 | 1/8 | 9/16 | 2000 | 0.085 | 17/.090 | 0.040 | 20/.110 | 37/.234 | 49/.341 | .011–.040 |
| 17059641 | 1/8 | 9/16 | 1800 | 0.085 | 17/.090 | 0.040 | 23.5/.132 | 37/.234 | 49/.341 | .011–.040 |
| 17059643 | 1/8 | 9/16 | 1800 | 0.085 | 17/.090 | 0.040 | 23.5/.132 | 37/.234 | 49/.341 | .011–.040 |
| 17059740 | 1/8 | 9/16 | 2000 | 0.085 | 17/.090 | 0.040 | 20/.110 | 37/.234 | 49/.341 | .011–.040 |
| 17059741 | 1/8 | 9/16 | 2100 | 0.085 | 17/.090 | 0.040 | 20/.110 | 37/.234 | 49/.341 | .011–.040 |
| 17058764 | 1/8 | 9/16 | 2100 | 0.085 | 17/.090 | 0.040 | 20/.110 | 37/.234 | 49/.341 | .011–.040 |
| 17059765 | 1/8 | 9/16 | 2100 | 0.085 | 17/.090 | 0.040 | 23.5/.132 | 37/.234 | 49/.341 | .011–.040 |
| 17059767 | 1/8 | 9/16 | 2100 | 0.085 | 17/.090 | 0.040 | 23.5/.132 | 37/.234 | 49/.341 | .011–.040 |
| 17080621 | 1/8 | 9/16 | 2000 | 0.085 | 17/.090 | 0.010 | 22/.123 | 35/.220 | 41/.269 | .011–.040 |
| 17080622 | 1/8 | 9/16 | 2200 | 0.085 | 17/.090 | 0.010 | 22/.123 | 35/.220 | 41/.269 | .011–.040 |
| 17080623 | 1/8 | 9/16 | 2000 | 0.085 | 17/.090 | 0.010 | 22/.123 | 35/.220 | 41/.269 | .011–.040 |
| 17080626 | 1/8 | 9/16 | 2200 | 0.085 | 17/.090 | 0.010 | 22/.123 | 35/.220 | 41/.269 | .011–.040 |
| 17080720 | 1/8 | 9/16 | 2200 | 0.085 | 17/.090 | 0.010 | 20/.110 | 35/.220 | 41/.269 | .011–.040 |
| 17080721 | 1/8 | 9/16 | 2000 | 0.085 | 17/.090 | 0.010 | 23.5/.132 | 35/.220 | 41/.269 | .011–.040 |
| 17080722 | 1/8 | 9/16 | 2200 | 0.085 | 17/.090 | 0.010 | 20/.110 | 35/.220 | 41/.269 | .011–.040 |
| 17080723 | 1/8 | 9/16 | 2000 | 0.085 | 17/.090 | 0.010 | 23.5/.132 | 35/.220 | 41/.269 | .011–.040 |

### ROCHESTER M2MC (1979–80)

| Carburetor Identification | Float Level (in.) | Choke Rod (in.) | Choke Unloader (in.) | Front Vacuum Break (in.) | Pump Rod (in.) | Choke Coil Lever (in.) | Automatic Choke (notches) |
|---|---|---|---|---|---|---|---|
| All 1979 | 15/32 | 0.243 | 0.243 | 0.171 | 13/32 ① | 0.120 | 1 Lean |
| All 1980 | 7/16 | 0.243 | 0.243 | 0.171 | 9/32 ① | 0.120 | ② |

① Inner hole
② Riveted cover; replacement kits contain setting instructions

## Carburetor Specifications (cont.)

*ROCHESTER 4MV*

| | 1970 | 1971 | 1972 | 1973 | 1974 | 1975 |
|---|---|---|---|---|---|---|
| Float Level (in.) | $^1/_4$ | $^1/_4$ ④ | ⑥ | ⑨ | ⑫ | ⑯ |
| Accelerator Pump (in.) | $^5/_{16}$ | $^5/_{16}$ | $^3/_8$ | $^{13}/_{32}$ | $^{13}/_{32}$ | 0.275 |
| Fast Idle (rpm) | 2400 | 2400 | ⑦ | 1600 | 1600 ⑬ | 1600 |
| Choke Rod (in.) | 0.100 | 0.100 | 0.100 | 0.430 | 0.430 | 0.430 |
| Choke Vacuum Break (in.) | 0.245 ① | 0.260 | 0.215 ⑧ | 0.215 ⑩ | 0.215 ⑭ | ⑰ |
| Choke Unloader (in.) | 0.450 | 0.450 | 0.450 | 0.450 | 0.450 | 0.450 |
| Thermostatic Choke Rod Setting | ② | ② | — | — | — | — |
| Air Valve Spring (in.) | $^7/_{16}$ ③ | — | — | $^1/_2$ ⑪ | $^7/_8$ ⑮ | ⑱ |
| Air Valve Dashpot | 0.020 | 0.020 | 0.020 | — | — | 0.015 |
| CEC Valve (rpm) | — | ⑤ | — | — | — | — |

—Not applicable

① 0.275 in. w/carb No. 7040511 and manual trans No. 7040509 and manual trans
② Top of rod should be even with bottom of hole
③ $^{13}/_{16}$ in. w/all 396 cu in. V8
④ $^{11}/_{32}$ in. w/carb No. 7041209
⑤ 350 V8 w/manual trans—900 rpm
402 V8 w/manual trans—850 rpm
350 V8 w/automatic trans—650 rpm
402 V8 w/automatic trans—650 rpm
⑥ $^1/_4$ in. w/carb No. 7042206, 218
$^3/_{16}$ in. w/carb No. 7042208, 210, 211, 910, 911
$^{11}/_{32}$ in. w/carb No. 7042207, 219
⑦ 1350—Manual transmission
1500—Automatic transmission
⑧ 0.250 w/carb No. 7042206, 207, 218, 219
⑨ $^7/_{32}$ in. w/carb No. 7043202, 203
$^5/_{16}$ in. w/carb No. 7043208, 215
$^1/_4$ in. w/carb No. 7043200, 216, 207, 507
⑩ 0.250 in. w/carb No. 7043200, 216
0.275 in. w/carb No. 7043507

⑪ $^{11}/_{16}$ in. w/carb No. 7043200, 216, 207, 507
⑫ $^1/_4$ in. w/carb No. 7044202, 502, 203, 503, 218, 518, 219, 519
$^{11}/_{32}$ in. w/carb No. 7044213, 513
0.675 in. w/carb No. 7044212, 217, 512, 517, 500, 520
⑬ 1700 rpm w/carb No. 7044212, 217, 512, 517
⑭ 0.220 in. w/carb No. 7044223, 227
0.230 in. w/carb No. 7044212, 217, 512, 517
0.250 in. w/carb No. 7044500, 520
⑮ $^7/_{16}$ w/carb No. 7044223, 227, 212, 217, 512, 517, 500, 520
⑯ $^3/_8$ in. w/carb No. 7045212
$^{11}/_{32}$ in. w/carb No. 7045213, 229, 583, 589
$^{15}/_{32}$ in. w/carb No. 7045229
⑰ 0.225 in. w/carb No. 7045212
0.210 in. w/carb No. 7045213
0.200 in. w/carb No. 7045229
0.230 in. w/carb No. 7045583, 589
⑱ $^7/_{16}$ in. w/carb No. 7Q45212
$^7/_8$ in. w/carb No. 7045213, 583
$^3/_4$ in. w/carb No. 7045229, 589

## Carburetor Specifications (cont.)

### ROCHESTER 4MV (1976)

| Carburetor Number | Float Level (in.) | Vacuum Break (in.) | Air Valve Spring Windup (in.) |
|---|---|---|---|
| 7045231 | $^{11}/_{32}$ | 0.145 | $^7/_8$ |
| 7045229 | $^{11}/_{32}$ | 0.138 | $^3/_4$ |
| 7045583 | $^{11}/_{32}$ | 0.155 | $^7/_8$ |
| 7045588 | $^{11}/_{32}$ | 0.155 | $^3/_4$ |
| 17056212 | $^3/_8$ | 0.155 | $^7/_{16}$ |

### ROCHESTER 4MV (1977)

| Carburetor Number | Float Level (in.) | Vacuum Break (in.) | Air Valve Spring Windup (in.) |
|---|---|---|---|
| 7045583 | $^{11}/_{32}$ | 0.120 | $^7/_8$ |
| 17056212 | $^3/_8$ | 0.120 | $^7/_{16}$ |
| 17057213 | $^{11}/_{32}$ | 0.115 | $^7/_8$ |

NOTE: Pump Rod: $^9/_{32}$ in. in all applications
Air Valve Dashpot: 0.015 in. in all applications
Choke Unloader: 0.295 in. except 17057213: 0.205 in.
Choke Rod (Fast Idle Cam): 0.290 in. except 17057213: 0.220 in.

### ROCHESTER M4MC, M4MCA (1975)

| Carburetor Number | Float Level (in.) | Choke Rod (Fast Idle Cam) (in.) | Front Vacuum Break (in.) | Rear Vacuum Break (in.) | Choke Unloader (in.) | Choke Setting |
|---|---|---|---|---|---|---|
| 7045202, 203 | $^{15}/_{32}$ | 0.300 | 0.180 | 0.170 | 0.325 | * |
| 7045220 | $^{17}/_{32}$ | 0.300 | 0.200 | 0.550 | 0.325 | * |
| 7045512 | $^{17}/_{32}$ | 0.300 | 0.180 | 0.550 | 0.325 | * |

### ROCHESTER M4MC (1976)

| Carburetor Number | Float Level (in.) | Choke Rod (Fast Idle Cam) (in.) | Front Vacuum Break (in.) | Rear Vacuum Break (in.) | Choke Unloader (in.) | Choke Setting |
|---|---|---|---|---|---|---|
| 17056208, 508 | ** | 0.325 | 0.185 | — | 0.325 | 2 NL |
| 17056209 | ** | 0.325 | 0.185 | — | 0.325 | 3 NL |
| 17056509 | ** | 0.325 | 0.185 | — | 0.325 | 1 NL |
| 17056512 | $^7/_{16}$ | 0.325 | 0.185 | — | 0.275 | Index |

### ROCHESTER M4MC (1977)

| Carburetor Number | Float Level (in.) | Choke Rod (Fast Idle Cam) (in.) | Front Vacuum Break (in.) | Rear Vacuum Break (in.) | Choke Unloader (in.) | Choke Setting |
|---|---|---|---|---|---|---|
| 17057202, 204 | $^{15}/_{32}$ | 0.325 | 0.160 | — | 0.280 | 2 NL |
| 17057209 | $^7/_{16}$ | 0.325 | 0.160 | — | 0.325 | 3 NL |
| 17057229 | $^{11}/_{32}$ | 0.285 | 0.160 | — | 0.280 | 2 NL |
| 17057502, 504 | $^{15}/_{32}$ | 0.325 | 0.165 | — | 0.280 | 2 NL |

## Carburetor Specifications (cont.)

### ROCHESTER M4MC (1977)

| Carburetor Number | Float Level (in.) | Choke Rod (Fast Idle Cam) (in.) | Front Vacuum Break (in.) | Rear Vacuum Break (in.) | Choke Unloader (in.) | Choke Setting |
|---|---|---|---|---|---|---|
| 17057503 | $^{15}/_{32}$ | 0.325 | 0.165 | — | 0.280 | 1 NL |
| 17057512 | $^{7}/_{16}$ | 0.285 | 0.165 | — | 0.240 | Index |
| 17057529 | $^{11}/_{32}$ | 0.285 | 0.175 | — | 0.280 | 2 NL |
| 17057582, 584 | $^{15}/_{32}$ | 0.385 | 0.180 | — | 0.280 | 2 NL |

### ROCHESTER M4ME (1976–77)

| Carburetor Number | Float Level (in.) | Choke Rod (Fast Idle Cam) (in.) | Front Vacuum Break (in.) | Rear Vacuum Break (in.) | Choke Unloader (in.) | Choke Setting |
|---|---|---|---|---|---|---|
| 17056221 | $^{7}/_{16}$ | 0.300 | — | 0.160 | 0.325 | 2 NR |
| 17057221 | $^{3}/_{8}$ | 0.385 | — | 0.160 | 0.280 | 2 Notches Counter-clockwise |

Inner Pump Rod Setting: 0.275 in.—1975; $^{9}/_{32}$ in.—1976; $^{9}/_{32}$ in.—1977 except: 17057582, 584: $^{3}/_{8}$ in. Outer Pump Rod only
Choke Coil Lever: 0.120 in. all years
Air Valve Dashpot: 0.015 in. all years

Air Valve Spring Windup: $^{7}/_{8}$ in. all years except: 7045220, 512: $^{9}/_{16}$ in. 1975 only
NL: Notches Lean
NR: Notches Rich
*Choke valve setting is at the top of the valve
**Needle seat with groove at upper edge: $^{5}/_{16}$ in.
  Needle seat without groove at upper edge: $^{7}/_{16}$ in.

### ROCHESTER M4MC, 4MV (1978)

| Float Adjustment: (in.) | |
|---|---|
| 17058212, 8218, 8219, 8222, 8525 | $^{7}/_{16}$ |
| 8500, 8501, 8520, 8521 | $^{3}/_{8}$ |
| 8512 | $^{13}/_{32}$ |
| All others | $^{15}/_{32}$ |

| Pump Adjustment: (in.) | |
|---|---|
| 17058509, 8510, 8586, 8588 | $^{11}/_{32}$ Outer |
| All others | $^{9}/_{32}$ Inner |

NOTE: *All other adjustments require special angle gauge.*

| Choke Coil: (in.) | |
|---|---|
| All | 0.120 |

| Choke Setting | |
|---|---|
| 17058512 | Index |
| 8201, 8219, 8500, 8501, 8520, 8521 | 3 NL |
| 8218, 8222, 8509, 8510, 8586, 8588 | 2 NL |
| All others | 1 NL |

| Air Valve Spring Windup: | |
|---|---|
| 17058525 | $^{3}/_{4}$ turn |
| All others | $^{7}/_{8}$ turn |

## Carburetor Specifications (cont.)

*ROCHESTER M4MC* (1979)

| Float Adjustment: (in.) | |
|---|---|
| 17059212 | $7/16$ |
| 512 | $13/32$ |
| 520, 521 | $3/8$ |
| All others | $15/32$ |

| Pump Adjustment: (in.) | |
|---|---|
| 17059212, 213, 215, 229, 510, 512, 513, 515, 520, 521, 529 | $9/32$ Inner |
| 377, 378, 527, 528 | $9/32$ Outer |
| All others | $13/32$ Inner |

| Choke Coil Lever: (in.) | |
|---|---|
| All | 0.120 |

| Choke Rod: (in.) | |
|---|---|
| 17059213, 215, 229, 513, 515, 529 | 0.234 |
| All others | 0.314 |

| Air Valve Rod: (in.) | |
|---|---|
| All | 0.015 |

| Unloader Adjustment: (in.) | |
|---|---|
| 17059212, 213, 215, 229, 512, 513, 515, 529 | 0.260 |
| All others | 0.277 |

| Front Vacuum Break: (in.) | |
|---|---|
| 17059213, 215, 229, 513, 515, 529 | 0.129 |
| 212, 512 | 0.136 |
| 501, 520, 521 | 0.164 |
| 509, 510, 586, 588 | 0.179 |

| Rear Vacuum Break: (in.) | |
|---|---|
| 17059363, 366, 368, 377, 378, 503, 506, 508, 527, 528 | 0.149 |
| All others | 0.129 |

| Air Valve Spring: (turns) | |
|---|---|
| 17059212, 512 | $3/4$ |
| 213, 215, 229, 513, 515, 529 | 1 |
| All others | $7/8$ |

| Choke Setting: | |
|---|---|
| 17059061, 201 | Index |
| 509, 510, 586, 588 | 2 Lean |
| 520, 521, 501 | 3 Lean |
| 212, 213, 215, 229, 512, 513, 515, 529 | 1 Rich |
| All others | 1 Lean |

## Carburetor Specifications (cont.)

### ROCHESTER M4MC (1980)

| Float Adjustment: (in.) | |
| --- | --- |
| 17080213, 215, 513, 515, 229, 529 | 3/8 |
| All others | 15/32 |

| Pump Adjustment: (in.) | |
| --- | --- |
| All | 9/32 Inner |

| Choke Coil Lever (in.) | |
| --- | --- |
| All | 0.120 |

| Choke Rod: (in.) | |
| --- | --- |
| 17080213, 215, 513, 515, 229, 529 | 0.234 |
| All others | 0.314 |

| Air Valve Rod: (in.) | |
| --- | --- |
| All | 0.015 |

| Unloader Adjustment: (in.) | |
| --- | --- |
| 17080212, 213 215, 512, 513, 515, 229, 529 | 0.260 |
| All others | 0.277 |

| Front Vacuum Break: (in.) | |
| --- | --- |
| 17080212, 512 | 0.136 |
| All others | 0.129 |

| Rear Vacuum Break: (in.) | |
| --- | --- |
| 17080290, 291, 292, 503, 506, 508 | 0.149 |
| 212, 213, 215, 512, 513, 515, 229, 529 | 0.179 |
| All others | 0.129 |

| Air Valve Spring: (turns) | |
| --- | --- |
| 17080212, 512 | 3/4 |
| 213, 215, 513, 515, 229, 529 | 1 |
| All others | 7/8 |

| Choke Setting: |
| --- |
| All models have a riveted choke cover; replacement kits contain setting instructions. |

## Diesel Fuel Injection

The General Motors Diesel engine uses a Roosa-master rotary distributor fuel injection pump. There are six adjustments possible in connection with this unit. Two of them require the use of a tachometer equipped with a magnetic pickup probe. Setting the timing requires the use of a special wrench to reach three pump retaining nuts located beneath the injection pump. Although this wrench is not particularly expensive, it may be difficult to obtain. It is suggested that these adjustments be left to a dealer equipped with the proper tools. However, if access to the special wrench and tachometer is available, proceed as follows.

### CHECKING OR ADJUSTING TIMING

For the engine to be properly timed, the lines on the top of the injection pump adapter and the flange of the injection pump must be aligned.

NOTE: *The engine must be off when the timing is reset.*

If the marks are not aligned, adjustment is necessary.

1. Loosen the three pump retaining nuts with the special tool described.

2. Align the mark on the injection pump with the line on the adapter and tighten the nuts. Torque to 35 ft lbs.

NOTE: *Use a ¾ in. end wrench on the boss at the front of the injection pump to aid in rotating the pump to align the marks.*

3. Adjust the throttle rod.

### LINKAGE ADJUSTMENTS

1. Check timing, adjust if necessary (engine off).

2. Throttle rod adjustment (engine off):

a. If equipped with cruise control, remove clip from cruise control rod then remove rod from bellcrank.

b. Remove throttle valve cable from bellcrank.

c. Loosen the locknut on the throttle rod, then shorten the rod several turns.

d. Rotate the bellcrank to the full throttle stop, then lengthen the throttle rod until the injection pump lever contacts the injection pump full throttle stop. Release the bellcrank.

e. Tighten the throttle rod locknut.

f. Connect the throttle valve cable and cruise control rod to bellcrank, then adjust.

3. Transmission Throttle Valve Cable Adjustment.

a. With the engine off, push the snap lock to disengaged position.

b. Rotate the injection pump lever to the full throttle stop and hold there.

c. Push in the snap lock until it is flush. Release the injection pump lever.

4. Slow Idle Speed Adjustment.

NOTE: *To check idle speed, it will be necessary to insert the probe of a magnetic pickup tachometer into the timing indicator hole.*

a. With the driving wheels blocked, parking brake on, transmission in Drive, and air conditioning off, start the engine and adjust the slow idle screw on the injection pump to 575 rpm.

5. Idle Solenoid Adjustment

a. With the driving wheels blocked,

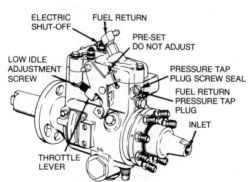

**Diesel fuel injection pump (© Chevrolet Motor Div.)**

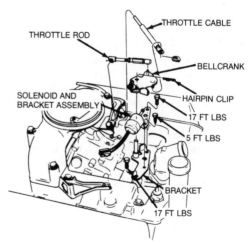

**Exploded view of the diesel throttle assembly (© Chevrolet Motor Div.)**

parking brake on, transmission in Drive, air conditioning on, and air conditioning compressor electrical wires disconnected at the compressor, adjust the idle solenoid plunger to 650 rpm.

6. Cruise Control Servo Relay Rod

a. With the engine off, adjust the rod to minimum slack, then put clip in the last free hole in the rod.

## FUEL TANK

### Draining

CAUTION: *Disconnect the battery before beginning the draining operation.*

If the vehicle is not equipped with a drain plug, use the following procedure to remove the gasoline.

1. Using a 10 foot piece of ⅜ in. hose cut a flap slit 18 in. from one end.

2. Install a pipe nipple, of slightly larger diameter than the hose, into the opposite end of the hose.

3. Install the nipple end of the hose into the fuel tank with the natural curve of the hose pointing downward. Keep feeding the hose in until the nipple hits the bottom of the tank.

4. Place the other end of the hose in a suitable container and insert an air hose pointing it in the downward direction of the slit and inject air into the line.

NOTE: *If the vehicle is to be stored, always drain the gasoline from the complete fuel system including the carburetor, fuel pump, fuel lines, and tank.*

### REMOVAL AND INSTALLATION

#### Cab-Mounted Tanks

1. Remove the seat back hold-down bolts and tilt the seat back forward.

2. If equipped, remove the tank cover.

3. Drain the tank.

4. Disconnect the fuel line, meter wire, and ground wire.

5. Remove the lug wrench and lug wrench mount.

6. Remove the bolts and fasteners securing the tank in place.

7. Remove the tank from the cab, and at the same time, disengage the filler neck from the rubber grommet in the cab opening.

8. Remove the meter assembly from the tank.

9. Installation is the reverse of removal.

#### All Other Tanks

1. Drain the tank.

2. Raise and secure the rear of the vehicle.

3. Remove the clamp on the filler neck and the vent tube hose.

4. Remove the gauge hose which is attached to the frame.

5. While supporting the tank securely, remove the support straps.

6. Lower the tank until the gauge wiring can be removed.

7. Remove the tank.

8. Install the unit by reversing the removal procedure. Make certain that the anti-squeak material is replaced during installation.

9. Lower the vehicle.

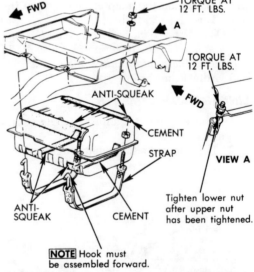

**Fuel tank installation, typical of most models (ⓒ Chevrolet Motor Div.)**

# Chassis Electrical

## HEATER

### Blower

#### REMOVAL AND INSTALLATION

1. Disconnect the battery leads, open the hood, and securely support it.

2. On 1970–72 models, scribe the hood and fender location of the right hood hinge. Remove the hinge.

3. Mark the position of the blower motor in relation to its case. Remove the electrical connection at the motor.

4. Remove the blower attaching screws

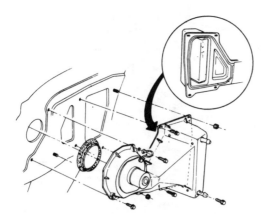

Heater blower assembly, 1970–72 (© Chevrolet Motor Div.)

and remove the assembly. Pry gently on the flange if the sealer sticks.

5. The blower wheel can be removed from the motor shaft by removing the nut at the center.

To assemble the unit:

6. Assemble the blower wheel to the motor with the open end of the wheel away from the motor and install the unit into the blower case. Connect the ground strap and the electrical connection.

7. Position the hood hinge using the scribe marks and check the hood alignment.

8. Connect the battery.

### Core

#### REMOVAL AND INSTALLATION

#### 1970–72 Without Air Conditioning

1. Drain the cooling system and disconnect the battery.

2. Remove the electrical connection at the blower.

3. Remove the heater hoses at the core tubes.

4. Remove the right front fender skirt. Remove enough screws so that the fender can be moved outward.

5. Working from under the instrument panel, remove the seal on the temperature

door cable and disconnect the cable from the temperature door.

6. Pull the case away from the mounting studs after removing the retaining bolts.

7. Remove the core retainers and remove the core.

The installation procedure is the reverse of removal.

### 1970–72 With Factory Installed Air Conditioning

NOTE: *Models with dealer installed air conditioning use the same procedure as those without air conditioning.*

1. Drain the coolant. Disconnect the battery ground cable.

2. Detach the heater hoses from the core tubes at the firewall.

3. Remove the stud nuts on the engine side of the firewall.

4. Remove the glove box.

5. Unplug the relay connector and remove the right ball outlet hose.

6. Remove the screw holding the panel outlet air distributor to the heater case. Remove the heater case retaining screws.

7. Pull the heater case away from the firewall; reach in and disconnect the resistor connector. Remove the resistor harness grommet and remove the harness.

8. Remove the heater case. Remove the core mounting straps. Reverse the procedure for installation.

### 1973–80 Without Air Conditioning

1. Disconnect the battery ground cable.

2. Disconnect the heater hoses at the core tubes and drain the engine coolant. Plug the core tubes to prevent spillage.

3. Remove the nuts from the distributor air ducts in the engine compartment.

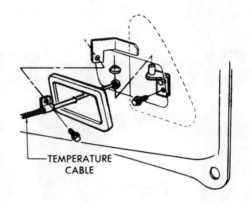

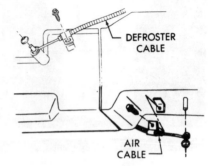

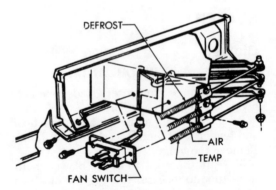

Heater controls, 1970–72 (© Chevrolet Motor Div.)

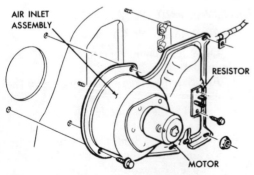

Heater blower assembly, 1973–80 (© Chevrolet Motor Div.)

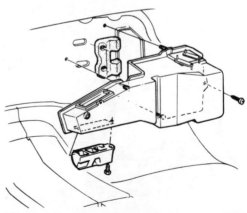

Heater distributor, 1973–80 (© Chevrolet Motor Div.)

4. Remove the glove compartment and door.

5. Disconnect the "Air-Defrost" and "Temperature" door cables.

6. Remove the floor outlet and remove the defroster duct-to-heater distributor screw.

7. Remove the heater distributor-to-instrument panel screws. Pull the assembly rearward to gain access to the wiring harness and disconnect the wires attached to the unit.

8. Remove the heater distributor from the truck.

9. Remove the heater core retaining straps and remove the core from the truck.

10. Installation is the reverse of removal. Be sure that the core-to-case and case-to-dash panel sealer is intact. Fill the cooling system and check for leaks.

### 1973–80 With Air Conditioning

1. Disconnect the battery ground cable.
2. Drain the coolant.
3. Remove the heater hoses from the core tubes. Plug the tubes to prevent spillage.
4. Remove the glove box and door.
5. Remove the screws holding the center duct to the selector duct and to the instrument panel. Remove the center upper and lower ducts.
6. Disconnect the control cable at the temperature door.
7. Remove the three stud nuts from the firewall. Remove the selector duct to firewall screw inside the truck.
8. Pull the selector duct assembly back until the core tubes clear the firewall, then

lower it to disconnect the vacuum and electrical connections.

9. Remove the selector duct assembly and remove the core mounting straps.

10. Reverse the procedure for installation.

## RADIO

### REMOVAL AND INSTALLATION

CAUTION: *Make certain that the speaker is attached to the radio before the unit is turned ON. If it is not, the output transistors will be damaged.*

#### 1970–72

1. Disconnect the negative battery cable and remove the flex hoses from the heater distributor duct under the dashboard.

2. Remove the heater control head by removing the attaching screws and pushing the unit back and down.

3. Remove the ash tray and the ash tray retainer.

4. Remove the electrical connections from the rear of the radio and also the front attaching screws and knobs.

5. Remove the mounting screw on the side of the radio chassis. Push the radio back and up before slipping it down and out of the instrument panel.

6. To install the radio, reverse the removal procedure.

#### 1973–80

1. Remove the negative battery cable and the control knobs and the bezels from the radio control shafts.

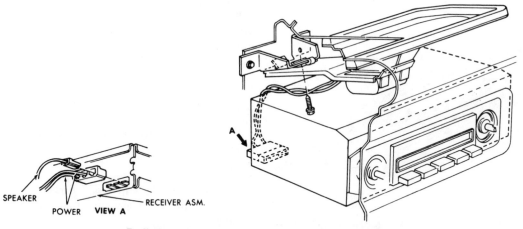

SPEAKER · POWER · VIEW A · RECEIVER ASM. · A

**Radio installation, 1970–72 (© Chevrolet Motor Div.)**

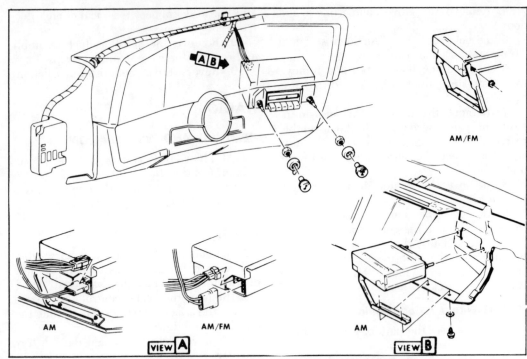

Radio installation, 1973–80 (© Chevrolet Motor Div.)

2. On AM radios, remove the support bracket stud nut and its lockwasher.

3. On AM/FM radios, remove the support bracket-to-instrument panel screws.

4. Lifting the rear edge of the radio, push the radio forward until the control shafts clear the instrument panel. Then lower the radio far enough so that the electrical connections can be disconnected.

5. Remove the power lead, speaker, and antenna wires and then pull out the unit.

6. To install the radio, reverse the above procedure.

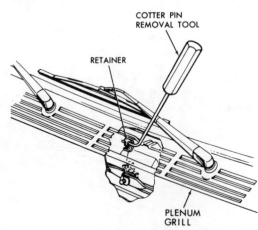

Removing the 1970–72 drive rod retainer (© Chevrolet Motor Div.)

# WINDSHIELD WIPERS

## Motor

### REMOVAL AND INSTALLATION

#### 1970–72

1. Disconnect the battery ground cable. Be sure the wipers are in the parked position.

2. Remove the wiper arms and blades.

3. Remove the plenum chamber grille.

4. Disconnect wiper drive rods from crank arm; remove crank arm nut and arm from motor shaft.

5. Working under the instrument panel, disconnect the wiper motor and washer wiring connections. Remove the parking brake assembly if it is in the way.

6. Remove the left hand defroster hose. Remove the washer hoses from the pump.

7. Remove the motor attaching screws and the motor.

8. To install, reverse the removal procedure.

#### 1973–80

1. Make sure the wipers are parked.

2. Disconnect the ground cable from the battery.

3. Disconnect the wiring harness at the

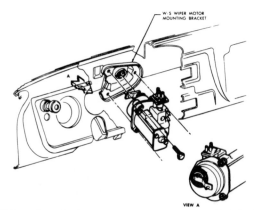

**Wiper installation, 1970–72 (© Chevrolet Motor Div.)**

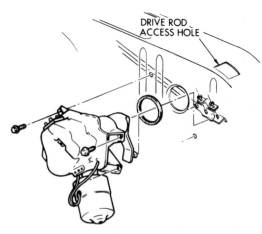

**Wiper motor installation, 1973–80 (© Chevrolet Motor Div.)**

wiper motor and the hoses from the washer pump.

4. Reach down through the access hole in the plenum and loosen the wiper drive rod attaching screws. Remove the drive rod from the wiper motor crank arm.

5. Remove the wiper motor attaching screws and the motor assembly.

6. To install, reverse the removal procedure.

NOTE: *Lubricate the wiper motor crank arm pivot before reinstallation.*

*Failure of the washers to operate or to shut off is often caused by grease or dirt on the electromagnetic contacts. Simply unplug the wire and pull off the plastic cover for access. Likewise, failure of the wipers to park is often caused by grease or dirt on the park switch contacts. The park switch is under the cover behind the pump.*

# INSTRUMENT CLUSTER

## REMOVAL AND INSTALLATION
### 1970–72

1. Disconnect the negative battery terminal. If equipped, remove the choke knob.

2. Remove the windshield wiper knob, the light switch rod, and the bezel. If equipped, disconnect and plug the oil pressure line to the gauge.

3. Disconnect the speedometer cable and the chassis wiring harness which is located at the rear of the instrument panel. Protect the mast jacket with a rag or other covering so that it doesn't become scratched.

4. Remove the cluster retaining screws and remove the cluster.

5. To install the cluster, reverse the removal procedure.

### 1973–76

1. Remove the negative battery cable.

2. Remove the steering column cover and the cluster bezel.

3. Remove the knob from the clock (if equipped).

4. Remove the lens retaining screws and the lens.

5. Remove the transmission gear indicator (PRNDL) and the cluster retainer.

6. Disconnect the speedometer cable by depressing the spring clip and pulling the cable out of the speedometer head. Disconnect and plug the oil pressure line, if so equipped.

7. Disconnect the cluster wiring harness and remove the cluster retaining screws and pull out the cluster.

8. To install, reverse the removal procedure.

### 1977–80

1. Disconnect battery ground cable.

2. Remove headlamp switch control knob and radio control knobs.

3. Remove eight screws and remove instrument bezel.

4. Reach up under instrument cluster and disconnect speedometer by first depressing tang on rear of speedometer head, then pulling cable free from head as tang is depressed.

5. Disconnect oil pressure gauge line at fitting in engine compartment.

6. Pull instrument cluster out just far enough to disconnect line from oil pressure gauge.

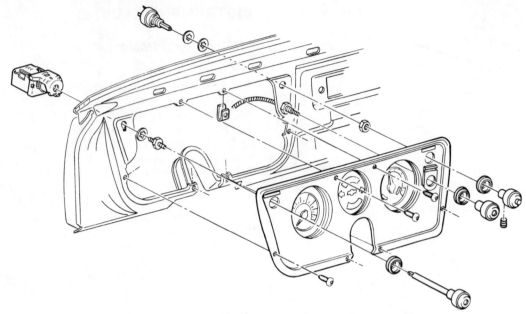

**Standard instrument cluster, 1970–72 (© Chevrolet Motor Div.)**

7. Remove cluster.

8. Install cluster in reverse order of removal.

## Speedometer Cable
### REMOVAL AND INSTALLATION
**1970–80**

1. Disconnect the speedometer cable from the rear of the speedometer head.

2. Remove the old cable by pulling it out from the speedometer end of the cable housing. If the old cable is broken, the speedometer cable will have to be disconnected from the transmission and the cable removed from the other end.

3. Lubricate the lower ¾ of the new cable with speedometer cable lubricant and feed the cable into the cable housing.

4. Connect the speedometer cable to the speedometer head and to the transmission if disconnected there.

## Ignition Switch
### REMOVAL AND INSTALLATION
**1970–72**

See Chapter 8 for "1973–80 Ignition Switch Removal and Installation."

1. Disconnect the battery ground cable.

2. Remove the lock cylinder by positioning the switch in "ACC" position and inserting a thin piece of wire in the small hole in the cylinder face. Push in on the wire and turn the key counterclockwise until the lock cylinder can be removed.

3. Remove the metal ignition switch nut.

4. Remove the ignition switch from under the dash and remove the wiring connector.

5. To remove the "theft-resistant" connector, the switch must be removed from under the dash. Use a small screwdriver, unsnap the locking tangs on the connector, and unplug the connector.

To install the switch:

6. Snap the connector into place on a new switch.

7. Install the switch in the dash and install the metal ignition switch nut.

8. Install the lock cylinder.

9. Connect the battery cable.

10. Test the operation of the switch.

## LIGHTING

## Headlights
### REMOVAL AND INSTALLATION

NOTE: *1970–72 GMC pick-ups have four headlights. Otherwise the following removal and installation procedures apply.*

1. Remove the headlight bezel by releasing the attaching screws.

2. Remove the spring (if any) from the retaining ring and turn the unit to disengage it from the headlamp adjusting screws.

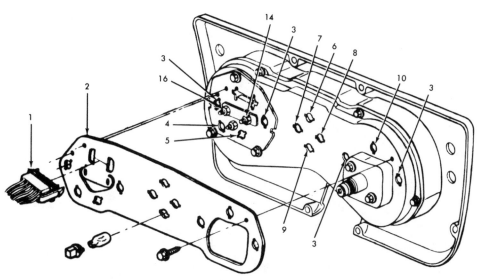

1. Instrument cluster connector
2. Laminated circuit
3. Instrument cluster lamp
4. Temperature indicator
5. Brake warning indicator
6. Generator indicator
7. RH directional indicator
8. LH directional indicator
9. Oil pressure indicator
10. High beam indicator
12. Generator (ammeter)
13. Battery (ammeter)
14. Ignition terminal
15. Temperature gauge
16. Fuel gauge

**Rear view of the standard cluster, 1970–72 (© Chevrolet Motor Div.)**

3. Disconnect the wiring harness connector.

NOTE: *Do not touch the adjusting screws.*

4. Remove the retaining ring and the headlamp from the mounting ring.

5. Position the new sealed beam unit in the mounting ring and install the retaining ring.

NOTE: *The number which is moulded into the lens must be at the top.*

6. Attach the wiring connection.

7. Install the headlamp assembly, twisting it slightly to engage the adjusting screws.

8. Install the retaining ring spring and check the operation of the unit. Install the bezel.

## FUSES AND FLASHERS

Fuses are located in the junction box below the instrument panel to the left of the steering column. The turn signal flasher and the hazard warning flasher also plug into the fuse block. Each fuse receptacle is marked as to the circuit it protects and the correct amperage of the fuse. In-line fuses are also used on the following circuits: 1970–75, ammeter; auxiliary heater and air conditioning 1973–74; and underhood lamp and air conditioning 1975–80.

NOTE: *A special heavy duty turn signal flasher is required to properly operate the turn signals when a trailer's lights are connected to the system.*

## CIRCUIT BREAKERS

A circuit breaker is an electrical switch which breaks the circuit in case of an overload. All models have a circuit breaker in the headlight switch to protect the headlight and parking light systems. An overload may cause the lamps to flicker or flash on and off, or in some cases, to remain off. 1974–80 windshield wiper motors are protected by a circuit breaker at the motor.

## FUSIBLE LINKS

Fusible links are sections of wire, with special insulation, designed to melt under electrical overload. Replacements are simply spliced into the wire in most cases. Circuits protected by fusible links, 1970–74, are: engine wiring, battery charging, alternator, and headlights. For 1975–80, the circuits are: high beam indicator, horn, ignition, and starter solenoid. 1979–80 models also have a fusible link in the air conditioning blower circuit (high speed setting).

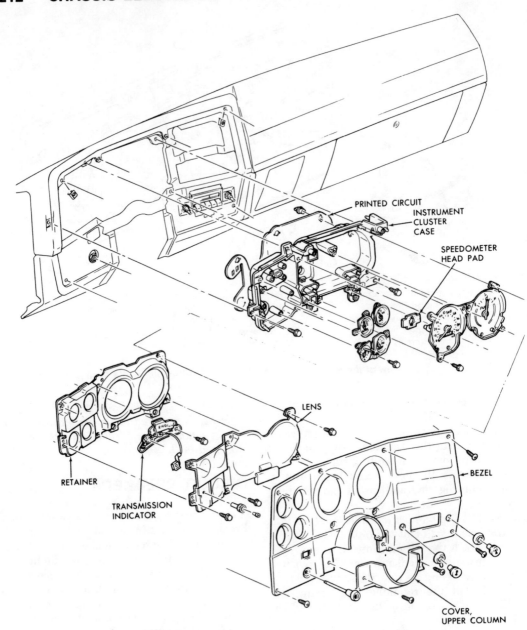

PRINTED CIRCUIT

INSTRUMENT
CLUSTER
CASE

SPEEDOMETER
HEAD PAD

LENS

BEZEL

RETAINER

TRANSMISSION
INDICATOR

COVER,
UPPER COLUMN

**1973–76 instrument cluster; 1977–80 similar (© Chevrolet Motor Div.)**

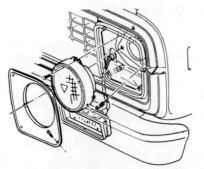

**Typical headlight, 1970–72; later models similar (© Chevrolet Motor Div.)**

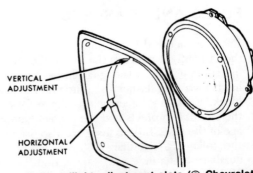

VERTICAL
ADJUSTMENT

HORIZONTAL
ADJUSTMENT

**Typical headlight adjustment slots (© Chevrolet Motor Div.)**

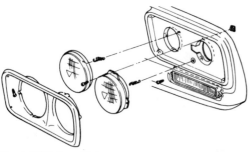

**Dual GMC headlight (© GMC Truck and Coach Div.)**

# Light Bulb Specifications

## 1970-71

| Use | Trade # | Power |
|---|---|---|
| Dome lamp | 211 | 12 CP |
| Parking lights | 67 | 4 CP |
| Oil pressure indicator lamp | 194 | 2 CP |
| Generator indicator lamp | 194 | 2 CP |
| Instrument cluster lamps | 194 or 1895 | 2 CP |
| Headlamp beam indicator lamp | 194 | 1 CP |
| Lamp assembly—tail & stop lamp | 1157 | 4-32 CP |
| License light | 67 | 4 CP |
| Directional signal (front park lamps) | 1157 | 4-32 CP |
| Headlamps | 6012 ① | 37.5–50 W |
| Temperature indicator lamp | 194 | 2 CP |
| Cigarette lighter lamp | 1445 | 1 CP |
| Glove box lamp | 57 | 2 CP |
| Tachometer gauge lamp | 1445 | 2 CP |
| Direction signal indicator lamp | 168 | 3 CP |
| Cab clearance and identification lamps | 01155 | 2 CP |
| Side marker lamps | 194 | 2 CP |
| Brake warning indicator | 194 or 1895 | 2 CP |

① 6014—1971

## 1972

| Use | Trade # | Power |
|---|---|---|
| Dome light | 211 | 12 CP |
| Oil pressure indicator lamp | 194 | 2 CP |
| Generator indicator lamp | 194 | 2 CP |
| Instrument cluster lamps | 194 or 1895 | 2 CP |
| Headlamp beam indicator lamp | 194 | 2 CP |
| Lamp assembly—tail & stop lamp | 1157 | 3-32 CP |
| License lamp | 67 | 4 CP |
| Directional signal (front park lamps) | 1157 | 3-32 CP |

## 1972 (cont.)

| Use | Trade # | Power |
|---|---|---|
| Headlamps | 6014 | 50–60 W |
| Temperature indicator lamp | 194 | 2 CP |
| Direction signal indicator lamp | 168 | 3 CP |
| Cab clearance and identification lamps | 194 | 2 CP |
| Marker lamps | 194 | 2 CP |
| Brake warning indicator | 194 or 1895 | 2 CP |
| Transmission control | 1445 | .7 CP |
| Backing lamp | 1156 | 32 CP |
| Heater or A/C | 1445 | .7 CP |

## 1973-74

| Use | Trade # | Power |
|---|---|---|
| Dome lamp | 212 | 6 CP |
| Oil pressure indicator lamp | 194 | 2 CP |
| Generator indicator lamps | 194 | 2 CP |
| Instrument cluster lamps | 194 or 1895 | 2 CP |
| Headlamp beam indicator lamp | 194 | 2 CP |
| Lamp assembly—tail & stop lamp | 1157 | 3-32 CP |
| License lamp | 67 | 4 CP |
| Directional signal (front park lamps) | 1157 | 3-32 CP |
| Headlamps | 6014 | 50–60 W |
| Temperature indicator lamp | 194 | 2 CP |
| Directional signal indicator lamp | 194 | 2 CP |
| Cab clearance and identification lamps | 194 | 2 CP |
| Roof marker lamps | 194 | 2 CP |
| Brake warning indicator | 194 | 2 CP |
| Transmission control | 1445 | .7 CP |
| Backing lamp | 1156 | 32 CP |
| Heater or A/C | 1445 | .7 CP |
| Corner marker lamps | 67 | 4 CP |
| Cargo lamp | 1142 | 21 CP |
| Radio dial lamp | 293 | 2 CP |
| Cruise control lamp | 53 | 1 CP |
| Courtesy lamp | 1003 | 15 CP |

## 1975-80

| Use | Trade # | Power |
|---|---|---|
| Dome lamps: Cab ② | 1003 | 15 CP |
| Oil pressure indicator lamp | 168 | 3 CP |
| Generator indicator lamp | 168 | 3 CP |
| Instrument cluster lamps | 168 | 3 CP |
| Headlamp beam indicator lamp | 168 | 3 CP |

## Light Bulb Specifications (cont.)

*1975–80 (cont.)*

| Use | Trade # | Power |
|---|---|---|
| Lamp assembly—tail & stop lamp | 1157 | 3-32 CP |
| License lamp | 67 | 4 CP |
| Directional signal (front park lamps) | 1157 NA | 2.2–24 CP |
| Headlamps | 6014 | 50–60 W |
| Temperature indicator lamp | 168 | 3 CP |
| Directional signal indicator lamp | 168 | 3 CP |
| Cab clearance and identification lamps | 168 | 3 CP |
| Roof marker lamps | 194 | 2 CP |
| Brake warning indicator | 168 | 3 CP |
| Transmission control | 1445 | .7 CP |
| Backing lamp | 1156 | 32 CP |
| Heater or A/C ③ | 1445 | .7 CP |
| Corner marker lamps | 67 | 4 CP |
| Cargo lamp | 1142 | 21 CP |
| Radio dial lamp—AM | 1816 | 3 CP |
| —AM/FM | 216 | 1 CP |
| Cruise control lamp | 53 | 1 CP |
| Courtesy lamp | 1003 | 15 CP |
| Windshield wiper switch | 161 | 1 CP |
| Clock | 168 | 3 CP |
| Rear identification ① | 1895 | 2 CP |
| Underhood lamp | 93 | 15 CP |
| Seat belt warning | 168 | 3 CP |
| Cargo/dome lamp | 211-2 | 12 CP |
| Four wheel drive indicator | 168 | 3 CP |

① Wideside pick-up
② 1004, 15 CP—1977–80
③ 161, 1 CP—1977–80

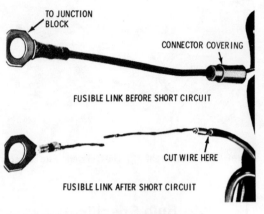

FUSIBLE LINK BEFORE SHORT CIRCUIT

FUSIBLE LINK AFTER SHORT CIRCUIT

**Fusible links (© Chevrolet Motor Div.)**

## WIRING DIAGRAMS

Wiring diagrams have been omitted from this book. As trucks have become more complex, and available with longer and longer option lists, wiring diagrams have grown in size and complexity as well. It has become impossible to provide a readable reproduction in a reasonable number of pages. Information on ordering wiring diagrams from Chevrolet or GMC can be found in the owner's manual.

# Clutch and Transmission

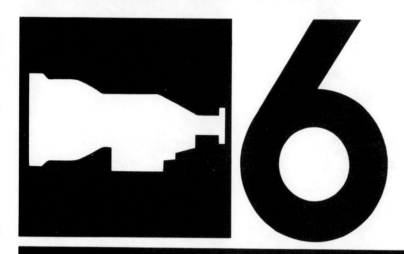

## MANUAL TRANSMISSION

Most three speed transmissions used are the very similar Saginaw and Muncie side cover units. These may be told apart by the shape of the side cover. The Saginaw has a single bolt centered at the top edge of the side cover, while the Muncie has two bolts along the top edge. Some 1976–80 models use the top cover Tremec three speed. All three speed transmissions use side mounted external linkage, with provision for linkage adjustment, and a column shift.

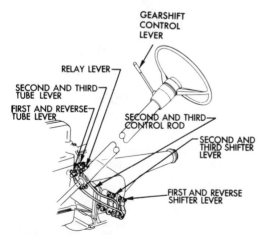

**Three speed column shift controls, 1970–72**
(© Chevrolet Motor Div.)

GEARSHIFT CONTROL LEVER
RELAY LEVER
SECOND AND THIRD TUBE LEVER
FIRST AND REVERSE TUBE LEVER
SECOND AND THIRD CONTROL ROD
SECOND AND THIRD SHIFTER LEVER
FIRST AND REVERSE SHIFTER LEVER

The Muncie CH465 with synchronized 2nd, 3rd and 4th gears is the standard four speed transmission for 1970–80. This is, more accurately, a three speed; 1st gear being an auxiliary, crawler low gear. The transmission is distinguished by its top cover and the absence of external linkage. In addition, the New Process 435CR close ratio four speed transmission was available on all C-10, C-1500, and C20, C-2500 models in 1970. It was also available in 1971 in those trucks, but only with the 350 engine. The 435CR is also a top cover unit, with no provision for linkage adjustment.

### LINKAGE ADJUSTMENT
#### 3-Speed Column Shift

1. Place the column lever in the neutral position.
2. Under the truck, loosen the shift rod clamps. These are at the bottom of the column on 1970–72 models, and at the transmission end for 1973–80.
3. Make sure that the two levers on the transmission are in their center, neutral positions.
4. Install a $^3/_{16}$ to $^7/_{32}$ in. pin or drill bit through the alignment holes in the levers at the bottom of the steering column. This holds these levers in the neutral position.

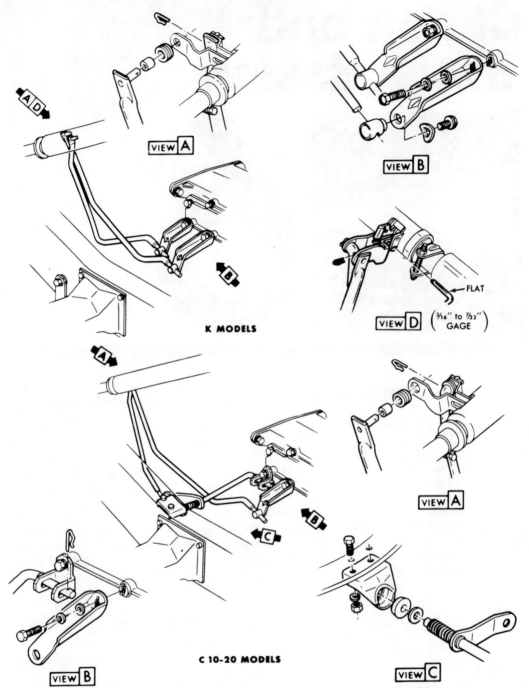

VIEW A

VIEW B

FLAT

VIEW D ( ³⁄₁₆″ to ⁷⁄₃₂″ GAGE )

K MODELS

VIEW A

VIEW B

VIEW C

C 10-20 MODELS

**Three speed column shift controls, 1973–80 (© Chevrolet Motor Div.)**

5. Tighten the shift rod clamps.

6. Remove the pin and check the shifting operation.

### REMOVAL AND INSTALLATION

#### Two Wheel Drive

1. Raise vehicle and support on jack stands.

2. Drain transmission.

3. Disconnect speedometer cable, TCS switch and back-up lamp wire at transmission.

4. Disconnect shift control levers or shift control from transmission. On 4-speeds, remove the gearshift lever by pressing down firmly on the slotted collar plate with a pair of channel lock pliers and rotating coun-

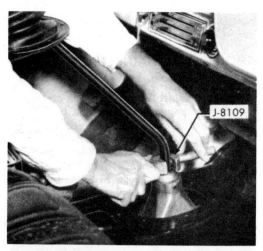

J-8109

The four speed gearshift lever can be removed with a pair of slip joint pliers in lieu of the special tool shown here (© Chevrolet Motor Div.)

terclockwise. Plug the opening to keep out dirt.

5. Disconnect parking brake lever and controls (if used).

6. Remove driveshaft after marking position of shaft to flange.

7. Position jack under transmission to support weight of transmission.

8. Remove crossmember. Visually inspect to see if other equipment, brackets or lines, must be removed to permit removal of transmission.

NOTE: *Mark position of crossmember when removing to prevent incorrect installation. The tapered surface should face the rear.*

9. Remove flywheel housing underpan.

10. Remove the top two transmission to housing bolts and insert two guide pins.

NOTE: *The use of guide pins will not only support the transmission but will prevent damage to the clutch disc. Guide pins can be made by taking two bolts, the same as those just removed only longer, and cutting off the heads. Slot for a screwdriver. Be sure to support the clutch release bearing and support assembly during removal of the transmission. This will prevent the release bearing from falling out of the flywheel housing.*

11. Remove two remaining bolts and slide transmission straight back from engine. Use care to keep the transmission drive gear straight in line with clutch disc hub.

NOTE: *Be sure to support release bearing when removing transmission to avoid having bearing fall into flywheel housing.*

12. When transmission is free from engine, move from under vehicle.

To install the transmission:

13. Place transmission on guide pins, slide forward starting main drive gear into clutch disc's splines.

NOTE: *Place transmission in gear and rotate transmission flange or output yoke to aid entry of main drive gear into disc's splines. Make sure clutch release bearing is in position.*

CAUTION: *Avoid springing the clutch when the transmission is being installed to the engine. Do not force the transmission into the clutch disc hub. Do not let the transmission hang unsupported in the splined portion of the clutch disc.*

14. Install two lower transmission mounting bolts, and flywheel lower pan (if equipped).

15. Remove guide pins and install upper mounting bolts. Torque to 55 ft lbs through 1972, and to 75 ft lbs for 1973–80.

16. Install driveshaft, watch align marks. Install crossmember according to align marks.

17. Connect parking brake, back-up lamp and TCS switch (if used).

18. Connect shift levers, or install the shifter, and adjust if needed.

19. Connect speedometer cable and refill transmission.

20. Lower vehicle and road test.

## Four Wheel Drive

### 3-SPEED

1. Jack up the vehicle and support it safely on stands. Remove the skid plate, if any.

2. Drain the transmission and transfer case. Remove the speedometer cable and the TCS switch from the side of the transmission.

3. Disconnect the driveshafts and secure them out of the way.

4. Remove the shifter lever by removing the pivot bolt to the adapter assembly. You can then push the shifter up out of the way.

5. On 1978 and later models, remove the bolts attaching the strut to the right side of the transfer case and to the rear of the engine, and remove the strut.

6. While supporting the transfer case securely, remove the attaching bolts to the adapter.

7. Remove the transfer case securing bolts from the frame and lower and remove the transfer case. (The case is attached to the right side of the frame.)

8. Disconnect the shift rods from the transmission.

9. While holding the rear of the engine with a jack, remove the adapter mounting bolts.

10. Remove the upper transmission bolts and insert two guide pins to keep the assembly aligned. See the two wheel drive procedure (Step 10) for details on making these.

11. Remove the flywheel pan and the lower transmission bolts.

12. Pull the transmission and the adapter straight back on the guide pins until the input shaft is free of the clutch disc.

13. The transmission and the adapter are removed as on assembly. The adapter can be separated once the assembly is out.

14. Installation is the reverse of removal. Place the transmission in gear and turn the output shaft to align the clutch splines. Transmission bolt torque is 55 ft lbs through 1972, and 75 ft lbs for 1973–80. See Transfer Case Removal and Installation for adapter bolt torques.

### 4-SPEED

1. Remove the shifter boots and the floor mat or carpeting from the front passenger compartment.

2. Remove the transmission shift lever. See Step 4 of the two wheel drive procedure for details on removing the lever. It may be necessary to remove the center floor outlet from the heater to complete the next step. Remove the center console, if so equipped.

3. Remove the transmission cover after releasing the attaching screws. It will be necessary to rotate the cover 90° to clear the transfer case shift lever.

4. Disconnect the transfer case shift lever link assembly and the lever from the adapter. Remove the skid plate, if any.

5. Remove the back-up light, the TCS switch, and the speedometer cable from the side of the transmission.

6. Raise and support the truck. Support the engine. Drain the transmission and the transfer case. Detach both drive shafts and secure them out of the way.

7. Remove the transmission-to-frame bolts. To do this, it will be necessary to open the locking tabs. Remove the transfer case-to-frame bracket bolts.

8. While supporting the transmission and transfer case, remove the crossmember bolts and the crossmember. It will be neces-sary to rotate the crossmember to remove it from the frame.

9. Remove the lower clutch housing cover.

NOTE: *On V8 engines it is necessary to remove the exhaust crossover pipe.*

10. Remove the transmission-to-clutch-housing bolts. Remove the upper bolts first and install guide pins. See Step 10 of the two wheel drive procedure for details.

11. Slide the transmission back until the main drive gear clears the clutch assembly and then lower the unit.

12. Install the transfer case on the transmission as an assembly. Attach the assembly to the clutchhousing. Put the transmission in gear and turn the output shaft to align the clutch splines. Torque the transmission bolts to 55 ft lbs through 1972, to 75 ft lbs 1973–80.

13. Install the clutchhousing cover and, on V8 models, the exhaust pipe.

14. Install the frame crossmember, the retaining adapter, and the transfer case.

15. The front and rear transfer case yoke locknuts must be torqued to 150 ft lbs.

16. Install the front and rear driveshafts.

17. Connect the speedometer cable, back-up lights, and TCS switches.

18. Fill the transmission and the transfer case to the proper level with the specified lubricant (Chapter 1).

19. Position the transfer case shift lever and the shift lever link on the shift rail bar.

20. Install the transmission floor cover and the center heating duct.

21. Install the center console, if so equipped.

22. Install the transmission shift lever.

## CLUTCH

Two types of clutches are used. Six cylinder engines use a single disc clutch with coil spring or diaphragm type pressure plates. V8 engines generally use a single disc with a coil spring pressure. Diaphragm type pressure plates operate with light pedal pressure, while coil spring pressure plates combine operating ease with high torque capacity.

The operating controls are mechanical.

### REMOVAL AND INSTALLATION
#### Diaphragm Clutch

1. Remove the transmission.

2. Disconnect the clutch fork pushrod and spring. Remove the clutch housing.

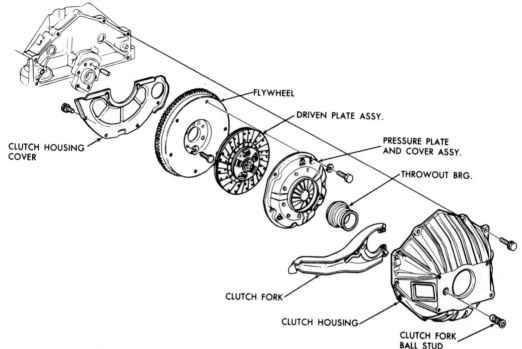

**Exploded view of a typical diaphragm clutch (© Chevrolet Motor Div.)**

3. Remove the clutch fork by pressing it away from the ball mounting with a screwdriver until the fork snaps loose from the ball or remove the ball stud from the clutch housing. Remove the throwout bearing from the clutch fork.

4. Install a pilot tool (an old mainshaft makes a good pilot tool) to hold the clutch while you are removing it.

NOTE: *Before removing the clutch from the flywheel, mark the flywheel, clutch cover (located under the pressure plate) and one pressure plate lug, so that these parts may be assembled in their same relative positions. They were balanced as an assembly.*

5. Loosen the clutch attaching bolts one turn at a time to prevent distortion of the clutch cover until the tension is released.

6. Remove the clutch pilot tool and the clutch from the vehicle.

Check the pressure plate and flywheel for signs of wear, scoring, overheating, etc. If the clutch plate, flywheel, or pressure plate is oil-soaked, inspect the engine rear main seal and the transmission input shaft seal, and correct leakage as required. Replace any damaged parts.

To install:

7. Install the pressure plate in the cover assembly, aligning the notch in the pressure plate with the notch in the cover flange. Install pressure plate retracting springs, lockwashers and drive strap to pressure plate bolts. Tighten to 11 ft lbs. The clutch is now ready to be installed.

8. Turn the flywheel until the X mark is at the bottom.

9. Install the clutch disc, pressure plate and cover, using an old mainshaft as an aligning tool.

10. Turn the clutch until the X mark or painted white letter on the clutch cover aligns with the X mark on the flywheel.

11. Install the attaching bolts and tighten them a little at a time in a crossing pattern until the spring pressure is taken up.

12. Remove the aligning tool.

13. Pack the clutch ball fork seat with a small amount of high temperature grease and install a new retainer in the groove of the clutch fork.

CAUTION: *Be careful not to use too much grease. Excessive amounts will get on the clutch fingers and cause clutch slippage.*

14. Install the retainer with the high side up with the open end on the horizontal.

15. If the clutch fork ball was removed, reinstall it in the clutch housing and snap the clutch fork onto the ball.

16. Lubricate the inside of the throwout

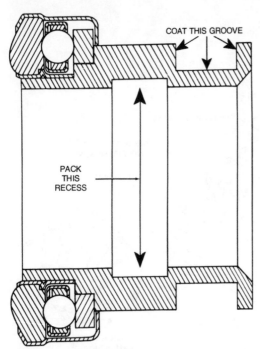

**Lubrication points of the throwout bearing (© Chevrolet Motor Div.)**

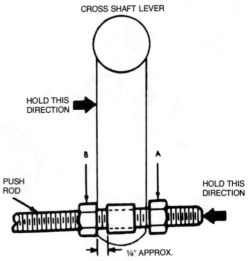

**Clutch pedal free-play adjustment, 1970–72 (© Chevrolet Motor Div.)**

bearing collar and the throwout fork groove with a small amount of graphite grease.

17. Install the throwout bearing. Install the clutch housing.

18. Install the transmission.

19. Further installation is the reverse of removal. Adjust the clutch.

**Coil Spring Clutch**

Basically, the same procedures apply to diaphragm clutch removal as to coil spring clutch removal.

1. Before removing the clutch, punch-mark the flywheel, clutch cover and one pressure plate lug so that the components can be reassembled in their original locations.

2. Loosen the attaching screws one turn at a time to prevent distortion.

3. When the clutch plate is removed, be sure to mark the flywheel side.

4. Place ⅜ in. wood or metal spacers between the clutch levers and the cover to hold the levers down as the holding screws are removed.

5. Adjust the clutch after installation.

## FREE PEDAL TRAVEL ADJUSTMENT

### 1970–72

Only one adjustment is necessary to assure that the clutch operates efficiently. This ad-

justment is for the amount of free clutch pedal travel before the throwout bearing contacts the clutch fingers. The pedal should be adjusted at periodic intervals to provide ¾–1 in. of free pedal travel.

1. Disconnect the clutch fork return spring at the fork.

2. Loosen the nut (A) and back it off approximately ½ in. from the swivel.

3. Hold the clutch fork pushrod against the fork to move the throwout bearing against the clutch fingers. The pushrod will slide through the swivel at the cross-shaft.

4. Rotate the lever until the clutch pedal contacts the bumper mounted on the parking brake support.

**Measure the clutch pedal free-play at the pedal (1970–72 shown) (© Chevrolet Motor Div.)**

5. Adjust nut (B) to obtain ³/₁₆–¼ in. clearance between nut (B) and the swivel.

6. Release the pushrod, connect the return spring and tighten nut (A) to lock the swivel against nut (B).

7. Check the free pedal travel at the pedal and readjust as necessary.

**1973–80**

1. Disconnect the return spring at the clutch fork.

2. Rotate the clutch lever and shaft assembly until the clutch pedal is firmly against the rubber bumper on the brake pedal bracket.

3. Push the outer end of the clutch fork rearward until the throwout bearing lightly contacts the pressure plate levers.

4. Loosen the locknut and adjust the rod length so that the swivel slips freely into the gauge hole. Increase the rod length until all lash is removed.

5. Remove the swivel from the gauge hole. Insert the swivel in the lower hole in the lever. Install two washers and the cotter pin. Tighten the locknut, being careful not to change the rod length. Reinstall the spring and check pedal free travel. It should be 1⅜–1⅝ in.

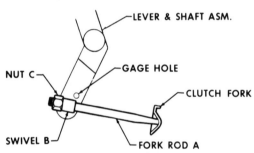

**1973–80 clutch linkage adjustment (© Chevrolet Motor Div.)**

NOTE: *If you have a problem with driveline chatter in reverse on an early 1973 model, this can be corrected with a service kit (no. 340607) containing a new clutch cross shaft and relocated clutch fork springs. The kit components were installed at the factory in later models.*

## AUTOMATIC TRANSMISSION

Three automatic transmissions are used. The aluminum Powerglide was used from 1970 through 1971, when it was discontinued for use in trucks. The Turbo Hydra-Matic 350 and 400 have been in use from 1970–80. No band adjustments are necessary or possible

on Turbo Hydra-Matic transmissions; they use clutches instead of bands. Pan removal, fluid and filter changes for all three transmissions are covered in Chapter 1.

### Powerglide
#### *LOW BAND ADJUSTMENT*

1. Raise and support the vehicle.

2. Place the selector lever in Neutral.

3. Remove the protective cap from the low band adjusting screw.

4. Loosen the adjusting screw locknut ¼ turn and hold it in this position with a wrench.

5. Using an in. lb torque wrench, adjust the band adjusting screw to 70 in. lbs, and back the screw off 4 complete turns for a band that has been in operation 6,000 miles or more; or, 3 complete turns for a band that has been in operation less than 6,000 miles.

NOTE: *The back-off figure is not approximate; it must be exact.*

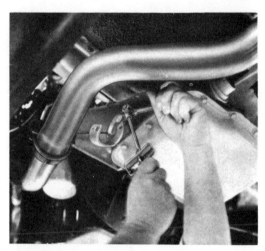

**Powerglide low band adjustment (© Chevrolet Motor Div.)**

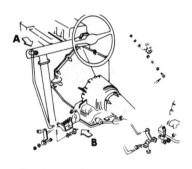

**Powerglide control rod adjustment (© Chevrolet Motor Div.)**

6. Tighten the adjusting screw locknut.

7. Lower the vehicle and road test.

### SHIFT LINKAGE

The shift tube and selector linkage must be free in the mast jacket.

1. Set the transmission lever in Drive (D). Do not be guided by the position of the needle. Determine Drive by shifting the lever all the way to the right to the Low (L) detent. Rotate it back to the left, one detent, to Drive (D).

2. Attach the control rod to the lever and inner lever of the shaft assembly with the retainers.

3. Assemble the swivel, clamp, grommet, bushing, washers and nut loosely on the selector lever.

4. Attach the control rod to the outer lever of the shaft assembly with the retainer.

5. Place the selector lever tang in the Neutral drive gate of the selector plate assembly and insert the control rod into the swivel.

6. Rotate the lever clockwise viewed looking down the steering column, until the tang contacts the drive side of the Neutral drive gate.

7. Tighten the nut.

### THROTTLE VALVE LINKAGE ADJUSTMENT

#### Six Cylinder Engines

1. With the accelerator depressed, the bellcrank on the engine must be in the wide-open throttle position.

2. The dash lever must be $1/64$–$1/16$ in. off the lever stop and the transmission lever must be against the transmission internal stop.

#### V8 Engines

1. Remove the air cleaner.

2. Disconnect the accelerator linkage at the carburetor.

3. Disconnect the accelerator return

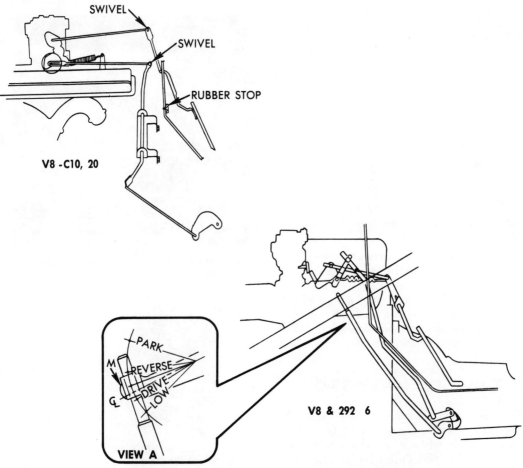

SWIVEL

SWIVEL

RUBBER STOP

V8 -C10, 20

PARK
REVERSE
DRIVE
LOW

V8 & 292 6

**VIEW A**

**Powerglide throttle valve adjustment (© Chevrolet Motor Div.)**

spring and throttle valve rod return springs.

4. Pull the throttle valve rod forward until the transmission is through the detent. Open the carburetor to the wide-open throttle position. The carburetor must reach the wide-open throttle position at the same time that the ball stud contacts the end of the slot in the upper throttle valve rod.

5. Adjust the swivel on the end of the upper throttle valve rod as per Step 4. The allowable tolerance is approximately $1/32$ in.

6. Connect and adjust the accelerator linkage.

7. Check for freedom of operation. Install the air cleaner.

### NEUTRAL SAFETY SWITCH ADJUSTMENT (1970–71)

1. Align the slot in the contact support with the hole in the switch and insert a $3/32$ in. pin to hold it in this position.

2. The switch is now in the drive position.

3. Place the contact support drive slot over the shifter tube drive tang and tighten the screws.

4. Remove the clamp pin.

5. Check the operation of the switch. The engine should not be able to be started in any drive gear.

## Turbo Hydra-Matic 350 and 400
### SHIFT LINKAGE ADJUSTMENT
**1970–72**

1. The shift tube and levers located in the mast jacket of the steering column must move freely and must not bind.

2. Pull the shift lever toward the steering wheel and allow the lever to be positioned in Drive by the transmission detent. The pointer may be out of adjustment, so don't

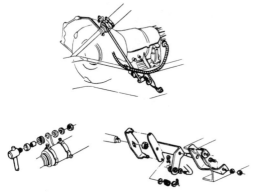

**Turbo Hydra-Matic shift linkage, 1970–72 (© Chevrolet Motor Div.)**

use the pointer on the column as a reference for positioning the lever. The pointer must be adjusted last.

3. Release the selector lever. The lever should not go into Low unless the lever is lifted.

4. Lift the lever toward the steering wheel and permit the lever to be placed in Neutral by the transmission detent.

5. Release the lever; it should not go into Reverse unless the lever is lifted.

6. If the linkage is adjusted correctly, the shift lever will not move past the Neutral detent and the Drive detent unless the lever is lifted so it can pass over the mechanical stop in the steering column.

7. If adjustment is necessary, place the lever in the Drive or High detent position. If the indicator pointer is out of alignment, you must rely upon the detent position to determine what gear you are in (see Steps 2 and 3).

8. Loosen the adjustment swivel or clamp at the cross-shaft and move the shift lever so that it contacts the drive stop in the column.

9. Tighten the swivel and recheck the adjustment (see Steps 2 and 6).

10. If the indicator pointer fails to line up properly with the gear symbol (P, R, N, D, L) or aligns with a wrong symbol (being in Reverse when the pointer indicates Neutral, etc.), the cause may be a bent indicator wire. Inspect it and repair.

11. If necessary, readjust the neutral safety switch to agree with the detent positions. The ignition key should move into "lock" only when the shift lever is in Park.

CAUTION: *The above adjustments must be made correctly to prevent early transmission failure caused by controls not being fully engaged with the detent. This results in a situation in which fluid pressure is reduced causing only partial engagement of the clutches. It may appear to run well but the pressure reduction may be just enough to cause clutch failure after only a few miles of operation.*

**1973–80**

1. The shift tube and lever assembly must be free in the mast jacket.

2. Lift the selector lever toward the steering wheel and allow the selector lever to be positioned in Drive by the detent. Do not use the selector lever pointer as a reference.

3. Release the selector lever. The lever

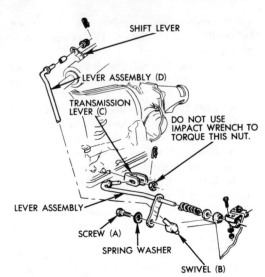

**Turbo Hydra-Matic shift linkage, 1973–80 (© Chevrolet Motor Div.)**

should not be able to go into Low unless the lever is lifted.

4. Lift the selector lever toward the steering wheel and allow the lever to be positioned in Neutral by the transmission detent.

5. Release the selector lever. The lever should not be able to engage Reverse unless the lever is lifted. A properly adjusted linkage will prevent the lever from moving beyond both the Neutral and Drive detents unless the lever is lifted.

6. If adjustment is required, remove the screw and spring washer from the swivel.

7. Set the transmission lever in Neutral by moving it counterclockwise to L and then three detents clockwise to Neutral.

8. Put the transmission selector lever in Neutral as determined by the mechanical stop in the steering column.

9. Do not use the pointer to determine these positions.

10. Assemble the swivel spring and washer to the lever and tighten to 20 ft lbs.

11. Readjust the Neutral safety switch if necessary.

12. Check the operation. With the key in RUN, and the transmission in Reverse, be sure that the key cannot be removed and the steering wheel is not locked.

With the key in LOCK and the shift lever in PARK, be sure that they key can be removed, the steering wheel is locked, and that the transmission remains in PARK when the steering column is locked.

NOTE: *Any inaccuracies in the above adjustments may result in premature trans-*

*mission failure, due to operation of the transmission with the controls not in the full detent. Partial engagement of clutches and other internal parts will result in transmission failure after only a few miles.*

## DETENT CABLE ADJUSTMENT (TURBO HYDRA-MATIC 350)

### 1970–71

1. Remove the air cleaner.

2. Loosen the detent cable screw.

3. With the choke off and the accelerator linkage adjusted, position the carburetor lever in the wide open position.

4. Pull the detent cable rearward until the wide open throttle stop in the transmission is felt. The cable must be pulled through the

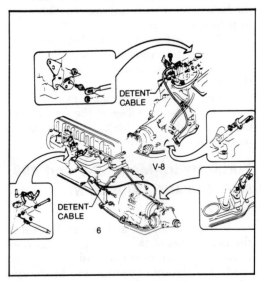

**Detent cable adjustment, 1970–72 (© Chevrolet Motor Div.)**

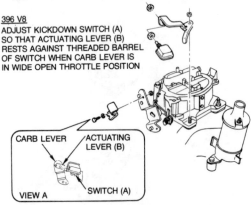

**Detent switch adjustment, 1970 396 V8 (© Chevrolet Motor Div.)**

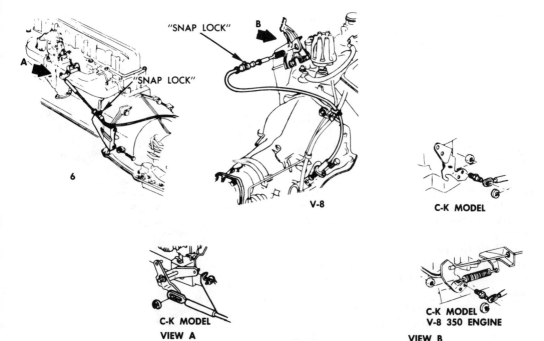

Detent cable adjustment, 1972–80 (© Chevrolet Motor Div.)

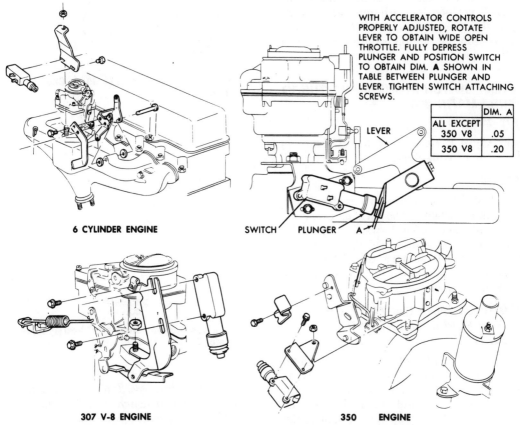

WITH ACCELERATOR CONTROLS PROPERLY ADJUSTED, ROTATE LEVER TO OBTAIN WIDE OPEN THROTTLE. FULLY DEPRESS PLUNGER AND POSITION SWITCH TO OBTAIN DIM. A SHOWN IN TABLE BETWEEN PLUNGER AND LEVER. TIGHTEN SWITCH ATTACHING SCREWS.

| | DIM. A |
|---|---|
| ALL EXCEPT 350 V8 | .05 |
| 350 V8 | .20 |

Detent switch adjustment, 1970–71 except 396 V8 (© Chevrolet Motor Div.)

detent position to reach the wide open throttle stop in the transmission.

5. Tighten the detent cable screw and check the linkage for proper operation.

### 1972

1. Remove the air cleaner.

2. Pry up on each side of the snap-lock with a screwdriver to release the lock.

3. Compress the locking tabs and disconnect the locking tabs from the bracket.

4. Attach the snap-lock to the accelerator control lever and install the retaining ring.

5. Pull the carburetor to the wide open throttle position against the stop on the carburetor.

6. With the carburetor held in this position, pull the cable housing rearward until the wide open throttle stop in the transmission is felt.

7. Push the snap-lock on the cable downward until it is flush with the cable.

8. Do not lubricate the cable. Install the air cleaner.

### 1973–80

1. With the snap-lock disengaged from the bracket, position the carburetor at the wide open throttle position. Push the snap-lock downward until the top is flush with the rest of the cable.

## DETENT SWITCH ADJUSTMENT (TURBO HYDRA-MATIC 400)

### 1970–71

1. Adjust the detent switch as shown in the accompanying illustrations.

### 1972–80

1. Install the detent switch as shown.

2. After installing the switch, press the switch plunger as far forward as possible. This will preset the switch for adjustment. The switch will automatically adjust itself with the first wide open throttle application of the accelerator pedal.

## NEUTRAL SAFETY/BACKUP LIGHT SWITCH REPLACEMENT AND ADJUSTMENT

This switch is on top of the steering column, behind the instrument panel. It prevents the starting circuit from being completed unless the shift lever is in Neutral or Park. The same switch causes the backup light to go on in Reverse.

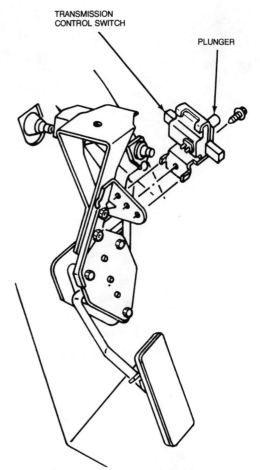

Detent switch adjustment, 1972–80 (© Chevrolet Motor Div.)

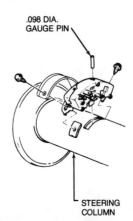

Neutral start switch adjustment, 1973–80 (© Chevrolet Motor Div.)

NOTE: *The three speed manual transmission backup light switch is on the column. On the four speed, it is on the transmission, near the top cover.*

### 1970-72

1. Disconnect the wiring plug. Remove the screws and the switch.

2. Place the shift lever in Drive. Locate the lever tang against the transmission selector plate.

3. Align the slot in the contact support with the hole in the switch and insert a $^3/_{32}$ in. drill bit to hold the support in place.

4. Place the contact support drive slot over the shifter tube drive tang and tighten the screws. Remove the bit.

5. Connect the wiring plug and check that the engine will start only in Neutral and Park (foot on the brake!) and that the backup lights work only in reverse. Loosen the screws and move the switch to correct.

### 1973-80

1. Disconnect the switch wiring plug. Remove the screws and the switch.

2. Place the shift lever in Neutral.

3. Insert a $^3/_{32}$ in. drill bit, $^3/_8$ in. into the switch hole on a used switch. A new switch is held in the Neutral position by a plastic shear pin, so the bit isn't needed.

4. Insert the switch tang into the column slot and install the screws.

5. Remove the locating bit. With a new switch, shift out of Neutral to shear the plastic pin.

6. Connect the wiring plug and check that the engine will start only in Neutral and Park (foot on the brake!) and that the backup lights work only in Reverse. Loosen the screws and move the switch to correct.

## TRANSMISSION REMOVAL AND INSTALLATION

NOTE: *It would be best to drain the transmission before starting.*

*It may be necessary to disconnect and remove the exhaust crossover pipe on V8s, and to disconnect the catalytic converter and remove its support bracket, on models so equipped.*

### Two Wheel Drive

1. Disconnect the battery ground cable. Disconnect the detent cable at the carburetor.

2. Raise and support the truck.

3. Remove the driveshaft, after matchmarking its flanges.

4. Disconnect the speedometer cable, downshift cable, vacuum modulator line, shift linkage, and fluid cooler lines at the transmission. Remove the filler tube.

5. Support the transmission and unbolt the rear mount from the crossmember. Remove the crossmember.

6. Remove the torque converter underpan, matchmark the flywheel and converter, and remove the converter bolts.

7. Support the engine and lower the transmission slightly for access to the upper transmission to engine bolts.

8. Remove the transmission to engine bolts and pull the transmission back. Rig up a strap or keep the front of the transmission up so the converter doesn't fall out.

9. Reverse the procedure for installation. Bolt the transmission to the engine first (30 ft lbs), then the converter to the flywheel (35 ft lbs). Make sure that the converter attaching lugs are flush and that the converter can turn freely before installing the bolts. Tighten the bolts finger tight, then torque to specification, to insure proper converter alignment.

NOTE: *Lubricate the internal yoke splines at the transmission end of the driveshaft with lithium base grease. The grease should seep out through the vent hole.*

### 1970-72 Four Wheel Drive

1. Disconnect the battery ground cable. Disconnect the detent cable at the carburetor.

2. Raise and support the truck.

3. Remove the driveshafts, after matchmarking their flanges.

4. Remove the transfer case shift lever.

5. Disconnect the speedometer cable, downshift cable, vacuum modulator line, shift linkage, and fluid cooler lines at the transmission. Remove the filler tube.

6. Support the transmission and transfer case separately. Remove the transmission to adapter case bolts. Unbolt the transfer case from the frame bracket and remove it.

7. Proceed with Steps 5 through 9 of the two wheel drive procedure. See transfer case Removal and Installation for adapter bolt torques.

### 1973-80 Four Wheel Drive

1. Disconnect the battery ground cable and remove the transmission dipstick. Detach the downshift cable at the carburetor. Remove the transfer case shift lever knob and boot.

2. Raise and support the truck.

3. Remove the skid plate, if any. Remove the flywheel cover.

4. Matchmark the flywheel and torque converter, remove the bolts, and secure the converter so it doesn't fall out of the transmission.

5. Detach the shift linkage, speedometer cable, vacuum modulator line, downshift cable, and cooler lines at the transmission. Remove the filler tube.

6. Remove the exhaust crossover pipe to manifold bolts.

7. Unbolt the transfer case adapter from the crossmember. Support the transmission and transfer case. Remove the crossmember.

8. Move the exhaust system aside. Detach the driveshafts after matchmarking their flanges. Disconnect the parking brake cable.

9. Unbolt the transfer case from the frame bracket. Support the engine. Unbolt

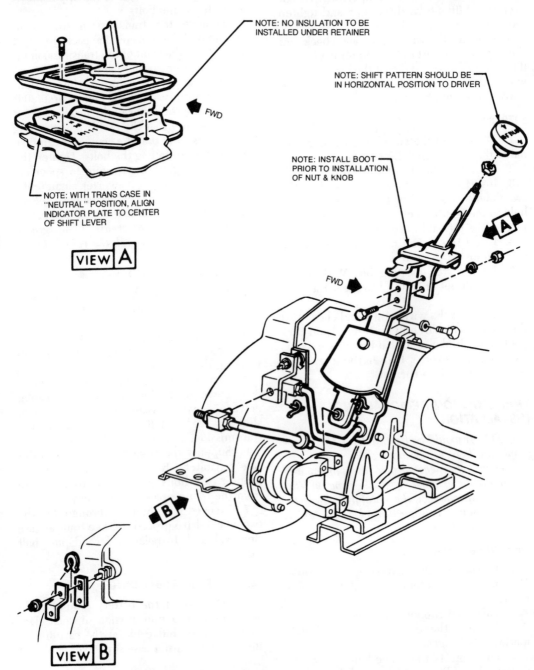

**New Process 203 shift linkage (© Chevrolet Motor Div.)**

the transmission from the engine, pull the assembly back, and remove.

10. Reverse the procedure for installation. Bolt the transmission to the engine first (30 ft lbs), then the converter to the flywheel (35 ft lbs). Make sure that the converter attaching lugs are flush and that the converter can turn freely before installing the bolts. See Transfer Case Removal and Installation for adapter bolt torques.

## TRANSFER CASE

There are two transfer cases used. The New Process 205 is used in part time systems with all transmissions through 1975, and in 1980, and with manual transmissions only 1976–79. It has a large New Process emblem on the back of the case. The full time New Process 203 is used with all transmissions in 1974 and early 1975, and only with automatics from mid-1975 to 1979. It can be identified by the H LOC and L LOC positions on the shifter.

NOTE: *Models with the New Process 203 full time four wheel drive transfer case, especially with manual transmissions, may give a front wheel "chatter" or vibration on sharp turns. This is a normal characteristic of this drivetrain combination. If it occurs shortly after shifting out of a LOC position, the transfer case is probably still locked up. This should correct itself after about a mile of driving, or can be alleviated by backing up for a short distance.*
CAUTION: *Owners of full time four wheel drive trucks (New Process 203 transfer case) often consider either removing the front driveshaft, or installing locking front hubs and operating in a LOC position, as a means of improving gas mileage. This practice will submit the transfer case to stresses beyond its design limits and will void all warranties. Use of any lubricant additive in the transfer case is also not recommended.*

### NEW PROCESS 203 SHIFT LINKAGE ADJUSTMENT

The full time four wheel drive transfer case is the only one on which linkage adjustment is possible.

1. Place the selector lever in the cab in the Neutral position.

2. Detach the adjustable rod ends from the transfer case levers.

3. Insert an $^{11}/_{64}$ in. drill bit through the alignment holes in the shifter levers. This will lock the shifter in the neutral position with both levers vertical.

4. Place the range shift lever (the outer lever) on the transfer case in the Neutral position.

5. Place the lockout shift lever (the inner lever) on the transfer case in the unlocked position. Both levers should now be vertical.

6. Adjust the rods so that the linkage fits together. The indicator plate can be moved to align with the correct symbol.

7. Remove the drill bit.

### REMOVAL AND INSTALLATION

1. Raise and support the truck.

2. Drain the transfer case.

3. Disconnect the speedometer cable, back-up light switch, and the TCS switch.

4. If necessary, remove the skid plate and crossmember support.

5. Disconnect the front and rear driveshafts and support them out of the way.

On New Process 205 models, disconnect the shift lever rod from the shift rail link.

On New Process 203 models, disconnect the shift levers at the transfer case.

**Manual transmission transfer case mounting, 1970–72 (© Chevrolet Motor Div.)**

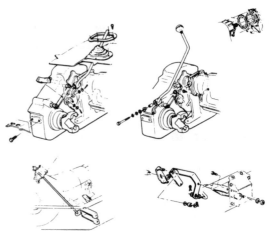

**Automatic transmission transfer case mounting, 1970–72 (© Chevrolet Motor Div.)**

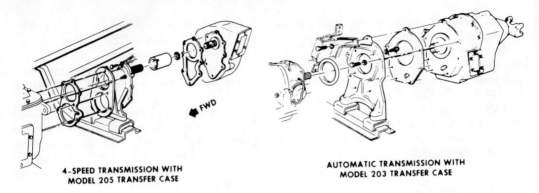

4-SPEED TRANSMISSION WITH
MODEL 205 TRANSFER CASE

AUTOMATIC TRANSMISSION WITH
MODEL 203 TRANSFER CASE

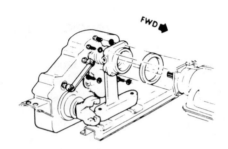

AUTOMATIC TRANSMISSION WITH
MODEL 205 TRANSFER CASE

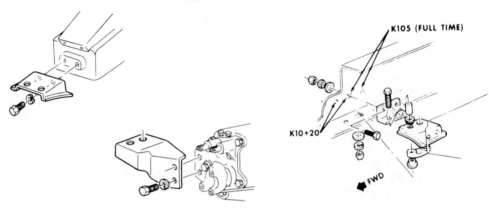

SUPPORT AND BRACKET ASSEMBLY (ALL MODELS)

**Transfer case installation, 1973–80 (© Chevrolet Motor Div.)**

## Adapter to Transfer Case Bolt Torque

| Model | Year | Torque (ft lbs) |
|---|---|---|
| NP 205 | '70–'72 | 35 |
| NP 205 | '73–'80 | 25 |
| NP 203 | '74–'79 | 38 |

## Adapter to Transmission Bolt Torque

| Model | Torque (ft lbs) |
|---|---|
| NP 205 | 22 manual |
| | 35 automatic |
| NP 203 | 40 |

## Adapter to Frame Bolt Torque

| Model | Torque (ft lbs) |
|---|---|
| NP 205 | 130 |
| NP 203 (bracket to frame) | 50 upper |
|  | 65 lower |

6. Remove the transfer case-to-frame mounting bolts.

7. Support the transfer case and remove the bolts attaching the transfer case to transmission adaptor.

8. Move the transfer case to the rear until the input shaft clears the adaptor and lower the transfer case from the truck.

To install the transfer case:

9. Lifting the transfer case on a transmission jack, attach the case to the adapter using through bolts. Torque to specification.

10. Remove the transmission jack and install the transfer case-to-frame rail bolts. Make certain to bend the locking tabs after installation.

11. Connect the shift linkage.

12. Connect the front driveshaft to the front transfer case output shaft and the rear drive shaft to the rear output shaft.

13. Install the crossmember and skid plate, if equipped.

14. Connect the speedometer cable, back-up light, and TCS switches.

15. Fill the transfer case to the proper level with lubricant.

16. Lower the vehicle.

NOTE: *Recheck all bolt torques. When attaching the driveshafts, make sure that the flange locknuts are torqued to specifications.*

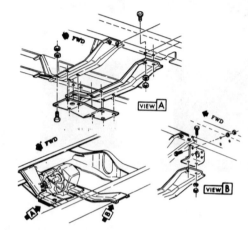

**Transfer case skid plate installation (© Chevrolet Motor Div.)**

# Drive Train

**7**

## DRIVELINE

Tubular driveshafts are used on all models, incorporating needle bearing U-joints. An internally splined sleeve at the forward end compensates for variation in distance between the rear axle and the transmission.

The number of driveshafts used is determined by the length of the wheelbase. On trucks that use two driveshafts there is a center support incorporating a rubber cushioned ball bearing mounted in a bracket attached to the frame crossmember. The ball bearing is permanently sealed and lubricated. 4 WD models use a front driveshaft with a constant velocity joint.

Extended life U-joints have been incorporated on most models and can be identified by the absence of a lubrication fitting.

## Front Driveshaft (4 WD Only)
### REMOVAL AND INSTALLATION

Chevrolet and GMC use U-bolts or straps to secure the driveshaft to the pinion flange. Use the following procedure to remove the driveshaft.

1. Jack the front of the vehicle so that the front wheels are off the ground. Block the rear wheels and safely support the truck on stands.

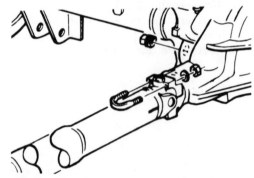

Rear driveshaft U-bolt attachment (© Chevrolet Motor Div.)

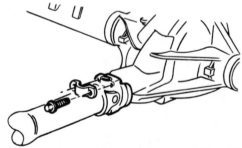

Rear driveshaft strap attachment (© Chevrolet Motor Div.)

2. Scribe aligning marks on the driveshaft and the pinion flange to aid in reassembly.

3. Remove the U-bolts or straps at the axle end of the shaft. Compress the shaft slightly

and tape the bearings into place to avoid losing them.

4. Remove the U-bolts or straps at the transfer case end of the shaft. Tape the bearings into place.

5. Remove the driveshaft.

6. Reverse the procedure for installation. Make certain that the marks made earlier line up correctly to prevent possible imbalances. Be sure that the constant velocity joint (the big double one) is at the transfer case end.

7. See Chassis Greasing in Chapter 1 for details on front driveshaft lubrication.

## Rear Driveshaft (All Models)
### REMOVAL AND INSTALLATION

1. Raise and safely support the rear of the truck as necessary. There is less chance of lubricant leakage from the rear of the transmission on two wheel drive models if the rear is raised. Block the front wheels.

2. Scribe alignment marks on the driveshaft and flange of the rear axle, and transfer case or transmission. If the truck is equipped with a two piece driveshaft, be certain to also scribe marks at the center joint near the splined connection. When reinstalling driveshafts, it is necessary to place the shafts into the same position from which they were removed. This is called phasing. Failure to reinstall the driveshaft properly will cause driveline vibrations and reduced component life.

3. Disconnect the rear universal joint by removing U-bolts or straps. Tape the bearings into place to avoid losing them.

4. If there are U-bolts or straps at the front end of the shaft, remove them. Tape the bearings into place. For trucks with two piece shafts, remove the bolts retaining the bearing support to the frame crossmember. Compress the shaft slightly and remove it. All four wheel drive trucks are of this type.

5. If there are no fasteners at the front end of the transmission, there will only be a splined fitting. Slide the shaft forward slightly to disengage the axle flange, lower the rear end of the shaft, then pull it back out of the transmission. Most two wheel drive trucks are of this type. For trucks with two

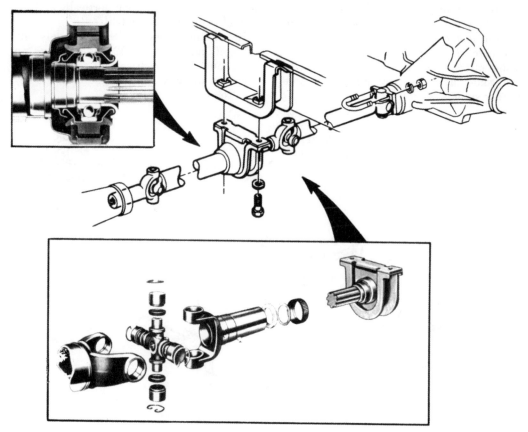

**Driveshaft, U-joint, and bearing support, 1971–80 (© Chevrolet Motor Div.)**

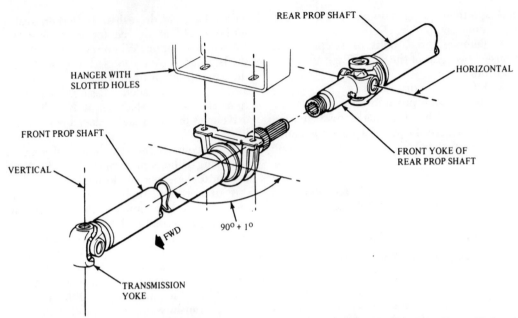

REAR PROP SHAFT

HANGER WITH
SLOTTED HOLES

HORIZONTAL

FRONT PROP SHAFT

FRONT YOKE OF
REAR PROP SHAFT

VERTICAL

90° + 1°

FWD

TRANSMISSION
YOKE

**U-joint alignment: 1977–80 K models with two piece driveshafts only (© Chevrolet Motor Div.)**

piece driveshafts, remove the bolts retaining the bearing support to the frame crossmember.

6. Reverse the procedure for installation. It may be tricky to get the scribed alignment marks to match up on trucks with two piece driveshafts. For those models only, the following instructions may be of some help. First, slide the grease cap and gasket onto the rear splines. Then:

1977–80 K models with 16 splines, after installing the front shaft to the transmission and bolting the support to the crossmember, arrange the front trunnion vertically and the second trunnion horizontally.

1973 C and K models, 1974 C models, and 1975–80 models with 32 splines have an alignment key. The driveshaft cannot be replaced incorrectly. Simply match up the key with the keyway.

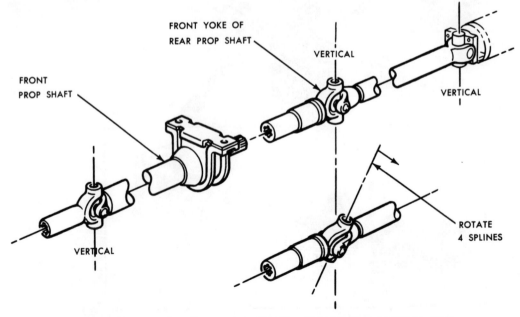

FRONT YOKE OF
REAR PROP SHAFT

VERTICAL

FRONT
PROP SHAFT

VERTICAL

ROTATE
4 SPLINES

VERTICAL

**U-joint alignment, 1971–72 C and K, 1974 K models (© Chevrolet Motor Div.)**

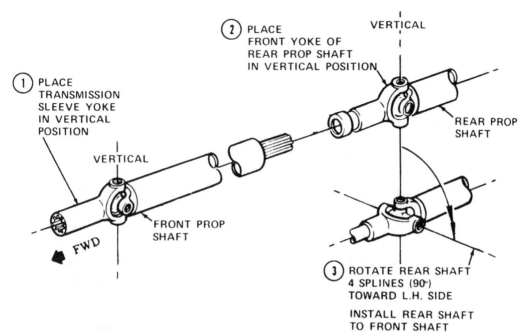

1 PLACE
TRANSMISSION
SLEEVE YOKE
IN VERTICAL
POSITION

VERTICAL

FWD

FRONT PROP
SHAFT

2 PLACE
FRONT YOKE OF
REAR PROP SHAFT
IN VERTICAL POSITION

VERTICAL

REAR PROP
SHAFT

3 ROTATE REAR SHAFT
4 SPLINES (90°)
TOWARD L.H. SIDE

INSTALL REAR SHAFT
TO FRONT SHAFT

**U-joint alignment, 1975–76 C models with 16 splines. 1975–76 K models steps 1 and 2 only (© Chevrolet Motor Div.)**

1975–76 K models with 16 splines, align the trunnions vertically. The shafts should not be rotated before installing the rear shaft to the front shaft.

1975–76 C models with 16 splines, after installing the front shaft to the transmission or transfer case, must align the trunnions vertically, then the rear shaft must be rotated four splines (90°) to the left (driver's) side before installing the rear shaft to the front shaft.

1971–72 C and K models and 1974 K models, after installing the front shaft to the transmission or transfer case and bolting the support to the crossmember, rotate all the U-joints so the trunnions are vertical, then rotate the rear shaft four splines towards the left (driver's) side of the truck before installing the rear shaft to the front shaft.

7. On two wheel drive automatic transmission models, lubricate the internal yoke splines at the transmission end of the shaft with lithium base grease. The grease should seep out through the vent hole.

NOTE: *A thump in the rear driveshaft sometimes occurs when releasing the brakes after braking to a stop, especially on a downgrade. This is most common with automatic transmission. It is often caused by the driveshaft splines binding and can be cured by removing the driveshaft, in-*specting the splines for rough edges, and carefully lubricating. A similar thump may be caused by the clutch plates in Positraction limited slip rear axles binding. If this isn't caused by wear, it can be cured by draining and refilling the rear axle with the special lubricant and adding Positraction additive, both of which are available from dealers.

1973 C-10 and C-1500 long wheelbase pickups equipped with either the Turbo Hydra-Matic 350 or 400 transmission may suffer from a driveline shudder during accel-

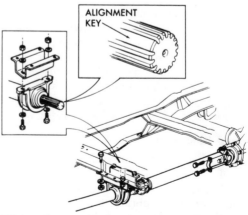

ALIGNMENT
KEY

**U-joint alignment keyway, 32 spline shaft (© Chevrolet Motor Div.)**

## Driveshaft Attachment Torque Specifications

| | |
|---|---|
| To Rear Axle (strap) | 12–17 ft lbs |
| To Rear Axle (U-bolt) | 18–22 ft lbs |
| Bearing Support to Hanger | 20–30 ft lbs |
| Hanger to Frame | 40–50 ft lbs |
| To Transfer Case | 70–80 ft lbs |

## Universal Joint Attachment Torque Specifications

| | |
|---|---|
| Strap Attachments | 15 ft lbs |
| U-bolt Attachments | 20 ft lbs |

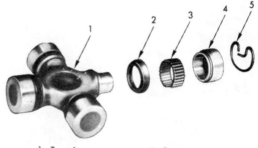

1. Trunnion    4. Cap
2. Seal       5. Snap Ring
3. Bearings

**U-joint overhaul kit for snap-ring types (© Chevrolet Motor Div.)**

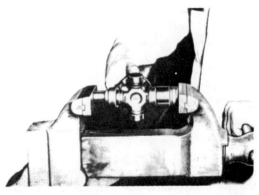

**U-joint bearing cup removal with a vise—snap-ring type (© Chevrolet Motor Div.)**

eration. This can be corrected by installing a spacer between the driveshaft center bearing support and the hanger to which it is attached. The spacer should measure 7¾ in. long and 1¼ in. wide, and be ½ in. thick. Two ½ in. diameter holes should be drilled at either end, centered ⁹/₁₆ from the end in the long dimension and ⅝ in. on the short dimension. This places the centers of the holes 6⅝ in. apart. Install the spacer between the center bearing support and the hangar using bolts ½ in. longer than the ones removed.

## U-Joint Overhaul

U-joint is mechanic's jargon for universal joint. U-joints should not be confused with U-bolts, which are U-shaped bolts used to hold U-joints in place to the axle or transfer case.

There are three types of U-joints used in these trucks. The first is held together by wire snap rings in the yokes. The second type, first used in 1975, is held together with injection molded plastic retainer rings. This type cannot be reassembled with the same parts, once disassembled. However, repair kits are available. The third type (four wheel drive models only) is the large constant velocity joint which looks like a double U-joint, located at the transfer case end of the front driveshaft.

### Snap Ring Type

1. Remove the driveshaft(s) from the truck.

2. Remove the lockrings from the yoke and remove the lubrication fitting.

3. Support the yoke in a bench vise. Never clamp the driveshaft tube.

4. Use a soft drift and hammer and drive against one trunnion bearing to drive the opposite bearing from the yoke.

NOTE: *The bearing cap cannot be driven completely out.*

5. Grasp the cap and work it out.

6. Support the other side of the yoke and drive the other bearing cap from the yoke and remove as in Steps 4 and 5.

7. Remove the trunnion from the driveshaft yoke.

8. If equipped with a sliding sleeve, remove the trunnion bearings from the sleeve yoke in the same manner as above. Remove the seal retainer from the end of the sleeve and pull the seal and washer from the retainer.

To remove the bearing support:

9. Remove the dust shield, or, if equipped with a flange, remove the cotter pin and nut and pull the flange and deflector assembly from the shaft.

10. Remove the support bracket from the rubber cushion and pull the cushion away from the bearing.

11. Pull the bearing assembly from the

shaft. If equipped, remove the grease retainers and slingers from the bearing.

Assemble the bearing support as follows:

12. Install the inner deflector on the driveshaft and punch the deflector on 2 opposite sides to be sure that it is tight.

13. Pack the retainers with special high melting grease.

Insert a slinger (if used) inside one retainer and press this retainer over the bearing outer race.

14. Start the bearing and slinger on the shaft journal. Support the driveshaft and press the bearing and inner slinger against the shoulder of the shaft with a suitable pipe.

15. Install the second slinger on the shaft and press the second retainer on the shaft.

16. Install the dust shield over the shaft (small diameter first) and depress it into position against the outer slinger or, if equipped with a flange, install the flange and deflector. Align the centerline of the flange yoke with the centerline of the driveshaft yoke and start the flange straight on the splines of the shaft with the end of the flange against the slinger.

17. Force the rubber cushion onto the bearing and coat the outside diameter of the cushion with clean brake fluid.

18. Force the bracket onto the cushion.

Assemble the trunnion bearings:

19. Repack the bearings with grease and replace the trunnion dust seals after any operation that requires disassembly of the U-joint. Be sure that the lubricant reservoir at the end of the trunnion is full of lubricant. Fill the reservoirs with lubricant from the bottom.

20. Install the trunnion into the driveshaft yoke and press the bearings into the yoke over the trunnion hubs as far as it will go.

21. Install the lockrings.

22. Hold the trunnion in one hand and tap the yoke slightly to seat the bearings against the lockrings.

23. On the rear driveshafts, install the sleeve yoke over the trunnion hubs and install the bearings in the same manner as above.

### Molded Retainer Type (1975–80)

An injection molded plastic retainer is used on some 1975–80 models. A service repair kit is available for overhaul.

1. Remove the driveshaft.

2. Support the driveshaft in a horizontal position. Place the U-joint so that the lower ear of the shaft yoke is supported by a 1⅛ in.

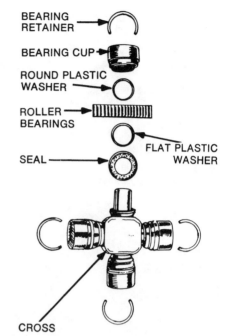

BEARING RETAINER

BEARING CUP

ROUND PLASTIC WASHER

ROLLER BEARINGS

SEAL

FLAT PLASTIC WASHER

CROSS

**Injected molded retainer U-joint repair kit**

socket. Press the lower bearing cup out of the yoke ear. This will shear the plastic retaining the lower bearing cup.

NOTE *Never clamp the driveshaft tubing in a vise.*

3. If the bearing cup is not completely removed, lift the cross, insert a spacer and press the cup completely out.

4. Rotate the driveshaft, shear the opposite plastic retainer, and press the other bearing cup out in the same manner.

5. Remove the cross from the yoke. Production U-joints cannot be reassembled. There are no bearing retainer grooves in the cups. Discard all parts that were removed and substitute those in the overhaul kit.

6. Remove the sheared plastic bearing retainer. Drive a small pin or punch through the injection holes to aid in removal.

7. If the front U-joint is serviced, remove the bearing cups from the slip yoke in the manner previously described.

8. Be sure that the seals are installed on the service bearing cups to hold the needle bearings in place for handling. Grease the bearings if they aren't pregreased.

9. Install one bearing cup partway into one side of the yoke and turn this ear to the bottom.

10. Insert the cross into the yoke so that the trunnion seats freely in the bearing cup.

11. Install the opposite bearing cup part-

**Installing the repair kit snap rings in the molded retainer type U-joint (© Chevrolet Motor Div.)**

STRIKE TUBE YOKE EAR IN THIS AREA

**Smack the tube yoke ear to seat the bearing and snap-ring (© Chevrolet Motor Div.)**

way. Be sure that both trunnions are started straight into the bearing cups.

12. Press against opposite bearing cups, working the cross constantly to be sure that it is free in the cups. If binding occurs, check the needle rollers to be sure that one needle has not become lodged under an end of the trunnion.

13. As soon as one bearing retainer groove is exposed, stop pressing and install the bearing retainer snap-ring.

14. Continue to press until the opposite bearing retainer can be installed. If difficulty installing the snap-rings is encountered, rap the yoke with a hammer to spring the yoke ears slightly.

15. Assemble the other half of the U-joint in the same manner.

16. Check that the cross is free in the cups. If it is too tight, smack the yoke ears again to help seat the bearing retainers.

## Constant Velocity Joint Overhaul

1. Remove the front driveshaft from the truck.

2. Remove the rear trunnion snap-ring from the center yoke.

3. Remove the grease fitting, if equipped.

4. Place the driveshaft in a vise as shown.

5. Drive one rear trunnion bearing cap from the center yoke until it protrudes approximately ⅜ in.

6. Release the vise and grasp the protruding portion of the cup in a vise and strike the center yoke until the cup is removed. Remove the cup seal with a thin screwdriver.

7. Repeat Steps 4, 5, and 6 for the remaining bearing cup.

8. When the center yoke cups have been removed, remove the rear yoke half bearing cups.

9. Remove the rear trunnion.

10. Remove the rear yoke half from the driveshaft by gently pulling it off. Remove all loose needle bearings and the spring seal.

11. Remove the front trunnion from the center yoke and the front yoke in the manner previously described. Remove all four bearing cups before the trunnions are removed.

12. Clean and inspect all needle bearings, cups, seals, trunnions, fitting, and yokes.

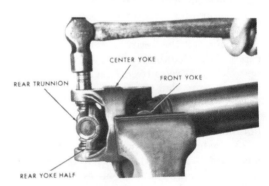

CENTER YOKE

FRONT YOKE

REAR TRUNNION

REAR YOKE HALF

**Driving out the bearing cup—constant velocity joint (© Chevrolet Motor Div.)**

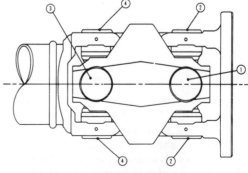

**Constant velocity joint disassembly sequence (© Chevrolet Motor Div.)**

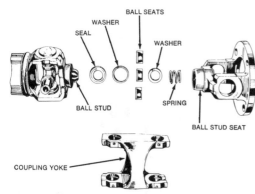

**Exploded view of a constant velocity joint**

13. Assemble the needle bearings in the cups. Assemble the needle bearings in the front yoke. Use heavy grease to retain the bearing rollers. Install the seals in the bearing cups.

14. Install the front trunnion in the driveshaft, and install the center yoke in the front trunnion.

15. Install one bearing cup and seal assembly in the front yoke. Drive it into position so that the snap-ring can be installed. Install the snap-ring and the remaining cup and seal in the front yoke. Install the other snap-ring.

16. Install the front trunnion bearing cups in the center yoke in the same manner.

17. With the front trunnion completely installed, install the seal on the driveshaft with the large face first. Gently slip the rear yoke half on the driveshaft using care not to disturb the rollers. Insert the rear trunnion into the center yoke.

18. Install the rear yoke half bearing caps on the rear trunnion. Install one rear trunnion bearing cap in the center yoke and press it into the yoke until the snap-ring can be installed. Install the remaining cap and snap-ring.

19. Grease the U-joint at the two conventional "zerk" fittings (if equipped) and the one in the rear yoke half which requires a needlenose grease gun adaptor.

20. Install the driveshaft with the constant velocity joint next to the transfer case.

# FRONT AXLE—4 WD

## Front Hub

Locking front hubs are standard equipment on 1975–80 four wheel drive models and op-

tional on earlier years, with the exception of 1973–79 full time four wheel drive trucks. The purpose of locking hubs is to reduce friction and wear by disengaging the front axle shaft, differential, and driveline from the front wheels when four wheel drive is not being used.

The engagement and disengagement of the hubs is a manual operation which must be performed to each hub assembly. Unlocking should only take place when the transfer case lever is in the two wheel drive position. The hubs should be placed in the full Lock or full Free position or damage will result.

CAUTION: *Do not use four wheel drive unless the hubs are in the Lock position.*
NOTE: *Locking hubs should be run in the Lock position for at least 10 miles each month to assure proper differential lubrication.*

### REMOVAL AND INSTALLATION

This procedure is covered in Chapter 1 under the heading of Wheel Bearings, Four Wheel Drive. Follow steps 1, 2, 3, 4, 16, 17, and 18.

## Axle Shaft
### REMOVAL AND INSTALLATION

NOTE: *The front spindles and universal joints were changed during the 1972 model year. You must know which one you have to order the correct parts. The early design is stamped 603351 or 603352 on the front of the left axle tube; the later design is 603333 or 603334. The only interchangeable part is the inner hub seal.*

1. Follow steps 1–9 of the Wheel Bearing section of Chapter 1, under Four Wheel Drive.

2. Pull out the axle shaft and universal joint assembly.

3. When installing the axle shaft, turn the shaft slowly to align the splines with the differential.

4. Reassemble everything and adjust the wheel bearings following steps 10–18 of the Wheel Bearing section of Chapter 1, under Four Wheel Drive.

### AXLE SHAFT U-JOINT OVERHAUL

1. Remove the axle shaft.

2. Squeeze the ends of the trunnion bearings in a vise to relieve the load on the snap rings. Remove the snap rings.

3. Support the yoke in a vise and drive

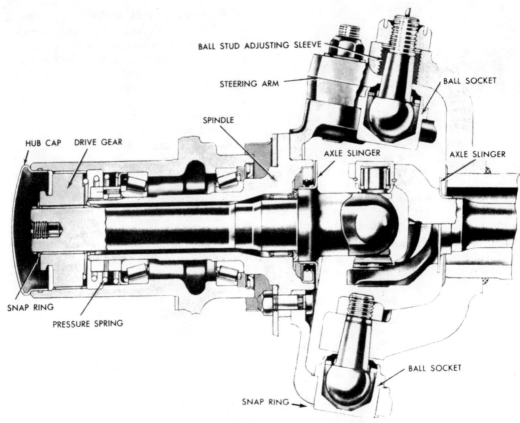

**Four wheel drive steering knuckle (© Chevrolet Motor Div.)**

on one end of the trunnion bearing with a brass drift enough to drive the opposite bearing from the yoke.

4. Support the other side of the yoke and drive the other bearing out.

5. Remove the trunnion.

6. Clean and check all parts. You can buy U-joint repair kits to replace all the worn parts.

7. Lubricate the bearings with wheel bearing grease.

8. Replace the trunnion and press the bearings into the yoke and over the trunnion hubs far enough to install the lock rings.

9. Hold the trunnion in one hand and tap the yoke lightly to seat the bearings against the lock rings.

10. The axle slingers can be pressed off the shaft.

NOTE: *Always replace the slingers if the spindle seals are replaced.*

You can use the spindle to start the slinger on the shaft.

11. Replace the shaft.

## BALL JOINT REPLACEMENT

The steering knuckle pivot ball joints may need replacement when there is excessive steering play, hard steering, irregular tire wear (especially on the inner edge), or persistent tie rod loosening.

This procedure requires a shop press. Your best bet would be to remove the steering knuckle and take it to the machine shop with the new parts.

1. Support the front axle on jackstands.

2. Remove the axle shaft as detailed earlier.

3. Remove the steering linkage. The best method is to use a tie rod end puller.

4. If you remove the steering arm from the top of the knuckle, the nuts cannot be reused.

5. Remove the cotter pin and ball joint stud nuts.

6. Remove the knuckle from the housing yoke by forcing a wedge between the lower ball stud and the yoke, then between the upper ball stud and the yoke.

NOTE: *If you have to loosen the upper ball stud adjusting sleeve to remove the knuckle, don't loosen it more than two threads. The soft threads in the yoke are easily damaged.*

7. Remove the lower ball joint snap-ring. Press the lower ball joint out first.

8. Press out the upper ball joint and un-screw the adjusting sleeve. A spanner wrench is required for the sleeve.

9. Press the new lower ball joint into the knuckle and install the snap-ring. The lower joint doesn't have a cotter pin hole.

10. Press the upper ball joint into the knuckle.

11. Position the knuckle to the yoke. In-stall new studs nuts finger tight.

12. Push up on the knuckle and tighten the lower nut to 70 ft lbs.

13. Using a spanner wrench, install and torque the upper ball stud adjusting sleeve to 50 ft lbs and install the cotter pin. Don't loosen the nut, but make it tighter to line up the cotter pin hole.

14. Replace the steering arm, using new nuts and torquing to 90 ft lbs.

15. Check the knuckle turning torque with a spring scale hooked to the tie rod hole in the steering arm. With the knuckle straight ahead, measure the right angle pull to keep the knuckle turning after initial breakaway, in both directions. The pull should be 25 lbs or less for axles assembled after Feb. 10, 1976, and 33 lbs for earlier models.

16. Replace the axle shaft and other com-ponents. Tighten the steering linkage nuts to 45 ft lbs.

## REAR AXLE

All models use conventional hypoid axles. Series 10 and 1500 trucks use semi-floating axles, while Series 20 and 2500 trucks use full floating axles. Semi-floating axles use one bearing at the end of the axle housing next to the wheel hub. These bearings do not require adjustment. Full floating axles use two bearings, and must be adjusted (in much the same manner as front wheel bearings) if removed or replaced. Full floating axle hous-ings carry the entire weight of the chassis and cargo, permitting the axle shafts to be removed without disturbing the differen-tial.

### AXLE SHAFT, BEARING, AND SEAL REMOVAL AND INSTALLATION

#### All Series 10 and 1500 Trucks Except 1974–80 Locking Differential

This procedure applies to all standard rear axles and to those with the optional Positrac-tion limited slip differential.

1. Support the axle on jackstands.

2. Remove the wheels and brake drums.

3. Clean off the differential cover area, loosen the cover to drain the lubricant, and remove the cover.

4. Turn the differential until you can reach the differential pinion shaft lockscrew. Remove the lockscrew and the pinion shaft.

5. Push in on the axle end. Remove the

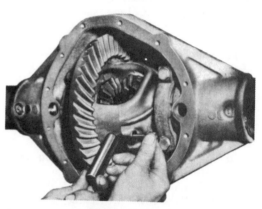

Removing the differential pinion shaft lockpin, all series 10 and 1500 except with locking differential (© Chevrolet Motor Div.)

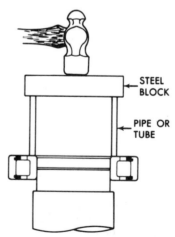

STEEL BLOCK

PIPE OR TUBE

The correct way to install a bearing. Note that the one illustrated is being driven down over a shaft. When installing the axle tube bearing, you would drive on the outer bearing race to prevent damag-ing the bearing rollers. The pipe exerts even pressure all around so that the bearing goes on straight (© Chevrolet Motor Div.)

C-lock from the inner (button) end of the shaft.

6. Remove the shaft, being careful of the oil seal.

7. You can pry the oil seal out of the housing by placing the inner end of the axle shaft behind the steel case of the seal, then prying it out carefully.

8. A puller or a slide hammer is required to remove the bearing from the housing.

9. Pack the new or reused bearing with wheel bearing grease and lubricate the cavity between the seal lips with the same grease.

10. The bearing has to be driven into the housing. Don't use a drift, you might cock the bearing in its bore. Use a piece of pipe or a large socket instead. Drive only on the outer bearing race. In a similar manner, drive the seal in flush with the end of the tube.

11. Slide the shaft into place, turning it slowly until the splines are engaged with the differential. Be careful of the oil seal.

12. Install the C-lock on the inner axle end. Pull the shaft out so that the C-lock seats in the counterbore of the differential side gear.

13. Position the differential pinion shaft through the case and the pinion gears, aligning the lockscrew hole. Install the lockscrew.

14. Install the cover with a new gasket and tighten the bolts evenly in a crisscross pattern.

15. Fill the axle with lubricant as specified in Chapter 1.

16. Replace the brake drums and wheels.

### 1974–80 Series 10 and 1500 With Locking Differential

This axle uses a thrust block on the differential pinion shaft.

1. Follow Steps 1–3 of the preceding procedure.

2. Rotate the differential case so that you can remove the lockscrew and support the pinion shaft so it can't fall into the housing. Remove the differential pinion shaft lockscrew.

3. Carefully pull the pinion shaft partway out and rotate the differential case until the shaft touches the housing at the top.

4. Use a screwdriver to position the C-lock with its open end directly inward. You can't push in the axle shaft till you do this.

5. Push the axle shaft in and remove the C-lock.

6. Follow Steps 6–11 of the preceding procedure.

Positioning the differential case for best clearance for pinion shaft removal, 1974–80 locking differential (© Chevrolet Motor Div.)

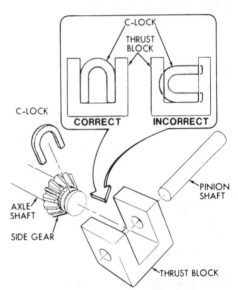

Correct C-lock positioning, 1974–80 locking differential (© Chevrolet Motor Div.)

7. Keep the pinion shaft partway out of the differential case while installing the C-lock on the axle shaft. Put the C-lock on the axle shaft and carefully pull out on the axle shaft until the C-lock is clear of the thrust block.

8. Follow Steps 13–16 of the previous procedure.

### 1970–80 Series 20 and 2500

These models all use axles of full floating design. The procedures are the same for locking and non-locking axles. Some 1970–72 trucks use Dana axles, but the same procedures should be used.

The best way to remove the bearings from the wheel hub is with an arbor press. Use of a press reduces the chances of damaging the bearing races, cocking the bearing in its

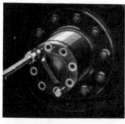

**Removing the full floating axle shaft, 1970–72; 1973 and later similar (© Chevrolet Motor Div.)**

bore, or scoring the hub walls. A local machine shop is probably equipped with the tools to remove and install bearings and seals. However, if one is not available, the hammer and drift method outlined can be used.

1. Support the axle on jackstands.
2. Remove the wheels.
3. Remove the bolts and lock washers that attach the axle shaft flange to the hub.
4. On 1970–72 trucks, install two ½ in. by 13 in. bolts in the threaded holes provided in the axle shaft flange. By turning these bolts alternately the axle shaft may be easily started and then removed from the housing.
5. On 1973–80 trucks, rap on the flange with a soft faced hammer to loosen the shaft. Grip the rib on the end of the flange with a pair of locking pliers and twist to start shaft removal. Remove the shaft from the axle tube.
6. The hub and drum assembly must be removed to remove the bearings and oil seals. You will need a large socket to remove and later adjust the bearing adjustment nut. There are also tools available which resemble the four wheel drive front wheel bearing adjusting tool in Chapter 1.
7. Disengage the tang of the locknut re-

**This tool is available for removing and adjusting the bearing locknut and adjusting nut (© Chevrolet Motor Div.)**

tainer from the slot or flat of the locknut, then remove the locknut from the housing tube, using the earlier mentioned tool.

8. Disengage the tang of the retainer from the slot or flat of the adjusting nut and remove the retainer from the housing tube.
9. Remove the adjusting nut from the housing tube with the tool mentioned earlier.
10. Remove the thrust washer from the housing tube.
11. Pull the hub and drum straight off the axle housing.
12. Remove the oil seal and discard.
13. Use a hammer and a long drift to knock the inner bearing, cup, and oil seal from the hub assembly.
14. Remove the outer bearing snap ring with a pair of pliers. It may be necessary to tap the bearing outer race away from the retaining ring slightly by tapping on the ring to remove the ring.
15. Drive the outer bearing from the hub with a hammer and drift.
16. To reinstall the bearings, place the outer bearing into the hub. The larger outside diameter of the bearing should face the outer end of the hub. Drive the bearing into the hub using a washer that will cover both the inner and outer races of the bearing. Place a socket on the top of this washer, then drive the bearing into place with a series of light taps. If available, an arbor press should be used for this job.
17. Drive the bearing past the snap ring groove, and install the snap ring. Then, turning the hub assembly over, drive the bearing back against the snap ring. Again, protect the bearing by placing a washer on top of it. You can use the thrust washer that fits between the bearing and the adjusting nut for this job.
18. Place the inner bearing into the hub. The thick edge should be toward the shoulder in the hub. Press the bearing into the hub until it seats against the shoulder, using a washer and socket as outlined earlier. Make certain that the bearing is not cocked and that it is fully seated on the shoulder.
19. Pack the cavity between the oil seal lips with the front wheel bearing grease specified in Chapter 1, and position it in the hub bore. Carefully press it into place on top of the inner bearing.
20. Pack the wheel bearings with the grease, and lightly coat the inside diameter of the hub bearing contact surface and the outside diameter of the axle housing tube.
21. Make sure that the inner bearing, oil

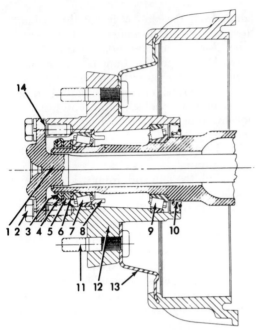

1. Axle Shaft
2. Shaft-to-Hub Bolt
3. Locknut
4. Locknut Retainer
5. Adjusting Nut
6. Thrust Washer
7. Hub Outer Bearing
8. Snap Ring
9. Hub Inner Bearing
10. Oil Seal
11. Wheel Bolt
12. Hub Assembly
13. Drum Assembly
14. Gasket

**Cross section of the hub and drum assembly for series 20 and 2500 trucks (© Chevrolet Motor Div.)**

seal, axle housing oil deflector, and outer bearing are properly positioned. Install the hub and drum assembly on the axle housing, exercising care so as not to damage the oil seal or dislocate other internal components.

22. Install the thrust washer so that the tang on the inside diameter of the washer is in the keyway on the axle housing.

23. Install the adjusting nut. Tighten to 50 ft lbs, at the same time rotating the hub to make sure that all the bearing surfaces are in contact. Back off the nut and retighten to 35 ft lbs, then back off ¼ of a turn.

24. Install the tanged retainer against the inner adjusting nut. Align the adjusting nut so that the short tang of the retainer will engage the nearest slot on the adjusting nut.

25. Install the outer locknut and tighten to 65 ft lbs. Bend the long tang of the retainer into the slot of the outer nut. This method of adjustment should provide .001 to .010 in. of end play.

26. Place a new gasket over the axle shaft and position the axle shaft in the housing so that the shaft splines enter the differential side gear. Position the gasket so that the holes are in alignment, and install the flange-to-hub attaching bolts. Torque to 90 ft lbs through 1975, 115 ft lbs 1976–80.

NOTE: *To prevent lubricant from leaking through the flange holes, apply a nonhardening sealer to the bolt threads. Use the sealer sparingly.*

27. Replace the wheels.

### DETERMINING AXLE RATIO

Axle ratios available in these trucks range from 2.56:1 to 4.57:1 with nine stops in between. However, not all ratios are available with all axles. If you are contemplating a change of axle ratios, your dealer can advise you as to what gears are available for your particular axle.

Front axle ratios installed on four wheel drive models are the same as the rear, or nearly so.

An axle ratio is obtained by dividing the number of teeth on the drive pinion gear into the number of teeth on the ring gear. For instance, on a 4.11 ratio, the driveshaft will turn 4.11 times for every turn of the rear wheel.

The most accurate way to determine axle ratios is to drain the differential, remove the cover, and count the number of teeth on the ring and pinion.

An easier method is to jack and support the truck so that both rear wheels are off the ground. Make a chalk mark on the rear wheel and the driveshaft. Block the front wheels and put the transmission in Neutral. Turn the rear wheel one complete revolution and count the number of turns made by the driveshaft. The number of driveshaft rotations is the axle ratio. You can get more accuracy by going more than one tire rotation and dividing the result by the number of tire rotations.

The axle ratio is also identified by the axle serial number prefix on the axles. See Chapter 1 for serial number location; the prefixes are listed in dealer's parts books. Dana axles usually have a tag under one of the cover bolts, giving either the ratio or the number of pinion/ring gear teeth.

Tire sizes will, to a certain extent, determine the effective axle ratio. Flotation type tires, for example, with wider sidewalls (increased distance between the wheel rim and the tread) will increase the effective ratio, as compared to lower profile tires.

# Suspension and Steering

## FRONT SUSPENSION

Conventional two wheel drive pick-ups use an independent front suspension with upper and lower control arms and coil springs. Four wheel drive pick-ups use tapered leaf springs and the traditional solid front axle.

CAUTION: *Springs, particularly coil springs, are under considerable tension. Be very careful when removing and installing them; they can exert enough force to cause serious injuries.*

## Coil Spring
### REMOVAL AND INSTALLATION

1. Raise and support the truck under the frame rails. The control arms should hang free.

2. Disconnect the shock absorber at the lower end and move it aside. Disconnect the stabilizer bar from the lower control arm.

3. Support the cross-shaft and install a spring compressor or chain the spring to the control arm as a safety precaution.

4. Raise the jack to remove the tension from the lower control arm cross-shaft and remove the two U-bolts securing the cross-shaft to the crossmember.

NOTE: *The cross-shaft and lower control arm keeps the coil spring compressed. Use care when you lower the assembly.*

5. Slowly release the jack and lower the control arm until the spring can be removed. Be sure that all compression is relieved from the spring.

6. Remove the spring.

7. To install, position the spring on the control arm and jack it into position. Use the spring compressor again as a precaution.

8. Position the control arm cross-shaft on the crossmember and install the U-bolts. Be sure that the front indexing hole in the cross-shaft is aligned with the crossmember attaching saddle stud. Torque the U-bolts to 45 ft lbs 1970–75 C-10 and C-1500s, 85 ft lbs 1976–80. Torque to 110 ft lbs 1970–72, 85 ft lbs 1973–80 C-20 or 2500s.

9. Further installation is the reverse of removal. Have the front suspension alignment checked.

## Leaf Spring
### REMOVAL AND INSTALLATION

1. Raise and support the vehicle so that all tension is taken off of the front suspension.

2. Remove the shackle upper retaining bolt and the front spring eye bolt.

3. Remove the spring-to-axle U-bolt nuts. Pull off the spring, the lower plate, and the spring pads.

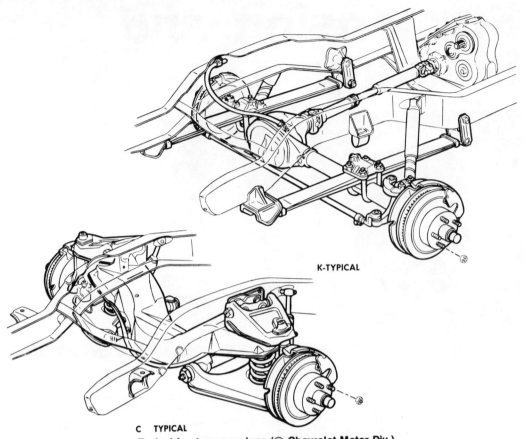

K-TYPICAL

C   TYPICAL

**Typical front suspensions (© Chevrolet Motor Div.)**

4. Remove the shackle-to-spring bolt, bushings, and shackle.

To replace the bushing, place the spring onto a press or vise and press out the bushing using suitable tools. Press in the new bushing. The new bushing should protrude evenly on both sides of the spring.

5. Install the spring shackle bushings into the spring and then attach the shackle. Do not tighten the bolt.

6. Place the upper spring cushion onto the spring.

7. Place the front of the spring into the frame and install the bolt but do not tighten it.

8. Position the shackle bushing into the frame and attach the rear shackle but do not tighten it.

9. Install the lower spring pad and the spring retainer plate. Torque the U-bolts to 120 ft lbs 1970–72, 150 ft lbs 1973–80.

10. Torque the spring shackle bolt to 50 ft lbs, the front eye bolt to 90 ft lbs, and the rear eye bolt to 50 ft lbs.

11. Lower the vehicle.

## Shock Absorbers

### REMOVAL AND INSTALLATION

1. Raise and support the truck.

2. Remove the nuts and eye bolts securing the upper and lower shock absorber eyes.

3. Remove the shock absorber and inspect the rubber eye bushings. If these are defective, replace the shock absorber assembly.

4. Installation is the reverse of removal.

### TESTING

Adjust the tire pressure before testing the shocks. If the truck is equipped with heavy-duty equipment, this can sometimes be misleading. A stiff ride normally accompanies a stiff or heavy-duty suspension. Be sure that all weight in the truck is distributed evenly.

#### Bounce Test

Each shock absorber can be tested by bouncing the corner of the truck until maximum up and down movement is obtained. Let go of the truck. It should stop bouncing in 1–2

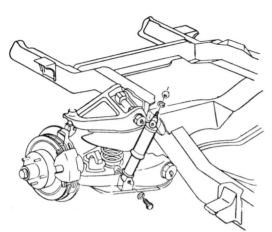

Two wheel drive front shock absorber (© Chevrolet Motor Div.)

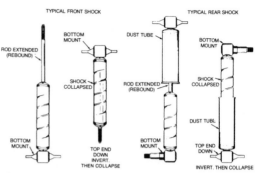

Purging air from the shock absorber (© Chevrolet Motor Div.)

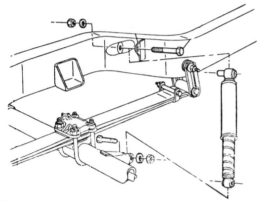

Four wheel drive front shock absorber (© Chevrolet Motor Div.)

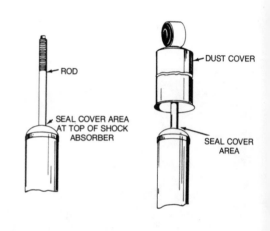

Seal cover area of the shock absorber (© Chevrolet Motor Div.)

bounces. If not, the shock should be inspected for damage and possibly replaced.

## Ball Joints

Service procedures for four wheel drive front axles are covered in Chapter 7.

### INSPECTION

#### Upper—1970–71

1. Raise and support the truck so that the control arms hang free.
2. Remove the wheel.
3. Support the lower control arm with a jackstand and disconnect the upper ball stud from the steering knuckle.
4. Reinstall the nut on the ball stud and measure the torque required to rotate the stud. If the torque is not within 1–10 ft lbs, replace the ball joint.
5. If no defects are evident, connect the steering knuckle to the upper stud and

torque the nut to 70 ft lbs. Tighten further to install the cotter pin, but don't exceed 90 ft lbs.

#### Upper—1972–80

1. Perform Steps 1–3 of the 1970–71 inspection procedure.
2. The upper ball joint is spring loaded in its socket. If it has any perceptible lateral shake or can be twisted in its socket, it should be replaced.
3. Go on with Step 5 of the 1970–71 inspection procedure.

#### Lower

1. Support the weight of the control arm at the wheel hub.
2. Measure the distance between the tip of the ball joint stud and the grease fitting below the ball joint.
3. Move the support to the control arm and allow the hub and drum to hang free. Measure the distance again. If the variation

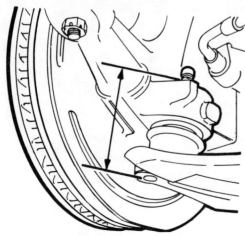

**Lower ball joint inspection**

**Loosening the ball joint stud with the special tool
(© Chevrolet Motor Div.)**

between the two measurements exceeds ³/₃₂ in. the ball joint should be replaced.

## REMOVAL AND INSTALLATION

### Lower

1. Raise and support the truck. Support the lower control arm with a floor jack.

2. Remove the tire and wheel.

3. Remove the lower stud cotter pin and loosen, but do not remove, the stud nut.

4. Loosen the ball joint with the tool illustrated or a commercial substitute. It may be necessary to remove the brake caliper and wire it to the frame to gain enough clearance.

5. When the stud is loose, remove the tool and ball stud nut.

6. Install a spring compressor on the coil spring for safety.

7. Pull the brake disc and knuckle assembly up and off the ball stud and support the upper arm with a block of wood.

8. Remove the ball joint from the control arm with a ball joint fork or another suitable tool.

To install:

9. Start the new ball joint into the control arm. Position the bleed vent in the rubber boot facing inward.

10. Turn the screw until the ball joint is seated in the control arm.

11. Lower the upper arm and match the steering knuckle to the lower ball stud.

12. Install the brake caliper, if removed.

13. Install the ball stud nut and torque it to 80–100 ft lbs plus the additional torque necessary to align the cotter pin hole. Do not exceed 130 ft lbs or back the nut off to align the holes with the pin.

14. Install a new lube fitting and lubricate the new joint.

15. Install the tire and wheel.

16. Lower the truck.

### Upper

1. Raise and support the truck. Remove wheel.

2. Support the lower control arm with a floor jack.

3. Remove the cotter pin from the upper ball stud and loosen, but do not remove, the stud nut.

4. Using the special tool or a commercial substitute, loosen the ball stud in the steering knuckle. When the stud is loose, remove the tool and the stud nut. It may be necessary to remove the brake caliper and wire it to the frame to gain clearance.

5. Drill out the rivets. Remove the ball joint assembly.

To install:

6. Install the service ball joint, using the nuts supplied or special hardened fasteners.

7. Torque the ball stud nut as follows:

10 Series: 60 ft lbs plus the additional torque to align the cotter pin. Do not exceed 90 ft lbs and never back the nut off to align the pin.

20 Series: 80–100 ft lbs plus additional torque necessary to align the cotter pin. Do not exceed 130 ft lbs and never back off the nut to align the pin.

8. Install a new cotter pin.

9. Install a new lube fitting and lubricate the new joint.

10. If removed, install the brake caliper.

11. Install the wheel and lower the truck.

## Upper Control Arm
### REMOVAL AND INSTALLATION

1. Raise and support the truck on jack-stands.

2. Support the lower control arm with a floor jack.

3. Remove the wheel and tire.

4. Remove the cotter pin from the upper control arm ball stud and loosen the stud nut until the bottom surface of the nut is slightly below the end of the stud.

5. Install a spring compressor on the coil spring for safety.

6. Loosen the upper control arm ball stud in the steering knuckle using a ball joint stud removal tool. Remove the nut from the ball stud and raise the upper arm to clear the steering knuckle. It may be necessary to remove the brake caliper and wire it to the frame to gain clearance.

7. Remove the nuts securing the control arm shaft studs to the crossmember bracket and remove the control arm.

8. Tape the shims and spacers together and tag for proper reassembly.

9. Installation is the reverse of removal. Place the control arm in position and install the nuts. Before tightening the nuts to 70 ft lbs for C-10 and C-1500, or 105 ft lbs for C-20 and C-2500 models, insert the caster and camber shims in the same order as when removed. Have the front end alignment checked, and as necessary, adjusted.

## Lower Control Arm
### REMOVAL AND INSTALLATION

1. Raise and support the truck on jack-stands.

2. Remove the spring (see "Spring Removal and Installation").

3. Support the inboard end of the control arm after spring removal.

4. Remove the cotter pin from the lower ball stud and loosen the nut one turn.

5. Loosen the lower ball stud in the steering knuckle using a ball joint stud removal tool. When the stud is loose, remove the nut from the stud. It may be necessary to remove the brake caliper and wire it to the frame to gain clearance.

6. Remove the lower control arm.

7. Installation is the reverse of removal. See the "Spring Removal and Installation" for bolt torques.

## Front End Alignment

Correct alignment of the front suspension is necessary to provide optimum tire life and for proper and safe handling of the vehicle. Caster and camber cannot be set or measured accurately without professional equipment. Toe-in can be adjusted with some degree of success without any special equipment.

### CASTER

Caster is the tilt of the front steering axis either forward or backward away from the vertical. A tilt toward the rear is said to be positive (+) and a forward tilt is negative (−). Caster is calculated with a special instrument but one can see the caster angle by looking straight down from the top of the upper control arm. You will see that the ball joints are not aligned if the caster angle is more or less than 0°. If the vehicle has positive caster, the lower ball joint would be ahead of the upper ball joint center line. Caster is designed into the four wheel drive front suspension. Small caster adjustments can be made on four wheel drive front axles by the use of tapered shims between the springs and the axle.

### CAMBER

Camber is the slope of the front wheels from the vertical when viewed from the front of the vehicle. When the wheels tilt outward at the top, the camber is positive (+). When the wheels tilt inward at the top, the camber is negative (−). The amount of positive and negative camber is measured in degrees from the vertical and the measurement is called camber angle. Camber is designed into the front axle of all four wheel drive vehicles. Small camber adjustments can be made on four wheel drive front axles by the use of an adjusting shim between the spindle and the steering knuckle. Any major corrections require axle straightening equipment.

### CASTER AND CAMBER ADJUSTMENTS
#### Two Wheel Drive

Caster and camber adjustments are made by removing or adding shims between the upper control arm shaft and the mounting bracket which is attached to the suspension crossmember.

Front wheel alignment on Chevrolet and GMC trucks is a complex operation. Specifications for camber and caster are given in

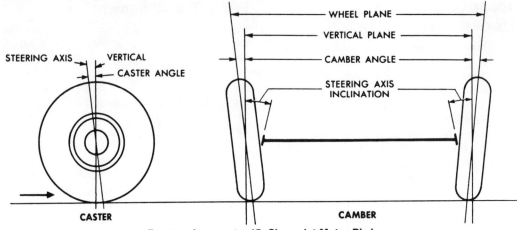

**Front end geometry (© Chevrolet Motor Div.)**

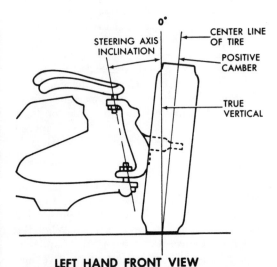

**LEFT HAND FRONT VIEW**

**Front wheel camber (© Chevrolet Motor Div.)**

**Independent front suspension alignment shims (© Chevrolet Motor Div.)**

relation to a measurement (the distance from the lower control arm to the bump stop bracket). This takes into account all sorts of individuality among trucks: heavy-duty suspensions, tires, spring rates, and even wear

on the front suspension. As a result specifications are not included in this book. Camber should not vary more than ½° from side to side.

## TOE-IN

Toe-in is the amount, measured in a fraction of an inch, that the wheels are closer together in front than at the rear.

Virtually all cars and trucks, except some with front wheel drive, are set with toe-in. Some front wheel drive cars, and some four wheel drive trucks, require toe-out to prevent excessive toe-in under power.

NOTE: *Some alignment specialists set toe-in to the lower specified limit on vehicles with radial tires. The reason is that radial tires have less drag, and therefore a lesser tendency to toe-out at speed. By the same reasoning, off-road tires would require the upper limit of toe-in.*

Toe-in must be checked after caster and camber have been adjusted, but it can be adjusted without disturbing the other two settings. You can make this adjustment without special equipment, if you make careful measurements. The adjustment is made at the

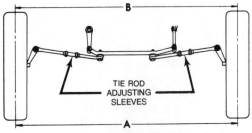

**Toe-in adjustment (© Chevrolet Motor Div.)**

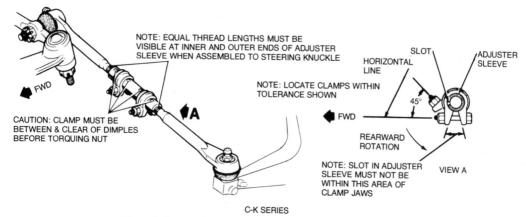

NOTE: EQUAL THREAD LENGTHS MUST BE
VISIBLE AT INNER AND OUTER ENDS OF ADJUSTER
SLEEVE WHEN ASSEMBLED TO STEERING KNUCKLE

NOTE: LOCATE CLAMPS WITHIN
TOLERANCE SHOWN

FWD

CAUTION: CLAMP MUST BE
BETWEEN & CLEAR OF DIMPLES
BEFORE TORQUING NUT

A

SLOT

HORIZONTAL
LINE

ADJUSTER
SLEEVE

45°

FWD

REARWARD
ROTATION

NOTE: SLOT IN ADJUSTER
SLEEVE MUST NOT BE
WITHIN THIS AREA OF
CLAMP JAWS

VIEW A

C-K SERIES

**Tie-rod sleeve clamp installation (© Chevrolet Motor Div.)**

tie-rod sleeves. The wheels must be straight ahead.

1. Toe-in can be determined by measuring the distance between the centers of the tire treads, front and rear. If the tread pattern of your tires makes this impossible, you can measure between the edges of the wheel rims, but make sure to move the truck forward and measure in a couple of places to avoid errors caused by bent rims or wheel runout.

2. Loosen the clamp bolts on the tie-rod sleeves.

3. Rotate the sleeves equally (in opposite directions) to obtain the correct measurement. If the sleeves are not adjusted equally, the steering wheel will be crooked.

NOTE: *If your steering wheel is already crooked, it can be straightened by turning the sleeves equally in the same direction.*

4. When the adjustment is complete, tighten the clamps.

## Toe-in (in.)

| Year | Model | Toe-In |
|------|-------|--------|
| 1970 | C-10, 1500, 20, 2500 | 1/8–1/4 |
| | K-10, 1500, 20, 2500 | 3/32–3/16 |
| 1971 | All | 1/8–1/4 |
| 1972–73 | All | 3/16 |
| 1974–80 | C-10, 1500, 20, 2500 | 3/16 |
| | K-10, 1500, 20, 2500 | 0 |

## REAR SUSPENSION

All two wheel drive trucks from 1970–72 use a coil spring with lateral control arm rear suspension. An auxiliary leaf spring is also used on C10 and 20 Series. In 1973 this was changed to a conventional leaf spring rear suspension. Four wheel drive trucks in all years use the traditional leaf springs in the rear. All models use one shock absorber at each rear wheel.

CAUTION: *Springs, particularly coil springs, are under considerable tension. Be careful when removing and installing them; they can exert enough force to cause very serious injuries.*

## Coil Spring
### REMOVAL AND INSTALLATION

1. Jack up the vehicle and support it from the frame. Position another jack under the control arm.

2. Remove the lower shock absorber bolt from its mounting on the lower control arm.

3. Remove the upper and lower clamps from the spring by releasing the lower bolt from the lower side of the control arm. The upper bolt is situated in the middle of the spring.

CAUTION: *Insert a safety chain through the spring and lower control arm to prevent the spring from flying out.*

4. Lower the jack under the control arm slowly until there is sufficient room to remove the spring.

To install the unit:

5. Using a spring clamp, place the clamp so that the end of the spring is within the area of the notch so that it will seat on the spring

Removing the upper clamp bolt from the rear coil spring (© Chevrolet Motor Div.)

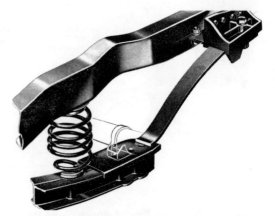

Auxiliary rear spring, 1970–72 C series (© Chevrolet Motor Div.)

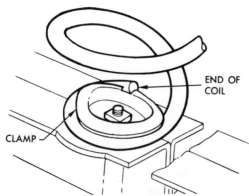

END OF COIL

CLAMP

Lower clamp bolt, rear coil spring (© Chevrolet Motor Div.)

end without any hangup. It will also align with the bolt hole in the control arm.

6. Position the clamp bolt with the washer up through the hole in the control arm and then loosely install the nut.

7. Place the upper clamp inside the spring and install the bolt and washer.

8. Raise the control arm and attach the shock absorber.

## Auxiliary Spring (1970–72)

### REMOVAL AND INSTALLATION

The auxiliary spring is attached to the frame and is removed as follows.

1. Remove all tension from the spring before attempting to remove it. Be certain that the spring leaf does not contact the bumper on the control arm.

2. Pull the cotter pin from the spring retaining bolt and then remove the nut. Remove the spring from the frame bracket.

3. If you are removing the contact bumper, support the axle with a jack, remove the U-bolts, and remove the bumper.

To install:

4. Place the spring bumper between the control arm and the axle housing. Make certain that the holes in the spring bracket are aligned with those in the control arm. Place the shock absorber bracket on the underside of the control arm. Place the U-bolt over the axle and through the auxiliary spring control arm and shock absorber bracket. Tighten the U-bolt retaining nuts alternately to 150 ft lbs.

5. Position the auxiliary spring assembly in the frame bracket so that the free end of the spring is above the bumper and aligned with the spring-to-bracket bolt holes. Place the bolt and washer through the top side of the bracket and then install the nut and washer on the bolt. The nut should be torqued to 370 ft lbs. Install the cotter pin.

## Leaf Spring

### REMOVAL AND INSTALLATION

1. Raise the vehicle and support it so that there is no tension on the leaf spring assembly.

2. Loosen the spring-to-shackle retaining bolts. (Do not remove these bolts.)

3. Remove the securing bolts which attach the shackle to the spring hanger.

4. Remove the nut and bolt which attach the spring to the front hanger.

5. Remove the U-bolt nuts and remove the spring plate.

6. Pull the spring from the vehicle.

7. It is important to inspect the spring and replace any damaged components such as bushings and springs.

NOTE: *If the spring bushings are defective, use the following procedures for re-*

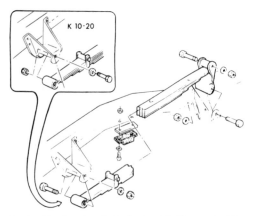

**Typical leaf spring installation (© Chevrolet Motor Div.)**

*moval and installation. 1975–80 C-20 and 2500 trucks use bushings that are staked in place. The stakes must first be straightened. When a new bushing is installed stake it in 3 equally spaced locations.*

*Using a press or vise, remove the bushing. Press in the new bushing.*

8. Place the spring assembly onto the axle housing.

NOTE: *The shackle assembly must be attached to the rear spring eye before the rear shackle is installed.*

9. Position the spring retaining plate and the U-bolts (loosely).

10. It will be necessary to jack the frame in some manner to align the spring and shackle with the spring hangers.

11. Install the shackle bolt and nut and reposition the spring if necessary in order to align the front eye. Position the front eyebolt and nut.

12. Torque the hanger and shackle fasteners to 110 ft lbs 1977–80, 90 ft lbs 1973–76.

NOTE: *Make sure that the bolts are free turning in their bushings prior to torquing.*

13. Lower the truck so that the weight is on the suspension components. Torque the U-bolt nuts to 140 ft lbs.

14. Lower the truck completely and remove the jacks.

## Shock Absorbers
### REMOVAL AND INSTALLATION

1. Raise and support the truck.
2. Support the rear axle with a floor jack.
3. If the truck is equipped with air lift shocks, bleed the air from the lines and disconnect the line from the shock absorber.

4. Disconnect the shock absorber at the top by removing the nut and washers.

5. Remove the nut, washers and bolt from the bottom mount.

6. Remove the shock from the truck.

7. Installation is the reverse of removal. If the truck is equipped with air lift shock absorbers, inflate them to 10–15 psi. Torque the upper mount to 140 ft lbs through 1977, or 150 ft lbs, 1978–80; the lower to 115 ft lbs.

### TESTING

See "Shock Absorber Testing" under "Front Suspension."

## STEERING

## Steering Wheel
### REMOVAL AND INSTALLATION

1. Disconnect the battery ground cable.
2. Remove the horn button and the receiving cap, belleville washer and bushing (if equipped).
3. Mark the steering wheel-to-steering shaft relationship.
4. On 1975–80 models, remove the snap ring from the steering shaft.
5. Remove the nut and washer from the steering shaft.
6. Remove the steering wheel with a puller.

CAUTION: *Don't hammer on the steering shaft.*

7. Installation is the reverse of removal. The turn signal control assembly must be in

**Steering wheel removal (© Chevrolet Motor Div.)**

the Neutral position to prevent damaging the cancelling cam and control assembly. Tighten the nut to 40 ft lbs 1970–72, 30 ft lbs 1973–80.

NOTE: *A steering wheel puller can be made by drilling two holes in a piece of steel the same distance apart as the two threaded holes in the steering wheel. Sometimes an old spring shackle will have the right dimensions. Drill another hole in the center. Place a center bolt with the head against the steering shaft and a nut against the bottom of the homemade puller bar. Thread the two outer bolts into the holes into the wheel. Unscrew the nut on the center bolt to draw the wheel off the shaft.*

## Turn Signal Switch

### REPLACEMENT

#### 1970–72

1. Disconnect the battery ground cable.
2. Remove the steering wheel, preload spring, and cancelling cam.
3. Remove the shift lever roll pin and shift lever (if applicable).
4. Remove the turn signal lever screw and the lever.
5. Push the hazard warning knob in. This must be done to avoid damaging the switch.
6. Disconnect the switch wire from the chassis harness located under the dash.
7. Remove the mast jacket upper bracket.
8. Remove the switch wiring cover from the column.
9. Unscrew the mounting screws and remove the switch, bearing housing, switch cover, and shift housing from the column.
10. Installation is the reverse of removal.

#### 1973–80

1. Remove the steering wheel as previously outlined.
2. Loosen the three cover screws and lift the cover off the shaft. On 1976–80 models, place a screwdriver in the cover slot and pry out to free the cover.
3. The round lockplate must be pushed down to remove the wire snap-ring from the shaft. A special tool is available to do this. The tool is an inverted U-shape with a hole for the shaft. The shaft nut is used to force it down. Pry the wire snap-ring out of the shaft groove. Discard the snap-ring.
4. Remove the tool and lift the lockplate off the shaft.

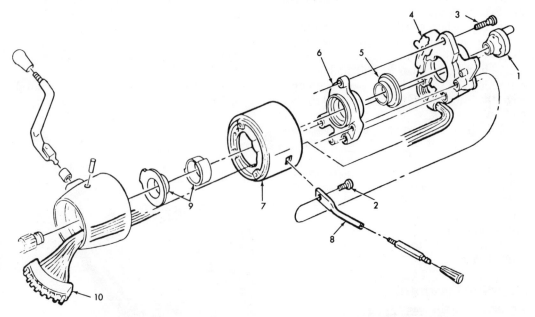

| | |
|---|---|
| 1. Cancelling cam | 6. Bearing support |
| 2. Directional lever retaining screw | 7. Switch cover |
| 3. Switch mounting screw | 8. Lever arm |
| 4. Switch | 9. Washer |
| 5. Upper bearing | 10. Wiring connector |

**1970–72 turn signal switch (© Chevrolet Motor Div.)**

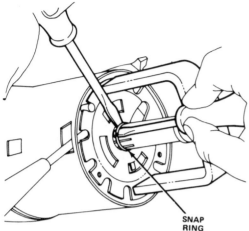

**Removing the lockplate retaining ring**

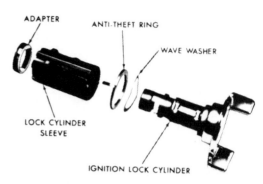

**Ignition lock cylinder, 1973–78; later models similar (© Chevrolet Motor Div.)**

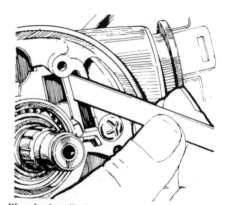

**Ignition lock cylinder removal, 1973–78**

5. Slip the cancelling cam, upper bearing preload spring, and thrust washer off the shaft.

6. Remove the turn signal lever. Push the flasher knob in and unscrew it.

7. Pull the switch connector out of the mast jacket and tape the upper part to facilitate switch removal. On tilt wheels, place the turn signal and shifter housing in Low position and remove the harness cover.

8. Remove the three switch mounting screws. Remove the switch by pulling it straight up while guiding the wiring harness cover through the column.

9. Install the replacement switch by working the connector and cover down through the housing and under the bracket. On tilt models, the connector is worked down through the housing, under the bracket, and then the cover is installed on the harness.

10. Install the switch mounting screws and the connector on the mast jacket bracket. Install the column-to-dash trim plate.

11. Install the flasher knob and the turn signal lever.

12. With the turn signal lever in neutral and the flasher knob out, slide the thrust washer, upper bearing pre-load spring, and cancelling cam onto the shaft.

13. Position the lockplate on the shaft and press it down until a new snap-ring can be inserted in the shaft groove.

14. Install the cover and the steering wheel.

## Ignition Switch

For procedures covering the 1970–72 ignition switch, see Chapter 5.

### LOCK CYLINDER REMOVAL AND INSTALLATION

#### 1973–78

1. Remove steering wheel and turn signal switch.

NOTE: *It is not necessary to completely remove the turn signal switch. Pull the switch over the end of the shaft—no further.*

2. Place lock cylinder in Run position.

CAUTION: *Do not remove the ignition key buzzer.*

3. Insert a small screwdriver into the turn signal housing slot. Keeping the screwdriver to the right-side of the slot, break the housing flash loose and depress the spring latch at the lower end of the lock cylinder. Remove the lock cylinder.

NOTE: *Considerable force may be necessary to break this casting flash, but be careful not to damage any other parts. When ordering a new lock cylinder, specify a cylinder assembly. This will save assembling the cylinder, washer, sleeve and adapter.*

4. To install, hold the lock cylinder sleeve

and rotate the knob clockwise against the stop. Insert the cylinder into the housing, aligning the key and keyway. Hold a 0.070 in. drill between the lock bezel and housing. Rotate the cylinder counterclockwise, maintaining a light pressure until the drive section of the cylinder mates with the sector. Push in until the snap-ring pops into the grooves. Remove drill. Check cylinder operation.

CAUTION: *The drill prevents forcing the lock cylinder inward beyond its normal position. The buzzer switch and spring latch can hold the lock cylinder in too far. Complete disassembly of the upper bearing housing is necessary to release an improperly installed lock cylinder.*

### 1979–80

1. Remove the steering wheel.
2. Remove the turn signal switch. It is not necessary to completely remove the switch from the column. Pull the switch rearward far enough to slip it over the end of the shaft, but do not pull the harness out of the column.
3. Turn the lock to Run.
4. Remove the lock retaining screw and remove the lock cylinder.

CAUTION: *If the retaining screw is dropped on removal, it may fall into the column, requiring complete disassembly of the column to retrieve the screw.*

5. To install, rotate the key to the stop while holding onto the cylinder.
6. Push the lock all the way in.
7. Install the screw. Tighten the screw to 3 ft lbs for regular columns, 2 ft lbs for adjustable columns.

8. Install the turn signal switch and the steering wheel.

### 1973–80 IGNITION SWITCH REMOVAL AND INSTALLATION

The switch is on the steering column, behind the instrument panel.

1. Lower the steering column, making sure that it is supported.

CAUTION: *Extreme care is necessary to prevent damage to the collapsible column.*

2. Make sure the switch is in the Lock position. If the lock cylinder is out, pull the switch rod up to the stop, then go down one detent.
3. Remove the two screws and the switch.
4. Before installation, make sure the switch is in the Lock position.
5. Install the switch using the original screws.

CAUTION: *Use of screws that are too long could prevent the column from collapsing on impact.*

6. Replace the column.

## Power Steering Pump

See Chapter 1 for fluid level checking and drive belt tension adjustments.

### REMOVAL AND INSTALLATION

#### All Models

1. Disconnect the hoses at the pump. When the hoses are disconnected, secure the ends in a raised position to prevent leakage. Cap the ends of the hoses to prevent the entrance of dirt.
2. Cap the pump fittings.

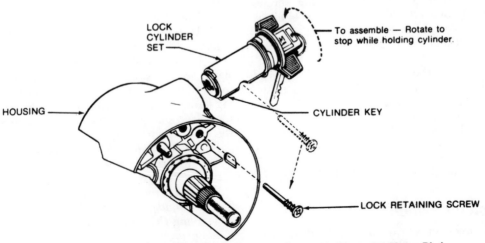

**1979–80 ignition lock cylinder removal and installation (© Chevrolet Motor Div.)**

3. Loosen the bracket-to-pump mounting nuts.

4. Remove the pump drive belt.

5. Remove the bracket-to-pump bolts and remove the pump from the truck.

6. Installation is the reverse of removal. Fill the reservoir and bleed the pump by turning the pulley counterclockwise (as viewed from the front) until bubbles stop forming. Bleed the system as outlined following. Adjust the belt tension.

### BLEEDING THE HYDRAULIC SYSTEM

1. Fill the reservoir to the proper level and let the fluid remain undisturbed for at least 2 minutes.

2. Start the engine and run it for only about 2 seconds.

3. Add fluid as necessary.

4. Repeat Steps 1–3 until the fluid level remains constant.

5. Raise the front of the vehicle so that the front wheels are off the ground. Set the parking brake and block both rear wheels front and rear. Manual transmissions should be in Neutral; automatic transmissions should be in Park.

6. Start the engine and run it at approximately 1,500 rpm.

7. Turn the wheels (off the ground) to the right and left, lightly contacting the stops.

8. Add fluid as necessary.

9. Lower the vehicle and turn the wheels right and left on the ground.

10. Check the fluid level and refill as necessary.

11. If the fluid is extremely foamy, let the truck stand for a few minutes with the engine off and repeat the above procedure. Check the belt tension and check for a bent or loose pulley. The pulley should not wobble with the engine running.

12. Check that no hoses are contacting any parts of the truck, particularly sheet metal.

13. Check the level and refill as necessary. This step and the next are very important. When filling, follow Steps 1–10 above.

14. Check for air in the fluid. Aerated fluid appears milky. If air is present, repeat the above operations. If it is obvious that the pump will not respond to bleeding after several attempts, refer it to a qualified shop for further service.

## Tie-Rod Ends

### REMOVAL AND INSTALLATION

1. Loosen the tie-rod adjuster sleeve clamp nuts.

2. Remove the tie-rod end stud cotter pin and nut.

3. You can use a tie-rod end ball joint removal tool to loosen the stud, or you can loosen it by tapping on the steering arm with a hammer while using a heavy hammer as a backup.

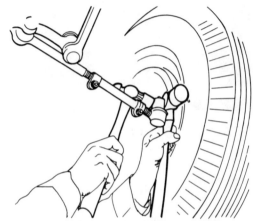

**Freeing the tie-rod end; use another hammer as a backup (© Chevrolet Motor Div.)**

4. Remove the inner stud in the same way.

5. Unscrew the tie-rod end from the threaded sleeve. The threads may be left or right hand threads. Count the number of turns required to remove it.

6. To install, grease the threads and turn the new tie-rod end in as many turns as were needed to remove it. This will give approximately correct toe-in. Tighten the clamp bolts.

7. Tighten the stud nuts to 45 ft lbs and install new cotter pins. You may tighten the nut to align the cotter pin, but don't loosen it.

8. Adjust the toe-in.

# Brakes

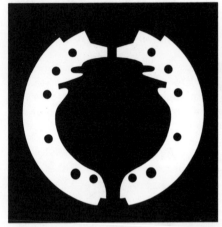

## BRAKE SYSTEM

All Chevrolet and GMC trucks from 1970 are equipped with a split hydraulic braking system. The system is designed with separate systems for the front and rear brakes using a dual master cylinder with separate reservoirs. If a wheel cylinder or brake line should fail in either the front or the rear system, the truck can still be stopped with reasonable control.

In 1970, trucks were equipped with drum brakes front and rear. The front brakes are duo-servo anchor pin type which are self-adjusting. The rear brakes are of the same basic type.

Beginning 1971, trucks were equipped with disc brakes at the front and drum brakes at the rear. The drum brakes are still of the duo-servo anchor pin self-adjusting type, while the front disc brakes are single-piston sliding caliper types. The front disc brakes are inherently self-adjusting.

The parking brake is either hand or foot operated, but in any event, acts upon the rear service brakes.

## Adjustment

### FRONT OR REAR DRUM BRAKES

These brakes are equipped with self-adjusters and no manual adjustment is necessary, except when brake linings are replaced.

### FRONT DISC BRAKES

These brakes are inherently self-adjusting and no adjustment is ever necessary or possible.

## HYDRAULIC SYSTEM

### Master Cylinder

#### REMOVAL AND INSTALLATION

1. Using a clean cloth, wipe the master cylinder and its lines to remove excess dirt and then place cloths under the unit to absorb spilled fluid.

NOTE: *Clean master cylinder parts in alcohol or brake fluid. Never use mineral-based cleaning solvents such as gasoline, kerosene, carbon-tetrachloride, acetone, or paint thinner as these will destroy rubber parts.*

2. Remove the hydraulic lines from the master cylinder and plug the outlets to prevent the entrance of foreign material.

3. Disconnect the brake pushrod from the brake pedal (non-power brakes).

4. Remove the attaching bolts and remove the master cylinder from the firewall or the brake booster. Remove the master cylinder from the booster.

5. Connect the pushrod to the brake pedal with the pin and retainer.

6. Connect the brake lines and fill the

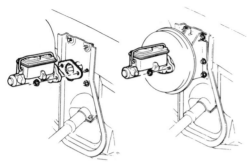

**Typical master cylinder installations (© Chevrolet Motor Div.)**

master cylinder reservoirs to the proper levels.

7. Bleed the brake system as outlined in this section.

8. If necessary, adjust the brake pedal free-play.

## OVERHAUL

In most years, there are two sources for master cylinders: Delco-Moraine and Bendix. The Bendix unit can readily be identified by the secondary stop bolt on the bottom, which is not present on the Delco-Moraine unit. Master cylinders bearing identifying code letters should only be replaced with cylinders bearing the same code letters. Secondary pistons are also coded by rings or grooves on the shank or center section of the piston, and should only be replaced with pistons having the same code. The primary pistons also are of two types. One has a deep socket for the pushrod and the other has a very shallow socket. Be sure to replace pistons with identical parts. Failure to do this could result in a malfunction of the master cylinder.

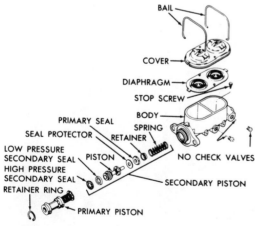

**Exploded view of a typical master cylinder (© Chevrolet Motor Div.)**

NOTE: *This is a tedious, time-consuming job. You can save yourself the trouble if you buy a rebuilt or new master cylinder.*

1. Remove the secondary piston stop screw (if equipped) which is located at the bottom of the master cylinder front reservoir.

2. Position the master cylinder in a vise covering the jaws with cloth to prevent damage. (Do not tighten the vise too tightly.)

3. Remove the lockring from the inside of the piston bore. Once this is done, the primary piston assembly may be removed.

4. The secondary piston, piston spring, and the retainer may be removed by blowing compressed air through the stop screw hole. If compressed air is not available, the piston may be removed with a small piece of wire. Bend the wire ¼ in. from the end into a right angle. Hook this end to the edge of the secondary piston and pull it from the bore. The brass insert should not be removed unless it is being replaced.

5. Inspect the piston bore for corrosion or other obstructions. Make certain that the outer ports are clean and the fluid reservoirs are free of foreign matter. Check the by-pass and the compensating ports to see if they are clogged.

6. Remove the primary seal, seal protector, and secondary seals from the secondary piston.

Clean all parts in denatured alcohol or brake fluid. Use a soft brush to clean metal parts and compressed air to dry all parts. If corrosion is found inside the housing, either a crocus cloth or fine emery paper can be used to remove these deposits. Remember to wash all parts after this cleaning. Be sure to keep the parts clean until assembly. If there is any doubt of cleanliness, wash the part again. All rubber parts should be clean and free of fluid. Check each rubber part for cuts, nicks, or other damage. If there is any doubt as to the condition of any rubber part, it is best to replace it.

NOTE: *Since there are differences between master cylinders, it is important that the assemblies are identified correctly. There is a two-letter metal stamp located at the end of the master cylinder. The stamp indicates the displacement capabilities of the particular master cylinder. If the master cylinder is replaced, it must be replaced with a cylinder with the same markings.*

7. Install the new secondary piston assembly.

NOTE: *The seal which is nearest the flat end has its lips facing toward the flat end.*

*On Delco units, the seal in the second groove has its lips facing toward the compensating holes of the secondary piston. On Bendix units, the seal is an O-ring.*

8. Install the new primary seal and seal protector over the end of the secondary piston opposite the secondary seals. It should be positioned so that the flat side of the seal seats against the flange of the piston with the compensating holes.

NOTE: *The seal protector isn't used on 1977–80 models.*

9. Install the complete primary piston assembly included in every repair kit.

10. Coat the master cylinder bore and the primary and secondary seals with brake fluid. Position the secondary seal spring retainer into the secondary piston spring.

11. Place the retainer and spring over the end of the secondary piston so that the retainer is placed inside the lips of the primary seal.

12. Seat the secondary piston. It may be necessary to manipulate the piston to get it to seat.

13. Position the master cylinder with the open end up and coat the primary and secondary seal on the primary piston with brake fluid. Push the primary piston into the bore of the master cylinder. Hold the piston and position the lockring.

14. Still holding the piston down, install and tighten the stop screw to a torque of 25 to 40 in. lbs.

15. Install the reservoir cover and also the cover on the master cylinder and its retaining clip.

16. Bleed the master cylinder of air. Do this by positioning the cylinder with the front slightly down, filling it with brake fluid, and working the primary piston until all the bubbles are gone.

## Bleeding the Brakes

The purpose of bleeding the brakes is to expel air trapped in the hydraulic system. The system must be bled whenever the pedal feels spongy, indicating that compressible air has entered the system. It must also be bled whenever the system has been opened or leaking. You will need a helper for this job.

NOTE: *Never bleed a wheel cylinder when a drum is removed. There are gadgets on the market which make it possible for one man to perform the bleeding operation.*

*Usually they consist of a bleeder hose with a one way check valve.*

Start with the wheel farthest from the master cylinder and work in. With disc brakes, the metering valve pin on the end of the combination valve must be held in slightly to allow fluid flow to the front disc brakes. If the master cylinder is equipped with bleed valves, these must be bled first.

1. Clean the master cylinder of dirt, and remove the cover and diaphragm.

2. Fill the master cylinder to the proper level and replace the cover and diaphragm.

NOTE: *Brake fluid picks up moisture from the air. Don't leave the master cylinder or fluid container uncovered for any longer than necessary. Be careful with the fluid; it eats paint.*

Check the fluid level often when bleeding. Do not allow all the fluid to drain out or you will have to start over.

3. Clean the bleeder screw at each wheel.

4. Attach a length of hose to the bleeder screw and submerge the other end in a container of clean brake fluid.

5. Have your assistant pump up the brake pedal and hold it.

To bleed the front disc brakes, you must hold in the metering valve pin on the end of the combination valve. Something similar to this tool can be fabricated from sheet stock (© Chevrolet Motor Div.)

Bleeding the brakes (© Chevrolet Motor Div.)

6. Open the bleeder screw about ¾ of a turn. Have your helper press down on the pedal. Close the bleeder screw before the pedal reaches the end of its travel. Have your helper slowly release the pedal. Continue until a solid stream of fluid, with no air bubbles, emerges from the hose.

7. Repeat the procedure on the remaining three brakes. Don't forget to refill the fluid in the master cylinder.

NOTE: *It sometimes helps to tap the disc brake caliper with a soft hammer while fluid is flowing when bleeding the front disc brakes.*

## Hydro-Boost

Diesel-engined trucks are equipped with the Bendix Hydro-boost system. This power brake booster obtains hydraulic pressure from the power steering pump, rather than vacuum pressure from the intake manifold as in most brake booster systems. Procedures for removing, overhauling, and replacing the master cylinder are the same as previously outlined. The master cylinder uses the same DOT 3 brake fluid recommended for other systems.

### HYDRO-BOOST BLEEDING

There are no separate fittings on the booster for system bleeding. Instead, the system is bled in conjunction with the power steering pump and hydraulic system. This procedure can be found in Chapter 8.

If, after bleeding the power steering pump, air is still trapped in the system, the booster may make a "gulping" noise when the brake is applied. Lightly pumping the brake pedal with the engine running should cause this noise to disappear. After the noise stops, check the pump fluid level and add fluid if necessary.

## FRONT DISC BRAKES

All models from 1971 have front disc brakes. This single-piston caliper is a sliding type. No brake adjustment is necessary once the brake pads have been seated against the rotor.

The single-piston system is a closed system with fluid pressure being exerted on two surfaces: on the piston itself and in the opposite direction against the bottom of the bore of the caliper housing. There is equal pressure

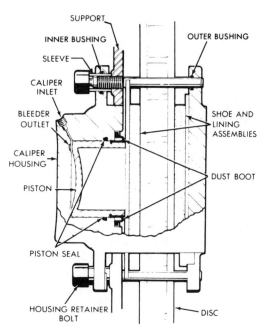

**Front disc brake and caliper cross section (© Chevrolet Motor Div.)**

since the area of the piston and the bottom of the caliper bore are equal.

When hydraulic pressure is applied to the piston, it is transmitted to the inner brake pad lining assembly which contacts the inner surface of the disc. This pulls the caliper assembly inboard as it slides on the four rubber bushings. As the caliper slides, the outer lining applies force to the outer surface of the disc and in this manner the two surfaces brake the vehicle.

Since the hydraulic pressure is equally applied to both brake pads there will be no flexing or distortion of the pad and if the unit is operating correctly, the pad wear should be equal.

This type of disc brake uses a very small running clearance between pad and rotor. As the brake linings wear, the caliper assembly moves inward and the brake fluid from the reservoir fills the area behind the piston so that brake pedal travel is not increased. Therefore, you will still have a high pedal even though the pad could be worn to the metal backing.

Because the brake pads are in close contact with the rotor, this gives the advantage of increased brake response, reduced brake pedal travel, and faster generation of hydraulic line pressure. The pad being close to the rotor disc also cleans it of foreign material.

The system is composed of the hub and

disc assembly, the shield, the support, the caliper assembly, and the linings. The disc is centrally vented with cooling fins which dissipate heat.

## Brake Pads

### INSPECTION

Support the front suspension or axle on jack stands and remove the wheels. Look in at the ends of the caliper to check the lining thickness of the outer pad. Look through the inspection hole in the top of the caliper to check the thickness of the inner pad. Minimum acceptable pad thickness is $1/32$ in. from the rivet heads on original equipment riveted linings and $1/32$ in. lining thickness on bonded linings.

NOTE: *These manufacturer's specifications may not agree with your state inspection law.*

All original equipment pads are the riveted type; unless you want to remove the pads to measure the actual thickness from the rivet heads, you will have to make the limit for visual inspection $1/16$ in. or more. The same applies if you don't know what kind of lining you have. 1974–80 original equipment pads and GM replacement pads have an integral wear sensor. This is a spring steel tab on the rear edge of the inner pad which produces a squeal by rubbing against the rotor to warn that the pads have reached their wear limit. They do not squeal when the brakes are applied.

CAUTION: *The squeal will eventually stop if the worn pads aren't replaced. Should this happen, replace the pads immediately to prevent expensive rotor (disc) damage.*

### REPLACEMENT

The caliper has to be removed to replace the pads, so go on to that procedure. Skip steps 8–10, as there is no need to detach the brake line.

## Disc Brake Caliper

Front disc brakes have inboard and outboard brake pads. The outboard shoe has ears which are bent over to keep the shoe in position while the inboard shoe has ears on the top end which fit over the caliper retaining bolts. A spring which is situated inside the brake piston holds the bottom edge of the inboard shoe.

NOTE: *Never use relined disc brake pads.*

### REMOVAL AND INSTALLATION

1. Remove the cover on the master cylinder and siphon enough fluid out of the reservoirs to bring the level to ⅓ full. This step prevents spilling fluid when the piston is pushed back. Discard the fluid.

2. Raise and support the vehicle. Remove the front wheels and tires.

3. Push the brake piston back into its bore using a C-clamp or other devices.

4. Remove the two Allen head bolts

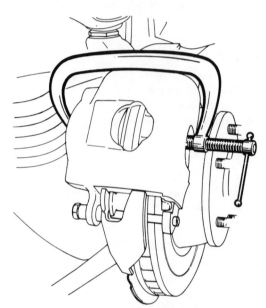

Use a C-clamp to retract the caliper piston (© Chevrolet Motor Div.)

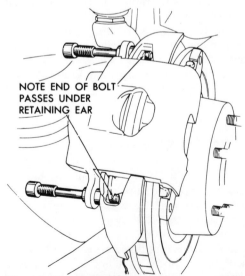

NOTE END OF BOLT PASSES UNDER RETAINING EAR

Disc brake caliper removal and installation (© Chevrolet Motor Div.)

which hold the caliper and then lift the caliper off the disc.

CAUTION: *Do not let the caliper assembly hang by the brake hose.*

5. Remove the inboard and outboard pads.

NOTE: *If the pads are to be reinstalled, mark them inside and outside.*

6. Remove the support spring from the piston. Be careful that it doesn't fly off.

7. Remove the two sleeves from the inside ears of the caliper and the four rubber bushings from the grooves in the caliper ears.

8. Remove the hose from the steel brake line and tape the fittings to prevent foreign material from entering the line or the hoses.

9. Remove the retainer from the hose fitting.

10. Remove the hose from the frame bracket and pull off the caliper with the hose attached.

NOTE: *Check the inside of the caliper for fluid leakage; if so, the caliper should be overhauled.*

CAUTION: *Do not use compressed air to clean the inside of the caliper as this may unseat the dust boot.*

The brake lining should be replaced if there is ⅛ in. of lining or less present on the shoe.

To install:

11. Lubricate the sleeves, rubber bushings, bushing grooves, and the end of the mounting bolts using silicone lubricant.

12. Install new bushings in the caliper ears along with new sleeves. The sleeve should be replaced so that the end toward

the pad is flush with the machined surface of the ear.

13. Position the support spring and the inner pad into the center cavity of the piston. The outboard pad has ears which are bent over to keep the pad in position while the inboard pad has ears on the top end which fit over the caliper retaining bolts. A spring which is inside the brake piston holds the bottom edge of the inboard pad.

14. Push down on the inner pad until it lays flat against the caliper. It is important to push the piston all the way into the caliper if new linings are installed or the caliper will not fit over the rotor.

15. Position the outboard pad with the ears of the shoes over the caliper ears and the tab at the bottom engaged in the caliper cutout.

16. With the two pads in position, place the caliper over the brake disc and align the holes in the caliper with those of the mounting bracket.

CAUTION: *Make certain that the brake hose is not twisted or kinked.*

17. Install the mounting bracket bolts through the sleeves in the inboard caliper ears and through the mounting bracket, making sure that the ends of the bolts pass under the retaining ears on the inboard pad.

18. Tighten the bolts into the bracket and torque to 35 ft lbs. Pump the brake pedal to seat the pads against the rotor. Don't do this unless both calipers are in place. Use a pair of channel lock pliers to bend over the upper ears of the outer pad so that it isn't loose.

19. Install the front wheel and lower the truck.

20. Add fluid to the master cylinder reservoirs so that they are ¼ in. from the top.

21. Test the brake pedal by pumping it to obtain a "hard" pedal. Check the fluid level again and add fluid as necessary. Do not move the vehicle until a "hard" pedal is obtained.

### OVERHAUL

Use only denatured alcohol or brake fluid to clean caliper parts. Never use any mineral based cleaning solvents such as gasoline or kerosene as these solvents will deteriorate rubber parts.

1. Remove the caliper, clean it and place it on a clean and level work surface.

2. Remove the brake hose from the caliper and discard the copper gasket. Check the

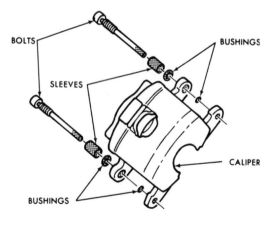

**BOLTS**

**BUSHINGS**

**SLEEVES**

**CALIPER**

**BUSHINGS**

▨ LUBRICATE AREAS INDICATED

**Caliper lubrication points at installation (© Chevrolet Motor Div.)**

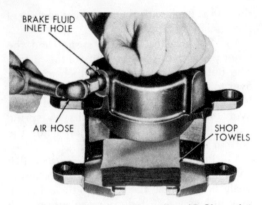

**Removing the piston from the caliper (© Chevrolet Motor Div.)**

**Caliper piston boot installation (© Chevrolet Motor Div.)**

brake hose for cracks or deterioration. Replace the hose as necessary.

3. Drain the brake fluid from the caliper.

4. Pad the interior of the caliper with cloth and then apply compressed air to the caliper inlet hose.

WARNING: *Do not place hands or fingers in front of the piston in an attempt to catch it. Use just enough air pressure to ease the piston out of the bore.*

5. Remove the piston dust boot by prying it out with a screwdriver. Use caution when performing this procedure.

6. Remove the piston seal from the caliper piston bore using a small piece of wood or plastic. DO NOT use any type of metal tool for this procedure.

7. Remove the bleeder valve from the caliper.

IMPORTANT: *Dust boot, piston seal, rub-*

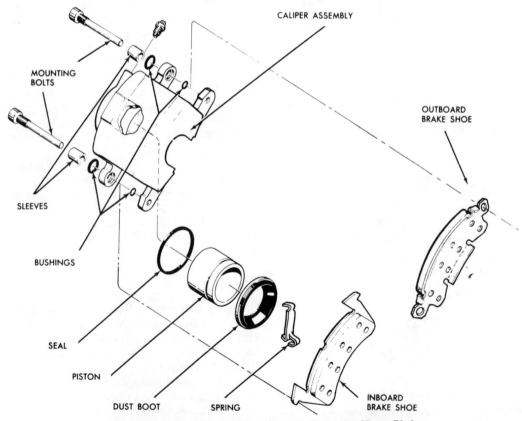

**Exploded view of the brake caliper (© Chevrolet Motor Div.)**

*ber bushings and sleeves are included in every rebuilding kit. These should be replaced at every caliper rebuild.*

8. Clean all parts in the recommended solvent and dry them completely, using compressed air if possible.

NOTE: *The use of shop air hoses may inject oil film into the assembly; use caution when using such hoses.*

9. Examine the mounting bolts for rust or corrosion. Replace them as necessary.

10. Examine the piston for scoring, nicks, or worn plating. If any of these conditions are present, replace the piston.

CAUTION: *Do not use any type of abrasive on the piston.*

11. Check the piston bore. Small defects can be removed with crocus cloth. (Do not use emery cloth.) If the bore cannot be cleaned in this manner, replace the caliper.

12. Lubricate the piston bore and the new piston seal with brake fluid. Place the seal in the caliper bore groove.

13. Lubricate the piston in the same manner and position the new boot into the groove in the piston so that the fold faces the open end of the piston.

14. Place the piston into the caliper bore using caution not to damage the seal. Force the piston to the bottom of the bore.

15. Place the dust boot in the caliper counterbore and seat the boot. Make sure that the boot is positioned correctly and evenly.

16. Install the brake hose in the caliper inlet using a new copper gasket.

NOTE: *The hose must be positioned in the caliper locating gate to assure proper positioning of the caliper.*

17. Connect the brake hose to the brake line at the frame bracket.

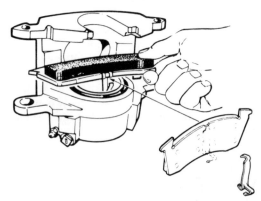

**Caliper support spring installation (© Chevrolet Motor Div.)**

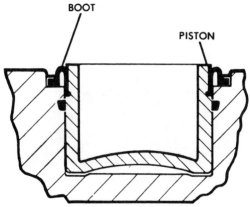

**Boot installation (© Chevrolet Motor Div.)**

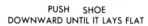
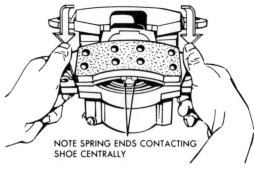

**Inner brake pad installation (© Chevrolet Motor Div.)**

18. Bleed the calipers. (See "Bleeding the Brakes," above.)

## Brake Disc (Rotor)

### REMOVAL AND INSTALLATION

#### Two Wheel Drive

1. Follow the procedures outlined for removing the caliper assembly.

2. Remove the bearing dust cap, cotter pin, center nut, and outer bearings.

3. Pull the rotor off the spindle and service it, as necessary.

To install the unit, reverse the removal procedure. Check the rotor before installing it. Pack the inner and outer bearings with the correct lubricant and torque the outer bearing to the proper specifications. (See Wheel Bearings, Chapter 1)

NOTE: *The minimum thickness allowable for the disc is stamped on the rotor.*

The rotor must meet the following specifications for use:

4. It must be radially flat within 0.002 in.

**Disc finish (© Chevrolet Motor Div.)**

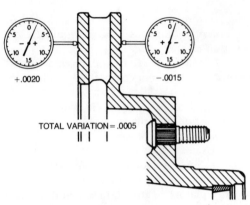

**Disc thickness variation measurement (© Chevrolet Motor Div.)**

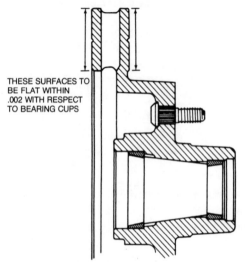

**Surface flatness measurement (© Chevrolet Motor Div.)**

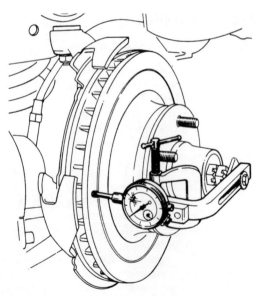

**Measure the disc run-out with a dial indicator (© Chevrolet Motor Div.)**

and the brake surfaces must be parallel to each other within 0.003 in.

5. Both inner and outer surfaces must be free of scratch marks or other defects.

NOTE: *Some discs have an anti-squeal groove. This should not be mistaken for scoring.*

6. The braking surfaces must be even with the bearing centerline to within 0.003 in.

7. When mounted on the bearings, the lateral run-out must not exceed 0.001 in. in 30°.

8. The variation in thickness over the 360° of the rotor must not vary more than 0.0005 in.

### Four Wheel Drive

Rotor removal and installation requires disassembly of the front hub components. This is covered in Chapter 1, under Wheel Bearings, Four Wheel Drive. The order for removal is:

1. Remove the caliper assembly following the procedures in this chapter.

2. Refer to Chapter 1 for disassembly of the hub.

3. Pull the hub and rotor assembly off the spindle.

Installation is the reverse, following the hub assembly and wheel bearing adjustments in Chapter 1. Check the rotor before installing it. Follow Steps 4–8 of the two wheel drive procedure of rotor removal and installation.

## Wheel Bearings

All front wheel bearing service is covered in Chapter 1.

# DRUM BRAKES

## Brake Drums

### REMOVAL AND INSTALLATION

Drums on all models can be removed by raising the vehicle, removing the wheel lugs and the tire, and pulling the drum from the brake assembly. If the brake drums have been scored from worn linings, the brake adjuster must be backed off so that the brake shoes will retract from the drum. Some drums are retained by two screws to the hub, and can be removed after removing the screws.

The adjuster can be backed off by inserting a brake adjusting tool through the access hole provided. In some cases the access hole is provided in the brake drum. A metal cover plate is over the hole. This may be removed by using a hammer and chisel.

NOTE: *Make sure all metal particles are removed from the brake drum before reassembly.*

To install, reverse the removal procedure.

CAUTION: *Do not blow the brake dust out of the drums with compressed air or lung power. The brake linings contain asbestos, a known cancer causing agent. Wipe the drums and linings with a clean, grease-free rag, and dispose of the rag immediately.*

### INSPECTION

#### Lining

Remove the drum and inspect the lining thickness on both brake shoes. A front brake lining should be replaced if it is less than ⅛ in. thick at the lowest point on the brake shoe. The limit for rear brake linings is ¹/₁₆. However, these lining thickness measurements may disagree with your state inspection laws.

NOTE: *Brake shoes should always be replaced in axle sets.*

#### Drum

When a drum is removed, it should be inspected for cracks, scores, or other imperfections. These must be corrected before the drum is replaced.

CAUTION: *If the drum is found to be cracked, replace it. Do not attempt to service a cracked drum.*

Minor drum score marks can be removed with fine emery cloth. Heavy score marks must be removed by "turning the drum."

This is removing metal from the entire inner surface of the drum in order to level the surface. Automotive machine shops and some large parts stores are equipped to perform this operation.

If the drum is not scored, it should be polished with fine emery cloth before replacement. If the drum is resurfaced, it should not be enlarged past 0.060 in. of the original diameter.

It is advisable, while the drums are off, to check them for out-of-round. An inside micrometer is necessary for an exact measurement; therefore unless this tool is available, the drums should be taken to a machine shop to be checked. Any drum which is more than 0.006 in. out-of-round will result in an inaccurate brake adjustment and other problems, and should be refinished or replaced.

NOTE: *If the micrometer is available, make all measurements at right angles to each other and at the open and closed edges of the drum machined surface.*

Check the drum with a micrometer in the following manner:

1. Position the drum on a level surface.

2. Insert the micrometer with its adapter bars if necessary.

3. Obtain a reading on the micrometer at the point of maximum contact. Record this.

4. Rotate the micrometer 45° and take a similar reading. The two readings must not vary more than 0.006 in.

## Brake Shoes

### REMOVAL AND INSTALLATION

1. Jack up and securely support the vehicle.

Measure the drum inside diameter with an inside micrometer (© Chevrolet Motor Div.)

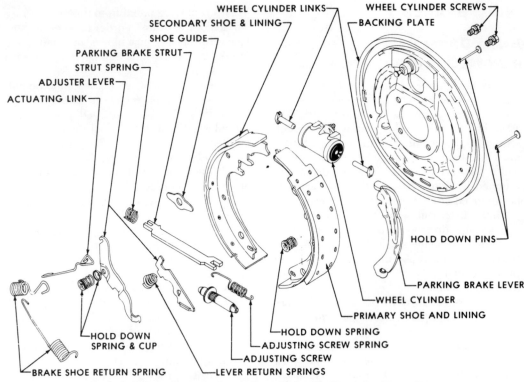

WHEEL CYLINDER LINKS

SECONDARY SHOE & LINING

SHOE GUIDE

PARKING BRAKE STRUT

STRUT SPRING

ADJUSTER LEVER

ACTUATING LINK

WHEEL CYLINDER SCREWS

BACKING PLATE

HOLD DOWN PINS

PARKING BRAKE LEVER

WHEEL CYLINDER

PRIMARY SHOE AND LINING

HOLD DOWN SPRING

ADJUSTING SCREW SPRING

ADJUSTING SCREW

LEVER RETURN SPRINGS

HOLD DOWN SPRING & CUP

BRAKE SHOE RETURN SPRING

**Exploded view of a typical rear drum brake (© Chevrolet Motor Div.)**

2. Remove the check nuts from the end of the parking brake equalizer bracket and remove all tension on the brake cable (rear brakes only).

3. Remove the brake drums.

CAUTION: *The brake pedal must not be depressed while the drums are removed.*

4. Using a brake tool, remove the shoe springs from their holder.

5. Remove the self-adjuster actuator spring.

6. Remove the spring from the secondary shoe by pulling it from the anchor pin.

7. Remove the hold-down pins. These are the brackets which run through the backing plate. They can be removed with a pair of pliers. Reach around the rear of the backing plate and hold the back of the pin. Turn the top of the pin retainer 45° with the pliers. This will align the elongated tang with the slot in the retainer. Be careful, as the pin is spring-loaded and may fly off when released. Use the same procedure for the other pin assembly.

8. Remove the adjuster actuating lever assembly by removing the holddown pin which is attached to the secondary brake shoe.

NOTE: *Since the actuator, pivot, and override spring are considered an assembly it is not recommended that they be disassembled.*

9. Remove the shoes from the backing plate. Make sure that you have a secure grip on the assembly as the bottom spring will still exert pressure on the shoes. Slowly let the tops of the shoes come together and the tension will decrease and the adjuster and spring may be removed.

NOTE: *If the linings are to be reused, mark them for identification.*

10. Remove the parking brake lever from the secondary shoe (rear brakes). Using a pair of pliers, pull back on the spring which surrounds the cable. At the same time, remove the cable from the notch in the shoe bracket. Make sure that the spring does not snap back or injury may result.

11. Use a cloth to remove dirt from the brake drum. Check the drums for scoring and cracks. Have the drums checked for out-of-round and service the drums as necessary.

12. Check the wheel cylinders by carefully pulling the lower edges of the wheel cylinder boots away from the cylinders. If there is excessive leakage, the inside of the cylin-

der will be moist with fluid. If there is any leakage at all, a cylinder overhaul is in order. DO NOT delay, as a brake failure could result.

NOTE: *A small amount of fluid will be present to act as a lubricant for the wheel cylinder pistons.*

13. Check the flange plate, which is located around the axle, for leakage of differential lubricant. This condition cannot be overlooked as the lubricant will be absorbed into the brake linings and brake failure will result. Replace the seals as necessary. See Chapter 7 for details.

NOTE: *If new linings are being installed, check them against the old units for length and type.*

14. Check the new linings for imperfections.

CAUTION: *It is important to keep your hands free of dirt and grease when handling the brake shoes. Foreign matter will be absorbed into the linings and result in unpredictable braking.*

15. Lightly lubricate the parking brake cable and the end of the parking brake lever where it enters the shoe. Use a high temperature waterproof grease or special brake lube.

16. Install the parking brake lever into the secondary shoe with the attaching bolt, spring washer, lockwasher, and nut. It is important that the lever move freely before the shoe is attached. Move the assembly and check for proper action.

17. Lubricate the adjusting screw and make sure that it works freely. Sometimes the adjusting screw will not move due to lack of lubricant or dirt contamination and the brakes will not adjust. In this case, the adjuster should be disassembled, thoroughly cleaned, and lubricated before installation.

18. Connect the brake shoe spring to the bottom portion of both shoes. Make certain that the brake linings are installed in the correct manner, the primary and secondary shoe in the correct position. If you are not sure remove the other brake drum and check it.

19. Install the adjusting mechanism below the spring and separate the top of the shoes.

NOTE: *Make the following checks before installation:*

a. Be certain that the right-hand thread adjusting screw is on the left-hand side of the vehicle and the left-hand screw is on the right-hand side of the vehicle;

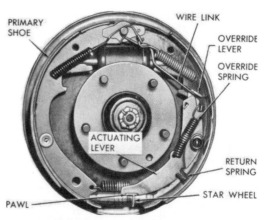

**Self-adjusting brake assembled (© Chevrolet Motor Div.)**

**Unhooking the pull-back springs (© Chevrolet Motor Div.)**

**Removing the hold-down springs (© Chevrolet Motor Div.)**

b. Make sure that the star adjuster is aligned with the hole in the flange plate;

c. The adjuster should be installed with the starwheel nearest the secondary shoe and the tension spring away from the adjusting mechanism;

d. If the original linings are being reused, position the linings in relation to the scribe marks which were made during disassembly.

20. Install the parking brake.

21. Position the primary shoe (the shoe with the short lining) first. Secure it with the hold-down pin and with its spring by pushing the pin through the back of the backing plate and, while holding it with one hand, install the spring and the retainer using a pair of needlenose pliers. Install the adjuster actuator assembly.

22. Install the parking brake strut and the strut spring by pulling back the spring with pliers and engaging the end of the cable onto the brake strut and then releasing the spring.

23. Place the small metal guide plate over the anchor pin and position the self-adjuster wire cable eye.

CAUTION: *The wire should not be positioned with the conventional brake installation tool or damage will result. It should be positioned on the actuator assembly first and then placed over the anchor pin stud by hand with the adjuster assembly in full downward position.*

24. Install the actuator return spring. DO NOT pry the actuator lever to install the return spring. Position it using the end of a screwdriver or another suitable tool.

**Lubricate the brake backing plate pads (© Chevrolet Motor Div.)**

NOTE: *If the return springs are bent or in any way distorted, they should be replaced.*

25. Using the brake installation tool, place the brake return springs in position. Install the primary spring first over the anchor pin and then place the spring from the secondary shoe over the wire link end.

26. Pull the brake shoes away from the backing plate and apply a *thin* coat of grease to the brake shoe contact points.

CAUTION: *Only a small amount is necessary. Keep the lubricant away from the brake facings.*

27. Once the complete assembly has been installed, check the operation of the self-adjuster mechanism by moving the actuating line by hand.

28. Adjust the brakes.

a. Turn the star adjuster until the drum slides over the brake shoes with only a slight drag. Remove the drum;

b. Turn the adjuster back one complete turn;

c. Install the drum and wheel and lower the vehicle;

NOTE: *If the adjusting hole in the drum has been punched out, make certain that the insert has been removed from the inside of the drum. Install a rubber hole cover to keep dirt out of the brake assembly. Also, be sure that the drums are installed in the same position as they were when removed—with the locating tang in line with the location hole in the axle shaft flange.*

**Checking the actuator (© Chevrolet Motor Div.)**

d. Make the final adjustment by backing the vehicle and pumping the brakes until the self-adjusting mechanisms adjust to the proper level and the brake pedal reaches satisfactory height.

NOTE: *Some drivers use a shift into the Drive position to slow the vehicle when backing slowly instead of the brakes. This will not operate the adjusting mechanisms.*

29. Adjust the parking brakes. (See "Parking Brake Adjustment.")

30. Make tests of the braking action and the parking brake. The brakes must not be severely applied immediately after installation of new brake linings, as this may permanently damage the linings and score the brake drums. When linings are new, they must be given moderate use for several hundred miles of burnishing.

## Brake Backing Plate

### REMOVAL AND INSTALLATION

1. Remove the complete brake mechanisms as outlined in "Brake Removal and Installation."

2. Remove the rear axles as outlined in "Rear Axle Shaft Removal."

3. Remove the attaching bolts and pull off the backing plate.

4. To install, reverse the removal procedure.

## Wheel Cylinders

### REMOVAL

1. Jack and support the axle.

2. Remove the wheel and tire.

3. Back off the brake adjustment and remove the drum.

4. Disconnect and plug the brake line.

5. Remove the brake shoe pull-back springs.

6. Remove the screws securing the wheel cylinder to the backing plate.

7. Disengage the wheel cylinder pushrods from the brake shoes and remove the wheel cylinder.

### Overhaul

As is the case with master cylinders, overhaul kits for wheel cylinders are readily available. When rebuilding and installing wheel cylinders, avoid getting any contaminants into the system. Always install clean, new high-quality brake fluid. If dirty or improper fluid has been used, it will be necessary to drain

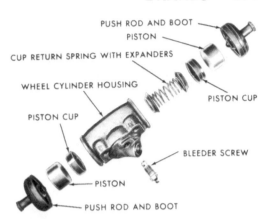

**Exploded view of a typical wheel cylinder (© Chevrolet Motor Div.)**

the entire system, flush the system with proper brake fluid, replace all rubber components, refill, and bleed the system.

1. Remove the rubber boots from the cylinder ends with pliers. Discard the boots.

2. Remove and discard the pistons and cups.

3. Wash the cylinder and metal parts in denatured alcohol or clean brake fluid.

CAUTION: *Never use a mineral-based solvent such as gasoline, kerosene, or paint thinner for cleaning purposes. These solvents will swell rubber components and quickly deteriorate them.*

4. Allow the parts to air dry or use compressed air. Do not use rags for cleaning since lint will remain in the cylinder bore.

5. Inspect the piston and replace it if it shows scratches.

6. Lubricate the cylinder bore and counterbore with clean brake fluid.

7. Install the rubber cups (flat side out) and then the pistons (flat side in).

8. Insert new boots into the counterbores by hand. Do not lubricate the boots.

### INSTALLATION

1. Installation is the reverse of removal. Adjust the brakes and bleed the system.

## Wheel Bearings

All front wheel bearing service is covered in Chapter 1. Rear wheel bearings are covered in Chapter 7.

## PARKING BRAKE

## Adjustment

The rear brakes serve a dual purpose. They are used as service brakes and as parking

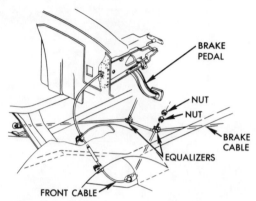

Typical parking brake system, 1971 shown. Adjustments are made at the equalizer nut (© Chevrolet Motor Div.)

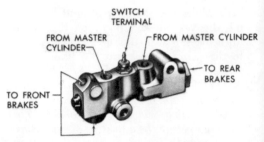

**Combination valve (© Chevrolet Motor Div.)**

brakes. To obtain proper adjustment of the parking brake, the service brakes must first be properly adjusted as outlined earlier.

1. Apply the parking brake 1 notch from the fully released position, 4 notches for 1976–80.

2. Raise and support the vehicle.

3. Loosen the jam nut at the equilizer.

4. Tighten or loosen the adjusting nut until a light drag is felt when the rear wheels are rotated forward.

5. Tighten the check nut.

6. Release the parking brake and rotate the rear wheels. No drag should be felt. If even a light drag is felt, readjust the parking brake.

7. Lower the vehicle.

NOTE: *If a new parking brake cable is being installed, prestretch it by applying the parking brake hard about three times before making adjustments.*

## COMBINATION VALVE

This valve is used on all models with disc brakes. The valve itself is a combination of: 1) the metering valve, which will not allow the front disc brakes to engage until the rear brakes contact the drum, 2) the failure warning switch, which notifies the driver if one of the systems has a leak, and 3) the proportioner which limits rear brake pressure and delays rear wheel skid.

## Testing and Centering the Switch

Whenever work on the brake system is done, it is possible that the brake warning light will come on and refuse to go off when the work is finished. In this event, the switch must be centered.

1. Raise and support the truck.

2. Attach a bleeder hose to the rear brake bleed screw and immerse the other end of the hose in a jar of clean brake fluid.

3. Be sure that the master cylinder is full.

4. When bleeding the brakes, the pin in the end of the metering portion of the combination valve must be held in the open position (with the tool described in the brake bleeding section installed under the pin mounting bolt). Be sure to tighten the bolt after removing the tool.

5. Turn the ignition key ON. Open the bleed screw while an assistant applies heavy pressure on the brake pedal. The warning lamp should light. Close the bleed screw before the helper releases the pedal.

To reset the switch, apply heavy pressure to the pedal. This will apply hydraulic pressure to the switch which will recenter it.

6. Repeat Step 5 for the front bleed screw.

7. Turn the ignition OFF and lower the truck.

NOTE: *If the warning lamp does not light during Step 5, the switch is defective and must be replaced.*

# Body

## DOORS

### REMOVAL AND INSTALLATION

The doors on all models can be removed by unscrewing the attaching bolts from the hinges. Installation is the reverse of removal.

### ADJUSTMENT

**1970–72**

The front doors can be adjusted at two points: at the hinge straps-to-door panel attachment and also the hinge cage-to-pillar point. Before adjusting any door, remove the door striker plate. The door can then be removed in any direction, up or down, in or out. In order to adjust the front side door assembly at the pillar, it is necessary to use a curved wrench.

The door should have equal clearance around its entire outer lip. The door should be adjusted so that the top edge and the side by the lock are parallel with the body opening as nearly as possible.

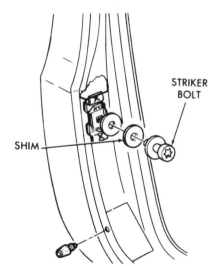

Typical striker bolt adjustment (© Chevrolet Motor Div.)

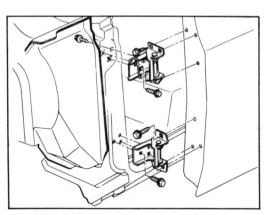

**Typical door hinge installation (© Chevrolet Motor Div.)**

Tighten the bolts and install and adjust the door striker plate. The plate is adjusted in the following manner.

1. Place the striker assembly onto the body locking pillar so that the rotor cover on the door swings into the striker with 0.10 in. clearance. Use special shims as required.

NOTE: *Under most conditions shims are not required.*

2. Slots are provided in the body panel lock pillar so that the lock rotor and the rotor cover assembly will swing smoothly into the opening between the teeth and strike the wedge block.

NOTE: *It is important that the lock rotor cover clear the striker plate as the lock enters the striker.*

3. To help with the correct adjustment, outline the striker in pencil as a base for adjustment. Place the striker assembly laterally in the slots provided so that the door's outer surface is flush with the body pillar at the rear edge of the door.

4. Tighten all bolts to 25 ft lbs.

### 1973–80

Door alignment adjustments are made at the door hinges and at the striker bolt. The hinge bolt holes on the door are oversize to allow adjustment. The striker bolt can be loosened and moved up and down or in and out. Shims can be used to adjust the striker forward and back.

The door should be adjusted so that the top edge and the lock side are parallel with the body opening as much as possible. There should be .25 in. clearance at the bottom and .19 in. at the top and sides.

## Door Panel

### REMOVAL AND INSTALLATION

#### 1970–72

1. Push in the panel and force the retaining clip off the window crank and the door handle. There is a special tool for these clips, available at auto parts stores, that makes their removal easier. If you don't have the tool, make do with a screwdriver.

2. Remove the armrest screws. Using a putty knife or screwdriver, carefully pry out the clips holding the edges of the panel.

3. Remove the panel.

4. After replacing the panel, install the clips on the handles and then rap them into place on their shafts.

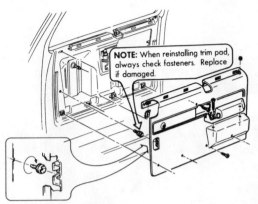

**Typical door panel; 1974 shown (© Chevrolet Motor Div.)**

### 1973–80

1. Remove the door lock knob, the armrest, and the panel retaining screws. Remove the screw at the door handle cover plate and the screw located under the armrest pad. If the door has an assist strap, remove the two screws retaining the strap.

2. Push in the panel and force the retaining clip off the window crank handle. There is a special tool for these clips, available at auto parts stores, that makes their removal easier. If you don't have the tool, make do with a screwdriver.

3. Carefully pull out the edges and bottom of the panel to detach the clips holding the panel.

4. Pull the panel up to disengage the clips at the top edge.

5. Remove the panel.

6. After replacing the panel, install the clip on the window handle and rap it into place on its shaft.

## Window

### REMOVAL AND INSTALLATION

1. Lower the window to the bottom of the door.

2. Remove the window handle.

3. Remove the armrest and the door panel.

4. Cover the upper portion of the door frame to guard against injury. Remove the vent window assembly.

   a. Open the vent window fully and remove the regulator handle clip and the door lock button;

   b. Remove the screws which attach the assembly to the door panel;

   c. Loosen the inner-to-outer panel attaching screws by reaching through the

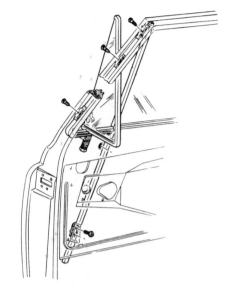

**Vent window installation (© Chevrolet Motor Div.)**

**Turn the vent window 90° for removal (© Chevrolet Motor Div.)**

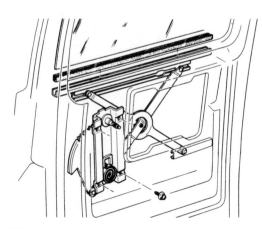

**Window glass and regulator assembly (© Chevrolet Motor Div.)**

access hole just behind the lower vent pivot;

d. Slide the door glass away from the ventilator and remove the three screws from the upper front of the door frame. Turn the vent assembly 90° and guide it carefully up and out of the door.

5. Slide the main window forward until the front roller is in line with the notch in the window channel and remove the roller from the channel.

6. Push the window forward and tilt the front up until the rear is disengaged.

7. Return the assembly to the level position and raise the window straight out.

8. To install, reverse the removal procedure.

## Lock Cylinder
### REMOVAL AND INSTALLATION

1. Raise the window to the very top.

2. Remove the regulator handle, locking button, and trim panel.

3. Using a screwdriver, push the lock cylinder retaining clip out of engagement with the lock cylinder.

4. Pull out the cylinder.

5. To install, reverse the removal procedure.

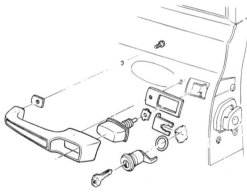

**Door handle and lock, 1970–72 shown; other years similar (© Chevrolet Motor Div.)**

## HOOD

### REMOVAL AND INSTALLATION

1. When removing the hood, scribe aligning marks on both the hood inside panels and on the hood brackets.

2. Remove the attaching screws and pull off the hood.

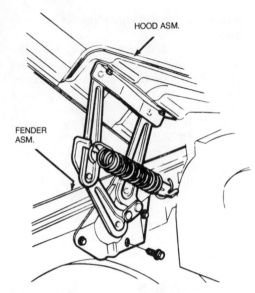

Hood hinge (© Chevrolet Motor Div.)

NOTE: *This should only be performed with the help of an assistant.*

3. To install the hood, align the scribe markings and tighten the attaching bolts.

If the alignment is not correct, make slight adjustments at each bracket and close the hood *slowly* while checking the alignment. There should be an equal gap around the perimeter of the hood. When this is obtained, tighten the attaching bolts and make a final check.

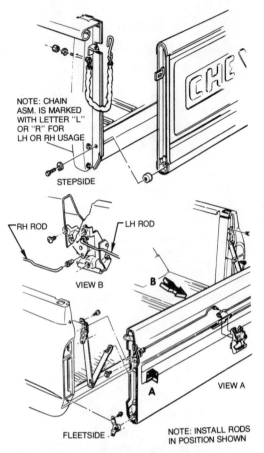

Typical tailgate assemblies. 1970 shown, later years similar (© Chevrolet Motor Div.)

## TAILGATE

### *REMOVAL AND INSTALLATION*

#### Stepside

1. Unhook the tailgate chain at each side.
2. Remove the bolt and lockwasher from each trunnion.
3. Remove the tailgate.
4. Reverse procedure for installation. Align the slot in the trunnion to coincide with the hole in the tailgate to permit using a screwdriver to hold the trunnion while tightening the nut.

#### Fleetside

1. Lower the tailgate half way.
2. Pull the center of the hinge upward and unlatch from the tailgate.
3. Lower the tailgate all the way.
4. Remove the two screws from the trunnions on each side and remove the tailgate.

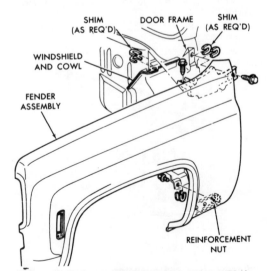

Front fender, 1973–80 (© Chevrolet Motor Div.)

# BODY REPAIR

You can repair most minor auto body damage yourself. Minor damage usually falls into one of several categories: (1) small scratches and dings in the paint that can be repaired without the use of body filler, (2) deep scratches and dents that require body filler, but do not require pulling, or hammering metal back into shape and (3) rust-out repairs. The repair sequences illustrated in this chapter are typical of these types of repairs. If you want to get involved in more complicated repairs including pulling or hammering sheet metal back into shape, you will probably need more detailed instructions. Chilton's *Minor Auto Body Repair, 2nd Edition* is a comprehensive guide to repairing auto body damage yourself.

## TOOLS AND SUPPLIES

The list of tools and equipment you may need to fix minor body damage ranges from very basic hand tools to a wide assortment of specialized body tools. Most minor scratches, dings and rust holes can be fixed using an electric drill, wire wheel or grinder attachment, half-round plastic file, sanding block, various grades of sandpaper (#36, which is coarse through #600, which is fine) in both wet and dry types, auto body plastic, primer, touch-up paint, spreaders, newspaper and masking tape.

Most manufacturers of auto body repair products began supplying materials to professionals. Their knowledge of the best, most-used products has been translated into body repair kits for the do-it-yourselfer. Kits are available from a number of manufacturers and contain the necessary materials in the required amounts for the repair identified on the package.

Kits are available for a wide variety of uses, including:
- Rusted out metal
- All purpose kit for dents and holes
- Dents and deep scratches
- Fiberglass repair kit
- Epoxy kit for restyling.

Kits offer the advantage of buying what you need for the job. There is little waste and little chance of materials going bad from not being used. The same manufacturers also merchandise all of the individual products used—spreaders, dent pullers, fiberglass

cloth, polyester resin, cream hardener, body filler, body files, sandpaper, sanding discs and holders, primer, spray paint, etc.

**CAUTION:** *Most of the products you will be using contain harmful chemicals, so be extremely careful. Always read the complete label before opening the containers. When you put them away for future use, be sure they are out of children's reach!*

Most auto body repair kits contain all the materials you need to do the job right in the kit. So, if you have a small rust spot or dent you want to fix, check the contents of the kit before you run out and buy any additional tools.

## ALIGNING BODY PANELS

### Doors

There are several methods of adjusting doors. Your vehicle will probably use one of those illustrated.

Whenever a door is removed and is to be reinstalled, you should matchmark the position of the hinges on the door pillars. The holes of the hinges and/or the hinge attaching points are usually oversize to permit alignment of doors. The striker plate is also moveable, through oversize holes, permitting up-and-down, in-and-out and fore-and-aft movement. Fore-and-aft movement is made by adding or subtracting shims from behind the striker and pillar post. The striker should be adjusted so that the door closes fully and remains closed, yet enters the lock freely.

#### DOOR HINGES

Don't try to cover up poor door adjustment with a striker plate adjustment. The gap on each side of the door should be equal and uniform and there should be no metal-to-metal contact as the door is opened or closed.

1. Determine which hinge bolts must be loosened to move the door in the desired direction.

2. Loosen the hinge bolt(s) just enough to allow the door to be moved with a padded pry bar.

3. Move the door a small amount and check the fit, after tightening the bolts. Be sure that there is no bind or interference with adjacent panels.

4. Repeat this until the door is properly positioned, and tighten all the bolts securely.

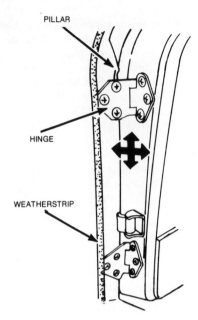

Door hinge adjustment

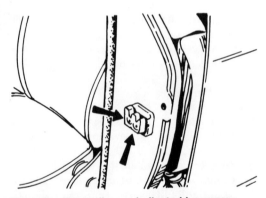

Move the door striker as indicated by arrows

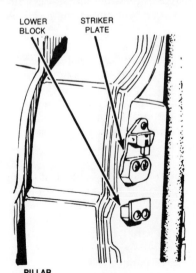

Striker plate and lower block

## Hood, Trunk or Tailgate

As with doors, the outline of hinges should be scribed before removal. The hood and trunk can be aligned by loosening the hinge bolts in their slotted mounting holes and moving the hood or trunk lid as necessary. The hood and trunk have adjustable catch locations to regulate lock engagement. Bumpers at the front and/or rear of the hood provide a vertical adjustment and the hood lockpin can be adjusted for proper engagement.

The tailgate on the station wagon can be

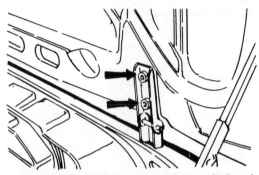

Loosen the hinge boots to permit fore-and-aft and horizontal adjustment

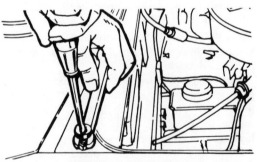

The hood is adjusted vertically by stop-screws at the front and/or rear

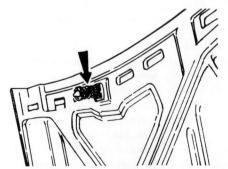

The hood pin can be adjusted for proper lock engagement

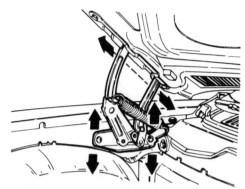

The height of the hood at the rear is adjusted by loosening the bolts that attach the hinge to the body and moving the hood up or down

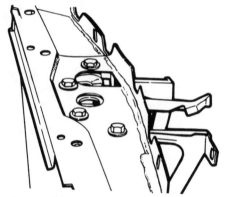

The base of the hood lock can also be re-positioned slightly to give more positive lock engagement

adjusted by loosening the hinge bolts in their slotted mounting holes and moving the tailgate on its hinges. The latchplate and latch striker at the bottom of the tailgate opening can be adjusted to stop rattle. An adjustable bumper is located on each side.

# RUST, UNDERCOATING, AND RUSTPROOFING

## Rust

Rust is an electrochemical process. It works on ferrous metals (iron and steel) from the inside out due to exposure of unprotected surfaces to air and moisture. The possibility of rust exists practically nationwide—anywhere humidity, industrial pollution or chemical salts are present, rust can form. In coastal areas, the problem is high humidity and salt air; in snowy areas, the problem is chemical

salt (de-icer) used to keep the roads clear, and in industrial areas, sulphur dioxide is present in the air from industrial pollution and is changed to sulphuric acid when it rains. The rusting process is accelerated by high temperatures, especially in snowy areas, when vehicles are driven over slushy roads and then left overnight in a heated garage.

Automotive styling also can be a contributor to rust formation. Spot welding of panels creates small pockets that trap moisture and form an environment for rust formation. Fortunately, auto manufacturers have been working hard to increase the corrosion protection of their products. Galvanized sheet metal enjoys much wider use, along with the increased use of plastic and various rust retardant coatings. Manufacturers are also designing out areas in the body where rust-forming moisture can collect.

To prevent rust, you must stop it before it gets started. On new vehicles, there are two ways to accomplish this.

First, the car or truck should be treated with a commercial rustproofing compound. There are many different brands of franchised rustproofers, but most processes involve spraying a waxy "self-healing" compound under the chassis, inside rocker panels, inside doors and fender liners and similar places where rust is likely to form. Prices for a quality rustproofing job range from $100–$250, depending on the area, the brand name and the size of the vehicle.

Ideally, the vehicle should be rustproofed as soon as possible following the purchase. The surfaces of the car or truck have begun to oxidize and deteriorate during shipping. In addition, the car may have sat on a dealer's lot or on a lot at the factory, and once the rust has progressed past the stage of light, powdery surface oxidation rustproofing is not likely to be worthwhile. Professional rustproofers feel that once rust has formed, rustproofing will simply seal in moisture already present. Most franchised rustproofing operations offer a 3–5 year warranty against rust-through, but will not support that warranty if the rustproofing is not applied within three months of the date of manufacture.

Undercoating should not be mistaken for rustproofing. Undercoating is a black, tar-like substance that is applied to the underside of a vehicle. Its basic function is to deaden noises that are transmitted from under the car. It simply cannot get into the crevices and seams where moisture tends to collect. In fact, it may clog up drainage holes and ventilation passages. Some undercoatings also tend to crack or peel with age and only create more moisture and corrosion attracting pockets.

The second thing you should do immediately after purchasing the car is apply a paint sealant. A sealant is a petroleum based product marketed under a wide variety of brand names. It has the same protective properties as a good wax, but bonds to the paint with a chemically inert layer that seals it from the air. If air can't get at the surface, oxidation cannot start.

The paint sealant kit consists of a base coat and a conditioning coat that should be applied every 6–8 months, depending on the manufacturer. The base coat must be applied before waxing, or the wax must first be removed.

Third, keep a garden hose handy for your car in winter. Use it a few times on nice days during the winter for underneath areas, and it will pay big dividends when spring arrives. Spraying under the fenders and other areas which even car washes don't reach will help

remove road salt, dirt and other build-ups which help breed rust. Adjust the nozzle to a high-force spray. An old brush will help break up residue, permitting it to be washed away more easily. It's a somewhat messy job, but worth it in the long run because rust often starts in those hidden areas.

At the same time, wash grime off the door sills and, more importantly, the under portions of the doors, plus the tailgate if you have a station wagon or truck. Applying a coat of wax to those areas at least once before and once during winter will help fend off rust.

When applying the wax to the under parts of the doors, you will note small drain holes. These holes often are plugged with undercoating or dirt. Make sure they are cleaned out to prevent water build-up inside the doors. A small punch or penknife will do the job.

Water from the high-pressure sprays in car washes sometimes can get into the housings for parking and taillights, so take a close look. If they contain water merely loosen the retaining screws and the water should run out.

## Repairing Scratches and Small Dents

**Step 1.** This dent (arrow) is typical of a deep scratch or minor dent. If deep enough, the dent or scratch can be pulled out or hammered out from behind. In this case no straightening is necessary

Step 2.  Using an 80-grit grinding disc on an electric drill grind the paint from the surrounding area down to bare metal. This will provide a rough surface for the body filler to grab

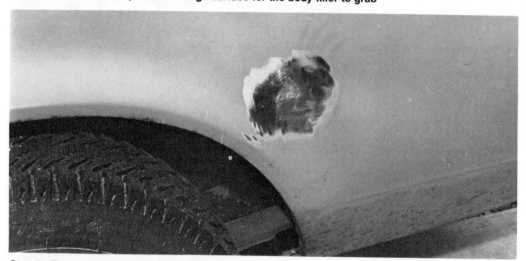

Step 3.  The area should look like this when you're finished grinding

Step 4.  Mix the body filler and cream hardener according to the directions

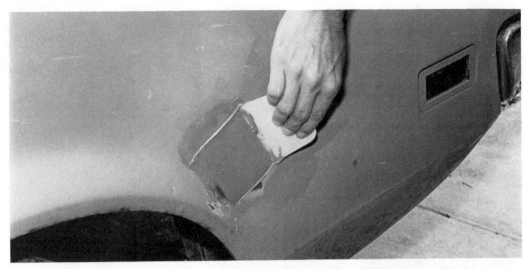

Step 5. Spread the body filler evenly over the entire area. Be sure to cover the area completely

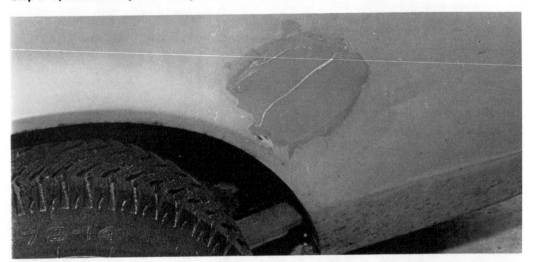

Step 6. Let the body filler dry until the surface can just be scratched with your fingernail

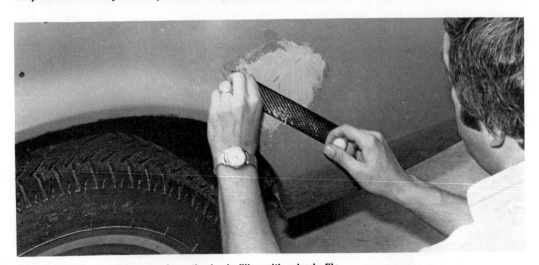

Step 7. Knock the high spots from the body filler with a body file

Step 8.  Check frequently with the palm of your hand for high and low spots. If you wind up with low spots, you may have to apply another layer of filler

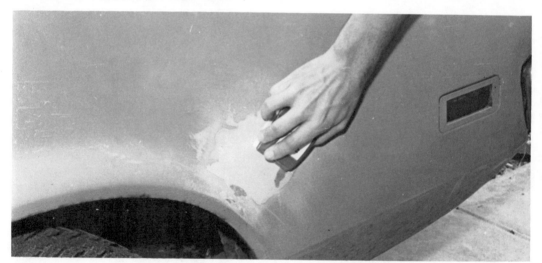

Step 9. Block sand the entire area with 320 grit paper

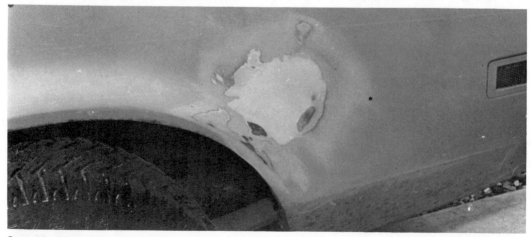

Step 10.  When you're finished, the repair should look like this. Note the sand marks extending 2—3 inches out from the repaired area

**Step 11. Prime the entire area with automotive primer**

**Step 12. The finished repair ready for the final paint coat. Note that the primer has covered the sanding marks (see Step 10). A repair of this size should be able to be spotpainted with good results**

## REPAIRING RUST HOLES

One thing you have to remember about rust: even if you grind away all the rusted metal in a panel, and repair the area with any of the kits available, *eventually* the rust will return. There are two reasons for this. One, rust is a chemical reaction that causes pressure under the repair from the inside out. That's how the blisters form. Two, the back side of the panel (and the repair) is wide open to moisture, and unpainted body filler acts like a sponge. That's why the best solution to rust problems

is to remove the rusted panel and install a new one or have the rusted area cut out and a new piece of sheet metal welded in its place. The trouble with welding is the expense; sometimes it will cost more than the car or truck is worth.

One of the better solutions to do-it-yourself rust repair is the process using a fiberglass cloth repair kit (shown here). This will give a strong repair that resists cracking and moisture and is relatively easy to use. It can be used on large or small holes and also can be applied over contoured surfaces.

**Step 1. Rust areas such as this are common and are easily fixed**

**Step 2. Grind away all traces of rust with a 24-grit grinding disc. Be sure to grind back 3—4 inches from the edge of the hole down to bare metal and be sure all traces of rust are removed**

## AUTO BODY CARE

There are hundreds—maybe thousands—of products on the market, all designed to protect or aid your car's finish in some manner. There are as many different products as there are ways to use them, but they all have one thing in common—the surface must be clean.

## Washing

The primary ingredient for washing your car is water, preferably "soft" water. In many areas of the country, the local water supply is "hard" containing many minerals. The little rings or film that is left on your car's surface after it has dried is the result of "hard" water.

Since you usually can't change the local water supply, the next best thing is to dry the surface before it has a chance to dry itself.

Into the water you usually add soap. Don't use detergents or common, coarse soaps. Your car's paint never truly dries out, but is always evaporating residual oils into the air. Harsh detergents will remove these oils, causing the paint to dry faster than normal.

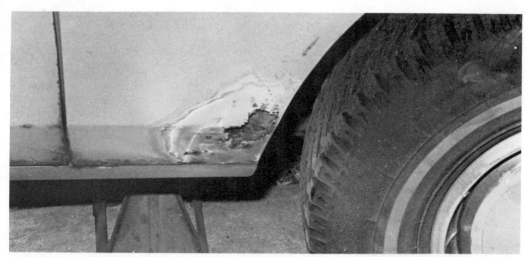

Step 3.  Be sure all rust is removed from the edges of the metal. The edges must be ground back to un-rusted metal

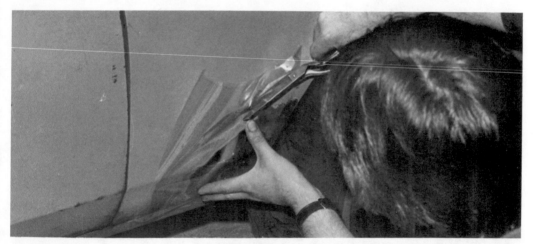

Step 4.  If you are going to use release film, cut a piece about 2″ larger than the area you have sanded. Place the film over the repair and mark the sanded area on the film. Avoid any unnecessary wrinkling of the film

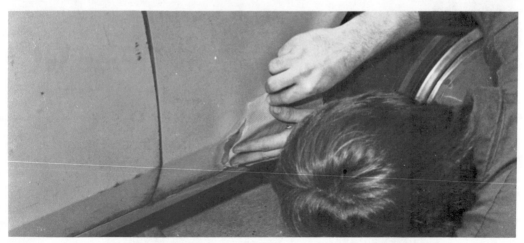

Step 5.  Cut 2 pieces of fiberglass matte. One piece should be about 1″ smaller than the sanded area and the second piece should be 1″ smaller than the first. Use sharp scissors to avoid loose ends

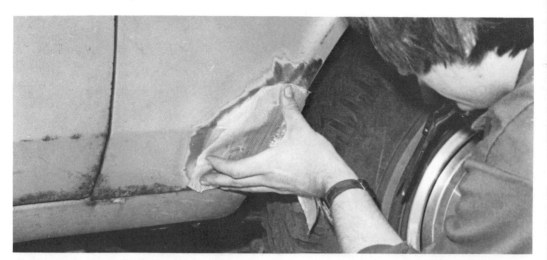

**Step 6.** Check the dimensions of the release film and cloth by holding them up to the repair area

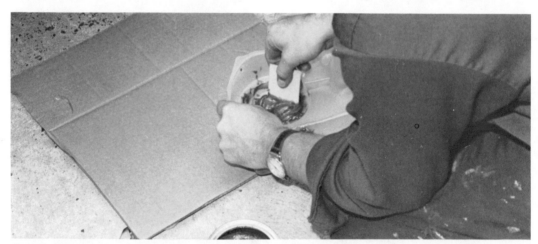

**Step 7.** Mix enough repair jelly and cream hardener in the mixing tray to saturate the fiberglass material or fill the repair area. Follow the directions on the container

**Step 8.** Lay the release sheet on a flat surface and spread an even layer of filler, large enough to cover the repair. Lay the smaller piece of fiberglass cloth in the center of the sheet and spread another layer of repair jelly over the fiberglass cloth. Repeat the operation for the larger piece of cloth. If the fiberglass cloth is not used, spread the repair jelly on the release film, concentrated in the middle of the repair

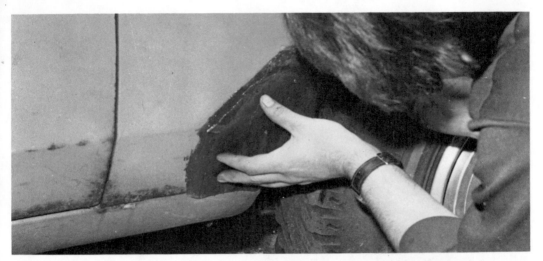

Step 9. Place the repair material over the repair area, with the release film facing outward

Step 10. Use a spreader and work from the center outward to smooth the material, following the body contours. Be sure to remove all air bubbles

Step 11. Wait until the repair has dried tack-free and peel off the release sheet. The ideal working temperature is 65—90° F. Cooler or warmer temperatures or high humidity may require additional curing time

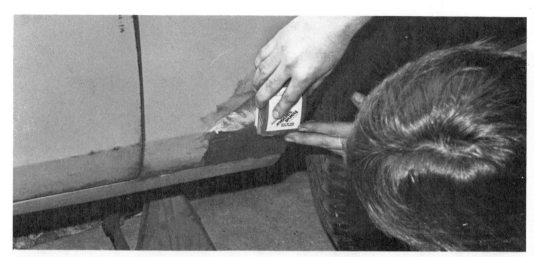

Step 12.  Sand and feather-edge the entire area. The initial sanding can be done with a sanding disc on an electric drill if care is used. Finish the sanding with a block sander

Step 13.  When the area is sanded smooth, mix some topcoat and hardener and apply it directly with a spreader. This will give a smooth finish and prevent the glass matte from showing through the paint

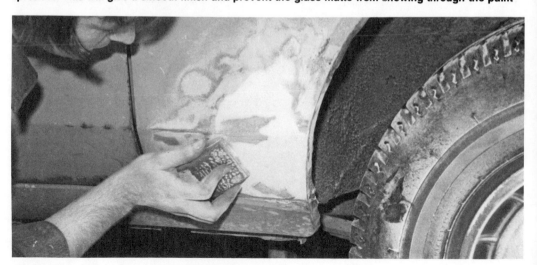

Step 14.  Block sand the topcoat with finishing sandpaper

Step 15. To finish this repair, grind out the surface rust along the top edge of the rocker panel

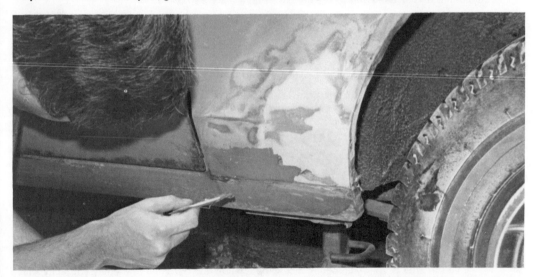

Step 16. Mix some more repair jelly and cream hardener and apply it directly over the surface

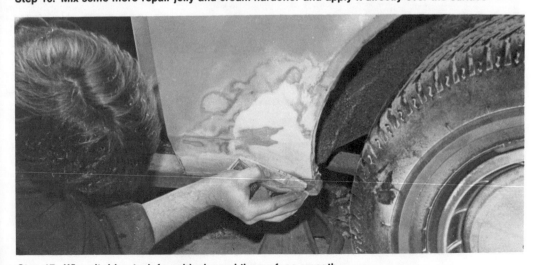

Step 17. When it dries tack-free, block sand the surface smooth

**Step 18.** If necessary, mask off adjacent panels and spray the entire repair with primer. You are now ready for a color coat

Instead use warm water and a non-detergent soap made especially for waxed surfaces or a liquid soap made for waxed surfaces or a liquid soap made for washing dishes by hand. Other products that can be used on painted surfaces include baking soda or plain soda water for stubborn dirt.

Wash the car completely, starting at the top, and rinse it completely clean. Abrasive grit should be loaded off under water pressure; scrubbing grit off will scratch the finish. The best washing tool is a sponge, cleaning mitt or soft towel. Whichever you choose, replace it often as each tends to absorb grease and dirt.

Other ways to get a better wash include:

• Don't wash your car in the sun or when the finish is hot.

• Use water pressure to remove caked-on dirt.

• Remove tree-sap and bird effluence immediately. Such substances will eat through wax, polish and paint.

One of the best implements to dry your car is a turkish towel or an old, soft bath towel. Anything with a deep nap will hold any dirt in suspension and not grind it into the paint.

Harder cloths will only grind the grit into the paint making more scratches. Always start drying at the top, followed by the hood and trunk and sides. You'll find there's always more dirt near the rocker panels and wheelwells which will wind up on the rest of the car if you dry these areas first.

## Cleaners, Waxes and Polishes

Before going any farther you should know the function of various products.

Cleaners—remove the top layer of dead pigment or paint.

Rubbing or polishing compounds—used to remove stubborn dirt, get rid of minor scratches, smooth away imperfections and partially restore badly weathered paint.

Polishes—contain no abrasives or waxes; they shine the paint by adding oils to the paint.

Waxes—are a protective coating for the polish.

### CLEANERS AND COMPOUNDS

Before you apply any wax, you'll have to remove oxidation, road film and other types of pollutants that washing alone will not remove.

The paint on your car never dries completely. There are always residual oils evaporating from the paint into the air. When enough oils are present in the paint, it has a healthy shine (gloss). When too many oils evaporate the paint takes on a whitish cast known as oxidation. The idea of polishing and waxing is to keep enough oil present in the painted surface to prevent oxidation; but when it occurs, the only recourse is to remove the top layer of "dead" paint, exposing the healthy paint underneath.

Products to remove oxidation and road film are sold under a variety of generic names—polishes, cleaner, rubbing compound, cleaner/polish, polish/cleaner, self-polishing wax, pre-wax cleaner, finish restorer and many more. Regardless of name there are two types of cleaners—abrasive cleaners (sometimes called polishing or rubbing compounds) that remove oxidation by grinding away the top layer of "dead" paint, or chemical cleaners that dissolve the "dead" pigment, allowing it to be wiped away.

Abrasive cleaners, by their nature, leave thousands of minute scratches in the finish, which must be polished out later. These should only be used in extreme cases, but are usually the only thing to use on badly oxidized paint finishes. Chemical cleaners are much milder but are not strong enough for severe cases of oxidation or weathered paint.

The most popular cleaners are liquid or paste abrasive polishing and rubbing compounds. Polishing compounds have a finer abrasive grit for medium duty work. Rubbing compounds are a coarser abrasive and for heavy duty work. Unless you are familiar with how to use compounds, be very careful. Excessive rubbing with any type of compound or cleaner can grind right through the paint to primer or bare metal. Follow the directions on the container—depending on type, the cleaner may or may not be OK for your paint. For example, some cleaners are not formulated for acrylic lacquer finishes.

When a small area needs compounding or heavy polishing, it's best to do the job by hand. Some people prefer a powered buffer for large areas. Avoid cutting through the paint along styling edges on the body. Small, hand operations where the compound is applied and rubbed using cloth folded into a thick ball allow you to work in straight lines along such edges.

To avoid cutting through on the edges when using a power buffer, try masking tape. Just cover the edge with tape while using power. Then finish the job by hand with the tape removed. Even then work carefully. The paint tends to be a lot thinner along the sharp ridges stamped into the panels.

Whether compounding by machine or by hand, only work on a small area and apply the compound sparingly. If the materials are spread too thin, or allowed to sit too long, they dry out. Once dry they lose the ability to deliver a smooth, clean finish. Also, dried out polish tends to cause the buffer to stick in one spot. This in turn can burn or cut through the finish.

## WAXES AND POLISHES

Your car's finish can be protected in a number of ways. A cleaner/wax or polish/cleaner followed by wax or variations of each all provide good results. The two-step approach (polish followed by wax) is probably slightly better but consumes more time and effort. Properly fed with oils, your paint should never need cleaning, but despite the best polishing job, it won't last unless it's protected with wax. Without wax, polish must be renewed at least once a month to prevent oxidation. Years ago (some still swear by it today), the best wax was made from the Brazilian palm, the Carnuba, favored for its vegetable base and high melting point. However, modern synthetic waxes are harder, which means they protect against moisture better, and chemically inert silicone is used for a long lasting protection. The only problem with silicone wax is that it penetrates all layers of paint. To repaint or touch up a panel or car protected by silicone wax, you have to completely strip the finish to avoid "fisheyes."

Under normal conditions, silicone waxes will last 4–6 months, but you have to be careful of wax build-up from too much waxing. Too thick a coat of wax is just as bad as no wax at all; it stops the paint from breathing.

Combination cleaners/waxes have become popular lately because they remove the old layer of wax plus light oxidation, while putting on a fresh coat of wax at the same time. Some cleaners/waxes contain abrasive cleaners which require caution, although many cleaner/waxes use a chemical cleaner.

### Applying Wax or Polish

You may view polishing and waxing your car as a pleasant way to spend an afternoon, or as a boring chore, but it has to be done to keep the paint on your car. Caring for the paint doesn't require special tools, but you should follow a few rules.

1. Use a good quality wax.
2. Before applying any wax or polish, be

sure the surface is completely clean. Just because the car looks clean, doesn't mean it's ready for polish or wax.

3. If the finish on your car is weathered, dull, or oxidized, it will probably have to be compounded to remove the old or oxidized paint. If the paint is simply dulled from lack of care, one of the non-abrasive cleaners known as polishing compounds will do the trick. If the paint is severely scratched or really dull, you'll probably have to use a rubbing compound to prepare the finish for waxing. If you're not sure which one to use, use the polishing compound, since you can easily ruin the finish by using too strong a compound.

4. Don't apply wax, polish or compound in direct sunlight, even if the directions on the can say you can. Most waxes will not cure properly in bright sunlight and you'll probably end up with a blotchy looking finish.

5. Don't rub the wax off too soon. The result will be a wet, dull looking finish. Let the wax dry thoroughly before buffing it off.

6. A constant debate among car enthusiasts is how wax should be applied. Some maintain pastes or liquids should be applied in a circular motion, but body shop experts have long thought that this approach results in barely detectable circular abrasions, especially on cars that are waxed frequently. They advise rubbing in straight lines, especially if any kind of cleaner is involved.

7. If an applicator is not supplied with the wax, use a piece of soft cheesecloth or very soft lint-free material. The same applies to buffing the surface.

## SPECIAL SURFACES

One-step combination cleaner and wax formulas shouldn't be used on many of the special surfaces which abound on cars. The one-step materials contain abrasives to achieve a clean surface under the wax top coat. The abrasives are so mild that you could clean a car every week for a couple of years without fear of rubbing through the paint. But this same level of abrasiveness might, through repeated use, damage decals used for special trim effects. This includes wide stripes, wood-grain trim and other appliques.

Painted plastics must be cleaned with care. If a cleaner is too aggressive it will cut through the paint and expose the primer. If bright trim such as polished aluminum or chrome is painted, cleaning must be performed with even greater care. If rubbing compound is being used, it will cut faster than polish.

Abrasive cleaners will dull an acrylic finish. The best way to clean these newer finishes is with a non-abrasive liquid polish. Only dirt and oxidation, not paint, will be removed.

Taking a few minutes to read the instructions on the can of polish or wax will help prevent making serious mistakes. Not all preparations will work on all surfaces. And some are intended for power application while others will only work when applied by hand.

Don't get the idea that just pouring on some polish and then hitting it with a buffer will suffice. Power equipment speeds the operation. But it also adds a measure of risk. It's very easy to damage the finish if you use the wrong methods or materials.

### Caring for Chrome

Read the label on the container. Many products are formulated specifically for chrome, but others contain abrasives that will scratch the chrome finish. If it isn't recommended for chrome, don't use it.

Never use steel wool or kitchen soap pads to clean chrome. Be careful not to get chrome cleaner on paint or interior vinyl surfaces. If you do, get it off immediately.

# Troubleshooting

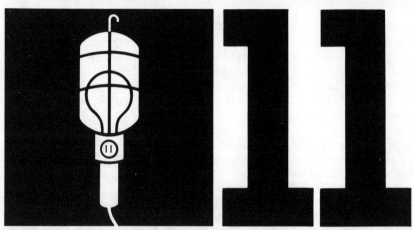

This section is designed to aid in the quick, accurate diagnosis of automotive problems. While automotive repairs can be made by many people, accurate troubleshooting is a rare skill for the amateur and professional alike.

In its simplest state, troubleshooting is an exercise in logic. It is essential to realize that an automobile is really composed of a series of systems. Some of these systems are interrelated; others are not. Automobiles operate within a framework of logical rules and physical laws, and the key to troubleshooting is a good understanding of all the automotive systems.

This section breaks the car or truck down into its component systems, allowing the problem to be isolated. The charts and diagnostic road maps list the most common problems and the most probable causes of trouble. Obviously it would be impossible to list every possible problem that could happen along with every possible cause, but it will locate MOST problems and eliminate a lot of unnecessary guesswork. The systematic format will locate problems within a given system, but, because many automotive systems are interrelated, the solution to your particular problem may be found in a number of systems on the car or truck.

## USING THE TROUBLESHOOTING CHARTS

This book contains all of the specific information that the average do-it-yourself mechanic needs to repair and maintain his or her car or truck. The troubleshooting charts are designed to be used in conjunction with the specific procedures and information in the text. For instance, troubleshooting a point-type ignition system is fairly standard for all models, but you may be directed to the text to find procedures for troubleshooting an individual type of electronic ignition. You will also have to refer to the specification charts throughout the book for specifications applicable to your car or truck.

## TOOLS AND EQUIPMENT

The tools illustrated in Chapter 1 (plus two more diagnostic pieces) will be adequate to troubleshoot most problems. The two other tools needed are a voltmeter and an ohmmeter. These can be purchased separately or in combination, known as a VOM meter.

In the event that other tools are required, they will be noted in the procedures.

# Troubleshooting Engine Problems

See Chapters 2, 3, 4 for more information and service procedures.

## Index to Systems

| System | To Test | Group |
|---|---|---|
| Battery | Engine need not be running | 1 |
| Starting system | Engine need not be running | 2 |
| Primary electrical system | Engine need not be running | 3 |
| Secondary electrical system | Engine need not be running | 4 |
| Fuel system | Engine need not be running | 5 |
| Engine compression | Engine need not be running | 6 |
| Engine vacuum | Engine must be running | 7 |
| Secondary electrical system | Engine must be running | 8 |
| Valve train | Engine must be running | 9 |
| Exhaust system | Engine must be running | 10 |
| Cooling system | Engine must be running | 11 |
| Engine lubrication | Engine must be running | 12 |

## Index to Problems

| Problem: Symptom | Begin at Specific Diagnosis, Number ___ |
|---|---|
| **Engine Won't Start:** | |
| Starter doesn't turn | 1.1, 2.1 |
| Starter turns, engine doesn't | 2.1 |
| Starter turns engine very slowly | 1.1, 2.4 |
| Starter turns engine normally | 3.1, 4.1 |
| Starter turns engine very quickly | 6.1 |
| Engine fires intermittently | 4.1 |
| Engine fires consistently | 5.1, 6.1 |
| **Engine Runs Poorly:** | |
| Hard starting | 3.1, 4.1, 5.1, 8.1 |
| Rough idle | 4.1, 5.1, 8.1 |
| Stalling | 3.1, 4.1, 5.1, 8.1 |
| Engine dies at high speeds | 4.1, 5.1 |
| Hesitation (on acceleration from standing stop) | 5.1, 8.1 |
| Poor pickup | 4.1, 5.1, 8.1 |
| Lack of power | 3.1, 4.1, 5.1, 8.1 |
| Backfire through the carburetor | 4.1, 8.1, 9.1 |
| Backfire through the exhaust | 4.1, 8.1, 9.1 |
| Blue exhaust gases | 6.1, 7.1 |
| Black exhaust gases | 5.1 |
| Running on (after the ignition is shut off) | 3.1, 8.1 |
| Susceptible to moisture | 4.1 |
| Engine misfires under load | 4.1, 7.1, 8.4, 9.1 |
| Engine misfires at speed | 4.1, 8.4 |
| Engine misfires at idle | 3.1, 4.1, 5.1, 7.1, 8.4 |

## Sample Section

| Test and Procedure | Results and Indications | Proceed to |
|---|---|---|
| 4.1—Check for spark: Hold each spark plug wire approximately ¼″ from ground with gloves or a heavy, dry rag. Crank the engine and observe the spark. | → If no spark is evident: | → 4.2 |
| | → If spark is good in some cases: | → 4.3 |
| | → If spark is good in all cases: | → 4.6 |

## Specific Diagnosis

This section is arranged so that following each test, instructions are given to proceed to another, until a problem is diagnosed.

## Section 1—Battery

| Test and Procedure | Results and Indications | Proceed to |
|---|---|---|
| **1.1**—Inspect the battery visually for case condition (corrosion, cracks) and water level. | If case is cracked, replace battery: | **1.4** |
| | If the case is intact, remove corrosion with a solution of baking soda and water (**CAUTION**: *do not get the solution into the battery*), and fill with water: | **1.2** |

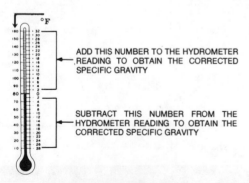

DIRT ON TOP OF BATTERY
CORROSION
PLUGGED VENT
LOOSE CABLE OR POSTS
CRACKS
LOW WATER LEVEL

**Inspect the battery case**

| Test and Procedure | Results and Indications | Proceed to |
|---|---|---|
| **1.2**—Check the battery cable connections: Insert a screwdriver between the battery post and the cable clamp. Turn the headlights on high beam, and observe them as the screwdriver is gently twisted to ensure good metal to metal contact. | If the lights brighten, remove and clean the clamp and post; coat the post with petroleum jelly, install and tighten the clamp: | **1.4** |
| | If no improvement is noted: | **1.3** |

TESTING BATTERY CABLE CONNECTIONS USING A SCREWDRIVER

| Test and Procedure | Results and Indications | Proceed to |
|---|---|---|
| **1.3**—Test the state of charge of the battery using an individual cell tester or hydrometer. | If indicated, charge the battery. **NOTE:** *If no obvious reason exists for the low state of charge (i.e., battery age, prolonged storage), proceed to:* | **1.4** |

°F

ADD THIS NUMBER TO THE HYDROMETER READING TO OBTAIN THE CORRECTED SPECIFIC GRAVITY

SUBTRACT THIS NUMBER FROM THE HYDROMETER READING TO OBTAIN THE CORRECTED SPECIFIC GRAVITY

### Specific Gravity ( @ 80° F.)

| Minimum | Battery Charge |
|---|---|
| 1.260 | 100% Charged |
| 1.230 | 75% Charged |
| 1.200 | 50% Charged |
| 1.170 | 25% Charged |
| 1.140 | Very Little Power Left |
| 1.110 | Completely Discharged |

**The effects of temperature on battery specific gravity (left) and amount of battery charge in relation to specific gravity (right)**

| Test and Procedure | Results and Indications | Proceed to |
|---|---|---|
| **1.4**—Visually inspect battery cables for cracking, bad connection to ground, or bad connection to starter. | If necessary, tighten connections or replace the cables: | **2.1** |

# Section 2—Starting System
See Chapter 3 for service procedures

| Test and Procedure | Results and Indications | Proceed to |
|---|---|---|
| **Note: Tests in Group 2 are performed with coil high tension lead disconnected to prevent accidental starting.** | | |
| **2.1**—Test the starter motor and solenoid: Connect a jumper from the battery post of the solenoid (or relay) to the starter post of the solenoid (or relay). | If starter turns the engine normally: | **2.2** |
| | If the starter buzzes, or turns the engine very slowly: | **2.4** |
| | If no response, replace the solenoid (or relay). | **3.1** |
| | If the starter turns, but the engine doesn't, ensure that the flywheel ring gear is intact. If the gear is undamaged, replace the starter drive. | **3.1** |
| **2.2**—Determine whether ignition override switches are functioning properly (clutch start switch, neutral safety switch), by connecting a jumper across the switch(es), and turning the ignition switch to "start". | If starter operates, adjust or replace switch: | **3.1** |
| | If the starter doesn't operate: | **2.3** |
| **2.3**—Check the ignition switch "start" position: Connect a 12V test lamp or voltmeter between the starter post of the solenoid (or relay) and ground. Turn the ignition switch to the "start" position, and jiggle the key. | If the lamp doesn't light or the meter needle doesn't move when the switch is turned, check the ignition switch for loose connections, cracked insulation, or broken wires. Repair or replace as necessary: | **3.1** |
| | If the lamp flickers or needle moves when the key is jiggled, replace the ignition switch. | **3.3** |

Checking the ignition switch "start" position

STARTER RELAY
(IF EQUIPPED)

| Test and Procedure | Results and Indications | Proceed to |
|---|---|---|
| **2.4**—Remove and bench test the starter, according to specifications in the engine electrical section. | If the starter does not meet specifications, repair or replace as needed: | **3.1** |
| | If the starter is operating properly: | **2.5** |
| **2.5**—Determine whether the engine can turn freely: Remove the spark plugs, and check for water in the cylinders. Check for water on the dipstick, or oil in the radiator. Attempt to turn the engine using an 18″ flex drive and socket on the crankshaft pulley nut or bolt. | If the engine will turn freely only with the spark plugs out, and hydrostatic lock (water in the cylinders) is ruled out, check valve timing: | **9.2** |
| | If engine will not turn freely, and it is known that the clutch and transmission are free, the engine must be disassembled for further evaluation: | **Chapter 3** |

## Section 3—Primary Electrical System

| Test and Procedure | Results and Indications | Proceed to |
|---|---|---|
| **3.1**—Check the ignition switch "on" position: Connect a jumper wire between the distributor side of the coil and ground, and a 12V test lamp between the switch side of the coil and ground. Remove the high tension lead from the coil. Turn the ignition switch on and jiggle the key. | If the lamp lights: | **3.2** |
| | If the lamp flickers when the key is jiggled, replace the ignition switch: | **3.3** |
| | If the lamp doesn't light, check for loose or open connections. If none are found, remove the ignition switch and check for continuity. If the switch is faulty, replace it: | **3.3** |

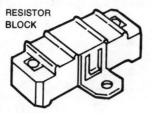

**Checking the ignition switch "on" position**

| | | |
|---|---|---|
| **3.2**—Check the ballast resistor or resistance wire for an open circuit, using an ohmmeter. See Chapter 3 for specific tests. | Replace the resistor or resistance wire if the resistance is zero. **NOTE:** *Some ignition systems have no ballast resistor.* | **3.3** |

 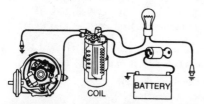

RESISTOR BLOCK

CALIBRATED RESISTANCE LEAD

**Two types of resistors**

| | | |
|---|---|---|
| **3.3**—On point-type ignition systems, visually inspect the breaker points for burning, pitting or excessive wear. Gray coloring of the point contact surfaces is normal. Rotate the crankshaft until the contact heel rests on a high point of the distributor cam and adjust the point gap to specifications. On electronic ignition models, remove the distributor cap and visually inspect the armature. Ensure that the armature pin is in place, and that the armature is on tight and rotates when the engine is cranked. Make sure there are no cracks, chips or rounded edges on the armature. | If the breaker points are intact, clean the contact surfaces with fine emery cloth, and adjust the point gap to specifications. If the points are worn, replace them. On electronic systems, replace any parts which appear defective. If condition persists: | **3.4** |

| Test and Procedure | Results and Indications | Proceed to |
|---|---|---|
| **3.4**—On point-type ignition systems, connect a dwell-meter between the distributor primary lead and ground. Crank the engine and observe the point dwell angle. On electronic ignition systems, conduct a stator (magnetic pickup assembly) test. See Chapter 3. | On point-type systems, adjust the dwell angle if necessary. **NOTE:** *Increasing the point gap decreases the dwell angle and vice-versa.* | ☞ **3.6** |
|  | If the dwell meter shows little or no reading; | **3.5** |
|  | On electronic ignition systems, if the stator is bad, replace the stator. If the stator is good, proceed to the other tests in Chapter 3. | |

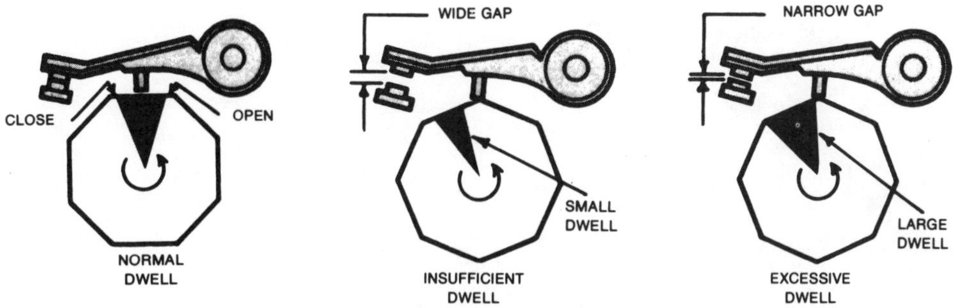

WIDE GAP    NARROW GAP

CLOSE    OPEN

NORMAL DWELL    INSUFFICIENT DWELL    EXCESSIVE DWELL

SMALL DWELL    LARGE DWELL

**Dwell is a function of point gap**

| | | |
|---|---|---|
| **3.5**—On the point-type ignition systems, check the condenser for short: connect an ohmeter across the condenser body and the pigtail lead. | If any reading other than infinite is noted, replace the condenser | **3.6** |

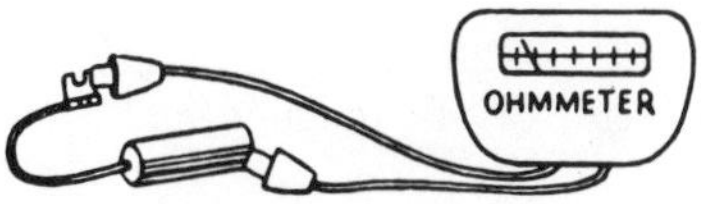

OHMMETER

**Checking the condenser for short**

| | | |
|---|---|---|
| **3.6**—Test the coil primary resistance: On point-type ignition systems, connect an ohmmeter across the coil primary terminals, and read the resistance on the low scale. Note whether an external ballast resistor or resistance wire is used. On electronic ignition systems, test the coil primary resistance as in Chapter 3. | Point-type ignition coils utilizing ballast resistors or resistance wires should have approximately 1.0 ohms resistance. Coils with internal resistors should have approximately 4.0 ohms resistance. If values far from the above are noted, replace the coil. | **4.1** |

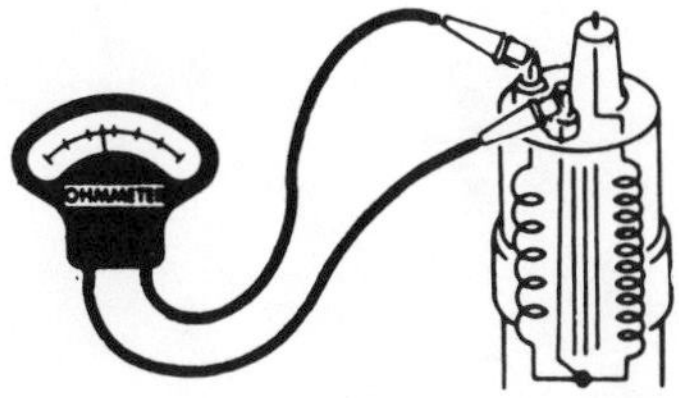

**Check the coil primary resistance**

## Section 4—Secondary Electrical System
See Chapters 2–3 for service procedures

| Test and Procedure | Results and Indications | Proceed to |
|---|---|---|
| **4.1**—Check for spark: Hold each spark plug wire approximately ¼″ from ground with gloves or a heavy, dry rag. Crank the engine, and observe the spark. | If no spark is evident: | **4.2** |
| | If spark is good in some cylinders: | **4.3** |
| | If spark is good in all cylinders: | **4.6** |

**Check for spark at the plugs**

| | | |
|---|---|---|
| **4.2**—Check for spark at the coil high tension lead: Remove the coil high tension lead from the distributor and position it approximately ¼″ from ground. Crank the engine and observe spark. **CAUTION:** *This test should not be performed on engines equipped with electronic ignition.* | If the spark is good and consistent: | **4.3** |
| | If the spark is good but intermittent, test the primary electrical system starting at 3.3: | **3.3** |
| | If the spark is weak or non-existent, replace the coil high tension lead, clean and tighten all connections and retest. If no improvement is noted: | **4.4** |
| **4.3**—Visually inspect the distributor cap and rotor for burned or corroded contacts, cracks, carbon tracks, or moisture. Also check the fit of the rotor on the distributor shaft (where applicable). | If moisture is present, dry thoroughly, and retest per 4.1: | **4.1** |
| | If burned or excessively corroded contacts, cracks, or carbon tracks are noted, replace the defective part(s) and retest per 4.1: | **4.1** |
| | If the rotor and cap appear intact, or are only slightly corroded, clean the contacts thoroughly (including the cap towers and spark plug wire ends) and retest per 4.1: | |
| | If the spark is good in all cases: | **4.6** |
| | If the spark is poor in all cases: | **4.5** |

**Inspect the distributor cap and rotor**

| Test and Procedure | Results and Indications | Proceed to |
|---|---|---|
| **4.4**—Check the coil secondary resistance: On point-type systems connect an ohmmeter across the distributor side of the coil and the coil tower. Read the resistance on the high scale of the ohmmeter. On electronic ignition systems, see Chapter 3 for specific tests. | The resistance of a satisfactory coil should be between 4,000 and 10,000 ohms. If resistance is considerably higher (i.e., 40,000 ohms) replace the coil and retest per 4.1. **NOTE:** *This does not apply to high performance coils.* | |

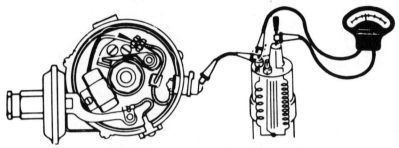

**Testing the coil secondary resistance**

| | | |
|---|---|---|
| **4.5**—Visually inspect the spark plug wires for cracking or brittleness. Ensure that no two wires are positioned so as to cause induction firing (adjacent and parallel). Remove each wire, one by one, and check resistance with an ohmmeter. | Replace any cracked or brittle wires. If any of the wires are defective, replace the entire set. Replace any wires with excessive resistance (over 8000 Ω per foot for suppression wire), and separate any wires that might cause induction firing. | **4.6** |

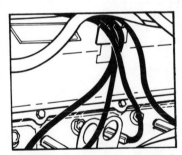

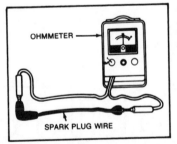

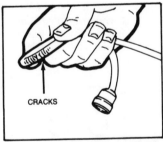

**Misfiring can be the result of spark plug leads to adjacent, consecutively firing cylinders running parallel and too close together**

**On point-type ignition systems, check the spark plug wires as shown. On electronic ignitions, do not remove the wire from the distributor cap terminal; instead, test through the cap**

**Spark plug wires can be checked visually by bending them in a loop over your finger. This will reveal any cracks, burned or broken insulation. Any wire with cracked insulation should be replaced**

| | | |
|---|---|---|
| **4.6**—Remove the spark plugs, noting the cylinders from which they were removed, and evaluate according to the color photos in the middle of this book. | See following. | **See following.** |

| Test and Procedure | Results and Indications | Proceed to |
|---|---|---|
| 4.7—Examine the location of all the plugs. | The following diagrams illustrate some of the conditions that the location of plugs will reveal. | **4.8** |

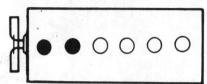

Two adjacent plugs are fouled in a 6-cylinder engine, 4-cylinder engine or either bank of a V-8. This is probably due to a blown head gasket between the two cylinders

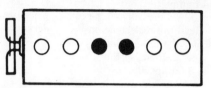

The two center plugs in a 6-cylinder engine are fouled. Raw fuel may be "boiled" out of the carburetor into the intake manifold after the engine is shut-off. Stop-start driving can also foul the center plugs, due to overly rich mixture. Proper float level, a new float needle and seat or use of an insulating spacer may help this problem

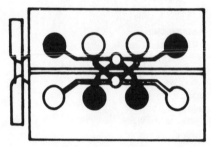

An unbalanced carburetor is indicated. Following the fuel flow on this particular design shows that the cylinders fed by the right-hand barrel are fouled from overly rich mixture, while the cylinders fed by the left-hand barrel are normal

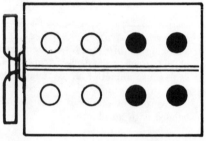

If the four rear plugs are overheated, a cooling system problem is suggested. A thorough cleaning of the cooling system may restore coolant circulation and cure the problem

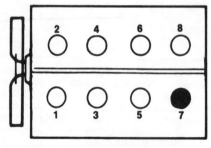

Finding one plug overheated may indicate an intake manifold leak near the affected cylinder. If the overheated plug is the second of two adjacent, consecutively firing plugs, it could be the result of ignition cross-firing. Separating the leads to these two plugs will eliminate cross-fire

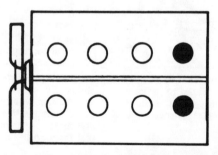

Occasionally, the two rear plugs in large, lightly used V-8's will become oil fouled. High oil consumption and smoky exhaust may also be noticed. It is probably due to plugged oil drain holes in the rear of the cylinder head, causing oil to be sucked in around the valve stems. This usually occurs in the rear cylinders first, because the engine slants that way

| Test and Procedure | Results and Indications | Proceed to |
|---|---|---|
| **4.8**—Determine the static ignition timing. Using the crankshaft pulley timing marks as a guide, locate top dead center on the compression stroke of the number one cylinder. | The rotor should be pointing toward the No. 1 tower in the distributor cap, and, on electronic ignitions, the armature spoke for that cylinder should be lined up with the stator. | **4.8** |
| **4.9**—Check coil polarity: Connect a voltmeter negative lead to the coil high tension lead, and the positive lead to ground (**NOTE:** *Reverse the hook-up for positive ground systems*). Crank the engine momentarily.<br><br>Checking coil polarity | If the voltmeter reads up-scale, the polarity is correct:<br><br>If the voltmeter reads down-scale, reverse the coil polarity (switch the primary leads): | **5.1**<br><br>**5.1** |

## Section 5—Fuel System
See Chapter 4 for service procedures

| Test and Procedure | Results and Indications | Proceed to |
|---|---|---|
| **5.1**—Determine that the air filter is functioning efficiently: Hold paper elements up to a strong light, and attempt to see light through the filter. | Clean permanent air filters in solvent (or manufacturer's recommendation), and allow to dry. Replace paper elements through which light cannot be seen: | **5.2** |
| **5.2**—Determine whether a flooding condition exists: Flooding is identified by a strong gasoline odor, and excessive gasoline present in the throttle bore(s) of the carburetor.<br><br>If the engine floods repeatedly, check the choke butterfly flap | If flooding is not evident:<br><br>If flooding is evident, permit the gasoline to dry for a few moments and restart.<br>If flooding doesn't recur:<br><br>If flooding is persistent: | **5.3**<br><br><br>**5.7**<br><br>**5.5** |
| **5.3**—Check that fuel is reaching the carburetor: Detach the fuel line at the carburetor inlet. Hold the end of the line in a cup (not styrofoam), and crank the engine.<br><br>Check the fuel pump by disconnecting the output line (fuel pump-to-carburetor) at the carburetor and operating the starter briefly | If fuel flows smoothly:<br><br>If fuel doesn't flow (**NOTE:** *Make sure that there is fuel in the tank*), or flows erratically: | **5.7**<br><br>**5.4** |

| Test and Procedure | Results and Indications | Proceed to |
|---|---|---|
| **5.4**—Test the fuel pump: Disconnect all fuel lines from the fuel pump. Hold a finger over the input fitting, crank the engine (with electric pump, turn the ignition or pump on); and feel for suction. | If suction is evident, blow out the fuel line to the tank with low pressure compressed air until bubbling is heard from the fuel filler neck. Also blow out the carburetor fuel line (both ends disconnected): | 5.7 |
| | If no suction is evident, replace or repair the fuel pump: **NOTE:** *Repeated oil fouling of the spark plugs, or a no-start condition, could be the result of a ruptured vacuum booster pump diaphragm, through which oil or gasoline is being drawn into the intake manifold (where applicable).* | 5.7 |
| **5.5**—Occasionally, small specks of dirt will clog the small jets and orifices in the carburetor. With the engine cold, hold a flat piece of wood or similar material over the carburetor, where possible, and crank the engine. | If the engine starts, but runs roughly the engine is probably not run enough. If the engine won't start: | 5.9 |
| **5.6**—Check the needle and seat: Tap the carburetor in the area of the needle and seat. | If flooding stops, a gasoline additive (e.g., Gumout) will often cure the problem: | 5.7 |
| | If flooding continues, check the fuel pump for excessive pressure at the carburetor (according to specifications). If the pressure is normal, the needle and seat must be removed and checked, and/or the float level adjusted: | 5.7 |
| **5.7**—Test the accelerator pump by looking into the throttle bores while operating the throttle. | If the accelerator pump appears to be operating normally: | 5.8 |
| | If the accelerator pump is not operating, the pump must be reconditioned. Where possible, service the pump with the carburetor(s) installed on the engine. If necessary, remove the carburetor. Prior to removal: | 5.8 |

**Check for gas at the carburetor by looking down the carburetor throat while someone moves the accelerator**

| Test and Procedure | Results and Indications | Proceed to |
|---|---|---|
| **5.8**—Determine whether the carburetor main fuel system is functioning: Spray a commercial starting fluid into the carburetor while attempting to start the engine. | If the engine starts, runs for a few seconds, and dies: | 5.9 |
| | If the engine doesn't start: | 6.1 |

| Test and Procedure | Results and Indications | Proceed to |
|---|---|---|
| **5.9**—Uncommon fuel system malfunctions: See below: | If the problem is solved:<br><br>If the problem remains, remove and recondition the carburetor. | **6.1** |

| Condition | Indication | Test | Prevailing Weather Conditions | Remedy |
|---|---|---|---|---|
| Vapor lock | Engine will not restart shortly after running. | Cool the components of the fuel system until the engine starts. Vapor lock can be cured faster by draping a wet cloth over a mechanical fuel pump. | Hot to very hot | Ensure that the exhaust manifold heat control valve is operating. Check with the vehicle manufacturer for the recommended solution to vapor lock on the model in question. |
| Carburetor icing | Engine will not idle, stalls at low speeds. | Visually inspect the throttle plate area of the throttle bores for frost. | High humidity, 32–40° F. | Ensure that the exhaust manifold heat control valve is operating, and that the intake manifold heat riser is not blocked. |
| Water in the fuel | Engine sputters and stalls; may not start. | Pump a small amount of fuel into a glass jar. Allow to stand, and inspect for droplets or a layer of water. | High humidity, extreme temperature changes. | For droplets, use one or two cans of commercial gas line anti-freeze. For a layer of water, the tank must be drained, and the fuel lines blown out with compressed air. |

## Section 6—Engine Compression

See Chapter 3 for service procedures

| | | |
|---|---|---|
| **6.1**—Test engine compression: Remove all spark plugs. Block the throttle wide open. Insert a compression gauge into a spark plug port, crank the engine to obtain the maximum reading, and record. | If compression is within limits on all cylinders: | **7.1** |
| | If gauge reading is extremely low on all cylinders: | **6.2** |
| | If gauge reading is low on one or two cylinders: (If gauge readings are identical and low on two or more adjacent cylinders, the head gasket must be replaced.) | **6.2** |

Checking compression

| | | |
|---|---|---|
| **6.2**—Test engine compression (wet): Squirt approximately 30 cc. of engine oil into each cylinder, and retest per 6.1. | If the readings improve, worn or cracked rings or broken pistons are indicated: | **See Chapter 3** |
| | If the readings do not improve, burned or excessively carboned valves or a jumped timing chain are indicated:<br>NOTE: *A jumped timing chain is often indicated by difficult cranking.* | **7.1** |

## Section 7—Engine Vacuum
See Chapter 3 for service procedures

| Test and Procedure | Results and Indications | Proceed to |
|---|---|---|
| 7.1—Attach a vacuum gauge to the intake manifold beyond the throttle plate. Start the engine, and observe the action of the needle over the range of engine speeds. | See below. | See below |

INDICATION: normal engine in good condition

Proceed to: 8.1

**Normal engine**
Gauge reading: steady, from 17–22 in./Hg.

INDICATION: sticking valves or ignition miss

Proceed to: 9.1, 8.3

**Sticking valves**
Gauge reading: intermittent fluctuation at idle

INDICATION: late ignition or valve timing, low compression, stuck throttle valve, leaking carburetor or manifold gasket

Proceed to: 6.1

**Incorrect valve timing**
Gauge reading: low (10–15 in./Hg) but steady

INDICATION: improper carburetor adjustment or minor intake leak.

Proceed to: 7.2

**Carburetor requires adjustment**
Gauge reading: drifting needle

INDICATION: ignition miss, blown cylinder head gasket, leaking valve or weak valve spring

Proceed to: 8.3, 6.1

**Blown head gasket**
Gauge reading: needle fluctuates as engine speed increases

INDICATION: burnt valve or faulty valve clearance. Needle will fall when defective valve operates

Proceed to: 9.1

**Burnt or leaking valves**
Gauge reading: steady needle, but drops regularly

INDICATION: choked muffler, excessive back pressure in system

Proceed to: 10.1

**Clogged exhaust system**
Gauge reading: gradual drop in reading at idle

INDICATION: worn valve guides

Proceed to: 9.1

**Worn valve guides**
Gauge reading: needle vibrates excessively at idle, but steadies as engine speed increases

White pointer = steady gauge hand              Black pointer = fluctuating gauge hand

| Test and Procedure | Results and Indications | Proceed to |
|---|---|---|
| **7.2**—Attach a vacuum gauge per 7.1, and test for an intake manifold leak. Squirt a small amount of oil around the intake manifold gaskets, carburetor gaskets, plugs and fittings. Observe the action of the vacuum gauge. | If the reading improves, replace the indicated gasket, or seal the indicated fitting or plug:<br><br>If the reading remains low: | **8.1**<br><br>**7.3** |
| **7.3**—Test all vacuum hoses and accessories for leaks as described in 7.2. Also check the carburetor body (dashpots, automatic choke mechanism, throttle shafts) for leaks in the same manner. | If the reading improves, service or replace the offending part(s):<br><br>If the reading remains low: | **8.1**<br><br>**6.1** |

## Section 8—Secondary Electrical System
See Chapter 2 for service procedures

| Test and Procedure | Results and Indications | Proceed to |
|---|---|---|
| **8.1**—Remove the distributor cap and check to make sure that the rotor turns when the engine is cranked. Visually inspect the distributor components. | Clean, tighten or replace any components which appear defective. | **8.2** |
| **8.2**—Connect a timing light (per manufacturer's recommendation) and check the dynamic ignition timing. Disconnect and plug the vacuum hose(s) to the distributor if specified, start the engine, and observe the timing marks at the specified engine speed. | If the timing is not correct, adjust to specifications by rotating the distributor in the engine: (Advance timing by rotating distributor opposite normal direction of rotor rotation, retard timing by rotating distributor in same direction as rotor rotation.) | **8.3** |
| **8.3**—Check the operation of the distributor advance mechanism(s): To test the mechanical advance, disconnect the vacuum lines from the distributor advance unit and observe the timing marks with a timing light as the engine speed is increased from idle. If the mark moves smoothly, without hesitation, it may be assumed that the mechanical advance is functioning properly. To test vacuum advance and/or retard systems, alternately crimp and release the vacuum line, and observe the timing mark for movement. If movement is noted, the system is operating. | If the systems are functioning:<br><br>If the systems are not functioning, remove the distributor, and test on a distributor tester: | **8.4**<br><br>**8.4** |
| **8.4**—Locate an ignition miss: With the engine running, remove each spark plug wire, one at a time, until one is found that doesn't cause the engine to roughen and slow down. | When the missing cylinder is identified: | **4.1** |

# Section 9—Valve Train
See Chapter 3 for service procedures

| Test and Procedure | Results and Indications | Proceed to |
|---|---|---|
| **9.1**—Evaluate the valve train: Remove the valve cover, and ensure that the valves are adjusted to specifications. A mechanic's stethoscope may be used to aid in the diagnosis of the valve train. By pushing the probe on or near push rods or rockers, valve noise often can be isolated. A timing light also may be used to diagnose valve problems. Connect the light according to manufacturer's recommendations, and start the engine. Vary the firing moment of the light by increasing the engine speed (and therefore the ignition advance), and moving the trigger from cylinder to cylinder. Observe the movement of each valve. | Sticking valves or erratic valve train motion can be observed with the timing light. The cylinder head must be disassembled for repairs. | **See Chapter 3** |
| **9.2**—Check the valve timing: Locate top dead center of the No. 1 piston, and install a degree wheel or tape on the crankshaft pulley or damper with zero corresponding to an index mark on the engine. Rotate the crankshaft in its direction of rotation, and observe the opening of the No. 1 cylinder intake valve. The opening should correspond with the correct mark on the degree wheel according to specifications. | If the timing is not correct, the timing cover must be removed for further investigation. | **See Chapter 3** |

# Section 10—Exhaust System

| Test and Procedure | Results and Indications | Proceed to |
|---|---|---|
| **10.1**—Determine whether the exhaust manifold heat control valve is operating: Operate the valve by hand to determine whether it is free to move. If the valve is free, run the engine to operating temperature and observe the action of the valve, to ensure that it is opening. | If the valve sticks, spray it with a suitable solvent, open and close the valve to free it, and retest. | |
| | If the valve functions properly: | **10.2** |
| | If the valve does not free, or does not operate, replace the valve: | **10.2** |
| **10.2**—Ensure that there are no exhaust restrictions: Visually inspect the exhaust system for kinks, dents, or crushing. Also note that gases are flowing freely from the tailpipe at all engine speeds, indicating no restriction in the muffler or resonator. | Replace any damaged portion of the system: | **11.1** |

# Section 11—Cooling System
See Chapter 3 for service procedures

| Test and Procedure | Results and Indications | Proceed to |
|---|---|---|
| **11.1**—Visually inspect the fan belt for glazing, cracks, and fraying, and replace if necessary. Tighten the belt so that the longest span has approximately ½″ play at its midpoint under thumb pressure (see Chapter 1). | Replace or tighten the fan belt as necessary: | **11.2** |

**Checking belt tension**

| Test and Procedure | Results and Indications | Proceed to |
|---|---|---|
| **11.2**—Check the fluid level of the cooling system. | If full or slightly low, fill as necessary: | **11.5** |
| | If extremely low: | **11.3** |
| **11.3**—Visually inspect the external portions of the cooling system (radiator, radiator hoses, thermostat elbow, water pump seals, heater hoses, etc.) for leaks. If none are found, pressurize the cooling system to 14–15 psi. | If cooling system holds the pressure: | **11.5** |
| | If cooling system loses pressure rapidly, reinspect external parts of the system for leaks under pressure. If none are found, check dipstick for coolant in crankcase. If no coolant is present, but pressure loss continues: | **11.4** |
| | If coolant is evident in crankcase, remove cylinder head(s), and check gasket(s). If gaskets are intact, block and cylinder head(s) should be checked for cracks or holes. If the gasket(s) is blown, replace, and purge the crankcase of coolant: | **12.6** |
| | NOTE: *Occasionally, due to atmospheric and driving conditions, condensation of water can occur in the crankcase. This causes the oil to appear milky white. To remedy, run the engine until hot, and change the oil and oil filter.* | |
| **11.4**—Check for combustion leaks into the cooling system: Pressurize the cooling system as above. Start the engine, and observe the pressure gauge. If the needle fluctuates, remove each spark plug wire, one at a time, noting which cylinder(s) reduce or eliminate the fluctuation. | Cylinders which reduce or eliminate the fluctuation, when the spark plug wire is removed, are leaking into the cooling system. Replace the head gasket on the affected cylinder bank(s). | |

**Pressurizing the cooling system**

| Test and Procedure | Results and Indications | Proceed to |
|---|---|---|
| **11.5**—Check the radiator pressure cap: Attach a radiator pressure tester to the radiator cap (wet the seal prior to installation). Quickly pump up the pressure, noting the point at which the cap releases. | If the cap releases within ± 1 psi of the specified rating, it is operating properly: | **11.6** |
| | If the cap releases at more than ± 1 psi of the specified rating, it should be replaced: | **11.6** |

Checking radiator pressure cap

| Test and Procedure | Results and Indications | Proceed to |
|---|---|---|
| **11.6**—Test the thermostat: Start the engine cold, remove the radiator cap, and insert a thermometer into the radiator. Allow the engine to idle. After a short while, there will be a sudden, rapid increase in coolant temperature. The temperature at which this sharp rise stops is the thermostat opening temperature. | If the thermostat opens at or about the specified temperature: | **11.7** |
| | If the temperature doesn't increase: (If the temperature increases slowly and gradually, replace the thermostat.) | **11.7** |
| **11.7**—Check the water pump: Remove the thermostat elbow and the thermostat, disconnect the coil high tension lead (to prevent starting), and crank the engine momentarily. | If coolant flows, replace the thermostat and retest per 11.6: | **11.6** |
| | If coolant doesn't flow, reverse flush the cooling system to alleviate any blockage that might exist. If system is not blocked, and coolant will not flow, replace the water pump. | |

## Section 12—Lubrication
See Chapter 3 for service procedures

| Test and Procedure | Results and Indications | Proceed to |
|---|---|---|
| **12.1**—Check the oil pressure gauge or warning light: If the gauge shows low pressure, or the light is on for no obvious reason, remove the oil pressure sender. Install an accurate oil pressure gauge and run the engine momentarily. | If oil pressure builds normally, run engine for a few moments to determine that it is functioning normally, and replace the sender. | — |
| | If the pressure remains low: | **12.2** |
| | If the pressure surges: | **12.3** |
| | If the oil pressure is zero: | **12.3** |
| **12.2**—Visually inspect the oil: If the oil is watery or very thin, milky, or foamy, replace the oil and oil filter. | If the oil is normal: | **12.3** |
| | If after replacing oil the pressure remains low: | **12.3** |
| | If after replacing oil the pressure becomes normal: | — |

| Test and Procedure | Results and Indications | Proceed to |
|---|---|---|
| **12.3**—Inspect the oil pressure relief valve and spring, to ensure that it is not sticking or stuck. Remove and thoroughly clean the valve, spring, and the valve body. | If the oil pressure improves:<br>If no improvement is noted: | —<br><br>**12.4** |
| **12.4**—Check to ensure that the oil pump is not cavitating (sucking air instead of oil): See that the crankcase is neither over nor underfull, and that the pickup in the sump is in the proper position and free from sludge. | Fill or drain the crankcase to the proper capacity, and clean the pickup screen in solvent if necessary. If no improvement is noted: | **12.5** |
| **12.5**—Inspect the oil pump drive and the oil pump: | If the pump drive or the oil pump appear to be defective, service as necessary and retest per 12.1:<br><br>If the pump drive and pump appear to be operating normally, the engine should be disassembled to determine where blockage exists: | **12.1**<br><br>**See Chapter 3** |
| **12.6**—Purge the engine of ethylene glycol coolant: Completely drain the crankcase and the oil filter. Obtain a commercial butyl cellosolve base solvent, designated for this purpose, and follow the instructions precisely. Following this, install a new oil filter and refill the crankcase with the proper weight oil. The next oil and filter change should follow shortly thereafter (1000 miles). | | |

## TROUBLESHOOTING EMISSION CONTROL SYSTEMS

See Chapter 4 for procedures applicable to individual emission control systems used on specific combinations of engine/transmission/model.

## TROUBLESHOOTING THE CARBURETOR

See Chapter 4 for service procedures

Carburetor problems cannot be effectively isolated unless all other engine systems (particularly ignition and emission) are functioning properly and the engine is properly tuned.

| Condition | Possible Cause |
|---|---|
| Engine cranks, but does not start | 1. Improper starting procedure<br>2. No fuel in tank<br>3. Clogged fuel line or filter<br>4. Defective fuel pump<br>5. Choke valve not closing properly<br>6. Engine flooded<br>7. Choke valve not unloading<br>8. Throttle linkage not making full travel<br>9. Stuck needle or float<br>10. Leaking float needle or seat<br>11. Improper float adjustment |
| Engine stalls. | 1. Improperly adjusted idle speed or mixture<br>**Engine hot**<br>2. Improperly adjusted dashpot<br>3. Defective or improperly adjusted solenoid<br>4. Incorrect fuel level in fuel bowl<br>5. Fuel pump pressure too high<br>6. Leaking float needle seat<br>7. Secondary throttle valve stuck open<br>8. Air or fuel leaks<br>9. Idle air bleeds plugged or missing<br>10. Idle passages plugged<br>**Engine Cold**<br>11. Incorrectly adjusted choke<br>12. Improperly adjusted fast idle speed<br>13. Air leaks<br>14. Plugged idle or idle air passages<br>15. Stuck choke valve or binding linkage<br>16. Stuck secondary throttle valves<br>17. Engine flooding—high fuel level<br>18. Leaking or misaligned float |
| Engine hesitates on acceleration | 1. Clogged fuel filter<br>2. Leaking fuel pump diaphragm<br>3. Low fuel pump pressure<br>4. Secondary throttle valves stuck, bent or misadjusted<br>5. Sticking or binding air valve<br>6. Defective accelerator pump<br>7. Vacuum leaks<br>8. Clogged air filter<br>9. Incorrect choke adjustment (engine cold) |
| Engine feels sluggish or flat on acceleration | 1. Improperly adjusted idle speed or mixture<br>2. Clogged fuel filter<br>3. Defective accelerator pump<br>4. Dirty, plugged or incorrect main metering jets<br>5. Bent or sticking main metering rods<br>6. Sticking throttle valves<br>7. Stuck heat riser<br>8. Binding or stuck air valve<br>9. Dirty, plugged or incorrect secondary jets<br>10. Bent or sticking secondary metering rods.<br>11. Throttle body or manifold heat passages plugged<br>12. Improperly adjusted choke or choke vacuum break. |
| Carburetor floods | 1. Defective fuel pump. Pressure too high.<br>2. Stuck choke valve<br>3. Dirty, worn or damaged float or needle valve/seat<br>4. Incorrect float/fuel level<br>5. Leaking float bowl |

| Condition | Possible Cause |
|---|---|
| Engine idles roughly and stalls | 1. Incorrect idle speed<br>2. Clogged fuel filter<br>3. Dirt in fuel system or carburetor<br>4. Loose carburetor screws or attaching bolts<br>5. Broken carburetor gaskets<br>6. Air leaks<br>7. Dirty carburetor<br>8. Worn idle mixture needles<br>9. Throttle valves stuck open<br>10. Incorrectly adjusted float or fuel level<br>11. Clogged air filter |
| Engine runs unevenly or surges | 1. Defective fuel pump<br>2. Dirty or clogged fuel filter<br>3. Plugged, loose or incorrect main metering jets or rods<br>4. Air leaks<br>5. Bent or sticking main metering rods<br>6. Stuck power piston<br>7. Incorrect float adjustment<br>8. Incorrect idle speed or mixture<br>9. Dirty or plugged idle system passages<br>10. Hard, brittle or broken gaskets<br>11. Loose attaching or mounting screws<br>12. Stuck or misaligned secondary throttle valves |
| Poor fuel economy | 1. Poor driving habits<br>2. Stuck choke valve<br>3. Binding choke linkage<br>4. Stuck heat riser<br>5. Incorrect idle mixture<br>6. Defective accelerator pump<br>7. Air leaks<br>8. Plugged, loose or incorrect main metering jets<br>9. Improperly adjusted float or fuel level<br>10. Bent, misaligned or fuel-clogged float<br>11. Leaking float needle seat<br>12. Fuel leak<br>13. Accelerator pump discharge ball not seating properly<br>14. Incorrect main jets |
| Engine lacks high speed performance or power | 1. Incorrect throttle linkage adjustment<br>2. Stuck or binding power piston<br>3. Defective accelerator pump<br>4. Air leaks<br>5. Incorrect float setting or fuel level<br>6. Dirty, plugged, worn or incorrect main metering jets or rods<br>7. Binding or sticking air valve<br>8. Brittle or cracked gaskets<br>9. Bent, incorrect or improperly adjusted secondary metering rods<br>10. Clogged fuel filter<br>11. Clogged air filter<br>12. Defective fuel pump |

# TROUBLESHOOTING FUEL INJECTION PROBLEMS

Each fuel injection system has its own unique components and test procedures, for which it is impossible to generalize. Refer to Chapter 4 of this Repair & Tune-Up Guide for specific test and repair procedures, if the vehicle is equipped with fuel injection.

# TROUBLESHOOTING ELECTRICAL PROBLEMS

See Chapter 5 for service procedures

For any electrical system to operate, it must make a complete circuit. This simply means that the power flow from the battery must make a complete circle. When an electrical component is operating, power flows from the battery to the component, passes through the component causing it to perform its function (lighting a light bulb), and then returns to the battery through the ground of the circuit. This ground is usually (but not always) the metal part of the car or truck on which the electrical component is mounted.

Perhaps the easiest way to visualize this is to think of connecting a light bulb with two wires attached to it to the battery. If one of the two wires attached to the light bulb were attached to the negative post of the battery and the other were attached to the positive post of the battery, you would have a complete circuit. Current from the battery would flow to the light bulb, causing it to light, and return to the negative post of the battery.

The normal automotive circuit differs from this simple example in two ways. First, instead of having a return wire from the bulb to the battery, the light bulb returns the current to the battery through the chassis of the vehicle. Since the negative battery cable is attached to the chassis and the chassis is made of electrically conductive metal, the chassis of the vehicle can serve as a ground wire to complete the circuit. Secondly, most automotive circuits contain switches to turn components on and off as required.

*Every complete circuit from a power source must include a component which is using the power from the power source.* If you were to disconnect the light bulb from the wires and touch the two wires together (don't do this) the power supply wire to the component would be grounded before the normal ground connection for the circuit.

Because grounding a wire from a power source makes a complete circuit—less the required component to use the power—this phenomenon is called a short circuit. Common causes are: broken insulation (exposing the metal wire to a metal part of the car or truck), or a shorted switch.

Some electrical components which require a large amount of current to operate also have a relay in their circuit. Since these circuits carry a large amount of current, the thickness of the wire in the circuit (gauge size) is also greater. If this large wire were connected from the component to the control switch on the instrument panel, and then back to the component, a voltage drop would occur in the circuit. To prevent this potential drop in voltage, an electromagnetic switch (relay) is used. The large wires in the circuit are connected from the battery to one side of the relay, and from the opposite side of the relay to the component. The relay is normally open, preventing current from passing through the circuit. An additional, smaller, wire is connected from the relay to the control switch for the circuit. When the control switch is turned on, it grounds the smaller wire from the relay and completes the circuit. This closes the relay and allows current to flow from the battery to the component. The horn, headlight, and starter circuits are three which use relays.

It is possible for larger surges of current to pass through the electrical system of your car or truck. If this surge of current were to reach an electrical component, it could burn it out. To prevent this, fuses, circuit breakers or fusible links are connected into the current supply wires of most of the major electrical systems. When an electrical current of excessive power passes through the component's fuse, the fuse blows out and breaks the circuit, saving the component from destruction.

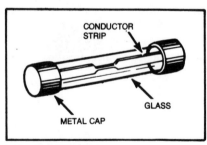

**Typical automotive fuse**

A circuit breaker is basically a self-repairing fuse. The circuit breaker opens the circuit the same way a fuse does. However, when either the short is removed from the circuit or the surge subsides, the circuit breaker resets itself and does not have to be replaced as a fuse does.

A fuse link is a wire that acts as a fuse. It is normally connected between the starter relay and the main wiring harness. This connection is usually under the hood. The fuse link (if installed) protects all the

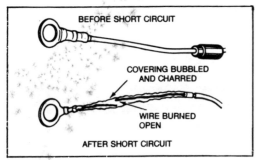

Most fusible links show a charred, melted insulation when they burn out

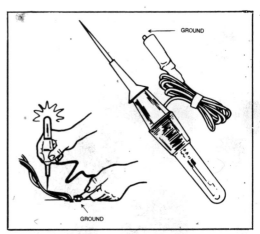

The test light will show the presence of current when touched to a hot wire and grounded at the other end

chassis electrical components, and is the probable cause of trouble when none of the electrical components function, unless the battery is disconnected or dead.

Electrical problems generally fall into one of three areas:

1. The component that is not functioning is not receiving current.

2. The component itself is not functioning.

3. The component is not properly grounded.

The electrical system can be checked with a test light and a jumper wire. A test light is a device that looks like a pointed screwdriver with a wire attached to it and has a light bulb in its handle. A jumper wire is a piece of insulated wire with an alligator clip attached to each end.

If a component is not working, you must follow a systematic plan to determine which of the three causes is the villain.

1. Turn on the switch that controls the inoperable component.

2. Disconnect the power supply wire from the component.

3. Attach the ground wire on the test light to a good metal ground.

4. Touch the probe end of the test light to the end of the power supply wire that was disconnected from the component. If the component is receiving current, the test light will go on.

**NOTE:** *Some components work only when the ignition switch is turned on.*

If the test light does not go on, then the problem is in the circuit between the battery and the component. This includes all the switches, fuses, and relays in the system. Follow the wire that runs back to the battery. The problem is an open circuit between the

battery and the component. If the fuse is blown and, when replaced, immediately blows again, there is a short circuit in the system which must be located and repaired. If there is a switch in the system, bypass it with a jumper wire. This is done by connecting one end of the jumper wire to the power supply wire into the switch and the other end of the jumper wire to the wire coming out of the switch. If the test light lights with the jumper wire installed, the switch or whatever was bypassed is defective.

**NOTE:** *Never substitute the jumper wire for the component, since it is required to use the power from the power source.*

5. If the bulb in the test light goes on, then the current is getting to the component that is not working. This eliminates the first of the three possible causes. Connect the power supply wire and connect a jumper wire from the component to a good metal ground. Do this with the switch which controls the component turned on, and also the ignition switch turned on if it is required for the component to work. If the component works with the jumper wire installed, then it has a bad ground. This is usually caused by the metal area on which the component mounts to the chassis being coated with some type of foreign matter.

6. If neither test located the source of the trouble, then the component itself is defective. Remember that for any electrical system to work, all connections must be clean and tight.

## Troubleshooting Basic Turn Signal and Flasher Problems

See Chapter 5 for service procedures

Most problems in the turn signals or flasher system can be reduced to defective flashers or bulbs, which are easily replaced. Occasionally, the turn signal switch will prove defective.

F = Front      R = Rear      ● = Lights off      ○ = Lights on

| Condition | Possible Cause |
|---|---|
| Turn signals light, but do not flash 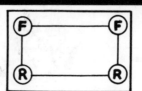 | Defective flasher |
| No turn signals light on either side 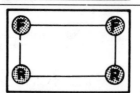 | Blown fuse. Replace if defective. Defective flasher. Check by substitution. Open circuit, short circuit or poor ground. |
| Both turn signals on one side don't work 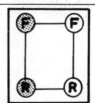 | Bad bulbs. Bad ground in both (or either) housings. |
| One turn signal light on one side doesn't work 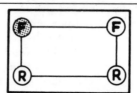 | Defective bulb. Corrosion in socket. Clean contacts. Poor ground at socket. |
| Turn signal flashes too fast or too slowly 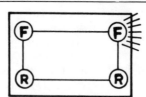 | Check any bulb on the side flashing too fast. A heavy-duty bulb is probably installed in place of a regular bulb. Check the bulb flashing too slowly. A standard bulb was probably installed in place of a heavy-duty bulb. Loose connections or corrosion at the bulb socket. |
| Indicator lights don't work in either direction  | Check if the turn signals are working. Check the dash indicator lights. Check the flasher by substitution. |
| One indicator light doesn't light  | On systems with one dash indicator: See if the lights work on the same side. Often the filaments have been reversed in systems combining stoplights with tail-lights and turn signals. Check the flasher by substitution. On systems with two indicators: Check the bulbs on the same side. Check the indicator light bulb. Check the flasher by substitution. |

## Troubleshooting Lighting Problems

See Chapter 5 for service procedures

| Condition | Possible Cause |
|---|---|
| One or more lights don't work, but others do | 1. Defective bulb(s)<br>2. Blown fuse(s)<br>3. Dirty fuse clips or light sockets<br>4. Poor ground circuit |
| Lights burn out quickly | 1. Incorrect voltage regulator setting or defective regulator<br>2. Poor battery/alternator connections |
| Lights go dim | 1. Low/discharged battery<br>2. Alternator not charging.<br>3. Corroded sockets or connections<br>4. Low voltage output |
| Lights flicker | 1. Loose connection<br>2. Poor ground. (Run ground wire from light housing to frame)<br>3. Circuit breaker operating (short circuit) |
| Lights "flare"—Some flare is normal on acceleration—If excessive, see "Lights Burn Out Quickly" | High voltage setting |
| Lights glare—approaching drivers are blinded | 1. Lights adjusted too high<br>2. Rear springs or shocks sagging<br>3. Rear tires soft |

## Troubleshooting Dash Gauge Problems

Most problems can be traced to a defective sending unit or faulty wiring. Occasionally, the gauge itself is at fault. See Chapter 5 for service procedures.

| Condition | Possible Cause |
|---|---|

### COOLANT TEMPERATURE GAUGE

| | |
|---|---|
| Gauge reads erratically or not at all | 1. Loose or dirty connections<br>2. Defective sending unit.<br>3. Defective gauge. To test a bi-metal gauge, remove the wire from the sending unit. Ground the wire for an instant. If the gauge registers, replace the sending unit. To test a magnetic gauge, disconnect the wire at the sending unit. With ignition ON gauge should register COLD. Ground the wire; gauge should register HOT. |

### AMMETER GAUGE—TURN HEADLIGHTS ON (DO NOT START ENGINE). NOTE REACTION

| | |
|---|---|
| Ammeter shows charge<br>Ammeter shows discharge<br>Ammeter does not move | 1. Connections reversed on gauge<br>2. Ammeter is OK<br>3. Loose connections or faulty wiring<br>4. Defective gauge |

| Condition | Possible Cause |
|---|---|

## OIL PRESSURE GAUGE

| | |
|---|---|
| Gauge does not register or is inaccurate | 1. On mechanical gauge, Bourdon tube may be bent or kinked.<br>2. Low oil pressure. Remove sending unit. Idle the engine briefly. If no oil flows from sending unit hole, problem is in engine.<br>3. Defective gauge. Remove the wire from the sending unit and ground it for an instant with the ignition ON. A good gauge will go to the top of the scale.<br>4. Defective wiring. Check the wiring to the gauge. If it's OK and the gauge doesn't register when grounded, replace the gauge.<br>5. Defective sending unit. |

## ALL GAUGES

| | |
|---|---|
| All gauges do not operate<br><br>All gauges read low or erratically<br>All gauges pegged | 1. Blown fuse<br>2. Defective instrument regulator<br>3. Defective or dirty instrument voltage regulator<br>4. Loss of ground between instrument voltage regulator and frame<br>5. Defective instrument regulator |

## WARNING LIGHTS

| | |
|---|---|
| Light(s) do not come on when ignition is ON, but engine is not started<br><br><br><br>Light comes on with engine running | 1. Defective bulb<br>2. Defective wire<br>3. Defective sending unit. Disconnect the wire from the sending unit and ground it. Replace the sending unit if the light comes on with the ignition ON.<br>4. Problem in individual system<br>5. Defective sending unit |

## Troubleshooting Clutch Problems

It is false economy to replace individual clutch components. The pressure plate, clutch plate and throwout bearing should be replaced as a set, and the flywheel face inspected, whenever the clutch is overhauled. See Chapter 6 for service procedures.

| Condition | Possible Cause |
|---|---|
| Clutch chatter | 1. Grease on driven plate (disc) facing<br>2. Binding clutch linkage or cable<br>3. Loose, damaged facings on driven plate (disc)<br>4. Engine mounts loose<br>5. Incorrect height adjustment of pressure plate release levers<br>6. Clutch housing or housing to transmission adapter misalignment<br>7. Loose driven plate hub |
| Clutch grabbing | 1. Oil, grease on driven plate (disc) facing<br>2. Broken pressure plate<br>3. Warped or binding driven plate. Driven plate binding on clutch shaft |
| Clutch slips | 1. Lack of lubrication in clutch linkage or cable (linkage or cable binds, causes incomplete engagement)<br>2. Incorrect pedal, or linkage adjustment<br>3. Broken pressure plate springs<br>4. Weak pressure plate springs<br>5. Grease on driven plate facings (disc) |

## Troubleshooting Clutch Problems (cont.)

| Condition | Possible Cause |
|---|---|
| Incomplete clutch release | 1. Incorrect pedal or linkage adjustment or linkage or cable binding<br>2. Incorrect height adjustment on pressure plate release levers<br>3. Loose, broken facings on driven plate (disc)<br>4. Bent, dished, warped driven plate caused by overheating |
| Grinding, whirring grating noise when pedal is depressed | 1. Worn or defective throwout bearing<br>2. Starter drive teeth contacting flywheel ring gear teeth. Look for milled or polished teeth on ring gear. |
| Squeal, howl, trumpeting noise when pedal is being released (occurs during first inch to inch and one-half of pedal travel) | Pilot bushing worn or lack of lubricant. If bushing appears OK, polish bushing with emery cloth, soak lube wick in oil, lube bushing with oil, apply film of chassis grease to clutch shaft pilot hub, reassemble. NOTE: Bushing wear may be due to misalignment of clutch housing or housing to transmission adapter |
| Vibration or clutch pedal pulsation with clutch disengaged (pedal fully depressed) | 1. Worn or defective engine transmission mounts<br>2. Flywheel run out. (Flywheel run out at face not to exceed 0.005″)<br>3. Damaged or defective clutch components |

## Troubleshooting Manual Transmission Problems
### See Chapter 6 for service procedures

| Condition | Possible Cause |
|---|---|
| Transmission jumps out of gear | 1. Misalignment of transmission case or clutch housing.<br>2. Worn pilot bearing in crankshaft.<br>3. Bent transmission shaft.<br>4. Worn high speed sliding gear.<br>5. Worn teeth or end-play in clutch shaft.<br>6. Insufficient spring tension on shifter rail plunger.<br>7. Bent or loose shifter fork.<br>8. Gears not engaging completely.<br>9. Loose or worn bearings on clutch shaft or mainshaft.<br>10. Worn gear teeth.<br>11. Worn or damaged detent balls. |
| Transmission sticks in gear | 1. Clutch not releasing fully.<br>2. Burred or battered teeth on clutch shaft, or sliding sleeve.<br>3. Burred or battered transmission mainshaft.<br>4. Frozen synchronizing clutch.<br>5. Stuck shifter rail plunger.<br>6. Gearshift lever twisting and binding shifter rail.<br>7. Battered teeth on high speed sliding gear or on sleeve.<br>8. Improper lubrication, or lack of lubrication.<br>9. Corroded transmission parts.<br>10. Defective mainshaft pilot bearing.<br>11. Locked gear bearings will give same effect as stuck in gear. |
| Transmission gears will not synchronize | 1. Binding pilot bearing on mainshaft, will synchronize in high gear only.<br>2. Clutch not releasing fully.<br>3. Detent spring weak or broken.<br>4. Weak or broken springs under balls in sliding gear sleeve.<br>5. Binding bearing on clutch shaft, or binding countershaft.<br>6. Binding pilot bearing in crankshaft.<br>7. Badly worn gear teeth.<br>8. Improper lubrication.<br>9. Constant mesh gear not turning freely on transmission mainshaft. Will synchronize in that gear only. |

| Condition | Possible Cause |
|---|---|
| Gears spinning when shifting into gear from neutral | 1. Clutch not releasing fully.<br>2. In some cases an extremely light lubricant in transmission will cause gears to continue to spin for a short time after clutch is released.<br>3. Binding pilot bearing in crankshaft. |
| Transmission noisy in all gears | 1. Insufficient lubricant, or improper lubricant.<br>2. Worn countergear bearings.<br>3. Worn or damaged main drive gear or countergear.<br>4. Damaged main drive gear or mainshaft bearings.<br>5. Worn or damaged countergear anti-lash plate. |
| Transmission noisy in neutral only | 1. Damaged main drive gear bearing.<br>2. Damaged or loose mainshaft pilot bearing.<br>3. Worn or damaged countergear anti-lash plate.<br>4. Worn countergear bearings. |
| Transmission noisy in one gear only | 1. Damaged or worn constant mesh gears.<br>2. Worn or damaged countergear bearings.<br>3. Damaged or worn synchronizer. |
| Transmission noisy in reverse only | 1. Worn or damaged reverse idler gear or idler bushing.<br>2. Worn or damaged mainshaft reverse gear.<br>3. Worn or damaged reverse countergear.<br>4. Damaged shift mechanism. |

# TROUBLESHOOTING AUTOMATIC TRANSMISSION PROBLEMS

Keeping alert to changes in the operating characteristics of the transmission (changing shift points, noises, etc.) can prevent small problems from becoming large ones. If the problem cannot be traced to loose bolts, fluid level, misadjusted linkage, clogged filters or similar problems, you should probably seek professional service.

## Transmission Fluid Indications

The appearance and odor of the transmission fluid can give valuable clues to the overall condition of the transmission. Always note the appearance of the fluid when you check the fluid level or change the fluid. Rub a small amount of fluid between your fingers to feel for grit and smell the fluid on the dipstick.

| If the fluid appears: | It indicates: |
|---|---|
| Clear and red colored | Normal operation |
| Discolored (extremely dark red or brownish) or smells burned | Band or clutch pack failure, usually caused by an overheated transmission. Hauling very heavy loads with insufficient power or failure to change the fluid often result in overheating.<br>Do not confuse this appearance with newer fluids that have a darker red color and a strong odor (though not a burned odor). |
| Foamy or aerated (light in color and full of bubbles) | 1. The level is too high (gear train is churning oil)<br>2. An internal air leak (air is mixing with the fluid). Have the transmission checked professionally. |
| Solid residue in the fluid | Defective bands, clutch pack or bearings. Bits of band material or metal abrasives are clinging to the dipstick. Have the transmission checked professionally. |
| Varnish coating on the dipstick | The transmission fluid is overheating |

# TROUBLESHOOTING DRIVE AXLE PROBLEMS

First, determine when the noise is most noticeable.

Drive Noise: Produced under vehicle acceleration.

Coast Noise: Produced while coasting with a closed throttle.

Float Noise: Occurs while maintaining constant speed (just enough to keep speed constant) on a level road.

## External Noise Elimination

It is advisable to make a thorough road test to determine whether the noise originates in the rear axle or whether it originates from the tires, engine, transmission, wheel bearings or road surface. Noise originating from other places cannot be corrected by servicing the rear axle.

### ROAD NOISE

Brick or rough surfaced concrete roads produce noises that seem to come from the rear axle. Road noise is usually identical in Drive or Coast and driving on a different type of road will tell whether the road is the problem.

### TIRE NOISE

Tire noise can be mistaken as rear axle noise, even though the tires on the front are at fault. Snow tread and mud tread tires or tires worn unevenly will frequently cause vibrations which seem to originate elsewhere; *temporarily, and for test purposes only,* inflate the tires to 40–50 lbs. This will significantly alter the noise produced by the tires, but will not alter noise from the rear axle. Noises from the rear axle will normally cease at speeds below 30 mph on coast, while tire noise will continue at lower tone as speed is decreased. The rear axle noise will usually change from drive conditions to coast conditions, while tire noise will not. Do not forget to lower the tire pressure to normal after the test is complete.

### ENGINE/TRANSMISSION NOISE

Determine at what speed the noise is most pronounced, then stop in a quiet place. With the transmission in Neutral, run the engine through speeds corresponding to road speeds where the noise was noticed. Noises produced with the vehicle standing still are coming from the engine or transmission.

### FRONT WHEEL BEARINGS

Front wheel bearing noises, sometimes confused with rear axle noises, will not change when comparing drive and coast conditions. While holding the speed steady, lightly apply the footbrake. This will often cause wheel bearing noise to lessen, as some of the weight is taken off the bearing. Front wheel bearings are easily checked by jacking up the wheels and spinning the wheels. Shaking the wheels will also determine if the wheel bearings are excessively loose.

### REAR AXLE NOISES

Eliminating other possible sources can narrow the cause to the rear axle, which normally produces noise from worn gears or bearings. Gear noises tend to peak in a narrow speed range, while bearing noises will usually vary in pitch with engine speeds.

## Noise Diagnosis

| The Noise Is: | Most Probably Produced By: |
|---|---|
| 1. Identical under Drive or Coast | Road surface, tires or front wheel bearings |
| 2. Different depending on road surface | Road surface or tires |
| 3. Lower as speed is lowered | Tires |
| 4. Similar when standing or moving | Engine or transmission |
| 5. A vibration | Unbalanced tires, rear wheel bearing, unbalanced driveshaft or worn U-joint |
| 6. A knock or click about every two tire revolutions | Rear wheel bearing |
| 7. Most pronounced on turns | Damaged differential gears |
| 8. A steady low-pitched whirring or scraping, starting at low speeds | Damaged or worn pinion bearing |
| 9. A chattering vibration on turns | Wrong differential lubricant or worn clutch plates (limited slip rear axle) |
| 10. Noticed only in Drive, Coast or Float conditions | Worn ring gear and/or pinion gear |

## Troubleshooting Steering & Suspension Problems

| Condition | Possible Cause |
|---|---|
| Hard steering (wheel is hard to turn) | 1. Improper tire pressure<br>2. Loose or glazed pump drive belt<br>3. Low or incorrect fluid<br>4. Loose, bent or poorly lubricated front end parts<br>5. Improper front end alignment (excessive caster)<br>6. Bind in steering column or linkage<br>7. Kinked hydraulic hose<br>8. Air in hydraulic system<br>9. Low pump output or leaks in system<br>10. Obstruction in lines<br>11. Pump valves sticking or out of adjustment<br>12. Incorrect wheel alignment |
| Loose steering (too much play in steering wheel) | 1. Loose wheel bearings<br>2. Faulty shocks<br>3. Worn linkage or suspension components<br>4. Loose steering gear mounting or linkage points<br>5. Steering mechanism worn or improperly adjusted<br>6. Valve spool improperly adjusted<br>7. Worn ball joints, tie-rod ends, etc. |
| Veers or wanders (pulls to one side with hands off steering wheel) | 1. Improper tire pressure<br>2. Improper front end alignment<br>3. Dragging or improperly adjusted brakes<br>4. Bent frame<br>5. Improper rear end alignment<br>6. Faulty shocks or springs<br>7. Loose or bent front end components<br>8. Play in Pitman arm<br>9. Steering gear mountings loose<br>10. Loose wheel bearings<br>11. Binding Pitman arm<br>12. Spool valve sticking or improperly adjusted<br>13. Worn ball joints |
| Wheel oscillation or vibration transmitted through steering wheel | 1. Low or uneven tire pressure<br>2. Loose wheel bearings<br>3. Improper front end alignment<br>4. Bent spindle<br>5. Worn, bent or broken front end components<br>6. Tires out of round or out of balance<br>7. Excessive lateral runout in disc brake rotor<br>8. Loose or bent shock absorber or strut |
| Noises (see also "Troubleshooting Drive Axle Problems") | 1. Loose belts<br>2. Low fluid, air in system<br>3. Foreign matter in system<br>4. Improper lubrication<br>5. Interference or chafing in linkage<br>6. Steering gear mountings loose<br>7. Incorrect adjustment or wear in gear box<br>8. Faulty valves or wear in pump<br>9. Kinked hydraulic lines<br>10. Worn wheel bearings |
| Poor return of steering | 1. Over-inflated tires<br>2. Improperly aligned front end (excessive caster)<br>3. Binding in steering column<br>4. No lubrication in front end<br>5. Steering gear adjusted too tight |
| Uneven tire wear (see "How To Read Tire Wear") | 1. Incorrect tire pressure<br>2. Improperly aligned front end<br>3. Tires out-of-balance<br>4. Bent or worn suspension parts |

# HOW TO READ TIRE WEAR

The way your tires wear is a good indicator of other parts of the suspension. Abnormal wear patterns are often caused by the need for simple tire maintenance, or for front end alignment.

Excessive wear at the center of the tread indicates that the air pressure in the tire is consistently too high. The tire is riding on the center of the tread and wearing it prematurely. Occasionally, this wear pattern can result from outrageously wide tires on narrow rims. The cure for this is to replace either the tires or the wheels.

This type of wear usually results from consistent under-inflation. When a tire is under-inflated, there is too much contact with the road by the outer treads, which wear prematurely. When this type of wear occurs, and the tire pressure is known to be consistently correct, a bent or worn steering component or the need for wheel alignment could be indicated.

Feathering is a condition when the edge of each tread rib develops a slightly rounded edge on one side and a sharp edge on the other. By running your hand over the tire, you can usually feel the sharper edges before you'll be able to see them. The most common causes of feathering are incorrect toe-in setting or deteriorated bushings in the front suspension.

When an inner or outer rib wears faster than the rest of the tire, the need for wheel alignment is indicated. There is excessive camber in the front suspension, causing the wheel to lean too much putting excessive load on one side of the tire. Misalignment could also be due to sagging springs, worn ball joints, or worn control arm bushings. Be sure the vehicle is loaded the way it's normally driven when you have the wheels aligned.

Cups or scalloped dips appearing around the edge of the tread almost always indicate worn (sometimes bent) suspension parts. Adjustment of wheel alignment alone will seldom cure the problem. Any worn component that connects the wheel to the suspension can cause this type of wear. Occasionally, wheels that are out of balance will wear like this, but wheel imbalance usually shows up as bald spots between the outside edges and center of the tread.

Second-rib wear is usually found only in radial tires, and appears where the steel belts end in relation to the tread. It can be kept to a minimum by paying careful attention to tire pressure and frequently rotating the tires. This is often considered normal wear but excessive amounts indicate that the tires are too wide for the wheels.

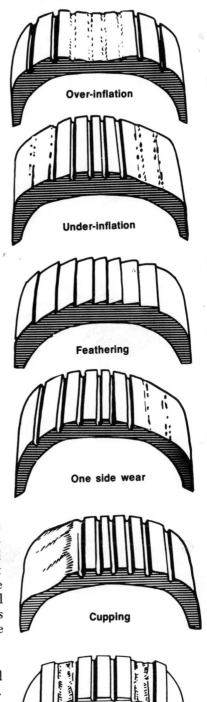

**Over-inflation**

**Under-inflation**

**Feathering**

**One side wear**

**Cupping**

**Second-rib wear**

## Troubleshooting Disc Brake Problems

| Condition | Possible Cause |
|---|---|
| Noise—groan—brake noise emanating when slowly releasing brakes (creep-groan) | Not detrimental to function of disc brakes—no corrective action required. (This noise may be eliminated by slightly increasing or decreasing brake pedal efforts.) |
| Rattle—brake noise or rattle emanating at low speeds on rough roads, (front wheels only). | 1. Shoe anti-rattle spring missing or not properly positioned.<br>2. Excessive clearance between shoe and caliper.<br>3. Soft or broken caliper seals.<br>4. Deformed or misaligned disc.<br>5. Loose caliper. |
| Scraping | 1. Mounting bolts too long.<br>2. Loose wheel bearings.<br>3. Bent, loose, or misaligned splash shield. |
| Front brakes heat up during driving and fail to release | 1. Operator riding brake pedal.<br>2. Stop light switch improperly adjusted.<br>3. Sticking pedal linkage.<br>4. Frozen or seized piston.<br>5. Residual pressure valve in master cylinder.<br>6. Power brake malfunction.<br>7. Proportioning valve malfunction. |
| Leaky brake caliper | 1. Damaged or worn caliper piston seal.<br>2. Scores or corrosion on surface of cylinder bore. |
| Grabbing or uneven brake action—Brakes pull to one side | 1. Causes listed under "Brakes Pull".<br>2. Power brake malfunction.<br>3. Low fluid level in master cylinder.<br>4. Air in hydraulic system.<br>5. Brake fluid, oil or grease on linings.<br>6. Unmatched linings.<br>7. Distorted brake pads.<br>8. Frozen or seized pistons.<br>9. Incorrect tire pressure.<br>10. Front end out of alignment.<br>11. Broken rear spring.<br>12. Brake caliper pistons sticking.<br>13. Restricted hose or line.<br>14. Caliper not in proper alignment to braking disc.<br>15. Stuck or malfunctioning metering valve.<br>16. Soft or broken caliper seals.<br>17. Loose caliper. |
| Brake pedal can be depressed without braking effect | 1. Air in hydraulic system or improper bleeding procedure.<br>2. Leak past primary cup in master cylinder.<br>3. Leak in system.<br>4. Rear brakes out of adjustment.<br>5. Bleeder screw open. |
| Excessive pedal travel | 1. Air, leak, or insufficient fluid in system or caliper.<br>2. Warped or excessively tapered shoe and lining assembly.<br>3. Excessive disc runout.<br>4. Rear brake adjustment required.<br>5. Loose wheel bearing adjustment.<br>6. Damaged caliper piston seal.<br>7. Improper brake fluid (boil).<br>8. Power brake malfunction.<br>9. Weak or soft hoses. |

## Troubleshooting Disc Brake Problems (cont.)

| Condition | Possible Cause |
|---|---|
| Brake roughness or chatter (pedal pumping) | 1. Excessive thickness variation of braking disc.<br>2. Excessive lateral runout of braking disc.<br>3. Rear brake drums out-of-round.<br>4. Excessive front bearing clearance. |
| Excessive pedal effort | 1. Brake fluid, oil or grease on linings.<br>2. Incorrect lining.<br>3. Frozen or seized pistons.<br>4. Power brake malfunction.<br>5. Kinked or collapsed hose or line.<br>6. Stuck metering valve.<br>7. Scored caliper or master cylinder bore.<br>8. Seized caliper pistons. |
| Brake pedal fades (pedal travel increases with foot on brake) | 1. Rough master cylinder or caliper bore.<br>2. Loose or broken hydraulic lines/connections.<br>3. Air in hydraulic system.<br>4. Fluid level low.<br>5. Weak or soft hoses.<br>6. Inferior quality brake shoes or fluid.<br>7. Worn master cylinder piston cups or seals. |

## Troubleshooting Drum Brakes

| Condition | Possible Cause |
|---|---|
| Pedal goes to floor | 1. Fluid low in reservoir.<br>2. Air in hydraulic system.<br>3. Improperly adjusted brake.<br>4. Leaking wheel cylinders.<br>5. Loose or broken brake lines.<br>6. Leaking or worn master cylinder.<br>7. Excessively worn brake lining. |
| Spongy brake pedal | 1. Air in hydraulic system.<br>2. Improper brake fluid (low boiling point).<br>3. Excessively worn or cracked brake drums.<br>4. Broken pedal pivot bushing. |
| Brakes pulling | 1. Contaminated lining.<br>2. Front end out of alignment.<br>3. Incorrect brake adjustment.<br>4. Unmatched brake lining.<br>5. Brake drums out of round.<br>6. Brake shoes distorted.<br>7. Restricted brake hose or line.<br>8. Broken rear spring.<br>9. Worn brake linings.<br>10. Uneven lining wear.<br>11. Glazed brake lining.<br>12. Excessive brake lining dust.<br>13. Heat spotted brake drums.<br>14. Weak brake return springs.<br>15. Faulty automatic adjusters.<br>16. Low or incorrect tire pressure. |

| Condition | Possible Cause |
|---|---|
| Squealing brakes | 1. Glazed brake lining.<br>2. Saturated brake lining.<br>3. Weak or broken brake shoe retaining spring.<br>4. Broken or weak brake shoe return spring.<br>5. Incorrect brake lining.<br>6. Distorted brake shoes.<br>7. Bent support plate.<br>8. Dust in brakes or scored brake drums.<br>9. Linings worn below limit.<br>10. Uneven brake lining wear.<br>11. Heat spotted brake drums. |
| Chirping brakes | 1. Out of round drum or eccentric axle flange pilot. |
| Dragging brakes | 1. Incorrect wheel or parking brake adjustment.<br>2. Parking brakes engaged or improperly adjusted.<br>3. Weak or broken brake shoe return spring.<br>4. Brake pedal binding.<br>5. Master cylinder cup sticking.<br>6. Obstructed master cylinder relief port.<br>7. Saturated brake lining.<br>8. Bent or out of round brake drum.<br>9. Contaminated or improper brake fluid.<br>10. Sticking wheel cylinder pistons.<br>11. Driver riding brake pedal.<br>12. Defective proportioning valve.<br>13. Insufficient brake shoe lubricant. |
| Hard pedal | 1. Brake booster inoperative.<br>2. Incorrect brake lining.<br>3. Restricted brake line or hose.<br>4. Frozen brake pedal linkage.<br>5. Stuck wheel cylinder.<br>6. Binding pedal linkage.<br>7. Faulty proportioning valve. |
| Wheel locks | 1. Contaminated brake lining.<br>2. Loose or torn brake lining.<br>3. Wheel cylinder cups sticking.<br>4. Incorrect wheel bearing adjustment.<br>5. Faulty proportioning valve. |
| Brakes fade (high speed) | 1. Incorrect lining.<br>2. Overheated brake drums.<br>3. Incorrect brake fluid (low boiling temperature).<br>4. Saturated brake lining.<br>5. Leak in hydraulic system.<br>6. Faulty automatic adjusters. |
| Pedal pulsates | 1. Bent or out of round brake drum. |
| Brake chatter and shoe knock | 1. Out of round brake drum.<br>2. Loose support plate.<br>3. Bent support plate.<br>4. Distorted brake shoes.<br>5. Machine grooves in contact face of brake drum (Shoe Knock).<br>6. Contaminated brake lining.<br>7. Missing or loose components.<br>8. Incorrect lining material.<br>9. Out-of-round brake drums.<br>10. Heat spotted or scored brake drums.<br>11. Out-of-balance wheels. |

## Troubleshooting Drum Brakes (cont.)

| Condition | Possible Cause |
|---|---|
| Brakes do not self adjust | 1. Adjuster screw frozen in thread.<br>2. Adjuster screw corroded at thrust washer.<br>3. Adjuster lever does not engage star wheel.<br>4. Adjuster installed on wrong wheel. |
| Brake light glows | 1. Leak in the hydraulic system.<br>2. Air in the system.<br>3. Improperly adjusted master cylinder pushrod.<br>4. Uneven lining wear.<br>5. Failure to center combination valve or proportioning valve. |

# Appendix

## General Conversion Table

| Multiply by | To convert | To | |
|---|---|---|---|
| 2.54 | Inches | Centimeters | .3937 |
| 30.48 | Feet | Centimeters | .0328 |
| .914 | Yards | Meters | 1.094 |
| 1.609 | Miles | Kilometers | .621 |
| .645 | Square inches | Square cm. | .155 |
| .836 | Square yards | Square meters | 1.196 |
| 16.39 | Cubic inches | Cubic cm. | .061 |
| 28.3 | Cubic feet | Liters | .0353 |
| .4536 | Pounds | Kilograms | 2.2045 |
| 4.226 | Gallons | Liters | .264 |
| .068 | Lbs./sq. in. (psi) | Atmospheres | 14.7 |
| .138 | Foot pounds | Kg. m. | 7.23 |
| 1.014 | H.P. (DIN) | H.P. (SAE) | .9861 |
| — | To obtain | From | Multiply by |

Note: 1 cm. equals 10 mm.; 1 mm. equals .0394".

## Conversion—Common Fractions to Decimals and Millimeters

| Common Fractions | Decimal Fractions | Millimeters (approx.) | Common Fractions | Decimal Fractions | Millimeters (approx.) | Common Fractions | Decimal Fractions | Millimeters (approx.) |
|---|---|---|---|---|---|---|---|---|
| 1/128 | .008 | 0.20 | 11/32 | .344 | 8.73 | 43/64 | .672 | 17.07 |
| 1/64 | .016 | 0.40 | 23/64 | .359 | 9.13 | 11/16 | .688 | 17.46 |
| 1/32 | .031 | 0.79 | 3/8 | .375 | 9.53 | 45/64 | .703 | 17.86 |
| 3/64 | .047 | 1.19 | 25/64 | .391 | 9.92 | 23/32 | .719 | 18.26 |
| 1/16 | .063 | 1.59 | 13/32 | .406 | 10.32 | 47/64 | .734 | 18.65 |
| 5/64 | .078 | 1.98 | 27/64 | .422 | 10.72 | 3/4 | .750 | 19.05 |
| 3/32 | .094 | 2.38 | 7/16 | .438 | 11.11 | 49/64 | .766 | 19.45 |
| 7/64 | .109 | 2.78 | 29/64 | .453 | 11.51 | 25/32 | .781 | 19.84 |
| 1/8 | .125 | 3.18 | 15/32 | .469 | 11.91 | 51/64 | .797 | 20.24 |
| 9/64 | .141 | 3.57 | 31/64 | .484 | 12.30 | 13/16 | .813 | 20.64 |
| 5/32 | .156 | 3.97 | 1/2 | .500 | 12.70 | 53/64 | .828 | 21.03 |
| 11/64 | .172 | 4.37 | 33/64 | .516 | 13.10 | 27/32 | .844 | 21.43 |
| 3/16 | .188 | 4.76 | 17/32 | .531 | 13.49 | 55/64 | .859 | 21.83 |
| 13/64 | .203 | 5.16 | 35/64 | .547 | 13.89 | 7/8 | .875 | 22.23 |
| 7/32 | .219 | 5.56 | 9/16 | .563 | 14.29 | 57/64 | .891 | 22.62 |
| 15/64 | .234 | 5.95 | 37/64 | .578 | 14.68 | 29/32 | .906 | 23.02 |
| 1/4 | .250 | 6.35 | 19/32 | .594 | 15.08 | 59/64 | .922 | 23.42 |
| 17/64 | .266 | 6.75 | 39/64 | .609 | 15.48 | 15/16 | .938 | 23.81 |
| 9/32 | .281 | 7.14 | 5/8 | .625 | 15.88 | 61/64 | .953 | 24.21 |
| 19/64 | .297 | 7.54 | 41/64 | .641 | 16.27 | 31/32 | .969 | 24.61 |
| 5/16 | .313 | 7.94 | 21/32 | .656 | 16.67 | 63/64 | .984 | 25.00 |
| 21/64 | .328 | 8.33 | | | | | | |

## Decimal Equivalent Size of the Number Drills

| Drill No. | Decimal Equivalent | Drill No. | Decimal Equivalent | Drill No. | Decimal Equivalent |
|---|---|---|---|---|---|
| 80 | .0135 | 53 | .0595 | 26 | .1470 |
| 79 | .0145 | 52 | .0635 | 25 | .1495 |
| 78 | .0160 | 51 | .0670 | 24 | .1520 |
| 77 | .0180 | 50 | .0700 | 23 | .1540 |
| 76 | .0200 | 49 | .0730 | 22 | .1570 |
| 75 | .0210 | 48 | .0760 | 21 | .1590 |
| 74 | .0225 | 47 | .0785 | 20 | .1610 |
| 73 | .0240 | 46 | .0810 | 19 | .1660 |
| 72 | .0250 | 45 | .0820 | 18 | .1695 |
| 71 | .0260 | 44 | .0860 | 17 | .1730 |
| 70 | .0280 | 43 | .0890 | 16 | .1770 |
| 69 | .0292 | 42 | .0935 | 15 | .1800 |
| 68 | .0310 | 41 | .0960 | 14 | .1820 |
| 67 | .0320 | 40 | .0980 | 13 | .1850 |
| 66 | .0330 | 39 | .0995 | 12 | .1890 |
| 65 | .0350 | 38 | .1015 | 11 | .1910 |
| 64 | .0360 | 37 | .1040 | 10 | .1935 |
| 63 | .0370 | 36 | .1065 | 9 | .1960 |
| 62 | .0380 | 35 | .1100 | 8 | .1990 |
| 61 | .0390 | 34 | .1110 | 7 | .2010 |
| 60 | .0400 | 33 | .1130 | 6 | .2040 |
| 59 | .0410 | 32 | .1160 | 5 | .2055 |
| 58 | .0420 | 31 | .1200 | 4 | .2090 |
| 57 | .0430 | 30 | .1285 | 3 | .2130 |
| 56 | .0465 | 29 | .1360 | 2 | .2210 |
| 55 | .0520 | 28 | .1405 | 1 | .2280 |
| 54 | .0550 | 27 | .1440 | | |

## Decimal Equivalent Size of the Letter Drills

| Letter Drill | Decimal Equivalent | Letter Drill | Decimal Equivalent | Letter Drill | Decimal Equivalent |
|---|---|---|---|---|---|
| A | .234 | J | .277 | S | .348 |
| B | .238 | K | .281 | T | .358 |
| C | .242 | L | .290 | U | .368 |
| D | .246 | M | .295 | V | .377 |
| E | .250 | N | .302 | W | .386 |
| F | .257 | O | .316 | X | .397 |
| G | .261 | P | .323 | Y | .404 |
| H | .266 | Q | .332 | Z | .413 |
| I | .272 | R | .339 | | |

## Conversion—Millimeters to Decimal Inches

| mm | inches | mm | inches | mm | inches | mm | inches | mm | inches |
|---|---|---|---|---|---|---|---|---|---|
| 1 | .039 370 | 31 | 1.220 470 | 61 | 2.401 570 | 91 | 3.582 670 | 210 | 8.267 700 |
| 2 | .078 740 | 32 | 1.259 840 | 62 | 2.440 940 | 92 | 3.622 040 | 220 | 8.661 400 |
| 3 | .118 110 | 33 | 1.299 210 | 63 | 2.480 310 | 93 | 3.661 410 | 230 | 9.055 100 |
| 4 | .157 480 | 34 | 1.338 580 | 64 | 2.519 680 | 94 | 3.700 780 | 240 | 9.448 800 |
| 5 | .196 850 | 35 | 1.377 949 | 65 | 2.559 050 | 95 | 3.740 150 | 250 | 9.842 500 |
| 6 | .236 220 | 36 | 1.417 319 | 66 | 2.598 420 | 96 | 3.779 520 | 260 | 10.236 200 |
| 7 | .275 590 | 37 | 1.456 689 | 67 | 2.637 790 | 97 | 3.818 890 | 270 | 10.629 900 |
| 8 | .314 960 | 38 | 1.496 050 | 68 | 2.677 160 | 98 | 3.858 260 | 280 | 11.032 600 |
| 9 | .354 330 | 39 | 1.535 430 | 69 | 2.716 530 | 99 | 3.897 630 | 290 | 11.417 300 |
| 10 | .393 700 | 40 | 1.574 800 | 70 | 2.755 900 | 100 | 3.937 000 | 300 | 11.811 000 |
| 11 | .433 070 | 41 | 1.614 170 | 71 | 2.795 270 | 105 | 4.133 848 | 310 | 12.204 700 |
| 12 | .472 440 | 42 | 1.653 540 | 72 | 2.834 640 | 110 | 4.330 700 | 320 | 12.598 400 |
| 13 | .511 810 | 43 | 1.692 910 | 73 | 2.874 010 | 115 | 4.527 550 | 330 | 12.992 100 |
| 14 | .551 180 | 44 | 1.732 280 | 74 | 2.913 380 | 120 | 4.724 400 | 340 | 13.385 800 |
| 15 | .590 550 | 45 | 1.771 650 | 75 | 2.952 750 | 125 | 4.921 250 | 350 | 13.779 500 |
| 16 | .629 920 | 46 | 1.811 020 | 76 | 2.992 120 | 130 | 5.118 100 | 360 | 14.173 200 |
| 17 | .669 290 | 47 | 1.850 390 | 77 | 3.031 490 | 135 | 5.314 950 | 370 | 14.566 900 |
| 18 | .708 660 | 48 | 1.889 760 | 78 | 3.070 860 | 140 | 5.511 800 | 380 | 14.960 600 |
| 19 | .748 030 | 49 | 1.929 130 | 79 | 3.110 230 | 145 | 5.708 650 | 390 | 15.354 300 |
| 20 | .787 400 | 50 | 1.968 500 | 80 | 3.149 600 | 150 | 5.905 500 | 400 | 15.748 000 |
| 21 | .826 770 | 51 | 2.007 870 | 81 | 3.188 970 | 155 | 6.102 350 | 500 | 19.685 000 |
| 22 | .866 140 | 52 | 2.047 240 | 82 | 3.228 340 | 160 | 6.299 200 | 600 | 23.622 000 |
| 23 | .905 510 | 53 | 2.086 610 | 83 | 3.267 710 | 165 | 6.496 050 | 700 | 27.559 000 |
| 24 | .944 880 | 54 | 2.125 980 | 84 | 3.307 080 | 170 | 6.692 900 | 800 | 31.496 000 |
| 25 | .984 250 | 55 | 2.165 350 | 85 | 3.346 450 | 175 | 6.889 750 | 900 | 35.433 000 |
| 26 | 1.023 620 | 56 | 2.204 720 | 86 | 3.385 820 | 180 | 7.086 600 | 1000 | 39.370 000 |
| 27 | 1.062 990 | 57 | 2.244 090 | 87 | 3.425 190 | 185 | 7.283 450 | 2000 | 78.740 000 |
| 28 | 1.102 360 | 58 | 2.283 460 | 88 | 3.464 560 | 190 | 7.480 300 | 3000 | 118.110 000 |
| 29 | 1.141 730 | 59 | 2.322 830 | 89 | 3.503 903 | 195 | 7.677 150 | 4000 | 157.480 000 |
| 30 | 1.181 100 | 60 | 2.362 200 | 90 | 3.543 300 | 200 | 7.874 000 | 5000 | 196.850 000 |

To change decimal millimeters to decimal inches, position the decimal point where desired on either side of the millimeter measurement shown and reset the inches decimal by the same number of digits in the same direction. For example, to convert 0.001 mm to decimal inches, reset the decimal behind the 1 mm (shown on the chart) to 0.001; change the decimal inch equivalent (0.039″ shown) to 0.000039″.

## Tap Drill Sizes

| Screw & Tap Size | National Fine or S.A.E.<br>Threads Per Inch | Use Drill Number |
|---|---|---|
| No. 5 | .44 | .37 |
| No. 6 | .40 | .33 |
| No. 8 | .36 | .29 |
| No. 10 | .32 | .21 |
| No. 12 | .28 | .15 |
| 1/4 | .28 | 3 |
| 5/16 | .24 | 1 |
| 3/8 | .24 | .Q |
| 7/16 | .20 | .W |
| 1/2 | .20 | 29/64 |
| 9/16 | .18 | 33/64 |
| 5/8 | .18 | 37/64 |
| 3/4 | .16 | 11/16 |
| 7/8 | .14 | 13/16 |
| 1 1/8 | .12 | 1 3/64 |
| 1 1/4 | .12 | 1 11/64 |
| 1 1/2 | .12 | 1 27/64 |

## Tap Drill Sizes

| Screw & Tap Size | National Coarse or U.S.S.<br>Threads Per Inch | Use Drill Number |
|---|---|---|
| No. 5 | .40 | .39 |
| No. 6 | .32 | .36 |
| No. 8 | .32 | .29 |
| No. 10 | .24 | .25 |
| No. 12 | .24 | .17 |
| 1/4 | .20 | 8 |
| 5/16 | .18 | .F |
| 3/8 | .16 | 5/16 |
| 7/16 | .14 | .U |
| 1/2 | .13 | 27/64 |
| 9/16 | .12 | 31/64 |
| 5/8 | .11 | 17/32 |
| 3/4 | .10 | 21/32 |
| 7/8 | .9 | 49/64 |
| 1 | .8 | 7/8 |
| 1 1/8 | .7 | 63/64 |
| 1 1/4 | .7 | 1 7/64 |
| 1 1/2 | .6 | 1 11/32 |

# Anti-Freeze Chart

Temperatures Shown in Degrees Fahrenheit +32 is Freezing

| Cooling System Capacity Quarts | Quarts of ETHYLENE GLYCOL Needed for Protection to Temperatures Shown Below | | | | | | | | | | | | | |
|---|---|---|---|---|---|---|---|---|---|---|---|---|---|---|
| | 1 | 2 | 3 | 4 | 5 | 6 | 7 | 8 | 9 | 10 | 11 | 12 | 13 | 14 |
| 10 | +24° | +16° | + 4° | −12° | −34° | −62° | | | | | | | | |
| 11 | +25 | +18 | + 8 | − 6 | −23 | −47 | | | | | | | | |
| 12 | +26 | +19 | +10 | 0 | −15 | −34 | −57° | | | | | | | |
| 13 | +27 | +21 | +13 | + 3 | − 9 | −25 | −45 | | | | | | | |
| 14 | | | +15 | + 6 | − 5 | −18 | −34 | | | | | | | |
| 15 | | | +16 | + 8 | 0 | −12 | −26 | | | | | | | |
| 16 | | | +17 | +10 | + 2 | − 8 | −19 | −34 | −52° | | | | | |
| 17 | | | +18 | +12 | + 5 | − 4 | −14 | −27 | −42 | | | | | |
| 18 | | | +19 | +14 | + 7 | 0 | −10 | −21 | −34 | −50° | | | | |
| 19 | | | +20 | +15 | + 9 | + 2 | − 7 | −16 | −28 | −42 | | | | |
| 20 | | | | +16 | +10 | + 4 | − 3 | −12 | −22 | −34 | −48° | | | |
| 21 | | | | +17 | +12 | + 6 | 0 | − 9 | −17 | −28 | −41 | | | |
| 22 | | | | +18 | +13 | + 8 | + 2 | − 6 | −14 | −23 | −34 | −47° | | |
| 23 | | | | +19 | +14 | + 9 | + 4 | − 3 | −10 | −19 | −29 | −40 | | |
| 24 | | | | +19 | +15 | +10 | + 5 | 0 | − 8 | −15 | −23 | −34 | −46° | |
| 25 | | | | +20 | +16 | +12 | + 7 | + 1 | − 5 | −12 | −20 | −29 | −40 | −50° |
| 26 | | | | | +17 | +13 | + 8 | + 3 | − 3 | − 9 | −16 | −25 | −34 | −44 |
| 27 | | | | | +18 | +14 | + 9 | + 5 | − 1 | − 7 | −13 | −21 | −29 | −39 |
| 28 | | | | | +18 | +15 | +10 | + 6 | + 1 | − 5 | −11 | −18 | −25 | −34 |
| 29 | | | | | +19 | +16 | +12 | + 7 | + 2 | − 3 | − 8 | −15 | −22 | −29 |
| 30 | | | | | +20 | +17 | +13 | + 8 | + 4 | − 1 | − 6 | −12 | −18 | −25 |

For capacities over 30 quarts divide true capacity by 3. Find quarts Anti-Freeze for the 1/3 and multiply by 3 for quarts to add.

For capacities under 10 quarts multiply true capacity by 3. Find quarts Anti-Freeze for the tripled volume and divide by 3 for quarts to add.

## To Increase the Freezing Protection of Anti-Freeze Solutions Already Installed

| Cooling System Capacity Quarts | Number of Quarts of ETHYLENE GLYCOL Anti-Freeze Required to Increase Protection | | | | | | | | | | | | | | |
|---|---|---|---|---|---|---|---|---|---|---|---|---|---|---|---|
| | From +20° F. to | | | | | From +10° F. to | | | | | From 0° F. to | | | |
| | 0° | −10° | −20° | −30° | −40° | 0° | −10° | −20° | −30° | −40° | −10° | −20° | −30° | −40° |
| 10 | 1¾ | 2¼ | 3 | 3½ | 3¾ | ¾ | 1½ | 2¼ | 2¾ | 3¼ | ¾ | 1½ | 2 | 2½ |
| 12 | 2 | 2¾ | 3½ | 4 | 4½ | 1 | 1¾ | 2½ | 3¼ | 3¾ | 1 | 1¾ | 2½ | 3¼ |
| 14 | 2¼ | 3¼ | 4 | 4¾ | 5½ | 1¼ | 2 | 3 | 3¾ | 4½ | 1 | 2 | 3 | 3½ |
| 16 | 2½ | 3½ | 4½ | 5¼ | 6 | 1¼ | 2½ | 3½ | 4¼ | 5¼ | 1¼ | 2¼ | 3¼ | 4 |
| 18 | 3 | 4 | 5 | 6 | 7 | 1½ | 2¾ | 4 | 5 | 5¾ | 1½ | 2½ | 3¾ | 4¾ |
| 20 | 3¼ | 4½ | 5¾ | 6¾ | 7½ | 1¾ | 3 | 4¼ | 5½ | 6½ | 1½ | 2¾ | 4¼ | 5¼ |
| 22 | 3½ | 5 | 6¼ | 7¼ | 8¼ | 1¾ | 3¼ | 4¾ | 6 | 7¼ | 1¾ | 3¼ | 4½ | 5½ |
| 24 | 4 | 5½ | 7 | 8 | 9 | 2 | 3½ | 5 | 6½ | 7½ | 1¾ | 3½ | 5 | 6 |
| 26 | 4¼ | 6 | 7½ | 8¾ | 10 | 2 | 4 | 5½ | 7 | 8¼ | 2 | 3¾ | 5½ | 6¾ |
| 28 | 4½ | 6¼ | 8 | 9½ | 10½ | 2¼ | 4¼ | 6 | 7½ | 9 | 2 | 4 | 5¾ | 7¼ |
| 30 | 5 | 6¾ | 8½ | 10 | 11½ | 2½ | 4½ | 6½ | 8 | 9½ | 2¼ | 4¼ | 6¼ | 7¾ |

Test radiator solution with proper hydrometer. Determine from the table the number of quarts of solution to be drawn off from a full cooling system and replace with undiluted anti-freeze, to give the desired increased protection. For example, to increase protection of a 22-quart cooling system containing Ethylene Glycol (permanent type) anti-freeze, from +20° F. to −20° F. will require the replacement of 6¼ quarts of solution with undiluted anti-freeze.

# Index